SOUTHEAST ASIAN AFFAIRS 2020

The **ISEAS – Yusof Ishak Institute** (formerly Institute of Southeast Asian Studies) is an autonomous organization established in 1968. It is a regional centre dedicated to the study of socio-political, security, and economic trends and developments in Southeast Asia and its wider geostrategic and economic environment. The Institute's research programmes are grouped under Regional Economic Studies (RES), Regional Strategic and Political Studies (RSPS), and Regional Social and Cultural Studies (RSCS). The Institute is also home to the ASEAN Studies Centre (ASC), the Singapore APEC Study Centre, and the Temasek History Research Centre (THRC).

ISEAS Publishing, an established academic press, has issued more than two thousand books and journals. It is the largest scholarly publisher of research about Southeast Asia from within the region. ISEAS Publishing works with many other academic and trade publishers and distributors to disseminate important research and analyses from and about Southeast Asia to the rest of the world.

SOUTHEAST ASIAN AFFAIRS 2020

EDITED BY
MALCOLM COOK
DALJIT SINGH

First published in Singapore in 2020 by
ISEAS Publishing
30 Heng Mui Keng Terrace
Singapore 119614

E-mail: publish@iseas.edu.sg
Website: http://bookshop.iseas.edu.sg

All rights reserved. No part of this publication may be reproduced, stored in a retrieval system, or transmitted in any form or by any means, electronic, mechanical, photocopying, recording or otherwise, without the prior permission of the ISEAS – Yusof Ishak Institute.

© 2020 ISEAS – Yusof Ishak Institute

The responsibility for facts and opinions in this publication rests exclusively with the authors and their interpretations do not necessarily reflect the views or the policy of the publisher or its supporters.

ISEAS Library Cataloguing-in-Publication Data

Title: Southeast Asian affairs 2020.
Description: Singapore : ISEAS – Yusof Ishak Institute, 2020.
Identifiers: ISSN 0377-5437 | ISBN 9789814881302 (hard cover) | ISBN 9789814881319 (pdf) | ISBN 9789814881326 (epub)
Subjects: LCSH: Southeast Asia—Periodicals.
Classification: LCC DS501 S72A 2020

Typeset by Superskill Graphics Pte Ltd

Contents

Introduction *Malcolm Cook*	vii

THE REGION

Southeast Asia in 2019: Adjustment and Adaptation to China's Regional Impact *Graham Ong-Webb*	3
Economic Overview of Southeast Asia *Manu Bhaskaran*	19
The Rise of the Right: Populism and Authoritarianism in Southeast Asian Politics *Kanishka Jayasuriya*	43
American Foreign Policy and Southeast Asia *Daljit Singh*	57
China's Belt and Road Initiative Financing in Southeast Asia *Xue Gong*	77

BRUNEI DARUSSALAM

Brunei Darussalam in 2019: Issues Revisited *Pushpa Thambipillai*	99

CAMBODIA

Cambodia in 2019: Entrenching One-Party Rule and Asserting National Sovereignty in the Era of Shifting Global Geopolitics *Kheang Un and Jing Jing Luo*	119

INDONESIA

Post-Election Politics in Indonesia: Between Economic Growth and Increased Islamic Conservatism *Amalinda Savirani*	137
Social Media and the 2019 Indonesian Elections: Hoax Takes the Centre Stage *Jennifer Yang Hui*	155

LAOS

Laos in 2019: Moving Heaven and Earth on the Mekong *Geoffrey C. Gunn*	175

MALAYSIA

Malaysia in 2019: A Change of Government without Regime Change 191
Ross Tapsell

Malaysia and the Pursuit of Sustainability 209
Serina Rahman

MYANMAR

Myanmar in 2019: Rakhine Issue, Constitutional Reform and Election Fever 235
Nyi Nyi Kyaw

The 2020 Myanmar General Election: Another Turning Point? 255
Ye Htut

THE PHILIPPINES

The Ones Who Don't Walk Away from the Philippines 275
Lowell Bautista

SINGAPORE

Singapore in 2019: In Holding Pattern 295
Khairulanwar Zaini

The Bicentennial Commemoration: Imagining and Re-imagining Singapore's History 323
Terence Chong

THAILAND

Thailand in 2019: The Year of Living Unpredictably 337
Kanokrat Lertchoosakul

Future—Forward? The Past and Future of the Future Forward Party 355
James Ockey

TIMOR-LESTE

Timor-Leste: Twenty Years after the Self-Determination Referendum 381
Rui Graça Feijó

VIETNAM

Vietnam in 2019: A Return to Familiar Patterns 393
Paul Schuler and Mai Truong

Succession Politics and Authoritarian Resilience in Vietnam 411
Nguyen Khac Giang

Introduction

Malcolm Cook

The twenty-two chapters in *Southeast Asian Affairs 2020* again highlight the dynamism and diversity of the eleven countries covered and Southeast Asia as a region.[1] Events ranged from the tragic deaths from overwork and poor conditions of many election workers in Indonesia during the national elections to the release on social media of a rap song supporting former Malaysian prime minister Najib Razak, the first leader of UMNO to lose a parliamentary election.

Six overarching themes each feature in many of the twenty-two chapters, and no chapter is devoid of all six. Two of these themes are global in nature, two relate to major powers outside of Southeast Asia, and two are domestic in nature. The enduring and definitive nature of these themes is underlined by the fact that many of them feature heavily in previous volumes of *Southeast Asian Affairs*, including those like major power competition and transitions in political leadership that have been constant themes since the first volume was published almost a half century ago. Others, like environmental degradation and the political ramifications of social media, are distinctly modern.

Environmental Degradation

In the thematic chapter for Malaysia, Serina Rahman looks at the ambitious environmental policy agenda of the Pakatan Harapan government and the political challenges it faces. Global pressure particularly from the European Union on the Malaysian palm oil industry, a major source of Malaysian exports, has led to a defensive response from Kuala Lumpur in contrast to the proactive position the government has taken against the export of trash to Malaysia from advanced Western economies. The Pakatan Harapan government has taken a regional lead in trying to address some of the causes and consequences of environmental degradation. Will others follow?

MALCOLM COOK is Senior Fellow at the ISEAS – Yusof Ishak Institute, Singapore.

Social Media Politics

The thematic chapter for Indonesia by Jennifer Yang Hui looks at the use and influence of social media in the 2019 elections in the largest country of Southeast Asia. In Indonesia, social media is now the predominant channel of political communication between politicians and voters and supporters of politicians and voters. A large industry of social media political communication has arisen that is changing the conduct of election campaigns fundamentally. In the 2014 and 2019 presidential campaigns, black propaganda against political opponents has proven to be widespread even if its effectiveness is questionable.

In the thematic chapter for Thailand, James Ockey's study of the rapid rise of the Future Forward Party shows a positive democratic-opening dimension to social media politics. The clever use of social media greatly aided the party's phoenix-like rise to become the third-largest party in Thailand, and one that is particularly popular among young urban voters. The country review chapters on Vietnam by Paul Schuler and Mai Truong and on Singapore by Khairulanwar Zaini highlight the concerns of the ruling regimes with the political impact of social media.

China

As with last year's volume, the chapters of *Southeast Asian Affairs 2020* underline that China is now the leading external power in Southeast Asia and its influence is expanding and becoming more politically salient. In the first chapter, the regional political and security outlook, Graham Ong-Webb goes into some detail on the centrality of China regionally. The regional thematic chapter on China's Belt and Road Initiative by Gong Xue evaluates President Xi Jinping's signature foreign policy endeavour and counters criticism from within Southeast Asia and internationally of the initiative's rationale and effects on host countries. The country review chapter for the Philippines by Lowell Bautista looks into President Duterte's close embrace of China. The country review chapter for Brunei by Pushpa Thambipillai, Cambodia by Kheang Un, and Laos by Geoffrey Gunn each show the growing asymmetrical importance of China for each of these countries. In the thematic chapter for Singapore on the Bicentennial commemorations, Terence Chong posits that concerns with China's growing influence was a major external factor in the ongoing recasting of Singaporean history reflected in the Bicentennial.

US-China Rivalry

In 2019, the nature and regional ramifications of the US-China major power rivalry became clearer and of greater concern. In his regional thematic chapter, Daljit Singh looks at changes in US foreign policy and grand strategy and what they mean for Southeast Asia. In the regional economic chapter, Jayant Menon analyses the economic fallout for Southeast Asia of the rivalry and how this is strengthening intraregional economic integration efforts. Most of the country-level chapters make no or only brief mention of this significant regional strategic development. This lack of juxtaposition suggests either that the domestic ramifications of this new rivalrous regional strategic order are still nascent or that the links between regional strategic and domestic political developments are fewer and weaker than many international relations scholars posit.

Infrastructure

Infrastructure development is a key political and performance-legitimacy focus of each of the eleven Southeast Asian governments, a source of domestic political debate, and a central component of Southeast Asian states' relationships with China. China is the predominant source of foreign financing for public infrastructure in Myanmar, Cambodia, Laos, Malaysia and Brunei Darussalam and a major source for Thailand, the Philippines, Indonesia, Vietnam and Timor Leste. In her country review chapter for Indonesia, Amalinda Savirani looks at the political importance of President Jokowi's infrastructure development agenda in an election year. Geoffrey Gunn, in his chapter on Laos, looks at the strong focus on delivering China-financed infrastructure projects by the ruling regime in Vientiane.

For both President Jokowi in Indonesia and President Duterte in the Philippines, infrastructure development is a central component of their focus on the delivery of public services as their source of political legitimation, and for Jokowi's successful re-election campaign. Lowell Bautista in his chapter on the Philippines contrasts this with the preceding Aquino administration's appeals to liberal values and good governance. In the most conceptual chapter in this volume, Kanishka Jayasuriya, using the cases of the Jokowi and Duterte administrations, looks at how this focus on service delivery (often at the cost of the loss of political rights and space) is part of the global shift towards conservative democratic politics and populism.

Political Transition

Transitions in political leadership and elections are the central theme for this volume's chapters on eight of the eleven states. It did not feature prominently for the Philippines, where President Duterte is halfway through his six-year term, for Brunei Darussalam, or for Laos. For Myanmar, Vietnam and Singapore, leadership transitions and national elections will take place in the near future. The two chapters on Myanmar by Ny Nyi Kyaw and Ye Htut focus on the upcoming national election that will most likely be held in 2020 and which will probably see the return of a National League of Democracy administration led by Aung San Suu Kyi. The thematic chapter for Vietnam by Nguyen Khac Giang highlights the outsized role the current president and general secretary of the Communist Party, Ngyuen Phu Trong, is to play in the leadership transition scheduled for 2021. The Vietnam country review chapter by Paul Schuler concurs.

For Thailand and Indonesia, 2019 saw elections that returned the incumbent leaders: for Indonesia, the re-election of President Jokowi with a larger majority; and for Thailand, Prayut Chan-o-cha, the head of the 2014 coup, as prime minister and leader of the ruling multiparty coalition. In the country review chapter for Thailand, Kanokrat Lertchoosakul analyses why the nineteen-party ruling coalition led by Prayut has remained together and has been able to pass legislation despite many forecasting its demise.

For Malaysia and Cambodia, it is about the political transition after the last election. In the case of Malaysia, this saw a truly historic result where UMNO lost power in 2018 for the first time. Ross Tapsell in his country review chapter for Malaysia looks at the challenges the new Pakatan Harapan government under Prime Minister Mahathir Mohammed is facing in living up to its campaign promises and the expectations its victory sparked. Cambodia's flawed election in 2018 saw the ruling Cambodian People's Party under Prime Minister Hun Sen win all the seats. Kheang Un's chapter looks at how the current Hun Sen government is taking steps to address domestic and international backlashes against the 2018 result and the emasculation of the political opposition and jailing of Kem Sokha that preceded it.

Timor Leste, the smallest and poorest democracy in the region, is a case of a failed transition that may lead to an unscheduled early election in 2020 to try to overcome the deadlock. Rui Feijo carefully dissects the causes of the current impasse between president and parliament and its likely future scenarios.

The year 2019 saw major worrying changes to the regional strategic order in Southeast Asia with the increasingly overt major power rivalry between the United States and China and significant domestic political change and tensions. The year 2020 promises more of the same.

Note

1. The authors were asked to submit their draft chapters in early December 2019 and were given only limited opportunity to update them after submission.

The Region

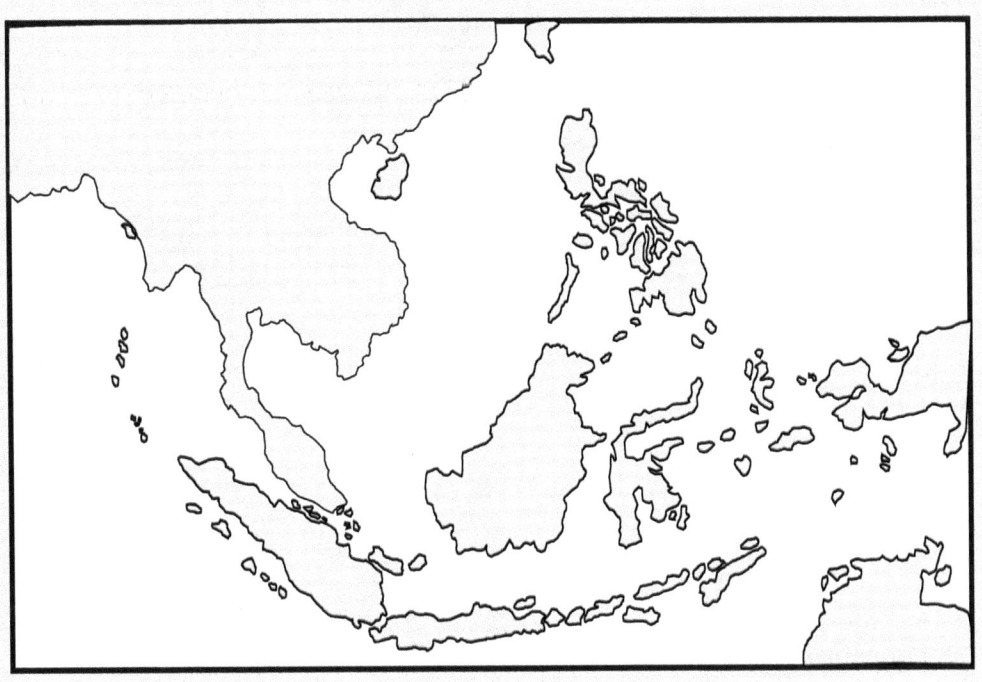

Southeast Asia in 2019: Adjustment and Adaptation to China's Regional Impact

Graham Ong-Webb

Trends in 2018 indicated that ASEAN regionalism was under pressure, putting into question the grouping's role and function. In contrast, developments in 2019 reflect the independent and collective resolve of Southeast Asian states to manage external political and economic risk, which has had the effect of shoring up cohesiveness of the ten-member grouping, or at least compelling members to put aside regionally divisive issues in order to deal with common challenges. Firstly, and perhaps most importantly, ASEAN and its member states have had to adjust to the realities and impact of the ongoing US-China trade war in a bid to ensure economic development and growth.

Secondly, they have sought to break out from the impasse of being sidelined in the regional power play of the United States and China. Despite adhering to a hedging strategy in dealing with China and the United States in the region's management of major power politics, ASEAN member states have telegraphed a heightened consideration of China as both a dialogue and free-trade partner. Thirdly, a stronger consideration of China's political and economic role in the region did somewhat mute the assertions of claimant states against China over disputed features and waters in the South China Sea for most of 2019 until the closing months of that year. Fourthly, in seeking to manage common external challenges in a united fashion, member states—as in previous years—remained unwilling to put more direct pressure on the Myanmar government for human rights violations relating to its Rohingya crisis; a problem that become internationalized since late 2017.

GRAHAM ONG-WEBB is Adjunct Fellow at the S. Rajaratnam School of International Studies, Nanyang Technological University, Singapore.

Adjusting to the US-China Trade War

The US-China Trade War, which began in July 2018 when the US government led by President Donald Trump implemented its first round of tariffs and other trade barriers on China—with the goal of forcing it to make changes to what the US says are "unfair trade practices"—has further impacted Asian countries whose supply chains have been closely linked to Chinese industries and are dependent on the US market as a significant export destination. Because of the US-China trade war—amidst the prospect of a global economic slowdown that is already dampening business confidence around the world—the year 2019 saw the worst twelve months for Asia-Pacific trade in goods and services by both volume and value since the global financial crisis ten years ago. The Bangkok-based UN Economic and Social Commission for Asia and the Pacific (ESCAP) recently estimated that, by volume, total exports could drop by 2.5 per cent and imports dip by 3.5 per cent. Under the pressure of lower prices, values of exports and imports could also fall by 3.6 per cent and 4.8 per cent respectively.[1] The forecast for 2020 does not appear to be much better.[2]

Recent data from the Asian Development Bank (ADB) suggests that Southeast Asia has grown less than anticipated, resulting in slight downward revisions to growth forecasts, which now stand at 4.8 per cent (2019) and 4.9 per cent (2020), down from 4.9 per cent and 5.0 per cent, respectively. In particular, Singapore, Thailand and the Philippines are among the regional economies that have seen cuts in their forecasted GDP growth rates for 2019. Weak manufacturing and external trade in Singapore have seen the country's GDP forecast for 2019 dip from 2.6 per cent to 2.4 per cent. In Thailand, the ADB forecasted the nation's economy to grow by 3.5 per cent, a drop from the original forecast of 3.9 per cent. Weaker global trade caused exports to contract by 4.5 per cent year-on-year in the first five months of 2019, weighing on growth. In the Philippines, the ADB cut the country's GDP forecast from 6.4 per cent to 6.2 per cent as growth in exports also slowed.[3]

To be sure, it is likely that this general downturn could have been even more significant if not for the efforts by a good number of Southeast Asian states to encourage transnational and homegrown companies to move their production out of China to Southeast Asia and other markets. With the expectation that the US-China trade war will likely continue for some years to come, some experts argue that this effort of trade diversion and inflow of foreign investment as a result of the trade war will confer net benefits on to Southeast Asian countries in the medium to long term.

Already, countries such as Vietnam and Malaysia seem to be coming out on top.[4] Towards the end of 2019, Vietnam has been projected to gain product orders diverted from China equivalent to 7.9 per cent of its GDP in 2020, as importers further attempt to avoid trade war tariffs. As it stands, Vietnamese exports to the United States surged 36 per cent in the first five months of 2019 compared with the same period in 2018. In the case of Malaysia, Chinese imports of liquefied propane from Malaysia grew 624 per cent year-on-year. Meanwhile, Chinese imports from the United States for liquefied butane and metal ores and concentrates dropped to zero in the first five months of 2019. Other countries such as Indonesia, the Philippines, Cambodia, Laos and Myanmar also saw noticeable gains in exports to the United States because of the US tariffs imposed on China, albeit on a smaller scale.[5]

However, these gains may be short-lived unless ASEAN and regional states overcome several existing challenges that stand in the way of not only unlocking further dividends but also of using the overall opportunity afforded by the trade war to transform Southeast Asia into a single production base. As one observer summed up the tasks ahead correctly, "For Southeast Asia to truly reap the benefits of the trade war and hedge against its attendant risks, it will have to step up its commitment to multilateralism, proactively invest in infrastructure and production capacity, and increase regional supply chain integration."[6]

Drift Towards China as an Economic Partner

Indeed, cognisant of what needs doing to transcend the impact of the trade war, ASEAN stepped up its efforts at preserving and even boosting economic multilateralism by pressing for the finalization of the Regional Comprehensive Economic Partnership (RCEP), which China had initiated at the 19th ASEAN Summit in 2011. At that time, Beijing proposed RCEP as a counterweight to the twelve-country Trans-Pacific Partnership (TPP) that was first mooted by the United States through the administration of then president Barack Obama in 2005 (as an expansion of the Trans-Pacific Strategic Economic Partnership Agreement signed by Chile, New Zealand, Brunei and Singapore) that would involve the inclusion of ASEAN member states Malaysia and Vietnam. Deemed to be the world's largest free trade agreement (FTA) if ever implemented, RCEP would link together ASEAN member states and their six FTA partners comprising China, Japan, South Korea, Australia, New Zealand and India. RCEP has the potential to bring significant opportunities for participating countries, as it is set to encompass about 45 per cent of the world's population (3.4 billion) and a third of global

GDP at about US$20 trillion. In addition, the bloc would account for total trade of US$10 trillion and 26 per cent of global FDI flows.

Currently, ASEAN has several "plus-one" trade agreements with its FTA partners. What RCEP would do is simplify the rules and procedures for each FTA within a single arrangement and reduce existing trade inefficiencies, hence providing concrete market access and investment commitments. In sum, RCEP entails lowering trade barriers and improving market access for goods and services, hence attracting foreign companies keen on entering into a more integrated ASEAN region. The plan would facilitate a greater inclusion of the region's small and medium-sized enterprises (SMEs) to global and regional supply chains. Likewise, technical cooperation with advanced industrialized countries like Japan, South Korea, New Zealand and Australia will assist Southeast Asian SMEs in developing better, more competitive products.

During the tenure of the Obama administration, most Asia-Pacific governments preferred the US-led TPP (that excluded China) over the China-backed RCEP (that excluded the United States). The collapse of the TPP through the withdrawal of the United States from the agreement by the newly formed administration of President Trump in his first week in office in January 2017 redefined RCEP into a bulwark against rising US-led protectionism driven by the Trump administration and as an agreement to preserve economic multilateralism in the Asia-Pacific and beyond. China certainly capitalized on the collapse of the TPP to advance its ambition of establishing a Chinese-centric multilateral order.[7] This outcome led geopolitical expert Ian Bremmer to assert in an article in *Time* magazine "How [President] Trump gave China a win on trade in Southeast Asia". He added that, "If the Belt and Road Initiative [BRI]—a Beijing-funded series of infrastructure projects throughout Asia and Europe—is the hardware of China's ambitious global plan, RCEP is the software much of it is supposed to run on."[8]

To be sure, ASEAN members, in the least, are generally aware that both the BRI and RCEP pose the risk of increasing the spread of Chinese influence across the region beyond economic matters. With this concern in mind, the grouping re-shaped China's 2011 proposition for RCEP into being an ASEAN-led project, underpinned by a set of "Guiding Principles and Objectives for Negotiating the Regional Comprehensive Economic Partnership" to preserve "ASEAN Centrality" during the negotiation process. However, there has always been the risk that signatories to RCEP would be subjected to China's significant negotiating leverage over its partners, facilitating its state-owned enterprises (SOEs) to occupy a hegemonic position in regional trade, because RCEP rules and processes are inherently non-stringent.

However, the onset of the trade war prosecuted by the United States against China in July 2018 has tilted ASEAN's risk calculus towards the merits offered by RCEP over the trade-offs. Furthermore, with the normalization of ties between Japan and China later that same year, Japanese prime minister Shinzo Abe encouraged the wider Asia-Pacific region to sign a deal to put the arrangement into motion.[9] With the Japanese government backing its Chinese counterpart, and with the sustainment and escalation of the US-China trade war across 2019, ASEAN intensified discussions and negotiations on RCEP in that year. In March 2019, a ministerial meeting of RCEP trade ministers was held in Cambodia as part of the agreement to intensify engagements for the year, including convening more inter-sessional meetings. In May, senior officials held their next inter-sessional meeting in Bangkok to iron out issues pertaining to the goods and services sector. The twenty-sixth and twenty-seventh rounds of negotiations were then held in Melbourne and Zhengzhou province in China, respectively, within the month of July, culminating in yet another ministerial meeting of RCEP trade ministers in Beijing in August. A 3rd RCEP summit was held on 31 October to 3 November in Thailand—which held the ASEAN Chairmanship for the year—with the 35th ASEAN summit on the latter day. During the RCEP Summit, fifteen out of the sixteen nations involved concluded "text-based" negotiations. While it is true that India's decision to opt out of RCEP at the ASEAN+3 Summit in November has stalled negotiations for now, China, Japan, South Korea, Australia, New Zealand and ASEAN are actively pushing for a formal signing to be completed in 2020.[10]

Overall, the salience of ASEAN's ramping up of discussions with China over both the BRI and RCEP in 2019 can be reflected by the grouping's description of this major power as its "most important" dialogue partner—amongst Australia, Canada, the European Union, India, Japan, South Korea, New Zealand, Russia and the United States as the others—during an ASEAN-China ministerial meeting in August. Philippine foreign secretary Teodoro Locsin added that ASEAN's dialogue relations with China "should be the most dynamic and substantive we have in the region". Thai foreign minister Don Pramudwinai backed Mr Locsin's sentiment, saying that it can safely be regarded as ASEAN's position.[11] ASEAN's pegging of its relationship with China stands in stark contrast to how ASEAN-US diplomatic ties soured in 2019.

At the US-ASEAN Summit in early November, President Trump decided to send his advisor on national security affairs, Robert C. O'Brien, to represent him at the meeting. This was a drastic downgrade from the presidents, vice presidents and secretaries of state that had attended this annual summit in previous years. In a bid to show the grouping's overall disappointment, only three ASEAN leaders showed up for the summit: the ASEAN Summit chair, Prime Minister Prayut Chan-o-cha of Thailand; Prime Minister Nguyen Xuan Phuc of Vietnam, who is chairing this year's US-ASEAN Summit; and Prime Minister Thongloun Sisoulith of Laos, the official ASEAN liaison for US officials—in other words, just a troika.[12] As an editorial on this event by the *Japan Times* put it, "ASEAN's displeasure was plain". The article further reported that "Unofficially, regional leaders called the low level of ASEAN representation a snub, noting that it was the first time any participating country had sent a representative lower ranked than foreign minister to the summit."[13] The protocol mismatch was clearly viewed as inappropriate for a summit, putting most members in a quandary.

To make matters worse, the US government positioned itself as a victim in this situation, as one US official described the snub as "an intentional effort to embarrass the President of the United States of America and this will be very damaging to the substance of the ASEAN-US relations". To be sure, the US government is attempting to blunt the damage of this incident in announcing that it is working towards a "special summit" with all ten leaders of ASEAN states on US soil this year—an apparent attempt to create a second iteration of Obama's February 2016 Sunnyland special leaders' summit.[14] Though, as one observer put it, "The message, however, will be unconvincing in Southeast Asia: after all, if Trump can't be bothered to come to the region himself or ensure cabinet-level representation at the ASEAN-US summit, why should ASEAN heads of state and government fly over to the United States?"[15] Overall, this diplomatic faux pas in 2019 has embellished the growing perception in Southeast Asia that the United States is disinterested in the affairs of the region, never mind that in reality the latter is ASEAN's fourth-largest trading partner in terms of goods—with bilateral trade reaching more than US$271 billion in 2018—and that it also continues to serve as the overall security guarantor for Southeast Asia.

Playing Down the South China Sea Dispute

It can be imagined that the approbation of China by ASEAN reported above was likely accorded through gritted teeth by ASEAN officials in what one observer has described as ASEAN's dilemma with China, especially in 2019. The grouping sought to reconcile with the major power's often-conflicting position as a growing economic partner on the one hand and its threat to the stability of the region on the other, specifically through the contention between China and claimant states Brunei, Malaysia, the Philippines and Vietnam over certain waters and features in the South China Sea; disputes that naturally draw in the rest of ASEAN's members, since the matter constitutes a regional issue with high stakes.[16] The South China Sea is of tremendous strategic importance, with one third of the world's shipping passing through it, carrying over US$3 trillion in trade each year. These waters also contain lucrative fisheries, and it is believed that large oil and gas reserves lie beneath the seabed.

In April, Chinese maritime militia—under the cover of fishing vessels—swarmed and blocked the Philippines from approaching Thitu Island.[17] In May, Chinese Coast Guard (CCG) vessel Haijing 35111 obstructed the activities of Malaysia's drilling rig in the area near Luconia Shoal, a thousand miles from the Chinese mainland but ninety miles from East Malaysia.[18] In June, a Chinese vessel rammed and sank a Philippine fishing boat near the disputed Reed Bank area. The Filipino crew were rescued by Vietnamese fishermen. On 3 July, Chinese survey ship Haiyang Dizhi 8 (HD8), escorted by the China Coast Guard and maritime militia, began surveying a large swath of seabed northeast of Vanguard Bank. The area sat within Vietnam's exclusive economic zone (EEZ) and continental shelf. Hanoi responded by sending its own coastguard and fisheries surveillance ships, resulting in a month-long standoff between the two countries. At the peak of the standoff, up to twenty armed vessels from both sides were involved, including China's Haijing 3901. The Haiyang Dizhi 8 briefly left the scene on 7 August, purportedly for a refuelling stop at Fiery Cross Reef, before returning to the disputed waters a week later.[19] Between 4 July and 24 October, China sent HD8 to conduct four seismic surveys in the waters within 200 nautical miles of Vietnam. Some reports indicate that HD8 came as close as around 65 nautical miles from the coast of Phu Yen Province and covered an area of roughly 110,000 square kilometres.[20] At the same time, the Haijing 35111 harassed the Japanese rig Hakuryu-5 chartered by a Vietnamese joint venture with Russia's Rosneft in Block 06.01 in waters about 190 miles southeast of Vietnam.[21]

Despite some voicing of consternation, ASEAN was relatively muted on China's overtures in the South China Sea, as it was the imperative of the grouping to focus on finalizing the Code of Conduct (CoC) within three years, starting from 2019.[22] Until 2017 the discussions and negotiations for a CoC—the concept of which was first raised in the 1990s and agreed upon in 2002—had made little progress while disputes intensified, driven by China's gradual militarization of the various features it had come to occupy: twenty-seven artificial military outposts scattered from the Paracels to the Spratlys by the end of 2019 by some accounts.[23] While fundamental expectations for an area code of conduct continue to differ between China and ASEAN—including on whether it would be legally binding—both sides were able to establish a draft framework at an ASEAN and China senior officials meeting in May 2017 that became the basis for a single draft put forth in August 2018. Chinese premier Li Keqiang himself urged Southeast Asian leaders at the 22nd ASEAN-China Summit held in Bangkok on 3 November to wrap up a "code of conduct" for the South China Sea by 2021.[24] He added that ASEAN's stable relations and "ever stronger" ties have helped them "cope with instability in other parts of the world", and an "ever important landmark is the completion of the first reading of the CoC".[25] A draft chairman's statement from the ASEAN-China Summit "commended" progress towards the code without directly mentioning the series of incidents above that actually sustained tensions.

ASEAN's decision to omit references to recent confrontations can be viewed as a diplomatic victory for China; an outcome assessed by some observers to be entirely possible because, on balance, the Chinese People's Liberation Army (PLA) possesses overwhelming military capabilities in the South China Sea.[26] However, developments after the ASEAN-China Summit belie the veneer of regional conviviality, as Malaysia and Indonesia hardened their positions on the issue of the South China Sea. On 12 December, Malaysia made a surprise submission to the Commission on the Limits of the Continental Shelf under the United Nations over its territorial sea limits in the northern part of the South China Sea.[27] The commission governs the implementation of the UN Convention on the Law of the Sea (UNCLOS) in respect of the establishment of the outer limits of the continental shelf beyond 200 nautical miles from the baselines from which the breadth of the territorial sea is measured. The Malaysian government is seeking to establish the outer limits of its legal continental shelf beyond the 200 nautical mile limit, which will encroach on China's claims over the entire South China Sea.[28] In response, China accused Malaysia of infringing on its sovereignty, saying that the submission "seriously infringed on China's sovereignty, sovereign rights and jurisdiction in the South China Sea".[29] On 30 December, Indonesia publicized that it had protested to China over the presence of a Chinese coastguard vessel in its territorial waters near the disputed South China Sea, saying it marked a "violation of sovereignty". According to Indonesia's foreign ministry, the vessel trespassed into Indonesia's exclusive economic zone off the coast of the northern islands of Natuna.[30]

Thus, it has made sense for ASEAN to continue its strategic prerogative in holding maritime security exercises not only with the United States but increasingly with China to preserve some regional autonomy on matters such as the South China Sea. Of the reported ten maritime exercises conducted between Southeast Asian countries and China in 2019, some of the more notable ones are described here. In April, China and six Southeast Asian countries took part in joint naval exercises off the east coast of Qingdao, Shandong province, called Joint Maritime Drill 2019.[31] The occasion, which coincided with the celebrations of the seventieth anniversary of the founding of the PLA Navy, included the participation of Vice-Admiral Shen Jinlong, commander of the PLA Navy, who promoted the event as part of Beijing's efforts at "building a maritime community with a shared future" with its southern neighbours.[32] In May, Singapore hosted the sea phase of an exercise conducted under the ASEAN Defence Ministers' Meeting-Plus (ADMM-Plus) comprising the ten ASEAN countries as well as Australia, China, Japan, India, South Korea, New Zealand, Russia and the United States. During the exercise, participating navies conducted maritime security drills, such as boarding operations and protection of key installations. Participating countries also practised the Code for Unplanned Encounters at Sea and shared information to track vessels-of-interest.[33] In October, a China-ASEAN Maritime Exercise was conducted off the coast of Zhanjiang in southern China's Guangdong province, which also included six ASEAN countries. This exercise saw an array of drills, with a focus on non-traditional security threats, as well as China's deployment of a 6,000-tonne Guangzhou multi-missile destroyer, the Huangshan type 054A-class frigate and the 10,000-tonne Junshanhu type 961 replenishment ship.

Discounting the Rohingya Crisis

On the 28 December, the UN General Assembly reflected world opinion in approving a resolution condemning human rights abuses against Muslim Rohingya and other minorities in Myanmar. The Myanmar military launched a counterinsurgency operation in 2017 after an insurgent attack. The campaign targeted Rohingya areas and allegedly saw atrocities committed against civilians who were driven from their homes. Thousands of Rohingya were killed and more than 700,000 fled to neighbouring Bangladesh during an army crackdown in the Buddhist-majority country in 2017. Myanmar has also been suspected of using rape and murder to persecute its Rohingya Muslim minority. The UN resolution also calls on Myanmar to stop the incitement of hatred against the Rohingya and other minorities. It highlighted the findings of an independent international mission "of gross human rights violations and abuses suffered by Rohingya Muslims and other minorities" by Myanmar's security forces, which the mission described as "the gravest crimes under international law". The resolution called on Myanmar to protect all groups and to ensure justice for all cases of violations of human rights. It was passed by a total of 134 countries in the 193-member world body, with 9 votes against and 28 abstaining.[34]

The UN resolution is also a reflection of ASEAN's continuing inability to exert significant pressure on Myanmar to curb its campaigns against the Rohingya. The perceived impotence of the grouping in dealing with what many quarters of the global community believe to be a case of genocide in its own backyard was already made very stark when Gambia, a small, Muslim-majority West African nation, filed a case to the International Court of Justice (ICJ) on 11 November—on behalf of dozens of other Muslim countries—accusing Myanmar of genocide against its Muslim-minority Rohingya people and urging the ICJ to order measures to "stop Myanmar's genocidal conduct immediately".[35] On 10 December, Myanmar's leader Aung San Suu Kyi was compelled to appear at the ICJ to defend her country against the accusations.

As in previous years, ASEAN member states remain committed to the association's cardinal principles of non-interference in the internal affairs of a member state and making any decision only by consensus, therefore leading to the overall avoidance of the Rohingya crisis. As in the case of previous countries holding the ASEAN Chair issuing the annual ASEAN statements and communiqués, Thailand, which held the seat for 2019, obfuscated on the Rohingya crisis, allowing the Myanmar government to hold on to its narrative that it is tackling an extremist threat. To be sure, Indonesian delegates during the ASEAN Inter-Parliamentary Assembly on 25 August did propose a resolution entitled "Responding to the Humanitarian Crisis of the Rohingya People". However, it was rejected because there was no consensus. As in past years, it will likely continue to be the case that paragraphs on the Rohingya issue will be placed in the social and cultural section of the ASEAN Summit and ministerial statements—positioning the matter as a social and cultural issue rather than a political, security or human rights issue—at Myanmar's insistence.[36]

In addition, a final statement from the 34th ASEAN Summit in July supported Myanmar's efforts to "facilitate the voluntary return of displaced persons in a safe, secure and dignified manner", omitting the term *Rohingya* altogether. In late August, ASEAN did attempt to put some teeth into this statement by deploying an observation team to Myanmar to witness the country's third attempt to facilitate the return of displaced Rohingya Muslims. The government dispatched buses to Cox's Bazaar tasked with bringing back some three thousand Rohingya refugees to their place of abode in Rakhine State. However, like the first and second attempts in November 2018 and July 2019, the refugees refused to board the buses for the return in the belief that it was unsafe for them to do so, that they would not be able to return to their original villages, and that they would not have a pathway to citizenship. To their defence each time, the

Myanmar authorities blamed the presence of the Arakan Rohingya Salvation Army (ARSA) for this outcome, arguing that the group was operating in Cox's Bazaar and deterring Rohingya from boarding the buses. The Myanmar authorities also accused the Bangladeshi government of not doing enough to facilitate the return of the Rohingya Muslims.

Prior to the 34th ASEAN Summit, Human Rights Watch (HRW) urged leaders of ASEAN not to rush to get involved in the repatriation of the Rohingya without addressing the root causes of their displacement. It also advocated that ASEAN countries "drastically rethink their response" to the plight of the Rohingya.[37] This was especially in the face of a fifty-six-page leaked ASEAN report entitled "Emergency Response and Assessment Team", which, according to the rights group, was developed without input from Rohingya refugees and which "almost entirely" disregards the Myanmar government's atrocities that led to the mass displacement.[38] The report predicted voluntary returns would be complete in two years and refused to acknowledge the Rohingya people. The executive director of HRW's Asia Division, Brad Williams, said that "ASEAN seems intent on discussing the future of the Rohingya without condemning—or even acknowledging—the Myanmar military's ethnic cleansing campaign against them. It's preposterous for ASEAN leaders to be discussing the repatriation of a traumatised population into the hands of the security forces who killed, raped, and robbed them."[39]

Strong statements on the Rohingya crisis by Malaysia's prime minister Dr Mahathir Mohamad after the 34th ASEAN Summit reinforced the assertions by human rights observers. This is not the first time the Malaysian government has broken ranks with its ASEAN counterparts on the Rohingya crisis. In November 2018, during the 33rd ASEAN Summit held in Singapore, Dr Mahathir castigated Myanmar civilian leader Aung San Suu Kyi for defending the military's crackdown on the Rohingya. In September of that year, Dr Mahathir gave an address at the UNGA in which he blamed Myanmar's authorities for closing their eyes to the fate of Muslims in Rakhine state. In September 2017, when the ASEAN Ministers meeting in New York issued a statement on the subject, Malaysia publicly disassociated itself from the document a few hours after it was released. The Malaysian government argued that the statement did not accurately reflect developments on the ground.

In general, despite the attempts by Indonesia and Malaysia to call out the Rohingya crisis for what it appears to be, ASEAN remains generally unable to effectively handle a serious human rights crisis manifested by one of its member countries. To be fair, individual ASEAN member states have made bilateral contributions to Myanmar, Bangladesh and international relief organizations to provide aid to displaced persons. Earlier in October 2017, ASEAN Ministers also agreed to dispatch eighty tons of relief aid to assist internally displaced persons in Rakhine State. Nevertheless, human rights observers continue to accuse ASEAN of prioritizing diplomacy over human rights concerns.

Conclusion

ASEAN and its member states have had to adjust to the realities and impact of the ongoing US-China trade war that has dampened economic growth, especially for countries dependent on Chinese supply chains. Trade diversion and the inflow of foreign investment as a result of the trade war are expected to confer net benefits to ASEAN countries in the medium to long term, provided they can hold on to existing multilateral endeavours and strengthen them, invest in infrastructure and production capacity, and increase regional supply chain integration. ASEAN members have sought to break out from the impasse of being sidelined in the regional power play of the United States and China. Despite adhering to a hedging strategy in dealing with China and the United States in the region's management of major power politics, ASEAN countries have telegraphed a heightened consideration of China as both a dialogue and a free-trade partner. Indeed, ASEAN stepped up its efforts in finalizing the RCEP linking ASEAN member states with their six FTA partners comprising China, Japan, South Korea, Australia, New Zealand and India. ASEAN member states are generally aware that both the BRI and RCEP pose a risk of increasing the spread of Chinese influence across the region beyond economic matters. Yet, the trade war prosecuted by the United States against China since July 2018 has tilted ASEAN's risk calculus towards the merits offered by RCEP over the trade-offs. A stronger consideration of China's political and economic role in the region muted the assertions of claimant states against China over disputed features and waters in the South China Sea for most of 2019 until the closing months of that year. Lastly, member states have sought to put aside ongoing challenges that invariably erode regional unity (such as the Rohingya problem emanating from Myanmar, as one of several examples discussed in this chapter) in order to capitalize on the potentially greater gains from tackling common external crises collectively. At the level of principle, the majority of Southeast Asian states, for now, have prioritized political and economic cohesion over certain social norms and aspirations (that have yet to be fully worked out), to avoid rocking the lifeboat that is ASEAN whose members rely on to help them navigate more effectively through a polarizing and fluid international environment.

Notes

1. ESCAP report cited in Sidney Leng, "Trade War Lands Asian Exports in Worst Condition since the Global Financial Crisis", *South China Morning Post*, 21 December 2019, https://www.scmp.com/economy/global-economy/article/3042989/trade-war-lands-asian-exports-worst-condition-global; see also "Global Trade War and Rising Protectionism Taking Toll on Asia Pacific, SEA Remains Bright Spot", *Business Times*, 13 December 2019, https://www.businesstimes.com.sg/asean-business/global-trade-war-and-rising-protectionism-taking-toll-on-asia-pacific-sea-remains.
2. Chad Bray, "Asian Markets Likely to Remain Volatile in 2020 as US-China Trade War Continues to Unnerve Investors", *South China Morning Post*, 30 November 2019, https://www.scmp.com/business/companies/article/3039957/asian-markets-likely-remain-volatile-2020-us-china-trade-war.
3. Asian Development Bank, "Asian Development Outlook Supplement", December 2019, https://www.adb.org/sites/default/files/publication/543066/ado-supplement-december-2019.pdf; "ASEAN Growth Slower Than Forecasted", *ASEAN Post*, 4 January 2020, https://theaseanpost.com/article/asean-growth-slower-forecasted.
4. Jason Thomas, "Vietnam Biggest Winner from US-China Trade War", *ASEAN Post*, 11 June 2019, https://theaseanpost.com/article/vietnam-biggest-winner-us-china-trade-war.
5. "Asean Countries Benefiting from Trade War: Maybank Kim Eng", *Business Times*, 10 July 2019, https://www.businesstimes.com.sg/asean-business/asean-countries-benefiting-from-trade-war-maybank-kim-eng.
6. Alec Lei, "Is Southeast Asia Winning the US-China Trade War? Not So Fast", *The Diplomat*, 5 September 2019, https://thediplomat.com/2019/09/is-southeast-asia-winning-the-us-china-trade-war-not-so-fast/.
7. "China Picks Up the U.S. Trade Fumble", *Wall Street Journal*, 17 November 2016, https://www.wsj.com/articles/china-picks-up-the-u-s-trade-fumble-1479404990.
8. Ian Bremmer, "How Trump Gave China a Win on Trade in Southeast Asia", *Time*, 7 November 2019, https://time.com/5720756/china-trade-trump-win-southeast-asia/.
9. Liu Zhen, "US Trade War and Japan Push Raise Prospects for China-Backed Asia Free-Trade Deal", *South China Morning Post*, 2 September 2018, https://www.scmp.com/news/china/diplomacy/article/2162395/japans-relations-china-back-normal-track-says-shinzo-abe.
10. "China, Japan, South Korea to Push for RCEP Signing in 2020", *Straits Times*, 24 December 2019, https://www.straitstimes.com/asia/east-asia/china-japan-south-korea-to-push-for-rcep-signing-in-2020.
11. Ronron Calunsod, "China Rises to Become ASEAN's 'Most Important' Dialogue Partner", *Kyodo News*, 5 August 2019, https://english.kyodonews.net/news/2019/08/a595858c0b1b-focus-china-rises-to-become-aseans-most-important-dialogue-partner.html

12. Natnicha Chuwiruch and Philip Heijmans, "Asean Leaders Snub U.S. Summit after Trump Skips Bangkok Meeting", Bloomberg, 4 November 2019, https://www.bloomberg.com/news/articles/2019-11-04/asean-leaders-snub-u-s-summit-after-trump-skips-bangkok-meeting.
13. "Troubling Developments at ASEAN Summit", *Japan Times*, 6 November 2019, https://www.japantimes.co.jp/opinion/2019/11/06/editorials/troubling-developments-asean-summit/#.XhayZxczYWo.
14. "Trump Invites ASEAN Leaders to 'Special Summit' in US after Skipping Bangkok Meet", Channel NewsAsia, 4 November 2019, https://www.channelnewsasia.com/news/asia/trump-invites-asean-leaders-special-summit-us-after-skip-bangkok-12061480.
15. Ankit Panda, "How Not to Win Friends and Influence the Indo-Pacific", *The Diplomat*, 6 November 2019, https://thediplomat.com/2019/11/how-not-to-win-friends-and-influence-the-indo-pacific/.
16. Trinh Le, "ASEAN's China Dilemma", *The Diplomat*, 29 October 2019, https://thediplomat.com/2019/10/aseans-china-dilemma/.
17. Andreo Calonzo and Ditas B. Lopez, "Philippines Alarmed by Roughly 200 Chinese Ships Near Disputed Island", Bloomberg, 9 April 2019, https://www.bloomberg.com/news/articles/2019-04-01/china-s-200-odd-ships-near-disputed-island-spur-philippine-alarm.
18. "China Attempts to 'Intimidate' its Neighbors' Offshore Drilling Rigs", *Maritime Executive*, 17 July 2019, https://www.maritime-executive.com/article/china-attempts-to-intimidate-its-neighbors-offshore-drilling-rigs.
19. Trinh Le, "China's Dominance on Display in the South China Sea", *The Diplomat*, 28 August 2019, https://thediplomat.com/2019/08/chinas-dominance-on-display-in-the-south-china-sea/.
20. Do Thanh Hai, "Vietnam Confronts China in the South China Sea", East Asia Forum, 6 December 2019, https://www.eastasiaforum.org/2019/12/06/vietnam-confronts-china-in-the-south-china-sea/.
21. Asia Maritime Transparency Initiative and the Center for Strategic and International Studies, "China Risks Flare-up over Malaysian, Vietnamese Gas Resources", 13 December 2019, https://amti.csis.org/china-risks-flare-up-over-malaysian-vietnamese-gas-resources/.
22. "Asean to Focus on COC while Playing Down South China Sea Dispute", *The Nation*, 1 November 2019, https://www.nationthailand.com/news/30377972.
23. Trinh Le, "China's Dominance on Display".
24. "Asean Summit: Beijing Says 'Ready to Work' with Asean on South China Sea Rules", *Straits Times*, 3 November 2019, https://www.straitstimes.com/asia/se-asia/beijing-says-ready-to-work-with-asean-on-south-china-sea-rules.
25. "Cliff Nenzon, Beijing Presses ASEAN Anew for South China Sea Code by 2021",

Nikkei Review, 3 November 2019, https://asia.nikkei.com/Politics/International-relations/Beijing-presses-ASEAN-anew-for-South-China-Sea-code-by-2021.
26. Yoji Koda, "Countering Beijing's South China Sea strategy", *Japan Times*, 10 December 2019, https://www.japantimes.co.jp/opinion/2019/12/10/commentary/japan-commentary/countering-beijings-south-china-sea-strategy/#.XhMNGBczYWo.
27. "Beijing Censures Malaysia over Fresh South China Sea Claim", *Straits Times*, 17 December 2019, https://www.straitstimes.com/asia/se-asia/china-objects-to-malaysias-un-submission-on-south-china-sea-report.
28. "Malaysia's Surprise Submission over Continental Shelf Limits Irks China", *The Independent*, 17 December 2019, http://theindependent.sg/malaysias-surprise-submission-over-continental-shelf-limits-irks-china/.
29. "Beijing Urges UN Commission Not to Consider Malaysian Claim in South China Sea", *South China Morning Post*, 17 December 2019, https://www.scmp.com/news/china/diplomacy/article/3042333/beijing-urges-un-commission-not-consider-malaysian-claim-south.
30. "Indonesia Protests 'Violation of Sovereignty' by Chinese Coastguard Vessel", *South China Morning Post*, 30 December 2019, https://www.scmp.com/news/asia/southeast-asia/article/3043998/indonesia-balks-violation-sovereignty-chinese-coastguard.
31. Minnie Chan, "China Begins Joint Naval Drills with Six Southeast Asian Nations", *South China Morning Post*, 26 April 2019, https://www.scmp.com/news/china/military/article/3007804/china-begins-joint-naval-drills-six-southeast-asian-nations.
32. Richard Heydarian, "Heavy Traffic in South China Sea: US Vies with China in Joint Naval Drills with Asean Members", *South China Morning Post*, 7 September 2019, https://www.scmp.com/news/china/diplomacy/article/3026142/heavy-traffic-south-china-sea-us-vies-china-joint-naval-drills.
33. "18-Country Maritime Exercise to Conclude at Changi Naval Base on Monday", *Straits Times*, 12 May 2019, https://www.straitstimes.com/singapore/multilateral-maritime-exercise-to-conclude-at-changi-naval-base-on-monday.
34. "Myanmar Rohingya: UN Condemns Human Rights Abuses", BBC, 28 December 2019, https://www.bbc.com/news/world-asia-50931565.
35. "Gambia Files Genocide Case against Myanmar", Deutsche Welle, 11 November 2019, https://www.dw.com/en/gambia-files-genocide-case-against-myanmar/a-51199168.
36. "The Rohingya Problem: Is There an ASEAN Solution in Sight?", *ASEAN Today*, 26 December 2019, https://www.aseantoday.com/2019/09/the-rohingya-problem-is-there-an-asean-solution-in-sight/.
37. "ASEAN Must Not Turn a Blind Eye to Rohingya Crisis: Rights groups", Al Jazeera, June 2019, https://www.aljazeera.com/news/2019/06/asean-turn-blind-eye-rohingya-crisis-rights-groups-190619091135258.html.
38. Sheith Khidhir, "Sending the Rohingya Home to Die?", *ASEAN Post*, 18 September 2019, https://theaseanpost.com/article/sending-rohingya-home-die.
39. "ASEAN Must Not Turn a Blind Eye", Al Jazeera.

ECONOMIC OVERVIEW OF SOUTHEAST ASIA

Manu Bhaskaran

This chapter provides an overarching view of macroeconomic trends in Southeast Asia in 2019.

The current state of the regional economies is first assessed. In general, the regional economies had to face a troubled global environment but demonstrated an encouraging degree of resilience in doing so.

The cyclical prospects are then considered. Two key factors will drive the outlook for next year. The first is how the global economy pans out—especially whether an improvement in the trade picture allows a recovery in business confidence and capital spending. A second factor is the impact of supportive monetary and fiscal policies.

Finally, a review of developments this year that shaped key drivers of the secular regional outlook is conducted. Four key drivers are identified and are likely to be supportive of an improved growth outlook in the medium term—infrastructure spending, synergies from economic integration initiatives, production relocation out of China and an improved business ecosystem.

Section 1: Recent Trends in the Regional Economies

Two contrasting themes characterized economic developments in Southeast Asia in 2019—growing challenges and a surprising degree of resilience. The regional economies had to contend with a turbulent global environment in 2019. Global demand for Asian exports was subdued, depressing economic growth and commodity prices in a region that remains heavily trade-dependent. Nevertheless, the region

---

MANU BHASKARAN is CEO of Centennial Asia Advisors, an independent economic research firm, and Adjunct Senior Fellow at the Institute of Policy Studies, Lee Kuan Yew School of Public Policy, National University of Singapore.

demonstrated a degree of resilience: economic growth continued, albeit modestly, while external stability was maintained. This relatively benign outcome was partly the payoff to the improved capacity for policy response in the region—and it builds a good base for future economic performance.

A confluence of disturbances hurt the global economy in 2019. Global economic activity began to weaken from around the middle of 2018 onwards and the decline persisted through 2019. As a result, global economic growth eased, from 3.8 per cent in 2017 to 3.6 per cent in 2018 and then to an estimated 3.0 per cent in 2019 according to the International Monetary Fund (Figure 1).[1] In parallel, the world economy saw a pronounced slowing in export demand (Figure 2). Not surprisingly, the World Trade Organization (WTO) became more cautious about world trade prospects. It revised down its expected growth of global trade flows in 2019 to 1.2 per cent from the earlier forecast of 2.6 per cent. It further concluded that the risks were to the downside given the headwinds created by more trade restrictions as well as the likelihood of slower growth in the developed economies.[2]

The Trade War, among Other Factors, Depressed Global Business Confidence

The most prominent disturbance was the trade friction between the United States and China, which grew in intensity as the year progressed. The tariffs imposed by each side on the other aroused concerns that the delicate supply chains throughout the region that exposed China's neighbouring economies to stresses in its economy could be damaged. Moreover, the United States also imposed restrictions on China's access to American technology, causing some anxiety over how disruptive a potential bifurcation of the technology world into separate American and Chinese spheres could be for regional countries caught between two contending superpowers.

Compounding the aggressive trade actions by the United States was the uncertainty over how and when this trade friction might be resolved. There were also concerns whether such a resolution would simply result in an increasingly aggressive American trade policy switching the focus of its trade to other Asian economies, many of which run large trade surpluses with the United States, and which the current American administration finds unacceptable. This concern was reinforced by the Trump administration's identification, during the course of the year, of certain Southeast Asian economies as potential "currency manipulators".

It was not only trade friction that depressed global business confidence. Many other factors also played a role. In the Middle East, a proliferation of political

Economic Overview of Southeast Asia

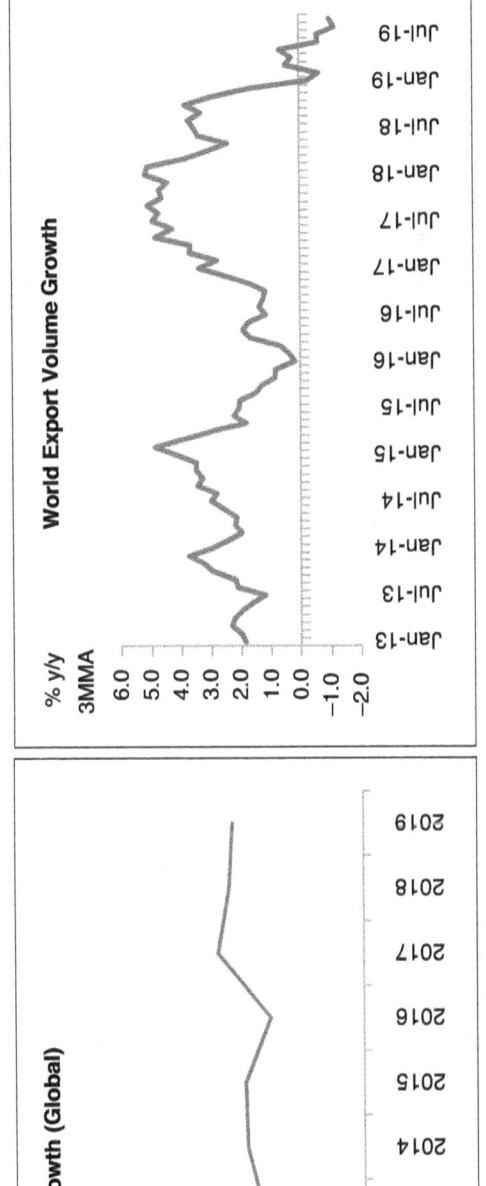

FIGURE 1
Slowing global growth...

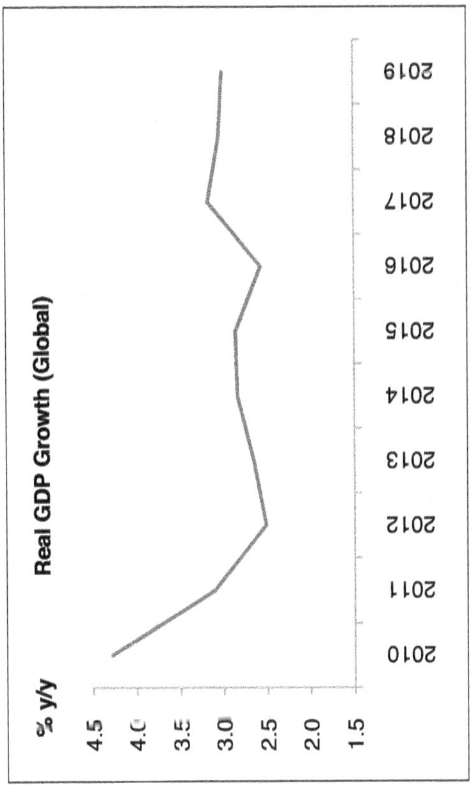

FIGURE 2
...led to weaker global trade

Source: IMF, CPB World Trade Monitor, Centennial Asia Advisors.

hot spots raised worries about the threat to oil prices and the supply of oil, a concern validated by the attack on Saudi Arabian oil facilities that temporarily took half of the latter's oil production out of the market. The unpredictability of Brexit and its potential damage to the European economies did not help either. And, quite apart from the impact of the trade war, China's economy was also hurt by financial stresses, the scale and threat of which were hard to quantify.

The result of these disturbances was to depress business confidence across the world. Corporate executives felt unable to assess the outlook for demand and, more fundamentally, whether their existing supply chains might need to undergo a painful restructuring as a result of the trade friction and the potential bifurcation of the technology world. In this context, few business leaders were prepared to make big bets such as adding sizeable new production capacity or leveraging as quickly as they would normally have on new technologies that were opening up new business opportunities. As a result, growth in capital spending eased considerably (Figure 3). As much of Southeast Asia's manufacturing capacity is oriented around the fabrication of components, especially electronic ones used in capital equipment, the deceleration of capital spending around the world hit regional exports of manufactured goods, causing trade growth to slow.

In addition to the problems created by trade friction, there were also sector-specific shocks in certain industries, which contributed to slower growth:

- In the electronics industry, an imbalance between supply and demand had led to an accumulation of inventories in certain segments, such as semiconductors. An inventory adjustment then depressed production activity for much of 2019. This impact was pronounced in the semiconductor industry (Figure 4).
- In the automobile sector, a number of one-off challenges related to policy changes affecting the sector emerged in major markets, such as Germany, China and India. These caused the industry—which the International Monetary Fund estimates at 5.7 per cent of global output—to undergo a correction that had a material impact on global growth. In addition to these transitory headwinds, the sector is undergoing the early stages of a major disruption caused by emerging new technologies. Major producers, such as some in Germany who had not invested in electric vehicle technology, have now been forced to restructure their businesses.
- The aviation sector also experienced a shock when Boeing Corporation's travails with its Boeing 737 MAX jetliner led to a sharp contraction in orders for new airliners.

Economic Overview of Southeast Asia 23

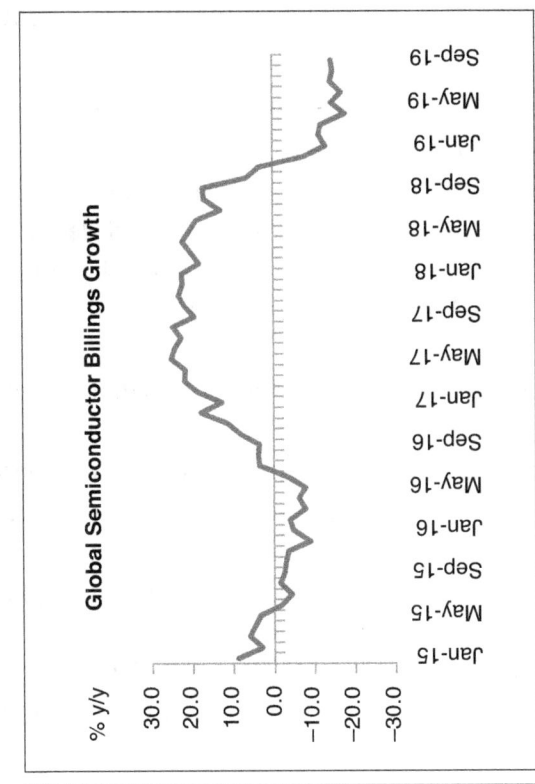

FIGURE 4
Global semiconductor billings growth

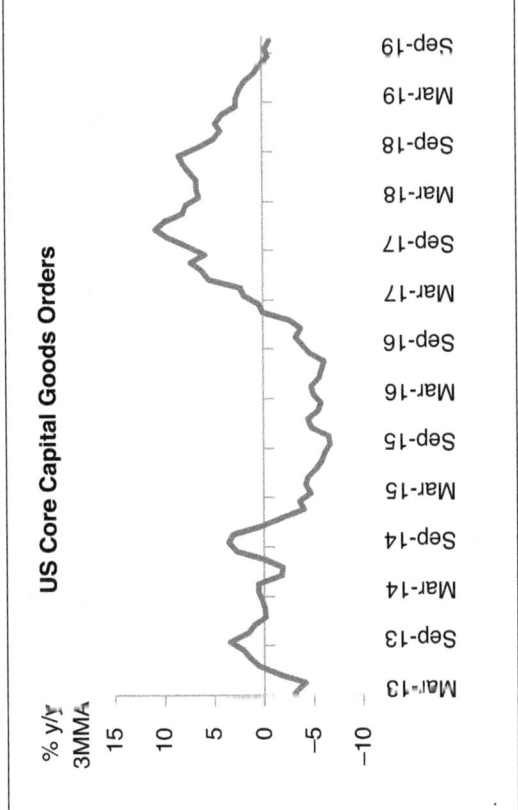

FIGURE 3
Weak capital spending

Source: CEIC, Centennial Asia Advisors.

However, Southeast Asian Economies Demonstrated a Degree of Resilience

Table 1 summarizes how the main Southeast Asian economies performed in 2019. A number of characteristics stood out in 2019's economic performance.

First, economic growth decelerated compared to 2018, with Singapore's heavily trade-dependent economy suffering the most marked deceleration. However, the slowdown in economic activity was not as substantial as many had feared, given the global headwinds. A number of factors explain this:

- **Domestic demand held up**: Consumer spending remained firm despite a small loss of momentum. Even in Singapore, where domestic demand usually plays a subordinate role, there were pockets of resilience in areas such as the increased spending on digitalization and in areas such as education and healthcare.
- **Export diversification**: Again, taking the example of the economy most sensitive to trade, Singapore, there were export segments such as pharmaceuticals whose prospects were less damaged by the trade friction and which therefore were able to provide a floor to export contraction.

TABLE 1
Overview of Economic Trends in Southeast Asia in 2019

Country	GDP Growth	Inflation	Current Account	Currency	Policy Stance
Indonesia	Firm but below potential	Decelerating	Deficit contained	Stable	Monetary easing; Fiscal stable
Malaysia	Firm; more resilient than expected	Stable	Surplus	Stable	Monetary easing; Fiscal more or less neutral
Philippines	Firm but below potential	Decelerating	Stable	Stable	Monetary easing; Fiscal neutral
Singapore	Weak, with pockets of resilience	Very low	Large surplus	Modest appreciation	Monetary policy eased
Thailand	Weak	Very low	Surplus	Strong	Monetary and fiscal easing
Vietnam	Firm	Up modestly	Surplus	Stabilizing	Easing

Source: Collated by Centennial Asia Advisors.

- **Trade diversion**: One response of manufacturers to increased American tariffs on Chinese-made goods was to switch the sourcing of goods exported to the United States from Chinese factories to other low-cost producers—countries in Southeast Asia were big winners from this trend. For example, media reports[3] quoted a report by Nomura that found that Vietnam's gain from the trade diverted from China is equivalent to 7.9 per cent of its GDP.

Second, while regional currencies weakened a little in response to a stronger US dollar and currency weakness in China, these currencies were generally stable (Figure 5) compared to most other emerging economy currencies. The performance of Southeast Asian currencies was a marked improvement compared to previous periods of global financial market turbulence, such as in mid-2013. As a result, inflation remained low, with Thailand and Singapore in particular experiencing markedly low inflation rates.

Third, one reason for this relatively good performance was the impact of improved policy capacity. Following the "taper tantrums" of 2013 (when hints of a possible tightening in United States' monetary policy caused financial markets in emerging economies to lose value sharply as a result of massive and abrupt capital outflows), regional policymakers made substantial efforts to boost their inflation-fighting credibility. Figure 6 shows the example of Indonesia—its inflation rate has begun to converge with the inflation rates of its main trading partners as Bank Indonesia came to grips with controlling domestic inflation. Their external deficits were also better contained, as seen in Figure 7—for instance, the Indonesian government took measures in 2018 to slow import-intensive investments, which helped to rein in the current account deficit. In addition, policymakers also pursued relatively cautious fiscal policies that kept public sector debt under control (Figure 8).

In short, 2019 was a difficult year for the regional economies but sound economic management helped to cushion the ill effects. Getting the basics of macro-economic policymaking right is not sexy but it produces outsized benefits in challenging times.

Section 2: The Cyclical Outlook – Prospects for 2020

The region's economic outlook hinges on two sets of factors—how the global economy pans out and the effectiveness of domestic policy responses.

FIGURE 5
Regional currencies remained firm

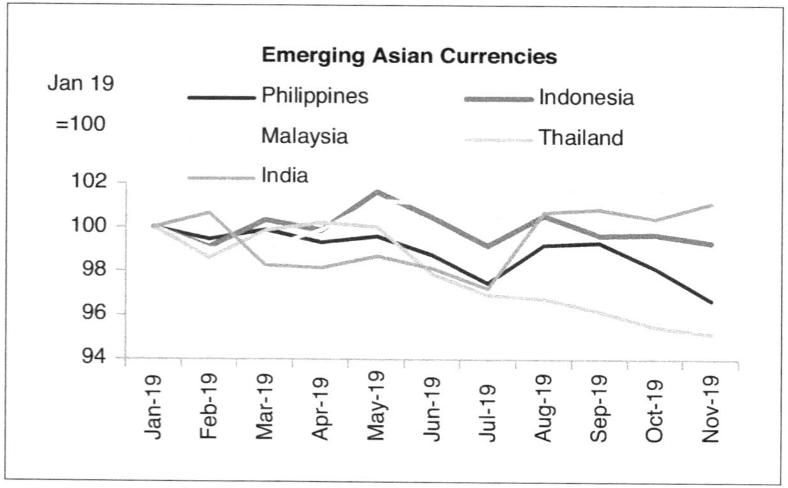

FIGURE 6
Inflation differentials narrowed

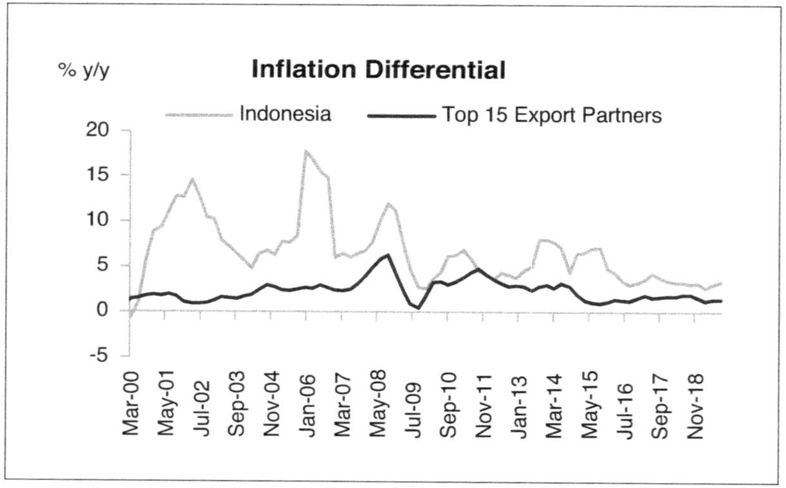

Source: CEIC, Centennial Asia Advisors.

Economic Overview of Southeast Asia

FIGURE 7
Current account deficits contained

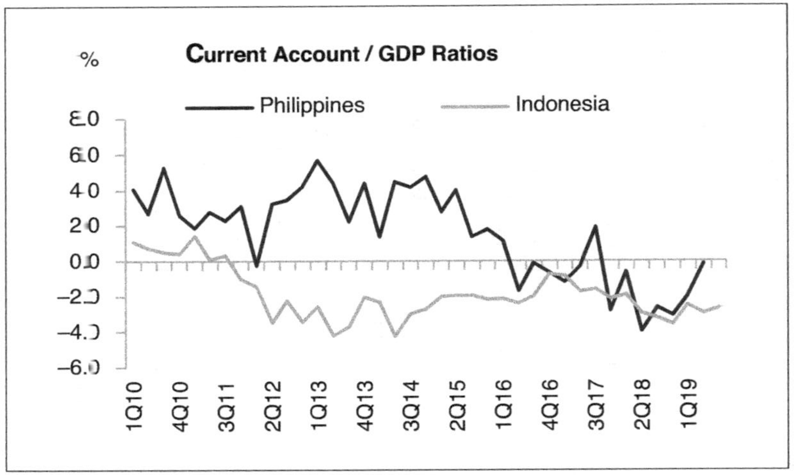

FIGURE 8
Public sector debt remains low

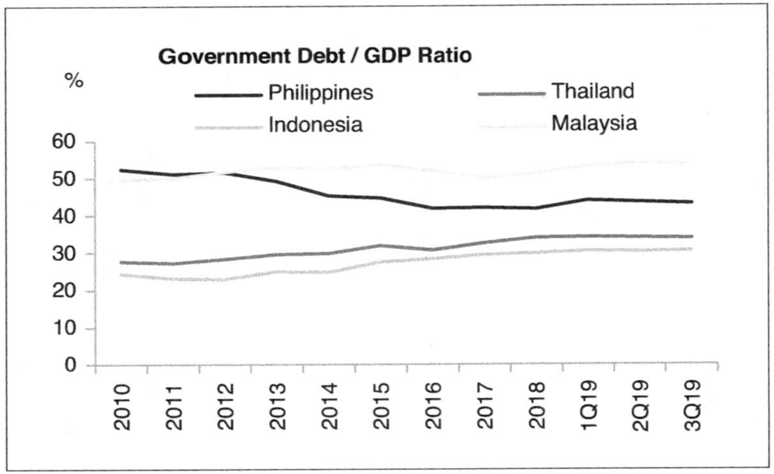

Source: CEIC, Bank of International Settlements, Centennial Asia Advisors.

Major Global Factors That Will Impact 2020 Performance

The single most important driver of regional performance will be what happens to global business confidence.

This in turn will depend on a number of factors, but the one that matters the most would be whether the United States and China can resolve their trade differences and so step back from an outright trade war. As this is written, both countries are negotiating a "phase one" trade deal that will address the more easily resolvable differences. If such an interim deal can be secured, it will prevent an unruly escalation of trade aggression, which will be a relief to businesses everywhere. That relief would be all the greater should such a deal then allow the two big powers to begin serious negotiations on a "phase two" deal that will delve into more difficult issues such as the alleged theft of intellectual property by China, reported instances of forced technology transfer, and China's industrial policy. Even if this "phase two" deal takes a long time to produce an agreement, the very fact that the two countries were talking rather than mounting tit-for-tat actions against each other would soothe business concerns.

Another factor would be demand for electronic components, since that segment carries an important weight in the region's manufacturing production. Two developments would support a rebound in demand. One is that the inventory adjustment is completed quickly, thus allowing production to again respond to growth in demand—the latest data suggests that destocking had progressed well in areas such as semiconductors and that a recovery was likely in 2020. An additional variable is how underlying demand in the sector might be bolstered, as rapid technological progress produced compelling improvements in the profitability of capital spending. There were signs in the recent trade data for South Korea and Taiwan that this was beginning to happen. For instance, the proliferation of data centres in the United States had led to an improvement in demand for semiconductors and computers.

Beyond the recovery in global business confidence, a number of other forces could help the region's prospects:

- A turnaround in the automobile and aviation sectors, which as explained above had suffered one-off shocks, would also help improve global economic activity and trade to the benefit of the region's manufacturers.
- An improvement in commodity prices: For the region's farmers, the key prices would be crude palm oil (Figure 9), rice and rubber. In the second half of 2019, a rebound in crude palm oil prices began, with many analysts confident that the recovery while modest could be sustained because of government policies in Indonesia and Malaysia to encourage use of crude palm oil in the

production of fuel. In Thailand, agricultural prices improved in the course of 2019, allowing a modest recovery in farm incomes. However, other key commodity prices such as thermal coal (Figure 10), which is important for Indonesia, remained lacklustre.

- Oil prices: Except for Malaysia, most of the countries in the region are net oil importers. With oil production in the United States continuing to expand because of the shale oil revolution and with new sources of supply coming on stream such as in Guyana, the oil price outlook will be sensitive to how effective the Organization of Petroleum Exporting Countries (OPEC) will be in securing an agreement among member countries to reduce oil supplies further. The International Energy Agency has upgraded its expectations of non-OPEC oil supply growth from 1.8 million barrels per day (mbpd) for 2019 to 2.3 mbpd in 2020.[4] This should help restrain oil prices to the current range or to slightly below the range that prevailed through 2019—a relief for the region.

Impact of Domestic Counter-cyclical Policies

Since the middle of 2019, a clear commitment by the systemically important central banks to ease monetary policies has given more room for Southeast Asian central banks to ease monetary policy. The Federal Reserve Bank of the United States has been cutting policy rates and has indicated that it might continue cutting rates if there were any warning signs of a slowdown. The European Central Bank has also cut rates and committed to continued quantitative easing.

As a result, Southeast Asian central banks have cut their policy rates and eased monetary conditions through other means such as reductions in reserve requirements. So long as inflation remains low and current account deficits well behaved, the region's central banks will retain the policy space to continue easing policy if they wish.

The governments of the region have also indicated that they will use fiscal policy more vigorously in 2020. In particular, infrastructure spending is likely to pick up momentum after one-off factors in 2019 caused such spending to slow in Indonesia, Thailand and the Philippines.

Section 3: Secular Forces Promoting Improved Development Prospects in the Region

The past year has seen signs of several drivers of long-term growth falling into place in the region. In particular, we would point to four such drivers that have

FIGURE 9
Palm oil beginning to turn around

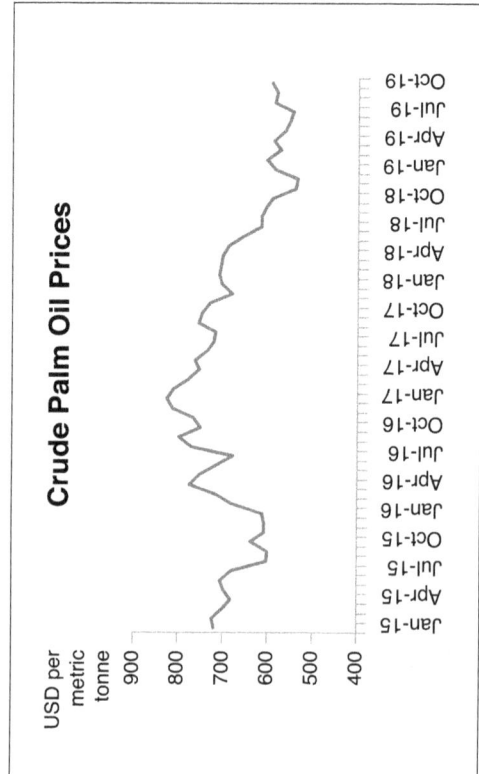

FIGURE 10
...but not others

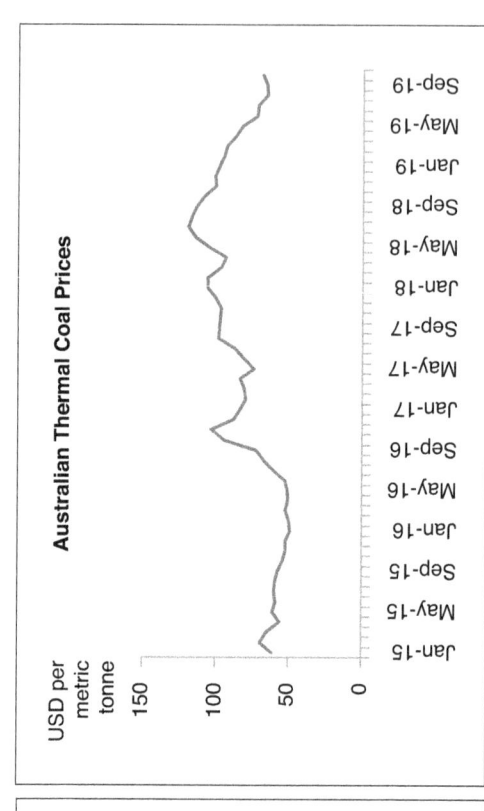

Source: World Bank Pink Sheet, Centennial Asia Advisors.

TABLE 2
Summary of Monetary Policy Moves in Southeast Asia

Country	Changes in Monetary Policy in 2019	Indications of further policy moves
Indonesia	Bank Indonesia has been aggressive in cutting policy rates (ytd: 100bps) to spruce up the economy. Bank Indonesia is also leaning on macroprudential tools (i.e., reserve requirement cuts or RRR and relaxing loan-to-value ratios) to boost liquidity and credit growth.	Further monetary accommodation in 1H20 by way of rate cuts and easing of macroprudential policy as growth comes under pressure, conditioned on stable rupiah and current account deficit.
Malaysia	Brief pause after a 25 basis points (bps) cut in May as economy remains resilient to date.	Another cut to follow in 1H20 to buoy the economy as uncertainty takes a toll on growth.
Philippines	The central bank is treading very carefully with policy rate cuts (75bps) and RRR reductions (200bps), which are being conducted in a staggered manner.	The central bank is to step up rate cuts in 1H20, along with more measured RRR cuts, as it remains wary of any upside surprise to price pressures.
Singapore	Modest reduction in rate of pace of appreciation of the nominal effective exchange rate in October.	Improving growth outlook will probably remove the need for further easing.
Thailand	Policy rate lowered by 25 bps in Aug 19 and again in Nov 19 to a record low of 1.25 per cent.	Central bank has taken a bearish view on growth; one more rate cut in 1H20 cannot be ruled out if the economy does not improve.
Vietnam	Four key policy rates were cut by 25 bps in Sep 19.	No further easing; policy rates are delinked from actual lending rates.

become prominent—infrastructure spending, production relocation, synergies from economic integration, and supply side improvements.

Infrastructure Spending

Governments across Southeast Asia are placing more emphasis on infrastructure as a driver of growth, and this was seen in rising public spending on infrastructure as a share of GDP (Figures 11 and 12). In Indonesia, the Philippines, Malaysia and Singapore, spending on public works projects as a share of GDP is on an uptrend.

Production Relocation

In the initial stages of the trade war, firms whose products were affected by tariffs responded by expanding production in existing manufacturing facilities in other jurisdictions—this was the trade diversion alluded to in Section 1. However, with the further deterioration in US-China relations, this trade diversion has now given way to actual reconfiguration of supply chains.

The relocation of production facilities is in full swing and is likely to accelerate. It is not just foreign firms that are packing; Chinese manufacturers that have been hit by US tariffs have also thrown in their lot with the exodus of firms out of China. A survey by the American Chamber of Commerce in Shanghai[5] showed that the optimism levels of American firms have fallen with respect to the medium- and long-term business outlook to the lowest levels in many years, despite the fact that actual business performance remained strong. Though the survey covered only American enterprises, the results probably reflect sentiment amongst foreign firms more broadly.

The survey showed that the share of firms that remain optimistic about the future fell by one fifth from the previous year to 61.4, against historical rates of 80–90 per cent. In addition, *pessimism* about the future shot up 14.0 percentage points—a significant increase (Figure 13). The report noted that non-consumer electronics and chemicals were among the most downbeat of industries. On the other hand, the pharmaceuticals and life sciences sector was among the most positive because of the accelerated approval of foreign drugs earlier in the year.

Table 3 provides a detailed list of examples of companies that have been moving production out of China and where they are moving to.

As US-China tensions persist and as Southeast Asian economies continue to improve their economic fundamentals, the pace of production relocation is set to accelerate. Production relocation is likely to be an important engine of regional growth.

Synergies from Economic integration

Over the course of 2019, two important economic integration processes were concluded.

First, the Comprehensive and Progressive Trans-Pacific Partnership (CPTPP) came into force at the end of December 2018 once a sufficient number of signatories

FIGURE 11
Improvements in key countries

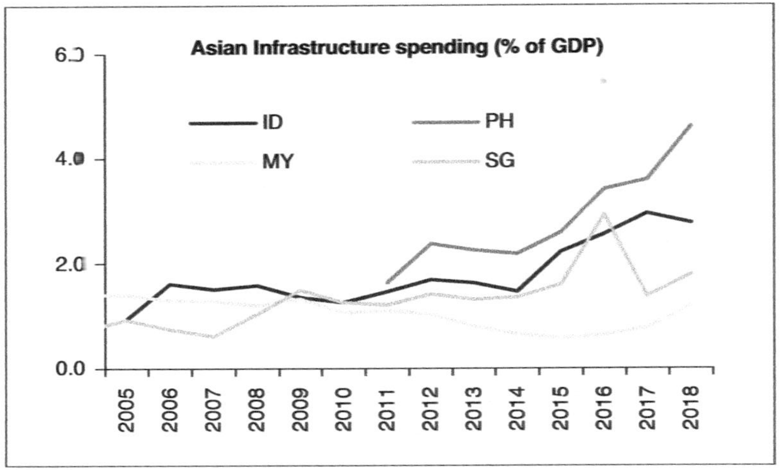

Asian Infrastructure spending (% of GDP)

— ID — PH
— MY — SG

FIGURE 12
...but others while lagging will pick up in 2020

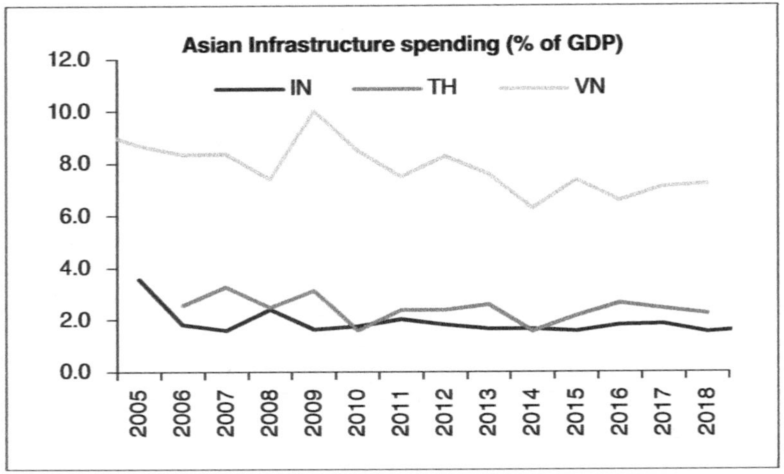

Asian Infrastructure spending (% of GDP)

— IN — TH — VN

Source: Calculated by Centennial Asia Advisors using CEIC.
Note: Data is based on allocations to infrastructure. If that was not possible, then capital expenditures and/or the allocations towards the relevant transport ministries were taken as a proxy for infra expenditure.

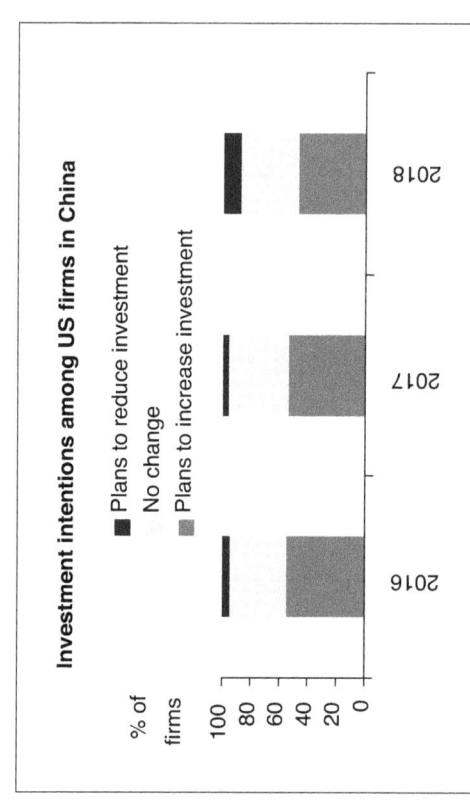

FIGURE 14
Firms increasingly hesitant to invest in China

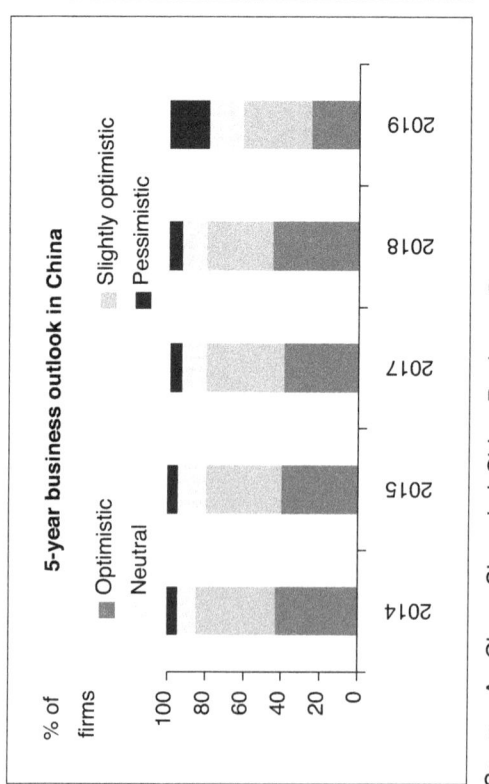

FIGURE 13
Sanguine no longer

Source: AmCham Shanghai China Business Report 2019.

TABLE 3
Evidence of Production Relocation as a New Engine of Growth

Company	Sector	New Production Site	Notable Comments from Media Reports
American/European firms (n=8)			
Google	Smartphones	Vietnam	Google "seeks to build a low-cost supply chain in SEA"
Apple	Smartphones	Mexico, Southeast Asia	Apex of supply chain; major suppliers to evaluate ideal locations for relocation
Dell	PCs	Taiwan, Philippines, Vietnam	Dell to move 30 per cent of laptop production out of China
HP	PCs	Thailand, Taiwan	"20-30 per cent of production to a new supply chain in either Thailand or Taiwan"
Nike, H&M, Gap	Apparel and garments	Vietnam	Halting expansion plans for fear of pushing up factor input costs
Japanese/Korean firms (n=15)			
Kyocera	Consumer, enterprise electronics	Vietnam	Chinese factories to produce for Europe; Vietnam facility to serve US demand
Nintendo	Gaming devices	Vietnam	Firm was considering diversifying production before trade tensions flared
Ricoh	Consumer electronics	Thailand	US-bound models shifted to Thailand; Chinese factory to continue serving Asia
Fast Retailing	Apparel and garments	Bangladesh, Vietnam	Still reliant on China for raw materials; may have to pass on costs to consumers

continued on next page

TABLE 3 – cont'd

Company	Sector	New Production Site	Notable Comments from Media Reports
Kasai Kyogo	Capital goods (automotive)	Japan	Previously shipped straight to United States; now sends to Japan for processing first
Yokowo	Industrial electronics (sensors)	Vietnam	Full relocation of production of US-bound exports by end-2019
Konica Minolta	Printers	Malaysia	Increasing manufacturing footprint in Malaysia; reducing it in China
Nidec	Automotive electronics	Mexico	Will retain investments in China because of new growth engines in electric vehicles
SK Hynix	Semiconductor (memory chips)	Korea	Moving production of certain chip components—not factories—back to Korea
Sharp	Consumer electronics	Indonesia, Vietnam, Mexico	Sees opportunity in the trade war by shifting production to lower-cost locations
LG	Consumer electronics	Indonesia	Further contingency plans are being made
Komatsu	Capital goods (construction)	Japan, US, Thailand	Re-shoring
Toshiba Machine	Capital goods (plastics)	Japan, Thailand	Re-shoring
Sumitomo Heavy Industries	Robotics	Japan	Re-shoring
Mitsubishi Electric	Capital goods (precision engineering)	Japan	Re-shoring

Asian/Taiwanese firms (n=6)			
Li & Fung	Consumer goods, retail	Diversified across SEA	CEO: "there is a trend to be less dependent on China"
Delta Electronics	Consumer electronics	Thailand	Shift production to Thailand via M&A
Inventec	Consumer electronics	Taiwan	Routing goods to Taiwan for final assembly before shipping to the United States
Foxconn	Original design manufacturer (ODM)	India, Vietnam	Behemoth says it has the capacity to make all US-bound goods outside of China
Pegatron	Original design manufacturer (ODM)	Indonesia, India, Vietnam	New facility in Taiwan to make non-Apple products, to offset trade war costs
Wistron	Original design manufacturer (ODM)	Taiwan, Philippines	Already has existing facilities in the country
Chinese firms (n=4)			
TCL	Consumer electronics	Mexico	Failed bid to acquire US tech firm on national security grounds (CFIUS)
Goertek	Advanced electronics	Vietnam	Expansion of existing facility in Vietnam
Zhejiang Hailide New Material	Chemicals	Vietnam	Setting up additional production centres outside China to "stabilize supply"
Hisense	Television	Mexico	Seeking closer proximity to the US market

Source: Centennial Asia Advisors, media reports.

had ratified the agreement. Over time, the four ASEAN members who are in the CPTPP—Brunei, Malaysia, Singapore and Vietnam—will gain from the enhanced market access that the CPTPP provides.

Second, the 35th ASEAN Summit in Bangkok concluded in early November with fifteen nations—including all the ASEAN members—agreeing on a final draft of an agreement to establish the Regional Comprehensive Economic Partnership (RCEP), a trade deal that would harmonize existing trade pacts in Asia. Having failed to secure the concessions it had demanded in terms of protection against a deluge of Chinese imports and services liberalization by ASEAN, India refused to go along with the rest. The fifteen remaining nations, having concluded negotiations on the full text of all twenty chapters of the agreement, will now forge ahead with signing the RCEP in early 2020.

RCEP brings many benefits. It will progressively lower tariffs across many areas—market access will therefore improve. The agreement will also create conditions for companies to export the same product anywhere within the bloc without having to meet separate requirements and fill out separate paperwork for each country. Thus, over time, it should encourage companies to build more extensive supply chains within the region. The agreement also makes a start in liberalizing services, though its provisions here are limited in scope. There are also provisions on protecting intellectual property.

Overall, the good news is that intraregional trade is gradually becoming more important to Southeast Asian economies, suggesting that efforts to improve regional integration, though stop-start at times, have paid off. Regional integration creates the potential for economies to leverage on scale economies; production costs tend to fall, which then translates into export competitiveness. This in turn serves as a buffer against the firming of external headwinds.

- Figure 15 shows that intraregional trade has gradually become more important in the Asian region, with Southeast Asia enjoying somewhat better integration than other parts of Asia. While intraregional trade as a ratio of total trade that Asia engages in rose from 55.6 per cent in 2014 to 57.5 per cent in 2018, the equivalent ratios for Southeast Asia in 2018 was 69.3 per cent of total trade.
- However, the above trends pertain mostly to trade in goods. Far from growing, intra-ASEAN services trade has waned in importance, suggesting that formidable barriers remain that impede services trade in the region (Figure 16).

Economic Overview of Southeast Asia

FIGURE 15
Slowly inching higher – mostly goods trade

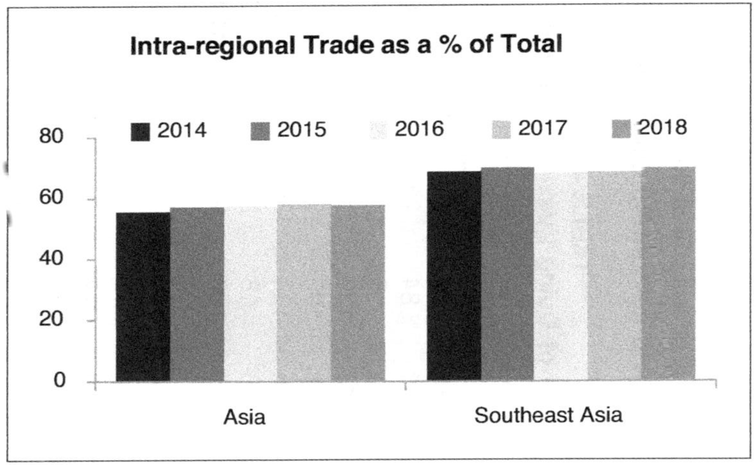

Intra-regional Trade as a % of Total

FIGURE 16
Much is left on the table for services

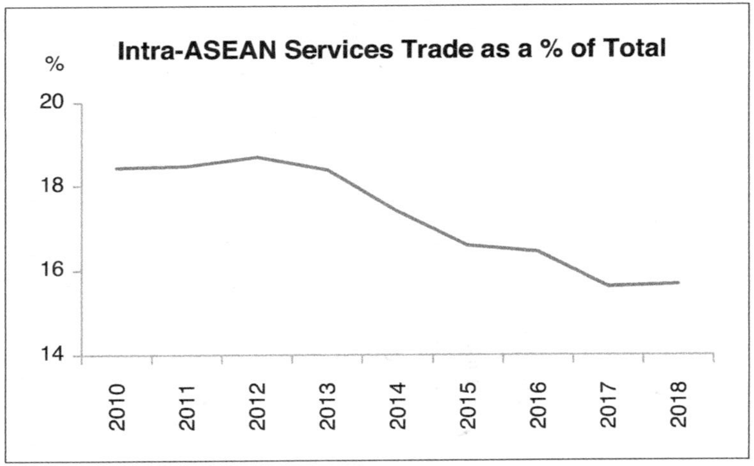

Intra-ASEAN Services Trade as a % of Total

Source: ADB, ASEAN Secretariat, Centennial Asia Advisors.
Note: SEA – Brunei, Cambodia, Indonesia, Laos, Malaysia, Myanmar, Philippines, Singapore, Thailand and Vietnam.

Thus, for a sustained pick-up in economic integration, ASEAN needs to focus more on the liberalization of services markets. Nevertheless, we expect trade in goods to continue benefiting from further integration, and that will boost the region's growth.

Continued Supply Side Improvements

The World Bank's Ease of Doing Business surveys provide a good measure of the impediments to business operations across the world and thus serve as a proxy indicator to the supply side of the economies. As Table 4 shows, Indonesia has made momentous leaps in these rankings. In fact, Indonesia is the only economy to have registered across-the-board improvement. Under a reformist administration, Indonesia is starting to make headway in improving the investment and business climate, though more has to be done to better consolidate the gains, which have slowed to a crawl on a year-on-year basis. Over the last five-year period, the ease of paying taxes under the stewardship of the competent finance minister (Table 4) has improved, while notable progress has also been seen in procuring electricity and construction permits, along with resolving insolvency.

Malaysia, Singapore and Thailand rank in the top twentieth percentile. Progress in other economies, such as Cambodia, the Philippines and Vietnam, has been more modest.

Overall, these improved rankings will flow through to an improved business ecosystem and eventually help raise investment and growth in the region.

TABLE 4
Ease of Doing Business Rankings

Country	2014	2015	2016	2017	2018	2019	y/y	5y
Cambodia	135	127	131	135	138	144	–6	–9
China	90	84	78	78	46	31	15	59
Hong Kong	3	5	4	5	4	3	1	—
India	142	130	130	100	77	63	14	79
Indonesia	114	109	91	72	73	73	—	41
Laos	148	134	139	141	154	154	—	–6
Malaysia	18	18	23	24	15	12	3	6
Philippines	95	103	99	113	124	95	29	—
Singapore	1	1	2	2	2	2	—	–1
Korea	5	4	5	4	5	5	—	—
Taiwan	19	11	11	15	13	15	–2	4
Thailand	26	49	46	26	27	21	6	5
Vietnam	78	90	82	68	69	70	–1	8

Source: Collated by Centennial Asia Advisors from *Ease of Doing Business Report 2020*.

Conclusion

Our overview of the regional outlook brings out some important features of Southeast Asia's economic picture.

First, the region has, through improved economic management, enhanced its resilience, and it was therefore able to sustain reasonable growth even in the face of a difficult world economy.

Second, if global business confidence improves and domestic monetary and fiscal policies yield the economic stimulus anticipated, economic growth prospects in 2020 should be positive. A small improvement over 2019 is likely.

Third, four drivers of an improved medium-term outlook are falling into place—infrastructure spending, production relocation, synergies from economic integration and an improved business ecosystem that can boost investment and growth.

Notes

1. International Monetary Fund, *World Economic Outlook October 2019*.
2. WTO, "Report on G20 Trade Measures", November 2019.
3. "ASEAN Caught in a Dilemma: China Daily Contributor", *Straits Times*, 16 November 2019.
4. International Energy Agency, "Oil 2019 – Analysis and Forecast to 2024".
5. American Chamber of Commerce in Shanghai, "2019 China Business Report", 2019, https://www.amcham-shanghai.org/sites/default/files/2019-09/2019%20China%20Business%20Report.pdf.

THE RISE OF THE RIGHT:
Populism and Authoritarianism in Southeast Asian Politics

Kanishka Jayasuriya

After the global economic crisis of 2008, there has been a trend towards a configuration of institutions and ideologies of state-society relations with a more intensified authoritarian form. At the heart of these political changes is the rise of right-wing political and ideological forces that seek to use religious, ethnic and/or national communities to build coalitions which are hostile to pluralist politics. This trend is combined with the deepening of the neoliberal market-reform agenda within a more authoritarian framework, especially in a further consolidation of politically linked domestic conglomerates. As such, it marks a shift from the technocratic governance—combined with the social forces that supported it—that had underpinned neoliberal reform over three decades. These mark the political changes that occurred over the long 1990s in Southeast Asia, which is a period that covers the implementation—albeit haltingly—of the Washington consensus and neoliberal policies, the establishment of the World Trade Organization (WTO), the collapse of the Soviet Union and the socialist project, as well as a push towards democratic polities.

In this chapter, I focus on Indonesia and the Philippines—two countries seen as the democratic benchmarks over the last two decades—as these nations now move in an increasingly authoritarian direction. The first term of President Jokowi's presidency saw a range of illiberal trends, such as the use of legislative means to criminalize political opposition, the passing of social conservative legislation, the increasing role of the security agencies in the political process, the growth of

---

KANISHKA JAYASURIYA is Professor of Politics and International studies at Murdoch University in Western Australia.

paramilitaries linked to right-wing parties, and the gutting of oversight institutions.[1] The recent elevation of his presidential election opponent Prabowo Subianto to the cabinet suggests that these trends will—if anything—intensify in Jokowi's second term. In the Philippines, the election of President Duterte has led to a spate of extrajudicial killings, the intimidation of political opponents and journalists, and the stacking of courts such as the Supreme Court of the Philippines.[2] As such, both Indonesia and the Philippines provide a window into the drivers of the new authoritarian climate in Southeast Asia. In Thailand, despite the attempt by the junta to provide some form of legitimacy to its rule—via its recent election—there has been only an intensification of the junta's authoritarian rule.[3]

Neoliberalism, Democratic Transitions and the Politics of Governance

The standard model of the transition to democracy has always been problematic in Southeast Asia. The influential transitions paradigm—now nearly three decades old—assumed that democracy once set in train would continue to be consolidated. There was a moment of optimism during the long 90s that the end of the Cold War period that had sustained the rule of strong authoritarian leaders such as Suharto would herald a more open and democratic reformism. It needs to be said that repressive measures and agencies were always crucial in the operation of political institutions, even in the relative open climate of political reform.

Certainly, the course of democratization in Indonesia, the Philippines and Thailand has not been anything like the smooth consolidation of democracy envisaged by that early transitions theory.[4] As the constitutional coup against President Estrada demonstrates, the Philippines has been far from an exemplar of democratic consolidation, and the country displays what Hutchcroft and Rocamora[5] term a persistent democratic deficit. Though this is not so much due to institutional failure as it is rooted in the form that the democratic transition took during the long 90s. In Indonesia, Hadiz and Robison[6] suggest that New Order political and economic elites remade themselves through the institution of reforms and managed to consolidate themselves by controlling access to key political and civil society institutions. In Thailand, the election of Thaksin, who bypassed the web of constitutional checks and oversight institutions, and the resulting ferocious authoritarian response of the royalist aligned—the "Yellow shirts"—shattered whatever legitimacy democratic institutions had in Thailand. The authoritarian right has been a part of political institutions—particularly through security apparatuses—of Southeast Asia even after democratic transitions.

Such democratic forms were the contingent outcomes of the defeat of key left-wing and radical forces during the Cold War. In particular, Hewison and Rodan[7] have argued that a pivotal element in the opening and closing of political contestation and opposition has been the crucial role played by left and radical groups. These groups were repressed—albeit less successfully in the Philippines—during the period of what could be termed the "long 1970s": the turbulent period from the late 60s to the end of the 70s. Hence they note that the opposition that emerged within civil society during the period of the long 90s was shaped in a political context where important elements of the middle class were supportive of the expansion of civil society. This was in contrast to earlier periods where "dominant classes were often supportive of authoritarian reversals, since they perceived the push for increased political space as being led by working class organisations, supported by communists and socialists".[8] Democratization in Southeast Asia was contingent on the repression of the left-wing oppositional movement of the Cold War. In short, the shift from the authoritarianism in key Southeast Asian states was shaped by what Bellin calls "contingent democrats".[9] I argue this was contingent on the containment of radical political opposition of the Cold War period.

This was not the only factor at play. Equally important was the shifting international political and economic order in a more market—or neoliberal—direction to drive economic policy away from the dirigiste policies that had marked economic and trade policy in the Cold War period. The Reagan and Bush presidencies strongly pushed this economic liberalization agenda across the globe, and in Southeast Asia. In some ways this was a reconstitution of the post-war security and economic order to promote particular market-oriented policies that included—often grouped together as the Washington consensus—trade and financial liberalization, a more legalized system of trade enforcement through the WTO, and the increasing regulatory pressure to comply with rules and standards in areas such as intellectual property rights.[10] In Southeast Asia the Asian economic crisis, particularly in Indonesia and Thailand, accelerated these changes.

External economic pressures consolidated and facilitated the dominance of key business groups whose interests were expressed and modified through the transition from authoritarian to democratic political institutions. At the same time, these political institutions incorporated other social forces—such as the middle class—within these regimes through programmes and institutions of good governance; what we refer to as modes of political disincorporation.[11] There was a shift towards a greater international focus on domestic conglomerates, and these corporate entities increasingly operated within the context of privatized and deregulated markets. This creates a "new alliance of politico bureaucrats and corporate moguls, with interests that extend beyond those of protecting and preserving state power to construct new corporate empires of private interest".[12] The neoliberal international order of the 90s was reproduced through the dominance of these segments of capital and the political and institutional forms through which political rule was secured.

In essence, permissive international conditions during the long 70s provided a domestic political environment for the consolidation of social forces—particularly powerful sectors of domestic capital—to be incorporated in the new, more open globalized economy. But the political management of this incorporation was undertaken within the context of democratic politics. This is the oligarchic democracy described by Robison and Hadiz, but this could just as easily apply to the Philippines.[13]

Other social forces have been incorporated within regimes through various technocratic forms of governance. Despite the fact that the "good governance" agenda was unevenly implemented across the region, it served an important political purpose; namely, to incorporate and contain the contestation of the middle class and other actors through the institutions of good governance. From this point of view, the governance paradigm was not only about technocratic policymaking but was also a way of shaping politics—managing opposition and contestation. It was "the way in which social arrangements are constructed as a result of the production of meanings and the repression, subordination or coordination of alternative meanings".[14] Hence, such technocratic forms of governance were crucial in providing avenues of political participation (such as consultative mechanisms), providing legitimacy for political institutions, including anti-corruption agencies and the Office of the Ombudsman, and thereby creating frameworks for the regulation of privatized markets such as water.

In the Philippines, a plethora of institutions was established to implement accountability and transparency, and these included a more robust Office of the Ombudsman and various anti-corruption agencies. One example is the emergence of new participatory budgeting institutions that help to incorporate local people in the implementation and design of budget policies.[15] In a similar way, the Supreme Court of the Philippines became more active on a range of governance-related issues, and this is emblematic of a trend towards the judicialization of politics.[16]

In Indonesia, in the wake of the Asian financial crisis, there was a considerable emphasis on the implementation of anti-corruption agencies. This includes the Corruption Eradication Commission, which goes by the acronym of KPK. It is a body that runs alongside the office of the Attorney General and the police. It has a robust set of powers to investigate public officials for any form of corruption. It has developed its own "brand", and signifies the commitment of the Indonesian government to combat corruption after the Asian financial crisis. Strikingly, the KPK's power is threatened by legislation passed by Parliament, and—as I write—is awaiting the signature of the president on this legislation. An embryonic pattern of judicialization of policymaking is evident in some of the decisions of the Constitutional Court of Indonesia, and it has been very active on a range of issues, including some pertaining to the governance of education.[17]

Thailand has witnessed the most extensive deployment of forms of technocratic governance, albeit in recent times this has been blatantly politicized. In 1997, the street protests in Thailand that brought the middle class on to the streets produced a new constitution. This constitution created the most elaborate governance and judicial mechanisms in Southeast Asia. Most crucially, one of the key elements was what Ginsburg[18] has described as a post-political set of mechanisms that created a range of guardianship institutions, including the Constitutional Court that has worked to constrain and contain political opposition. The Asian financial crisis and the subsequent election of Thaksin Shinawatra were characterized by populist politics that challenged the social forces that had underpinned the constitution of 1997. In turn, the counter-revolution to this populist programme witnessed an early manifestation of the tensions of the "governance political project" that is now evident across Southeast Asia. The military junta that seized power in 2014 has drafted a new constitution. But post political mechanisms in Thailand continue to be crucial in containing the red shirts and other oppositional elements. In Thailand, it is not so much that "post political" institutions have become marginal, but that they have been used in an overtly political way by the junta—and by its supporters, which include significant numbers of the middle class—to reinforce the containment of the red shirts.

The Crisis of Technocratic Governance

These various forms of technocratic governance are increasingly in crisis. The middle class that was so central to the forms of democratic rule that emerged after the long 90s are no longer as supportive of, and are even hostile to, these technocratic forms of governance. This has led to growing dissatisfaction and resentment, on which populist politicians and political parties have capitalized. The particular models of democratic contestation and engagement that emerged in Asia during the long 90s have been fractured by new forms of authoritarian populist politics.

This has been most evident in the Philippines, where the commitment to—if not the implementation of—the good governance agenda has been crucial. A key element of Duterte's election was the articulation of a populist programme that challenged this governance project. Thompson[19] has articulated this in the form of what he calls the disjunctive nature of liberal reformism in the Philippines. Liberal reformism—particularly the work of the Benigno Aquino administration—was challenged by the populist politics of Duterte. He argues that this has led to the weakening of the "once dominant political order—due to the discrediting of the good governance narrative, the weakening influence of key 'strategic groups' backing it (particularly the Church and social democrats), and the vulnerability of key institutions".[20] In short, the coalitions that had underpinned the "governance reform project" had lost legitimacy.

There are three important elements in this crisis of governance. First is the growing contradiction between corruption and cronyism and the good governance agenda. For example, while Aquino started out with reform credentials, his agenda was beset by allegations of pork-barrelling, particularly through the use of the Priority Development Assistance Fund (PDAF). The fund was used to provide benefits for legislators in return for their support for legislation and other initiatives.[21] The tension between the governance projects and the often systematic nature of patronage underlines one of the central contradictions of the relationship between the governance political project and neoliberalism. This is a political economy dependent on the access of powerful business groups to particular political and legislative rents, and this in turn financed political parties and politicians. It is the contradiction that fuelled the anti-political sentiment that Duterte was able to exploit.

Second, exacerbating such contradictions—and fuelling the populist resurgence—was the question of ineffective and often poor delivery of government services, including the delays of relief for disaster-hit areas. In consequence, the anger and resentment at the poor distribution and management of services became an increasing source of political contestation during Benigno Aquino's tenure. It seems to have led to the increasing disaffection of the middle class—particularly the lower middle class—with governance. In contrast to an earlier populist campaign by Estrada, Thompson argues that "Duterte's strongest support did not come from the poorest voters but rather from the elite and the middle class."[22] It is also clear that he drew significant support from the new lower middle classes—what Jafferlot[23] calls, in the Indian context, the "neo-neo middle class". These include self-employed individuals as well as those who have returned to the country after working overseas. These groups are disengaged with existing modes of incorporation through governance, and are likely to be most adversely affected by poor service delivery. However, it needs to be pointed out that the high approval rates that Duterte has received during his tenure does suggest that he has been able to construct a broad cross coalition of support.

Thirdly, there is an ideological dimension in this new authoritarian populism that is crucial to understanding its appeal to right-wing populists such as Duterte. The governance project pursued by politicians such as Benigno Aquino was framed by Duterte as a programme for the pursuit of human rights and liberal reform for the benefit—in typical populist language—of "corrupt elites". Against the political pluralism—limited as it might have been—the populist-used notions of justice are hostile to rectifying human rights violations, but relate more to the effective provision of services, particularly law and order in urban areas. Here, authoritarian populism is recognized as a directive for the provision of law and order and the securing of the interests of the "majority" from dangerous forces, which in the case of the Philippines was identified with drug users. This was a form of populism that Curato argues is a

> penal populism [that] draws its discursive power from its capacity to attribute blame to both offenders and the political establishment that perpetuate shared anxieties. Duterte was able to render visible concerns that used to lurk in the background and was able to give a voice to a public that felt victimised by illegal drugs.[24]

It was the ability of this authoritarian populism to frame this "order" in terms of its capacity to fight drug problems, but it was also an attack on the political establishment that is complicit in the perpetuation of this drug problem. On these terms, this right wing does not challenge existing power relationships or the neoliberal agenda—indeed it has deepened it. However, these economic programmes are more aligned with this authoritarian populist movement and the emphasis on order.

The recent presidential election in Indonesia pitted the Islamic-inclined populism of Prabowo with Jokowi. Although he has been identified as technocratic, and therefore more likely to pursue a more liberal governance project, Jokowi has in fact turned his back on key governance reforms. Perhaps the most striking evidence of this is the current legislative attempt to curtail the powers of the KPK, the anti-corruption agency. He has also instituted a range of illiberal measures—such as the broad anti-pornography law as well as increased the role and influence of security agencies. There has been an increasing use of repressive measures to target opposition politicians, and, according to Power, a "widespread view in elite circles was that government actors had threatened these individuals with legal charges, typically relating to corruption, unless they realigned with the incumbent".[25] In fact he goes on to note that anticorruption charges have been used to harass opposition politicians. Under the presidential administration of Jokowi, there has been an attempt to undermine key governance institutions—such as the KPK—that were so central to the democratic accommodation after the long 90s. Furthermore, there are also broader anti-pluralist measures and rhetoric that have increasingly taken on a coercive and illiberal turn. It may well be that during Jokowi's second term these tendencies will be further intensified.

When first elected, Jokowi was viewed as a reformer, but even in his first term his policies were tilting in an illiberal direction and the making of a right-wing populist programme. In the middle of his first term, Jokowi dismissed some reformist members of his cabinet, moving further away from the governance reform project of the long 90s. This populist project contrasted with technocratic ones designed to reinforce liberal institutions of accountability or the "rule of law". So what kind of populism is this? While Curato describes the Philippines as exemplifying a form of penal populism, Warburton describes Jokowi's programme in Indonesia as a kind of developmental populism, and one focused on effective forms of service delivery such as those through infrastructure development. She notes that "in 2016 there was a notable shift away from Jokowi's previous focus on pro-poor and populist policies and towards a growth-focused developmentalist agenda".[26] Warburton underlines the echoes of the New Order in this populism, though I would argue this is a rhetoric which is now linked to neoliberalism. While law and order issues might not be as central to this developmental populism—though it does figure in his political message—there is a common thread that links Duterte and Jokowi in their hostility to liberal reform, as well as their emphasis on order, political stability and development through the intensification of neoliberal programmes.

Hence, as with the Philippines, there is in this right-wing movement a complex relationship between authoritarianism, neoliberalism and populist politics. In Indonesia, Jokowi has pushed hard on deregulation to "cut red tape" and make it easier for business, and his deregulation projects are designed to facilitate investment in infrastructure. At the core of this developmentalism is a form of infrastructural populist politics designed to appeal to the developmental strand emphasized in Warburton's analysis, that the infrastructural projects are often ideologically framed in economic nationalism. However, these project also serve to intensify the project of market reform. For example, it is argued that "services costs are higher in Indonesia's outer islands because of poor infrastructure, and that improvements in physical infrastructure will bring down costs and therefore price".[27] To the extent that state-owned enterprise and investment is encouraged, it is within the framework of this infrastructural populist project that it also aligns—as Hadiz and Robison astutely note—with the network of corporate elites and bureaucratic allies who are the backbone of Jokowi's support.[28] Yet, it should be underlined that this is not the standard liberal market reform advocated by proponents of the Washington Consensus; it is, rather, like Duterte in the Philippines or indeed Orban in Hungary. It is an eclectic mix of market reform and state intervention that favours certain domestic firms. It is a specific form of authoritarian neoliberalism that—in contrast to the governance reform agenda—provides a dose of state intervention with deepening market reform and with a strong nationalist and religious hue.

In this context, Hadiz and Robison[29] argue that the difference between Jokowi and Prabowo in the recent election lies in a conflict between two forms of populism: a more modernist one for Jokowi and a more Islamic one for Prabowo. Certainly, there are important differences between these competing variants of populism, but they do have certain elements in common—an economic nationalist rhetoric, a suspicion of pluralist politics and human rights, and an emphasis on infrastructure—that suggest that what is important in this contest is not so much their differences but their departure from, and response to, the contradictions and tensions of programmes of neoliberalism and governance that emerged during the long 90s. Nevertheless, the Islamic populism promoted by Prabowo has a different constituency and draws on fringe Islamic groups such as the Islamic Defenders Front. This is a rhetoric that lays stress on how Muslims have been marginalized, and it builds on a deeply racist resentment of Indonesian Chinese conglomerates. It is this alliance that claimed one of Jokowi's key allies, Basuki Tjahaja Purnama (aka Ahok), who was ousted for supposedly blasphemous comments. After this, Jokowi's response has been to co-opt some elements of this Islamic populism, particularly after he selected a highly conservative cleric as his running mate. This snapshot of the competing populisms of Jokowi and Prabowo can be discerned as a complex relationship between neoliberalism, authoritarianism and populist politics.

Intriguingly, one of the features of the emergent right-wing populism is nostalgia for conservative themes of stability, security and the political order of previous authoritarian regimes, but re-cast within a neoliberal material framework. In Duterte's case this rests on an explicit appeal to the previous Marcos regime in the political language he has used and the alliances he has formed. In Indonesia, as the arguments of developmental populism have shown, there has been an effort to harness the language of "order and stability" of the New Order regime during the Jokowi administration.[30] Prabowo has been even more explicit in seeking to draw on the political language of the New Order regime. Jokowi has, for example, introduced a new training programme called Bela Negara. The programme was founded on ideological warfare against, and with the aim of protecting the nation from, ideological adversaries identified as communist and "liberals".[31] Such campaigns against a slew of enemies labelled as liberal or communist now follow familiar far-right attacks in countries such as Brazil and Hungary. In both these states, political leaders have adopted anti-pluralist and organic corporatist language borrowed from previous fascist traditions (as in Hungary) or far-right military regimes (as in Brazil) to reinforce new attacks on liberal institutions. In the case of Indonesia and the Philippines, there has been a conscious return to the older language—if not the political allies—of the previous Marcos and New Order regimes. It is a curious language because while it uses elements of the previous ideological language of order and stability—unmoored from the programme of authoritarian developmentalism—it is now linked to programmes of market reform or neoliberalism and business groups that benefit from these programmes.

In Thailand the situation is somewhat different. The last decade and a half has seen protracted political struggles between red shirts and yellow shirts. The durability of the contingent democratic transition has proved short-lived. It is also a case where liberal governance institutions have, as Ginsburg[32] suggested, an afterlife as instruments of overtly illiberal military and royalist forces to entrench authoritarian rule. More importantly, as in Indonesia and the Philippines, there has been an explicit use of the political language of previous authoritarian regimes of the 1960s to shore up an authoritarian junta. The key lesson from the case of Thailand—as Kanchoochat and Hewison so cogently argue—is that it requires

> not so much an analysis of the network monarchy, but of the contending social forces and class conflict that produced a political situation that permitted a reinvigoration of royalist discourse, the strengthening of rightist and anti-democratic politics and the circumstances that permitted a group associated with the monarchy to become politically significant.[33]

In conclusion, we have distilled some of the longer-term trends in Southeast Asian states, with a particular focus on the Philippines, Indonesia and Thailand. At stake is the fact that the governance project that sought to combine neoliberalism and—albeit limited—democratic contestation has been challenged by a rejuvenated set of right-wing and authoritarian forces with strong links to key domestic business groups and sections of the middle class that in many cases have sought to establish cross-class alliances. An important element of the rise of these right-wing authoritarian regimes lies in the failure of governance institutions—in the absence of effective political parties—to provide mediating institutions that could connect social groups with the political system. There has been broad political disincorporation of groups within these governance systems. A consequence of this dissatisfaction has been the rise of an overtly authoritarian and right-wing response to the failure of this system of technocratic governance. At the core of this renewed right-wing movement is the language of order and stability that seeks to cleanse the state of "liberal institutions" in favour of religious, ethnic or national communities that would build cross-class coalitions which would work to deepen market reform. It is the complex triangle of authoritarianism, neoliberalism and illiberal communities of faith, ethnicity or nation that makes this distinctive brand of political regime.

Notes

1. T. Powers, "Jokowi's Authoritarian Turn and Indonesia's Democratic Decline", *Bulletin of Indonesian Economic Studies* 54, no. 3 (2018): 307; E. Warburton and E. Aspinall, "Explaining Indonesia's Democratic Regression: Structure, Agency and Public Opinion", *Contemporary Southeast Asia* 41, no. 2 (2019): 255–85; V.R. Hadiz and R. Robison, "Competing Populisms in Post-Authoritarian Indonesia", *International Political Science Review* 38, no. 4 (2017), 488–502, https://doi.org/10.1177/0192512117697475.
2. M. Thompson, "Bloodied Democracy: Duterte and the Death of Liberal Reformism in the Philippines", *Journal of Current Southeast Asian Affairs* 35, no. 3 (2016): 39–68; V. Santos, "The Philippines Just Became More Authoritarian Thanks to the People", *New York Times*, 24 May 2019, https://www.nytimes.com/2019/05/24/opinion/philippines-duterte-election-senate.html.
3. K. Hewison, "Thailand: Contestation over Elections, Sovereignty and Representation", *Representation* 51, no. 1 (2015): 51–62.
4. K. Jayasuriya and G. Rodan, "Beyond Hybrid Regimes: More Participation, Less Contestation in Southeast Asia", *Democratization* 14, no. 5 (2007): 773–94; See also G. Rodan, *Participation without Democracy: Containing Conflict in Southeast Asia* (Cornell University Press, 2018).
5. P. Hutchcroft and J. Rocamora, "Strong Demands and Weak Institutions: The Origins and Evolution of the Democratic Deficit in the Philippines", *Journal of East Asian Studies* 3 (2003): 259–92.
6. Hadiz and Robison, "Competing Populisms".
7. K. Hewison and G. Rodan, "The Decline of the Left in Southeast Asia", *Socialist Register* 30 (1994): 235–62.

8. Ibid., p. 258.
9. E. Bellin, "Contingent Democrats: Industrialists, Labor, and Democratization in Late-Developing Countries", *World Politics* 52, no. 2 (2000): 175–205.
10. K. Jayasuriya, "Embedded Mercantilism and Open Regionalism: The Crisis of a Regional Political Project", *Third World Quarterly* 24, no. 2 (2003): 339–55.
11. P. Chacko and K. Jayasuriya, "Asia's Conservative Moment: Understanding the Rise of the Right", *Journal of Contemporary Asia* 48, no. 4 (2018): 529–41; K. Jayasuriya, "Authoritarian Statism and the New Right in Asia's Conservative Democracies", *Journal of Contemporary Asia* 48, no. 4 (2018): 584–605.
12. R. Robison and V. Hadiz, "Indonesia: Crisis, Oligarchy, and Reform", in *The Political Economy of Southeast Asia*, 3rd ed., edited by G. Rodan, K. Hewison, and R. Robison (Sydney: Oxford University Press, 2006), p. 19.
13. W. Bello, H. Docena, M. de Guzman, and M. Malig, *The Anti-Development State: The Political Economy of Permanent Crisis in the Philippines* (London: Zed Books, 2005).
14. J. Newman, *Modernising Governance: New Labour, Policy and Society* (London: Sage, 2001), p. 6.
15. Jayasuriya and Rodan, "Beyond Hybrid Regimes".
16. B. Dressel, "Governance, Courts, and Politics in Asia", *Journal of Contemporary Asia* 44, no. 2 (2014): 259–78.
17. A. Rosser and J. Curnow, "Legal Mobilisation and Justice: Insights from the Constitutional Court Case on International Standard Schools in Indonesia", *Asia Pacific Journal of Anthropology* 15, no. 4 (2014): 303–18.
18. T. Ginsburg, "Constitutional Afterlife: The Continuing Impact of Thailand's Post-Political Constitution", *International Journal of Constitutional Law* 1 (2009): 83–105.
19. Thompson, "Bloodied Democracy".
20. Ibid., p. 59.
21. Ibid.
22. Ibid., p. 9.
23. C. Jaffrelot, "Quota for Patels? The Neo-middle-class Syndrome and the (Partial) Return of Caste Politics in Gujarat", *Studies in Indian Politics* 4, no. 2 (2016): 218–32.
24. N. Curato, "Flirting with Authoritarian Fantasies? Rodrigo Duterte and the New Terms of Philippine Populism", *Journal of Contemporary Asia* 47, no. 1 (2017): 100.
25. Powers, "Jokowi's Authoritarian Turn".
26. Eve Warburton, "Jokowi and the New Developmentalism", *Bulletin of Indonesian Economic Studies* 52, no. 3 (2016): 307.
27. Ibid., p. 308.
28. Hadiz and Robison, "Competing Populisms".
29. Ibid.

30. Thompson, "Bloodied Democracy"; Warburton, "Jokowi and the New Developmentalism".
31. D. Bourchier, "Two Decades of Ideological Contestation in Indonesia: From Democratic Cosmopolitanism to Religious Nationalism", *Journal of Contemporary Asia* 49, no. 5 (2019): 713–33, https://doi.org/10.1080/00472336.2019.1590620.
32. Ginsburg, "Constitutional Afterlife".
33. V. Kanchoochat and K. Hewison, "Introduction: Understanding Thailand's Politics", *Journal of Contemporary Asia* 46, no. 3 (2016): 381.

AMERICAN FOREIGN POLICY AND SOUTHEAST ASIA

Daljit Singh

The decline of America's relative strategic and economic power is reflected in adjustments to its global policy and strategy. This has in fact been apparent since the Obama administration's unwillingness to become involved in the Syrian conflict, and its calls for "burden sharing" and more partnerships. The tendency towards retrenchment has continued under the Trump administration, with officials seeking to review foreign involvement with the question "What is in it for us?" and seeking ways out of the conflicts in the Middle East and Afghanistan as the country tries to focus on the Indo-Pacific region.

American primacy after World War II was a historical anomaly brought about by very special circumstances of the post-war world. For many years before World War II the United States relied on a balance-of-power strategy to secure its interests in Asia, often in a multipolar geopolitical setting. This is the likely direction for the future. It is not clear yet what form a balance-of-power strategy will take in the Indo-Pacific. Alliances, partnerships and "burden sharing" will be important elements.

This chapter first addresses the big change in US foreign policy—in particular, policy towards China—during the Trump administration. It describes the mood in US policy circles as well as in the wider foreign policy community towards China and President Trump's role, which is not always in tandem with that of the relevant bureaucracies and Congress. It then goes on to examine the policy towards Southeast Asia, the region's importance to US interests, the current US

DALJIT SINGH is Senior Fellow and Coordinator of the Regional Strategic and Political Studies Programme at the ISEAS – Yusof Ishak Institute in Singapore. This chapter is an abridged and updated version of an ISEAS Trends paper published in November 2019 that was based on fieldwork conducted in Washington DC in April–May 2019, as well as subsequent research in Singapore. The author is indebted to Khairulanwar Zaini of the ISEAS – Yusof Ishak Institute for research assistance.

"influence deficiency" in Southeast Asia and the prospects of the United States augmenting its influence and standing. Finally, there is a section making some concluding observations.

The New Turn in US Foreign Policy

A new phase in US foreign policy has begun, propelled mainly by three factors. First, the hubris and overreach during the immediate post–Cold War period, correctly seen in hindsight as a "unipolar moment", led to wasteful and costly wars in the Middle East. Second, domestic policy failures to cope with the negative effects of globalization resulted in significant damage to US manufacturing industries and sections of the white working class. The global financial crisis of 2008–9 only accentuated the economic distress.

A reaction to these two developments was bound to come sooner or later—and it came, if rather surprisingly, in the form of Trump with his "America First" rhetoric. Trump's Jacksonian ideas of self-reliance, isolationism, and denigrating external commitments are not new in the American foreign policy tradition. Movements advocating them have existed in other periods of US foreign policy history, particularly in the years between the two world wars.

According to Trumpism, liberal internationalism led the United States to be bled and exploited by the outside world and thus, in his view, a more transactional foreign policy with American interests foremost and more narrowly, if more selfishly, defined was required. Though the American security and foreign policy establishments often do not agree with the Trumpist prescriptions, they have been unable to prevent damage to US interests by actions like the scrapping of the Trans-Pacific Partnership and the callous and high-handed treatment of allies and partners.

A third major development, and perhaps the most consequential one shaping US foreign policy, is the rise of China. While the United States was mired in Middle Eastern conflicts and the war on terrorism, China's power grew exponentially. In 2000 China's GDP was US$1.21 trillion, by 2011 it had risen to US$7.57 trillion, a sixfold increase in little more than a decade. In 2018 it was US$13.6 trillion and is expected to surpass the US economy in the early 2030s in nominal dollar terms.[1] In terms of purchasing power parity, China's economy became the world's largest by 2014. China also made rapid advances in military power, which has made it more costly for the United States to fight a war in the vicinity of China. These developments mean a significant decline in the margin of US strategic preponderance, to which US foreign and security policies have to adjust.

It was not just the growth of China's power but more importantly its intentions, as seen by the United States, that convinced US policymakers that China had emerged as a powerful strategic competitor and a threat to vital US interests. Contributing to this belief were the direction and pace of China's military modernization, complaints of the US business community about China's unfair business practices, increased repression of human rights, harassment of US surveillance ships in the South China Sea (SCS), cyber espionage of US commercial secrets and other technology thefts, the building and militarization of artificial islands in the SCS, and Beijing's contemptuous rejection of the 2016 Hague Tribunal ruling on the Philippines case relating to the South China Sea. After Xi Jinping's ascent to power in Beijing in 2012, it seemed clear that US hopes and expectations about China had been misplaced. China was not going to be a partner of the United States in preserving the existing rules-based international order; instead, it seemed to seek dominance in Asia with its own regional agenda. Domestically, instead of liberalizing, China was becoming more authoritarian and repressive.

The net result was that by the end of the Obama administration there was a widespread view in the US security and foreign policy community that policy towards China had to change and a push-back was badly needed. However, this was not shared at the highest levels of the Obama administration, and the policy to sustain a cooperative relationship, "manage" the differences and avoid tensions continued, even as China became more assertive, even aggressive. Trump changed all this. He linked the issues, was unpredictable, did not mince his words about China, and was not afraid to create tensions. He rallied the government bureaucracies and public to stand up to China.

With the change in policy towards China under the Trump administration, the relatively benign era of US-China relations for nearly half a century, which has powered East and Southeast Asian prosperity, is now ending, and a new phase marked by deep distrust and intensified economic and strategic competition has begun.

The Mood in the United States

Within the US administration and Congress, the prevalent thinking is that China seeks to oust the United States from Asia and become the pre-eminent global power. Some go further to say that China constitutes an existential challenge to US economic and security well-being coupled with an ideological challenge because an increasingly powerful China will seek to foist its own authoritarian governance model and values on the world. Douglas Paal of the Carnegie Endowment for International Peace observed: "We are not in a new Cold War yet, in my opinion, but there is definitely a Cold War mentality at work that may diminish both sides' capacity to manage crises effectively."[2]

Two things in particular have caused genuine alarm in the United States. First, there is China's advances in certain areas of high technology and its plans to become the leading technology power with its Made in China 2025 industrial policy. This is seen as a dire threat to US economic well-being and prosperity and also to its military security. Second, there is the feeling that China has infiltrated the whole US system with spies, agents of influence, cyberespionage, and influence operations. The Federal Bureau of Investigation (FBI) has been publicizing what China has been doing in these areas. It is going to universities to brief university administrators on the dangers. Visas for STEM (Science, Technology, Engineering and Mathematics) students or researchers are more carefully screened. Chinese funding for universities and research institutes is under scrutiny, as is collaboration between US and Chinese scientific and research institutes.[3]

In addition to the strong anti-China mood in Congress (and it is bipartisan), in the security and intelligence services, the military and in the US Trade Representative's Office (USTR), a broad coalition is developing in the country. It includes those who lost their jobs or businesses and blame China for it; Christian conservatives; the annual Conservative Political Action Conference (CPAC) hosted by the American Conservative Union, with its anti-China stance; and the activities of the Committee on Present Danger, which has been revived recently to raise awareness of the danger from China, with prominent members including the likes of Steve Bannon and Newt Gingrich.[4] And then there are the human rights advocacy groups incensed about the human rights situation in China, including mass internment of Uighurs in Xinjiang province. Developments in Hong Kong are further incensing these groups, as are China's pressures on Taiwan in recent years. The old Taiwan lobby is starting to make a comeback.[5] All these forces are coming together.

American public opinion has also been shifting. According to a Chicago Council on Global Affairs poll conducted from 22 to 24 February 2019, a majority of Americans (63 per cent) now describe the United States and China as mostly rivals, up from 49 per cent who said the same in March 2018. Only one in three (32 per cent) say the two are mostly partners, down from 50 per cent in March 2018. An August 2019 Pew poll shows 60 per cent of Americans now have an unfavourable view of China.[6]

The supply chains and links were already affected by rising wages in China. Now they are being disrupted because of the great uncertainty and distrust. The arrest of Meng Wanzhou of Huawei has added impetus to breaking links. After her arrest and the subsequent arrests of the two Canadians in China, people from US high-tech companies are more reluctant to travel to China. The arrest of the two Canadians is regarded as taking of hostages, who have been ill-treated in detention compared to the luxury in which Meng Wanzhou is allowed to live in Vancouver while she awaits a decision on extradition to the United States. Such actions, as well as others that are expected from the US side, may also affect the sentiments of Asian investors who want to invest in China. Export controls to China, which will be a sensitive issue for US companies that derive significant profits from the Chinese market, are likely to be further tightened in the future.

Meanwhile the US military is being turned around to focus more on preparing for the contingency of high-intensity conventional warfare with China and Russia after focusing on low-intensity anti-terrorism for the last two decades. The defence budget has been increased and new weapons systems are being developed. Military cooperation with Japan, Australia and India has been stepped up in recent years.

The strategic competition with China, by all accounts, is long-term, which will continue well beyond the Trump administration. One senior official of the first Obama administration, who personally believes in both a push-back against China as well as engagement in some areas, said, "The present course has been set irreversibly for future administrations. Change will be very difficult."[7]

In the midst of the hawkish thinking and policies within the US administration, an intense debate on China and US policy to China is going on in the broader US foreign policy community comprising primarily former officials and scholars in think tanks and universities.[8] Members of the previous administration have been very much on the defensive because they have been made to feel that they had allowed all this to happen and had not taken action. Over a hundred of them published an "Open Letter" in 2019 criticizing the Trump administration for unnecessarily damaging US-China relations.[9] While a broadly agreed upon new consensus has yet to emerge, and the China policy debates in Washington and across the foreign policy community nationally remain contested and divisive, there has been an evident and widely shared shift towards advocating a "tougher" and more "competitive" strategy.[10] One group of specialists and former officials sought out a less confrontational and more middle-ground approach of "smart competition" in a recent task force report.[11]

Policy Coherence and Strategy

Trump dislikes anything that constrains him. So he does not want to be bound by the institutional process within government. The inter-agency meetings of previous administrations are not functioning. Under Trump, often officials try to work around this problem by arranging de facto inter-agency meetings quietly among themselves, while sometimes each agency acts on its own.[12]

Trump hovers above the anti-China attitude in the bureaucracies and Congress, and has at times actually been a restraint on it, at least tactically, because his approach to China has often seemed more transactional and related to his perceived domestic political needs. But, because he is not always on the same wavelength as his officials in the bureaucracies on strategic and security issues, and because of his capriciousness and unpredictability and his lack of in-depth understanding of issues, he introduces great uncertainty into the US foreign policy equation.

On China, there is a view that Trump is interested only in the economic side of the relationship and the domestic political benefits he can derive from it. However, this may be a superficial interpretation. According to Marvin C. Ott of the Woodrow Wilson Center, "Pushing back against China is central to Trump's foreign policy. Trump may be transactional with other countries, but not with China. He is convinced that China is out to harm the US and his concern about China is echoed throughout the Administration."[13]

Given Trump's worldview, his working style and the lack of inter-agency co-ordination, it is not surprising that the overall approach to China and other policy issues lacks coherence and appears erratic.

There are the hawks—in the defence, security, intelligence and trade bureaucracies—who want a full-spectrum, all-of-government push-back against China;[14] and they tend to look at the outside world through the prism of US-China relations. As Douglas Paal of the Carnegie Endowment for International Peace describes the situation, younger and younger people have filled posts in various departments, many of whom do not have a deep understanding of the issues or history of US policy, and thus are prone to acting unwisely. He observes: "Across the board, responsible American officials have lost patience with and understanding for China. When combined with a vainglorious and shallow leader and his chorus, it is a dangerous combination."

Michael Green at the Center for Strategic and International Studies (CSIS), when asked whether the present hawkish approach will be successful, said: "The way they are doing it now, it will not succeed or be sustained. It undermines allies and friends. There is a need to calibrate the push-back with other US interests, both domestic and international, such as interests of farmers in the US and interests of allies, friends and multilateralism. Even Japan is not standing up for a trade war with China."[15] He felt that adjustments will eventually have be made, arguing that historically it has taken time for the United States to adjust to a major strategic change and challenge. Initially it has tended to overreact, but after some time the pieces of policy fall together and a more sensible strategy is shaped.

There are those in policy circles who would desire comprehensive economic "decoupling" from China, which will not be possible. Hank Paulson, former US secretary of the treasury, in a speech at the Bloomberg Forum in Singapore on 6 November 2018, addressed the dangers of attempting a comprehensive decoupling: "It would result in the erection of an Economic Iron Curtain that closes large parts of the global economy to the free flow of trade and investment and impede innovation". "Decoupling", he said, "is easier when you are actually a couple, but this is not the case because many other countries are involved in trading and investing with China. These countries will not follow the US in restricting the flow of goods, technology capital and people to China. So in its efforts to isolate China, the US risks isolating itself."[16]

Yet, decoupling was proceeding even as the debates raged. The Commerce Department in the US added more companies to its blacklist (the Entity List).

On the geopolitical front, the broad direction the United States is heading towards is its Free and Open Indo-Pacific (FOIP) concept. Embodied in it are all the important principles that the United States has sought to adhere to in its Asia policy for more than a century: openness of Asia to all powers for commerce, free and fair trade, freedom of navigation and overflight, and a rules-based international order. The Defence Department is paying considerable attention to giving more substance to the FOIP.

However, the FOIP has yet to marshal an economic response to a crucial dimension of the China challenge; namely, economic and infrastructural matters. The US government is not in the infrastructure-building business, which is the responsibility of the private sector. Some initial steps have been taken to try to remedy this shortcoming—such as the BUILD (Better Utilization of Investment Related to Development) Act. However, it is still unclear how these will work out (see discussion below). Secondly, policy towards Southeast Asia, a vital component of the Indo-Pacific region, is still not clear. This is discussed further below.

Still, it would be a mistake to dismiss the FOIP as just a shell or skeleton without any flesh. A careful look will show much that has been going on informally and below the radar. For instance, a military dimension already exists in the form of the Quad. Military forces of the Quad countries have been training together bilaterally or trilaterally and have acquired interoperability to come together in a crisis. James Przystup of the National Defence University in Washington DC described the FOIP as follows: "At present it is like pieces of a jig-saw puzzle moving around: US alliances, TPP 11 multilateralism; British and French naval moves in South China Sea; evolution of the US alliance structure like mini-laterals even without the US; the Quad; and India. Eventually these floating pieces will come closer together. With more co-ordination there will be more leverage."[17] Engaging ASEAN and Southeast Asian states is also part of the FOIP strategy.

The United States and Southeast Asia

What are the implications of this big shift in American thinking about, and policy towards, China for Southeast Asia?

The Obama and Trump Administrations

President Obama's response to China's assertiveness was his pivot or "rebalance" to Asia, which prominently included Southeast Asia. It entailed a number of policy moves. First, enhanced multilateral and bilateral diplomacy with ASEAN and Southeast Asia, with the president meeting ASEAN leaders at summits. Second, continuation of the strong defence diplomacy that the Defence Department maintained with the militaries of key Southeast Asian countries, and stepping-up of capacity building in maritime domain awareness, exercises, sale of equipment and training. Third, improving the US military's access to the region. The 2014 Enhanced Defence Cooperation Agreement (EDCA) with the Philippines and the 2015 Defence Cooperation Agreement (DCA) signed with Singapore provided for more access. Finally, President Obama recognized the critical importance of economic engagement and had a clear economic prong to his pivot to Asia, including Southeast Asia, in the form of the Trans-Pacific Partnership (TPP). However, he flunked it by not acting fast enough to get it through Congress.

These were all good moves. However, President Obama lacked the will to use US power to check Chinese advances in the South China Sea. There were no red lines drawn and the Chinese just moved in.[18]

After the relatively high-profile diplomatic attention to ASEAN under President Obama, the regional organization has been receiving less attention from the Trump administration. However, Obama's high-profile stance was an aberration in the post–Vietnam War history of US-ASEAN relations. One way to look at the new change may be to regard it as a return to normal.[19]

In the first year of his administration, President Trump received a few Southeast Asian leaders in the White House and talked to a few on the phone. He was also present at the ASEAN summit in Manila in 2017. However, the degree of summit-level attention decreased in 2018 when Secretary of State Pompeo represented the president at the ASEAN summit meeting in Singapore in November. US representation at the Bangkok ASEAN summit in 2019 declined further when National Security Advisor Robert C. O'Brien attended the meetings in place of President Trump. He was accompanied by Commerce Secretary Wilbur Ross. ASEAN states were dismayed, to say the least, by the unprecedented despatch of a non-cabinet level official, even if dubbed the "Special Representative" of the president, to attend meetings of leaders, including the East Asian Summit. In response, most ASEAN states downgraded their own representation at the ASEAN Plus One Summit with the US in Bangkok to the level of foreign ministers. Only three countries—Thailand, the 2019 ASEAN Chair; Vietnam, the 2020 ASEAN Chair; and Laos, the US-ASEAN coordinator—sent their leaders to the meeting. President Trump's surprise invitation to ASEAN leaders for a summit with him in the United States in the first quarter of 2020 did not assuage ruffled sentiments.

US officials have expressed support for ASEAN centrality against the backdrop of reduced interest in multilateralism, but there seems to be less interest in working with ASEAN. Among US officials and most knowledgeable experts there are considerable frustrations with ASEAN's lack of coherence and unity, especially in regard to the South China Sea. From the American perspective, ASEAN could not even come together to support the Hague ruling on the Philippines case against China on the South China Sea, i.e., to support a ruling of international law.

However, this diplomatic turbulence should not obscure the fact that the Defence Department has continued with its robust engagement with Southeast Asian states, especially in the maritime sphere. The US defence secretary has also been attending the ADMM plus meetings of defence ministers.

How Important is Southeast Asia to the United States?

Northeast Asia has traditionally been much more important to the United States than Southeast Asia. It is the part of Asia where the United States has a staunch ally, Japan, with the world's third-largest economy and which provides the United States with bases for forward deployment of US military forces. There are no strong or reliable allies in Southeast Asia capable of military "burden sharing". US trade with northeast Asia has always surpassed its trade with Southeast Asia.

The US also has substantial investments in Northeast Asia, though US investments in Southeast Asia are larger.

However, despite frustrations with Southeast Asia—lack of ASEAN unity, lack of reliable allies, authoritarian governments and human rights violations (governance and human rights issues remain important to the US Congress)—there seems to be growing recognition of the greater strategic and economic importance of this sub-region of Asia, perhaps greater than at any time since the Vietnam War in the 1960s–1970s. Michael Green of CSIS and Georgetown University has argued that "Southeast Asia and the Korean Peninsula can no longer be considered strategically important only because they form the frontlines against the hegemonic aspirations of America's adversaries. Korea is the world's twelfth largest economy, and ASEAN as a whole constitutes America's fifth largest trading partner. These states must today be viewed as essential 'strong points' in the same way Kennan saw Germany and Japan in his early concepts of containment."[20] David Shambaugh of George Washington University also sees Southeast Asia becoming "an epicentre" of the escalating US-China competition and Southeast Asian countries likely becoming increasing *objects* of this competition".[21]

Southeast Asia's importance is both strategic and commercial. A number of narrow straits in Southeast Asia connect the Indian and Pacific oceans through which commerce, including oil, vital to the economies of Northeast Asia, and the navies of the major powers pass, endowing great strategic importance to maritime Southeast Asia and especially Indonesia.

Southeast Asia had a total stock of US$329 billion of US investments in 2018, which is more than investments from China, Japan, India and South Korea combined.[22] The amount of these investments has increased by an average annual rate of 10 per cent over the past decade. US exports to Southeast Asia presently support over half a million US jobs. Southeast Asia's economy, supported by favourable demographics, is expected to continue to grow by an average of 5 per cent a year, becoming the fourth-largest economy in the world by 2050. The region's middle class is expected to double from 135 million to 334 million in 2030 (51 per cent of the population).[23] With the ongoing trend to reduce supply chain links with China or to diversify to avoid overdependence on it, Southeast Asia has the opportunity to take advantage of the situation to attract more investments. Hence the need for Southeast Asian states to expedite regulatory and other reforms to improve their investment climate.

An important reason why the United States cannot afford to neglect Southeast Asia is that it and the sea routes through it are critically important to America's most important Asian ally, Japan.[24] The danger is that if the United States was to abandon Southeast Asia, Japan could become unnerved enough to reach an accommodation with China. Such an eventuality would undermine the United States' position in Asia as it relies on Japan for bases and forward deployment of its forces in Asia.

The emergence of a closed Chinese sphere of influence embracing Southeast Asia would be inimical to the fundamental US commercial and strategic interest of keeping the Indo-Pacific region open to all states, a principle underlying US foreign policy since the Open Door Notes of 1899 and 1900. This is an increasing concern in Washington—as China increases its presence and interactions with Southeast Asian states and societies.

What Resources can the United States Commit to Southeast Asia?

While the perceived importance of Southeast Asia is increasing, it is still not clear to what extent the United States will contest China in this region. The gap between President Trump's priorities and interests and those of the national security community persists. There is also the gap between what is being said about China (and Southeast Asia) and the level of resources, including attention, that the administration is willing to commit to Southeast Asia. Will the United States engage in a full spectrum competition with China or adopt a lesser strategy? This remains unsettled as the administration continues to be preoccupied with problems in northeast Asia and the Middle East. To focus more on the Indo-Pacific, the United States will need to reduce its entanglements in the Middle East. Yet, US military deployments to the Gulf States have in fact been increasing.

One important challenge is to provide countries with the option of an alternative to infrastructure projects under China's Belt and Road Initiative (BRI). The BRI is much more than an infrastructure or economic initiative. Packed into it are levers of political influence and strategic advantage over a large swathe of the Indo-Pacific. The Maritime Silk Road is, in fact, a Chinese Indo-Pacific strategy. The United States and its allies recognize the broad challenge posed by the BRI and the need to compete more effectively with it. The US government cannot match China in dollar-to-dollar investments in Southeast Asia for infrastructure construction, which in any case can be done only by the US private sector. So it is likely to try to work more with the private sector and with like-minded countries to focus on investments that can help Southeast Asia as well as make a difference to American standing in Southeast Asia.

Some initial steps have been taken. In October 2018 President Trump signed into law the United States BUILD Act, and the agency set up under it, the United States Development Finance Corporation (USDFC), became operational on 1 October 2019. The USDFC will double US development finance capacity to US$60 billion for infrastructure projects on a sustainable public-private partnership basis, possibly also with the participation of allies like Japan and Australia.[25] The USDFC will liaise closely with the State Department and the security agencies to push the American response to the BRI through infrastructure development. When properly staffed and resourced, it will have the potential to compete with the BRI. But uncertainties remain about how this will work out and how the reluctant private sector can be brought into the game.

Also, in December 2018 the Asia Reassurance Act (ARIA) was passed with a budget of US$1.5 billion annually over five years for the Indo-Pacific, part of which is likely earmarked for Southeast Asia. Among other things, it calls for closer US engagement with ASEAN and support for ASEAN centrality. It also calls upon the president to negotiate economic and strategic engagement frameworks with ASEAN and to report annually to Congress on the implementation. ARIA further requires the US administration to push Southeast Asian states to improve human rights, democracy and good governance and to urge them to support the July 2016 ruling of the Permanent Court of Arbitration on the Philippines case against China's expansive claims in the South China Sea. These are touchy subjects in Southeast Asia, and the US administration would be well advised to broach them with sensitivity and behind closed doors. Their utility should be viewed in the broader context of the high-stakes strategic game with China in which the latter wins merit points by respecting the existing political systems of states.[26] The US Congress in particular needs to have a more sophisticated understanding of the stakes involved.

Making an Impact

Some American observers have argued that the United States is already deeply and comprehensively engaged in Southeast Asia in various spheres.[27] Yet the irony is that the United States is not making enough of a political impact on the region compared to China. A survey of elite attitudes in Southeast Asia conducted by the ISEAS – Yusof Ishak Institute at the beginning of 2019 demonstrates this. When asked which country has the most political and strategic influence in Southeast Asia, 45.2 per cent of the respondents said China, while 30.5 per cent said the United States. The response to economic influence was even more striking: 73 per cent said China had the most economic influence and only 7.9 per cent said the United States, while 6.2 per cent chose Japan and 1.7 per cent the European Union.[28] This was way out of proportion to the facts on the ground: While China is the largest trading partner of Southeast Asia, the United States is by far the largest investor and also a substantial trading partner. And both the European Union and Japan are bigger investors than China in Southeast Asia and major trading partners. The survey results show the impact China is making on elite minds in Southeast Asia. The 2020 survey, published in January 2020, confirmed this trend in perceptions: in terms of both economic and political/strategic power in the region, the gaps between the United States and China in fact increased in China's favour.[29]

As a result of this reputational "influence deficit", the US government is becoming aware of the need to step up its public diplomacy in Southeast Asia. David Shambaugh points out that the extensive US presence is not well appreciated or reported by regional media—whereas China's presence and influence is presented as pervasive. He says, "The United States maintains a comprehensive and robust presence throughout Southeast Asia that has grown dramatically since the 1980s. It includes the commercial, security, education and diplomatic, and other domains. America's strengths and contributions to the region lie particularly in both hard and soft power, but the U.S. economic footprint is both broad and deep." Washington is likely to address this shortcoming by stepping up its public diplomacy to better promote its own narrative in Southeast Asia. An important agency for this task will be the Global Engagement Centre in the State Department, which has dedicated funds for the purpose.

However, public diplomacy, while important, may not suffice to bridge the US "influence deficit" in Southeast Asia. Southeast Asian countries are being drawn into China's orbit not because they trust or like China (indeed the ISEAS surveys show that China is the least trusted among the major countries) but because of the economic opportunities China offers and the high economic cost of opposing China's agenda. The message that China will use economic punishment against countries perceived to be unwilling to accommodate its interests has been driven home by past acts of such punishment in Asia and elsewhere.[30] China has also skilfully managed to create the impression of an unstoppable expansion of its power and influence in the region. Its expansion and militarization in the South China Sea without any real opposition from the Obama administration and the negative image of the United States resulting from the governance style and conduct of President Trump and his perceived pro Israel policies (nearly half the population of Southeast Asia is Muslim) are among the important factors that have contributed to the relative decline of US influence. The latter point was also illustrated in the ISEAS – Yusuf Ishak Institute's 2020 survey of elite attitudes in Southeast Asia. When asked if confidence in the United States as a regional security provider will increase if there is a change in the US leadership, on average over 60 per cent of the Southeast Asian policy elites, including in the three Muslim-majority countries (Brunei, Malaysia and Indonesia), responded in the affirmative.[31] Recent Pew Center public opinion polling in six Asian countries (Indonesia, the Philippines, Japan, South Korea, India and Australia) also echo the ISEAS results. All six countries expressed more favourable views of the United States than confidence in President Trump to "do the right thing in world affairs".[32]

On the military front, China now has facilities on its reclaimed land features in the South China Sea from which it can fly its fighter planes to some Southeast Asian states. This military reach will expand if reports that it is building an air and naval base complex in Cambodia turn out to be correct.[33] Chinese warplanes flying close to their borders will be a new phenomenon for many Southeast Asian states that have long been accustomed to US military dominance in the region. Its psychological effect could be considerable. This is happening at a time when it is uncertain whether the United States will be able to have enough access to Philippine bases in view of President Duterte's anti-American attitude. Yet hardly any other Southeast Asian country is today prepared to provide more access for the US military—for fear of offending China.

Nothing less than a sustained long-term and multidimensional US engagement, together with its allies, and with the requisite public diplomacy, can help to restore US credibility vis-à-vis what is seen as a consistent, growing and long-term Chinese presence. Many in Southeast Asia are still sceptical of the US ability to do this.

At least privately, many Southeast Asian officials express support for a continued American security presence in the region. Public statements of support would be most welcome to the United States, but these have become fewer or weaker in recent years. In part for reasons of domestic public support, traditionally the United States likes to rationalize its foreign deployments and wars in terms of helping local friends who face aggression or bullying.

The South China Sea

The South China Sea (SCS) is viewed in Washington not as a "Southeast Asian" issue but rather as a maritime theatre for the wider contest against China over who controls the Western Pacific, though Southeast Asia benefits from efforts to keep the sea open. This contrasts with the perception sometimes encountered in Southeast Asia that the SCS is already "lost" to China. In the United States the SCS is viewed very much as a contested sea in the context of the new tougher policy towards China. Freedom of Navigation Operations (FNOPS) have increased significantly under the Trump administration and the United States has also multilateralized the problem by getting other "outside" powers like the United Kingdom, France, Japan and Australia to send their naval ships into the SCS. According to Marvin Ott, the South China Sea is a core interest of the United States and indeed it is the most likely place where the confrontation between the rising power and the established one will take place, if and when it does.[34]

In terms of military power, China has significantly narrowed the military gap with the US—but it has not bridged it. Its anti-access strategy has made it more costly for the United States to fight China in the vicinity of Taiwan or in the South China Sea. However, the United States is now gearing up to meet the challenge, led with increases in its military budget. Marvin Ott again:

> George Kennan years ago observed that Americans tend to be slow in recognizing threats and committing forces to deal with them. But once the process starts it becomes a massive effort with few restraints. I think we are seeing something like this occurring with regard to China's strategic reach into the South China Sea and Western Pacific. Since the 9/11 attacks the US, collectively, has been preoccupied with perceived challenges in the Middle East and southwest Asia. But now the switch has been thrown and attention is shifting to China's maritime power play. Over the next few years we will see a very large commitment to upgrade and strengthen the American military presence in that arena. The current balance of power is temporary and the future trajectory highly dynamic.[35]

Conclusion

After almost half a century of relatively benign relations in which engagement usually trumped rivalry, US-China relations have deteriorated and entered a period of long-term strategic and economic competition with profound implications for the rest of the world, especially Asia. Southeast Asian countries are not being openly asked to take sides, but pressures, subtle or not so subtle, are bound to come to support specific policies or actions.

Instead of a more integrated world, "decoupling" is in progress between the United States and China. It was started not by the United States but by China through moves like the building of the "great firewall", but it is being accelerated by actions seen by Washington as necessary to safeguard its security and economic well-being. The two economies have been so integrated with each other and also integrated with other economies that there are clearly limits to how far decoupling can be taken without also damaging US interests. It is possible that in the end decoupling will be confined to military-related products and systems and other sensitive technologies of security and commercial importance. However, given the hawkish sentiments within key US security and trade bureaucracies, it is not clear how far it will be taken. And the trend towards bifurcation, with separated supply chains and separate technological systems—for example, for 5G—is in progress, and it is not clear how far it will go.

Meanwhile, Trump's unilateralism, capriciousness and shabby treatment of allies and friends have damaged US interests and its reputation abroad. This will make it more difficult to build a broad coalition of countries that is needed for the contest with China. In Southeast Asia it may be accelerating the shift towards China.

America post-Trump will feel different without Trump's histrionics and unpredictability. But it is unlikely to return entirely to the pre-Trump America—generous and pursuing enlightened self-interest that also benefited others—because the focus on America's own interests, more narrowly defined, started by Trump is likely to continue, since resources are likely to be more limited and the security challenges in the Indo-Pacific region more acute.

In Southeast Asia the United States faces a formidable political, economic and military challenge from China that will require an effective multidimensional response, together with US allies. It is still not clear whether the United States will be prepared to commit the necessary resources to counter China's influence in Southeast Asia in a comprehensive way. Many in Southeast Asia remain sceptical.

Though America's relative strategic and economic power has declined, it will still remain a powerful strategic actor in Asia and, together with its allies, capable of balancing China. It can be expected to move towards a balance of power strategy to preserve its interests, a strategy it employed successfully for many years before World War II. However, it is uncertain whether a balance will be attainable in the whole of Southeast Asia because of China's advantages in areas closer to it.

A balance of power will be good for Southeast Asian states, as it will help to preserve their sovereignty and independence, which in turn should be an important US strategic interest. Hopefully one day China will also accept it instead of wanting to replace the declining US dominance with its own.

Notes

1. World Development Indicators, World Bank.
2. Opinion, *South China Morning Post*, 30 May 2019.
3. FBI Director Christopher Wray said at an event at CSIS, Washington DC, on 6 February 2020, that Beijing was seeking to steal American technology "by any means necessary" and that his bureau currently had about a thousand open investigations of Chinese technology thefts in the United States. The investigation spanned "just about every industrial sector". China was also exploiting US academic openness to steal technology, using "campus proxies" and establishing "institutes on our campuses".
4. In its old incarnation during the Cold War it was used to arouse awareness of the danger of communism.
5. Much of this paragraph is from a conversation with Robert Sutter on 7 May 2019 in Washington DC. He is Professor of Practice of International Affairs, George Washington University.
6. Laura Silver, Kat Devlin, and Christine Huang, "U.S. Views of China Turn Sharply Negative Amid Trade Tensions", Pew Research Center, 13 August 2019, https://www.pewresearch.org/global/2019/08/13/u-s-views-of-china-turn-sharply-negative-amid-trade-tensions/.
7. Interview in Washington DC, 8 May 2019.
8. For summaries of the evolving debate, see Gilbert Rozman, "The Debate on China Policy Heats Up: Doves, Hawks, Superhawks, and the Viability of the Think Tank Middle Ground", *Asan Forum*, 16 July 2019, http://www.theasanforum.org/the-debate-over-us-policy-toward-china-heats-up-doves-hawks-superhawks-and-the-viability-of-the-think-tank-middle-ground/.
9. M. Taylor Fravel et al., "China is Not an Enemy", *Washington Post*, 3 July 2019.
10. See, for example, Aaron Friedberg, "Competing with China", *Survival* 60, no. 3 (2018); Robert D. Blackwill and Ashley J. Tellis, *Revising U.S. Grand Strategy towards China*, Council on Foreign Relations Special Report No. 72 (March 2015), http://carnegieendowment.org/files/Tellis_Blackwill.pdf; Nikki Haley, "How to Win against Beijing: Getting Tough on Trade is Just the First Step toward Countering China", *Foreign Affairs*, 18 July 2019, https://www.foreignaffairs.com/articles/china/2019-07-18/how-confront-advancing-threat-china.
11. Orville Schell and Susan L. Shirk, eds., *Course Correction: Toward an Effective and Sustainable China Policy*, https://asiasociety.org/sites/default/files/inline-files/CourseCorrection_FINAL_2.7.19_1.pdf.
12. Interview with a think tank scholar in Washington DC on 2 May 2019.
13. Interview with Marvin C. Ott, 16 May 2019. He is Visiting Professor, Johns Hopkins University; Senior Scholar, Woodrow Wilson International Center; and a former Professor of National Security Policy at the National War College.
14. See Robert Sutter, "Washington's 'Whole-of-Government' Pushback against Chinese

Challenges: Implications and Outlook", *Pacnet*, no. 26 (2019), https://www.pacforum.org/analysis/pacnet-26-—-washingtons-whole-government-pushback-against-chinese-challenges—implications.

15. Interview in Washington DC, 7 May 2019. Michael J. Green is Senior Vice-President for Asia and Japan Chair at CSIS, Washington DC. He was senior director for Asian affairs in the National Security Council under President George W. Bush.

16. See Edna Curran, "Paulson Warns of 'Economic Iron Curtain' between US, China", Bloomberg, 6 November 2018, https://www.bloomberg.com/news/articles/2018-11-07/paulson-warns-of-economic-iron-curtain-between-u-s-china.

17. Interview with James J. Przystup, Centre for Strategic Research, Institute for National Strategic Studies, National Defence University, 3 May 2019.

18. For a Leninist state well versed in the power game, this must have been a surprising gift. A senior Chinese scholar with connections with the Chinese authorities described President Obama as a "dreamer" in a private conversation in Singapore in 2016. Wrong signals were sent in leaked reports that the US would not go to war with China over "rocks in the South China Sea". Bonnie Glaser of CSIS, in a discussion in Singapore in January 2019, noted that China desisted from reclamation at Scarborough Shoal after Obama warned President Xi in April 2016 of "very severe consequences" if China proceeded to do so, suggesting that the outcome in the South China Sea might have been different if handled differently from the start.

19. Joseph Liow describes US engagement with Southeast Asia after the Cold War as "episodic". See Joseph Chinyong Liow, *Ambivalent Engagement: The United States and Regional Security in Southeast Asia after the Cold War* (Washington, DC: Brookings Institution Press, 2017).

20. See Michael J. Green, *By More than Providence: Grand Strategy and American Power in the Asia Pacific since 1783* (New York: Columbia University Press, 2017), p. 546.

21. David Shambaugh, "US-China Rivalry in Southeast Asia: Power Shift or Competitive Coexistence?", *International Security* 42, no. 4 (Spring 2018).

22. A large portion of US investment in Southeast Asia goes to Singapore, where it supports "hundreds of thousands" of jobs, according to Singapore Prime Minister Lee Hsien Loong; part of it is re-invested from Singapore to other Southeast Asian countries as Singapore investments.

23. The statistics in this paragraph are from the East-West Centre and the US-ASEAN Business Council, *ASEAN Matters for America, America Matters for ASEAN (2019)*.

24. The United States itself is now self-sufficient in oil and it can possibly bypass the sea routes through Southeast Asia.

25. On 12 November 2018, Australia's Department of Foreign Affairs and Trade (DFAT) and Export Finance and Insurance Corporation (Efic), the Japan Bank for International Cooperation (JBIC), and the US Overseas Private Investment Corporation (OPIC)

signed a Trilateral Memorandum of Understanding to operationalize the Trilateral Partnership for Infrastructure Investment in the Indo-Pacific announced in Washington DC on 30 July. Their stated intention is to work together to mobilize and support the deployment of private sector investment capital to deliver major new infrastructure projects, enhance digital connectivity and energy infrastructure, and achieve mutual development goals in the Indo-Pacific.

26. The United States opened up new pathways for an expansion of China-Thailand cooperation, especially in the military sphere, through its actions in relation to the military coup in Thailand in 2014. The traditional Thai ruling elite saw the threat from former premier Thaksin as an existential one needing extreme measures to neutralize. To them the US insensitivity contrasted sharply with China's assurances that it would not interfere in the domestic politics of Thailand.

27. See, for example, David Shambaugh, *US Relations with Southeast Asia in 2018: More Continuity than Change*, Trends in Southeast Asia, no. 18/2018 (Singapore: ISEAS – Yusof Ishak Institute, 2018).

28. *The State of Southeast Asia: 2019 Survey Report*, ISEAS – Yusof Ishak Institute, 29 January 2019.

29. *The State of Southeast Asia 2020: Survey Report*, ISEAS – Yusof Ishak Institute, 16 January 2020.

30. Examples in Asia include the cessation of imports of bananas from the Philippines and boycotts of Japanese businesses and of Korean goods in retaliation for acts by these countries deemed as unfriendly to China. Tourists from China make an important contribution to the economies of a number of Asian states. Turning off and on the tourist tap to provide alternative pain and relief serves not only as an economic weapon but also a psychological one.

31. *The State of Southeast Asia: 2020 Survey Report*, p. 41.

32. See Malcolm Cook, "America's Polling Problems", ISEAS Commentaries, 2020/11, 23 January 2020, https://www.iseas.edu.sg/medias/commentaries/item/11224-americas-polling-problems-by-malcolm-cook.

33. "A Jungle Strip Stirs Suspicion about China's Plans for Cambodia", *New York Times*, nytimes.com, 22 December 2019.

34. Marvin Ott, email communication, 29 September 2019.

35. Ibid.

CHINA'S BELT AND ROAD INITIATIVE FINANCING IN SOUTHEAST ASIA

Xue Gong

As an infrastructure financier in many parts of the developing world, China has built hydroelectric plants, railroads, roads, airports and telecommunication networks on a global scale. Southeast Asia occupies a significant place in China's Belt and Road Initiative (BRI). Situated at the very centre of the Indo-Pacific region, Southeast Asia has long been a strategically important region for China's foreign relations and security.[1] A stable and positive relationship with the region will serve several of China's interests, such as the development of its maritime economy, energy security, and maritime claims in the South China Sea. Moreover, the centrality of ASEAN in regional multilateralism and its stated neutrality in great power competition adds to the geostrategic importance for China.[2]

To incentivize Southeast Asian states to participate in the BRI, China highlighted the long-term economic benefits of the BRI that could be gained through cooperation on policy coordination, trade facilitation, financial integration, infrastructure development and societal-level exchanges. To counter anti-globalization sentiments, the BRI can be used to sustain and revitalize globalization, to improve infrastructure connectivity, and to promote regional and global trade as part of Chinese efforts to provide public goods. Two corridors pass through Southeast Asia: the China-Indochina Peninsular Economic Corridor and the Sino-Myanmar Economic Corridor (originally Bangladesh-China-India-Myanmar Economic Corridor). In addition, China's proposed Maritime Silk Road includes marine industry cooperation, port alliances and logistics. China has also proposed the Lancang-Mekong Cooperation (LMC) in Southeast Asia. The LMC has supported some projects that reduce poverty and others that promote small

---

XUE GONG is Research Fellow with the China Programme of the S. Rajaratnam School of International Studies, Singapore.

and medium-sized enterprises, agriculture, training in water resource management, and education.

It is undeniable that the vision of infrastructure connectivity is targeted at economic growth and regional development. According to the World Bank, connectivity projects in the BRI will increase the trade of countries along the route by 4.1 per cent. The United Nations Development Programme also suggests that the initiative can help BRI-participating countries accelerate industrial diversification and economic growth to achieve the Sustainable Development Goals (SDG).[3] With Chinese companies having set up more than fifty-six economic cooperation zones in more than twenty countries, generating US$1.1 billion in tax revenues and 180,000 jobs during the 2014–16 period, the hubs for capital and manufacturing investment may trigger broader market reforms and spur local employment, export earnings and growth.[4]

Considered as the vehicle for the provision of public goods, initially China's BRI had potential for enhancing regional connectivity. It appealed to Southeast Asian countries with infrastructure bottlenecks that hindered economic growth.[5] However, the proliferation of BRI projects has encountered considerable regional setbacks, as seen in the cancellation and renegotiation of projects in Malaysia and in the downgrading of the deep-sea port by the Myanmar government. During local elections in Indonesia, Malaysia and Thailand, China's BRI-related investments became easy targets for criticism and accusations.[6] In this regard, amid an image crisis, China is also vulnerable because of domestic political changes in BRI host countries.[7]

According to a report by the Organisation for Economic Co-operation and Development (OECD), troubled global Chinese investments are associated with about US$369.5 billion worth of global transactions. The largest problem area is the BRI's US$101.8 billion of troubled assets.[8] Troubled Chinese infrastructure investment is evidenced by the increasing number of suspended, renegotiated or cancelled BRI projects, including those in Malaysia. Nonetheless, the majority of projects seem to be progressing without significant problems.

The observation above has led to the research question: Is there a specific set of conditions that can lead China's infrastructure investment into trouble in Southeast Asia? The main challenge in studying China's large-scale official infrastructure investment is its opacity. Although Beijing claims to collect data on China's overseas aid and investments through the new International Development and Cooperation Agency, it still has not released data on lending, interest rates or borrowing parties of its overseas projects. Under such constraints, the author has used data from China Global Investment Tracker (CGIT) by the American

Enterprise Institute (a verifiable database), the World Bank, the Asian Infrastructure Investment Bank and ASEAN Secretariat Statistics. As the BRI appears to be a vague concept[9] that even counts amongst its projects those announced or started before it was launched in 2013, the author has analysed the infrastructure investment of China between 2005 and 2019. The research outcome will not only provide an assessment of China's project implementation but will also help a wider readership understand the factors that ensure the success and sustainability of infrastructure investment. Furthermore, if China intends to rise as a provider of regional/international public goods, policymakers need to identify the areas in which both China and Southeast Asian states need to improve.

To achieve this goal, the next section provides a literature review on Chinese narratives of infrastructure for development. It is followed by an analysis of China's investment patterns (including infrastructure investments) and financing in Southeast Asia. The chapter also introduces the concept of a meme in the BRI that may impact developmental efforts in the region. The conclusion shows the implications of China's BRI for Southeast Asia and makes recommendations for China's policymakers.

China's Economic Presence in Southeast Asia

As a rising power experienced in addressing development issues such as poverty, infrastructure shortages, disease epidemics and education, China aspires to provide a solution to global underdevelopment.[10] When Chinese President Xi visited the coastal province of Guangxi, he said: "We often say that if you want to be rich, build a road first; while in the coastal areas, build a port first."[11] With this narrative based on China's own success in infrastructure investment,[12] the Chinese government encourages investments in industrial parks and economic zones in recipient countries. In addition, China also proposes to enhance ocean-based prosperity through marine resource utilization, marine industry cooperation, maritime connectivity, maritime transport, and the connectivity of information infrastructures and networks.[13] Beijing claims to "advance the development of multi-modal transportation that integrates expressways, railways, waterways, and airways, build international logistics, and strengthen infrastructure development along major routes and major ports of entry".[14] Other than physical investment projects, China has also shown interest in exporting the port-park-city (PPC) development model known as the Shekou Model:[15] China transformed the backward fishing village Shenzhen into a place more prosperous than Hong Kong. For example, China has been a significant partner in many ports and connected industrial park-related projects in Southeast

Asia (see Figure 1). The PPC model ties China's economic interests even more closely to the economic development of recipient countries.[16]

After the announcement of the BRI in 2013, China's investments in Southeast Asia between 2014 and 2018 were concentrated mostly in such sectors as financial services, real estate and manufacturing (see Figure 2). In contrast, China's investments in infrastructure sectors such as transport and storage, telecommunications, electricity and water supply are of far less value. Table 1 shows that China's investments in the logistics sector in Southeast Asia (with the exception of Singapore) are almost negligible. According to recent research on sectoral investment growth, the BRI has not generated a big-bang effect in connectivity yet.[17] Figure 3 shows that from 2005 to 2019, Indonesia, Malaysia and Singapore were the top three destinations for Chinese total investments and contracts.

The data in Table 1 and Figures 2 and 3 shows that China's investments, regardless of whether they belong to the BRI or not, are a continuation of its overseas investment flow into Southeast Asia. The investments in sectors such as financial services and manufacturing, which are more influenced by markets, are believed to bring employment opportunities to the investing destinations. Largely driven by market forces, these sectors are not really linked to loans between states.

FIGURE 1
BRI Connnectivity Projects in Southeast Asian Countries

- China–Thai Railway
- Jakarta–Bandung Railway (Indonesia)
- Melaka Gateway (Malaysia)
- Kuantan Industrial Park (Malaysia)
- Malaysian East Coast Rail Line (construction started in August 2017 but was renegotiated in 2018)
- China–Myanmar Economic Corridor (MOU of feasibility studies was signed in March 2018)
- Kyaukpyu deepsea port (Myanmar)
- Sihanoukville Special Economic Zone (Cambodia)
- Sino-Lao railway

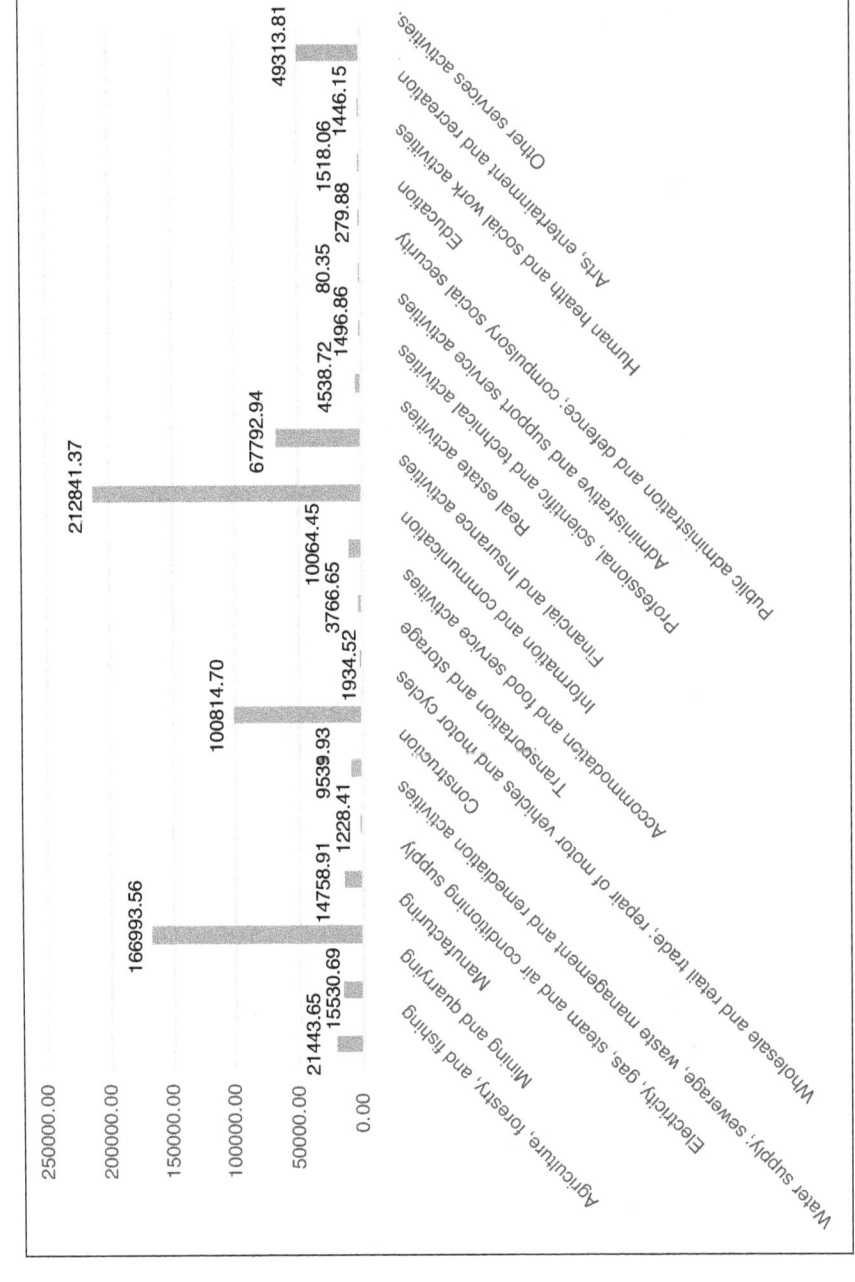

FIGURE 2
China's Investment by Sector (2014–18), USD million

Source: ASEAN Secretariat Database.

TABLE 1
China's Investment Patterns by Sector in Southeast Asia (2005–19), USD billion

Country	Transport	Energy	Chemicals	Agriculture	Health	Entertainment	Logistics	Metals	Finance	Real estate	Tourism	Utilities	Technology	Other
Brunei	0.67	3.44												
Cambodia	6.11	3.83		0.68		0.4		0.5	0.17	1.65	0.11			
Indonesia	7.03	27.1	0.44					8.61		3.87			0.2	
Laos	5.37	17.01		1.5	0.11			0.28		0.95	0.1	0.34		0.6
Malaysia	11.9	12.29	0.58	0.28				5.25	0.12	7.8	2.44	0.63	0.81	1.27
Myanmar	1.49	4.46						2.39		0.4			0.38	2.33
Singapore	5.83	5.59	0.11	0.38		1.45	11.37	0.33	2.49	5.86	0.52	1.08	2.15	4
Thailand	3.81	1.3	0.69	0.64				0.13	0.53	0.5			1.21	0.55
Philippines	0.87	9.72	0.17							0.51	0.8	0.11	1.21	
Vietnam	3.06	16.63	1.33	0.17				3.19		0.48			0.37	0.8

Source: China Going Global Tracker (accessed 31 December 2019).

FIGURE 3
China's Total Investments and Contracts in ASEAN Member States (2005–19), USD billion

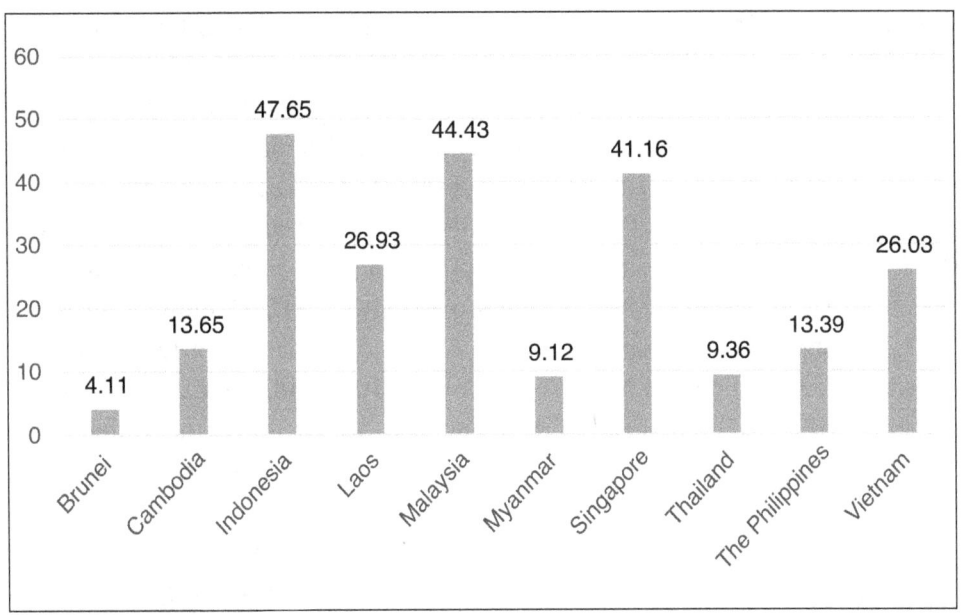

Source: China Going Global Tracker (accessed 31 December 2019).

Financing Is Where Problems Arise

Unlike services or industry production activities, China's state-level sponsored infrastructure investment has always been questioned. One of the reasons for this is the opacity of China's overseas lending for infrastructure investment. In 2010, China set up the China-ASEAN Investment Cooperation Fund (CAF), an offshore quasi-sovereign equity fund sponsored by the Export-Import Bank of China (EXIM Bank).[18] CAF, despite its commitment to responsible investments across infrastructure sectors, only provided updates and information on its official website up to 2014.[19] Another of China's funding sources, the Silk Road Fund (SRF), was created in 2014 to serve the BRI. However, the SRF provides minimal project information, such as the amounts, actors in the projects and interest rates. Similar to the situation with the CAF and SRF, another fund supported by China—the China-ASEAN Maritime Cooperation Fund—provides limited information on its projects.

Given the challenges of identifying specific and verifiable data sources for China's bilateral financing towards infrastructure investments and other related projects, this paper assesses the China-led Asian Infrastructure Investment Bank (AIIB) as a benchmark to understand China's lending activities. Table 2 shows that five ASEAN member states received AIIB-sponsored infrastructure investments, with Indonesia being the largest recipient. The total value of AIIB funded projects in Southeast Asia was US$3.5665 billion as of 31 December 2019.

The total investment value from the AIIB in Southeast Asia appears insignificant compared to China's unilaterally funded projects. For example, the suspended Myitsone Dam of 2011 in Myanmar reportedly was to cost US$3.6 billion. The ongoing Sino–Lao railway will cost about RMB37.4 billion (US$5.38 billion). In the recent renegotiated ECRL project, the originally agreed cost was MYR65.5 billion (approximately US$15.97 billion). In April 2019, Beijing and Kuala Lumpur finally agreed to implement a revised ECRL project at a reduced cost of MYR44 billion (US$10.73 billion). Concerned about overborrowing, the Myanmar government also scaled down the Chinese-led Kyaukpyu deep-sea port project in the western state of Rakhine, slashing the initial cost from US$7.2 billion to US$1.3 billion.

This analysis shows that the multilateral AIIB plays a minimal role in financing the current BRI projects, compared to China's state policy banks. Not only in Southeast Asia but also on a global scale, AIIB only has initial funds of US$10 billion. AIIB, with more prudence in assessment and the realization of limited funding, has funded only a small number of projects, such as clean energy programmes in Pakistan and an LNG integration project in Russia.[20] In contrast, just one of China's policy banks alone, China EXIM Bank, has been involved in more than a thousand BRI projects such as highways, railways, ports, power plants, pipelines, industrial parks and global communication.[21]

Moreover, China has been active in financing large-scale infrastructure investment in the region, largely through bilateral or China-sponsored funds. Owing to the opaqueness in the two approaches, more countries are becoming concerned about China's BRI infrastructure financing. Some researchers argue that unsustainable debt to China can lead to more public funds being used to salvage infrastructure that has fallen into a state of disrepair. Host governments may find it challenging to service their debts and cover their recurrent expenditures, compromising financial and economic returns. Hambantota Port in Sri Lanka and its debt for equity swap is usually used as an example of this risk. The Sri Lankan government failed to service its loans and gave a ninety-nine-year lease to a Chinese state-owned enterprise (SOE) in 2017.

Indebtedness to China has become a rising concern in the region. A few developing ASEAN member states with high debt to China to GDP ratios may

TABLE 2
AIIB-Financed Projects in Southeast Asia to 31 December 2019, USD million

Country	Project Name	Sector	Amount
Brunei	n/a		
Cambodia	Fibre-optic Communication Network	Digital infrastructure	75
Indonesia	National Slum Upgrading Project	Multi-sectoral infrastructure	1743
	Regional Infrastructure Development Fund Project	Multi-sector	406
	Dam Operational Improvement and Safety Project	Dams and Water Resource Management	300
	Strategic Irrigation Modernisation and Urgent Rehabilitation Project	Water/irrigation	578
	Mandalika Urban and Tourism Infrastructure Project	Multi-sectoral infrastructure	316.5
Laos	National Road 13 Improvement and Maintenance Project	Transport	128
Malaysia	n/a		
Myanmar	Myingyan 225 MW Combined Cycle Gas Turbine Power Plant Project	Energy	20
Thailand	n/a		
Philippines	Metro Manila Flood Management Project	Water/flood Management	500
Singapore	n/a		
Vietnam	n/a		
Grand total			3566.5

Source: Compiled by author from AIIB data.

suffer from debt distress in BRI-related financing. According to a recent study, the approximately US$6 billion figure for the Sino–Lao railway amounts to almost half of the GDP of Laos, bringing the country under considerable pressure to cover losses.[22] Another example is Cambodia, whose debt to China accounts for 48.4 per cent of the country's total outstanding debt as of the first half of 2018.[23] Although studies on the risks of debt distress in Southeast Asia indicate that Laos is the most debt-reliant on China,[24] several Southeast Asian countries, concerned about over-reliance on China's lending, have begun to reassess BRI projects or renegotiate the related project loans.

Before we assess the extent of China's financing that will lead to debt distress in the region, we should look at the environment where China's infrastructure investment flows. It is often argued that China's investment projects are implemented in countries with less stability and more corruption. In these countries, deals are vulnerable to domestic political changes and corruption.[25] Indeed, the institutional capacity of the host country generally plays a determining role in ensuring the implementation of foreign investments.[26] The member states of ASEAN are a diverse group, each with very different governance capabilities. Some ASEAN member states lack the institutional capacity to negotiate mutually beneficial investment arrangements with more powerful states. As a result, these states with perverse economic policies and a lack of alternative financing sources become easily "exploitable".[27] For some ASEAN member states, the inability to curb corruption is eroding the confidence of investors. However, China's corporate actors involved in infrastructure investment appear to be more adaptable to the local environment. Therefore, when the governance capacity of the host country is low, especially when political corruption is rife, Chinese companies are susceptible to corruption; for example, the reported use by Malaysian Prime Minister Najib of Chinese investment in the ECRL to bail out the 1MDB scandal.[28] Therefore, when there is a lack of transparency of investment procedures and when the investing destination undergoes a political transition, China's infrastructure investments can quickly become a target for attack during elections.

While some countries may not have the same level of knowledge and experience, other countries may have more information on financial techniques and better resources for financing in the midst of negotiations over complicated transactions. For example, the Thai government secured loans from the EXIM Bank of China at a 2.3 per cent interest rate, a lower rate than the domestic financial institutions, which offer an average of 2.86 per cent.[29] Another example is the Indonesian government securing the Jakarta–Bandung railway project through loans from China even without a sovereign debt guarantee. Concerned

TABLE 3
Governance Indicators of ASEAN Member States (1996–2018)

Country	Voice and accountability	Political stability	Government efficiency	Regulatory quality	Rule of law	Corruption control
Brunei	−0.76285	1.182262	1.082881	0.822855	0.552152	0.637693
Cambodia	−1.11591	0.059853	−0.70258	−0.45994	−1.02871	−1.19968
Indonesia	0.141864	−0.49256	−0.04137	−0.13677	−0.38353	−0.42292
Laos	−1.73094	0.408563	−0.51835	−0.78902	−0.81171	−0.9276
Malaysia	−0.33231	0.177989	0.972146	0.717478	0.510449	0.238696
Myanmar	−1.09589	−1.09855	−1.18535	−1.09174	−1.08684	−0.74886
Singapore	−0.10044	1.416273	2.194301	2.148598	1.806126	2.106393
Thailand	−0.89194	−0.94782	0.335506	0.202048	−0.06625	−0.41015
Philippines	0.099196	−1.05672	0.068934	−0.01523	−0.38512	−0.46335
Vietnam	−1.38704	0.17058	−0.0405	−0.49157	−0.17873	−0.47694

Notes: The global governance indicators use −2.5 to 2.5 as a range of measurement. The higher value tilting towards 2.5, the better governance it implies.
Source: Daniel Kaufmann and Aart Kraay, "Worldwide Governance Indicators", World Bank, https://info.worldbank.org/governance/wgi/.

about hefty debts to China in the ECRL project, the newly elected Prime Minister Mahathir managed to reduce the costs of the ECRL project.[30] According to the study, eight ASEAN member states, excluding Laos and Cambodia, were not even ranked among the top fifty BRI borrowers from China.[31] Statistical studies have shown that the BRI is not likely be "plagued with widescale debt sustainability problems". As shown in this chapter, out of the eight member states with BRI loans, only Laos is likely to be vulnerable to debt distress.

Despite this reality, the leaders of Southeast Asian countries are wary of the domestic economic effects of massive debts. In early July 2018, Myanmar's Minister of Planning and Finance U Soe Win warned: "[To] avoid falling into the debt trap, Myanmar seeks to scale down the size of Kyaukphyu special economic zone."[32] Malaysian Prime Minister Mahathir even warned the Philippines against "overborrowing" to "regulate or limit influences from China".[33]

Geopolitical Meme

Arguably, Chinese overseas financing has vexed India, the United States and other major powers because of developmental and geopolitical concerns. Even Chinese scholars have begun to acknowledge that geopolitics has become a "disruptive factor" in the implementation of BRI projects.[34] For example, pundits on geopolitics concur that China's 99-year lease of Hambantota Port is a form of "debt for equity swap" that serves the strategic motivation of "debt trap" diplomacy along the string of pearls in the Indian Ocean.[35] Starting from New Delhi, the "debt trap" narrative warnings have been shared with and propagated in Washington political circles.[36] Furthermore, the narrative has been circulated and amplified by both the former and current US secretary of state.[37] This effect is called the meme of "debt trap", in the sense that the narrative has become a popular belief. Media coverage of such narratives has led to rising global concern over Chinese overseas infrastructure financing. By analysing data from 14,596 documents, the author found that the BRI is closely related to the topic of the "debt trap" in the media (see Figure 4).

To major powers, the meme of the "debt trap" is that the BRI is not merely about commerce but is also about the party that sets the rules. The narrative is justifiable in geopolitical analysis. First, Chinese overseas lending and infrastructure investments are generally conducted by Chinese SOEs and state policy banks. Chinese SOEs, as political and economic entities, have a dual identity, which leads to Chinese infrastructure investments being mistrusted. Second, infrastructure investments entail not only construction but also standard-setting.[38] Many standards

FIGURE 4
Most Mentioned Topics Related to "Debt Trap" (September 2013 – December 2019)

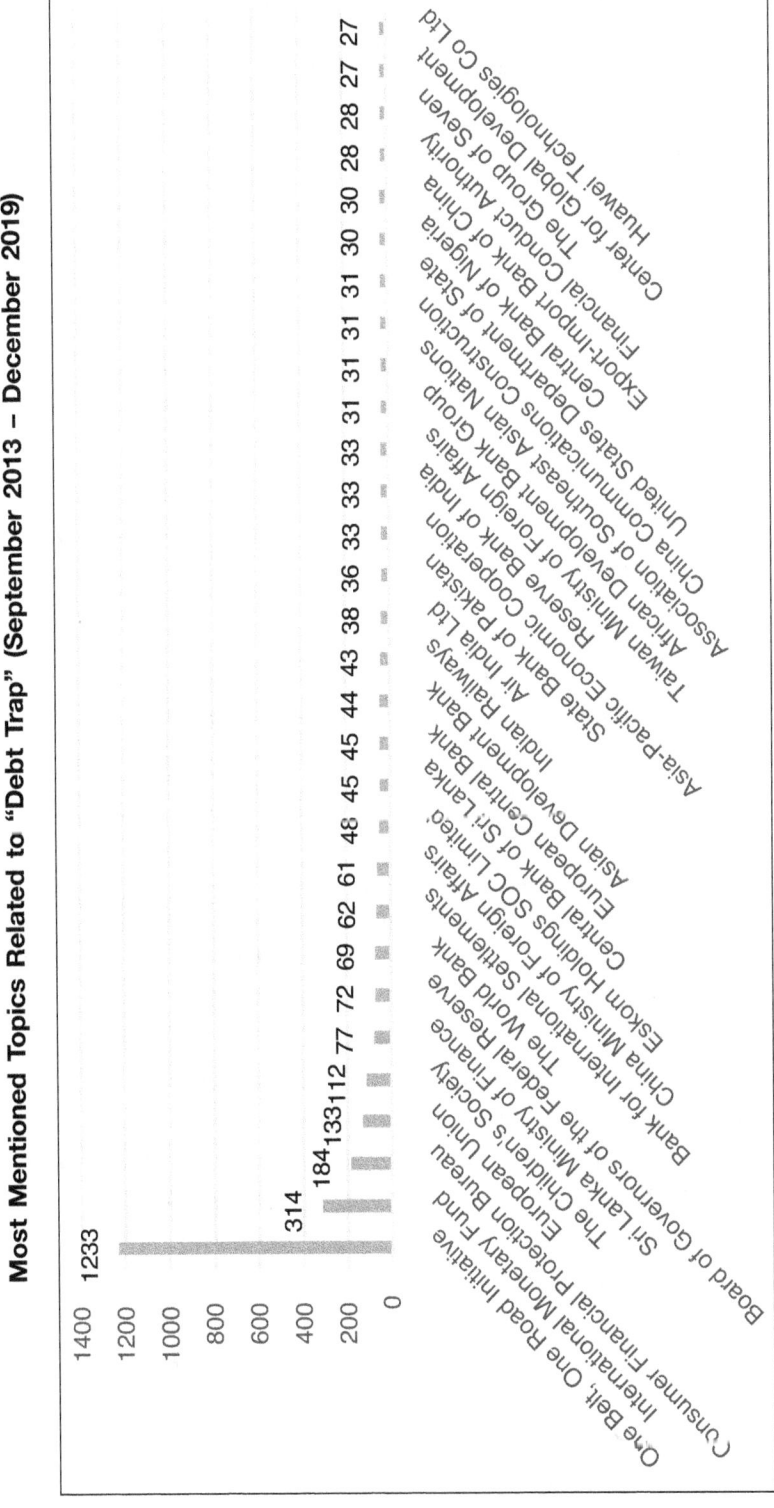

Source: Data analysis from Factiva by author, 21 December 2019.

of infrastructure investments can be used as a strategic tool during wartime. For example, "peace" goods such as water utilities and food storage facilities could be used as strategic materials during a war. Infrastructure projects such as railways and deep-sea ports bring about even more strategic implications because they can serve military troops.

Clearly, these negative narratives have cast an enduring shadow on China's promise and ability to deliver a win-win solution as pledged in the official BRI narrative. Some countries have turned to external powers for assistance. For example, Myanmar's government turned to a team of American advisors to reassess the project, resulting in a scaling down of the investment value of the Kyaukpyu deep-sea port. As the United States is constantly strategizing to counter China's growing influence through the BRI, China can expect an increasing presence of consulting and advisory services provided by international groups.[39]

Whither the BRI

Scholars have warned that the growing meme of the debt trap of the BRI is undesirable for development. Despite the setbacks, many more Chinese infrastructure investments provide conditions that favour the fulfilment of the Sustainable Development Goals (SDG), where traditional donors have begun to retreat from providing infrastructure investment public goods,[40] as many research results show.[41]

Despite highlighting the "debt-trap" hype in disrupting the development elements of the BRI, the backlash manifests several significant problems for the financing of China's BRI. The first issue is the lack of both commercial viability and transparency of bilateral financing agreements between the Chinese government and the host governments, resulting in speculation by observers about the purpose and practices of the financing. Second, China's elite-oriented approach to overseas lending is often associated with the "corrupt" image of China's BRI infrastructure investment. When the governance capacity of the host country is weak, China's BRI projects are subject to the scrutiny of both local society and the international community. Third, China's financing sources are abundant but are not well coordinated or utilized in the region, where Beijing has the AIIB, CAF, SRF and China-ASEAN Maritime Cooperation Fund. Observers do not understand why China elected to establish different sources of financing instead of pooling the resources to form a single multilateral financing institution.

Considering the resistance and involvement of other countries, China realizes that current financing practices could drive up the costs of China's implementation of the BRI in Southeast Asia and beyond as Chinese companies may be forced to make concessions. China has also begun to recognize that current financing practices have undermined its strategic interests in the region. Some participating countries have already demanded the renegotiation of loan terms with China or have bargained with China by inviting in economic competitors. To ease geopolitical tensions, China played down the BRI hype by redefining the commercial aspects of the initiative at the second Belt and Road International Cooperation Forum in April 2019. At the forum, Chinese President Xi Jinping repeatedly called for "high-quality" projects and higher standards by encouraging other developed countries to engage in "third market cooperation" (in other words, to participate in the BRI). By emphasizing the commercial gains, Xi claims to be building a "clean, green and lean" BRI, a claim aimed at addressing concerns about China's investment and reducing the growing apprehensions about Beijing's political and economic influence in BRI regions.

To make the BRI a catalyst for reforming regional and global development and governance, China would have to create a level playing field for both domestic and foreign companies involved in the BRI. As China claims to be building a "clean, green and lean" BRI, the Chinese government needs to establish a standard that can increase transparency and motivate private sector actors to take part in financing. Beijing also needs to reassess its "hands-off" infrastructure approach in the host country by regulating corporate practices and behaviour in overseas investments. In addition, China should also help the host country improve governance and strengthen its institutional capacity. Effective governance of the host government can optimize the distribution of benefits to the host country and ensure a smooth implementation of China's investments and flagship BRI projects. To attract investments and provide a friendly investment environment, Southeast Asian governments also need to develop strong regulatory capabilities to identify viable projects while establishing regulatory credibility among investors.

Observers who generalize about Chinese infrastructure investments should be aware that Chinese financing is far more complicated[42] because China's engagement is "multivariate".[43] China's BRI can potentially be more developmental than suggested by the current hype generated by the "debt trap" meme. Therefore, the intellectual and policy communities in the region should also evaluate the "debt trap" meme very carefully. To be fair, this meme has arisen for a reason. If China wants to provide regional and international public goods, Beijing needs to consider the concerns of regional countries. One such concern is whether China's engagement in the region can create a fair and open market for others if China abides by existing standards and rules. The more benefits the regional countries can gain from China's projects, the more likely China's investments will be well-received by regional states. Multilateral financing can reduce political and financial risks for China. Furthermore, if China aspires to provide public goods to the region and the world, Beijing must take steps to improve its overseas financing.

Notes

1. Xue Gong, "The Belt & Road Initiative and China's Influence in Southeast Asia", *Pacific Review* 32, no. 4 (2019): 635–65.
2. Joshua Kurlantzick, *Charm Offensive: How China's Soft Power Is Transforming the World* (New Haven: Yale University Press, 2008).
3. UNDP, China Development Bank, and Peking University, *The Economic Development along the Belt and Road 2017*, https://issuu.com/undp-china/docs/the_economic_development_along_the_.
4. Jan Zhang, "Will the Manufacturing Growth Cycle Continue in China? Part 1, *Interact Analysis*, 14 November 2017, https://www.interactanalysis.com/china-manufacturing-growth/.
5. Xue, "The Belt & Road Initiative", pp. 635–65.
6. Huileng Tan, "The Specter of Chinese Investment Looms over Indonesia's Election", CNBC, 15 April 2019, https://www.cnbc.com/2019/04/16/indonesia-elections-jokowi-prabowo-and-the-topic-of-china.html; James Griffith, "China Is Becoming an Election Issue in Asia. And That Is Bad News for Beijing", CNN, 5 April 2019, https://edition.cnn.com/2019/04/04/asia/china-indonesia-election-influence-asia-intl/index.html; Bhavan Jaipragas and Coco Liu, "Is Chinese Money an Issue? In Malaysia, Only at Election Time", *South China Morning Post*, 28 May 2018, https://www.scmp.com/week-asia/politics/article/2144779/chinese-money-issue-malaysia-only-election-time; Natnicha Chuwiruch, "Thai Politicians Criticize China as Election Comes into Focus", Bloomberg, 31 August 2018, https://www.bloomberg.com/news/articles/2018-08-31/thai-politicians-criticize-china-as-election-comes-into-focus.
7. OECD, "China's Belt and Road Initiative in the Global Trade, Investment and Finance Landscape", in *OECD Business and Finance Outlook 2018* (Paris: OECD Publishing, 2018), p. 29, https://www.oecd.org/finance/Chinas-Belt-and-Road-Initiative-in-the-global-trade-investment-and-finance-landscape.pdf.
8. Ibid., p. 87.
9. Xue, "The Belt & Road Initiative", pp. 635–65.
10. Sun Degang and Yahia Zoubir, "Development First: China's Investment in Seaport Constructions and Operations along the Maritime Silk Road", *Asian Journal of Middle Eastern and Islamic Studies* 11, no. 3 (2017): 35–47.

11. Xi Jinping, "Guangxi kaocha: Xiehao xinshiji haishang sichou zhilu xin pianzhang" [Xi Jinping visited Guangxi: write a new chapter on new century Maritime Silk Road well], Xinhuanet, 19 April 2017.
12. The Belt and Road Research Group, "A Strategic Analysis on China's Overseas Port Projects under the Belt and Road Initiative", Center for Policy Studies, Grandview Institution, April 2019.
13. "Full Text: Vision for Maritime Cooperation under the Belt and Road Initiative, NDRC and National Oceanic Administration", Xinhuanet, 20 June 2017, http://www.xinhuanet.com//english/2017-06/20/c_136380414.htm.
14. Ibid.
15. "Zhaoshangju: Dazao siluyizhan zhili jiejue zhongguo qiye zouchuqu hexin tongdian" [China Merchants Group: Create a Silk Road courier station devoted to solving the core problems of Chinese companies going out], *China Youth*, 20 June 2017.
16. "Zhang Jie, Haishang tongdao anquan yu zhongguo zhanlve zhidian de goujian" [SLOC security and construction of china's strategic support points], *International Security Studies (China)*, no. 2 (2015): 100–18.
17. Xue, "The Belt & Road Initiative", pp. 635–65.
18. China-ASEAN Investment Cooperation Fund, "Vision and Mission", http://www.china-asean-fund.com/about-caf.php?slider1=1.
19. China-ASEAN Investment Cooperation Fund, "News and Press Release", http://www.china-asean-fund.com/news.php?slider1=1.
20. "Jin Qi tan jinrong ruhe zhichi yidaiyilu jianshe" [Jin Qi speaks on financial support for Belt and Road], *Jingrong shibao*, 23 May 2016; "Sichou zhilu jijin jihua: Zijin congheerlai?" [Silk Road Fund plan: Where the money comes from], *Jingrong shibao*, 13 May 2016.
21. "Jinchukou yinhang yidaiyilu daikuan yu'er chao 5200 yi" [EXIM Bank loans to BRI projects exceeded RMB520 billion], *Zhongguo zhengguan bao*, 15 January 2016.
22. John Hurley, Scott Morris, and Gailyn Portelance, "Examining the Debt Implications of the Belt and Road Initiative from a Policy Perspective", CGD Policy Paper 121, March 2018.
23. *Cambodia Economic Update: Recent Economic Developments and Outlook. Selected Issue: Investing in Cambodia's Future: Early Childhood Health and Nutrition* (World Bank Group, May 2019).
24. Hurley, Morris, and Portelance, "Examining the Debt Implications".
25. OECD, "China's Belt and Road Initiative, p. 87.
26. Jenny Rebecca Kehl, *Foreign Investment and Domestic Development: Multinationals and the State* (Boulder, CO: Lynne Rienner, 2009); Colin Kirkpatrick, David Parker, and Yin-Fang Zhang, "Foreign Direct Investment in Infrastructure in Developing Countries: Does Regulation Make a Difference?", *Transnational Corporations* 15, no. 1 (2006): 143–71; Thomas Brewer, "Effects of Government Policies on Foreign

Direct Investment as a Strategic Choice of Firms: An Expansion of Internalization Theory", *International Trade Journal* 7, no. 1 (1992): 111–29.

27. Agatha Kratz, Allen Feng, and Logan Wright, "New Data on the 'Debt Trap' Question", *Rhodium Group*, 29 April 2019.
28. Danson Cheong, "China's Belt and Road Initiative Faces Fresh Backlash", *Straits Times*, 15 June 2019, https://www.straitstimes.com/asia/east-asia/chinas-bri-faces-fresh-backlash.
29. "Thailand Resisting Falling into Rail Debt Trap", *Bangkok Post*, 25 April 2019, https://www.bangkokpost.com/thailand/special-reports/1667000/thailand-resisting-falling-into-rail-debt-trap.
30. Raul Dancel, "Beware of China 'Debt Trap', Malaysia's Mahathir Tells the Philippines", *Straits Times*, 7 March 2019, https://www.straitstimes.com/asia/se-asia/beware-of-china-debt-trap-malaysias-mahathir-tells-the-philippines.
31. Hurley, Morris, and Portelance, "Examining the Debt Implications".
32. "Myanmar Scales Back China-Funded Kyauk Pyu Port Project in Rakhine State due to Debt Concerns", *South China Morning Post*, 2 August 2018, https://www.scmp.com/news/asia/southeastasia/article/2158015/myanmar-scales-back-china-funded-kyauk-pyu-port-project.
33. Dancel, "Beware of China 'Debt Trap'".
34. Sun Degang, "Zhongguo gangkou waijiao de lilun yu shijian" [China port diplomacy: Theory and practice], *World Politics and Economics*, no. 5, 2018.
35. Zahih Ali Khan, "China's Gwadar and India's Chahbahar: An Analysis of Sino-India Geostrategic and Economic Competition", *Strategic Studies* 32, no. 4 (2013); Virginia Marantidou, "Revisiting China's 'Strings of Pearls' Strategy: Places with Chinese Characteristics and Their Security Implications", *Issues & Insights* 14, no. 7 (2014).
36. US Embassy in Paraguay, "Speech of Secretary of State Michael R. Pompeo: The China Challenge", 30 October 2019, https://py.usembassy.gov/speech-of-secretary-of-state-michael-r-pompeo-the-china-challenge/.
37. US Department of Defense, "Summary of the 2018 National Defense Strategy of the United States of America", 29 January 2018, https://dod.defense.gov/Portals/1/Documents/pubs/2018-National-Defense-Strategy-Summary.pdf.
38. Jonathan E. Hillman, "Influence and Infrastructure: The Strategic Stakes of Foreign Projects", *CSIS*, 22 January 2019.
39. Ben Kesling and Jon Emont, "U.S. Goes on the Offensive against China's Empire-Building Funding Plan", *Wall Street Journal*, 9 April 2019, https://www.wsj.com/articles/u-s-goes-on-the-offensive-against-chinas-empire-building-megaplan-11554809402.
40. Deborah Brautigam, "A Critical Look at Chinese 'Debt-Trap Diplomacy': The Rise of a Meme, *Area Development and Policy* 5, no. 1 (2019): 1–14, https://doi.org/10.1080/23792949.2019.1689828.
41. Maggie Xiaoyang Chen and Chuanhao Lin, "Foreign Investment across the Belt and

Road Patterns, Determinants and Effects", Policy Research Working Paper no. 8607 (World Bank Group, October 2018).

42. Min Ye, "Fragmentation and Mobilization: Domestic Politics of the Belt and Road in China", *Journal of Contemporary China* 28, no. 119 (2019): 696–711, https://doi.org/10.1080/10670564.2019.1580428.

43. Jing Gu, Zhang Chuanhong, Alcides Vaz, and Angton Mukwereza, "Chinese State Capitalism? Rethinking the Role of the State and Business in Chinese Development Cooperation in Africa", *World Development* 81 (2016): 24–34; Ye Min, "Economy in Command: Unpacking the Domestic Politics of China's Belt and Road Initiative", GEGI Working Paper no. 16 (Boston University Global Development Policy Center, 2018).

Brunei Darussalam

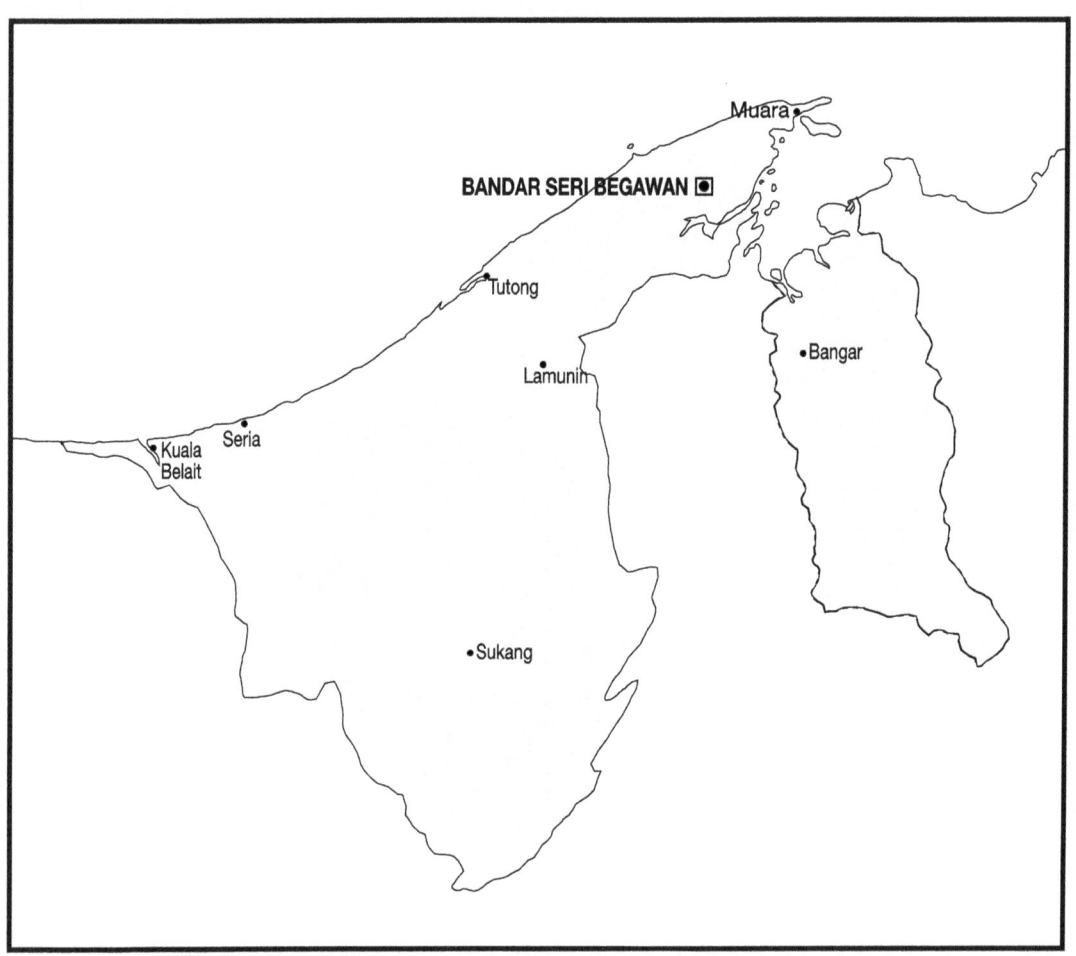

BRUNEI DARUSSALAM IN 2019:
Issues Revisited

Pushpa Thambipillai

It was generally a busy year for Brunei Darussalam in 2019 as it continued to focus on developmental issues while experiencing peace and political stability. Recurring concerns for the economy and administration surfaced periodically in line with fresh assessments towards the one major national goal—Wawasan 2035 (Brunei Vision 2035). Except for intense but short-lived global attention on its *syariah* system of jurisprudence, Brunei's domestic affairs were not of much concern for foreign observers. The effects of the preceding years' reduced income from the country's hydrocarbon exports were still felt by the domestic economy, although global prices for oil had moderately improved in early 2019. Any increase in prices for the period under study was only speculative given the uncertainty of global economic trends. Increasing down-stream hydrocarbon activities provided diversification, while improved productive capacities in agriculture and agroindustry were sought. The recurring national concerns had familiar undertones—except that relevant policymakers appeared more committed to advancing the social and economic development of the state—with frequent admonishment from the Head of State and Government, Sultan Haji Hassanal Bolkiah.

Managing the State

As a small state, Brunei is politically and economically manageable in accordance with the stated priorities embodied in its philosophy of Melayu Islam Beraja (MIB; Malay Islamic Monarchy) and Vision 2035, which promotes socio-economic

---

Pushpa Thambipillai is Associate Fellow at the ISEAS – Yusuf Ishak Institute, Singapore. She was previously Senior Lecturer at the Faculty of Business, Economics and Policy Studies, Universiti Brunei Darussalam (now renamed School of Business and Economics, UBD).

developmental goals. At an average growth rate of 3 per cent, the 2018 population was 442,400, a bane for large-scale economic activities.[1] However, guided by the twin pillars of Vision 2035 and the UN Agenda for Sustainable Development 2030, the policymakers are mindful of the directions that uphold the national aspirations of growth amidst austerity in providing a satisfactory quality of life for Bruneians. The annual economic growth rate is of concern. In his speech on the occasion of the New Year 2019, Sultan Haji Hassanal Bolkiah expected better economic growth for the year. However, he reminded his subjects that they had to "march forward … with full spirit and determination" and not be plagued with "lazy syndrome". He urged them to be "a more proactive and productive society" in light of the economic challenges faced by Brunei.[2] On another occasion, at the commencement of the Legislative Council meeting, he called for concerted action by all, as GDP growth had been "less favourable" with the drop in global oil prices, and there was thus a need for emphasis on the non–oil and gas sectors and preparedness for the inevitable surge in the Fourth Industrial Revolution.[3] Given the nature of Brunei's economy—with the oil and gas sector accounting for between 73 and 75 per cent of the whole—ascertaining GDP growth for the year is not straightforward. Various international agencies have offered their assessments. For example, the IMF expected economic growth in 2019 to reach 1.8 per cent based on stronger oil and gas activities, while the ADB forecast a 1 per cent growth rate. The EIU sees an average growth of between 1 and 1.5 per cent. The most optimistic assessment, at 2.1 per cent, was given by AMRO, the ASEAN+3 Macroeconomic Research Office.[4] Bruneians are generally "cash-rich", at a GDP per capita of BN$41,366, with generous subsidies and welfare programmes. Other than through natural increase, the number of citizens enlarged by only a small amount, given the tough requirements. For instance, in 2019, 222 residents were granted Brunei citizenship, while the total from January 2017 to October 2019 was 1,262.[5]

One of the tasks of the Legislative Council, which meets in March of each year, is to pass the budget for the financial year from April to March of the following year. The Minister of Finance and Economy II (concurrently Minister at the Prime Minister's Office) presented the year's budget, themed "Investing in our Future". The budget allocation of BN$5.86 billion for 2019/20 was only BN$560 million more than that of the previous year. The minister pointed out that he expected another budget deficit, as has been the case over the last few years, because of low GDP growth. The expected revenue for 2019/20 was BN$4.36 billion, made up of BN$3.18 billion from the oil and gas sector and BN$1.18 billion from the non–oil and gas sector, resulting in a deficit of BN$1.50 billion. The allocations are for four main activities: increase investments, facilitate business, produce competent and relevant human capital, and sustain public welfare.[6]

Digital technology is spreading globally, and Brunei has not been spared. One of the current emphases is on digital applications in the public and business sector to facilitate trade and investment. Thus, digital usage has been incorporated into the economic strategy, with civil servants, entrepreneurs and youths exposed to its potentials. Brunei's old refrain on diversification has now taken on a more serious adage with the Fourth Industrial Revolution, calling for new approaches. Diversification is still very much the bedrock of the national economic policy, as the presence of a cross section of new industries indicates incremental steps in diversifying the economy away from relying predominantly on the hydrocarbon sector. There is no question of the role of oil and gas in Brunei's economy. The country plans to drill for oil offshore to depths of two kilometres or more using new deep-water drilling technologies.[7] It is inevitable that, with foreign input, drilling and oil exploration will continue to dominate the economic life of Brunei.

In the last few years, downstream activities have taken on an important role. This includes the large petrochemical complex that began its maiden production in the third quarter of 2019. The Hengyi Brunei Pulau Muara Besar (PMB) project, one of the largest FDI projects in Brunei, began construction of its oil refinery and petrochemical plant in early 2017, after undertaking basic infrastructural projects on the island. Trial production had already produced fuels such as diesel, JetA-1, petroleum, and liquefied petroleum gas (LPG). The plant's first cargo of LPG has been exported. Full operation of the complex is expected by the end of 2019 or early 2020. In the meantime, Brunei Shell Petroleum Company (BSP) and Brunei Shell Marketing Co (BSM) signed an agreement with Hengyi Industries on the supply of crude oil (by BSP) and the distribution of refined fuel products for the local market (by BSM). According to initial agreements on the first phase of Hengyi Industries, 40 per cent of its workforce would be local by the end of 2019, but it was only likely to meet 50 per cent of the target by the end of the year. Under its skilled workforce programme, since 2014, 68 Bruneians have completed their studies under the Hengyi scholarship at Universiti Brunei Darussalam and Zhejiang University in China. They are employed in various departments of the PMB project.[8]

Meanwhile, at the Sungei Liang Industrial Park, a consortium of Japanese companies has set up a plant that produces hydrogen from natural gas. Over 200 metric tonnes of the liquefied hydrogen is expected to be exported to Japan during a one-year period in 2020. The initial export of hydrogen from Muara port to Kawasaki city in Japan commenced in November 2019 and will be continued on a weekly basis. The hydrogen is to fuel Toa Oil Company's gas turbine power generator. It is reported to be part of Japan's "hydrogen supply chain demonstration project", which will run from January to December 2020. According to Brunei's Ministry of Energy, Manpower and Industry, there are potential uses for the demonstration plant beyond 2020; the transport sector may explore the possibility of supplying hydrogen fuel cells to electric vehicles such as cars and buses to sustain a cleaner environment.[9] With the increase in industrial activities in Brunei Darussalam, there has been a corresponding increase in demand for energy, especially in the demand for gas. Thus, energy security is of concern to decision makers, and alternate sources of renewable energy have been considered, notably in the development of solar photovoltaic power plants.[10]

Development Issues

While the downstream oil and gas sector has been targeted for further expansion through FDI and joint ventures, the non–oil and gas sector has seen renewed focus. Sectors such as food industries, tourism-related services, and agro and aquatic industries have seen increasing input. Lacking in capital, technology and skilled manpower, the sultanate relies on foreign direct investment for its industrial activities. Two recent reports have given it a slight boost: the World Bank's annual Doing Business 2020 has placed Brunei 66th out of 190 economies in its Ease of Doing Business ranking, an improvement of four places over the previous year. The World Economic Forum, meanwhile, has ranked Brunei 56th out of 141 countries in the Global Competitiveness Index 2019. Both agencies have cited some improvements in domestic policies that have contributed to the upward movement in the rankings. However, more reforms and changes to some policy practices may encourage a positive perception and hence participation by potential investors, both local and foreign. The ranking exercises are also significant in that past rankings have pointed out specific areas of successes and failures that policy planners have taken into consideration to lead to improvements.

Available data on net FDI (2017) indicates BN$635.3 million—manufacturing attracted the highest FDI at BN$680.2 million, followed by construction at BN$663.9 million. Malaysian sources accounted for the largest inflow at BN$674.7 million for the year. While the balance of trade has been in Brunei's favour, it has declined over the years as the prices of its vital exports have fallen. For example, the total trade in August 2019 saw a decrease of 12 per cent compared to August 2018 (year-on-year). One of its lowest receipts was in mid-

2019, when total exports decreased by 20 per cent compared to the previous year. This was mainly due to a decrease in exports of crude oil and liquefied natural gas. The export prices of crude oil and LNG had decreased by 10.5 per cent and 0.6 per cent, respectively. Thus, Brunei's income from its main exports is a direct consequence of international markets, while its other merchandise exports only constitute a small portion.[11]

Food security is of paramount concern, as Brunei imports most of its food needs, including its staple, rice. Local rice production meets only about 5 per cent of the country's increasing demand. Over the past decade various schemes have been introduced to increase production. Agricultural land has been distributed to farmers, subsidies have been implemented, and high yield rice varieties have been employed. However, the results have been modest. Undaunted, more efforts are being made to promote rice cultivation in all the districts. The latest such move has been phase one of the 500-hectare commercial paddy plantation project at Kandol Agricultural Development Area in Belait District, undertaken by a government-linked company. The initial phase of planting 20 hectares will be completed by the end of 2019. It is projected that by 2025, when the entire area will be under cultivation, it will supply about 11–15 per cent of the country's rice needs.[12] Special projects for youths have also been introduced. Brunei Shell Petroleum, through Live WIRE Brunei (its entrepreneurship and social investment programme), has allocated funds to support the AgroBiz Padi Agropreneur scheme at the Institute of Brunei Technical Education (IBTE). At the IBTE Agro-Technology Campus in Kampong Wasan, 10 hectares of land has been provided for paddy planting, using modern farming methods and technology. It is expected that the sponsored project will be continued beyond the 2019 planting cycle, attracting more students and viable research to be shared with local farmers to improve farming methods.[13]

Issues related to employment are of concern to policymakers. The Labour Force Survey of 2018 identified the working age population (aged 15 years and above) at 337,900. The labour force totalled 221,000, of whom 201,700 were employed and 19,200 unemployed. The foreign labour force came to 117,000. Unemployment stood at about 9 per cent, with youths making up a significant component. The Department of Economic Development conducted the second phase of the Labour Force Survey during October and November 2019. Information from the survey on the size, structure, distribution and other characteristics of the labour force is expected to assist in various aspects of decision-making. Unemployment and the issue of the replacement of foreign labour are not the only concerns; job creation by new industries and services and the promotion of self-employment are also national priorities. An encouraging trend has been the number of locals entering the private sector instead of waiting for the preferred public sector. According to the last Annual Census of Enterprises, conducted in December 2017, there was an increase of 2.2 per cent of locals entering the private sector over the previous year. The research was able to identify 6,047 enterprises: 2,442 micro (with less than 5 workers), 2,490 small (with 5–19 workers), 944 medium (with 20–99 workers) and 171 large enterprises (with 100 or more workers). The data (from the Department of Economic Planning and Development) also compared information from earlier annual surveys. The increase in the number of enterprises over the years provides some positive opportunities for the local labour force.

A worrisome issue for policymakers is the imminent Fourth Industrial Revolution (4IR) and the commensurate need to develop competent human resources to manage the new technologies and innovation. The minister in charge of manpower noted that the country would approach the issue from a national strategic focus, as it required human and capital resources. The Minister of Energy, Manpower and Industry and the Minister of Transport and Info-communications fielded questions on this topic at the Legislative Assembly in March 2019. They expressed that a prudent approach would ensure changes would have a minimum impact on workers and employment. Stakeholders including the government, education providers and industry players are in consultation as to how best be prepared with the appropriate ICT infrastructure and a skilled workforce to meet the demands of 4IR.[14] In relation to this, the Civil Service Institute organized a two-day roundtable on understanding 4IR issues in order to share the knowledge of experts from within and outside Brunei Darussalam.[15]

Social Policies

The year saw a number of youth-focused policies under consideration. Demands for employment opportunities, the increase in the number of graduates from tertiary institutions, and changes to the economic environment affecting job opportunities have prompted reviews of existing educational policies and the future employability of the country's citizens. The Ministry of Education introduced its New Strategy Plan 2018–22 to emphasize quality education in addressing preparedness for the Fourth Industrial Revolution. In a presentation at the UNESCO General Conference in Paris in November 2019, the Minister of Education stated that Brunei was embarking on efforts towards developing and integrating educational technologies in the curriculum. Such efforts will not only take place at the tertiary level but will also encompass those who have demonstrated an aptitude for technical training at the high school level. The scattering of technical schools has been strengthened under the new Institute of Brunei Technical Education, while Politeknik Brunei is also providing post-secondary-level training.[16] Education related to components of the Malay Islamic Monarchy philosophy have not been neglected. The Sultan announced the establishment of a centre to promote Jawi script (Malay language written in Arabic script) as a representation of national identity and that all higher education institutions were to promote Jawi as having the same importance as the Malay language.[17]

Another area with heavy government subsidies is the health sector. As the Brunei population has a high level of disposable income, a major portion of it goes into the purchase of food items—leading to one of the negative effects on health— as well as encouraging a sedentary lifestyle, where car ownership is generally affordable. According to the Ministry of Health, the increasing incidences of heart ailments, kidney failure and diabetes have been brought about by unhealthy eating habits. In September 2019 the Minister of Health (at the launch of the Strategic Plan 2019–2023) cited non-communicable disease as the major cause of death in the country, with cancer, heart disease and diabetes accounting for 44 per cent of deaths in 2018. The plan aims to strengthen the healthcare system through the provision of quality and accessible services.[18] The minister also noted that there was an increase in the suicide rate, from 1.9 cases per 100,000 population in 2015 to 2.6 cases per 100,000 population in 2018. Although the rate was considered low compared to some other countries, he called for effective measures to address mental health problems within society to prevent adverse consequences.[19] The World Health Organization in the meantime has given a positive evaluation of Brunei's capacity to prevent, detect and respond to public health threats, including epidemics and chemical or radiation emergencies. Housing needs for citizens have continued to be met by the government. Ownership is approved under various national housing schemes, and each year several hundred people receive their plot of land or a built house, ranging from low to middle price brackets. The latest distribution under the National Housing Scheme was in Temburong District, where the Sultan, during his visit to the district capital Bangar, handed out keys to 234 house owners.[20]

As the chief executive, Sultan Hassanal Bolkiah takes an astute interest in the affairs of the state. He appears well informed by his cabinet and other advisers. Complaints and negative assessments of public policies in the print and social media also do not escape his attention, as his occasional scathing remarks indicate. On at least three occasions during the year he reprimanded government officials for specific inadequacies. He was disappointed that some civil servants "lacked the necessary effort and drive in working for the benefit of society".[21] Speaking at the annual Civil Service Day celebrations, he pointed out weaknesses in implementing certain policies or laws, for example in enforcing anti-dumping, anti-polluting of public areas, prohibition of smoking in certain areas, and a case of an eight-year-old issue that had yet to be resolved. But, as is the norm, he went on to present merit awards to deserving individuals in various categories of the civil service.

A national issue that has implications for the labour and immigration sectors is that of foreign workers. During an unscheduled visit to the Immigration and National Registration Department and the Labour Department, the Sultan queried the enforcement of regulations on foreign workers. Contrary to regulations, foreign workers without the sponsorship of employers had entered and stayed in the sultanate for indefinite periods, while there were also "visa rackets" of individuals who sponsored foreign nationals for a certain fee. The Labour Department was queried on the granting of increased quotas to employment agents who invariably misused their permits to allow foreign workers to work for a certain fee or used counterfeit company licences, presumably registered with the Labour Department, to acquire foreign workers. Issues of security, the employment of local labour, and entrepreneurship were at stake as more foreign nationals set up their businesses under dubious work visas.

The Sultan asked, "How can the management and administration be so poor? There are plenty of reasons for this. Among them is insufficient manpower, or it could also be due to laziness and lack of focus. Or worst of all, corruption." He warned that corruption should not be allowed to "taint government management and administration".[22] In a *titah* during a visit to the Royal Brunei Police Force (RBPF), the Sultan (who is the Inspector General of Police) raised the matter of a lack of firm leadership and of inefficiency in the management and administration of the RBPF. He expressed that such a situation should not occur, as the RBPF is a security agency and the members of the police force must seek excellence in their careers in preventing crime in the nation. According to police statistics, the crime rate was on the rise, especially property crimes such as general theft, car/house break-ins, vehicle theft and robbery (in 2017 about 3,090 cases related to property were recorded; there was a total of 5,192 cases in 2018). Drug related incidents have also been on the increase, with the sultanate potentially becoming a transit or sale point for illicit drugs. According to the Narcotics Control Bureau (NCB), it had intercepted two attempts to smuggle in drugs. At a meeting between the NCB and the Narcotics Criminal Investigation Department of the Malaysian Police Force, in Bandar Seri Begawan, both sides expressed their plans to share information and cooperate. Meanwhile, the Immigration and National Registration Department stated that 9,975 foreign nationals charged with various offences had been deported between 2014 and 2019.[23]

Strengthening Islamic Identity

The Proclamation of Independence of Brunei Darussalam on 1 January 1984 identified the sultanate to be "for ever a sovereign, democratic and independent Malay, Muslim Monarchy". Over the past three decades, more stringent expectations from the dominant faith have been visible in the country. This has manifested not just in the outward acceptance of such symbols of faith as dressing and ritual, but also in the stringent policies that have emerged to accord Islam the central position. *Syariah*, or the Islamic legal system, has in some form or another been in practice throughout the sultanate's history. As a British protectorate, a dual system of English Common Law and *syariah* law was present, the latter only applying to certain practices among the Muslim population. *Syariah* law had its own specialized group of legal practitioners. The intention to introduce *syariah*-based criminal jurisprudence, or *hudud*, was first announced by the Sultan in 2013. It was to be implemented in stages over a number of years, as it had to be instituted and experts trained in its application. The initial phase reviewed and strengthened the existing *syariah* laws. These included legal matters affecting the institutions of the family, property, marriage, divorce and the requirements of certain obligations such as joining Friday prayers and fasting during Ramadan. Under phase one of the new law that came into effect in 2014 there would be stricter enforcement and increased penalties of fines and imprisonment compared to the previous legal regime. The culmination of the revisions resulted in the Syariah Penal Code (*hudud*), which includes severe punishments for a variety of crimes, such as severing the hands of thieves and stoning to death those guilty of gay sex or adultery. The implementation of *hudud* was slated for early 2019.

International reaction to the proposed Syariah Penal Code began during the initial announcements in 2013 and rose to a crescendo in early April 2019 as the date for implementation neared. The launch date itself was not highlighted within Brunei. Domestic reactions were muted, except on some social media or where apprehensive locals (like the LGBT community) had been quoted in foreign media. Negative reactions came from some Western governments, NGOs, international personalities and student groups, who took up the cause to show their disapproval. They viewed the punishments under *hudud* as "inhuman", especially those affecting the LGBT community. Critics proposed a boycott of Brunei-owned hotels and properties (about nine properties were listed as located in the United Kingdom, the United States and Europe; a high-profile celebrity event that was to be held in one of the venues was cancelled). Meanwhile, Brunei stood its ground and called for foreign agitators to respect its laws. In a nationally televised speech in early May to mark the beginning of the fasting month of Ramadan, the Sultan announced that there was a moratorium on the death penalty in Brunei, as no offenders had been sent to the gallows over the past two decades, thus implying the *hudud* system would not hand down any death sentences.[24] A related consequence to the *hudud* saga was the step taken by Sultan Hassanal Bolkiah of returning an honorary law degree he was awarded by Oxford University in 1993. Reportedly nearly 120,000 people had signed a petition by April 2019 calling on the university to withdraw the degree. As the university undertook the review process (informing the Sultan of its intention), the Sultan pre-empted any decision by Oxford by returning the degree.[25]

In another development, Malaysia's Universiti Teknologi MARA (UiTM) presented the Sultan an honorary doctorate (in Islamic Leadership) during its ninetieth convocation ceremony.[26] Subsequently, Malaysia's Ministry of Education proposed a Sultan Hassanal Bolkiah Chair for Islamic Leadership to be set up at UiTM, and the proposal was submitted to the Sultan. The chair would focus on the study of the Malay sultanate, Islamic leadership, and *syariah* law, among others.[27] As 2019 drew to a close there were no reported cases of severe punishments under the new *syariah* law. In fact, a couple of cases of theft judged at the Syariah High Court were handed prison terms: the theft of BN$100 from a friend landed the offender a five-month prison term, while a man who stole his mother's gas cylinder spent four months in jail. Another offender who stole a mosque donation box escaped the *syariah* law; following his trial in the civil court he was given a jail term and was whipped.[28] Other reported cases of burglary, armed robbery, rape and car theft were dealt with under the prevalent common law of Brunei.

While the international uproar over *hudud* caused some distraction, there were plenty of occasions for Brunei to push for greater Islamization. Several of the Sultan's speeches dwelt on the subject of enhancing the teachings of Islam and giving the religion greater prominence in society. He noted that religious education based on the Qur'an should not be limited to religious or Arabic schools, but that all government and private secondary schools ought to adopt such subjects.[29] A permanent building to propagate Islamic knowledge, called Balai Khazanah Islam Sultan Haji Hassanal Bolkiah, was inaugurated in October 2019. It is to be managed by the Prime Minister's Office. Since 2001 it had been temporarily located at another site. It has to date attracted 100,000 visitors from both home and abroad. Not only will the Balai Khazanah be active in promoting knowledge through academic activities, but it also has the potential of becoming an Islamic tourism destination.[30]

External Linkages: Defence, Economics and Politics

While the main task of the police force is to ensure a crime-free domestic environment, the armed forces are entrusted with the defence of the state and its sovereignty. With a coastline facing the South China Sea, Brunei is wary of international security issues relating to rival claims over the sultanate's exclusive economic zone. It prefers, however, not to deliver any public statements on such issues. The country has to ensure the security of its extensive oil fields and keep poachers from its rich fishing grounds. There were reported intrusions by foreign fishermen into Brunei waters; they were apprehended by the navy and turned over to the marine police. Poaching not only occurs in deep waters but also nearer to the coast and along inland waterways rich in marine and forest products. Coastal patrols by the navy and the police have been active against offenders, though there does not seem to be an end to the intrusions.

The RBAF (Royal Brunei Armed Forces) have established strong ties with several partner countries at the bilateral, regional and international levels. Brunei continues to participate in UNIFIL (United Nations Interim Forces in Lebanon), embedded with the peacekeeping operations of the Malaysian Battalion. A thirty-man contingent left for Lebanon in September 2019 to replace the previous team for a twelve-month assignment. Another group of nine personnel went to Mindanao as part of the ongoing International Monitoring Team to secure a peace deal between warring factions in Muslim Mindanao. Brunei continues its close defence ties with the United Kingdom; a visit by the Vice Chief of the Defence Staff in February was only one of several contacts between the United Kingdom and the sultanate's Ministry of Defence and the RBAF. Meanwhile, Brunei's security forces participated in several bilateral exercises during 2019. As usual, the largest exercise involved the RBAF and the US Navy/US Marine Corp in CARAT (Cooperation Afloat Readiness and Training), the twenty-fifth in the series. Another large bilateral exercise—Exercise PELICAN—involved about 420 personnel from the Brunei and Singapore navies. Brunei-Japan defence ties were boosted with a joint maritime exercise in April, augmented with a visit by a Japanese coastguard patrol vessel in June to exchange knowledge and share experiences with the marine police.³¹ The Russian Pacific Fleet Task Force was also at the navy port as part of bilateral cooperation. In an apparent increase in ties between the two navies, the commander of the Brunei Navy had earlier visited St Petersburg to attend Russian Navy Day and naval parade celebrations together with other foreign chiefs of navies. Other meetings included one with the leaders of ASEAN navies, the Brunei Darussalam–Australia Joint Defence Working Committee Meeting, the ASEAN Ministerial Meeting on Transnational Crime, and the Defence Ministers Meeting and related meetings with Dialogue Partners in Bangkok.³²

Multisectoral relations with Malaysia and Singapore were prominent in 2019. Sociocultural, economic and diplomatic exchanges between leaders and amongst other strata of society were evident. The Sultan's delegation was in Malaysia on several occasions; for instance, at the Annual Leaders' Consultation in Putrajaya, where a number of issues—including the ongoing land demarcation exercise, collaboration between Petronas and PetroleumBRUNEI and an MOU on transfers of prisoners to and from Sabah/Sarawak through Brunei territory—were covered.³³ Cooperation between the armed forces of the two countries and trade and investment links were also referred to in the joint statement. Sharing close ties with the Malaysian royalty, the Sultan was in Malaysia on a number of other occasions: at the installation of the Sultan of Pahang as the Yang Di-Pertuan Agong, and to pay respects upon the deaths of the former Sultan of Pahang and the former Sultan of Kelantan. Official delegations from Malaysia to Brunei included, among others, that of the Agong and his spouse in August (his first foreign visit after his installation as king in July), the Deputy Prime Minister, Minister of Education, and the Chief of Defence Force of the Malaysian Armed Forces, who was bestowed with a state decoration by the Sultan, signifying the military links.

Singapore's special relations with Brunei were strengthened with the visit of Senior Minister and Coordinating Minister for National Security of Singapore, Teo Chee Hean, who led a delegation of young office holders for the Seventh Young Leaders' Programme in Brunei, part of the exchange between younger leaders of both countries. During the Senior Minister's visit, both countries announced the establishment of a working group in the agri-food sector to attract more investment and create employment opportunities. Particular interest was expressed in aquaculture, given the demand for such products in both countries. Subsequently, Brunei and Singapore signed an MOU to produce Atlantic salmon at a land-based farming facility, which will be a venture between a Brunei GLC and a private enterprise from Singapore.³⁴ Besides the strong military ties (Singapore has a long-standing jungle training facility and a helicopter detachment in Brunei), there were several exchanges of students and youths under various programmes. Singapore professionals are also engaged in a number of educational, business and service sectors in Brunei. The interchangeability of the two currencies eases economic interactions between the two states.

Other official delegations to Brunei included that of the Prime Minister of Bangladesh, Sheikh Hasina, in April; the first such visit from the country, which has a sizeable number of workers in Brunei. Several MOUs were signed, including on collaboration in the halal food industry, agriculture and skills training in petroleum geoscience by the University of Dhaka, and the sale of LNG to Bangladesh. Another significant visitor was President Moon Jae-In of South Korea in March. MOUs were signed in areas of scientific and technological cooperation and in investment promotion. He visited the Temburong Bridge that is under construction— portions of which have been undertaken by a Korean-Brunei joint venture—to address the Korean workers on site. South Korea is one of the main importers of Brunei's oil and gas. Brunei is also the country coordinator of ASEAN–Korea Dialogue Relations for the period 2018–21. Prior to the ASEAN–Republic of Korea Commemorative Summit in Seoul, Sultan Hassanal Bolkiah undertook a state visit to South Korea, holding a bilateral summit with President Moon. Three MOUs were signed: in the areas of information and communication technology, electronic governance systems, and building smart cities.[35] Joining other leaders at the enthronement ceremony in Tokyo for the new Emperor, the Sultan had an opportunity to hold talks with the Japanese Prime Minister Shinzo Abe. Japan is an important trade and investment partner for Brunei, in addition to cooperating in education, culture and youth exchanges. Nearer to home, the Sultan attended the inauguration ceremony of Indonesia's re-elected President, Joko Widodo. While there he held discussions with Australian Prime Minister Scott Morrison. Enjoying sports diplomacy, the Brunei leader visited the Philippines to lend support to his young representatives during the opening ceremony of the Southeast Asia (SEA) Games, and he also took time there to hold talks with President Duterte. The Philippines, like Indonesia, is an important source for trade, investment and human resources. Other diverse sources of linkages include countries as far away as Egypt, where, during a state visit in August, MOUs were signed in cultural, economic and technical cooperation. Russia is another country keen to explore ties with Brunei. An exchange of ministerial visits took place, including the Fifth Bilateral Consultation Meeting in Brunei in December.

A number of important visits between Brunei and China spanned the year. Towards the end of 2018, President Xi Jinping had made his first state visit to

Brunei, immediately after the APEC summit in Papua New Guinea. The visit reaffirmed the growing close ties between the smallest and the biggest Asian states, elevating the bilateral relations to a strategic partnership. This was followed by several Chinese delegations to the sultanate throughout 2019, underscoring the fact that China is the country's leading trade and investment partner. The biggest presence of Chinese capital and manpower in Brunei is on the island of Pulau Muara Besar, about twenty miles from the capital Bandar Seri Begawan, where a large petrochemical complex is nearing completion. China has participated in the development of Brunei's infrastructure (including the construction of highways, bridges and the port) as well as in industrial joint ventures, which had commenced even before the Belt and Road Initiative (BRI) had been popularized. Brunei was one of the first countries to respond positively to Xi's BRI—it welcomed Chinese participation in its domestic development. Underscoring the importance of the ties, the Sultan, as one of several Asian leaders, attended the Second Belt and Road Forum for International Cooperation in Beijing in April 2019, followed by a bilateral meeting with President Xi Jinping.

As in previous years, Brunei participated in the Sixteenth China-ASEAN EXPO in Nanning in September, whereby Brunei's industries were showcased to visitors from China, ASEAN member countries, and other nations. Brunei-China relations are not limited to just trade and investment sectors. Nanjing in fact holds a special historical link to Brunei—one of the sultans of Brunei died during a visit to China in 1408. The environs of his tomb have been accorded the status of a Memorial Park by the local Chinese authorities. Brunei's Ambassador-at-Large from the Ministry of Foreign Affairs officiated at the newly constructed "History Exhibition Hall of the King of Boni" during her official visit to Nanjing. China-Brunei ties are also set to expand further. For instance, Huawei is already present in the sultanate, and it may be in the lead to offer 5G networks for Brunei's telecommunications sector.

At the global level, the Sultan skipped the UN General Assembly meetings in September 2019. The assembly was instead attended by the Foreign Minister II, who spoke of the need for a settlement to the Palestinian problem, among other matters. As has been his practice with ASEAN summits, the Sultan participated in both summits hosted by Thailand: the 34th in June and the 35th in November, as well as at the special meeting of the heads of the sub regional grouping BIMP-EAGA during the 34th Summit. Brunei is an active member of EAGA, providing opportunities to the country's micro and small industries to expand beyond its national borders through trade and other services. President Joko Widodo's announcement that the new Indonesian capital would be built in East

Kalimantan has provided encouragement to neighbouring EAGA states looking at potential business opportunities. Brunei's national carrier, Royal Brunei, has already expanded its services to four new destinations in Sabah and Sarawak with the collaboration of Malindo Air of Malaysia. Other destinations in Borneo are being planned. The expanded network would undoubtedly contribute to Brunei's tourism and trade sector. Brunei is also looking ahead to 2021 when it will take on the role of ASEAN Chair and host several related meetings.

Conclusion

The year saw a number of familiar and long-standing issues and policies, but approached with a renewed sense of determination. This was especially portrayed by a set of younger ministers appointed within the past two years, and a rejuvenated stance towards energy, industry and human resource development under a progressive-oriented ministry. There are still several challenges, both domestic and external: expanding the industrial and agricultural base, providing adequate employment opportunities, reassessing the direction of education and technical training to meet new demands, and sustaining the quality of life that Bruneians have taken for granted for a long time. Security and defence are challenging areas, with the increase in petty crimes, while vigilance against transnational terrorist groups calls for concerted regional and international cooperation. As a MIB state, the country has chosen its own path and it occasionally has to explain and defend some of the policies it has adopted to the wider international community. As the developments of 2019 have shown, the small state has the tenacity to address various areas of national concern.

Notes

1. This is the mid-year population estimate for 2018, according to the Economic Planning and Development (JPKE) branch of Brunei's Ministry of Finance and Economy, http://www.depd.gov.bn.
2. *Borneo Bulletin*, 1 January 2019. The Sultan's official speech is called *titah*. For the official transcripts of his speeches, see http://www.pmo.gov.bn.
3. Speech at the commencement of the Legislative Council Meeting. *Borneo Bulletin*, 8 March 2019.
4. For the IMF source, see *Borneo Bulletin*, 14 October 2019; for ADB, see *Borneo Bulletin*, 28 September 2019; for AMRO, see *Borneo Bulletin*, 26 July 2019. The EIU report is available at http://www.eiu.com (accessed 5 December 2019).
5. *Borneo Bulletin*, 25 October 2019.

6. For the full text of the proposed budget by the Minister at the Prime Minister's Office and Minister of Finance and Economy II, Dr Awang Haji Mohd Amin Liew bin Abdullah, *Budget Speech FY 2019–2020* (in Malay), see http://www.mofe.gov.bn.
7. As stated by a senior official of the Ministry of Energy, Manpower and Industry (MEMI) while officiating at the Borneo Deepwater Symposium, Bandar Seri Begawan. *Borneo Bulletin*, 30 July 2019.
8. For various reports by local reporters on Hengyi Industries, see, among others, *Borneo Bulletin*, 15 November 2019 (exports), 19 September (agreements), 14 November (workforce) and 11 July (scholarships).
9. Rasidah Hj Abu Bakar, "Brunei Exports First Shipment of Hydrogen to Japan", https://thescoop.co/2019/11/27.
10. Brunei's renewable energy programme is still in its early stages. See Nadhilah Shani and Pradyito Bagas Wicaksono, ASEAN Centre for Energy, "Brunei Has Potential to Go Big with Renewable Energy", *Borneo Bulletin*, 27 July 2019.
11. For data on the country's FDI and international merchandise trade, see http://www.depd.gov.bn.
12. *Borneo Bulletin*, 29 October 2019.
13. *Borneo Bulletin*, 16 November 2019.
14. The annual *Borneo Bulletin Yearbook 2019*, published by Brunei Press, gave special emphasis on the theme, "Unlocking Brunei's Digital and Diverse Economy". It highlighted some of the FDI projects that help diversify the economy and transform the country.
15. *Borneo Bulletin*, 14 November 2019.
16. http://www.moe.gov.bn.
17. https://thescoop.co/2019/10/16. Refer to the Sultan's *titah* at KUPU convocation on 15 October 2019. KUPU refers to Kolej Universiti Perguruan Ugama Seri Begawan (Religious Teachers University College).
18. More information is available from the Ministry of Health at http://www.moh.gov.bn.
19. *Borneo Bulletin*, 10 October 2019; https://thescoop.co/2019/11/11 (on WHO).
20. *Borneo Bulletin*, 19 November 2019.
21. *Borneo Bulletin*, 13 November 2019. Also refer to the Sultan's *titah* at http://www.pmo.gov.bn.
22. *Borneo Bulletin*, 9 October 2019.
23. *Borneo Bulletin*, 6 September 2019 (on crime statistics); 23 November 2019 (on NCB); 19 October 2019 (on deportation).
24. *Titah* of His Majesty Sultan Haji Hassanal Bolkiah in conjunction with the month of Ramadan 1440 Hijriah at Istana Nurul Iman, 5 May 2019, http://www.pmo.gov.bn.

25. *The Sun Daily* (KL), 24 May 2019.
26. http://www.pmo.gov.bn, 23 March 2019. Noteworthy is the fact that the Malaysian Agong (king) is the Chancellor of UiTM.
27. From Bernama, as quoted in http://www.freemalaysiatoday.com, 6 May 2019.
28. *Borneo Bulletin*, 22 August 2019 (BND100 theft); 15 October 2019 (gas cylinder theft); 6 October 2019 (donation theft).
29. *Titah* at the Nusul Al Quran celebrations, 22 May 2019, http://www.pmo.gov.bn.
30. *Titah* at the opening of the 2019 Knowledge Convention, 12 October 2019, http://www.majlisilmu.gov.bn.
31. *Borneo Bulletin*, 24 October 2019 (CARAT); 6 November 2019 (PELICAN); 27 April 2019 (with Japan).
32. *Borneo Bulletin*, 2 November 2019 (Russian fleet); 31 July 2019 (Russia Navy Day); 29 November 2019 (ADMM).
33. *The Star* (Malaysia), 3 March 2019.
34. *Borneo Bulletin*, 3 October 2019 (aquaculture); 11 December 2019 (salmon).
35. *Borneo Bulletin*, 25 November 2019.

Cambodia

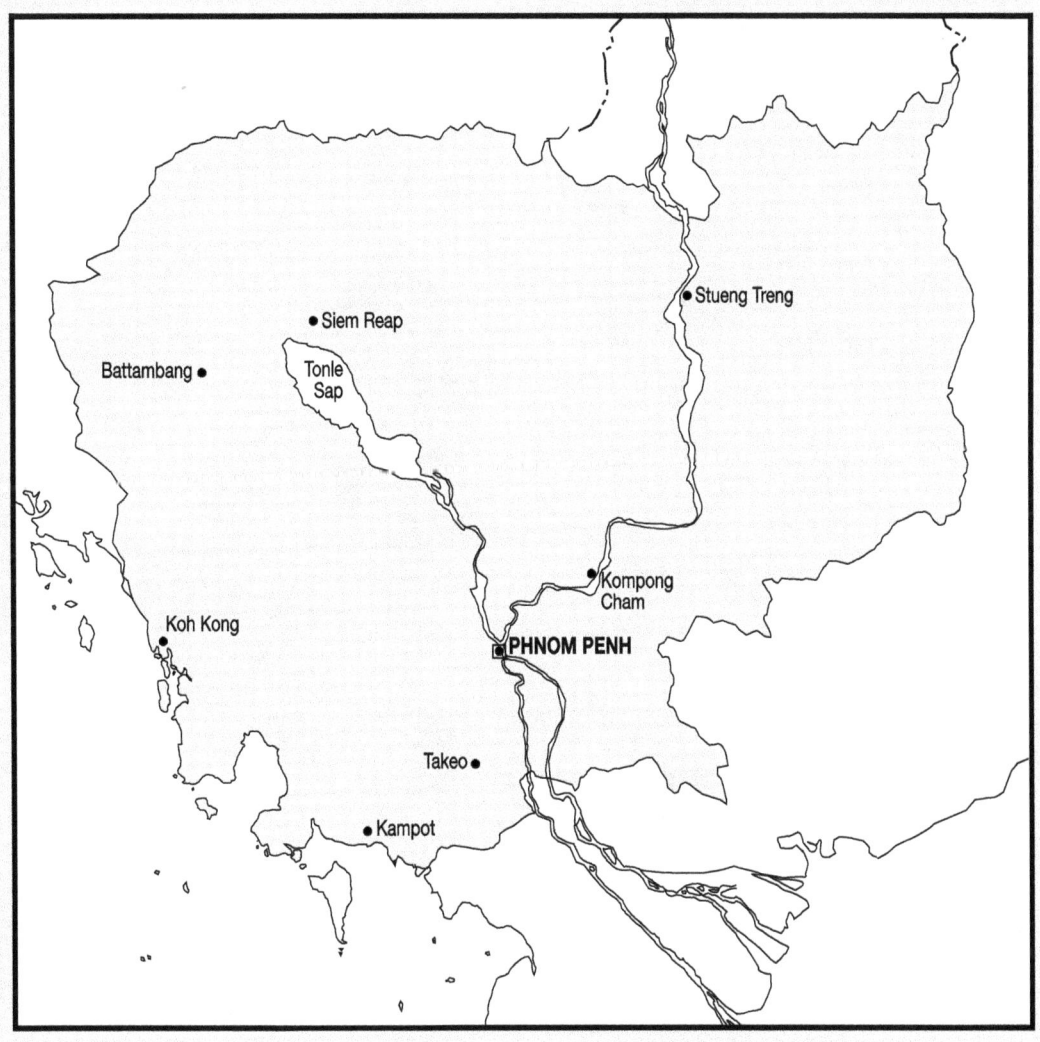

CAMBODIA IN 2019:
Entrenching One-Party Rule and Asserting National Sovereignty in the Era of Shifting Global Geopolitics

Kheang Un and Jing Jing Luo

On 29 December 2018, Prime Minister Hun Sen presided over the inauguration of the Win-Win Monument, constructed on the outskirts of Phnom Penh to commemorate the end of civil war in Cambodia some twenty years ago when the Khmer Rouge was finally defeated in 1998. Achieving total peace is a source of pride for Prime Minister Hun Sen, signalling his triumph over the neoliberal global order, especially since even the United Nations (UN) failed in this task, despite the mission's expensive price tag. The ceremony was also a testimony to the pre-eminence of the ruling Cambodian People's Party (CPP) following the dissolution of the opposition Cambodia National Rescue Party (CNRP) and the party's comprehensive victory in the 2018 general elections that transformed Cambodia into a de facto one-party state. In many ways, Prime Minister Hun Sen and the CPP have reasons to be proud of Cambodia's achievements. The economy continued to expand sustainably at a rate of around seven per cent, elevating Cambodia to one of the fastest-growing economies in the world. Its international geopolitical position has also been strengthened with the political and economic support of China. However, despite these successes, the CPP faces challenges to its legitimacy, both on the international and domestic fronts, as it embarks on further

---

KHEANG UN is Associate Professor of Political Science at Northern Illinois University.

JING JING LUO is a doctoral candidate at the School of International Relations and the Center for Southeast Asian Studies, Xiamen University, China.

power consolidation. This chapter analyses the CPP's successes and challenges in 2019 in the domains of politics, economics and foreign affairs. The first section will discuss the domestic political developments surrounding Sam Rainsy's attempt to return from self-imposed exile and the reactions of the Cambodian government. The second section will address economic developments in 2019 as well as possible future trends. The third section will discuss Cambodia's external relations, particularly Western concerns over its recent democratic regression and its bilateral relations with China and Vietnam.

Politics

The CPP's electoral victories since the UN-organized elections in 1993 have occurred largely because of the divisions within the opposition camp. The merger between the Sam Rainsy Party and the Human Rights Party into the CNRP had initially posed an electoral challenge to the CPP, as evidenced by the former's strong performance in both rural and urban areas in the 2013 general election and the 2017 local elections. In 2017 the Cambodian government arrested the CNRP leader Kem Sokha, while the Supreme Court dissolved the CNRP and barred its senior leaders from political activities for five years on charges of plotting a "colour revolution" to overthrow the government. Many observers, however, characterized the government's action as a pre-emptive measure to preserve the CPP's political dominance. Immediately thereafter, many senior CNRP leaders fled the country. Ongoing efforts by the CNRP to reconstitute itself with the help of international partners, as well as reactions to this by the government, have dominated Cambodian political news throughout 2019.

With Kem Sokha under house arrest, Sam Rainsy assumed the role of acting president of the CNRP. On several occasions he vowed to return to Cambodia to lead a "people power movement" to oust Prime Minister Hun Sen, only to backtrack. Eventually, Sam Rainsy chose 9 November 2019 as the date for his return to Cambodia. Even though the government has clipped the CNRP of its leadership, the party's grass-roots networks are still intact, although currently dormant. As a result, the CPP remains concerned about a "colour revolution", however remote the possibility. Consequently, the Cambodian government imposed close surveillance on CNRP activists[1] and declared a zero-tolerance policy for any activity in support of the CNRP.[2] When some CNRP cells were reactivated following news of Sam Rainsy's planned return, the authorities arrested over seventy CNRP activists who were planning to mobilize supporters to accompany Sam Rainsy when he crossed the Thai-Cambodian border.

Sam Rainsy and Prime Minister Hun Sen traded fierce political barbs. Sam Rainsy fantasized that hundreds of thousands would rise up while members of the armed forces would turn their guns on the government.[3] In response, Prime Minister Hun Sen mobilized troops to the Thai-Cambodian border in a show of force, while deploying his elite bodyguard units on the streets of Phnom Penh. Sam Rainsy's plan was foiled when the Thai government, citing the ASEAN principle of non-interference, denied Sam Rainsy the right to board any Bangkok-bound flight. Although Sam Rainsy's planned return to Cambodia was foiled, it drew international attention to Cambodia. This was indeed the CNRP's strategy. Since multiparty democracy in Cambodia was the product of international intervention and engagement, the expectation is that similar international pressure on the Cambodian government will help to restore that state of affairs. However, the imposition of democracy in Cambodia in the 1990s occurred at the historical juncture of euphoria over the end of the Cold War and the supposed triumph of Western-style democracy.[4] Given the recent global geopolitical shift precipitated by China's economic rise and global assertiveness, Western pressure on Hun Sen's government may not yield the level of concessions the CNRP is hoping for.

Moreover, the dissolution of the CNRP, which received 45 per cent of the vote in the 2013 and 2017 elections, did not trigger mass protests, demonstrating that most Cambodians were somewhat satisfied with the CPP's handling of the economy, if not the politics, of the country. The lack of popular demonstrations against the CPP permits it to pursue its policy of developmental authoritarianism, which prioritizes economic development over civil and political liberty.[5]

The government's ability to continue delivering sustained economic growth has contributed to rising standards of living in Cambodia, although inequality persists and the provision of public goods remains sub-optimal. These latter developments, if left unaddressed, will undermine the CPP's claim to performance-based legitimacy. The ruling party seems to be aware of this issue as Prime Minister Hun Sen announced the launch of "surgical strikes" in the form of government action to address the problems of corruption, illegal logging and land grabbing.[6] While the government has made similar declarations previously, the efforts have largely been unsuccessful in the face of the entrenched system of neo-partrimonialism centred on the symbiotic relationship between big businesses and the ruling party and the nepotism within the ruling elite.[7] Consequently, in the past the gap between policy pronouncements and actual implementation damaged the CPP's credibility. However, 2019 saw some tangible evidence of the government's commitment to fight corruption and the illegal expropriation of natural resources A few *Oknha*[8] and senior government officials were arrested on charges of illegal logging and land grabbing.[9] The government also advanced initiatives to ensure a more responsive and effective provision of public goods. For instance, the government abolished various fees for residency books, marriage certificates and national identity cards. The introduction of a one-window service—one-stop access to multiple government agencies—for small and medium-sized enterprises also showed signs of improvement.[10]

Sustained Growth ... Some Uncertainties

Cambodia's economy has increasingly been integrated into the regional and global economy, enabling it to experience a sustainable rate of growth. The projected economic growth for 2019 is around seven per cent, comparable to the level in 2018. However, the sources of growth remain based on three sectors: tourism, construction and garments.

The number of tourists visiting Cambodia rose in 2019. In 2018, more than 6.2 million tourists visited Cambodia, generating over US$4.3 billion in revenues. For the first nine months of 2019, 4.8 million tourists visited Cambodia. While the number of tourists visiting the Angkor Archaeological Park has decreased slightly because of a decline in Western tourists, Phnom Penh and Sihanoukville continue to receive more tourists.[11] This shifting trend signifies the attractiveness of the seaside and, more importantly, the popularity of the gambling industry in Sihanoukville among Chinese tourists. The number of Chinese visitors to Cambodia for the first nine months of 2019 reached 1.8 million—surpassing the 1.44 million figure for the whole of 2018.[12]

The construction sector has also rapidly expanded on account of two factors. The first is the growth of the Cambodian middle class. Facilitated by the expansion of the credit market, the middle class has contributed to a rising demand for housing, including both cheap apartments as well as higher-end gated communities. The second factor is the influx of Chinese nationals seeking to invest their capital. There is a Khmer saying that goes, "Where there is water, there are fish. Where there is land, there are Chinese." Nowhere is this more evident than the coastal city of Sihanoukville and Phnom Penh, where the influx of Chinese investments and people have caused considerable shock to both Cambodians and foreign observers, who are upset at the degree to which Chinese nationals have come to completely dominate certain industries. The skyline of the capital city of Phnom Penh is rapidly changing with the construction of multiple high-rise buildings, financed by Chinese companies and geared towards Chinese buyers, who have the right to own condominiums under Cambodian law.

In Sihanoukville, Chinese companies have literally taken over the city. Chinese companies have invested prolifically in the special economic zone, taking advantage of tax holidays as well as the availability of cheap labour to construct and operate resorts and casinos. To date, Chinese companies have built and operate over 156 hotels and guesthouses and approximately 88 casinos—with many more still under construction. Although no exact figures are available, the estimated total number of Chinese nationals in Cambodia is around 300,000.[13] The considerable influx of Chinese investment and nationals into Cambodia has presented both benefits and challenges. Cambodians with links to foreign capital and landowners have benefited disproportionately from the influx of the Chinese. As Chinese investors purchased land in Sihanoukville from Cambodians, the latter were able to use their abundant cash to speculate on land and real estate in other parts of Cambodia, further feeding the construction boom. However, for many other locals, the Chinese nationals and cash flooding into Sihanoukville have had the result of pushing the values of city properties and services "high into the cloud" and beyond their reach.

Resentment against the Chinese presence is on the rise among many Cambodians living in Sihanoukville and beyond. Many Sihanoukville residents have been affected by high inflation and the loss of employment opportunities. Previously, Sihanoukville's tourism economy catered to Cambodians and Westerners. Although the number of Chinese tourists has swelled significantly, the Chinese visitors are largely confined to the bubble of Chinese-owned and -operated tours and hotels, thus preventing local residents from benefitting from the tourism boom. Across the country, many Cambodians are worried about the risk of their country losing its national identity and possible sovereignty, high crime rates, widespread money laundering, the drug trade, and the many social ills associated with the gambling industry. The speed and comprehensiveness of the changes brought about by the Chinese is also of ongoing public concern. Facebook posts on Chinese gang activities and the apparent lawlessness in Sihanoukville by concerned Cambodians went viral, making the city a no-go zone for many Cambodian tourists.[14] Furthermore, as shocking as it may be, anecdotal evidence suggests that resentment against Chinese among some segments of the Cambodian population has become as intense as the long-held historical antipathy towards the Vietnamese.

Are the issues associated with the influx of Chinese capital and nationals inevitable? Deng Xiaoping, the former paramount leader of China, once famously said, in reference to the potential negative ramifications of China's opening-up policy, that "when you open the door for fresh air, flies naturally come in". This is a vivid reminder for Cambodia about the need to safeguard against the negative impacts as it welcomes foreign investment. The primary challenge accompanying the influx of Chinese money is the weak state capacity in Cambodia. Despite the government's efforts to improve state capacity, weaknesses persist. Corruption remains high, with Transparency International scoring Cambodia 20 out of 100 and ranking it 161 out of 180 countries.[15] Similarly, the rule of law is weak—with a score of 0.32/1 and a rank of 125 out of 126 countries worldwide.[16] These conditions have weakened the government's regulatory capability, allowing opportunities for corrupt elements within the Cambodian patronage networks to collude with bad elements among Chinese investors for personal gain.

The disorderly sprawl of construction activities and the lack of enforcement of construction codes in Sihanoukville is a testimony to Cambodia's weak state capacity. For example, in June 2019 a Chinese-funded structure in Sihanoukville collapsed, killing twenty-five Cambodian workers. Subsequent inspections exposed the alarming scale of dangerously sub-standard construction, prompting the authorities to order the demolition of at least fourteen buildings.[17] The increasingly anarchical nature of life in Sihanoukville today—as crime, drugs and money laundering grow unabated—is an additional indicator of Cambodia's weak state capacity. The rise in the number of casinos and associated money laundering activities in Cambodia appears to correspond to China's 2014 crackdown on money laundering in Macau,[18] which forced criminal groups to seek shelter elsewhere. Cambodia's embrace of Chinese investment and the country's weak state capacity thus presented an opportunity for transnational crime networks. The sudden inflow of Chinese capital and the rise in money laundering led the Financial Action Task Force in 2019 to place Cambodia on the "grey list" of suspected countries where money laundering is prevalent, which might affect the country's external trade and inflows of international investment and finance.[19]

The problems arising from the Chinese influx has led many people to question the necessity of Chinese investment in particular and closer Sino-Khmer relations in general. Whether Cambodia should continue to be open to Chinese investments is not up for debate. However, what should be debated is how Cambodia can most effectively capitalize on China's investments. Both theoretical and empirical studies have demonstrated how many developing countries, particularly those in Africa, had missed the boat of globalization in the 1980s and 1990s because of their inward-looking policies, depriving them of the economic gains associated with globalization.[20] China's current economic expansion, intensified recently by the Belt and Road Initiative (BRI), is akin to a new wave of globalization presenting potentially huge benefits for developing countries like Cambodia. However, many of the issues identified above are not merely the result of Cambodia's limited state capacity but are also a by-product of the lack of proactive bilateral coordination in long-term development planning between the Chinese and Cambodian authorities. It is apparent that China intends to use Cambodia as its beachhead in Southeast Asia and as a showcase for Chinese soft power. China's objective presents great opportunities for both governments to collaborate closely to achieve a mutually sustainable and beneficial outcome for both countries.

In 2019, however, there were signs that Cambodia has been putting greater emphasis on the orderly development of Sihanoukville. For one, the Cambodian government appointed Khouch Chamroeun—who has a reputation as a "can-do" man—as the governor of Sihanoukville. The Cambodian government also closed down online gambling operations in Sihanoukville because of its association with criminal activities such as money laundering and its limited capacity to generate employment for local Cambodians. Such measures resulted in the exodus of roughly 120,000 Chinese nationals from the city, while also causing a drop in property values.[21] At the bilateral level, authorities in Cambodia and China have increased their law enforcement cooperation to tackle the city's high crime rate, while also collaborating to address the disorderly development of the city. The Chinese have provided support for the long-term urban planning of the city, with the aim of transforming Sihanoukville into a hub for manufacturing, finance and seaport shipping.[22]

The garment industry remains the most important sector of the Cambodian economy. It employs approximately 800,000 workers and provides benefits, either directly or indirectly, to approximately three million Cambodians. In 2018 the export value of the sector was US$8 billion, which is a phenomenal figure for an economy with a gross domestic product of roughly US$20 billion. In 2018, garment exports from Cambodia to the European Union (EU) accounted for 45 per cent, or US$5.8 billion, of the country's total exports.[23] Cambodia's high export volume to the EU was made possible by the European Union's trade scheme known as Everything But Arms (EBA), which allows developing countries to export their goods to the EU duty-free on the condition that they respect labour rights and human rights. The Cambodian government and other stakeholders in the garment sector are currently anxious over the EU's decision to link the extension of the EBA scheme with the issue of Cambodia's deteriorating human rights and conditions for democracy. After six months of monitoring and consultation with the Cambodian government, the EU submitted its assessment to the Cambodian government in November 2019; the latter, at the time of this writing, will have one month to respond to the EU's recommendations. The EU report states that the

Cambodian government has not taken sufficient and concrete steps to address the "systematic and severe" violations of human rights and democracy in Cambodia.[24] The EU is expected to render a final decision on whether to suspend Cambodia's EBA trade privileges in February 2020.

Should the withdrawal of the EBA by the EU take place it is estimated that it would cost Cambodia's export industry around US$600 million per year and 90,000 jobs.[25] The government's decision to release on bail all political prisoners, including former CNRP leader Kem Sokha, suggests that the pressure applied by the EU has had some effect. Kem Sokha, who was arrested in 2017 on charges of conspiring with the United States government to launch "a colour revolution" to overthrow the Cambodian government, is still awaiting trial and does not have freedom to engage in political activities or to leave the country. However, the hope that the CPP will permit Cambodia to return to a competitive multiparty system as a result of EU pressure is overblown. Other than being determined to maintain one-party rule, Prime Minister Hun Sen is also committed to pursuing a path of developmental authoritarianism that prioritizes social peace, stability and continuing economic growth over human rights and democracy.[26] Furthermore, as the next section demonstrates, the current global geopolitics favours the CPP in resisting the pressure of Western countries and its domestic political opponents. The Cambodian government appears to have already devised plans to mitigate the possible termination of the EBA through the reduction of taxes, port inspection fees and electricity fees as well as further expansion of bilateral trade with China. The Cambodian government also announced at the end of November 2019 that it had set aside US$3 billion of its reserves to cushion the impact of an EBA withdrawal.[27]

Foreign Relations

Cambodia's foreign relations with major powers is a predictable mix of tension and close collaboration. Since the crackdown on the opposition party and civil society in 2017, Cambodia's relations with the United States and the European Union have declined precipitously. The United States is in a dilemma. On the one hand, for strategic reasons, the United States wants to keep an open channel of contact with Cambodia, including in military-to-military cooperation. The United States is concerned that alienating Cambodia will push the latter even closer into China's orbit. On the other hand, the United States is keen to see some semblance of democracy being re-established in Cambodia, such as the reconstitution of the CNRP. Pressure by lobby groups forced the US House of Representatives to pass the Cambodia Democracy Act, which includes provisions for freezing the assets of and denying visas to senior political and economic elites involved in undermining democracy and human rights in Cambodia.[28] This followed legislation introduced in the Senate in 2018 that would have suspended Cambodia's preferential trade status with the United States.[29] These developments have caused considerable strain in US-Cambodia relations.

Sino-Cambodian relations—which jumpstarted in 1997 when the CPP was searching for a sympathetic patron in the midst of Western political and economic pressure following its military move against its then coalition partner the National United Front for an Independent, Neutral, Peaceful and Cooperative Cambodia (FUNCINPEC)—have deepened on all fronts and reached a pinnacle in 2019 with the signing of a Comprehensive Strategic Partnership of Cooperation. Close Sino-Khmer relations have once again placed Cambodia at the front and centre of global geopolitical rivalry. Given China's assertiveness in the South China Sea and its "String of Pearls" strategy, speculations abound over China's planned construction of a naval base at Ream in Preah Sihanouk province and an airfield in Koh Kong province. In June 2019, the *Wall Street Journal* reported that the US Indo-Pacific Command confirmed the existence of a secret agreement between the Cambodian and Chinese governments over the lease of the naval base at Ream.[30] Cambodia has vehemently denied this allegation.

Amidst the political and economic pressure applied by the United States and European Union on Cambodia, China's support has become increasingly salient for the Cambodian government's survival. Indeed, while promising to further aid Cambodia in the event that the EU imposes trade sanctions, China pledged US$588 million in aid to Cambodia for the period 2019–21. The two countries also agreed to increase the volume of bilateral trade and have started to negotiate a Sino-Khmer free trade agreement. China has also become Cambodia's largest creditor. By 2019, Cambodia's total debt was US$6.9 billion (equivalent to 28.6 per cent of its GDP), of which 48.4 per cent is owed to China. Despite some concerns about Cambodia falling into China's debt trap diplomacy, the level of debt Cambodia owes China and other creditors remains at manageable levels. The 2019 World Bank report states, "The debt distress level remained low as per 2018 World Bank/IMF Debt Sustainability Analysis."[31]

A less publicized state of affairs, though pertinent to Cambodia's foreign affairs, is its relations with Vietnam. Overall, Cambodian-Vietnamese relations have generally been warm. The close relationship between the two countries derives partly from the historically close collaboration between the two countries' ruling parties—the Cambodian People's Party (CPP) and the Vietnamese Communist

Party (VCP). The two parties share common interests in preserving their political dominance and have therefore worked closely to combat, according to Steve Heder, "hostile and 'unfriendly' forces" towards their respective governments.[32] Ground in special historical developments, cooperation between the two parties is broad and comprehensive. This is reflected, since the Vietnamese military withdrawal from Cambodia in 1989, in the frequent exchanges of top party and government officials as well as Vietnam's aid to Cambodian security forces in terms of training and free healthcare services to senior army and police officers.[33]

Commercial ties between Vietnam and Cambodia remain strong. Vietnam is Cambodia's third-largest source of exports, with them growing in value from US$2.2 billion in 2016 to US$2.77 billion in 2017 to over US$3.4 billion in 2018.[34] Cambodia's exports to Vietnam also increased substantially, from US$20 million in 2000 to 46 million in 2005, 96 million in 2010 and 326 million in 2017, according to the Cambodian Ministry of Commerce. Trade turnover between Cambodia and Vietnam reached US$4.7 billion in 2018 and is expected to reach US$5 billion by the end of 2019.[35] In 2019, Vietnam was one of the top five investors in Cambodia. The number of Vietnamese visitors to Cambodia has also increased substantially, with them now constituting the second-largest group behind Chinese tourists.[36]

Despite the strong ties, there are still some tensions over national boundaries and the status of Vietnamese immigrants in Cambodia. Cambodia's electoral politics has further exacerbated these issues. In past elections, opposition parties have politicized Cambodia's close relations with Vietnam by accusing the ruling CPP of being subordinate to Vietnam and of not doing enough to rebuff "Vietnam's intention of swallowing Cambodia".[37] Arguably, the CNRP's anti-Vietnamese rhetoric is a strategy to counter the CPP's campaign messages that portray the CPP—with the support of the Vietnamese army—as the liberator of Cambodians from the atrocities of the Khmer Rouge regime and as the guarantor of peace and stability. However, this claim has lost political traction as the memory of the Khmer Rouge has faded. In the meantime, however, the opposition's campaign to arouse the deeply rooted historical animosity towards Vietnam continues to resonate and appeal politically to a large segment of the Cambodian population.

The politicization of the border and Vietnamese immigrants has pressured the Cambodian government to find a lasting solution. The governments of Vietnam and Cambodia have continued their negotiations over the final border demarcation and the planting of border posts. By 2019, reports indicated that approximately 84 per cent of the land border demarcation and marker planting had been completed.

However, the two sides remained in disagreement over the remaining 16 per cent of the 1,245 kilometre shared border.[38] Now, with the main opposition CNRP banned, the border issue might not be as politically contentious as it once was. It is likely therefore that land boundary tensions may be resolved in the near future. However, tension will remain for the foreseeable future over maritime boundaries, especially the status of an island off the coast of Cambodia known to the Vietnamese as Phu Wuco and to the Cambodians as Koh Tral, as well as exploration rights in contested waters of the Gulf of Thailand.

Given asymmetrical historical power relations, Vietnam's past domination over Cambodia has been apparent. However, to allege, as the Cambodian opposition does, that the CPP subordinates Cambodian national interests to Vietnam is problematic. The Cambodian government has recently reasserted its sovereignty in its foreign affairs vis-à-vis Vietnam. The Cambodian government's decision not to support an ASEAN communiqué that was critical of China's assertiveness in the South China Sea in recent years is a case in point.[39] Cambodia exercising its sovereignty vis-à-vis Vietnam has also been evident in the former's close collaboration with China. Such close Sino-Cambodian relations have posed security concerns for Vietnam. Vietnam, like the United States, is concerned about rumours of a planned Chinese naval base in Cambodia. Given its ongoing territorial dispute with China in the South China Sea, and past Chinese encirclement of Vietnam through its backing of the Khmer Rouge regime, the Vietnamese government fears that history might repeat itself. The Vietnamese-Cambodian summit initiated by the Vietnamese government in February 2019 is testimony to the Vietnamese government's efforts to balance China in Cambodia, or at least to limit China's influence on Cambodia. The summit's joint communiqué, undoubtedly in reference to Vietnamese concerns over a potential Chinese military presence in Cambodia, states that both sides will seek "to pursue the principle of not allowing any forces to use one country's territory to conduct acts against the other's security and stability".[40]

Close Sino-Cambodian relations arguably offer the Cambodian government the confidence to address the sensitive issue of Vietnamese immigrants in Cambodia. The number of Vietnamese immigrants living in Cambodia is estimated to be around 750,000.[41] Some are descendants of Vietnamese migrants who have lived in Cambodia for generations (though most fled to Vietnam during the Khmer Rouge regime); others came to Cambodia during the Vietnamese occupation of Cambodia from 1979 to 1989. But the greatest number of ethnic Vietnamese in Cambodia today were born in Cambodia after the 1970s. The majority of these Vietnamese live on the water along the Mekong River and the Tonle Sap Lake.

As discussed above, Vietnamese immigrants have been a political liability for the CPP. In 2019 the Cambodian government took concrete steps to address the issue of Vietnamese immigrants, including the systematic registration of Vietnamese immigrants in Cambodia and the relocation of those living on the Tonle Sap Lake.

A more fundamental issue is the citizenship status of Vietnamese immigrants in Cambodia. Approximately ninety per cent of the ethnic Vietnamese in Cambodia do not possess birth certificates, subjecting them to the denial of citizenship by both Vietnam and Cambodia, thus rendering them essentially stateless. The Vietnamese government has lobbied Cambodia to grant them Cambodian citizenship. However, the Cambodian government has resisted this proposal, offering instead residency status that can be renewed every three years for a fee. The Vietnamese government did not publicly protest these policies of the Cambodian government; rather, it extended its collaboration by assisting poor Vietnamese to pay the residency card fees and creating employment opportunities for those resettled from Tonle Sap Lake through Vietnamese companies operating in Cambodia.[42] In sum, the Cambodian government's firm stance on Vietnamese immigrants signals a new era of Vietnamese-Cambodian relations, one that no longer fits the CNRP's characterization of the CPP as a Vietnamese "puppet".

Conclusion

"Men make their own history", Karl Marx once wrote, "but they do not make it just as they please; they do not make it under circumstances chosen by themselves, but rather circumstances found, given, and transmitted."[43] Marx's thought sheds light on modern Cambodian history, which has been closely intertwined not only with its immediate neighbours but also with complex global geopolitics. Political developments in Cambodia in 2019 appeared to turn to a rendezvous with history in which Cambodia could once again become the site of global geopolitical contest between great powers. The optimal outcome for Cambodia is to maintain positive relations with both China and the West. However, ideological differences between the West and the Cambodian government have soured their relations, particularly with the European Union, such that it would consider withdrawing Cambodia's preferential trade status with the union. As one of the co-authors of this chapter articulates elsewhere with reference to international leverage and counter-leverage associated with such recent global-geopolitical shifts:

> The EU has in 2018 issued an ultimatum for the Cambodian government to restore democracy and the respect for human rights or face EU's

suspension of Cambodia's preferential trade status under the "Everything But Arms" scheme. If China's aid, investment, and trade cannot cover the loss associated with EU's sanctions, then the electoral authoritarian pendulum can swing back, though it is unlikely to reach pre-2017 levels.[44]

This chapter demonstrates that in 2019, China's aid to, investment in and trade with Cambodia increased. The increase means that China's aid, investment and trade can cover the economic fallout associated with the EU's withdrawal of Cambodia's EBA status, rendering the Cambodian government undeterred by the EU's ultimatum. Consequently, 2019 set the firm foundation for further entrenchment of one-party rule and the beginning of Cambodia's assertion of its sovereignty vis-à-vis the West and, increasingly, Vietnam. Some analysts argue that while having freed itself from the West, Cambodia could well fall into China's trap. Regardless of one's view of China's role in Cambodia, it remains the elephant in the room. If managed well, Cambodia can continue to benefit from China's economic engagement, creating a long-term win-win relationship. But, as this chapter suggests, to maximize the benefits from China's engagement and to mitigate its negative impact requires that the Cambodian state consistently and forcefully strengthens its capacity. Serious and sustained strikes on the cancer of corruption and bureaucratic incompetence, as Prime Minister Hun Sen initiated in 2019, are crucial at this current juncture. The challenge for the Cambodian government is to maintain sustainable reforms. Their absence will encourage booty capitalism wherein the political and capital classes will enrich themselves with rent-seeking activities, which would further perpetuate the current levels of inequality and social discontent. These developments will negatively affect the CPP's claim to performance-based legitimacy. The social order and stability that the ruling party intends to maintain through popular consent will then have to be implemented by force.

Notes

1. Human Rights Watch, "Cambodia: Former Opposition Official Detained: Drop Politically Motivated Case, Release Nuth Pich", 19 August 2019, https://www.hrw.org/news/2019/08/19/cambodia-former-opposition-official-detained.
2. Niem, Chheng, "CNRP Support Will Not Be Tolerated", *Phnom Penh Post*, 29 August 2019, https://www.phnompenhpost.com/national-politics/cnrp-support-will-not-be-tolerated (accessed 20 November 2019).
3. "Cambodian Opposition Leader Sam Rainsy Vows to Lead 'Tsunami' of Supporters to Arrest PM Hun Sen", Radio Free Asia, 18 October 2019, https://www.rfa.org/english/news/cambodia/tsunami-10182019164229.html (accessed 20 November 2019).

4. See, for example, Francis Fukuyama, *The End of History and the Last Man* (Simon and Schuster, 2006).
5. Kheang Un, "Cambodia in 2012: Towards Developmental Authoritarianism", in *Southeast Asian Affairs 2013*, edited by Daljit Singh (Singapore: Institute of Southeast Asian Studies, 2013): 73–86.
6. "New Momentum to Fight against Corruption", *Khmer Times*, 31 July 2019, https://www.khmertimeskh.com/50628790/new-momentum-to-fight-against-corruption (accessed 30 November 2019).
7. Kheang Un and Sokbunthoeun So, "Land rights in Cambodia: How Neopatrimonial Politics Restricts Land Policy Reform", *Pacific Affairs* 84, no. 2 (2011): 289–308; Alice Baban, Sokbunthoeun So, and Kheang Un, "From Force to Legitimation: Rethinking Land Grab in Cambodia", *Development and Change* 48, no. 3 (2017): 590–612.
8. *Oknha* is a honourable title given to any Cambodian who has contributed at least US$100,000 to the government for national development. In recent years the government raised the qualifying amount for a contribution to US$500,000. Many sought this title, however, for access to the government and for protection for illegal business activities.
9. Soth Koemsoeun, "Three Nabbed over $100K Payment", *Phnom Penh Post*, 29 July 2019, https://www.phnompenhpost.com/national/three-nabbed-over-100k-payment (accessed 30 November 2019); "Soth Sam Ol in Court for Mondulkiri Illegal Logging", *Phnom Penh Post*, 12 July 2019, https://www.phnompenhpost.com/national/oknha-sam-ol-court-mondulkiri-illegal-logging (accessed 15 November 2019); Sokhean Ben, "Official Sacked for Land Grabbing", *Khmer Times*, 24 August 2019, https://www.khmertimeskh.com/50636812/official-sacked-for-land-grabbing/ (accessed 15 November 2019).
10. Author's field notes, August 2019.
11. Chea Vannak, "Over 3m Tourists Visit Cambodia in H1 with Big Rise in Chinese Visitors", *Khmer Times*, 8 August 2019, https://www.khmertimeskh.com/631306/over-3m-tourists-visit-cambodia-in-h1/ (accessed 15 November 2019).
12. Nem Sopheakpanha, "Tourist Arrivals Continue to Rise, Buoyed by Chinese Tourists", VOA Cambodia, 20 November 2019, https://www.voacambodia.com/a/tourist-arrivals-continue-to-rise-buoyed-by-chinese-tourists/5173741.html (accessed 23 November 2019).
13. James Massola, "China's Takeover of Sihanoukville is Almost Complete Despite Base Row", *Sydney Morning Herald*, 9 August 2019, https://www.smh.com.au/world/asia/china-s-takeover-of-sihanoukville-is-almost-complete-despite-base-row-20190805-p52e44.html (accessed 5 November 2019).
14. Author's monitoring of Facebook.
15. Transparency International, Cambodia, https://www.transparency.org/country/KHM (accessed 30 October 2019).

16. World Justice Project, Rule of Law Index 2019, http://data.worldjusticeproject.org/ (accessed 30 October 2019).
17. Ben Sokhean, "Demolition of 14 Unsafe Buildings in Sihanoukville Ordered", *Khmer Times*, 27 August 2019, https://www.khmertimeskh.com/50637496/demolition-of-14-unsafe-buildings-in-sihanoukville-ordered/ (accessed 1 November 2019).
18. UNODC, "Transnational Organized Crime in Southeast Asia: Evolution, Growth and Impact, 2019", https://www.unodc.org/documents/southeastasiaandpacific/Publications/2019/SEA_TOCTA_2019_web.pdf (accessed 27 November 2019).
19. "Global Watchdog to Put Cambodia on its Money Laundering Watchlist", Reuters, 22 February 2019, https://www.reuters.com/article/us-cambodia-moneylaundering/global-watchdog-to-put-cambodia-on-its-money-laundering-watchlist-idUSKCN1QB0N0 (accessed 27 November 2019).
20. Paul Collier, *The Bottom Billion* (Oxford: Oxford University Press, 2007).
21. "Some 120,000 Chinese Nationals Depart Cambodia following Ban on Online Gambling", Radio Free Asia, 6 September 2019, https://www.rfa.org/english/news/cambodia/depart-09062019172808.html (accessed 29 November 2019).
22. Khmer Times Staff, "Schenzen Institute of Planning to Undertake Sihanoukville Masterplan", *Khmer Times*, 15 November 2019, https://www.khmertimeskh.com/660033/shenzhen-institute-of-planning-to-undertake-sihanoukville-masterplan/ (accessed 29 November 2019).
23. Chheng Niem, "GMAC Makes EU Plea to Consider Job Losses", *Khmer Times*, 11 August 2019, https://www.phnompenhpost.com/national-politics/gmac-makes-eu-plea-consider-job-losses.
24. Turton, Shawn, "Hun Sen Rival Faces Trail Even as EU Threatens Cambodia Sanctions", 19 November 2019, https://asia.nikkei.com/Spotlight/Hun-Sen-s-Cambodia/Hun-Sen-rival-faces-trial-even-as-EU-threatens-Cambodia-sanctions (accessed 23 November 2019).
25. Zazithorn Rungchida, "H&M Consider Leaving Cambodia due to EU Trade Sanction", 10 November 2019, https://scandasia.com/hm-consider-leaving-cambodia-due-to-eu-trade-sanctions/ (accessed 23 November 2019).
26. Kheang Un, "Cambodia in 2012", pp. 71–86.
27. Vireak Thou, "$3 Billion in Reserve ahead of Possible EBA Withdrawal", *Phnom Penh Post*, 28 November 2019, https://phnompenhpost.com/national-politics/3-billion-reserve-ahead-possible-eba-withdrawal (accessed 29 November 2019).
28. Men Kimseng, "US House Passes Bill to Sanction Cambodia's Top Officials", 18 July 2019, https://www.voanews.com/east-asia-pacific/us-house-passes-bill-sanction-cambodias-top-officials (accessed 27 November 2019).
29. Men Kim Seng, "U.S. Senators Proposes Cambodia Sanction Bill", VOA Cambodia, 16 February 2019, https://www.voacambodia.com/a/us-senators-propose-cambodia-sanctions-bill/4256301.html (accessed 29 November 2019).
30. Jeremy Page, Gordon Lubold, and Rob Taylor, "Deal for Naval Outpost in Cambodia

Furthers China's Quest for Military Network", *Wall Street Journal*, 22 July 2019, https://www.wsj.com/articles/secret-deal-for-chinese-naval-outpost-in-cambodia-raises-u-s-fears-of-beijings-ambitions-11563732482 (accessed 23 November 2019).
31. World Bank, *Cambodia Economic Update: Recent Economic Developments and Outlook* (Phnom Penh: World Bank, 2019), https://www.worldbank.org/en/country/cambodia/publication/cambodia-economic-update-may-2019 (accessed 26 November 2019).
32. Steve Heder, "Cambodia–Vietnam: Special Relationship against Hostile and Unfriendly Forces", In *Southeast Asian Affairs 2018*, edited by Malcolm Cook and Daljit Singh (Singapore: ISEAS – Yusof Ishak Institute, 2018), pp. 113–32.
33. Author's field notes, June 2012 and August 2017.
34. VNA, "Vietnam Sees Export, Trade Opportunities in Cambodian Market", Vietnam+, 8 January 2019, https://en.vietnamplus.vn/vietnam-sees-export-trade-opportunities-in-cambodian-market/144797.vnp (accessed 26 November 2019).
35. "Forum Promotes Vietnam – Cambodia Trade and Investment Cooperation", *Nhân Dân*, 10 July 2019, https://en.nhandan.org.vn/business/item/7676002-forum-promotes-vietnam-%E2%80%93-cambodia-trade-and-investment-cooperation.html (accessed 23 November 2019).
36. "Vietnam Ranks Second in Number of Visitors to Cambodia", Vietnam Net, 8 June 2019, https://vietnamnet.vn/en/travel/vietnam-ranks-second-in-number-of-visitors-to-cambodia-585433.html (accessed 26 November 2019).
37. Kheang Un, "The Cambodian People Have Spoken", *New York Times*, 9 August 2019, https://www.nytimes.com/2013/08/10/opinion/global/the-cambodian-people-have-spoken.html (accessed 23 November 2019).
38. Long Kimmarita, "National Border Committee to Clarify Treaty with Vietnam", *Phnom Penh Post*, 9 October 2019, https://www.phnompenhpost.com/national-politics/national-border-committee-clarify-treaty-vietnam (accessed 23 November 2019).
39. See, for example, Thearith Leng, "2016: A Promising Year for Cambodia?", in *Southeast Asian Affairs 2017*, edited by Daljit Singh and Malcolm Cook (Singapore: ISEAS – Yusof Ishak Institute, 2017): 133–46.
40. "Vietnam, Cambodia Issue Joint Statement", *Viêt Nam News*, 6 October 2019, https://vietnamnews.vn/politics-laws/536461/viet-nam-cambodia-issue-joint-statement.html#XjTqKxiAhhvuTIXP.97 (accessed 26 November 2019).
41. Minority Rights Groups, "Ethnic Vietnamese", https://minorityrights.org/minorities/ethnic-vietnamese/ (accessed 29 November 2019).
42. Author's conversation with Vietnamese academic Hoang Minh Vu, 3 October 2019.
43. Cited in Gideon Rose, "A Review Essay: Democracy Promotion and American Foreign Policy", *International Security* 25 (2000/2001): 202.
44. Kheang Un, *Cambodia: Return to Authoritarianism* (Cambridge: Cambridge University Press, 2009), p. 61.

Indonesia

POST-ELECTION POLITICS IN INDONESIA:
Between Economic Growth and Increased Islamic Conservatism

Amalinda Savirani

The year 2019 was publicly labelled an election year in Indonesia, as mammoth elections were conducted, accompanied by a media and social media frenzy that absorbed the attention of the country's citizens. The year was also a milestone from which to look back on and reflect upon the first term of President Joko Widodo (popularly known as Jokowi), as well as to look forward to his second five-year term. In April 2019 more than 140 million citizens went to the ballot box to elect their president and vice-president, 575 members of the House of Representatives, 2,000 provincial representatives for 33 provinces, and 17,610 district and city representatives in more than 500 city and district councils. The total number of candidates running for legislative election was 245,000. The presidential election in 2019 was the fourth election after the New Order era, while the parliamentary election was the twelfth in Indonesian history. With an expenditure of more than 25 trillion rupiah (US$1.78 million), this year's elections also led to the death of 144 election ad-hoc committee members due to overwork, fatigue and stress.[1] More than 7,385,500 personnel were distributed across 809,500 polling stations. These figures demonstrate how electoral democracy has become institutionalized in the country.

Yet, democracy in Indonesia is not perfect. A successful electoral process does not directly result in "substantial democracy", which emphasizes the guarantee of civil liberties, freedom of expression, protection for minority groups, as well as social and economic rights. It is with respect to the substantive aspects of

---

AMALINDA SAVIRANI is Associate Professor and Head of the Department of Politics and Government, Universitas Gadjah Mada, Indonesia.

democracy that many observers and pundits on Indonesian politics have expressed worries about the "stagnation",[2] "regression",[3] "illiberal turn",[4] and "decline"[5] of democracy in the country, with reasons that will be explored in the sections that follow. Such observers are concerned that after two decades Indonesia has entered another version of the New Order regime, one marked by ignorance of basic human rights and which neglects the political rights of minority groups, all for the ambition of economic development. A more empathetic view though suggests that Indonesia is a young democratic country and that it will need time to nurture a vibrant democracy beyond formal elections.[6]

As an election year, Indonesia in 2019 was coloured by sharp social polarization between the groups following the two presidential candidates: the supporters of Jokowi and Ma'ruf Amin on the one hand, and those of Prabowo Subianto and his running mate Sandiaga Uno on the other. The majority of Islamic conservative groups supported Prabowo-Sandi, whilst nationalist, liberal and pluralist groups supported Jokowi-Amin. This political contestation in the elections is an expression of ideological divisions that "echo deep historical patterns and point toward underlying social cleavages",[7] similar to the ideological divisions in the 1955 election. The divisions in the 1955 election though were centred on control of the legislature, while in 2019 the focus was on the presidential race. Also, in 1955 there were five major competing ideologies, consisting of traditional Islam, socialism, communism, nationalism, and modern Islam. In 2019 it was between conservative Islam and nationalism, which was backed by the forces of moderate Islam in the form of the Nahdlatul Ulama (NU). Another difference is that in 2019 the social division appeared more tense because of the role of social media such as Facebook, Twitter and WhatsApp, which were able to greatly amplify the political differences between citizens.

This chapter discusses Indonesian politics in 2019. It addresses the elections, Indonesia's economic and foreign policies, and the security issues the country faced. Each of these topics will be explored in the sections that follow. Since it was an election year, the chapter will give particular focus to what happened in 2019, evaluate Jokowi's policies between 2014 and 2019, and his plans for his second tenure. I will also explore two significant emerging political trends: the rise of conservative Islam in politics and the apparent democratic "decline". The economic section will highlight Jokowi's focus on economic growth and infrastructure projects, while highlighting the resulting inequality and impact on human rights. The next section will look at the continued focus on economic diplomacy in 2019 and in the coming years. And the conclusion will offer some thoughts and reflections on Indonesia's future trajectory.

Power Balance after the Election

In the 2019 elections, a coalition of nine political parties supported the presidential slate of Jokowi and Ma'ruf Amin. These parties were Partai Demokrasi Indonesia Perjuangan (PDI-P), Golongan Karya (Golkar), Nasional Demokrat (Nasdem), Partai Persatuan Pembangunan (PPP), Hanura, Partai Persatuan Indonesia (Perindo), Partai Keadilan dan Persatuan Indonesia (PKPI) and Partai Solidaritas Indonesia (PSI). The first five of these parties secured more than 4 per cent of the popular vote, thus passing the threshold to garner seats in the Indonesian parliament. The remaining four parties were unable to gain enough votes, although individual candidates from parties such as the PSI were able to attract substantial numbers of voters. Between them, the five parties gathered a majority of 344 seats (or 54.9 per cent) in parliament. PDI-P, to which Jokowi belongs, managed to secure the largest number of seats (125 seats, or 19.3 per cent) and succeeded in making Puan Maharani the Speaker of the house. Puan Maharani is the daughter of former president Megawati Sukarnoputri, who currently heads PDI-P. As the first female house Speaker in Indonesian history, this helps to position Puan Maharani as a prospective candidate for the 2024 presidential election, with the full support of PDI-P.[8] In contrast, the parties supporting the Prabowo-Sandiaga slate only secured 45.1 per cent of the seats in parliament.

With the legislature already thinking about the 2024 election, the new Jokowi cabinet is busy with its development plan for the next five years. The second Jokowi cabinet consists of thirty-eight positions, including the attorney general and the head of the main government investment body. Almost half of the appointments are party cadres, while the rest are drawn from the professional class or supporters of the president during the campaign. Golkar cadres were chosen as ministers for industry and economic coordination; Nasdem controls the Agriculture, Spatial Planning, Environment, and Forestry ministries; PKB holds power in the Manpower, Trade, and Village and Transmigration ministries. Other ministries were divided equally between PPP and Gerindra. Two military officers, Lieutenant Terawan Agus Purwanto and General Fachrul Razi, were appointed as the minister of healthcare and the minister of religious affairs, respectively. Prabowo Subianto, Jokowi's erstwhile rival for the presidency, was given the post of defence minister. Prior to the entry of these four into the government, there was also the presence of retired general Luhut Binsar Pangaribuan in Jokowi's cabinet. This cabinet profile shows how Jokowi has sought to achieve a power balance by distributing ministerial positions, including to Jokowi's political rival, Prabowo Subianto. Meanwhile, Jokowi has also recruited professional figures to support his economic programme over the next five years. The professionals who supported Jokowi during the presidential contest now have control over the ministries of Education, Tourism and Creative Economy, as well as state-owned enterprises.

Two other cabinet appointments merit attention. Jokowi has chosen the former national chief of the Indonesian Police, Tito Karnavian, as the minister of home affairs, and has selected a retired general to serve as the minister of religious affairs. This combination of having the Ministry of Home Affairs in the hands of the former chief of police and the Ministry of Religious Affairs in the hands of a former military officer reflects Jokowi's efforts to manage the domestic politics of Indonesia, which has increasingly become more conservative and 'radical', and is thus evolving into a security issue. The decision to appoint an official with a security background as the minister of home affairs harks back to the New Order tradition in which this ministry was always headed by a military officer. During his rule, Soeharto approached domestic politics through a security framework, which also informed how he handled domestic challenges. In the previous two cabinets—under President Yudhoyono and during Jokowi's first term—the home affairs ministers (Gamawan Fauzi and Tjahjo Kumolo) were civilians. This revived security approach seems to anticipate two things: increased Islamic conservatism, and increased protests from civil society organizations against Jokowi's accelerated infrastructure projects. A security approach is likely to be used widely to deal with these two issues.

Increased Islamic Conservative Politics

Jokowi's decision to select Ma'ruf Amin as his running mate in the 2019 presidential election reflected his strategy to gain support from traditional Muslim voters. The so-called "Islamic card" played a role in his victory. Jokowi had to confront the challenge posed by major conservative Islamist groups such as Front Pembela Islam (FPI, or Islamic Defenders Front), and Gerakan Nasional Pengawal Fatwa Ulama (GNPF-Ulama, or Ulama Movement for Guiding Fatwa), which were in support of the Prabowo-Sandi pair. These groups were alleged to have used religious sentiments to mobilize voters. In selecting Ma'ruf Amin as his vice presidential nominee, Jokowi was able to cultivate the support of more moderate Muslim organizations such as the NU, which was headed by Ma'ruf.

The increased role of conservative groups in Indonesian electoral politics took root during the blasphemy proceedings against Jakarta's former governor Basuki Tjahaja Purnama (popularly known as Ahok) in 2016 and the ensuing Jakarta gubernatorial election in 2017.

Ironically, Ma'ruf Amin, as head of the Indonesian Ulama Council, was among those calling for Ahok to be jailed. During the race for the governorship, many conservative Muslim groups backed the campaign of Anies Baswedan and Sandiaga Uno, who were running against Ahok and his running mate, PDI-P cadre Djarot Saeful Hidayat. (These same groups later transferred their support to Prabowo-Sandi in the 2019 presidential race.) Through sermons at Friday prayers, religious leaders asked residents of the city to not vote for a non-Muslim leader during the Jakarta campaign period in 2016. The Anies-Sandi campaign won significantly, with a 15 per cent margin over Ahok. The election showed how to effectively use primordial sentiments as a tool to mobilize voters.

What happened during the Jakarta gubernatorial election influenced the mood of the 2019 presidential election, and will perhaps also affect the coming September 2020 local elections. In 2020 there will be 270 local elections to select 9 governors (4 in Sumatra, 3 in Kalimantan, 2 in Sulawesi), 224 district heads, and 37 city mayors. Islam is likely to be instrumentalized to mobilize voters, especially in areas with a more plural background.

The politics of intolerance is not limited to social media but has spread to the everyday lives of citizens, particularly in arenas where inclusivity and tolerance should be practised, as Indonesia is a secular state. In public schools, for instance, there has been an increase in instances of informal instructions from headmasters and teachers for girls to wear headscarves at school. While it is doubtful whether the participants of the Aksi Bela Islam (Action for Defending Islam) rally in 2017 actually support the establishment of an Islamic country (which there was chanting for during the demonstration), the event testifies to the consolidation of the Islamic conservative movement in Indonesian.[9] The demonstration articulated the strength of the Islamic movement and its ability to mobilize the masses in defence of its interests. The event may have been attended by Jakartans from a mixture of backgrounds, but it sent a message to Muslim groups that mass gatherings are an effective means of advancing their demands.

The increased Islamic conservatism and Islamic radicalism have resulted in some victims. Retired general Wiranto, who also served as a minister in Jokowi's first cabinet, was stabbed in his thigh during a visit to Banten Province, a neighbourhood of the capital Jakarta, on 10 October 2019. Police believe he was attacked by a member of Jamaah Ansharut Daulah, a network with links to Islamic State.[10] This attack increased the government's awareness of the existence of this network and of security concerns related to domestic politics in general.

Growth, Investment and Infrastructure Politics

Jokowi consistently prioritized economic growth during his first term, and he will do the same during his second. As the seventh-largest world economy in purchasing power parity terms, the latest World Bank data[11] shows that the growth rate of Indonesia's GDP has increased from 4 per cent between 2000 and 2017 to 5.1 per cent in the first quarter of 2019. In Asia, the only two countries with higher GDP growth rates are China (9 per cent) and India (5.5 per cent). Jokowi has pushed for growth through investments and infrastructure projects in the belief that improved infrastructure will increase Indonesia's competitiveness in Southeast Asia in attracting foreign investments.

Infrastructure is at the heart of Jokowi's economic policy, and this will continue over the next five years.[12] The infrastructure projects are aimed at supporting growth and solving problems of connectivity, power shortages, congestion and sanitation in the country. In the National Medium-term Development Plan for 2014–19, the Jokowi government had set a target of building 5,000 kilometres of railway tracks, 2,600 kilometres of roads, 1,000 kilometres of toll roads, 49 dams, 24 harbours, and power plants with a capacity of 35 thousand megawatts. These are all part of the "National Strategic Program".

TABLE 1
Infrastructure Projects under Jokowi, 2016–19

Year	Projects Completed	Type of Projects	Fund Allocation, IDR (USD)
2016	20	1 toll road, 7 airports, 6 dams, 1 harbour, 1 gas pipeline, and 4 PLBN (National Border Posts)	33.3 trillion (2.4 billion)
2017	10	2 toll roads, 1 airport, 1 gas pipeline, 1 dam, 1 irrigation channel, 3 PLBN	61.4 trillion (4.4 billion)
2018	32	10 toll roads, 1 airport for industrial area, 2 railway tracks, 4 dams, 1 irrigation channel, 4 smelters, 5 integrated economic areas, and 1 fish centre auction facility	207.4 trillion (15 billion)
2019	19	3 airports, 5 roads, 4 integrated areas, 3 dams, and 2 technology projects	7.7 trillion (550 million)

Source: S.M. Jannah, "Realisasi Pembangunan Infrastruktur Periode I Jokowi Cuma Capai 46%" [Jokowi's realization of infrastructure reaches 46% in his first period], Tirto. ID, 2 October 2019, https://tirto.id/realisasi-pembangunan-infrastruktur-periode-i-jokowi-cuma-capai-46-ei7e (accessed 25 November 2019).

According to data from the National Budget Plan, there will be a 4.9 per cent increase in the budget for infrastructure for 2020, to 419.2 trillion rupiah (US$30 billion). A target of the construction of 837 kilometres of roads has been set, which is almost double the length for 2019. In 2018 and 2019 a total of 8 airports were completed, and a further 3 are expected to be ready in 2020. More than 600 kilometres of train tracks were completed between 2018 and 2019, and a target of 238.8 kilometres is set for 2020. The number of new dams constructed between 2018 and 2019 came to 97, with 49 more expected in 2020. These projects are distributed all over the archipelago, with the train tracks laid in South Sulawesi (Makassar-Parepare), a harbour in Gorontalo, North Sulawesi and in Bau-bau, Central Sulawesi, and a road in Sumatra.[13] Despite these impressive statistics, only 46 per cent of the targeted infrastructure projects (103 units) were completed in 2019. In the capital, the long wait for the mass rapid transit (MRT) ended when the MRT began operations in March 2019. By 2023 the MRT network is projected to carry 173,000 passengers daily.[14] Compared to the Yudhoyono era, the growth of infrastructure under Jokowi has been significant.

Investment is another key issue to support infrastructure policies. So far, the majority of infrastructure projects have been financed from the government budget and state-owned enterprises (SOEs), with only very minimal amounts coming from the private sector. This has put pressure on the Indonesian budget deficit, which has soared in recent years. Data from Bank Indonesia reveal that the budget deficit had reached US$2 billion by the second quarter of 2019.[15] The ratio of infrastructure stock-to-GDP in Indonesia has fallen consistently since the Asian financial crisis two decades ago, although recent efforts had increased investment from 3 per cent of GDP to 4 per cent by 2016. Yet, Sri Mulyani has assured the public the Indonesian economy is in an acceptable position, because having a deficit amounting to 3 per cent of GDP is sustainable.[16]

Foreign direct investment into Indonesia is still low compared to other Southeast Asian countries such as Malaysia, Vietnam and Cambodia. One economist has suggested the problem is not restricted to the limited rate of foreign investment but to the way these funds are spent in sectors that do not boost Indonesian productivity. Moreover, institutional weaknesses in the planning, budgeting, implementation and execution of policies persist.[17] As a result, Jokowi's infrastructure programme has not significantly boosted the economy yet, with growth stuck at 5 per cent.[18]

In the global context, Jokowi's development priorities have had to contend with a global economic slowdown as a result of the US-China trade war and the protectionist economic policies introduced by the two countries. Indonesian imports of raw material, capital goods and consumer goods had declined drastically by

June 2019. The decline in raw material imports is a sign of declining investment. Exports also declined by 8.57 per cent between January and June 2019 compared to the same period the previous year.[19]

The Cost of Economic Growth: Inequality

Jokowi's relentless pursuit of growth has also contributed to the rise in inequality. Indonesia's Gini coefficient in 2019 was 0.4. For comparison, in the period between 1976 and 1990 under the New Order regime, the Gini coefficient was 0.32, while the economy was growing at a rate of 7 per cent annually.[20] The rise in inequality has been witnessed since the end of the Yudhoyono era. Credit Suisse reported in 2017 that the top one per cent of the richest Indonesians control 49.3 per cent of the national wealth. Indonesia ranks as the sixth most unequal country in the world. In 2012, in a survey on Indonesian perceptions of inequality conducted by the World Bank and the Indonesian Survey Institute, most respondents agreed that inequality was increasing and highlighted the need for the government to act quickly to resolve it. Additionally, the survey also indicated that a majority of Indonesians are "willing to accept slower economic growth in exchange for less inequality".[21]

The Jokowi government has tried hard to mitigate the rise in inequality through many poverty-alleviation programmes. These include sectoral policies related to poverty, such as agrarian reform and social forestry programmes, subsidies for public services such as healthcare and education, and direct cash transfers through Program Keluarga Harapan (PKH, or Family Hope Programme) for the poor. The infrastructure projects are also expected to improve connectivity and communication with the remote areas of Indonesia. This could help in mitigating inequality by allowing for better human resources development, which should eventually boost Indonesia's Human Development Index.[22]

Guaranteeing the security of land ownership is one of the administration's strategies to address inequality. Millions of Indonesian farmers have benefitted from the land-titling programme. In 2018 the National Land Agency issued more than 9.3 million land certificates, exceeding the target of 7 million. In 2019 Jokowi set a target of 9 million certificates for Indonesians to ease the land-titling programme.[23] Along with the land certificate programme, farmers have been given access to state-owned forests through the social forestry programme, which was established in 2014. Under this programme, local communities will manage 12.7 million hectares of social forests. As of July 2018, the Ministry of Environment and Forestry has only managed to issue permits for 1.75 million hectares of forests, which amounts to only 15 per cent of the target. Despite the slow process, social forestry remains an important programme to address economic inequality in the forest sector.[24]

Another major welfare programme to mitigate poverty has been the cash transfers under the PKH. Introduced in 2007 during the Yudhoyono era, the PKH adopted a conditional cash transfer model based on the experience of Brazil's Bolsa Familia programme. The programme provides a fixed annual sum of 550,000 rupiah (US$32.90) to each family, with supplementary conditional transfers for children to cover their school fees and for other family members who are disabled, elderly or pregnant.[25] In addition to the conditional cash transfers, there are other welfare programmes for the poor; namely, the Unconditional Cash Transfer programme and Rice for the Poor (Beras Miskin, or Raskin). Since 2016 the budget allocation for PKH has consistently been increased. In 2016 the programme distributed 10 trillion rupiah (US$710 million). By 2019 the amount had increased by more than threefold to 32 trillion rupiah (US$2.3 billion), with coverage expanded from 6 million to 10 million poor families.

While these programmes have contributed to decreasing the poverty rate in Indonesia, the level of economic inequality remains high.[26] In all, the present efforts have resulted in a decrease of absolute poverty from affecting almost 11.6 per cent of the population (28 million people) in 2014 to 9.41 per cent (25 million people) by July 2018. The Gini coefficient also fell from 0.42 to 0.39, with a target of a further reduction to 0.36. However, these incremental results in reducing poverty cannot be expected to resolve the wider problem of inequality.[27]

As such, the presidential ticket of Prabowo-Sandi turned economic inequality into a political issue during the presidential campaign.[28] The pair harnessed economic dissatisfaction among citizens to gain popularity. Their campaign materials on economic inequality brought back the "classic" issue of the political economy being cornered by Chinese Indonesians, who were presented as controlling a majority of wealth at the expense of the *pribumi*. This overlapped with another longstanding political cleavage framed around religion, especially in terms of Muslims against non-Muslims. This framing of economic discourse around such majority-minority lines can carry over to other issues concerning vulnerable minority groups, such as the Ahmadiyah and LGBT groups. Government protection is essential here, although in reality it has been very limited.

Economy First, Democracy Later

In his ten-page inauguration speech delivered on 20 October 2019, Jokowi described his plan for his second term. Infrastructure, the provision of jobs, entrepreneurship and other economic programmes will be his priorities. There was no mention of addressing corruption or of protecting human rights. On top of exacerbating inequality, the pursuit of economic growth has other unavoidable costs, such as violating human rights. To pave the way for development, members of the *adat* community have been displaced from their habitats. The media have also reported on increasing intimidation of social activists. An environmental activist was killed in Medan, North Sumatera, allegedly by individuals on behalf of palm oil corporate interests.[29] The president also has some homework to do in reviewing old human rights cases, such as the killing of Trisakti student protestors, or the unsolved murder of human rights advocate Munir in 2004.

Anti-corruption efforts have increasingly been seen as inhibiting factors that limit development. Any legal constraints, including strict monitoring from the Corruption Eradication Commission (KPK), are regarded as having slowed investments. In the spirit of creating a business-friendly environment, important regulations—such as the one requiring an environmental impact analysis before a permit is issued—are now in the process of being annulled.[30] Moreover, the government plans to pass an "omnibus law" covering many issues and sectors in order to facilitate investment. For instance, under the new law, workers rights will be restricted in order to pave the way for increased investment. While Indonesia currently ranks 73rd out of 190 countries in terms of the ease of doing business,[31] Jokowi wants the country to reach 40th in 2020.

Members of the House of Representatives have similar interests to those of the president. They want to limit the authority of the KPK, which has been active in prosecuting corruption over the past decade. The house supported legislative revisions that basically minimize the powers and role of the KPK. This is despite the House of Representatives being, according to a recent survey, the least trusted public institution.[32] In 2018, of 260 corruption cases, almost half involved members of parliament.[33] In passing the law that weakened the KPK, on 24 September 2019, the house argued that the KPK had become a "super body" without any institutional oversight.

The public was very critical of these legislative manoeuvres, and protests continued for weeks. Shortly after the passage of the law, students in seventeen cities across Indonesia took to the streets in protest, between 24 and 29 September 2019. In Yogyakarta around 150,000 students gathered at the Gejayan crossroads. Using the hashtag #GejayanMemanggil (Gejayan Calling) on Twitter, along with a media campaign #ReformasiDiKorupsi (or "The reformation has been corrupted"), the protesters demanded the president issue a decree to annul the revised KPK Law.[34] During the protests, two students were shot dead by police officers in Kendari in Southeast Sulawesi, while a further twelve died in Jakarta during similar protests.³⁵ While Jokowi invited public figures for an advisory meeting to gather their inputs, he eventually decided not to stop the KPK Law. This represents a setback for the agenda of public transparency and accountability in Indonesia.

The House of Representatives also supported a revision to the country's Criminal Code (KUHP) that introduced articles that threatened basic civil rights such as freedom of expression and removed protection for minority groups. The revision also contains articles against defaming the president, as well as against adultery, cohabitation and premarital sex. These "morality" articles raised public concerns.³⁶ Although the bill was supposed to be passed in early September 2019, it was eventually halted to allow the newly elected batch of parliamentarians begin work.

These developments have caused civil society activists to worry about the emerging trend under Jokowi of "investment first, human rights later", especially if—as is likely—it will continue over the next five years. In 2019, for instance, forty-four people died for the cause of freedom of expression.³⁷ This has sparked concerns that Indonesia has returned to an authoritarian era, with the only difference being that the president was elected democratically, unlike the case with Soeharto.

Economic Diplomacy as a Core: Indonesian Foreign Policy in 2019

Indonesian foreign policy in 2019 was marked by at least three features: its continued focus on economic diplomacy, the West Papuan protests for independence, and the establishment of the Agency for International Development. Differing from Yudhoyono, Jokowi is known to give less priority to formal diplomacy unless it relates to his domestic economic agenda. He attended the World Economic Forum not long after his inauguration in his first term, but since then he has carefully selected which international forums he would attend based on their potential economic impact. He has attended the G20 meetings and all the forums related to international trade and investment, but has often been absent from forums related to political diplomacy. Apart from economic diplomacy, Indonesia's role on the global stage in 2019 can be said to be more of routine performance than any strategic manoeuvre responding to global challenges.³⁸

Retno Marsudi continues to serve as minister of foreign affairs into Jokowi's second term. In a meeting with the House of Representatives in October 2019, she shared the five Diplomatic Priorities for the period 2019 to 2024. The future of Indonesian diplomacy is formulated in terms of a "4+1 policy". The first four items in this equation are economic diplomacy, protection diplomacy, sovereign diplomacy, and nationality diplomacy. The "plus one" is infrastructure diplomacy.[39] The first priority of economic diplomacy and the "plus one" are oriented towards Jokowi's domestic infrastructure policy (see below). International trade and investment negotiation forums and agreements are the arena for this, such as CEPA/FTA/PTA. Protection diplomacy is about protecting Indonesian citizens abroad, including migrant workers. A system called "one single data", which aims to facilitate protection, is currently being established. The programme aims for "reconstruction of migration governance for *safe, orderly and regular* migration; and building focus on preventive actions for crises through education and community empowerment". Sovereign diplomacy relates to a standing position that Indonesia will not "give any room for separatist groups to utilize various international forums in campaigning their separatist agendas". Indonesia will sit on the United Nations Human Right Council from 2020 to 2022, will chair ASEAN in 2023, and in the future will chair the G20. The Bali Democracy Forum established by President Yudhoyono is also still conducted regularly.

In pursuit of Indonesia's infrastructure diplomacy, the president has tasked Mahendra Siregar, Indonesian ambassador to the United States, and Foreign Minister Marsudi to make use of economic diplomacy to attract foreign investments. Economic and infrastructure diplomacy will be key to Indonesian foreign policy during Jokowi's second term. In addition, and related to the economic agenda, what will perhaps be new in the next five years of Jokowi's foreign affairs orientation will be the use of "Muslim Identity". The president intends to expand Indonesia's halal market globally,[40] which means increased interaction with Muslim countries in the Middle East. The Global Halal Summit will be held in Indonesia in 2020.

The second feature of Indonesian foreign policy is sovereign diplomacy. This relates to the recent scaling up of activities in West Papua calling for independence from Indonesia. The issue escalated in August 2019 after the racial slur incident in Surabaya, East Java. A local police officer is reported to have insulted the Papuan student community by calling them "monkeys". This triggered great anger among Papuans both inside and outside the country. After that incident, a wave of protests occurred in cities in West Papua, all of which ended with violence and atrocities, such as in Manokwari and Wamena. The death toll was twenty-seven people, and hundreds of buildings were burnt.[41] The central government decided to isolate West Papua from the world for a time by cutting the Internet connection. Papuan activists were also jailed. Veronika Koman, a public defender and advocate for West Papuan Independence Movement activists, was accused of being involved in the protest by spreading fake news.[42] She has been very active on

Twitter sharing updates on Papua during the outbreaks. The Indonesian government threatened to revoke her passport and has asked Interpol to locate her. She is now in Australia and she recently received a Sir Ronald Wilson human rights award from the non-governmental Australian Council for International Development.[43]

The Indonesian government, through coordinating minister for law and security affairs Machfud MA, has accused Koman of being an "irresponsible citizen". He commented that she received a scholarship from the Indonesian government but she is now staying in Australia. He also said that Australia should respect Indonesian law regarding Koman.[44] The Pacific Islands Forum, consisting of Pacific Island countries, supports West Papua independence. The forum managed to express its support during the UN General Assembly in September 2019.

Related to this, the third feature of Indonesian foreign policy to take note of for 2019 may be seen in the Indonesian Agency for International Development, which was launched in October. Foreign Minister Retno Marsudi said the agency "is a very precious tool for Indonesian diplomacy [that we can use] to strengthen our presence on the international stage".[45] Indonesia established an endowment fund of US$238 million for the project. Its aim is to boost South-South cooperation. The initiative though has been criticized. Indonesia still receives developmental aid from developed countries such as Australia. In 2018–19, total official development assistance from Australia to Indonesia came to A$331 million.[46] Thus, there is an irony here that Indonesia, as a donor recipient country, is now aspiring to become a donor country itself. The agency is seen as a potential means of mitigating increased support for West Papuan independence from Pacific Island countries. Criticism over the motives of the aid is situated within this context, although the official statement has refuted this accusation.[47]

Conclusion: What Will Happen Next Year?

The year 2019 has been a crucial one for Indonesia on account of the elections, which determined the government plans for 2019–24. Despite all the criticism about the declining quality of Indonesian democracy, the elections generally went on without any political complication, and elite consolidation was established immediately after them. It is likely in Jokowi's second term that growth will be a continuing focus of economic development, through infrastructure projects and investment. Increased competition among countries in Southeast Asia is also a pressing concern that the government must address. Institutional aspects of economic development, including regulations that may constrain and block investments, are being streamlined. This is to boost Indonesia's ease of doing business ranking.

An "Omnibus law", a grouping of regulations related to investment activities, is on the way, which aims to provide a friendly economic environment to welcome foreign investors.

Jokowi is also prepared to deal with the interrelated issues of inequality, security and increased Islamic conservatism. He has positioned figures with a background in national security in related ministries to deal with domestic politics. These moves are all aimed at supporting his economic development programmes, focusing on growth, infrastructure and investments. He seems to be of the opinion that there will always be an unavoidable cost to growth in social and political life. And it is understandable that many observers are of the opinion that Jokowi is no different from Soeharto during the New Order era. Critical activists that support human rights are ignored. A tension between economic development and political development (democracy), which was widely debated during the New Order era, has re-emerged. In 2019, as with the previous years of the Jokowi era, economics was prioritized over democracy. And this approach will likely continue during his second term.

Notes

1. Reality Check Team, "Indonesia Election in 2019: Why Did Many Officials Die?", CNN Indonesia, 16 May 2019, https://www.bbc.com/news/world-asia-48281522 (accessed 10 December 2019).
2. Marcus Mietzner, "Indonesia's Democratic Stagnation: Anti-Reformist Elites and Resilient Civil Society", *Democratization* 19, no. 2 (2006): 209–29.
3. Eve Warburton, "Explaining Indonesia's Democratic Regression: Structure, Agency and Popular Opinion", *Contemporary Southeast Asia* 41, no. 2 (August 2019): 225–85.
4. Rachael Diprose, Dave McRae, and Vedi Hadiz, "Two Decades of *Reformasi* in Indonesia: Its Illiberal Turn", *Journal of Contemporary Asia* 49, no. 5 (2019): 691–712.
5. Edward Aspinall, Diego Fossati, Burhanuddin Muhtadi, and Eve Warburton, "Elites, Masses, and Democratic Decline in Indonesia", *Democratization* (2019): 1–23.
6. Ibid.
7. Edward Aspinall, "Indonesia's Election and the Return of Ideological Competition", *New Mandala*, 22 April 2019, https://www.newmandala.org/indonesias-election-and-the-return-of-ideological-competition/ (accessed 26 November 2019).
8. Dewi Nurita, "PDIP Optimistic to Introduce the Next Jokowi in 2024 Election", *Tempo.co*, 3 July 2019, https://en.tempo.co/read/1220879/pdip-optimistic-to-introduce-the-next-jokowi-in-2024-election (accessed 20 November 2019).
9. Greg Fealy, "Bigger than Ahok: Explaining 2 December Mass Rally", *Indonesia at Melbourne*, 7 December 2016, https://indonesiaatmelbourne.unimelb.edu.au/bigger-than-ahok-explaining-jakartas-2-december-mass-rally/ (accessed 19 November 2019).

10. "Wiranto: Indonesia Security Minister Stabbed by 'IS' Radical", BBC News, 10 October 2019, https://www.bbc.com/news/world-asia-49997210 (accessed 18 December 2019).
11. World Bank, *Indonesian Economic Quarterly: Oceans of Opportunity*, June 2019, https://www.worldbank.org/en/country/indonesia/publication/june-2019-indonesia-economic-quarterly.
12. Aichiro Prabowo, "Building a Better Infrastructure Policy after Indonesia's Election", *New Mandala*, 7 March 2019, https://www.newmandala.org/building-a-better-infrastructure-policy-after-indonesias-elections (accessed 15 November 2019).
13. "Deretan Proyek Infrastruktur Fantastis Rp 400 T Jokowi 2020" [Here's the list of Jokowi's IDR 400 billion infrastructure project in 2020], CNBC Indonesia, 17 August 2019, https://www.cnbcindonesia.com/news/20190817114500-4-92714/deretan-proyek-infrastruktur-fantastis-rp-400-t-jokowi-2020 (accessed 25 November 2019).
14. "MRT Jakarta Targets 173,000 Daily Users in 2023", *Tempo.co*, 18 November 2019, https://en.tempo.co/read/1273570/mrt-jakarta-targets-173000-daily-users-by-2023 (accessed 11 December 2019).
15. "Indonesia's Balance of Payments Falls to Deficit in Q2 amid the Slowing Growth", *Jakarta Post*, 9 August 2019, https://www.thejakartapost.com/news/2019/08/09/indonesias-balance-of-payments-falls-to-deficit-in-q2-amid-slowing-growth.html (accessed 11 December 2019).
16. Rachmadea Aisyah, "Data Points Slowdown in Indonesian Economy amid Ongoing Trade War", *Jakarta Post*, 16 July 2019, https://www.thejakartapost.com/news/2019/07/16/data-points-to-slowdown-in-indonesian-economy-amid-ongoing-trade-war.html (accessed 22 November 2019).
17. Roland Rajah, "Indonesia Economy: Between Growth and Stability", Lowy Institute, 15 August 2019, https://www.lowyinstitute.org/publications/indonesia-economy-between-growth-and-stability (accessed 11 December 2019).
18. Ibid.
19. Rachmadea Aisya, "Data Points to Slow Down in Indonesian Economy amid Ongoing Trade War", *Jakarta Post*, 17 July 2019, https://www.thejakartapost.com/news/2019/07/16/data-points-to-slowdown-in-indonesian-economy-amid-ongoing-trade-war.html/ (accessed in 21 January 2020).
20. Asep Suharyadi, "Is Higher Inequality the New Normal in Indonesia?", *Indonesia at Melbourne*, 27 November 2018, https://indonesiaatmelbourne.unimelb.edu.au/is-higher-inequality-the-new-normal-for-indonesia/ (accessed in 19 November 2019).
21. Vincent Lingga, "Commentary: Reducing Inequality Cracking Wealth Concentration in Indonesia", *Jakarta Post*, 2 April 2018, https://www.thejakartapost.com/academia/2018/04/02/commentary-reducing-inequality-cracking-wealth-concentration-in-indonesia.html (accessed 19 November 2019).
22. Yenny Tjoe, "Two Decades of Economic Growth Benefited Only the Richest 20%.

How Severe is Inequality in Indonesia?", *The Conversation*, 28 August 2018, https://theconversation.com/two-decades-of-economic-growth-benefited-only-the-richest-20-how-severe-is-inequality-in-indonesia-101138 (accessed 15 November 2019).

23. Vindry Florentin, "Jokowi: Land Certificate Issuance Passed Targets", *Tempo.co*, 4 January 2019, https://en.tempo.co/read/1161644/jokowi-land-certificate-issuance-in-2018-surpasses-target (accessed 22 November 2019).
24. Nabiha Shahab, "Taking Stock of Indonesia's Social Forestry Program", CIFOR *Forest News*, 29 October 2018, https://forestsnews.cifor.org/58344/taking-stock-of-indonesias-social-forestry-program?fnl=en (accessed 22 November 2019).
25. Ministry of Social Affairs, "Apa itu Program Keluarga Harapan?", *Program Keluarga Harapan*, 2018, https://pkh.kemsos.go.id/?pg=tentangpkh-1 (accessed 17 December 2019).
26. "Poverty Rate Falls but Disparity Remains High", *Jakarta Post*, 16 July 2019, https://www.thejakartapost.com/news/2019/07/16/poverty-rate-falls-but-disparity-remains-high.html (accessed 17 December 2019).
27. Lingga, "Commentary: Reducing Inequality".
28. Eve Warburton and Burhanudin Muhtadi, "Politicizing Inequality in Indonesian Election", Brookings Institution, 8 April 2019, https://www.brookings.edu/blog/order-from-chaos/2019/04/08/politicizing-inequality-in-indonesian-elections/ (accessed 20 November 2019).
29. "Journalist cum Activist Found Dead in North Sumatera", *Jakarta Post*, 3 November 2019, https://www.thejakartapost.com/news/2019/11/03/journalist-cum-activists-found-dead-in-north-sumatra.html (accessed 9 December 2019).
30. "Property Developers Need Legal Certainty More Than IMB Abolishment", *Jakarta Post*, 25 September 2019, https://www.thejakartapost.com/news/2019/09/25/property-developers-need-legal-certainty-more-than-imb-abolishment.html (accessed 28 November 2019).
31. World Bank, *Doing Business in 2019: Training for Reform: Comparing Business Regulations for Domestic Firms in 190 Economies*, 16th ed., 2019, https://www.doingbusiness.org/content/dam/doingBusiness/media/Annual-Reports/English/DB2019-report_web-version.pdf.
32. Dwi Hadya Jayani, "KPK dan Presiden adalah lembaga yang paling dipercaya publik", *Databoks Katadata*, 30 August 2019, https://databoks.katadata.co.id/datapublish/2019/08/30/survei-lsi-kpk-dan-presiden-jadi-lembaga-yang-paling-dipercaya-publik (accessed 18 December 2019).
33. Irma Garnesia, "Kasus Korupsi: 2018 Terbanyak, Anggota DPR & DPRD Paling Korup", *Tirto.id*, 17 October 2019, https://tirto.id/kasus-korupsi-2018-terbanyak-anggota-dpr-dprd-paling-korup-ejTv (accessed 25 November 2019).
34. Kharishar Kahfi and Karina Maharani Tehusirajana, "Protests Set to Continue as House Holds Final Preliminary Meeting", *Jakarta Post*, 30 September 2019, https://www.thejakartapost.com/news/2019/09/30/protests-set-to-continue-as-house-holds-final-plenary-meeting.html (accessed 18 December 2019).

35. "Second Indonesian Students Dies in Legal Reform Protest", Channel NewsAsia, 27 September 2019, https://www.channelnewsasia.com/news/asia/second-student-dies-indonesia-reform-protests-11948922 (accessed 18 December 2019).
36. Nurul Fitri Ramadhani, "House Keeps 'Morality' Article in KUHP Bill", *Jakarta Post*, 1 July 2019, https://www.thejakartapost.com/news/2019/07/01/house-keeps-morality-articles-kuhp-bill.html (accessed 28 November 2019).
37. Dewi Nurita, "YLBHI: 44 orang tewas misterius akibat utarakan pendapat", *Tempo.co*, 27 October 2019, https://nasional.tempo.co/read/1265042/ylbhi-44-orang-tewas-misterius-akibat-utarakan-pendapat-di-2019/full&view=ok (accessed 9 December 2019).
38. S.F. Muhibat and M.W. Karisma, "Jokowi's Second Term Needs Innovative Foreign Policy", *East Asia Forum*, 4 September 2019, https://www.eastasiaforum.org/2019/09/04/jokowis-second-term-needs-innovative-foreign-policy/ (accessed 20 November 2019).
39. Ministry of Foreign Affairs, "Indonesian FM Presents the Diplomacy Priorities 2019–2024 to the House of Representative", 14 November 2019, https://kemlu.go.id/portal/en/read/786/berita/indonesian-fm-presents-the-diplomacy-priorities-2019-2024-to-the-house-of-representatives (accessed 20 November 2019).
40. Ibid.
41. "West Papua: Day of Violence Sees at Least 27 dead", BBC News, 24 September 2019, https://www.bbc.com/news/world-asia-49806182 (accessed 18 December 2019).
42. "Indonesia Police Named Suspect in West Papua Unrest", Al Jazeera, 4 September 2019, https://www.aljazeera.com/news/2019/09/indonesia-police-suspect-west-papua-unrest-190904063940855.html (accessed 18 December 2019).
43. Tasia Wibawa, "Veronica Koman Received Australian Human Rights Awards for West Papuan Activism", *ABC News*, 24 October 2019, https://www.abc.net.au/news/2019-10-24/veronica-koman-west-papua-human-rights-lawyer-activist-awards/11633222 (accessed 18 December 2019).
44. Deti Mega Purnamasari, "Mahfud MD Nilai Veronica Koman WNI yang Ingkar Janji" [Mahfud MD sees Veronica Komas as a traitor], *Kompas.com*, 19 November 2019, https://nasional.kompas.com/read/2019/11/19/21120341/mahfud-md-nilai-veronica-koman-wni-yang-ingkar-janji (accessed 21 November 2019).
45. Nivell Rayda, "Indonesia Denies Aid Fund Aimed at Dampening Support for Papuan Independence", Channel NewsAsia, 23 October 2019, https://www.channelnewsasia.com/news/asia/indonesia-aid-agency-fund-pacific-nations-papua-independence-12023670 (accessed 21 November 2019).
46. Department of Foreign Affairs and Trade, "Overview of Australia's Aid Program in Indonesia: How We Are Helping", 2019, https://dfat.gov.au/geo/indonesia/development-assistance/pages/development-assistance-in-indonesia.aspx (accessed 9 December 2019).
47. Rayda, "Indonesia Denies Aid Fund".

SOCIAL MEDIA AND THE 2019 INDONESIAN ELECTIONS:
Hoax Takes the Centre Stage

Jennifer Yang Hui

On 17 April 2019, elections were held across Indonesia, the third-largest democracy in the world. The 2019 elections were significant as the first-ever simultaneous presidential and legislative elections in the nation's history, all held within the same day. The complexity of the 2019 elections meant that effective communication strategies were more vital than ever in reaching out to electoral constituents. Social media, which has become an integral part of everyday social and economic life in the nation, is a natural channel to publicize political visions and missions and to galvanize support for parties and candidates.

As a digital commons, however, social media is inevitably weaponized as well. Concerns over the "dark side" of social media in the form of disinformation (popularly called "hoax", referring to the general phenomenon of falsehoods) received outsized attention throughout the campaigning period of the 2019 elections. The low barrier to entry and ease of sharing user-generated content means that social media is more easily used for all kinds of purposes, including negative ones. Aksi Bela Islam 212 (the 2 December 2016 Defend Islam Action), combined with intense political mudslinging in past elections, resulted in "hoax" becoming a term that means division to many Indonesians, potentially tearing apart the young democracy.

This chapter examines how social media interplayed with electoral politics in Indonesia's 2019 elections. The first part of the paper outlines the role of social media in the nation's past elections. Social media has been weaponized for use

---

JENNIFER YANG HUI is Associate Research Fellow at the Centre of Excellence for National Security (CENS), a constituent unit of the S. Rajaratnam School of International Studies (RSIS), Nanyang Technological University (NTU), Singapore.

in political smear campaigns since its introduction on to the nation's political landscape in 2012. Aksi Bela Islam 212 gave rise to fears that hoaxes could further split the nation and affect subsequent elections. Combined with worldwide events such as the 2016 US presidential election, it changed Indonesia's understanding of the so-called "fake news" phenomenon. The second part of the paper discusses how the notion of hoax was central to campaign discourses in the 2019 elections. Social media was the dominant means, although not the only one, by which hoaxes were disseminated.

Social Media and Political Contestation in Past Indonesian Elections

Indonesia is nicknamed the "Social Media Nation". In terms of numbers, active social media users comprise 48 per cent of the country's total population.[1] Indonesian netizens on average spend three hours and twenty-six minutes on social media.[2] The average number of social media accounts per Internet user is 11.2.[3] The video-sharing site YouTube is the most active social media platform (88 per cent) in Indonesia, followed by instant messaging app WhatsApp (83 per cent).[4] Social networking platform Facebook (81 per cent), photo-sharing site Instagram (80 per cent) and microblogging platform Twitter (52 per cent) are also widely used.[5] The majority of these apps are accessed via mobile devices.

While political campaigns have long utilized traditional media such as television and radio,[6] social media is a relative newcomer in Indonesian elections. Social media was first incorporated into Indonesia's electoral politics during the 2012 Jakarta gubernatorial elections.[7] During this early expansion of social media usage in elections, optimism regarding its potential for enhancing political participation and civic engagement prevailed. Twitter hashtags (for example #ReplaceTitleSongWithJOKOWI) and YouTube music videos in support of candidates were first shared during this time.[8] Experiments in election result prediction using social media analytics were also first conducted during the 2012 elections, some of which triumphed over opinion polls.[9]

The increasing ubiquity of social media during this time, however, made traditional political mudslinging more apparent than ever. The term "black campaigns"—campaigns that seek to undermine the image of electoral candidates through rumours, half-truths or completely fabricated information—was coined then. Joko Widodo (Jokowi) and running-mate Basuki Tjahaja Purnama (Ahok), in seeking election, found themselves the target of smear campaigns that sought to paint them as communists, foreigners, proselytizers and so on. Much of these smears were spread via Blackberry Messenger.[10]

In the 2014 presidential elections, in which current president Joko Widodo and former army general Prabowo Subianto first ran against each other, social media played a central role in electoral campaigning. For Jokowi, who was then supported by a vast network of grass-roots volunteers, social media was instrumental in marketing his candidacy, being still a relative unknown to the wider Indonesian public despite his successful stints as the mayor of Solo and the governor of Jakarta. The Jokowi Advanced Social Media Volunteers (JASMEV), a group of volunteers who had first championed Jokowi and Ahok in the 2012 elections, actively campaigned for him. Realizing the importance of social media in targeting voters, Prabowo also relied on a highly structured social media team in his campaigns.

The intensity of black campaigns during the 2014 elections, however, also meant that it was one of the most divisive elections in Indonesian history. On one side, Jokowi was accused of being a communist, Chinese, non-Muslim and a puppet of a political party, among others.[11] Meanwhile, Prabowo's citizenship, temperament and state of the business he owned were questioned.[12] Some of the black campaigns began on social media. For example, a Twitter account, @triomacan2000, actively spread anti-Jokowi messages. Jokowi's electability fell in the months leading up to the elections,[13] and black campaigns were seen as a contributing factor.

Black campaigns reached a fevered pitch in the lead-up to the 2017 gubernatorial elections in Jakarta. Then-governor Ahok was placed on trial for blasphemy after a video of him accusing his political opponents of using religion as a campaign tool was shared on Facebook in October 2016. Protests against Ahok, the biggest of which was Aksi Bela Islam 212, subsequently took place across many parts of Indonesia. Along with the protests, conspiracy theories and rumours against him took the form of memes and all sorts of edited photos and videos, mostly circulated via social media. For instance, during the 2017 governor elections in Jakarta, edited posters of a sword-wielding man in white religious garb with the message "If Anies Baswedan [the current governor of Jakarta who was then contending for election] lost, there will be an Islamic Revolution"[14] could be found all over the Internet. Fostered by algorithms and the online echo chamber, sectarian and racist themes were the substance of much of these online campaigns, encouraging what media scholar Merlyna Lim called the "freedom to hate".[15]

Disinformation was even monetized; the police cybercrime unit reported the existence of a Saracen Cyber Team, an online syndicate that created social media accounts to spread hate speech for clients willing to pay for them, some of whom were believed to be organizers of the anti-Ahok rallies.[16]

During this time, those deemed to have insulted Islamic leaders and organizations were subjected to doxing (putting out personally identifiable information online, usually for public shaming) and *digilantism* (cyber-vigilantism or real-life attacks after having been identified online).[17] An online movement calling itself the Muslim Cyber Army (MCA) identified people whom they deemed to have insulted Muslims and Islamic leaders online and subjected them to real-life attacks and police reports.[18] Some social media posts were even falsified to get the MCA to attack the individuals in question.[19] These were all made possible by the surveillance capabilities of social media.

Ahok conceded defeat at the second round of the polls and was later imprisoned for blasphemy. The anti-Ahok campaigns shocked many Indonesians. The events resulted in a turning point in the public perception of hoax, which was now seen as detrimental to the nation's hard-won democracy, which had only been consolidated as recently as 1999. Coupled with worldwide concerns over "fake news", as illustrated by the alleged Russian interference in the 2016 US presidential election, among others, Indonesia began to take the threat of hoax seriously in preparation for the 2019 elections. Many concerted efforts to counter hoaxes began to be put in place around this time; the Indonesian authorities implemented measures to restrict the spread of hoaxes online, those spreading hate speech were arrested, and grass-roots initiatives against hoaxes were established.

It is against the backdrop of the Aksi Bela Islam 212 and the 2017 elections that Indonesia's understanding of hoax in the 2019 elections was formed. The subsequent section will discuss the role of social media in spreading hoaxes during the 2019 elections.

The 2019 Elections

The 2019 elections in Indonesia were not only the most logistically challenging[20] but they also saw a very long campaign period—seven months to be exact. In contrast, campaigning during the 2014 election only lasted a month. This meant that the 2019 elections generated arguably more election-related discussion in the digital space than previously. With the abundance of information online, official or otherwise, voters faced the challenge of finding accurate information on the election: candidates, political parties, as well as logistics for voting such as the location of polling stations, etc.

Although the social media landscape in Indonesia has changed since the previous election campaigns, it is still an indispensable avenue for netizens to find out about real-time updates on campaign issues. Platforms like Instagram and WhatsApp played a bigger role in disseminating campaign messages and discussion on the election. For example, Instagram had collaborated with comic artist Reza Mustar to launch a series of election-themed stickers.[21] The presidential and vice-presidential debates were closely followed by viewers via live-streaming on the Internet and social media platforms like Twitter and Facebook. Instant messaging platforms like WhatsApp, which have become an indispensable part of ordinary Indonesians' daily lives, have been used by supporters of both candidates for communication and information sharing.

There were also significant efforts at winning support from some segments of the population through social media. The millennials (those born between 1981 and 1996), widely viewed as digital natives, are one such segment. Eighty-one per cent of the combined advertising audiences of Facebook, Instagram and Facebook Messenger are aged under thirty-four years old.[22] Efforts were made by political parties to circumvent the political apathy of millennials through savvy digital strategies.[23] The term *emak-emak* (mothers) also became a trending topic on Twitter since the end of August 2018, showing the desire among campaigners to target the simple, everyday mother figure among voters.[24]

Political campaigning teams and the supporters of candidates and parties sought to outdo one another on social media. This took the form of the "Hashtag War". One prominent hashtag, #2019GantiPresiden (Change the President in 2019), was pro-opposition in nature. It was popularized by Mardani Ali Sera, the chairman of the PKS (Partai Keadilan Sejahtera, or the Prosperity and Justice Party), who used the term to create a movement that is seemingly grass-roots and neutral, relying on, among others, WhatsApp chat groups to mobilize activities such as rallies.[25] A competing, pro-Jokowi hashtag was #01JokowiLagi. As the two sides crossed swords online, care was taken to keep the discourse to the limits of "positive campaigning" and "negative campaigning"—emphasizing the strengths and pointing out the weaknesses of election candidates and proposed policies—without resorting to false allegations.

From Black Campaign to Hoax Campaign

Driving around Jakarta's main thoroughfare of the Bundaran HI (Hotel Indonesia roundabout) during the campaign period, one could see a plaque reminding voters to reject hoaxes and expressions of SARA (any public expression deemed to violate ethnic, racial, religious or inter-group relations).

Hoax was clearly at the forefront of the consciousness of Indonesians during the 2019 elections. With the elections being a rematch between the incumbent and Prabowo for the presidential seat, hoax was seen as a tool that could lend strategic advantage in garnering votes for the candidates. During a campaign gathering in Surabaya, East Java in February 2019, Jokowi complained that his opponent resorted to "Russian propaganda" in a systematic attempt to "produce non-stop slander, lies and hoaxes" to mislead the public.[26] One of the smears he had in mind was certainly the claims of assault made by former human rights activist and Prabowo campaign team member Ratna Sarumpaet, who admitted that she was the "best hoax creator" after her injuries were later found to have been the result of plastic surgery.[27] After a strong rebuttal from the Russian Embassy in Jakarta,[28] the president clarified that he was not referring to Russia as a nation but to a technique called the "firehose of falsehoods" coined by the RAND Corporation, an American think-tank.[29]

Regardless, hoaxes continued to spread throughout the election campaign period and after, affecting all election candidates and institutions. Indonesian voters were aware that social media could be a tool for *pencitraan* (engineering), and the creation of hoaxes is one such illustration of this.

Actors behind hoax campaigns take advantage of online anonymity and the shift to horizontal trust in the digital age. As the popular meme goes: "On the internet, nobody knows you're a dog." Similarly, on social media, anonymity allows users to lie about their identities, despite the community guidelines of some platforms that require users to create accounts and post with their real names. On the other hand, there has been a general decline of trust towards formal institutions and a corresponding rise of "peer-to-peer influence", whereby close ones are deemed more trustworthy in decision-making.[30] The combination of the ability to be anonymous online and the rise of horizontal trust means that partisanship towards online echo chambers and opinion leaders that fit into them can be exploited.

Compounded by the inability to critically evaluate online formation,[31] hoax campaigns gained traction among some people during the 2019 elections. For example, the vote counting system (*situng*) of the KPU (Indonesian General Election Commission) became the subject of hoaxes in the 2019 elections because it was the first time that the vote tabulation was put online in a national election; some Indonesians did not understand that vote-counting was in fact still computed manually before the results were uploaded on to the KPU website.[32] Hoax campaigns therefore thrive where there are existing gaps in the media and digital literacy in society.

Buzzers and Cyber Troops/Armies

Terms like "buzzers" and "cyber troops/armies" were thrown about during the 2019 election period.

Cyber troops/armies refer to actors representing the interests of political parties who are responsible for manipulating public opinion online.[33] The Jokowi-Ma'ruf social media campaign team was estimated to have around 8,000 social media "soldiers" all over Indonesia, 500 of whom were based in West Java.[34] The Prabowo-Sandi team was also believed to be employing the services of cyber troops in their campaigning.[35]

Buzzers, on the other hand, is a term unique to Indonesia's context, referring to digital influencers who are hired to strategically amplify online messages. They are commonly used for promotional branding purposes in the commercial sector, but they have been increasingly making headway in political campaigning since the 2012 Jakarta elections.[36]

The two terms, which are sometimes used interchangeably, show that there is increasing public awareness that behind seemingly organic expressions of support online a much more deliberate attempt at shaping voter sentiment is at play. Communications scholar Muninggar Sri Saraswati argued that social media usage during Indonesia's elections was very much the result of professional political campaigners such as buzzers who have skilfully turned the potential for online activism of social media to the electoral arena.[37]

During the 2019 election campaign, investigative journalism uncovered teams of buzzers who were in charge of framing public opinion on the behalf of candidates.[38] These buzzer teams relied on fake social media accounts, which were maintained to make them seem like they belonged to real-life users, to spread their clients' messages.[39]

While buzzers have often been accused of being digital mercenaries who create and disseminate disinformation for financial gain, in reality the situation is much more complex. Most buzzers are reluctant to be seen to be creating or spreading hoaxes because of the intense scrutiny of their roles, particularly in the lead-up to the election. They tend to take advantage of the terminological ambiguity of what the term "hoax" means, and they only admit to spreading negative campaign messages, rather than falsehoods.[40]

Some buzzers also truly believe in their political cause, using social media to garner wider support for their candidate of choice, sometimes at the expense of the truth. For this type of buzzer, the line between personal activism and their legally grey paid work is a fine one. This category of buzzers cannot be dismissed as mere mercenaries for the candidates.

Hoax Campaigns: Platforms and Modalities

Social media platforms and technological applications were used to disseminate hoaxes before and after the 2019 elections.

Bots are automated software applications that are used to do tasks such as organizing online content and disseminating alerts over social media accounts. Research by the Oxford Internet Institute demonstrates that bots can be used to operate many fake accounts and spread disinformation.[41] Twitter bots,[42] for instance, were instrumental in September 2018 in publicizing a website[43] that tried to cast the personal life of Prabowo's running mate, Sandiaga Uno, in a negative light. Seventy million Twitter accounts were found to be employing bots during the campaign period in mid-2018.[44]

A fake Twitter account, @opposite 6890, claimed that the police created a network of pro-Jokowi buzzers.[45] Twitter hashtag campaigns also questioned the neutrality of the KPU: #INAelectionObserverSOS, #KPUtidaknetral (the KPU is not neutral) and #IndonesiaCallsObservers.

The Indonesian Anti-Slander Society (Mafindo), a civil society organization that has spearheaded many fact-checking activities, observed that Facebook was the platform that was most popularly used to spread hoaxes, accounting for 49.54 per cent of those reported to them in January 2019.[46] A fake Facebook account, for example, was first used to spread a video showing ballots that had supposedly been cast in North Sumatra before voting day.[47] In the technology giant's operations against "coordinated, inauthentic behaviour", twice in early 2019, accounts, pages, groups and followers on its platform and Instagram related to the Saracen Group, a movement linked to an online syndicate accused of peddling fake news, were removed.[48] These online networks mostly attacked President Jokowi and sought to amplify support for Prabowo.[49]

WhatsApp was also used in hoax campaigns. One example of falsehoods spread through WhatsApp claimed that the police criminal intelligence unit is the base from where the KPU vote-counting system is controlled.[50] A voice message spread through WhatsApp claimed that seventy million fake ballots cast for the incumbent had arrived from China.[51]

Another platform used to spread hoaxes was Instagram. For instance, an Acehnese man was arrested for running an Instagram account used to disseminate the hoax that Jokowi is a communist.[52]

Impact of Hoaxes on the 2019 Elections

Assessing the impact of attempts to use hoaxes for political gain in Indonesia's 2019 elections is challenging.

For one, the link between fake news consumption and electoral behaviour is inconclusive. To date, there is insufficient analysis that examines the relationship between the growing amount of information and the psychology of information processing.[53] According to researchers from think tanks such as the Indonesian Political Indicator (IPI) and the Center for Strategic and International Studies (CSIS), hoaxes in Indonesia had little effect on changing the minds of the strong supporters of either presidential candidate.[54] Instead, hoaxes confirm existing biases on their preferred election candidates and against those they do not support.[55] Despite some claims that most of the hoaxes targeted the incumbent,[56] the Jokowi-Ma'ruf pair still won the 2019 election decisively.

Also, despite the assessment by some experts that hoaxes could increase vote abstinence, especially among undecided voters,[57] voter turnout in Indonesia's 2019 election was at a historic high of more than 80 per cent.[58] This suggested that hoaxes could have less impact on voter turnout than other factors such as existing political identification.

Public trust in Indonesia's electoral institutions, however, has been affected. A 2017 survey by the ISEAS – Yusof Ishak Institute reported that Indonesians' trust in their electoral commission was at 79.3 per cent.[59] A January 2019 survey by the Saiful Mujani Research Center (SMRC), however, showed that while the majority (56 per cent) of respondents maintained trust in the professionalism of the KPU, at least 13 per cent did not believe the organization was neutral during the elections.[60] The number of those who doubted the neutrality of the KPU in organizing the elections rose to 27–28 per cent after the post-election riots took place.[61]

Hoaxes established a climate of distrust during the campaign period. Civil conversation regarding choices of election candidates had been challenging since Jokowi and Prabowo first contested against each other in the 2014 presidential elections. Anecdotal examples, from online acquaintances who deleted each other from their friends' lists to couples who divorced because of political differences, had existed back in 2014, and they continued to crop up in 2019. Even as the rhetorical contest has ended post-election and with there likely being no serious opposition in the new parliament, political division from Indonesia's recent elections could be long-standing and have an effect on future elections and other political events.[62]

Conclusion

Following the official announcement of the re-election of President Joko Widodo on 21 May 2019, two nights of rioting took place in the Indonesian capital of Jakarta. The riots were significant because they followed months of campaigning riddled with hoaxes against election candidates and institutions. Furthermore, hoaxes also accompanied the riots: allegations that some of the anti-riot police were from China and purported evidence that they had conversed in the Chinese language flooded various social media platforms during the riots. Other post-election conspiracies such as rumours that many election workers had been killed to cover up for helping a particular candidate also circulated online. The climate of distrust that had developed now served as the backdrop to the worst national election-related violence to take place in Indonesia since 1999.

To manage the riots, besides tactical security measures on the ground, the authorities implemented an unprecedented three-day curb on social media. The Indonesian Ministry of Communication and Information Technology announced that some features, particularly sending and receiving photos and videos, had been restricted on six social media platforms to prevent the spread of hoaxes.[63] Some social media accounts and websites were also shut down in a bid to calm the situation.[64]

Given the centrality of hoaxes in the election discourse, the role of social media as a medium of dissemination will continue to be probed, not only in Indonesia but also regionally. Some positive steps, such as identifying and disrupting "coordinated, inauthentic behaviour" and limiting the forwarding function, had been taken by the global tech giants in Indonesia's 2019 elections. But more must be done by the social media companies to identify and remove false accounts used for disinformation in future elections and during other incidents such as local conflicts.

Calls for greater regulation, especially in the form of legislation, have been made in neighbouring countries like Singapore, Malaysia, the Philippines and Vietnam. Given the challenges that hoaxes pose during and after elections, calls for digital regulation in Indonesia may surface at some point as Jokowi settles into his second term.

Beyond social media, the prominence of hoaxes in Indonesia's domestic politics has highlighted the danger of a political culture that thrives on rumours, conspiracies and falsehoods. Going forward, more needs to be done to prevent hoaxes from being a regular feature of the campaign cycle that sees a "race to the bottom" competition between domestic politicians and interest groups.

The answer lies neither in the regulation of digital architecture nor in the cultivation of digital literacy alone. Instead, a combination of different measures from diverse stakeholders across society may offer a more practical solution. On one hand, efforts must be made to foster better public trust in legitimate efforts to combat hoaxes. As subsequent events showed, some believed that the government was using buzzers to promote its agenda and suppress dissenting speech. More effective and transparent public dialogue could be conducted to engage citizens. In general, the Indonesian public has already accepted that hoaxes are detrimental to democracy and the country as a whole. Despite criticism of the Electronic Transactions Law (UU ITE),[65] many are in fact highly supportive of law enforcement efforts to tackle hoaxes and the peddlers of fake news. The implementation of legitimate measures to tackle hoaxes is something that could be better communicated for public buy-in in future public engagement against hoaxes.

On the other hand, grass-roots-led initiatives against hoaxes remain important for roles the authorities cannot fill in Indonesia. Establishing trustworthy fact-checkers, educating the public in digital literacy, and the overall establishment of pro-social norms such as responsible information sharing are all indispensable in fighting hoaxes. Successful endeavours must be encouraged and scaled up, and ways need to be found to apply them to other events with potentially far-reaching consequences, especially in parts of Indonesia with a history of separatist tendencies and ethnic tensions.

In short, efforts to combat hoaxes in Indonesia need to incorporate a whole-of-society approach that leverages the strengths of all segments across society.

Notes

1. "Digital 2019: Indonesia", *We are Social*, https://datareportal.com/reports/digital-2019-indonesia (accessed 26 July 2019).
2. Ibid. See also Fernando Duarte, "Berapa banyak waktu yang dihabiskan rakyat Indonesia di media sosial?" [How much time do Indonesians spend on social media?], BBC Indonesia, 9 September 2019, https://www.bbc.com/indonesia/majalah-49630216.
3. "Digital 2019: Indonesia".
4. Ibid.

5. Ibid.
6. See Andreas Ufen, "Electoral Campaigning in Indonesia: The Professionalization and Commercialization after 1998", *Journal of Current Southeast Asian Affairs* 29, no. 4 (2010): 11–37.
7. Nyarwi Ahmad and Ioan Lucian Popa, "The Social Media Usage and the Transformation of Political Marketing and Campaigning of Emerging Democracy in Indonesia", in *Social Media in Politics*, edited by Bogdan Pătrut and Monica Pătrut (Cham: Springer, 2014), pp. 97–125.
8. #ReplaceTitleSongWithJOKOWI was a prominent Twitter hashtag used in the election to support Jokowi. Many music videos in support of candidates were also shared on YouTube during this period. For example, parodies of popular songs highlighting Jokowi and Ahok's use of checked shirts were the substance of music videos created by the CAMEO Project, a Jakarta-based group of YouTube entertainers that began their career that same year.
9. Most opinion polls had predicted that the pair of Fauzi Bowo (Foke) and Nachrowi Ramli (Nara) would win the election, only to be proven wrong by the victory of Joko Widodo (Jokowi) and Basuki Tjahaja Purnama (Ahok). The event raised doubts among some quarters about the methodology employed by traditional opinion polls. Provetic, a Jakarta-based data consultancy, noted that from April to July 2012 during the gubernatorial election, the percentage of people talking about the different candidates on social media correlated very closely with the actual results. Another social media consultancy company, Politicawave, predicted a Jokowi-Ahok victory with 40.6 per cent of the votes in round one and 53.9 per cent in the second round. These results corroborated very closely with the actual election results, raising optimism about the predictive potential of social media in Indonesian elections.
10. Mr Jaim, "Pilkada DKI: Jokowi-Ahok Dihajar 'Black Campaign' Berbau SARA" [The Jakarta Gubernatorial Elections: Jokowi-Ahok attacked by sectarianist "black campaigns"], Ciricara.com, 16 July 2012, http://ciricara.com/2012/07/16/pilkada-dki-jokowi-ahok-dihajar-black-campaign-berbau-sara/.
11. "Ini Tiga 'Black Campaign' yang Serang Jokowi" [Three "black campaigns" against Jokowi], Republika.com, 1 July 2014, https://www.republika.co.id/berita/pemilu/hot-politic/14/07/01/n80t0d-ini-tiga-black-campaign-yang-serang-jokowi.
12. Ibid.
13. Desi Purnamasari, "Pada 2014, Tren Elektabilitas Jokowi Turun Meski Menang pada Hari-H" [In 2014, Jokowi's electability fell even though he won], *Tirto.id*, 15 January 2019, https://tirto.id/desJ.
14. Christine Franciska, "Tentang Ahok, Anies, dan Pilkada Jakarta yang dibumbui 'seribu hoax'" [Regarding Ahok, Anies and the Jakarta Gubernatorial Election that was filled with hoaxes], BBC Indonesia, 18 April 2017, https://www.bbc.com/indonesia/trensosial-39618703.

15. Merlyna Lim, "Freedom to Hate: Social Media, Algorithmic Enclaves, and the Rise of Tribal Nationalism in Indonesia", *Critical Asian Studies* 49, no. 3 (2017): 411–27.
16. Wahyudi Soeriaatmadja, "Indonesian Police Probe Alleged Fake News Factory's Protest Links", *Straits Times*, 26 August 2017, http://www.straitstimes.com/asia/se-asia/indonesian-police-probe-alleged-fake-news-factorys-protest-links.
17. Wishnugroho Akbar and Lalu Rahadian, "The Ahok Effect, Warga Agresif Buru 'Penista Agama'" [The Ahok effect, citizens aggressively hunt down blasphemers], BBC Indonesia, 27 May 2017, http://www.cnnindonesia.com/nasional/20170527151727-20-217678/the-ahok-effect-warga-agresif-buru-penista-agama.
18. Damar Juniarto, "The Muslim Cyber Army: What Is It and What Does It Want?", *Indonesia at Melbourne*, 20 March 2018, https://indonesiaatmelbourne.unimelb.edu.au/the-muslim-cyber-army-what-is-it-and-what-does-it-want/; Kate Lamb, "Muslim Cyber Army: A 'Fake News' Operation Designed to Derail Indonesia's Leader", *The Guardian*, 13 March 2018, https://www.theguardian.com/world/2018/mar/13/muslim-cyber-army-a-fake-news-operation-designed-to-bring-down-indonesias-leader.
19. Damar Juniarto, "The Muslim Cyber Army".
20. Ben Bland, "The Mind-Boggling Challenge of Indonesia's Election Logistics", *Lowy Interpreter*, 3 April 2019, https://www.lowyinstitute.org/the-interpreter/mind-boggling-challenge-indonesian-election-logistics.
21. "'Nyoblos Yuk': Instagram Taps @komikazer to Launch First Election Stickers", *Jakarta Post*, 15 April 2019, https://www.thejakartapost.com/life/2019/04/15/nyoblos-yuk-instagram-taps-komikazer-to-launch-first-electionstickers.html.
22. "Digital 2019: Indonesia".
23. Budi Irawanto, "Young and Faithless: Wooing Millennials in Indonesia's 2019 Presidential Election", *ISEAS Perspective*, no. 2019/1, 4 January 2019.
24. "Istilah 'emak-emak' dan 'ibu bangsa': Cara Jokowi dan Prabowo memikat pemilih perempuan" [The terms 'emak-emak' and 'ibu bangsa': How Jokowi and Prabowo wooed female voters], BBC Indonesia, 19 September 2018, https://www.bbc.com/indonesia/trensosial-45563444.
25. "Anti-Ahok to Anti-Jokowi: Islamist Influence on Indonesia's 2019 Election Campaign", *IPAC Report No. 55*, 15 March 2019.
26. Wahyudi Soeriaatmadja, "Jokowi Hits Out at 'Russian Propaganda' in Polls Run-up", *Straits Times*, 7 February 2019, https://www.straitstimes.com/asia/se-asia/jokowi-hits-out-at-russian-propaganda-in-polls-run-up.
27. Gilang Ramadhan, "Kronologi Kasus Hoaks Ratna Sarumpaet: Bikin Prabowo Minta Maaf" [The chronology of the Ratna Sarumpaet Hoax case: Causing Prabowo to apologise], *Tirto.id*, 28 February 2019, https://tirto.id/dhXd.
28. Russian Embassy, IDN (@RusEmbJakarta), "Kami menggarishawahi bahwa posisi prinsipil Rusia adalah tidak campur tangan pada urusan dalam negeri dan proses-

proses elektoral di negara-negara asing, termasuk Indonesia yang merupakan sahabat dekat dan mitra penting kami" [We state that the principal position of Russia is not to interfere in the domestic politics and electoral processes in foreign countries, including Indonesia which is our close friend and important partner], Twitter post, 4 February 2019, https://twitter.com/RusEmbJakarta/status/1092275344151728129.

29. "Jokowi Clarifies the Meaning of His 'Russian Propaganda' Comment", *Tempo*, 6 February 2019, https://en.tempo.co/read/1172584/jokowi-clarifies-the-meaning-of-his-russian-propaganda-comment.
30. Interview with Mohamad Rinaldi Camil, Research Associate at the Centre for Innovation Policy and Governance (CIPG), 26 April 2019.
31. Lugina Setyawati and Daisy Indira Yasmine, "Digital Literacy and Social Network: Its Impact on Political Activism and Participation", paper presented at the 11th International Convention of Asian Scholars, Leiden, The Netherlands, 15–19 July 2019.
32. Interview with Septiaji Eko Nugroho, Founder and Chairman of Masyarakat Anti-Fitnah Indonesia (Mafindo), 27 April 2019.
33. Samantha Bradshaw and Philip N. Howard, "Troops, Trolls and Troublemakers: A Global Inventory of Organized Social Media Manipulation", *The Computational Propaganda Project*, 2017, http://comprop.oii.ox.ac.uk/research/troops-trolls-and-trouble-makersa-global-inventory-of-organized-social-media-manipulation/.
34. "The Hashtag Spectre", *Tempo*, 4 December 2018, https://magz.tempo.co/read/35032/the-hashtag-spectre.
35. "Pendukung Prabowo di Medsos Diduga 'Cyber Troops'" [Social media supporters of Prabowo are believed to be "Cyber Troops"], CNN Indonesia, 17 December 2018, https://www.cnnindonesia.com/nasional/20181216203415-32-354098/pendukung-prabowo-di-medsos-diduga-cyber-troops.
36. "Di Balik Fenomena Buzzer: Memahami Lanskap Industri dan Pengaruh Buzzer di Indonesia" [Behind the buzzer phenomenon: Understanding the industrial landscape and influence of buzzers in Indonesia], Centre for Innovation Policy and Governance, 2017.
37. Muninggar Sri Saraswati, "Social Media and the Political Campaign Industry in Indonesia", *Jurnal Komunikasi ISKI* 3, no. 1 (2018): 51–65.
38. Adi Renaldi, "'I'm Like a Lawyer Defending My Political Clients': A Profile of a Social Media Puppet Master", *Vice News*, 22 December 2018, https://www.vice.com/en_asia/article/nepmyq/indonesia-meet-social-media-puppet-master-presidential-election-political-fake-news-hoax-black-campaign; Fanny Potkin and Agustinus Beo Da Costa, "In Indonesia, Facebook and Twitter are 'Buzzer' Battlegrounds as Elections Loom", Reuters, 13 March 2019, https://www.reuters.com/article/us-indonesia-election-socialmedia-insigh/in-indonesia-facebook-and-twitter-are-buzzer-battlegrounds-as-elections-loom-idUSKBN1QU0AS.

39. Adi Renaldi, "'This Is Pure Business. It Has Nothing to Do With Personal Politics': Inside the Hoax Industry", *Vice News*, 21 December 2018, https://www.vice.com/en_asia/article/pa58g7/inside-indonesia-hoax-black-campaign-industry-presidential-elections-jokowi-prabowo.
40. Ibid.
41. Lisa-Maria Neudert, "Future Elections May Be Swayed by Intelligent, Weaponized Chatbots", *MIT Technology Review*, 22 August 2018, https://www.technologyreview.com/s/611832/future-elections-may-be-swayed-by-intelligent-weaponized-chatbots/.
42. "Analisis Drone Emprit: Membedah Robot dalam #SkandalSandiagaUno" [Drone Emprit analysis: Dissecting the role of bots in #SkandalSandiagaUno)", *Drone Emprit*, 28 September 2018, https://pers.droneemprit.id/analisis-drone-emprit-membedah-robot-dalam-skandalsandiagauno/.
43. Mawa Kresna, "Jejaring Akun Robot Pendukung Jokowi Tersangkut Situs Skandal Sandi" [Pro-Jokowi bot network involved in the Sandi Scandal website], *Tirto.id*, 1 October 2018, https://tirto.id/jejaring-akun-robot-pendukung-jokowi-tersangkut-situs-skandal-sandi-c3XZ.
44. Marguerite Afra Sapiie and Kharishar Kahfi, "Facebook, Twitter Try to Safeguard Indonesian Elections", *Jakarta Post*, 1 February 2019, https://www.thejakartapost.com/news/2019/02/01/facebook-twitter-try-to-safeguard-indonesian-elections.html.
45. A. Santoso, "Polri Profiling Akun Opposite6890 yang Sebar Tuduhan Polisi Buzzer Jokowi" [The Police profiles Opposite6890 account that claims that the police are Jokowi's buzzers], *Detik.com*, 10 March 2019, https://news.detik.com/berita/4461040/polri-profiling-akun-opposite6890-yang-sebar-tuduhan-polisi-buzzer-jokowi.
46. "Siaran pers 'Meningkatnya Dominasi Hoaks Politik Jelang Pemilu'" [Press release: Rise in hoax in the lead-up to the elections], Mafindo website, accessed 29 May 2019, https://www.mafindo.or.id/2019/03/16/siaran-pers-meningkatnya-dominasi-hoaks-politik-jelang-pemilu/.
47. "KPU juga jadi korban hoaks" [The Elections Commission has also become a victim of hoax], *Metro TV News*, 9 March 2019, http://www.metrotvnews.com/metro-highlight/8Ky4Ar2k-kpu-juga-jadi-korban-hoaks.
48. Nathaniel Gleicher, "Taking Down Coordinated Inauthentic Behaviour in Indonesia", *Facebook Newsroom*, 11 April 2019, https://newsroom.fb.com/news/2019/01/taking-down-coordinated-inauthentic-behavior-in-indonesia/.
49. Nika Aleksejeva, Kanishk Karan, and Ben Nimmo, "#ElectionWatch: Facebook Takes Down Network Supporting Indonesian Presidential Candidate Prabowo Subianto", *Medium*, 12 April 2019, https://medium.com/dfrlab/electionwatch-facebook-takes-down-network-supporting-indonesian-presidential-candidate-prabowo-18b8792e9529.
50. Audrey Santoso, "Penyebar Hoax 'Bareskrim Jadi Pusat Kendali Situng KPU' Ditangkap" [Disseminator of 'Cybercrime division is the centre of election vote

counting' has been arrested], *Detik.com*, 10 May 2019, https://news.detik.com/berita/4543802/penyebar-hoax-bareskrim-jadi-pusat-kendali-situng-kpu-ditangkap.

51. "Tackling a New Disinformation Threat on WhatsApp in Indonesia", ICFJ.org, 4 February 2019, https://www.icfj.org/news/tackling-new-disinformation-threat-whatsapp-indonesia.

52. Indra Subagja, "Polisi Tangkap Admin IG Suara Rakyat 23, Pernah Posting Jokowi PKI" [The police arrested the administrator of the Instagram account Suara Rakyat 23 which once claimed that Jokowi is a communist], MSN.com, 23 November 2018, https://www.msn.com/id-id/berita/nasional/polisi-tangkap-admin-ig-suara-rakyat-23-pernah-posting-jokowi-pki/ar-BBQ0yjj.

53. Norman Vasu, Benjamin Ang, Terri-Anne Teo, Shashi Jayakumar, Muhammad Faizal, and Juhi Ahuja, "Fake News: National Security in the Post-Truth Era", *RSIS Policy Report*, January 2018, https://www.rsis.edu.sg/wp-content/uploads/2018/01/PR180313_Fake-News_WEB.pdf.

54. "Hoaxes Not Affecting Electability, Analysts Say", *Tempo*, 8 March 2019, https://en.tempo.co/read/1183107/hoaxes-not-affecting-electability-analysts-say.

55. Ibid.

56. "Digitroops: Hoaks di Medsos terkait Jokowi Jauh Lebih Banyak" [Digitroops: Jokowi-related hoax dominates on social media], *Kompas*, 12 April 2019, https://nasional.kompas.com/read/2019/04/12/06505861/digitroops-hoaks-di-medsos-terkait-jokowi-jauh-lebih-banyak?page=all; Ihsanuddin, "Kominfo: Presiden Jokowi Paling Banyak Diserang Hoaks", Suara.com, 15 January 2019, https://www.suara.com/news/2019/01/15/171540/kominfo-presiden-jokowi-paling-banyak-diserang-hoaks; "Politicawave: Ada 10 Isu Hoaks di Media Sosial Serang Jokowi" [PoliticaWave: 10 Hoaxes attacking Jokowi on social media], *Tempo*, 7 February 2019, https://nasional.tempo.co/read/1173282/politicawave-ada-10-isu-hoaks-di-media-sosial-serang-jokowi.

57. Arkhelaus Wisnu, "CSIS Expert: Rampant Hoax Spread Can Increase Nonvoters", *Tempo*, 6 March 2019, https://en.tempo.co/read/1182349/csis-expert-rampant-hoax-spread-can-increase-nonvoters.

58. "Indonesia Sees Record Turnout in Historic Election, Braces for Fallout", *Jakarta Globe*, 17 April 2019, https://jakartaglobe.id/context/indonesia-sees-record-turnout-in-historic-election-braces-for-fallout.

59. Diego Fossati, Hui Yew-Foong, and Siwage Dharma Negara, *The Indonesia National Survey Project: Economy, Society and Politics*, Trends in Southeast Asia, no. 10/2017 (ISEAS – Yusof Ishak Institute), p. 31.

60. Ryan Dwiky Anggriawan, "SMRC Survey: Some Believe KPU Not Neutral in Election", *Tempo*, 11 March 2019, https://en.tempo.co/read/1183904/smrc-survey-some-believe-kpu-not-neutral-in-election?https://en.tempo.co/index&campaign=https://en.tempo.co/index_Click_8.

61. "Mayoritas Rakyat Percaya Pemilu 2019 Berlangsung Jurdil" [Most citizens believed

that the 2019 election was conducted in an honest, transparent manner], Saiful Mujani Research and Consulting, 16 June 2019, https://saifulmujani.com/mayoritas-rakyat-percaya-pemilu-2019-berlangsung-jurdil/.
62. Max Lane, "President Joko Widodo's New Cabinet: Some Implications for Indonesian Politics", *ISEAS Perspective*, no. 2019/99, 27 November 2019; Liam Gammon, "Understanding Indonesia's 2019 Election Riots", seminar held at ISEAS – Yusof Ishak Institute, 10 June 2019.
63. "Kominfo Sebut 6 Medsos yang Terkena Pembatasan", CNN Indonesia, 23 May 2019, https://www.cnnindonesia.com/teknologi/20190523204246-185-397935/kominfo-sebut-6-medsos-yang-terkena-pembatasan.
64. Rudiantara (@rudiantara_id), "4. Sebelum dan selama pembatasan akses fitur image dan video di media sosial, Kominfo jg telah menutup ribuan sumber baik URL (alamat situs) dan/atau akun. Berikut daftarnya: FB: 551, IG: 640, Twitter: 848, Youtube: 143, Website: 1, Linked In: 1, Total: 2184" [Before and during the restriction of image and video features on social media, the Ministry of Communication and Information Technology had also shut down thousands of sites such as URLs and/or accounts. This is the list: Facebook: 551, Instragram: 640, Twitter: 848, YouTube: 143, website: 1, LinkedIn: 1, Total: 2184], Twitter post, 27 May 2019, https://twitter.com/rudiantara_id/status/1132898409399169024.
65. Usman Hamid, "Indonesia's Information Law Has Threatened Free Speech for More Than a Decade. This Must Stop", *The Conversation*, 25 November 2019, https://theconversation.com/indonesias-information-law-has-threatened-free-speech-for-more-than-a-decade-this-must-stop-127446.

Laos

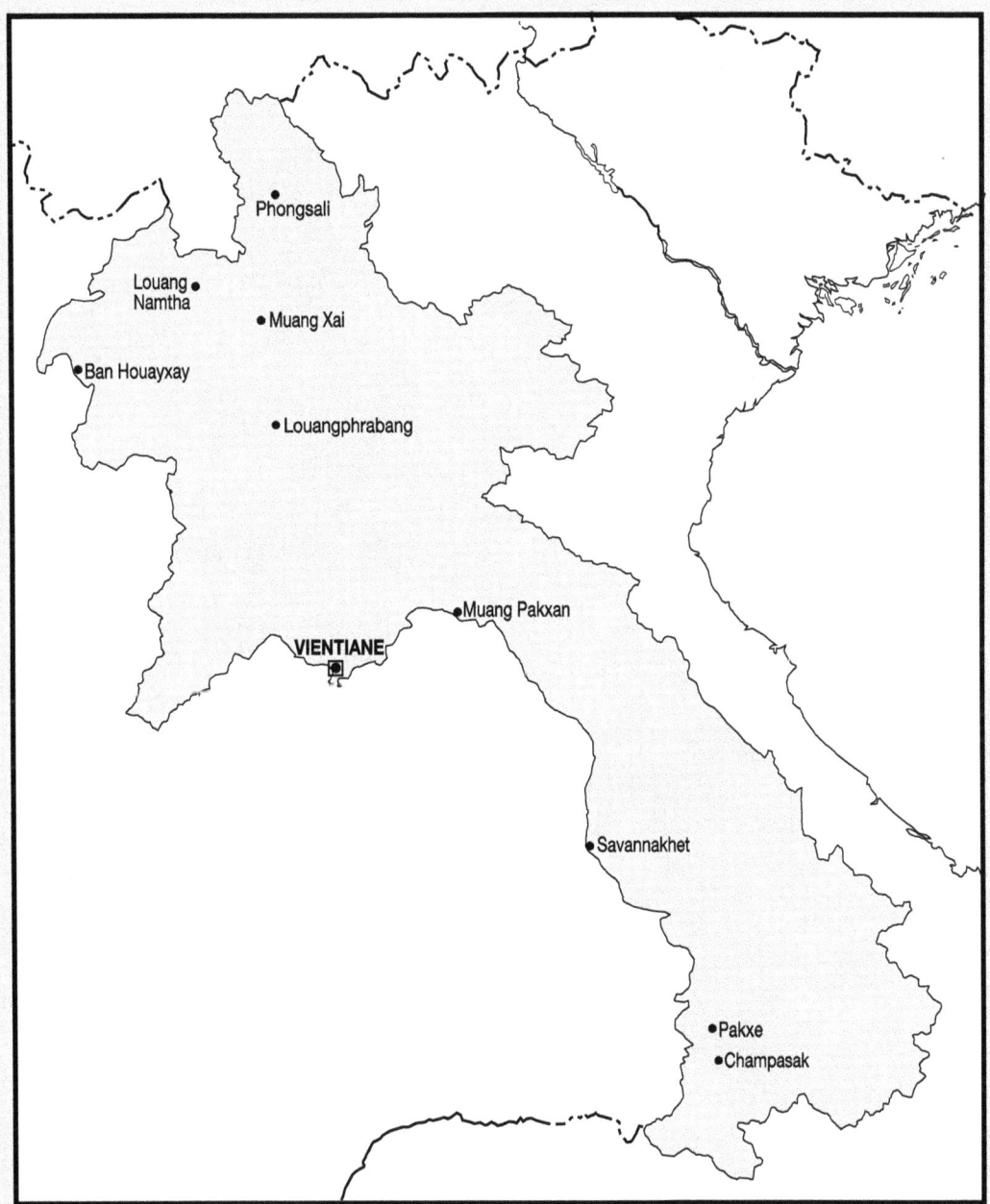

LAOS IN 2019:
Moving Heaven and Earth on the Mekong

Geoffrey C. Gunn

While the year saw some venting of concern at official corruption in the National Assembly, remarkable in itself, it is rent-seeking activities that define the Lao People's Democratic Republic (Lao PDR) party-state. A market economy operating under a Leninist system, events in 2019 did not detract from the general trajectory of a state hell-bent on prioritizing major projects such as hydro-electricity generating dams and the Chinese-built railroad, moving heaven and earth on the Mekong River, whatever the social and ecological consequences locally or downstream. But the practice of issuing licences and concessions for casinos and/or agribusiness ventures also creates market distortions. Drought, disease and human dislocation stemming from mega projects or disasters (as with the 2018 dam collapse in Attapeu Province), land alienation and compensation issues all came to national and/or international attention during the year. Various serious human rights cases, including disappearances, suggest the longevity of the Lao PDR authoritarian developmental model, one that brooks no domestic challenge or even external scrutiny.

Governance

Typically, draft laws and amendments to laws are discussed at monthly sessions of the nation's National Assembly, which is invariably chaired by the prime minister. Notably, at the 7th Ordinary Session of the Assembly's 8th legislature held in Vientiane on 23–24 July in the presence of National Assembly president Mrs Pany Yathortou, Lao PDR president Bounnhang Vorachit, and other party

---

GEOFFREY C. GUNN is Emeritus Professor, Nagasaki University, Japan and Adjunct Professor, Center for Macau Studies, University of Macau, China.

and government leaders, Prime Minister Thongloun Sisoulith called for the sectors responsible to shoulder more responsibility in finding solutions to six pressing issues that were seen as affecting socio-economic development. The first major issue was an outbreak of dengue fever, which had claimed 37 lives and saw at least 16,690 people falling sick. The second topic was an epidemic of African swine fever. Third on the list was the infestation of sweetcorn crops by a plague of caterpillars in Xayaboury Province, which had destroyed 30 per cent of 35,000 hectares of the crop. The fourth issue concerned persistent drought, which resulted in low river levels and affected rice and other crops. The fifth matter of concern was the fluctuating exchange rate, the falling value of the national currency, the kip, and the depletion of foreign-exchange reserves, seen as driving up commodity import prices and hindering economic growth. The sixth issue related to posts on social media by members of the public commenting negatively on state administration and management. Other issues debated included the development and management of special and specific economic zones, a draft decree on the policy for economic development in Xaysomboun Province, and a draft decree relating to climate change.[1]

At the 8th Ordinary Session of the National Assembly running from 7 November until 6 December, Assembly president Pany Yathotou highlighted the progress made in the 8th five-year National Socio-economic Development Plan for 2016–20, and the challenges posed by the global economy, the trade war, natural disasters and climate change. Assembly members approved the appointment of Deputy Prime Minister Sonexay Siphandone to a second post as minister of planning and investment, following the retirement of Souphanh Keomixay. Also approved was the appointment of Kikeo Khaykhamphithoune as incoming minister of information, culture and tourism following the retirement of Bosengkham Vongdara. In his address, Prime Minister Thongloun maintained that the key focus of the government the following year would be to maintain political stability, security and social order (a set of priorities not inconsistent with a party-state under siege, even if the threat is only from its own people). On his part, Sonexay delivered a report on the implementation of the socio-economic development plan, the state budget and fiscal plan, while also alluding to "macroeconomic difficulties" for the year ahead and to the impact of recent floods. According to schedule, Assembly members then prepared to debate a draft of a Law on Cinema and the draft Law on Gender Equality. Draft amendments to six laws already promulgated were scheduled to be debated. These comprised the Laws on Bankruptcy, Hygiene, Disease Prevention, Health Promotion, Laws on Insurance and Securities, a Law on Sports and Gymnastics, and a Law on Investment Promotion.[2]

Economy

Citing a report presented at the 7th Ordinary Session of the National Assembly's 8th legislature on 5 June, Prime Minister Thongloun pointed out difficulties and shortcomings facing the economy. In particular he noted that although the national economy grew at a rapid rate of 6.5 per cent over the past four months, it was slower than the rate recorded in recent years, blaming a lower contribution of energy, mining and agriculture owing to natural disasters. Revenue collection in the first four months reached 6.32 trillion kip, representing 24 per cent of the target set for fiscal year 2019, with a revenue deficit of 347 billion kip. Though the service sector enjoyed a growth in the first four months, the tourism sector experienced a slight decrease of 0.5 per cent compared to the same period in the previous year.[3] Moreover, because of drought and severely reduced water levels in the Mekong River region, along with the delay of seasonal monsoon rains, Lao farmers had planted rice on less than half the country's cultivable land in 2019, or just 40 per cent of the country's 850,000 cultivable hectares.[4] Not only was the dry season longer than usual but also the area of wet season rice affected by natural disasters was almost 172,000 hectares. This led to rising prices for rice and to shortages.[5]

According to a World Bank *Lao Economic Monitor* released on 12 August, the economic growth of Laos was expected to rebound to 6.5 per cent in 2019, higher than the figure of 6.3 per cent recorded in 2018. The report noted that economic growth was supported by a resilient service sector led by wholesale and retail growth associated with robust construction driven by strong investment inflows to large construction projects, including the Laos–China railway and an associated service sector. It commented that the Lao PDR government remained committed to fiscal consolidation to contain public debt in the medium term by tightening public spending and improving revenue administration. If carried through, this could result in a decline in the fiscal deficit from 4.4 per cent of GDP in 2018 to 4.3 per cent in 2019. The report also noted that the government had suspended public projects with low economic returns and that it had "instituted a moratorium on all new hydropower projects"[6] (although, as mentioned below, this decision was reversed within the year).

The World Bank country manager for Laos, Nicola Pontara, made it known that although economic growth had rebounded after declining in 2018, partly as a result of floods, the country was still at high risk of debt distress unless measures were undertaken to deal with the situation, such as strengthening revenue collection and improving the business environment to support private sector development, including the growth of small-and medium-sized enterprises. He advised that these measures could contribute to maintaining a stable macroeconomic environment, in promoting job creation and in reducing poverty and inequality. As Somneuk Davading, Lao senior economist at the World Bank Lao Office elaborated, its economic growth placed the nation among the top five fastest growing economies in the region. Nevertheless, he advised that the government should continue its reform measures and to further improve the investment climate in order to attract more capital. The depreciation of the kip against the US dollar and Thai baht was another concern for Laos impacting on debt serviceability.[7]

As revealed in July 2019 by the minister of finance Somdy Duangdy, the government will sell its stake in loss-making state enterprises and turn them into joint ventures, or will even sell the whole company if necessary, with Lao Airlines and Électricité du Laos among them. Reportedly, some National Assembly members had previously questioned the executive structure of state enterprises, noting that key personnel remained in place despite their poor performance resulting in consistent losses. According to the State-Owned Enterprise Development and Insurance Department under the Ministry of Finance, the reform of state enterprises will focus on three main areas—business, finance and personnel.[8] While ostensibly a good move, not mentioned here is the practice of issuing licences, some dubiously, for the construction of casinos in so-called special economic zones, of which there are fourteen, and with local residents sidelined. A case in point is the one awarded to Chinese businessman and former wildlife trader Zhao Wei, whose casino was built by some forty thousand illegal Myanmar migrant workers and which can be seen across the Mekong River from Chiang Saen, Chiang Rai Province, Thailand.[9] Another case, involving land seized by the government with inadequate compensation, is the Savan-Seno special economic zone located on the "East-West Economic Corridor" notionally linking south-central Laos to Danang in Vietnam, which also hosts a casino resort run by a company called Macau Legend Development.[10]

Journalist David Hutt has drawn attention to the government's reliance on energy and infrastructure at the expense of other parts of the economy. He is of the opinion that the government has put all its eggs in one basket. Notably, Laos lacks a real export sector in comparison to its neighbours. Whereas medium-sized enterprises make up two-fifths of GDP in Thailand, they comprise just a fifth of GDP in Laos. Tourism is growing but it has its limits as well. The risk of Laos falling into a "debt trap" laid by China has been well canvassed but, as Hutt points out, "it is the Lao government that has saddled the country with debt through its own bet on megaprojects that could turn into white elephants".[11]

Corruption

Since coming to power in 2016, Prime Minister Thongloun gave the impression that he would break with the past and move to end official corruption.[12] Nevertheless, weak laws and lack of enforcement by authorities have clearly stymied Thongloun's drive, revealing the depth of the problem. Remarkably, given the top-down character of the party-state, on 14 June members of the National Assembly openly criticized corruption in the country's judiciary and political system. Among those speaking out were an assemblyman from Xaysomboun Province, one from Champassak Province, and another from Houapanh, who was quoted as saying "Punishments for government workers who break the law are also ineffective. In fact, they are not strict at all."[13] According to Radio Free Asia, the government disciplined more than two hundred officials involved in taking bribes or embezzling state funds during this period, albeit with only a few of them being held criminally accountable for their actions.[14] Hutt is undoubtedly correct in asserting that "The nature of corruption is tied to the operation of the one-party political system in Laos. Following from that, it is unlikely to be solvable in its entirety unless we see some sort of political change accompanying it as well." To be sure, he estimates, nothing is likely to happen soon without less control by the party over the courts and media, a greater role for civil society, and more control over the economy by the private sector than by the state sector. Neither, he points out, do we actually hear from the United Nations, the World Bank or the International Monetary Fund how Laos is to achieve rule of law or solve its corruption problem.[15]

Moving Heaven and Earth on the Mekong—
The China-built Railroad and other Projects

The most ambitious project under way in Laos and the one that challenges basic economics is the China–Laos railroad. Part of China's Belt and Road Initiative, its planned 250-plus miles of track are meant to connect China's southern Yunnan Province with the capital of Laos, Vientiane. The project includes the 1,458.9-metre Luang Prabang cross-Mekong bridge built by China Railway No. 8 Engineering Group, with the first bridge span completed in May. As the Lao PDR deputy prime minister Sonexay Siphandone announced in September, nearly 80 per cent of the construction of the railway has been completed, and it is expected to be fully operational in 2021. According to Sonexay, from 1988 until the end of June this year, China had invested a total of US$12.5 billion in 782 projects in Laos, mostly to do with infrastructure, making it the biggest investor in the country.[16]

While touted as a win-win infrastructure project by Lao PDR officials, not all observers agree. According to Brian Eyler, Southeast Asia programme director at the Stimson Center in Washington, DC, the rail link is not necessarily intended to link China to the rest of the world but rather serves "to create channels to bring natural resources and commercial inputs back to China so that China's economy can keep growing". Few local jobs have been generated. Neither had there been much consultation with locals. Residents have told journalists that thousands were ordered off their land to make way for the railway and they are not being compensated as promised. Neither is the promise of more tourists coming to Luang Prabang necessarily appealing, especially as tourist arrivals, predominately Chinese, stay in Chinese-owned hotels. Conservationists also add their concerns as to the habitat fragmentation effect of big infrastructure projects impacting the natural world.[17] According to freelance writer Skylar Lindsay, with the government requisitioning 3,832 hectares of land for the project, those local residents affected were left with little means of supporting themselves. Out of 4,411 families negatively affected by the project, only about 230 of them have been compensated.[18] The United Nations special rapporteur on extreme poverty and human rights, Philip Alston, in summing up following his visit to Laos in March 2019, gave what might be seen as a veiled indictment of the regime: "The Government's single-minded focus on large infrastructure projects (such as dams and railways), land acquisition, resource extraction, and foreign investment has created all too few jobs for Lao people, generated very large debt repayment obligations, and disproportionately benefited wealthy elites. Those living in poverty, ethnic minorities, and people in rural areas have seen very few of the benefits of the economic boom."[19]

Borrowing and Debt

As echoed by Lindsay, debt continues to siphon economic gains away from Laos. Built by the Laos China Railway Company—a joint venture in which China owns a 70 per cent stake and Laos owns 30 per cent—the total project cost is US$6 billion, over a third of the country's US$17 billion GDP. Laos has agreed to pay US$720 million within the next five years, but to fulfil that promise it will borrow US$470 million from the Export Import Bank of China at a rate of interest of 2.3 per cent. Laos has yet to figure out how it will fund its remaining US$1.1 billion share of the project. The Lao government may be planning to raise the capital through land concessions. In 2018 the Lao PDR's public debt was 65 per cent of its GDP, and the government is already struggling to generate revenue: taxes account for only 12 per cent of GDP, and the country's copper and silver mines may be nearing exhaustion.[20]

For his part, Prime Minister Thongloun claims that Laos borrows from China and other countries only for projects that are both necessary and economically viable. Speaking to *Nikkei Asian Review* in a rare press interview in Tokyo in May, he pushed back against international warnings about his government's debt to Asia's emerging superpower. "If we don't borrow", he declared, "Laos, as a least-developed country, won't develop further." In regard to the railroad, he asserted that the government has "its own measures to manage the debt and ensure balance in the public debt sector". Moreover, he insisted, Laos sticks to "high-efficiency projects which are long-term, with low interest rates." Defensively, he continued, "The observers who have concern for Laos in terms of debt repayment ... may not have enough or sufficient information on how the government assesses those projects", adding that China's Belt and Road Initiative (BRI) was a valuable new mechanism for international cooperation. Through cooperation, Thongloun said, countries will be able to "overcome complex situations" and "handle the challenges" they now face.[21]

As journalist John Pennington has pointed out, the level of borrowing is indeed alarming, and China is both the Lao PDR's leading investor and provider of significant aid assistance. The country's gross debt is forecast to rise to more than 70 per cent of its GDP. The World Bank recommends that governments aim for less than 40 per cent; the International Monetary Fund (IMF) suggests 50 per cent. Furthermore, in 2017 the IMF raised its perception of the Lao PDR's debt distress from medium to high as a result of its borrowing from China. In 2018 the Center for Global Development, a non-profit organization based in both London and Washington, ranked Laos as one of the eight most vulnerable countries participating in the BRI. And in addition to the China-built railroad, Laos has reportedly borrowed US$600 million for a hydropower project. There are thus concerns about just how much money is flowing out of the country to Beijing. The mounting debt to China leaves Vientiane heavily reliant on Beijing and raises the question—one which Prime Minister Thongloun has studiously avoided—of what happens if Laos falls short on its payments?[22]

The Attapeu Dam Disaster

On 23 July 2018, Laos experienced the worst dam disaster in its history when, following heavy rains, an auxiliary dam at Xe Pian Xe Namnoy in Attapeu Province collapsed inundating twelve villages, killing at least forty people and leaving many more missing (a disaster that also saw the rare entry into Laos of international relief teams). Each survivor is entitled to a government dispensation of US$12 per month for food and other living expenses. Nevertheless, some victims had not received any material support or, if they did, it was long delayed. Speaking in June, Attapeu provincial governor Leth Xayaphone complained that the province was "having a problem with the funding. We are not able to payout [allowances] right now. But the provincial government is trying to get more funding from the [central] government and other sources."[23] In the words of Philip Alston, who visited the three temporary camps for survivors, "Regarding Attapeu, a senior official of the Ministry of Energy and Mines described the elaborate and very positive conditions which would govern resettlement and ensure enhanced livelihood opportunities. On the ground, I saw and heard nothing that remotely resembled that description." This experience, among others, led him to conclude, "Both in relation to the situation in Attapeu, but also more generally in the Government's overall approach, one thing stands out. It is the stark contrast between the theory and the reality."[24] According to a senior spokesperson of the National Investigation Committee formed by the Lao government to conduct an inquiry into the cause of the disaster, even if rainfall was quite heavy on the days leading to the tragedy, the reservoir was still below its maximum operating level and well below the crest level when the failure began. "Thus, the failure incident cannot be considered as 'force majeure'" or an unforeseeable act of god.[25] With compensation and insurance claims for the victims in the balance, the implication of the ruling for the South Korean builder of the hydropower project could be significant if it means that construction problems were the primary cause of the dam collapse.

New Mainstream Mekong Dam in Luang Prabang

In September the government of Laos officially informed the intergovernmental Mekong River Commission of its plan to build a new dam in Luang Prabang. This was despite warnings about the environmental effects of the project (and despite an earlier government assertion of a moratorium on further dam building). A state-owned Vietnamese company, PetroVietnam Power Corp, holds the largest share in the project.[26] Also involved is Chart Karnchang Thai, the Thai company behind the construction of the Xayaburi Dam further downstream. According to a Radio Free Asia report, if the dam goes ahead it would be the fifth Laos is planning on the mainstream of the Mekong and potentially the largest so far among nine slated for development.[27] With the Xayaburi Dam entering service in 2019, photographs reveal more sandbars than water in the Mekong, suggesting major ecological change upstream, as critics had long warned.

Human Rights

Various serious human rights cases received international attention in 2019, including the detention of a man who refused to cede ownership of inherited land and the arrest of a woman for online criticism of the government's handling of a flooding disaster in the south of the country. As Philip Alston noted, "A series of high-profile arrests and disappearances have contributed to a climate of fear that forecloses much-needed discussion."[28] One, albeit symbolic, case involves a Lao villager, Sy Phong, detained since 2011 over a land protest and who died in jail.[29] With the discovery in the Mekong River in 2018 of the concrete-stuffed bodies of two Thai activists who had disappeared from Laos still a recent memory, members of the exiled Thai protest band Faiyen also looked to their safety. Reuters, which has investigated this and other "missing" cases, claims that both Lao *and* Thai officials are in denial about the allegations.[30] In August, after five years of hiding in Laos, Faiyen arrived in France to perform its first street performance since escaping Thailand. Pro-democracy activists are not able to find sanctuary across the border either. This was demonstrated with the case of Od Sayavong, a prominent pro-democracy activist from Laos who went missing from his Bangkok home on 26 August and with no progress in the Thai police investigation of his disappearance.[31] On 12 November the Lao authorities arrested eight activists who are part of a loose network of an unregistered pro-democracy group called Lao National Unity, which reportedly planned to stage a protest in Vientiane calling for free speech and condemning land grabs and dam projects—which would have been an extremely rare case of demonstrating opposition to the government. Six of the eight have subsequently been released but the fate of the two others remains a matter of concern.[32]

On the positive side, according to Alston, the government has taken some steps to engage with international human rights mechanisms, such as by inviting Special Rapporteurs to the country after years of not receiving any such visits. Likewise, the National Assembly appears to have taken a more robust approach to its auditing role. Nevertheless, Alston found "a near-total lack of space for freedom of expression, strict limitations on media and civil society, and a history of reprisals, arrests, and disappearances [which] have shut down space for the exchange of ideas and solutions, and [which] prevent people from raising grievances and seeking accountability". Indeed, he claims to have experienced this restrictive approach first-hand, "when it strongly resisted [his] requests to move freely within the country so [he] could visit Attapeu".[33]

International Relations

There is a strong sense that since its admittance to ASEAN in 1997 the Lao PDR has ritually played off its membership to its advantage by gaining regional legitimacy on the one hand yet being shielded against interference in its internal affairs on the other. Nowhere else is this better demonstrated than in its relationship with close neighbour Thailand where, as commented on above, the newly elected military-dominated regime is not above hunting down critics of the Lao PDR, just as domestic critics of the Bangkok regime find no space in Laos. But when it comes to issues of security, close socialist allies in the party-state's victory over the Kingdom of Laos in 1975—China and Vietnam—are placed on a pedestal, whether for the legacy of revolutionary solidarity and past sacrifices or as investors and partners in development. While, as already discussed, the China-built railroad and economic impacts appear to dominate discussions about the Lao PDR's current international relations, we should not neglect the particular way Laos triangulates among its traditional socialist allies, with China on one side and Vietnam on the other. On various occasions throughout 2019, leaders of Laos and Vietnam came together to reiterate long-standing bonds of solidarity.

For example, on 23 May Lao party general secretary and president Bounnhang Vorachith and National Assembly chairwoman Pany Yathotou hosted a reception for Truong Thi Mai, head of the Communist Party of Vietnam's Central Committee's Commission for Mass Mobilisation, affirming their "great friendship and special solidarity".[34] Speaking in Vientiane on 24 and 25 June, Vietnamese deputy prime minister Trinh Dinh Dung and his Lao counterpart Sonexay Siphandone promised to continue promoting bilateral cooperation in security, defence and trade, including agreements relating to their shared border, agreements on justice and cooperation on education, and in developing human resources. As noted, Vietnam remains the third-largest investor in Laos, with 410 projects worth US$4.22 billion. Notably, the two sides signed off on a power purchase agreement between Vietnam Electricity and Phongsubthavy Group of Laos (linked to the Namxam 3 Power dam). Vietnam also pledged to build the new National Assembly House of Laos.[35] In mid-year the defence aspect of relations between the two countries was in the headlines again with what was officially termed the first-ever Vietnam-Laos defence policy exchange. Held in Vientiane on 25 July, the "exchange" was co-chaired between Lao deputy defence minister Onsi Sensuk and his visiting Vietnamese counterpart Nguyen Chi Vinh.[36]

While the Russian Federation hardly rivals the influence once asserted in the Lao PDR by its Soviet forerunner, still the visit to Moscow in July by Lao

PDR minister of planning and investment Souphanh Keomixay led to the signing of cooperation agreements in digital development, a treaty on legal assistance in criminal matters, cooperation in the use of nuclear energy for peaceful purposes, and cooperation in geological exploration and subsoil development.[37] Neither are such other fraternal allies as North Korea and Cuba neglected, with exchanges and remembrances ritually celebrated. In March, top North Korean diplomat Ri Su Yong led a delegation of the Workers' Party of Korea to Laos, part of a regular exchange between the two states.[38] Between 8 and 9 September, a high-ranking Cuban trade delegation visited Vientiane.[39] On 11 November, the foreign ministers of Cuba and Laos, Bruno Rodriguez and Saleumxay Kommasith, respectively, met in Havana, ostensibly to strengthen bilateral relations on the occasion of the 45th anniversary of their establishment.

Notwithstanding a de-escalation of tensions across the partly demarcated 540-kilometre land border between Laos and Cambodia, misunderstandings and low-level tensions continued to simmer in 2019. As Cambodian prime minister Hun Sen made it known in September, following a telephone conversation with his Lao PDR counterpart, both sides had agreed to withdraw troops from the undemarcated area and would continue bilateral negotiations. In the meantime, representatives from the defence committees of the legislatures of Cambodia, Laos and Vietnam (CLV) entered into discussions in August on not only security issues but also on what they term a CLV Growth Triangle.[40] Even so, there has been little to show given the basic lack of infrastructure, the boundary issues, and the recent history.

Conclusion

As exemplified by the mid-year session of the National Assembly bringing together ruling communist party and government officials, along with the familiar cycle of visits and exchanges with fraternal parties and governments, the Lao PDR ritually resorts to foundational narratives around suffering and sacrifice to shore up its historical legitimacy. Such appeals are not unique to socialist states—and Laos is but one of three countries in the world where the hammer and sickle emblazons national emblems, just as it continues to invoke the thirty-year, mostly military, struggle against the royalist government, the ruling families and cliques in the Mekong River towns and their Western backers as a legitimizing device (and nowhere else is this bitter memory of American bombing better invoked than by the grim statistics yielded by yearly fatalities produced by unexploded ordinance) As a market economy operating under a Leninist system, major projects such as the hydro-electricity generating dams and the Chinese-built railroad, along with the practice of issuing licences and concessions for casinos and/or agribusiness ventures, create market distortions. While the year saw some venting of concern at official corruption, it is but an epiphenomenon of rent-seeking activities that define the party-state. Neither has the ruling party taken steps to reinvent itself with respect to popular grievances—of which there are many. No Zhao Ziyang has emerged in the Lao PDR; and Laos has yet to have its Tiananmen, or even its Hong Kong, moment. Hell-bent on development in the form of big infrastructure—indeed seeking to move heaven and earth on the Mekong—neither is the regime noted for listening to public, much less international, opinion. Drought, disease and human dislocation stemming from mega projects or disasters are not new in Laos, but one senses that more inclusion in governance would lead to better management practices with respect to land alienation and compensation issues, as indeed would transparency as the spectre of public debt ratchets up.

Notes

1. Somsack Pongkhao, "Laos Takes Steps to Tackle Six Urgent Issues", *Vientiane Times*, 26 July 2019, https://elevenmyanmar.com/news/laos-takes-steps-to-tackle-six-urgent-issues.
2. "NA Session Kicks Off with Govt Post Approvals, Socio-Economic Report", *Vientiane Times*, 8 November 2019, http://www.vientianetimes.org.la/freeContent/FreeConten_NA245.php.
3. "PM Highlights Economic Difficulties at NA's 7th Ordinary Session", Khaosan Pathet Lao (KPL), 5 June 2019, http://kpl.gov.la/En/Detail.aspx?id=46374/; "National Assembly Opens its 7th Ordinary Session", Khaosan Pathet Lao (KPL), 5 June 2019, http://kpl.gov.la/En/Detail.aspx?id=46375.
4. "Severe Drought in Mekong Region Reduces Rice Planting in Laos", reliefweb, 26 July 2019, report by Radio Free Asia's Lao Service, https://reliefweb.int/report/lao-peoples-democratic-republic/severe-drought-mekong-region-reduces-rice-planting-laos\.
5. "Rice Prices in Laos Likely to Rise Next Year", Xinhua, 14 November 2019, http://www.xinhuanet.com/english/2019-11/14/c_138554434.htm.
6. *Lao Economic Monitor*, August 2019, http://pubdocs.worldbank.org/en/339961565582635355/Lao-Economic-Monitor-August-2019-Summary.pdf.
7. "World Bank Optimistic about Laos' Economic Growth", VNA, 13 August 2019, https://en.vietnamplus.vn/world-bank-optimistic-about-laos-economic-growth/157758.vnp.
8. "Govt to Shed Stake in Loss Making State Enterprises", *Vientiane Times*, 16 July 2019, http://www.vientianetimes.org.la/freeContent/FreeConten_Govt.php.

9. Ye Ni, "A Visit to the Chinese Casino City in Laos Built by Myanmar Workers", *The Irrawaddy*, 21 October 2019, https://www.irrawaddy.com/news/burma/visit-chinese-casino-city-laos-built-myanmar-workers.html.
10. Ms Pakhem, "Who is Laos' First Special Economic Zone Benefitting?", chinadialogue, 25 October 2019, https://chinadialogue.net/article/show/single/en/11609-Who-is-Laos-first-special-economic-zone-benefitting-.
11. David Hutt, "The Only Way to End Corruption in Laos", *The Diplomat*, 10 July 2019, https://thediplomat.com/2019/07/the-only-way-to-end-corruption-in-laos/.
12. See Geoffrey C. Gunn, "Laos in 2016: Difficult History, Uncertain Future", *Asian Survey* 57, no. 1 (January/February 2017): 206–10.
13. "Lao National Assembly Members Call Out Pervasive Corruption", Radio Free Asia, 17 June 2019, https://www.rfa.org/english/news/laos/corruption-06172019142019.html.
14. "Laos 'Disciplines' Hundreds of Corrupt Officials in Recent Months, Jails Few", Radio Free Asia, 17 May 2019, https://www.rfa.org/english/news/laos/corruption-05172019151426.html.
15. Hutt, "The Only Way to End Corruption".
16. "Nearly 80 pct of China-Laos Railway Construction Completed", Xinhua, 22 September 2019, http://www.xinhuanet.com/english/2019-09/22/c_138412982.htm.
17. Ashley Westerman, "In Laos, a Chinese-Funded Railway Sparks Hope For Growth—And Fears of Debt", NPR, 26 April 2019, https://www.npr.org/2019/04/26/707091267/in-laos-a-chinese-funded-railway-sparks-hope-for-growth-and-fears-of-debt.
18. Skylar Lindsay, "China-Laos Railway Marred by Compensation Issues and Pollution", *Asean Today*, 11 June 2019, https://www.aseantoday.com/2019/06/china-laos-railway-marred-by-compensation-issues-and-pollution/.
19. OHCHR, "Statement by Professor Philip Alston, United Nations Special Rapporteur on Extreme Poverty and Human Rights on His Visit to Lao PDR, 18–28 March 2019 United Nations Human Rights Office of the High Commissioner", https://www.ohchr.org/EN/NewsEvents/Pages/DisplayNews.aspx?NewsID=24417&LangID=E.
20. Lindsay, "China-Laos Railway Marred".
21. Eri Sugiura, "Laos Can 'Manage' Debt to China, PM Insists", *Nikkei Asian Review*, 31 May 2019, https://asia.nikkei.com/Spotlight/The-Future-of-Asia-2019/Laos-can-manage-debt-to-China-PM-insists.
22. John Pennington, "Can Laos Manage its Debt to China?", *ASEAN Today*, 28 October 2019, https://www.aseantoday.com/2019/06/can-laos-manage-its-debt-to-china/.
23. "Local Government in Laos Again Falls Behind on Living Allowances for Dam Collapse Survivors", Radio Free Asia, 13 June 2019, https://reliefweb.int/report/lao-peoples-democratic-republic/local-government-laos-again-falls-behind-living-allowances.
24. OHCHR, "Statement by Professor Philip Alston".
25. "Attapeu Dam Collapse in Laos Not Force Majeure Event; Investigator", Xinhua, 29 May 2019, http://www.xinhuanet.com/english/2019-05/29/c_138099872.htm.

26. Andrew Nachemson, "Laos to Go Ahead with Luang Prabang Dam Project Despite Warnings", https://www.aljazeera.com/news/2019/09/laos-luang-prabang-dam-project-warnings-190924102523452.html.
27. "Villagers Brace for Resettlement amid Signs Laos Wants to Build Another Mainstream Mekong Dam", Radio Free Asia, 19 June 2019, https://www.rfa.org/english/news/laos/mekong-dam-06182019172127.html.
28. OHCHR, "Statement by Professor Philip Alston".
29. Ounkeo Souksavanh, Sidney Khotpanya, and Max Avary, "Lao Villager Dies after 8 Years in Jail over Land Grab Protest", Radio Free Asia, 20 June 2019, https://www.rfa.org/english/news/laos/villager-05202019154307.html.
30. "Thai Exiles in Fear after Murders and Disappearances", Reuters, 24 May 2019, https://www.straitstimes.com/asia/se-asia/thai-exiles-in-fear-after-murders-and-disappearances.
31. "Thai Government Pressed over Missing Lao Activist Od Sayavong", *The Guardian*, 7 September 2019, https://www.theguardian.com/world/2019/sep/07/thai-government-pressed-over-missing-lao-activist-od-sayavong.
32. "Police Detain Eight Would-be Protesters in Lao Capital Vientiane", Radio Free Asia, 15 November 2019, https://www.rfa.org/english/news/laos/vientiane-protest-11152019160135.html; Human Rights Watch, "Laos: Democracy Activists Arrested", 16 November 2019, https://www.hrw.org/news/2019/11/16/laos-democracy-activists-arrested.
33. OHCHR, "Statement by Professor Philip Alston".
34. "Laos Vows to Preserve Relationship with Vietnam", *Nhan Dan*, 23 June 2019, https://en.nhandan.org.vn/politics/item/7499202-laos-vows-to-preserve-relationship-with-vietnam.html.
35. *Viet Nam News*, "VN, Laos Continue to Foster Co-operation", 25 June 2019, http://vietnamnews.vn/politics-laws/521784/vn-laos-continue-to-foster-co-operation.html#IhvuZKbps9VcVklW.99.
36. Prashanth Parameswaran, "Defense Policy Exchange Spotlights Vietnam-Laos Military Cooperation", *The Diplomat*, 29 July 2019, https://thediplomat.com/2019/07/defense-policy-exchange-spotlights-vietnam-laos-military-cooperation/.
37. "Laos, Russia Announce Cooperation in Numerous Fields", *Vientiane Times*, 16 July 2019, https://elevenmyanmar.com/news/laos-russia-announce-cooperation-in-numerous-fields.
38. Colin Zwirko, "Top North Korean Diplomat Leading Delegation to Laos This Week: KCNA", NK News, 26 March 2019, https://www.nknews.org/2019/03/top-north-korean-diplomat-leading-delegation-to-laos-this-week-kcna/.
39. "Laos, Cuba Set New Heights for Economic and Trade Cooperation", *Inquirer.net*, 10 September 2019, https://business.inquirer.net/278645/laos-cuba-set-new-heights-for-economic-and-trade-cooperation#ixzz5zACz9irY.
40. Prashanth Parameswaran, "What's Next after the New Cambodia-Laos Border Tensions?", *The Diplomat*, 28 August 2019, https://thediplomat.com/2019/08/whats-next-after-the-new-cambodia-laos-border-tensions/y.

Malaysia

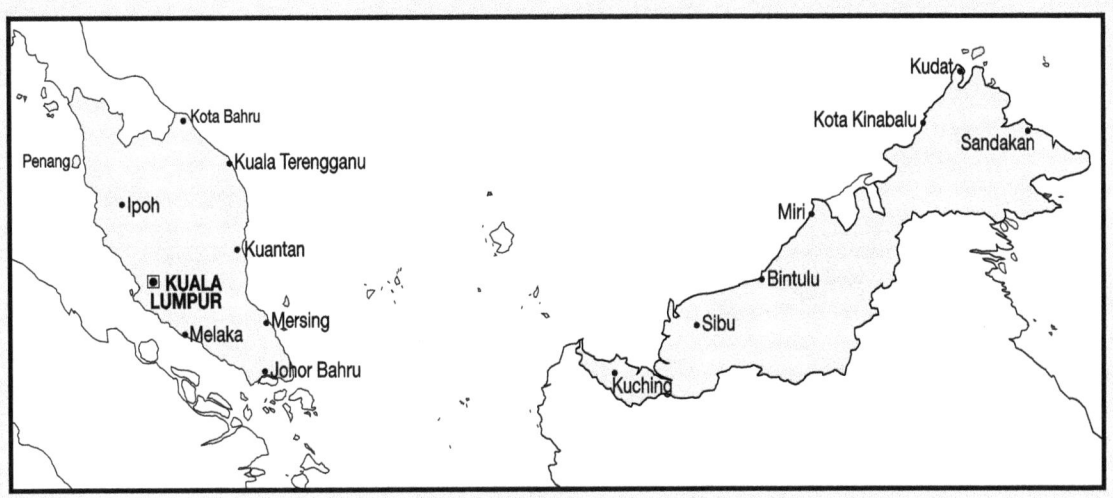

MALAYSIA IN 2019:
A Change of Government without Regime Change

Ross Tapsell

The year 2019 was potentially the most important one in Malaysia's political history since the creation of the Federation in 1963. While the historic change in government which ended the sixty-year reign of the Barisan Nasional (BN) coalition government the previous year was indeed momentous, the transition of power would have far less meaning if the promises of broader national transformation are not fulfilled by the new Pakatan Harapan (PH) government led by former prime minister Mahathir Mohamad. PH's 194-page *Buku Harapan* ("book of hope") manifesto included sixty pledges, from reforming the Anti-Corruption Commission to ensuring "transparency and robustness of our election system", along with promises to "abolish oppressive laws" and "enhance the transparency and integrity of the budget and budgeting process". Other bold promises included the "decentralisation of power to Sabah and Sarawak", "making government schools the best choice for its people" and for Malaysia to "lead efforts to resolve the Rohingya and Palestine crises."[1]

It would be easy, then, to highlight the various unfulfilled promises of the manifesto in order to determine 2019 as an abject disappointment for the fledgling PH government. Indeed, it has become a well-worn path for many analysts to measure the new government against its manifesto pledges, especially after the first hundred days of the PH administration and the one-year anniversary of its electoral victory.[2] The slow pace of reform is not only limited to the political sector. The economy remains buffeted by stock outflows and a weak ringgit as global funds signalled their concerns about the lack of reforms.[3] Elina Noor has written

---

Ross Tapsell is Senior Lecturer at the Australian National University's College of Asia and the Pacific, and Associate Fellow at the ISEAS – Yusof Ishak Institute, Singapore.

that while Malaysia "faced myriad challenges" in terms of foreign and security policies, "not much is likely to change" under Mahathir's "new Malaysia".[4] There has also been no major reform of education at any level, no progress on promises of decentralization, and only limited attempts to address the issues relating to the Orang Asli (indigenous peoples). Many Malaysians have thus become despondent when discussing national politics in 2019, including those who were initially part of the reform process themselves. Opinion polls throughout the year from the Merdeka Centre (Figure 1) reflect the growing public disappointment with the PH government. In the face of these criticisms, senior PH politicians have spent much of the year defending their track record. Some of them have argued that "reform takes time",[5] while others have chosen to blame the unrealistic "high expectations" of voters.[6] Mahathir himself conceded that the PH government are "victims of our own manifesto".[7]

However, to dismiss Pakatan Harapan in 2019 as a government of broken promises misses the deeper, and more important, question of *why* many significant reforms have not yet been pursued or implemented. Usually, when a change in government occurs after decades of rule by a singular party, the country will experience both rapid reform and political turmoil. One only has to think of Malaysia's next-door neighbour, Indonesia, after the fall of Suharto's New Order regime in 1998. Unlike the dramatic and violent contestations that occurred in Indonesia, Malaysia's change of government in 2018 occurred peacefully through the ballot box. Thus, the new PH government could claim a mandate from the people to implement a list of bold promises. It also faced no post-election outbursts of racial and ethnic violence, nor regional conflict, that could have distracted it. To be sure, there were some reforms passed in Parliament in 2019, such as abolishing the draconian Anti-Fake News Law and lowering the voting age from 21 to 18. New parliamentary committees were established, with some effort to ensure parliamentary oversight of institutions such as the Malaysian Anti-Corruption Commission. But, for most Malaysians, 2019 felt more of the same. Why? While this will remain a puzzle for social scientists to interrogate in the years to come, this chapter will probe some possible answers by examining key political issues and events that have occurred in PH's first full calendar year in power.

In with the Old: Mahathir's Leadership

The biggest question mark around Mahathir's return to the prime ministership was his commitment to reform. When Mahathir formed the Partai Pribumi Bersatu Malaysia (hereafter Bersatu), sceptics were already characterizing the party as

Malaysia in 2019: A Change of Government without Regime Change

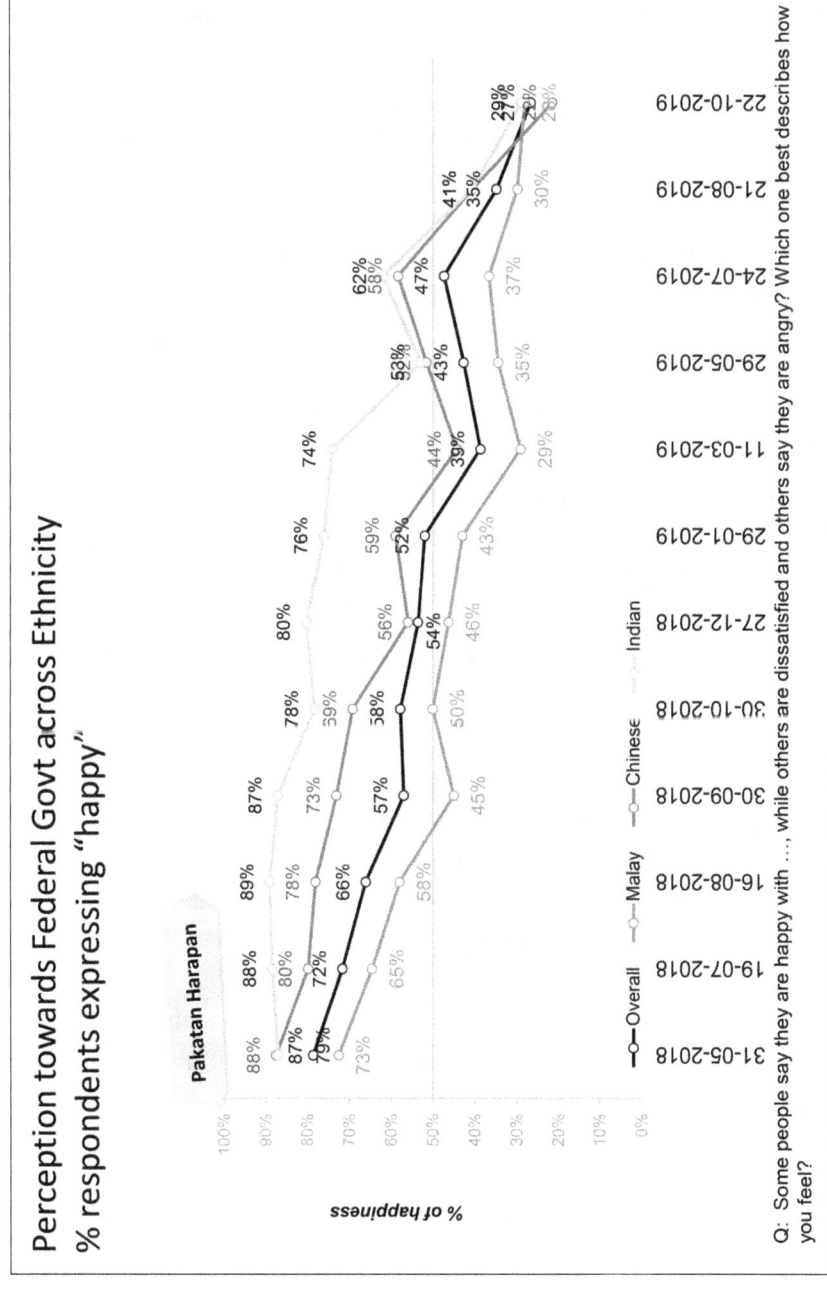

FIGURE 1
Perception towards the Federal Government

Source: Merdeka Centre, "Malaysia Political Developments and Trajectories Updates", 26 November 2019.

an "UMNO 2.0". Mahathir's record during his leadership of the United Malays National Organisation (UMNO) and as prime minster from 1981 to 2003 also raised concerns that he was not interested in the democratic reforms that other component parties in PH and in civil society movements like Bersih had envisaged once the BN was ousted from power. Moreover, the developments in 2019 rebutted any suggestion that Mahathir was simply warming the seat for the heir-apparent Anwar Ibrahim, as Mahathir set about consolidating his own party while playing rivals off one another within the PH coalition.

The inevitable revival of the decades-long competition for leadership between Mahathir and his promised successor, Anwar Ibrahim, was the focus of many discussions surrounding Malaysian politics throughout 2018, but they gained more significance in 2019 for two reasons. The first was that Mahathir continued to be vague about the dates and details of the succession. The initial plan seems to suggest that Mahathir would step down for Anwar after around two years at the helm. However, individuals within Mahathir's circle have denied such a timeframe for a handover,[8] while Mahathir himself has suggested that he may need three years to allow him sufficient time to correct major problems.[9] In November 2019 he indicated in a *Financial Times* interview that he would not be stepping down in 2020.[10] Released from the shackles imposed by the previous government on reportage over intra-party strife and leadership tensions, the Malaysian media covered the internal factional machinations within PH and the Mahathir-Anwar succession story with vigour throughout the year. Any statement by any politician on any aspect of the leadership transition became a "clickbait" headline for readers. The BN opposition also encouraged the story as it added to the general sense of an unstable PH government, most notably in October when six UMNO MPs publicly urged for Mahathir's party to keep him as prime minister until the next general election in 2023.[11] Despite turning ninety-four years old in July, Mahathir has managed to keep support of key allies within and without his coalition. Perhaps more importantly he seems to be enjoying his second tenure as prime minister and keen to continue in the role. In August he showed off his physical prowess by riding a bicycle for over eleven kilometres around Putrajaya. Photos of him doing so were widely spread and discussed on Malaysian social media platforms.[12] In September he went horse riding during the smog, and also received yet another honorary doctorate, this time from Japan's Doshisha University.

The second reason for the dominance of the leadership transition issue in 2019 was the potential for a third candidate to be the next prime minister. Mahathir has long adopted a strategy of making political rivals play off one another in order to elevate himself as the ultimate key to power. Mahathir remained stubbornly noncommittal on details of the succession, prompting pundits and others to look for an alternative Mahathir-endorsed candidate as his eventual successor. The result was a roll call of Malaysian politicians being floated as the next possible prime minister. The minister of economic affairs Azmin Ali, Anwar's most formidable rival from within his own party, is considered to be Mahathir's favourite, although others were said to be quietly staking their claims, including Bersatu's Muhyiddin Yassin and UMNO's Hishammudin Hussein and Khairy Jamaluddin. The narrative that others were being considered as successors has prompted Anwar to become increasingly concerned—perhaps even paranoid—about his support within the ruling coalition, going as far as claiming that "traitors" are trying to keep him from being Malaysia's next prime minister.[13]

The factional infighting within his own party, Parti Keadilan Rakyat (PKR), became more pronounced in 2019. This reached a sensational height when a series of sex tapes surfaced in July allegedly involving Azmin Ali, leading Anwar to state that Azmin should resign if it is proven to be him in the clip. Azmin responded by telling Anwar to "look at the man in the mirror".[14] The factionalism within the PKR became so overt that there were moves towards rival party gatherings at the National Congress in December. On the day of the Congress, Azmin and his supporters sensationally walked out, claiming speeches from pro-Anwar members were attacking them, and with Azmin claiming he was being portrayed as a "traitor" to the party. One former PKR member has described the factionalism dominating the PKR in 2019 as "tearing [the party] apart", which "will likely mean PH losing power" in the next election.[15] An alternative and more positive take here is that Malaysia is witnessing a "decentralisation of political power", which, while indeed "messy", is ultimately good for democracy.[16] For instance, the party chiefs of the PH coalition have regular meetings with Mahathir to discuss and formulate policies, far more than Najib used to do with the BN coalition government. The establishment of parliamentary committees also reveals efforts towards a more consultative policymaking process. The open conflict between political factions could be a sign of a more open and transparent politics, even if it means a decline in the opinion polls for the PH.

There is no doubt the factionalism and infighting in PKR and the PH coalition have detracted from effective and efficient governance. This had electoral repercussions for the PH government in a November by-election in Tanjung Piai, Johor, which was called after the incumbent Pakatan MP passed away in September. PH was represented by the sixty-six-year-old Karmaine Sardini from Bersatu, a former UMNO divisional treasurer who had previously been defeated when contesting the nearby seat of Pontian in GE14. During the campaign's final weeks, non-governmental organizations such as Bersih 2.0 accused PH of vote-buying and abusing government machinery, especially in announcing a slew of projects in the constituency worth about RM7.3 million.[17] The eventual result was however a damning one for PH, as BN's candidate from the Malaysian Chinese Association (MCA) won 25,466 votes to Karmaine Sardini's 10,380 votes. The defeat raised questions over Bersatu's inflated influence within the PH coalition and whether the result was a "referendum" of Mahathir's leadership. Furthermore, in nominating a Chinese candidate, BN proved to be more innovative than PH; the former had also successfully fielded an Orang Asli candidate in Cameron Highlands in a January 2019 by-election. The Tanjung Piai result is likely to exacerbate the tensions between the Mahathir and Anwar factions. For instance, following the electoral defeat, Lim Kit Siang of the Democratic Action Party (DAP), a component party of PH, tweeted that the "DAP and Pakatan Harapan accept the devastating result of the Tanjong Piai voters who spoke not only on behalf of themselves but of the country at their frustration and unhappiness at the pace of reforms since May 9, 2018".[18] This message could be read as a subtle criticism against Mahathir for not pursuing reform more vigorously. Azmin Ali, meanwhile, described the by-election as a "resounding wake up call" and blamed the partisan in-fighting for the defeat, urging instead for "every member and leader of Pakatan Harapan to continue to give our undivided support to YAB Tun Dr Mahathir Mohamad, Prime Minister of Malaysia and Chairman of Pakatan Harapan to continue to lead the country and the coalition".[19]

A longer-term concern about the second Mahathir administration is the lack of a clear policy framework. Also absent are strict safeguards to reduce corruption and patronage politics, or institutional mechanisms to make politicians and political parties more accountable for the way they acquire and spend money. Mahathir came to power in 2018 with a reputation for rapid economic growth during his previous tenure and a promise to reduce government corruption that had significantly permeated under Najib's rule. As economist E. Terence Gomez and others explored in the book *Minister of Finance Incorporated*, a key conduit for corruption and patronage politics under the BN government was the Ministry of Finance, which was under Najib's jurisdiction as finance minister.[20] Although the DAP's Lim Guan Eng is the current finance minister, Gomez noted that "covert" reconfigurations have allowed the Prime Minister's Department under Mahathir to control key government enterprises. According to Gomez, the "entire corporate sector is under control of PPBM [Bersatu] and with Azmin [as minister of economic affairs]", while "the Prime Minister's department controls big businesses".[21] Along with the ability to place political appointees as heads of government-linked companies (GLCs), the arrangement suggests that the new PH government, and Mahathir's Bersatu in particular, is retaining the same system of patronage used by UMNO in order to channel resources to key constituents. In response to such criticisms, a deputy minister from Bersatu declared that the new government never committed to getting rid of political appointees in GLCs, while arguing that people should "not pluck words and phrases" from the *Buku Harapan*'s list of promises.[22] As an analyst privately shared, "When the fox is in charge of the sheep, why change anything when it's good for the fox?"

Being "Malay": What is Old is New Again

The year 2019 was also a momentous one for UMNO. For the first time in its history, the party started the year as the opposition. In Malaysia, this means not only losing access to the support of government agencies and the levers of decision-making in the country but also the loss of funds and resources to allocate in order to keep the party machine running. This was evident when Utusan Melayu (Malaysia) Berhad, the printing press behind *Utusan Malaysia*, the country's oldest Malay-language newspaper, which generally served as a mouthpiece for UMNO, ceased operations in October. The chairman was upfront in attributing the newspaper's demise to the lack of funding from UMNO following its electoral loss in 2018, stating that "the company went downhill after May last year".[23] The loss of access to state resources also meant that many UMNO cadres were tempted by overtures to join Mahathir's Bersatu in 2019, with seven doing so in February.

The question in 2019 was gauging to what extent UMNO felt they needed to reform. The party's president, Zahid Hamidi, remained loyal to ousted PM Najib, and both are under criminal investigation in connection with 1MDB. Many UMNO cadres blame Najib for the GE14 loss. In a suggestion there was some factional divergence, UMNO postponed its general assembly in 2019, apparently to focus on the Tanjung Piai by-election, but UMNO held their general assembly in December without any major incident. UMNO was in need of a compelling narrative and direction in the hope to return to government in 2023. Khairy Jamaluddin, for example, argued for a more inclusive, multiracial UMNO, but by his own admission was part of a "minority" of thinking inside the party.[24] In September, UMNO and the Islamic Parti Islam Se-Malaysia (PAS) signed a unity pact, the *Muafakat Nasional* (or National Cooperation Charter). Over the years, PAS and UMNO have gone through various stages of official and unofficial alliances (PAS actually competed under the Barisan banner in the 1974 elections). This latest "marriage" marked a more concerted focus on the rights and privileges of

Malay-Muslims, which the two parties claim have been increasingly threatened under the PH government. This narrative has clearly attracted support of the Malay community, as evinced by the fifty-thousand-strong prayer rally held at the National Mosque in Kuala Lumpur in late 2018 calling for Malay rights to be preserved and Islam to continue as the national religion. However, while this "marriage" might make sense ideologically, the practical details remain to be negotiated, since it seems to lead to more questions than solutions electorally. For example, in October, PAS administrators in Kelantan and Terengganu stated that despite the cooperation between the two parties, there was "no space" for UMNO lawmakers to join the respective state governments.[25] Nevertheless, the decision by UMNO and PAS to focus on Malay identity politics has raised concerns for many Malaysians about the potential for greater ethnic and religious tensions in the future. These concerns were heightened further when four public universities organized the highly controversial "Malay Dignity Congress" in October. The congress advanced ideas associated with Malay racial supremacy and featured speeches demanding the abolishment of vernacular schools and the reservation of top government posts for Malays. Mahathir himself attended, delivering a speech about non-Malay foreigners and lamenting how his ability to defend the Malays has been weakened by the PH coalition, while denying hearing the lead organizer proclaiming that "Malaysia is for Malays".[26] Significantly, the congress was not a partisan affair limited to UMNO and PAS, as some Bersatu MPs were involved in key organizing roles. Notably absent was Anwar Ibrahim, while Azmin Ali stood shoulder-to-shoulder with Mahathir and the top Malay opposition figures in PAS and UMNO.

The issue of Malay support is clearly a pre-eminent concern for Mahathir and many of his fellow Bersatu cadres. In late 2018, Mahathir reversed the PH government's earlier decision to ratify the International Convention on the Elimination of All Forms of Racial Discrimination (ICERD) after weeks of protests organized by UMNO and PAS and fear-mongering about the loss of bumiputra rights. In the 2019 national budget, the government also increased funds to JAKIM (Malaysia Islamic Development Department) from 1.2 billion ringgit to 1.3 billion ringgit (US$31 million) to provide for a one-off special allowance of 500 ringgit (US$120) for each *imam*, *bilal*, mosque custodian and *takmir* teacher "as a show of appreciation of their role in society".[27] The 2019 budget also increased funding to assist bumiputra institutions and entrepreneurs from 7.6 billion ringgit to 8.0 billion ringgit (US$20 million), while continuing the policy of tax exemptions for fund management companies managing Shariah-compliant funds until after the next election.[28] The government also continued to promise that at least 30 per cent of tenders for each ministry would be reserved for only bumiputra contractors. Other than maintaining a hard line against the LGBTQ community, the PH government denied India's request to extradite controversial preacher Zakir Naik on charges of money laundering and hate speech. (In a speech in August in Kelantan, Zakir Naik called on Malaysian Chinese to "go back", as they were "old guests" of the country.) In short, Mahathir was careful to ensure that there was nothing concrete for UMNO or PAS to latch on to in order to claim that the Malays are being disadvantaged under the PH government, especially since the important post of finance minister is currently occupied by a member of the Chinese-dominated DAP. This means that everything that was old was thus new again.

While such allocations of priorities and resources makes tactical sense for Mahathir and Bersatu, it raises bigger issues for the reformist potential of the governing coalition. Mahathir's own speeches and activities throughout the year have provoked the concern of the reformists. Overseas, he has continued to rail against the Jews,[29] while defending palm oil interests at the United Nations.[30] At home, his attendance at the Malay Dignity Congress had caused some upset with the reformists within his coalition, as well as among conservative Malays, since his speech "condemned the Malays" for being disunited and accepting cash handouts.[31]

While no one would expect Mahathir to become an advocate for racial equality and the environment, his speeches are notable because they highlight the ideological diversity of the PH coalition and its supporters as well as Mahathir's commitment to an old narrative that had served him in the past. The most impactful campaign video of the 2018 election involved a tearful Mahathir telling two Malaysian children that he had returned to politics in order to "rebuild the country because of mistakes I made in the past".[32] Political theatre it may have been, but the message of "good governance" and "a Malaysia for all where everybody lives happily and in peace" resonated widely. A more pluralist Malaysia seemed to have beckoned with PH, even if the choice of Mahathir as leader was strategically made to woo conservative and older Malay voters. However, the country post-GE14 appears to have evolved into four different Malaysias: a pluralist domain concentrated around the west coast of the Peninsula, a conservative Malay heartland based along the east coast of the Peninsula, Sabah and Sarawak.[33] Rather than uniting under Mahathir, Malaysia has seemingly become more fractured and divided.

The overarching theme for Malaysia in 2019 was a PH government predominantly concerned with defending itself against the charge of being "anti-Malay", a narrative promoted by the opposition UMNO and PAS as they coalesced around the issue of Malay-Muslim identity politics. This resulted in a government reluctant to upset the status quo in terms of how money is collected and distributed, particularly the New Economic Policy. Thus, deliberations about reforms to major sectors of Malaysian society—schools, university admissions, government scholarships, poverty, rural development, state-federal relations and so on—continue to be narrowly framed in terms of race, or more specifically whether a policy would be beneficial for the Malays. While no one expected these racial and religious frames to disappear once PH assumed power, there were hopes for more mature policy discussions premised on the idea of racial equality. However, many Malay leaders and scholars have persisted with the argument that Malays needed special privileges not because of their supposed racial superiority but because they were the poorest group in society, and a race-based affirmative action policy would thus help with poverty reduction. In contrast, some PH leaders have regularly tried to shift the focus to the fact that poverty exists among all ethnic communities. The issues of whether poverty in Malaysia is exclusive to the Malays, and whether employing race-based policies is the most effective way to alleviate poverty, will be common themes of contestation in the years to come as PH looks to defend its legacy from the opposition PAS and UMNO.

Sabah and Sarawak: Out with the New

The often-neglected Borneo states of Sabah and Sarawak are increasingly becoming key in determining the balance of power in Putrajaya. Sabah's Shafee Apdal played the role of kingmaker following GE14 as his party, Warisan, joined the PH coalition to secure a parliamentary majority. Unlike on the Peninsula, the binary categories of "Malay" and "non-Malay" have always been more alien to the religiously, ethnically and linguistically diverse Sabah and Sarawak.[34] Thus, the BN's various attempts over the years (through UMNO in particular) to replicate the political discourse and identity politics of the Peninsula in Borneo did not always succeed; the issue of which peninsular party or prime minister would assume office has always been of far less concern to the residents of Sabah and Sarawak. While the leadership tensions and factional fighting within PKR, as well as the pro-Malay rallies and Dignity Congress, made for great headlines for media companies based in Kuala Lumpur, these issues and events were derided by Sabahans and Sarawakians as the typical melodrama of peninsular politics.

For East Malaysians, the issue of state autonomy garnered the most attention, fuelled as it was by rising state nationalism amidst increasing state-periphery tensions. As James Chin had written in the 2019 issue of *Southeast Asian Affairs*, "historical grievances" relating to the marginalization of the two states and the 1976 constitutional amendment erasing the "special status" of Sabah and Sarawak as enshrined in the Malaysia Agreement of 1963 (MA63) took precedence in the GE14 campaigns, with terms like "Sabah for Sabahans" and "Sarawak for Sarawakians" coming to the fore.[35] On its part, PH had promised Borneo greater autonomy in their manifesto, with pledges to restore the special status of Sabah and Sarawak and devolve powers on education and health. The PH coalition also vowed to return 20 per cent of oil royalties and 50 per cent of state revenue to the two states.

In April 2019, PH tabled a constitutional amendment in parliament to have Sabah and Sarawak listed separately from the other eleven peninsular states as constituent members of Malaysia. This was a return to the original formulation of Malaysia in the 1963 constitution. However, the terminology used by PH meant the amendment was criticized as "cosmetic".[36] The amendment was also rushed through parliament without extensive discussions or consideration of its legal implications, leading to the loss of support from many Borneo MPs. For instance, the Gabungan Partai Sarawak (GPS) abstained from the vote as it wanted the terms "Borneo" (representing Sabah and Sarawak) and "Malaya" (representing the other eleven peninsular states) to be explicitly mentioned.[37] The proposed amendment was ten votes short of the required two-thirds majority as lawmakers from BN chose to abstain. The failure of the amendment added to the list of undelivered promises for PH in 2019, leading to consistent calls through the year by opposition politicians in Sabah and Sarawak for the government to "fulfil MA63 vows".[38] As the year closes, little progress appears to have been made on this issue.

The inability of PH to return more oil revenues to Sabah and Sarawak has created perhaps the most local angst, given the substantial and tangible impact it would have had on the state coffers. Admittedly, there is no guarantee that the money would be funnelled to programmes that would benefit the people. It may be the case that the diversion of oil revenues to the two states would simply enrich the Borneo political elite. However, Mahathir's excuse for breaking the promise—that returning 20 per cent of the oil royalties to Sabah and Sarawak would weaken Petronas as an international oil company—did not go down well among the local residents.[39]

The federal government also ran into conflict with the Sarawak state government, which is led by the GPS, a coalition of four former BN component parties that currently sits on the opposition benches in the federal parliament. The Sarawak state government is resisting attempts by the federal government to establish a Village Community Management Council (MPKK) that will replace the state government's control of village funds under the Village Security and Development Committee (JKKK). The GPS state government has accused the

MPKK of being an example of "political colonisation" by the federal Pakatan government, while PH has countered that the JKKK has been abused to ensure that longhouse chiefs vote for the GPS. In short, the fight is over the control of funds for political patronage and vote buying between the federal and state governments, rather than over the best interests of the villagers and their future.[40]

Meanwhile, broader problems that have plagued Borneo for decades such as the lack of development, housing, clean water and schooling as well as the migration of millions of Sabah and Sarawak youths to West Malaysia in search of greater employment opportunities remain unaddressed by the PH government. These issues of inequality lie at the heart of the local autonomy movement, which will not be abated by "cosmetic" constitutional amendments.

In Sarawak, the issue of greater autonomy gained more traction through the year. In November 2019, the Chinese-dominated party within the GPS coalition, the Sarawak United People's Party (SUPP), took the bold step of calling for a referendum to determine Sarawak's future in Malaysia. Although this was seen as political posturing intended for the ethnic Chinese constituencies of Sarawak, the escalation also indicates how the GPS will continue to adopt an anti-federal and anti-Pakatan stance as they mount a campaign claiming to be the voice for Sarawakians. Local PH candidates, forced to defend the national government's decisions and unfulfilled promises, will find it difficult to defeat the GPS in the next state election, which is likely to be held in 2020. At the same time, the argument that "nothing has changed under PH" is perhaps most prevalent in Sarawak, given that the ruling party of the state remains run by four component parties of the former Barisan Nasional. In Kuching, local newspapers are still beholden to advertising and ownership pressures of local elites, while NGOs continue to complain that the domestic intelligence agency, or Special Branch, still attends their events. There has also been no attempt by any tier of government to promote the "cultural practices of democracy" in governance.[41] The activity of vote buying through cash or goods is likely to continue as an entrenched practice of all political parties in the state.

In GE14, the promises of *Sabah baharu* ("New Sabah") were regularly made by Warisan, the party that eventually emerged victorious in the state. Yet, the same issues of patronage politics and a lack of policy changes continue in Sabah. Chief Minister Shafee Apdal was appointed (or appointed himself) as the state's minister of finance, allowing him unfettered control of the state coffers in the same way that Najib did at the federal level and Shafee's predecessor in Sabah, Musa Aman, did from 2003 to 2018. The Warisan state government also backtracked on its election promise to scrap a number of unpopular development initiatives in the state, specifically the Kaiduan dam and the Tanjung Aru beach development projects. These projects were instead approved, albeit with some variations to the original proposals. (The dam would have a new site and would now be a hydroelectric dam; the Tanjung Aru development would be scaled down from its original plans.) There were however no clear explanations forthcoming from the state government justifying these decisions, prompting opponents to label the Warisan coalition as a "U-turn government".[42] Yet, unlike in Sarawak, the politics in Sabah appears to be more dynamic, as the media in the state is more open to criticizing the state government.

Another significant development in the politics of Sabah is Bersatu's entry to the state, thus fuelling discussion over its potential to displace Warisan as the dominant party in the coalition should MPs switch from Warisan to Bersatu, as some UMNO MPs had done earlier in the year. This move was made partly to reduce the power of "kingmaker" Shafee Apdal, whose decision to back PH on election night proved pivotal in helping to push the coalition over the threshold to secure a parliamentary majority. Bersatu's efforts are indicative of Mahathir's focus on consolidating his party throughout the country, while portending more fractures in the ruling coalition in the near future.

Conclusion: A Change of Government without a Regime Change

It is the argument of this chapter that Malaysia in 2019 was not a place of drastic change and bold reforms. This does not mean nothing has changed in Malaysia since PH came to power. The restrictions on speech and politicized prosecutions of opposition leaders—features of Najib's BN—are now less prevalent in Malaysian society. Malaysia in 2019 seems to be a place where the law is becoming more impartial. The ongoing delays in Najib's corruption trial throughout the year suggest that Mahathir and PH want an independent, evidence-based judicial proceeding over a political show trial. There were also moves undertaken to make the Attorney General's Chambers and the Anti-Corruption Commission more professional and therefore more independent from the government. Malaysia's journalists can speak and write more freely thanks to the abolition of the Anti-Fake News Law. Moreover, they are less concerned about running afoul of the Printing, Presses and Publications Act, even if this law has yet to be repealed by the PH. There were signals for reform in electoral and parliamentary procedures, including in December a recommendation from the Electoral Reform Committee for a proportional representation voting system for parliamentary seats. These incremental changes have led Freedom House to assess Malaysia in its 2019 report as being freer, but still only "partly free".[43]

Nevertheless, as the government remains distracted by factional wars and the issue of the post-Mahathir leadership, the political will to undertake further reforms is weak. The lack of progress in reforming the justice sector is most noticeable: little effort has been made to abolish or amend draconian laws, and the reform of the police proceeds at a glacial pace. The government still continues to use the sedition law and the Security Offences (Special Measures) Act (SOSMA), such as in the case of the detention of twelve people, including two ruling coalition politicians, in October 2019 for alleged links to a defunct Sri Lankan armed group.

For Mahathir and many others within the PH coalition, politics remain an arena to hold power and win elections by maintaining the status quo. While PH has eschewed the blatant corruption that defined the Najib era, the system of local patronage politics still thrives. PH came to power because of the protest vote against Najib's corruption, the opportunity presented by "three-corner fights" (BN coalition government; PH coalition opposition; PAS as independent—with PAS and BN voters splitting Malay Muslim votes, meaning PH ultimately won the seat) in certain constituencies, and the decisive shift of Warisan in Sabah. Many voters had chosen Mahathir not for the prospects of a "new" Malaysia but because he represented the promise of the "old" Malaysia from during his first tenure: a time of economic growth and pro-Malay policies, of which local patronage systems and cronyism were a feature. Of course, the undercurrents of the Bersih movement and the legacies of the Anwar-led *reformasi* movement played a role in the GE14 campaign. But as Larry Diamond argued in 2010, "if a transition occurs" in Malaysia, it will be because of "the coalescence of an effective opposition and the blunders of an arrogant regime". And so it was in May 2018. The problem for PH in 2019 was its inability to consolidate in the absence of an "arrogant regime" to oppose.

The year 2019 will be remembered as one where more Malaysians believed (as some did in 2018) that Malaysia had undergone a change of government but not a regime change. In future, scholars will need to examine more closely the nature of the PH "regime" and whether serious reforms of institutions are possible. This however will be difficult to determine until PH's five years in office come to a close. What seems to be the most pressing matter currently is the significant decline in support for Mahathir as prime minister. Mahathir has spent most of 2019 manoeuvring over his succession, blocking the reform of draconian laws, and reiterating his support for Malay rights. Despite all this politicking, however, Mahathir has failed to increase his support among the Malays and has instead alienated a large percentage of the non-Malay electorate. As a result, PH lost four by-elections in the Peninsula in 2019. Questions will soon be asked as to who will be the first among Mahathir, Anwar and Azmin to step down, and whether PH can indeed last the full five-year term.

Notes

1. Pakatan Harapan, *Buku Harapan: Rebuilding Our Nation Fulfilling Our Hopes*, 10 March, 2018, https://kempen.s3.amazonaws.com/manifesto/Manifesto_text/Manifesto_PH_EN.pdf.
2. Serina Rahman, "Pakatan Harapan Government Approaches 100 Days in Office", CNA, 5 August 2018, https://www.channelnewsasia.com/news/commentary/pakatan-harapan-hundred-days-in-office-promises-unrealised-10585592; Bloomberg, "Malaysians Turn away from Mahathir after Year of Failed Promises", *Business Times*, 10 May 2018, https://www.businesstimes.com.sg/government-economy/malaysians-turn-away-from-mahathir-after-year-of-failed-promises; Emmanuel Smarathisa, "Did Pakatan Harapan Overpromise?", *Focus Malaysia* no. 294, http://www.focusmalaysia.my/Mainstream/did-pakatan-harapan-overpromise.
3. "Global Funds Lose Patience with Malaysia, Fail to See Reform", *Malaysiakini*, 14 May 2019, https://www.malaysiakini.com/news/476041.
4. Elina Noor, "Foreign and Security Policy in the New Malaysia", Lowy Institute Paper, November 2019, https://www.lowyinstitute.org/publications/foreign-and-security-policy-new-malaysia.
5. Azura Abas and The Athira Yusof, "Reform Takes Time, But We Are on It", *New Straits Times*, 31 March 2019, https://www.nst.com.my/news/nation/2019/03/474539/reform-takes-time-we-are-it-nsttv.
6. "Progress Was Made but Many Promises Unfulfilled", *The Star*, 10 May 2019, https://www.thestar.com.my/news/nation/2019/05/10/progress-was-made-but-many-promises-unfulfilled.
7. "Dr M Doing What He Can to Fulfil PH Manifesto, Says Anwar", *Free Malaysia Today*, 4 October 2019, https://www.freemalaysiatoday.com/category/nation/2019/10/04/dr-m-doing-what-he-can-to-fulfil-ph-manifesto-says-anwar/.
8. "No Two-Year Timeline for Malaysian PM Succession Plan: Mukhriz Mahathir", *CAN Online*, 12 July 2019, https://www.channelnewsasia.com/news/asia/no-two-year-timeline-for-mahathir-succession-anwar-mukhriz-11715378.
9. "Dr M Won't Stay as Malaysian PM 'beyond Three Years': Report, *Today World*, 24 June 2019, https://www.todayonline.com/world/dr-m-wont-stay-malaysian-pm-beyond-three-years-report.
10. Jessica Lin, "Mahathir Tells FT There are No Plans to Step Down in 2020 – and Admits he May Be the Best Person to Run Malaysia Right Now", *Business Insider*,

6 November 2019, https://www.businessinsider.sg/mahathir-tells-ft-there-are-no-plans-to-step-down-in-2020-and-admits-he-may-be-the-best-person-to-run-malaysia-right-now/.
11. "Anwar Says 'Traitors' Trying to Keep Him from Being Malaysia's Next Prime Minister", *Straits Times*, 29 October 2019, https://www.straitstimes.com/asia/se-asia/anwar-says-traitors-trying-to-keep-him-from-being-malaysias-next-prime-minister.
12. Zanariah Abd Mutalib, "Dr M Cycles around Putrajaya Lake on Tandem Bike", *New Straits Times*, 6 January 2019, https://www.nst.com.my/news/nation/2019/01/447624/dr-m-cycles-around-putrajaya-lake-tandem-bike.
13. "Anwar Says 'Traitors' Trying to Keep Him".
14. Bhavan Jaipragas, "'Tell Him to Look in the Mirror': Malaysia's Anwar Ibrahim and Azmin Ali Trade Barbs as Sex Video Scandal Escalates", *South China Morning Post*, 17 July 2019, https://www.scmp.com/week-asia/politics/article/3018944/anwar-ibrahims-top-aide-detained-malaysian-police-sex-video.
15. FMT Reporters, "For PKR, Power Divides and Unites", *Free Malaysia Today*, 17 July 2019, https://www.freemalaysiatoday.com/category/nation/2019/07/17/for-pkr-power-divides-and-unites/.
16. Ooi Kok Hin, "Messy is the New Order: Succession Time in Malaysia", *The Interpreter*, 29 October 2019, https://www.lowyinstitute.org/the-interpreter/messy-new-order-succession-time-malaysia?fbclid=IwAR2p9bvy-N7asC-qObcXeZFscTnoOpLQHH-pCBLjoZH0Tzc3pZFG8N313TI.
17. "KOk: Pakatan Vote-Buying ahead of Tanjung Piai By-election? I'm Disappointed with Such Accusations", *Malay Mail*, 26 October 2019, https://sg.news.yahoo.com/kok-pakatan-vote-buying-ahead-094333546.html.
18. https://twitter.com/limkitsiang/status/1195871399061012480.
19. https://twitter.com/AzminAli/status/1196266200562487296.
20. Terence Gomez, T. Padmanabhan, N. Kamaruddin, S. Bhalla, and F. Fisal, *Minister of Finance Incorporated: Ownership and Control of Corporate Malaysia* (IDEAS, 2018).
21. Nicholas Chung, "Corporate Sector, Big Business in Mahathir's Grip, Says Economist", *Free Malaysia Today*, 30 October 2019, https://www.freemalaysiatoday.com/category/nation/2019/10/30/corporate-sector-big-business-in-mahathirs-grip-says-economist/.
22. Nicholas Chung, "PH Never Promised to End Political Appointments, Says Deputy Minister", 31 October 2019, https://www.freemalaysiatoday.com/category/nation/2019/10/31/ph-never-promised-to-end-political-appointments-says-deputy-minister/.
23. "Utusan Officially Closes its Doors", *New Straits Times*, 9 October 2019, https://www.nst.com.my/news/nation/2019/10/528302/utusan-officially-closes-its-doors.
24. https://www.newmandala.org/qa-khairy-jamaluddin/.
25. Radzi Razak, "PAS Says No Room for Umno in Kelantan, Terengganu Governments,

Malay Mail, 29 October 2019, https://sg.news.yahoo.com/pas-says-no-room-umno-070607079.html.

26. "Malaysia is for Malays? Mahathir Says He Didn't Hear That at Congress", *Malaysiakini*, 6 October 2019, https://www.malaysiakini.com/news/494676.
27. Yuen Meikeng, "Budget 2020: Jakim Welcomes Increase in Allocations for Islamic Affairs", *Star Online*, 11 October 2019, https://www.thestar.com.my/news/nation/2019/10/11/budget-2020-jakim-welcomes-increase-in-allocations-for-islamic-affairs.
28. "Full Budget 2020 Speech", *The Edge Markets*, 11 October 2019, https://www.theedgemarkets.com/article/full-budget-2020-speech.
29. "Malaysian PM Mahathir Sparks Controversy over Anti-Semitic Remarks at Cambridge University", CNA, 18 June 2019, https://www.channelnewsasia.com/news/asia/malaysia-mahathir-anti-semitic-controversy-cambridge-union-11638054.
30. Bernama, "Dr Mahathir Defends Palm Oil in UN Address", *The Star*, 28 September 2019, https://www.thestar.com.my/news/nation/2019/09/28/dr-mahathir-defends-palm-oil-in-un-address.
31. Shannon Teoh, "Mahathir Says It's up to Malays to Reclaim Their Dignity by Grasping Opportunities", *Straits Times*, 6 October 2019, https://www.straitstimes.com/asia/se-asia/mahathir-says-its-up-to-malays-to-reclaim-their-dignity-by-grasping-opportunities.
32. KiniTV, "I Will Work Together with My Friends to Rebuild Malaysia, Says Mahathir in Emotional Video", *Youtube*, 29 April 2018, https://www.youtube.com/watch?v=XzXWBLDstJw.
33. Kai Ostwald, "Four Arenas: Malaysia's 2018 Election, Reform, and Democratization", paper presented at the ISEAS – Yusof Ishak Institute, Singapore, 15 August 2019.
34. Barbara and Leonard Andaya, *A History of Malaysia*, 3rd ed. (Palgrave Macmillan, 2017), p. 295.
35. James Chin, "GE14 in East Malaysia: MA63 and Marching to a Different Drum", in *Southeast Asian Affairs 2019*, edited by Daljit Singh and Malcolm Cook, pp. 211–21 (Singapore: ISEAS – Yusof Ishak Institute, 2019).
36. Muguntan Vanar, "Bill to Amend Constitution to Make Sabah, Sarawak as Equal Partners Merely 'Cosmetic' Says Activist", *The Star*, 4 April 2019, https://www.thestar.com.my/news/nation/2019/04/04/bill-to-amend-constitution-to-make-sabah-sarawak-equal-partners-merely-cosmetic/.
37. Minderjeet Kaur, "Sabah, Sarawak MPs Clash with Speaker over Bill to Amend Constitution", *Free Malaysia Today*, 4 April 2019, https://www.freemalaysiatoday.com/category/nation/2019/04/04/sabah-sarawak-mps-clash-with-speaker-over-bill-to-amend-constitution/; MT Webmaster, "Sarawak MP Tells Why Constitutional Amendment Bill Failed", *Malaysia Today*, 10 April 2019, https://www.malaysia-today.net/2019/04/10/sarawak-mp-tells-why-constitutional-amendment-bill-failed/.
38. Muguntan Vanar, "Fulfil MA63 Vows, Pakatan Told", *The Star*, 17 September 2019,

https://www.thestar.com.my/news/nation/2018/09/17/fulfil-ma63-vows-pakatan-told-liow-deliver-manifesto-promises-to-sabah-sarawak-now.

39. Avila Geraldine, "Sabah Stands Firm on 20 Per Cent Oil Royalty", *New Straits Times*, 28 September 2019, https://www.nst.com.my/news/nation/2019/09/525367/sabah-stands-firm-20-cent-oil-royalty.

40. Larissa Lumandan, "Appointing MPKK Community Leaders Part of Political Colonisation of Sarawak", *Free Malaysia Today*, 23 October 2019, https://www.freemalaysiatoday.com/category/nation/2019/10/23/appointing-mpkk-community-leaders-part-of-political-colonisation-of-sarawak/.

41. Interview with political analyst, Kuching, 12 November 2019.

42. Julia Chan, "PBS Slams Sabah Government for U-turn on Dam and Beachfront Projects", *Malay Mail*, 27 June 2019, https://www.malaymail.com/news/malaysia/2019/06/27/pbs-slams-sabah-government-for-u-turn-on-dam-and-beachfront-projects/1766153.

43. Freedom House Malaysia Report 2019, https://freedomhouse.org/report/freedom-world/2019/malaysia.

MALAYSIA AND THE PURSUIT OF SUSTAINABILITY

Serina Rahman

In the build-up to Malaysia's 14th General Elections (GE14), the then-opposition Pakatan Harapan (PH) coalition campaigned on multiple reform platforms—including that of sustainability and inclusivity. *Buku Harapan* (The Book of Hope), the coalition's much-lauded manifesto, was written to encapsulate the grievances of an electorate hankering for change (with a little less regard to the practicality of the promises within), and it had all the right sustainability targets. The publication won praise from non-governmental organizations (NGOs), with a coalition of twenty NGOs releasing the results of a survey indicating that 69 per cent of those who intended to vote considered the environment a factor in their choice of government.[1]

The Promise

The PH coalition promised to govern "based on principles of sustainability and sustainable development", pledging that development projects would comply with international environmental protection standards, that logging quotas would be strictly enforced and that a PH government would support the United Nation's Sustainable Development Goals (UN SDGs). The coalition also vowed it would focus on the development of green technology and renewable energy, and that it would set up a "National Coordination Council for Climate Adaptation and Mitigation". Promise 39 of the *Buku Harapan* declared that a PH government would be "an environmentally friendly government". For the indigenous peoples of

---

SERINA RAHMAN is Visiting Fellow at the ISEAS – Yusof Ishak Institute, Singapore, where her research includes sustainable development, rural politics, political ecology, and women and radicalization.

Malaysia, whose lives, identities and livelihoods depend entirely on the preservation of natural habitats, the manifesto's Promise 38 was an assurance that the coalition would advance "the interests of Orang Asal in Peninsular Malaysia" and "recognise, uphold and protect the dignity and rights" of the indigenous people.[2]

The Action

Immediately after the wholly unexpected outcome of the elections, media announcements designed to demonstrate the new regime's commitment to environmental and indigenous causes came thick and fast. A new Ministry of Energy, Science, Technology, Environment and Climate Change (MESTECC) was established. The MESTECC minister Yeo Bee Yin announced in September 2018 that a 20 per cent renewable energy production target would be achieved by 2030.[3] In October she launched the Roadmap towards Zero Single-Use Plastic 2018–2030, declaring that Malaysia will have done away with single-use plastics by 2030.[4] In January 2019 the federal government announced it would file a civil suit against the Kelantan state government because of its failure "to protect and preserve the welfare of the Temiar Orang Asli".[5] This was in response to the state's deliberate refusal to recognize their native land rights in Pos Simpor, having instead distributed logging and mining rights to private entities.

In March 2019, Minister Yeo Bee Yin declared that the federal government would no longer consider approvals for environmental impact assessments (EIAs) on Ramsar sites, in line with Prime Minister Mahathir Mohamed's GE14 campaign against the Forest City developments in Johor.[6] Ramsar sites are wetland areas recognized as having international importance under the Ramsar Convention, an intergovernmental environmental treaty established by UNESCO in 1975; Malaysia has seven of these sites. In the same month, following the minister's October 2018 announcement of renewable energy targets, the Sustainable Energy Development Authority (SEDA) published the Renewable Energy Transition Roadmap 2035, which aims to balance environmental targets, affordability, economic benefits and system stability. The outcome of the roadmap will be part of the 12th Malaysia Plan (2021–2025). SEDA also announced the Supply Agreement for Renewable Energy programme, which allows consumers to lease and install solar panels at no upfront cost in an effort to make renewable energy accessible to the general public.[7]

In the following month, the minister of the Water, Land and Natural Resources Ministry (KATS), Dr Xavier Jayakumar, declared that the Wildlife Conservation Act 2010 would be amended to enforce a minimum penalty of RM1 million and five years in jail for poaching. He declared his intention to get "2000 boots on the ground" through collaboration between the Wildlife Department, the Johor National Park Corporation, Perak State Park, the police and the army. He also indicated he wanted to implement a shoot-on-sight policy, similar to the one in India.[8] The Johor sultan echoed his call, declaring that wildlife poachers and hunters, whether local, foreign or Orang Asli, would be hunted "if they illegally hunt tigers". This was in response to the sighting of four tigers in Kota Tinggi, Johor, two of which were albino cubs.[9]

In May 2019, Minister Yeo Bee Yin took questions from the press in front of shipping containers of plastic waste from the United Kingdom that were about to be returned to the country. This was the result of Malaysia's success in 2018 at amending a clause in the Basel Convention to require the recipient country to approve the import of plastic waste. She criticized the "recycling myth" of developed nations and encouraged state governments to enforce the National Land Code against landowners that allowed illegal plastic recycling factories on their properties.[10] In the same month, she launched the Climate Governance Initiative – Malaysian Chapter at the Securities Commission, a project hosted by the World Economic Forum that provides oversight and assists businesses with the long-term risks of climate change.[11] This is intended to translate sustainability requirements and reporting from mere talk of compliance to "built in" action embedded within the companies' psyches.[12] These efforts are in line with the earlier announcement of a green financing roadmap to support the many MESTECC initiatives in motion, including energy research and development, tenders for solar energy generation, a Climate Change Centre and exploring ways to create wealth through science and technology.[13]

The Ministry of Primary Industry, helmed by Minister Theresa Kok, is the third ministry with some purview over environmental issues, in particular agriculture. In July 2019 she announced that the PH government would maintain the previous government's goal of achieving Malaysian Sustainable Palm Oil (MSPO) certification for all oil palm plantations in the country. This declaration was followed up with a reminder in November 2019 that growers' licences would be revoked if they were not certified by the end of the year.[14]

The 10th International Greentech & Eco Products Exhibition & Conference Malaysia (IGEM 2019) in October 2019 and the Malaysia SDG Summit 2019 in November closed the year with further demonstrations of Malaysia's commitments to the environment. Both events were inaugurated by the prime minister. At IGEM 2019, he stated that Malaysia is a "longstanding proponent of balancing environmental conservation, technological innovation and economic prosperity

... [that is] underpinned by a dynamic innovative ecosystem and affirmative institutional support".[15] At the SDG Summit, he reiterated that sustainability and inclusivity are hallmarks of Malaysia's development and he spoke of how the new Shared Prosperity Vision (SPV 2030) would continue this policy with roadmaps underpinned by sustainable development.[16] At both events, he emphasized Malaysia's commitment to achieving the SDG goals, "including ending poverty, improving global health, ensuring universal education and mitigating climate change". At the IGEM, Minister Yeo Bee Yin again announced a raft of new initiatives and programmes, such as the green tariff and the Malaysian Green Attribute Tracking System, to encourage green investments.

The Reality

All in all, then, it looks like the new PH government is truly achieving its sustainability targets and has taken concrete steps to walk the talk. However, tiny details from the ground have prompted some questions.

Renewable Energy

While the renewable energy goals are commendable and while several other initiatives, plans and policies have been launched in support of this initiative, Minister Yeo Bee Yin conceded that Malaysia would need RM33 billion worth of investments for the plan to work. The government is relying on private-public partnerships and private financing to supplement government expenditure in renewable energy. Although solar has been advanced as the main component of this renewable energy plan, the minister has also admitted that because solar is intermittent it might be necessary to depend on solar energy only in the day and to rely on gas at night. Discussions with energy experts and strategists have also revealed that the costs of renewable energy may derail these plans, especially given the difficulties of bringing solar energy to rural areas. Hydropower from large dams is not included in the renewable energy plans as it has well-documented drawbacks, ranging from environmental damage, community displacement and loss of ancestral lands.[17]

The Loss of Indigenous Lands and Lives

While the announcement of the suit against the Kelantan state government for its neglect of the Orang Asli and its misappropriation of native lands elicited whoops of joy from those affected by or fighting for the Orang Asli cause, the celebrations were short-lived. One month after the National Orang Asli Convention was graced by the prime minister—during which 136 resolutions to improve the lives of the community, especially on issues related to land, education, health, the economy, leadership, infrastructure and culture were declared—threats to the lives and lands of the Orang Asli in Kampung Cunex, Perak arose.[18] A wooden blockade was built by the indigenous people of this village to prevent loggers from removing timber from their customary lands. This blockade was dismantled with the support of Perak's chief minister, and no charges were made against the individuals who had threatened the indigenous people in the process. These actions seem designed to "silence and intimidate" both the indigenous communities and their advocates who are seeking to peacefully protect indigenous land. These developments are not unique to the current regime. In 2016, Bill Kayong, a vocal advocate for indigenous rights in Sarawak, was shot dead as he rode to work; the attacker has been charged with murder but no charges have yet been filed against the individuals who ordered the killing.[19]

More than 50 per cent of Peninsular Malaysia's Orang Asli population of 217,000 are categorized as poor, with an additional 33 per cent suffering from hard-core poverty.[20] In comparison, the national average rate of hard-core poverty is 0.7 per cent. Destruction of indigenous land results in the complete annihilation of livelihoods, identities and lives; environmental damage can mean the end of an indigenous community. Even if the federal government intended to help these marginalized citizens, the overlaps in ministerial jurisdiction over environmental affairs make the endeavour difficult. Beyond the fact that there are three federal ministries with oversight of matters related to the environment, as previously discussed, there is also the added complication of the Ninth Schedule in the Federal Constitution, which determines that state governments have the right to legislate, govern and rule over matters related to land (and mining), agriculture and forests. As such, the state (and not the federal government) has the final say.[21] Some researchers have noted that federal economic policies are also partially to blame for the misuse of land by state governments; when the states are cash-strapped, they have no choice but to make use of their best available resource to generate income. In the case of Kelantan and East Malaysia, this has historically resulted in the distribution of land titles and plantation or mining licences.[22] For instance, the Kelantan's People's Farm programme, launched in 2006, set aside 600,000 hectares of forest reserve (including native customary lands) for monoculture plantations.[23]

Reports of mysterious deaths among the nomadic Batek tribe in Kuala Koh of Kelantan emerged in June 2019, revealing that not only were their lands razed for oil palm and logging but also that nearby mining (all approved by the state government) had resulted in manganese pollution of their only water source. However, the federal government announced that measles was the cause of the deaths, while Deputy Prime Minister Wan Azizah declared that the water supply in Kuala Koh, especially near the Batek village, had been tested and found to be normal, meeting all national drinking water specifications for a raw water source. This finding was disputed by the Federation of Private Medical Practitioners Association of Malaysia, whose independent study of the issue noted that, with no piped water available to the community, the Batek's only source of water from nearby rivers and streams contained twenty-five times the accepted amount of manganese, as well as faecal content.[24]

Colin Nicholas, the director of the Centre for Orang Asli Concerns, explained the circumstances confronting the Batek; after a forest is cut down, first comes plantations, and then mining. The indigenous people are left in poverty and stripped of their means of survival, and thereafter they become susceptible to deadly illnesses: "without an intact resource base for their subsistence needs, without the ability to practise their traditional way of life, without full control of their lives, they became malnourished, underweight, and depressive. And their body resistance dropped."[25] Upon the destruction of their homes in the forest, indigenous tribes are also sometimes "rehomed" in isolated concrete houses located far from towns or jungle, often with no running water, electricity or even a paved road.[26] In the case of the Batek, the final affront was the reburial of their dead according to Islamic rights, which was done after the bodies were exhumed from their traditional graves in order to determine the cause of death.[27] Lim Teck Wyn, technical director of Resource Stewardship Consultants, refers to this as "structural genocide".[28]

In the case of oil palm, plantations have been found to encroach on areas gazetted as indigenous lands or national parks. In the absence of a clear buffer zone, fringe areas adjacent to plantations can suffer from collateral damage. Because "forest reserves" are defined by the United Nations to include monoculture,[29] a country can still fulfil its declared SDGs by labelling a plantation with a crop of trees of the same age and species as a "forest", even if that plantation replaced a richly biodiverse primary (or secondary) jungle full of wildlife. Beyond logging and oil palm plantations, there are also new threats; as in the case of the Batek, the Orang Asli will suffer as a result of new plans for Malaysia to become the Asian centre of manganese mining and production.[30] The recent trend of meeting China's demand for durians has also impacted Malaysia's forest reserves and indigenous lands. Malaysia currently aims to export 8,000 tonnes of durians to

China annually. In pursuit of this lucrative US$111.6 million trade, the Kelantan state government has already approved the use of 10,000 acres of forested land in Gua Musang for the farming of *Musang King* durians. Peaceful blockades by the Orang Asli to prevent the encroachment of their lands was met with physical intimidation and violence; one particular businessman has filed a suit against the Orang Asli for millions of ringgit, claiming this was the amount he lost from not being able to cultivate and export durians.[31]

The Case of Lynas

Prior to the 13th and the 14th General Elections, a few of the current PH politicians were on the ground in Gebeng, Pahang together with non-governmental activists campaigning to shut down the Lynas Advanced Materials Plant, a rare-earth refinery under the control of the Australian rare-earth mining company, Lynas Corporation.[32] A 2013 report by the Malaysian Physicians for Peace and Social Responsibility highlighted the potential health risks posed by the Lynas refinery by drawing a parallel to the Asian Rare Earth (ARE) refinery by Mitsubishi Chemical in Bukit Merah and Papan, Perak that was forced to shut down in 1992. In the Bukit Merah case, there were eight leukaemia cases amongst workers and members of the surrounding community: seven of these were fatal. There were also several recorded cases of birth defects related to radioactive poisoning from the refinery. The out-of-court settlement and the costs of the subsequent clean-up came to US$10 million.[33]

However, with PH now in power, Malaysia renewed its deal with Lynas subject to a number of conditions, including finding an appropriate site and getting approval for a permanent deposit facility (PDF) for water leach purification residue and stopping all research related to the use of that radioactive residue in agriculture. Concerns regarding the safety of the PDF and possible health impacts on workers and the surrounding community were inadequately addressed. Instead, the government pointed out that Malaysia stands to benefit from the US-China trade war as the United States seeks alternative sources of rare-earth elements. The Lynas plant is the largest rare-earth producer outside of China. The prime minister has noted that the plant provides seven hundred high-quality and high-paying jobs and that the renewal of the licence was important for investments into Malaysia.[34] Other media reports have captured the sense of "relief" among local residents that around a thousand jobs at the plant would be preserved. Some residents have expressed confidence that the plant runs "in a safe and orderly manner", stating that while they are aware of possible health risks from rare-earth manufacturing, there has been no instances of anyone falling ill as a result of the plant over the past seven years.[35] Even more recently, the Perak state government has signed a memorandum of understanding with China's Chinalco GXNF Rare Earth Development company to explore the possibility of mining rare earth minerals in Perak, thirty years after the ARE refinery disaster. This venture has received the approval of the KATS ministry.[36]

Development Approvals

In arguing against the Forest City developments in southwest Johor, PH politicians and environmentalists cited the damage caused to critical wetland habitats (mangroves and seagrass) from the construction of a golf resort and the reclamation of several islands for mixed development. These were examples given by Mahathir during the GE14 campaign in accusations that UMNO had failed to protect the environment and livelihoods of local fishermen. There were also claims that Malaysia's national sovereignty was being undermined as the properties in Forest City were sold under freehold terms.

However, just a little over a year after GE14, the chief minister of Penang announced that the federal government has approved the Penang South Reclamation project. This development entails the reclamation of three artificial islands totalling 1821.1 hectares of new land off Penang Island's southern coast. A revised EIA was accepted by the Department of the Environment with seventy-two conditions.[37]

While the chief minister insists that reclamation will not start until the conditions are met, and has argued that the project was necessary to fund the RM46 billion (about US$11 billion) Penang Transport Master Plan,[38] environmentalists have drawn parallels between this Penang project and the Forest City developments in Johor. The Penang reclamation would similarly impact seagrass beds—which serve as nursery grounds for fisheries species—and would smother substantial fishing grounds around the island. Several academic and NGO publications have flagged the environmental, biological, socio-economic and physical impacts on land, sea and society caused by such large-scale reclamation. A study of similar seagrass ecosystems in southwest Johor calculated that an economic loss of US$57,731.80 is sustained for every hectare of seagrass damaged per year.[39] This conservative estimate does not yet take into account the economic value of fish catch to Penang fishermen or coastal habitat damage to the mangroves, mudflats and shoreline as a result of the planned reclamation.

While the Penang reclamation project is the outcome of a long-brewing plan by the Democratic Action Party state government, which has been in power since 2008, the return of Mahathir Mohamad as prime minister spells uncertainty given his historical preference for physical infrastructure over environmental conservation. Recognized as *Bapa Pembangunan* (the Father of Development), his first stint as prime minister was marked by the clearing of almost five million hectares of forests and the extensive physical change of previously undisturbed natural habitats in the name of modernization and infrastructural advancement.[40] The New Economic Policy also created a cohort of new *bumiputra* elites whose corporate ventures sometimes came at the expense of local community land and traditional livelihoods, particularly if those communities were dependent upon the natural habitats that were forsaken for physical development. The combination of these factors quickly took Malaysia to "little tiger" status at the time, but it also entrenched vertical inequalities and huge divisions between rich and poor across all ethnicities, which are further aggravated when the poor are displaced from traditional habitat-based livelihoods.[41]

Yet another undertaking that emerged soon after the new government came into power was the swift cabinet approval of a new airport on Tioman Island. This was a project backed by a large private developer that had been rejected in 2009 by the then-transport minister Ong Tee Keat. The project is expected to involve substantial coastal reclamation and damage to the natural habitat. The cost of the damage is estimated to be at least US$15.66 million per year because of losses in ecosystem services and US$1.13 billion from biodiversity loss. Construction of the airport may lead to an increase in the island's water and electricity shortages and aggravate waste and sewage issues, which potentially could reduce tourism revenue in the long run.[42] Authentic sustainable development entails the consideration of both environmental concerns and social inclusivity; the Tioman airport project is yet another example of the exact opposite.

Beyond the Plastic Roadmap

While the initiative to eliminate single-use plastics is a commendable effort, there are several obstacles that could stand in its way. Malaysia is the world's eighth largest producer of mismanaged waste, generating 1.52 kilogrammes of waste per person per day, amounting to 0.94 million tonnes of waste per year. Of this waste, 2.9 per cent is mismanaged plastic waste, meaning that it does not go into a proper waste receptacle or is not properly disposed of or processed; the waste will most likely end up in a drain, river or the sea as marine debris. In 2018 Malaysians (overall) produced 236,000 tonnes of waste per month on average, of which only 0.06 per cent was recycled. An average of 300 plastic bags are thrown away per person every year. Penang, Selangor and Kedah have initiated plastic bag bans on specific days of the week, while in Selangor straws are only distributed to those with a disability or who are unwell, but there is still much to be done.[43]

Progress on this front revolves around public education and in instilling understanding in children (in schools) and adults (especially at home), not only by providing education on the proper ways of recycling and disposing rubbish but also in encouraging less consumption. The days of repairing products for reuse disappeared with the rise of the middle class and the ease of disposable goods. This alone has had a tremendous impact on the environment. Malaysia's economic ties to plastic production must also be noted: it is a global player in the plastic industry and is home to 1,300 plastic manufacturers. In 2016, plastic exports amounted to RM30 billion (US$7.18 billion)—a substantial contribution to the national economy. Yeo Bee Yin's plans to build a circular economy for plastic manufacturers will need to be realized to reduce the negative impacts of this industry.[44]

Palm Oil, Wildlife and Haze

Palm oil has always been the bogeyman of the Malaysian agricultural industry. As the second-largest producer of palm oil in the world, Malaysia has been the target of European Union boycotts and myriad other international anti–palm oil campaigns. The new federal government has set a limit to the nation's oil palm estates at 6 million hectares (a 2.5 per cent increase from the industry's current acreage). But with current rates of forest loss and with minimal enforcement, it remains to be seen whether this ruling will have any impact, especially as state governments have the final say on land-use allocation.[45] Orangutans are emblematic of the campaigns against palm oil, a charismatic species used to highlight the industry's destruction of their forest habitats. A 2019 study by the World Wide Fund for Nature–Malaysia (WWF-Malaysia) revealed that while large orangutan population groups in Sabah are stable, especially within logged or unlogged managed forests, fragmented populations in areas surrounded by oil palm plantations are on the decline. The study also showed that there are more orangutans than previously documented, as a result of improvements in survey techniques.[46] Unfortunately, four pygmy elephants were found dead around oil palm estates in Sabah in 2019, one riddled with gunshot wounds and at least two with their tusks sawn off.[47] While elephant-human conflicts are not uncommon around oil palm estates or smallholdings, this was the worst in a series of incidents to have arisen in the state.

The goal to enforce 100 per cent MSPO certification has also faced countless problems. Even as the ministry battled wave after wave of negative publicity—including the allegation that four companies certified by the Malaysian RSPO (Roundtable for Sustainable Palm Oil) were responsible for transboundary haze[48]—it eventually had to admit that the 100 per cent goal was unattainable. By October 2019 only 60 per cent of oil palm planted areas had attained MSPO certification. Minister Theresa Kok was forced to both reduce and extend the goal; the government now targets 70 per cent MSPO certification by February 2020.[49] Smallholders, especially the indigenous people of the Peninsula and East Malaysian natives, have had many difficulties in providing the Malaysian Palm Oil Board the land title documents needed for MSPO certification. Minister Kok has clarified that these individuals only need to produce the land title to get the MSPO certification, while reassuring them that their licences would not be revoked as long as their smallholding remains below 100 acres.[50] Notwithstanding the need to protect community livelihoods, there is then the question of how stringent the regulations are in ensuring quality standards.

Climate Change

The inclusion of climate change under MESTECC's ambit is an indication of how far the nation has come in putting environmental problems up front and centre. Minister Yeo Bee Yin's nonstop announcements of new programmes and initiatives signal her ministry's attempts to fulfil PH promises. A Climate Change Act is to be tabled in parliament by 2023, but the ministry is only examining comprehensive risk scenarios that come with a rise in temperature by 2 degrees Celsius above pre-industrial levels. The stipulated benchmark necessary to avert climate disaster is a rise of 1.5 degrees Celsius; the ministry's modelling, which anticipates a higher rise in temperature, indicates that the government is not prepared to make the necessary economic and developmental sacrifices to meet this benchmark. MESTECC's efforts at pursuing sustainability and managing climate change is seemingly hampered by the fact that Malaysia continues to insist on the right of developing nations to exploit natural resources, given the failure of developed nations to pay their dues in the fight against climate change; the prioritizing of resource extraction and use over environmental conservation in the KATS and Primary Industries ministries; and Mahathir's legacy of choosing economic growth over environmental concerns.[51]

Much of climate change research in Malaysia is focussed on examining its impacts on agriculture given the industry's major contribution to the national GDP. Palm oil is the industry's largest sector, with rice paddy in second place. While agriculture is highly dependent on climatic factors, palm oil is seen as contributing to climate change because of its record of deforestation and cultivation on carbon-dense ecosystems such as peat swamps. Some researchers report, however, that while conversion of peatlands is a serious problem, the palm oil sector is not solely responsible for deforestation, especially before 1985.[52]

Figures from 2014 show that Malaysia is ranked third in the region in terms of per capita carbon dioxide emissions (8 tonnes). Brunei and Singapore, respectively, ranked higher. Malaysia's energy industry is responsible for most of the emissions (76 per cent), followed by waste disposal (12 per cent) and industry (6 per cent). The agriculture industry contributes 5 per cent of total carbon emissions. Calculations in 2011 reveal that forestlands are significant carbon sinks, removing 85 per cent of greenhouse gases (GHGs) generated, while croplands remove only 5.3 per cent of GHGs.[53] While there are clear efforts towards mitigating climate change, researchers note that more work needs to go into the protection of terrestrial, freshwater and, especially, coastal marine habitats. Sustainable agricultural policies also need to be put into place, with more public education (especially of farmers and fishermen) about disaster management and the connection between their broad environmental understanding and climate change.

A study by the Centre for Governance and Political Studies projected that Muar, Pekan, Bagan Datoh, Teluk Intan and Kuala Selangor will be severely affected by the rise in sea levels by 2050, with Alor Setar expected to become an island. The KATS ministry has responded by dismissing these calculations as an overestimation.[54] The government needs to be cognisant, however, of the potential health problems that can arise as a result of extreme weather conditions precipitated by climate change. These include the spread of climate sensitive diseases endemic to Malaysia such as cholera, malaria, meningococcal meningitis, dengue, Japanese encephalitis, leptospirosis and rickettsial infections.[55] Care for the environment and the mitigation of climate change are undoubtedly intertwined with human health and well-being.

Attaining the SDGs

The United Nations 2030 Agenda for Sustainable Development effectively illustrated how true sustainability cannot be achieved without an equal focus on both the environment and inclusivity, which will then balance economic considerations. This chapter has shown that for many communities, human survival and livelihoods are often mutually dependent on the health of land, forests and seas. While Malaysia's new PH government has taken many positive steps towards improving its concern and action for the environment, there have been many occasions over the past year in which little connection has been made between preservation of natural habitats or climate change mitigation and the marginalized communities' right to good health, pristine environments and physical, mental and spiritual well-being. The final section of this paper will examine ways in which authentic sustainability might be achieved.

The Way Forward
Involving Local Communities

Long before the UN SDGs were launched and ratified, Local Agenda 21 (LA21) was introduced across the world. First announced in Malaysia in 1999, LA21 is meant to encourage public participation in attaining sustainable development through a programme that forges partnerships between local authorities (town, city and municipal councils) and local communities.[56] Involving the local community in planning, decision-making and implementation of the UN SDGs follows the ground-up approach of LA21, which is meant to empower a community to make a real contribution to a country's achievement of its SDG targets.[57]

Since GE14, the voice of civil society has become a force to be reckoned with. In the fields of environmental sustainability and community inclusivity, there are countless NGOs working on myriad issues. However, not all NGOs have authentic engagement and experience on the ground; those who do are usually less capable of promoting their successes, or do not have time to work on self-promotion. In order to effectively harness these forces for good, it is important to identify genuine entities and to support them in their work.[58] Collaborations with sincere organizations that have the right objectives and are actually engaged on the ground can go a long way to attaining both LA21 goals and the SDGs. Community empowerment has been proven to enable people to shape and improve their own lives and neighbourhoods, as they know best how to engage their communities to make a difference and alleviate poverty.[59]

In the southwest of Johor, a community organization that trains youth as citizen scientists to document and monitor natural habitats has been recognized by local developers, local and municipal councils and the state government as local habitat experts. As pilot partners in the Iskandar Regional Development Authority's (IRDA) multi-stakeholder coastal documentation and monitoring programme (PESISIR), the organization has also been appointed as ecological experts by the state education department. All schools in Johor are to visit the area to learn about

Johor's unique marine habitats from these youths as part of an enhancement of the state's primary and secondary school syllabus. The organization is working with the Johor Port Authority and the Port of Tanjung Pelepas to map coastal mangrove habitats in order to determine vital areas that should not be disturbed by the port's expansion plans. They are also working with other large developers in the area to devise a collaborative community-private habitat conservation and management plan.[60] This is a model of an authentic and community-grounded approach that can be adapted and applied to the many other biodiverse areas of Malaysia that are facing similar development threats.

Education has often been mentioned as necessary for individuals, businesses and even government agencies to better understand the urgent need to act to mitigate climate change and gross environmental destruction. Johor has included issues related to carbon emissions and ecology in its primary and secondary school syllabi. Both these themes have been holistically incorporated, ensuring that environmental empathy and comprehension is present in all aspects of a child's education. The RCE Iskandar (UN Regional Centre of Excellence), with the support of IRDA, has numerous programmes to ensure that schools and students in Johor are active participants in pursuing low-carbon initiatives. The programme has also since been expanded to encourage similar initiatives by local councils.[61]

Changing the Patterns of Agriculture

One way to reduce global carbon emissions is to plant trees. While the biodiversity and carbon-sequestration capacities of primary and secondary forests are undoubtedly more beneficial to the planet than monocultures, the latter remains a far better option for the environment than acres upon acres of carbon-emitting manufacturing or chemical processing factories. It is also possible to ensure economic progress and sustainability in agriculture through multiple or inter-cropping, organic treatments and ensuring that seeds and saplings are locally sourced and not genetically modified. A recent study showed that transforming the land sector by implementing more sustainable measures in agriculture, forestry, wetlands and bioenergy can contribute to 30 per cent of the global mitigation of carbon emissions needed by 2050.[62]

Johor's independent oil palm smallholders are an example of an industry that grew out of converted farmland, hence producing low-risk, "no deforestation" palm oil that can meet sustainability certification standards.[63] Smallholder rubber plantations, for example, have historically combined their crops with other low-canopy produce such as vegetables. Johor's state investment corporation has also expressed an interest in moving agriculture towards coconut farming, which has multiple uses and benefits. These are examples that can be adopted and adapted by other Malaysian states.

Supporting smallholders goes a long way towards ensuring community and environmental sustainability, especially if farmer cooperatives are created to ensure stable and continuous supplies to the market on the back of international collaboration.[64] The Malaysian government has already launched several initiatives to encourage college graduates to return to agriculture with the use of financial incentives.[65] If these initiatives could be spread to the rural poor, with land set aside on a minimum-cost lease-to-buy scheme, this would also enable the government to demonstrate its commitment to enhancing incomes and nurturing the practical skills of a sizeable voting bloc. Only when farmers are convinced they will have long-term access to and ownership of land will they be willing to convert to organic practices.[66] Government initiatives in this direction will hence have a substantial positive impact on smallholders' sustainability.

Even as Malaysia's palm oil industry tackles myriad challenges, some companies have assumed responsibility to become more environmentally friendly. The Sabahmas Plantation, part of the Wilmar group in Lahad Datu, for example, has its own Wildlife Protection Unit where members of staff are trained under the Wildlife Ranger Programme. Initiated because of the plantation's proximity to the Tabin Wildlife Reserve, fifteen Honorary Wildlife Wardens work to strengthen biodiversity conservation and the prevention of poaching, especially in plantation areas. The wardens also use camera-traps to study and monitor the wildlife that use these riparian corridors.[67]

Improving Environmental Legislation and Enforcement

Since Malaysia is a signatory to the 2002 ASEAN Agreement on Transboundary Haze Pollution, Minister Yeo Bee Yin has mentioned that her ministry will communicate with the ASEAN Secretariat on the need to enforce a uniform transboundary haze law across the region. Some lawyers however believe that Malaysia needs to follow in the footsteps of Singapore in passing domestic legislation that will enable it to take legal action against both domestic and international individuals or companies who add to the haze.[68]

Tackling corruption was a big part of the Pakatan Harapan electoral campaign, with it being mentioned twice in their manifesto and recently affirmed by Mahathir's unilateral appointment of Latheefa Koya as Chief Commissioner of the Malaysian Anti-Corruption Commission (MACC).[69] If true to the ambition, this alone could ensure that developers in Malaysia are not able to bypass environmental regulations with illicit payments. Moreover, it will also guarantee that compensation for communities disrupted by development works reaches the affected individuals rather than being diverted by middlemen and the village hierarchy.[70]

While the Pakatan Harapan government has pledged numerous institutional and policy changes to ensure transparency and integrity, amendments to environmental legislation and regulations are still needed. In response to the incidents of toxic waste in the Johor River around Pasir Gudang, experts have noted that the Environmental Quality Act must be updated to take into account the accumulative contaminant loading of river pollutants. They also advocate for stronger action to be taken by the Department of the Environment (DOE) on errant factory owners, as well as on DOE officers who fail to act upon obvious breaches of the law.[71] The severe pollution events in Pasir Gudang and their effects on many schoolchildren in the area are a clear illustration of how a lack of care in environmental protection and regulation can have tragic consequences on community health and well-being.

Relying on Religious Beliefs on Environmental Sustainability

If all other ways fail, perhaps one solution to advance environmental conservation is through an emphasis on Islamic dictates on sustainability, given increasing conservatism among the Malaysian public. In his analysis of the Islamic perspective on sustainability, Zubair Hasan states:

> The insistence of Shari'ah on preservation of the progeny is intended for ensuring inter-generational equity in the distribution of wealth and prosperity, conservation of resources, and sustenance of the environment, all links in one chain.[72]

> Shari'ah alone provides the natural law for mankind to regulate social behaviour. In a comparative vein, this regulation demands spiritual growth not material, contentment not greed, patience not haste, moderation not maximisation, balance, not tilt, cooperation not competition and spread of equity not corruption in His land. Thus seen, sustainable development essentially poses a moral, ethical, social and political issue. Economists or economics alone cannot resolve it.[73]

WWF-Malaysia has already begun to use this approach to encourage more concern for the environment through collaborations with the Kelantan religious department to feature environmental topics in sermons at mosques. The organization also worked with the Institute of Islamic Understanding Malaysia to produce a handbook entitled *Islam, Wildlife Conservation and You*.[74]

Last Words

Malaysia is a country known for its unrivalled biodiversity and vast natural resources. However, after many decades of mismanagement, rampant exploitation and gross environmental destruction by elites on both sides of the political divide, the Pakatan Harapan government has its work cut out to meet the expectations of an increasingly vocal and highly demanding electorate. While media announcements of new initiatives, programmes and policies for sustainability and sustainable development have been consistently rattled off since GE14, the realities on the ground indicate that there remains a long way to go to achieve the lofty goals set out in its *Buku Harapan*. Not only does sustainability require environmental preservation, but it also entails the protection of marginalized communities, especially those who rely entirely on natural habitats for their survival.

Malaysia's indigenous people, fishermen and rural farmers are in need of more support and care to ensure that they do not completely lose the very ecosystems that keep them alive. Unfortunately, in too many cases, too much has already been lost; from native customary lands in Kelantan to wildlife in Sabah or traditional fishing heritage and livelihoods all around Malaysia. There is an urgent need to act immediately to prevent further damage and loss. Even as it works to improve the nation's economy and attract more foreign investment, Pakatan Harapan has no choice but to fulfil the promises in its manifesto before climate disaster strikes. The federal government will need to find a way to balance environmental priorities with the need to boost a struggling economy—and on top of that, garner the support of the individual states to achieve environmental goals. There are no clear answers and very little hope on the ground, but a way must be found; every tiny step towards inclusivity and sustainability will make a difference.

Notes

1. Refer to A. Sia, "Include Environmental Needs in GE14 Agendas, Politicians Urged", *Star Online*, 11 April 2018, https://www.thestar.com.my/news/nation/2018/04/11/include-environmental-needs-in-ge14-agendas-politicians-urged (accessed 28 November 2019); and M.M. Chu, "Pakatan Manifesto on Environmental Protection More Specific, Say Activists", *Star Online*, 15 April 2018, https://www.thestar.com.my/news/nation/2018/04/15/pakatan-manifesto-on-environmental-protection-more-specific-say-activists (accessed 28 November 2019).

2. Pakatan Harapan, *Buku Harapan – Rebuilding Our Nation, Fulfilling Our Hopes* (Kuala Lumpur: Pakatan Harapan, 2018), https://kempen.s3.amazonaws.com/pdf/Buku_Harapan.pdf (accessed 28 November 2019).
3. N.S. Eusoff, "Malaysia Sets New Goal of 20% Clean Energy Generation by 2030", *The Edge Markets*, 18 September 2018, https://www.theedgemarkets.com/article/malaysia-sets-new-goal-18-clean-energy-generation-2030 (accessed 1 December 2019).
4. L.L. Sim, "M'sia to Do Away with Single-Use Plastics", *Star Online*, 18 October 2018, https://www.thestar.com.my/news/nation/2018/10/18/msia-to-do-away-with-singleuse-plastics-country-set-to-ban-straws-and-carrier-bags-by-2030 (accessed 1 December 2019). For more information on the roadmap, refer to Ministry of Energy, Science, Technology, Environment and Climate Change (MESTECC), "Malaysia's Roadmap towards Zero Single-use Plastics 2018–2030: Towards a Sustainable Future" (Putrajaya, 2018), https://www.mestecc.gov.my/web/wp-content/uploads/2019/03/Malaysia-Roadmap-Towards-Zero-Single-Use-Plastics-2018-20302.pdf (accessed 28 November 2019).
5. "Federal Govt Sues Kelantan", *Star Online*, 19 January 2019, https://www.thestar.com.my/news/nation/2019/01/19/federal-govt-sues-kelantan-legal-action-sought-to-protect-orang-asli-land-rights/ (accessed 28 November 2019).
6. Ramsar sites are wetlands recognized as being of international importance under the Ramsar Convention, an intergovernmental environmental treaty established in 1971 by UNESCO. Malaysia has seven Ramsar sites, including Sungai Pulai, where one of the Forest City developments is located. Refer to "No More Approval for EIAs on Ramsar Sites", Bernama, 28 March 2019, http://www.bernama.com/en/news.php?id=1710169 (accessed 28 November 2019).
7. Suruhan Tenaga, *Energy Malaysia* 18 (2019), https://www.st.gov.my/contents/files/download/112/Energy_Malaysia_18_(Online).pdf (accessed 28 November 2019).
8. M.M. Chu, "We Are Coming for You, Xavier Tells Poachers as Minimum Penalty Set To Be Increased", *Star Online*, 30 April 2019, https://www.thestar.com.my/news/nation/2019/04/30/we-are-coming-for-you-xavier-tells-poachers-as-minimum-penalty-set-to-be-increased (accessed 28 November 2019).
9. "Johor Sultan Warns Poachers They Will Be Hunted Down", *Straits Times*, 27 October 2019.
10. A.F. Othman and S.U. Ariff, "Yeo: Plastic Dumped Here To Be Shipped Back Today", *New Straits Times*, 28 May 2019, https://www.nst.com.my/news/nation/2019/05/491970/yeo-plastic-dumped-here-be-shipped-back-today (accessed 28 November 2019).
11. Institute of Corporate Directors Malaysia, "YB Yeo Bee Yin Launches Malaysian Chapter of Climate Governance Initiative", press release, 2019, https://icdm.com.my/media/yb-yeo-bee-yin-launches-malaysian-chapter-of-climate-governance-initiative (accessed 1 December 2019).
12. J. Cheam, "Sustainability in Malaysia: Bolted On, or Built In?", Eco-Business,

25 January 2017, https://www.eco-business.com/opinion/sustainability-in-malaysia-bolted-on-or-built-in/ (accessed 28 November 2019).
13. L.L. Sim, "Ministry to Take on 80 Initiatives", *Star Online*, 4 May 2019, https://www.thestar.com.my/news/nation/2019/05/04/ministry-to-take-on-80-initiatives (accessed 1 December 2019).
14. Refer to S. Ling, "Govt to Maintain Target of 100% MSPO Certification by Year-End, Says Theresa Kok", *Star Online*, 3 July 2019, https://www.thestar.com.my/news/nation/2019/07/03/govt-to-maintain-target-of-100-mspo-certification-by-year-end-says-teresa-kok (accessed 1 December 2019); and A. Yusof, "Oil Palm Growers' Licences Will Be Revoked If Not MSPO Certified", *New Straits Times*, 19 November 2019, https://www.nst.com.my/business/2019/11/540067/oil-palm-growers-licenses-will-be-revoked-if-not-mspo-certified (accessed 28 November 2019).
15. PR Newswire, "Malaysian Green Technology Corporation Unveils 10th IGEM", 11 October 2019, https://finance.yahoo.com/news/malaysian-green-technology-corporation-unveils-220000646.html (accessed 1 December 2019).
16. Prime Minister's Office of Malaysia, Keynote address by YAB Tun Dr Mahathir bin Mohamad Prime Minister of Malaysia at the Malaysia SDG Summit 2019, Kuala Lumpur Convention Centre (KLCC), Kuala Lumpur, Malaysia, 6 November 2019, https://www.pmo.gov.my/2019/11/malaysia-sdg-summit-2019/ (accessed 1 December 2019).
17. X.Y. Tan, "Malaysia Needs RM33b to Achieve 2025 Green Energy Target", 4 September 2019, *The Edge Financial Daily*, https://www.theedgemarkets.com/article/malaysia-needs-rm33b-achieve-2025-green-energy-target (accessed 28 November 2019). Interviews were held with energy experts and staff of Malaysian energy production corporations between June and November 2019 for a forthcoming production (names withheld at this point).
18. K.H. Ooi, "Poverty, Inequality and the Lack of Basic Rights Experienced by Orang Asli in Malaysia", Malaysian CARE, 2019, https://www.ohchr.org/Documents/Issues/Poverty/VisitsContributions/Malaysia/MalaysiaCare.pdf (accessed 28 November 2019).
19. "Malaysia Has 'Window of Opportunity' on Indigenous Land Rights", Al Jazeera, 30 November 2018, http://aljazeera.com/news/2018/11/malaysia-window-opportunity-indigenous-land-rights-181130071817555.html (accessed 28 November 2019).
20. Ooi, "Poverty, Inequality".
21. S. Rahman, S., "The Struggle for Balance: Johor's Environmental Issues, Overlaps and Future", in *Johor, the Adobe of Development?*, edited by F. Hutchinson and S. Rahman (Singapore: ISEAS – Yusof Ishak Institute, forthcoming 2020).
22. A.A. Bari, "Provisions for Environment and Sustainable Development in the Federal Constitution: A Preliminary Study", in *Land Use Planning and Environmental Sustainability in Malaysia: Policies and Trends*, edited by H.A. Kadouf and S.Z. Al Junid (Kuala Lumpur: International Islamic University Malaysia, 2006), pp. 19–40.

23. H.E. Peterson, "Out of the Jungle and into a Death Trap: The Fate of Malaysia's Last Nomadic People", *The Guardian*, 7 September 2019, https://www.theguardian.com/world/2019/sep/07/from-jungle-to-death-trap-fate-of-malaysia-last-nomads (accessed 28 November 2019).
24. Y. Palansamy, "Medical Group Accuses Govt of Covering Up Batek Tribe Deaths Using Measles Outbreak Reason", *Malay Mail*, 8 September 2019, https://www.malaymail.com/news/malaysia/2019/09/08/medical-group-accuses-govt-of-covering-up-batek-tribe-deaths-using-measles/1788465 (accessed 28 November 2019).
25. C. Humphrey, "Indigenous Communities, Nat'l Parks Suffer as Malaysia Razes its Reserves", *Mongabay*, 23 August 2019, https://news.mongabay.com/2019/08/indigenous-communities-natl-parks-suffer-as-malaysia-razes-its-reserves/ (accessed 28 November 2019).
26. Peterson, "Out of the Jungle".
27. E. Mirante, "Death amid Oil Palms: Malaysia's Batek Orang Asli Health Crisis", *New Mandala*, 24 June 2019, https://www.newmandala.org/death-amid-oil-palms-malaysias-batek-orang-asli-health-crisis/ (accessed 1 November 2019).
28. Humphrey, "Indigenous Communities".
29. Ibid.
30. Peterson, "Out of the Jungle".
31. M. Lakshana, "China's Appetite for Durian Puts Malaysia's Forests under Pressure", China Dialogue, 28 August 2019, https://www.chinadialogue.net/article/show/single/en/11471-China-s-appetite-for-durian-puts-Malaysia-s-forests-under-pressure (accessed 28 November 2019).
32. S.M. Kamal, "A Radioactive Political Football: So What is All the Fuss with Lynas?", *Malay Mail*, 8 July 2019, https://www.malaymail.com/news/malaysia/2019/07/08/a-radioactive-political-football-so-what-is-all-the-fuss-with-lynas/1769221 (accessed 28 Nov 2019).
33. R. McCoy, "Report on Lynas Environmental Hazard", Malaysian Physicians for Peace and Social Responsibility, 2013, http://mpsr.org/wp/2013/03/09/report-on-lynas-environmental-hazard/ (accessed 28 November 2019).
34. T. Sukumaran, "Malaysia Signs New Rare Earths Deal with Australian Miner Lynas Despite Environmental Fears", *South China Morning Post*, 4 November 2019, https://www.scmp.com/news/asia/southeast-asia/article/3036266/malaysia-signs-new-rare-earths-deal-australian-miner-lynas (accessed 28 November 2019).
35. "Residents Optimistic Lynas will Fulfil Govt Conditions", Bernama, 18 August 2019, http://www.bernama.com/state-news/berita.php?id=1758109 (accessed 1 December 2019).
36. J. Bunyan, "After MoU Signed, Green Group Asks Perak Not to Mine Rare Earths", *Malay Mail*, 27 November 2019, https://www.malaymail.com/news/malaysia/2019/11/27/after-mou-signed-green-group-asks-perak-not-to-mine-rare-earths/1813757 (accessed 1 December 2019).

37. M. Li, "Penang Reclamation Stirs Up Controversy", *Dredging and Port Construction*, 8 October 2019, https://dredgingandports.com/news/2019/penang-reclamation-stirs-up-controversy/ (accessed 28 November 2019).
38. O. Mok, "Penang CM: Three-island Reclamation Won't Start before 72 Conditions Met", *Malay Mail*, 5 November 2019, https://www.malaymail.com/news/malaysia/2019/11/05/penang-cm-three-island-reclamation-wont-start-before-72-conditions-met/1806996 (accessed 28 November 2019).
39. S. Rahman and S.M. Yaakub, "Socio-economic Valuation of Seagrass Meadows in the Pulai River Estuary, Peninsular Malaysia, through a Well-being Lens", in *Marine and Freshwater Research* (forthcoming 2020). Also refer to Sahabat Alam Malaysia, *Impacts of Coastal Reclamation in Malaysia* (Penang, 2019); and N. Mohd Nadzir, M. Ibrahim, and M. Mansor, "Impacts of Coastal Reclamation to the Quality of Life: Tanjung Tokong Community, Penang", AMER International Conference on Quality of Life, Sutera Harbour, Kota Kinabalu, Sabah, Malaysia 4–5 January 2014, *Procedia Social and Behavioural Sciences* 153 (2014): 159–68.
40. T. Tang, "Mahathir is Back – Good News or Bad for Sustainability in Malaysia?", *Eco-Business*, 13 May 2018, https://www.eco-business.com/opinion/mahathir-is-backgood-news-or-bad-for-sustainability-in-malaysia/ (accessed 15 October 2019).
41. A. Aiman and N. Wong, "Malaysia was Never an Asian Tiger, says Economist", *Free Malaysia Today*, 1 April 2019, https://www.freemalaysiatoday.com/category/nation/2019/04/01/malaysia-was-never-an-asian-tiger-says-economist/ (accessed 28 November 2019).
42. S. Rahman, "Airports on Islands: Boon or Potential Bust?", *ISEAS Perspective*, no 2019/53, 27 June 2019.
43. S. Rahman, "Plastic Fantastic – Solving the Problem We Created for Ourselves", Heinrich Böll Stiftung, 31 October 2019, http://th.boell.org/en/2019/10/31/plastic-fantastic-solving-problem-we-created-ourselves (accessed 10 November 2019).
44. Malaysia should follow the examples of the Nordic countries as outlined in the following report: N. Kiørboe, H. Sramkova, and M. Krarup, "Moving Towards a Circular Economy – Successful Nordic Business Models", Green Growth Knowledge Platform, 2015, https://www.greengrowthknowledge.org/resource/moving-towards-circular-economy-%E2%80%93-successful-nordic-business-models (accessed 1 December 2019).
45. Humphrey, "Indigenous Communities".
46. D. Simon, G. Davies, and M. Ancrenaz, "Changes to Sabah's Orangutan Population in Recent Times: 2002–2017". *PLoS ONE* 14, no. 7 (2019), https://doi.org/10.1371/journalpone.0218819.
47. "Calf Elephant's Drowning Makes it 4 deaths in 5 weeks in Sabah", *Daily Express* (East Malaysia), 8 November 2019, http://www.dailyexpress.com.my/news/142968/calf-elephant-s-drowning-makes-it-4-deaths-in-5-weeks-in-sabah/ (accessed 1 December 2019).
48. "Indonesia Claims Four Malaysian Firms behind Open Burning", *Star Online*,

14 September 2019, https://www.thestar.com.my/news/nation/2019/09/14/indonesia-claims-four-malaysian-firms-behind-open-burning (accessed 1 December 2019).
49. "Govt Targets 70% MSPO Certification by February 2020", *Free Malaysia Today*, 19 November 2019, https://www.freemalaysiatoday.com/category/nation/2019/11/19/the-goal-is-70-mspo-certification-by-2020-says-teresa-kok/ (accessed 1 December 2019).
50. "Orang Asli Smallholders Only Need Land Documents to Apply MSPO Certification", Bernama, 5 November 2019, https://www.malaysiakini.com/news/498749 (accessed 1 December 2019).
51. H. Varkkey, "Winds of Change in Malaysia: The Government and the Climate", Heinrich Böll Stiftung, 27 February 2019, https://th.boell.org/en/2019/02/27/winds-change-malaysia-government-and-climate (accessed 21 January 2019).
52. K.H.D. Tang and H.M.S. Al Qahtani, "Sustainability of Oil Palm Plantations in Malaysia", *Environment, Development and Sustainability*, 2019, https://doi.org/10.1007/s10668-019-00458-6 (accessed 28 November 2019).
53. K.H.D. Tang, "Climate Change in Malaysia: Trends, Contributors, Impacts, Mitigation and Adaptations", *Science of the Total Environment* 650 (2019): 1858–71.
54. "Cities Gone Underwater by 2050? Rising Sea Levels Study an 'Overestimation' Malaysian Authorities Say", *Today Online*, 10 November 2019, https://www.todayonline.com/world/cities-gone-underwater-2050-rising-sea-levels-study-overestimation-malaysian-authorities-say (accessed 28 November 2019).
55. World Health Organisation – Western Pacific, "Climate Change Country Profile: Malaysia", n.d., http://www.wpro.who.int/environmental_health/documents/docs/MAA_3FB0.pdf (accessed 28 November 2019).
56. S. Mat Nurudin, R. Hashim, S. Akma Hamik, S. Rahman, N. Zulkifli, and A.S.P. Mohamed, "Public Participation in Local Agenda 21 Programs Implemented by Seremban Municipal Council", *Procedia – Social and Behavioural Sciences* 219 (2016): 555–61.
57. B.S. McCoy, Facilitator, Proceedings of the Environmental Protection Society Malaysia, Seminar on Local Communities and the Environment, "I Can Make a Difference", 25–26 October 1997.
58. S. Rahman, "Orienting ASEAN towards its People: Enabling Engagement with Local NGOs", S. Rajaratnam School of International Studies (RSIS) Working Paper No. 298 (2016).
59. N. Aung, "Poverty Alleviation and Community Empowerment in the Bagan-Nyaung-U Area of Central Myanmar", in *Population, Development, and the Environment: Challenges to Achieving the Sustainable Development Goals in the Asia-Pacific*, edited by H. James (Singapore: Palgrave Macmillan, 2019).
60. Refer to S. Rahman, "Overcoming the Challenges of Sustainable Coastal Development in Southeast Asia", Heinrich Böll Foundation, 2018, https://th.boell.org/en/2018/09/28/overcoming-challenges-sustainable-coastal-development-southeast-asia; S. Rahman,

"Using Citizen Science for Community Empowerment and Beyond: The Case of Kelab Alami", *CitizenScience.Asia*, 19 April 2019, https://medium.com/citizenscience-asia/using-citizen-science-for-community-empowerment-and-beyond-the-case-of-kelab-alami-8b57234de3a3; PESISIR, n.d., http://iskandarmalaysia.com.my/green/pesisir.php (accessed 3 July 2018); and UPEN Johor, "Johor Sustainability Policy 2017–2021" (Iskandar Puteri, 2016), p. 70.

61. "Low Carbon Initiative to Expand", *Star Online*, 31 October 2018, https://www.thestar.com.my/metro/metro-news/2018/10/31/low-carbon-initiative-to-expand/ (accessed 1 December 2019).

62. S. Roe, C. Streck, M. Obersteiner, S. Frank, B. Griscom, L. Drouet, O. Fricko et al., "Contribution of the Land Sector to a 1.5°C World", *Nature Climate Change* 9 (2019): 817–28.

63. G.K. Pakiam, "Johor's Oil Palm Economy: Past, Present and Future", in *Johor: Abode of Development?*, edited by F. Hutchinson and S. Rahman (Singapore: ISEAS – Yusof Ishak Institute, forthcoming 2020).

64. A.S. Bujang, "Technical Empowerment of Agricultural Cooperatives in Malaysia", FFTC Agricultural Policy Platform (FFTC-AP), 3 October 2017, http://ap.fftc.agnet.org/ap_db.php?id=790 (accessed 28 November 2019).

65. S.N.N. Koris and S. Ismail, "Salahuddin Calls on Youth to Get Involved in Agriculture", *New Straits Times*, 31 July 2018, https://www.nst.com.my/news/nation/2018/07/396611/salahuddin-calls-youth-get-involved-agriculture (accessed 1 December 2019); and "Budget 2020 Highlights", *The Edge Markets*, 11 October 2019, https://www.theedgemarkets.com/article/budget-2020-highlights (accessed 1 December 2019).

66. N. Tiraieyari, A. Hamzah, and B. Abu Samah, "Organic Farming and Sustainable Agriculture in Malaysia: Organic Farmers' Challenges towards Adoption", *Asian Social Science* 10, no. 4 (2014), http://dx.doi.org/10.5539/ass.v10n4p1 (accessed 28 November 2019).

67. M. Doksil, "Plantation Commits to Producing Sustainable Palm Oil", *Borneo Post*, 19 September 2017, https://www.pressreader.com/malaysia/the-borneo-post-sabah/20170919/281822873973477 (accessed 16 October 2019).

68. W.J. Soo, "Tackling Transboundary Haze: Does Malaysia Need its Own Laws When ASEAN Has a Deal?", *Malay Mail*, 18 September 2019, https://www.malaymail.com/news/malaysia/2019/09/18/tackling-transboundary-haze-does-malaysia-need-its-own-laws/1791632 (accessed 28 November 2019).

69. Refer to *Buku Harapan*, Pillar 2 (Institutional and Political Reform) Promise 14: Reform the MACC and Strengthen Anti-corruption Efforts (p. 41) and Pillar 5 (Create a Malaysia That Is Inclusive, Moderate and Respected Globally) Promise 57: Malaysia Must Be Known for its Integrity, Not Corruption (p. 118); and E. Paulsen, "Fearless Latheefa is Exactly What the MACC Needs", *Malaysiakini*, 9 June 2019, https://www.malaysiakini.com/news/478939 (accessed 28 November 2019).

70. S. Rahman, "The Failure of the Middlemen: The Scourge of Development

Compensation", *Ecodaily*, 13 July 2017, https://ecodaily.org/featured/the-failure-of-the-middlemen-the-scourge-of-development-compensation/ (accessed 10 June 2018).
71. V. Devi, "Law on Discharge of Contaminants into Rivers Needs Improvement", *Star Online*, 29 August 2019, https://www.thestar.com.my/news/nation/2019/08/29/039law-on-discharge-of-contaminants-into-rivers-needs-improvement039 (accessed 15 September 2019); See also comments by Dr Japareng during the Bait Al-Amanah forum on the Pasir Gudang pollution incident on 29 August 2019; Also refer to N. Shafeq and E. Suresh, "Pasir Gudang Pollution: Knowing and Realising", *CJ-truthnews*, 21 October 2019, http://www.cj-truthnews.com/2019/10/21/pasir-gudang-pollution-knowing-and-realising/ (accessed 28 November 2019).
72. Z. Hasan, "Sustainable Development from an Islamic Perspective: Meaning, Implications and Policy Concerns", in *Land Use Planning and Environmental Sustainability in Malaysia: Policies and Trends*, edited by H.A. Kadouf and S.Z. Al Junid (Kuala Lumpur: International Islamic University Malaysia, 2006), p. 49.
73. Ibid., p. 64.
74. WWF-Malaysia, "WWF-Malaysia's 'Islam, Wildlife Conservation and You' Handbook to Boost Muslims' Environmental Participation", press release, 18 February 2014, http://www.wwf.org.my/media_and_information/publications_main/?uNewsID=17066 (accessed 1 December 2019); and WWF-Malaysia, "Eco-Islam: Malaysia's Imams to Preach against Poaching", press release, 14 April 2009, https://wwf.panda.org/wwf_news/?162082/Eco-Islam-Malaysias-Imams-to-preach-against-poaching (accessed 1 December 2019).

Myanmar

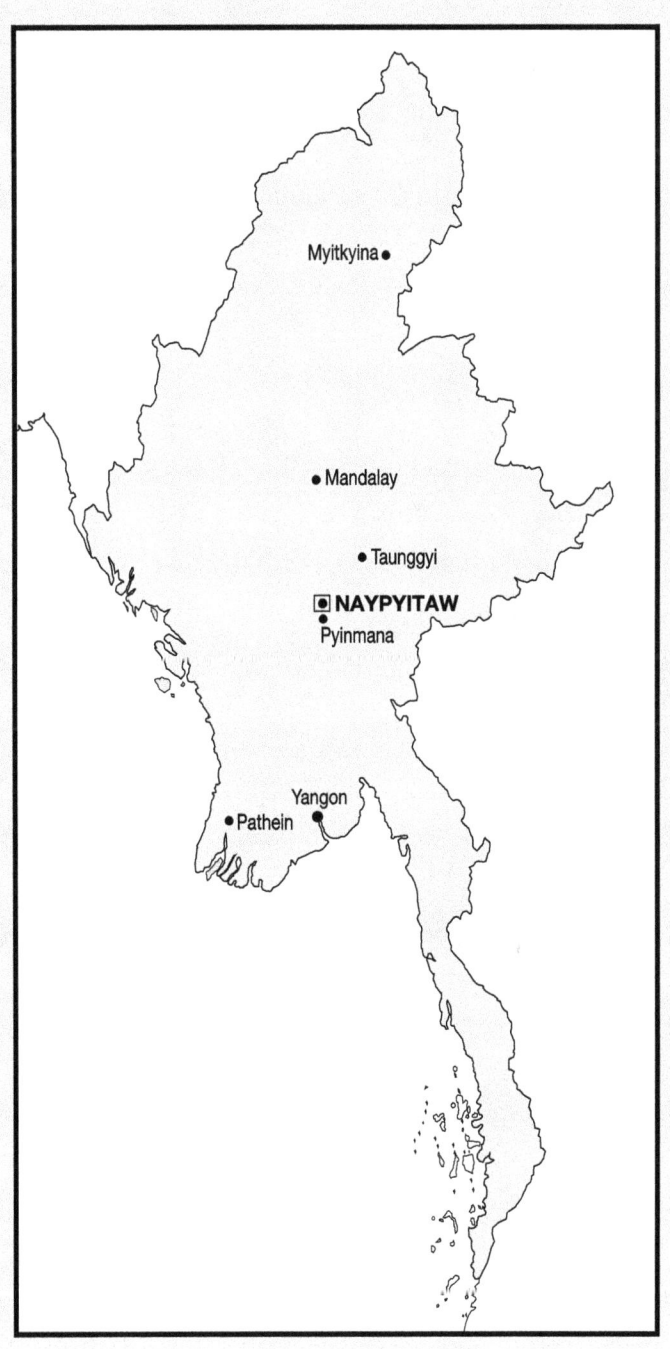

MYANMAR IN 2019:
Rakhine Issue, Constitutional Reform and Election Fever

Nyi Nyi Kyaw

Since it came to power in March 2016 after winning in a 2015 election landslide, 2019 has perhaps been the most problematic year thus far for Myanmar's National League for Democracy (NLD) government. The long-standing Rakhine issue, the initiation of a parliamentary constitutional reform process, and early election fever are some of the key developments to have dominated Myanmar's political attention in 2019. These high-level political events, mainly involving the executive and legislative branches, were accompanied by growing public distrust in the judiciary and the police. All these factors posed challenges for Myanmar in 2019, with considerable implications on the country's domestic and international fronts. Economically, Myanmar was working quite well, though some challenges remain.

The Rakhine Problem: Domestic and International Aspects

The Dual Rakhine Problem

Until early 2019, the "Rakhine problem", both within and outside Myanmar, was almost exclusively Rohingya-centric. Before the eruption of inter-communal violence in Rakhine State in 2012, the problem had not been envisaged as a Rakhine problem. The issue was merely referred to as *the* "Rohingya problem", "conundrum" or "crisis". After the 1990s, the Rohingya problem was framed internationally as an insurmountable crisis of forced migration and statelessness. Following the first and second Rohingya mass exoduses in 1978 and 1991–92,

---

Nyi Nyi Kyaw is Visiting Fellow in the Myanmar Studies Programme of the ISEAS – Yusof Ishak Institute. He is also Assistant Professor (adjunct) in the Department of Southeast Asian Studies at the National University of Singapore.

the Rohingya problem was respectively constructed by the Burma Socialist Programme Party (BSPP) government (1974–88) and the State Law and Order Restoration Council (SLORC) government (1988–97) as a colossal problem of (illegal) colonial migration, armed insurgency, and secession.

The dominant issue among Rakhine affairs remained the Rohingya problem, even after the outbreak of inter-communal violent and non-violent conflicts between Rohingya/non-Rohingya Muslims and Rakhine Buddhists from 2012 onwards, the emergence of a Rohingya "insurgency" led by the Arakan Rohingya Salvation Army (ARSA) from 2016 onwards, and the third Rohingya mass exodus from August 2017 onwards. These new problems have added two more layers to the Rohingya problem. First is the internal displacement of more than 100,000 Muslims in camps in Rakhine state. Second is a *new* protracted refugee situation that saw 909,000 Rohingyas being stranded in camps in Bangladesh as of March 2019, after about 745,000 Rohingyas fled following the Myanmar military's "clearance operation" in response to the ARSA attacks in August 2017.[1]

However, in January 2019 the Rakhine problem became more complex after the Rakhine ethnonationalist Arakan Army (AA) launched attacks on 4 January—the date on which Myanmar's Independence Day fell. The Rakhine problem now concerns two main parties: Rohingyas and Rakhines. Undeniably, the Rakhine people began to be embroiled with the Rakhine problem from 2012 onwards after Rakhines criticized the international community for the Rohingya-centric worldview and advocacy for Rohingyas' rights. However, the Rakhines were treated more as a nationalist, anti-Rohingya "troublemaker" than as an important actor or decision-maker, not just by the government and people of Myanmar but by the larger international community. The AA insurgency changed that, with the Rakhines now constituting a serious player on the political chessboard that must be satisfied.

Rohingyas and Rakhines have experienced inter-communal tensions and episodic violence with each other before, but since 2012 their relations have grown more inter-communal, riotous and identitarian. More importantly, their respective relations with the military and state of Myanmar have gradually become increasingly armed, violent and rebellious, leading to domestic and international repercussions.

The Rohingya Problem: Domestic and International Repercussions

The situation of the Rohingyas considerably deteriorated following the spate of inter-communal violence in 2012, as Myanmar underwent its transition from military dictatorship (1988–2011) to electoral democracy. The situation further deteriorated after the ARSA carried out attacks on police outposts in 2016 and 2017 that sparked the clearance operation by the Myanmar military and the consequent third Rohingya exodus. In a repeat of the aftermaths of the first two exoduses, Myanmar initially issued a blanket denial of wrongdoing and repression, but later acceded to repatriation because of pressure from Bangladesh and the larger international community. However, repatriation this time has been largely unsuccessful because of delays, the globalization of the Rohingya problem in which numerous actors have become embroiled in the issue (willingly or otherwise), and the unwillingness of Rohingyas to return "home" without promises of citizenship and other rights.

Although there is considerable variation in the views and perspectives on the Rohingya issue, there are, in general, two largely opposite perspectives on the issue: one held and produced by the state and society of Myanmar and the other by the international community. The positions are seemingly irreconcilable, and they have posed serious challenges to any well-meaning and serious efforts to solve the problem since as early as the early 1990s.

From Myanmar's perspective, there are five features of the Rohingya problem that the international community must be aware of and accept *first* before going further. Most importantly, this view asserts that the Rohingya are not the victims and that it is the Rohingyas' own actions that have resulted in the present crisis. Keeping in mind a high degree of variation within each, the five features are as follows:

- the colonial migration of Bengalis from then India to Burma in the nineteenth and twentieth centuries;
- secessionist attempts of those Bengali Muslims to include Rohingya-majority northern Rakhine in the future Pakistan in the late 1940s;
- the deliberate "creation" in the 1950s by Bengali Muslims of a "Rohingya" ethnic identity in order to demand recognition and rights as a native or indigenous group;
- the Rohingyas' violent racial attacks upon Rakhine Buddhists or intercommunal violence between the two groups in 1942 and 2012, as well as in the intervening years;
- Bengali "terrorism" that was manifested in attacks by the ARSA upon Myanmar police posts in Rakhine State in 2016 and 2017.

In contrast, from the global perspective, there are four features of the Rohingya problem that Myanmar has failed to recognize, intentionally or otherwise. The global perspective considers the Rohingya to be the victims, and not the other way around. Again, keeping in mind a high variation within each, the four features are as follows:

- successive Myanmar governments, intentionally or otherwise, have failed to give the Rohingya their due recognition and rights of citizenship, regardless of when they "migrated to" or "arrived in" Myanmar;
- the Myanmar military engaged in forced migration, extrajudicial killings and the large-scale deportation of hundreds of thousands of Rohingya in the late 1970s, the early 1990s and the late 2010s;
- the Myanmar government has, rather successfully, convinced the people of Myanmar that the Rohingya "belong" more to Bangladesh than to Myanmar by racial origin and citizenship;
- the ongoing Rohingya humanitarian crisis since 2017 does not seem solvable yet and the Rohingyas may not be repatriated soon despite repeated promises made by Myanmar to Bangladesh and the international community.

There is *some* truth to all these claims made by both sides. More importantly, such competitive, contradictory narratives, especially those rooted in questionable historical reasoning and arguments, are effectively acts of blame displacement, and they do not help to solve the structural issue relating to Rohingya refugees, asylum seekers and illegal migrants. This affects not only Myanmar and Bangladesh but also countries such as Thailand, Malaysia and even Australia that Rohingyas have fled to.

The protracted Rohingya refugee crisis has caused political and diplomatic repercussions, especially over the past two years. But, as of December 2019, Rohingyas remain displaced. In response to international condemnation and warnings of economic sanctions and the removal of preferential access to foreign markets such as the European Union, several international and domestic investigative bodies have been formed.[2] The most important ones are the Rakhine Inquiry Commission formed by the Myanmar government (2012–13); the Advisory Commission on Rakhine State, known as the "Annan Commission", jointly formed by the Myanmar government and the Kofi Annan Foundation (2016–17); the Advisory Board for the Committee for Implementation of the Recommendations on Rakhine State formed by the Myanmar government (2017–18); the Independent International Fact-Finding Mission on Myanmar (IIFFMM) (2017–19); and the Independent Commission of Enquiry formed by the Myanmar government (ICOE) (2018–).

By December 2019, the mandates of all these bodies except that of the ICOE have ended, and they have submitted their respective reports. The most damning finding, made by the IIFFMM, stipulated that the clearance operations by the Myanmar military had "genocidal" intent.[3] This allegation has catalysed two international criminal processes. First has been the ongoing International Criminal Court (ICC) proceedings to investigate alleged crimes against Rohingyas that began on 14 November 2019, although Myanmar has rejected the proceedings and has additionally questioned the jurisdiction of the court.[4] However, Myanmar responded to the lawsuit brought by The Gambia at the International Court of Justice (ICJ) at The Hague on 11 November. The Gambia, apparently at the behest of the Organization of Islamic Cooperation, alleges the Rohingya face genocide, and requested provisional measures that would prevent this from continuing. State Counsellor Daw Aung San Suu Kyi herself led the Myanmar delegation to defend the country against the charges of genocide at the public hearings on 11 and 12 December. She however denied any wrongdoing with "genocidal intent" as such on the part of the Tatmadaw (the Myanmar military) before or during its so-called clearance operation, although she admitted that serious crimes might have been committed by the Tatmadaw in "clearing" the area.[5] In addition to ICC and ICJ proceedings, a private lawsuit was also filed in November by the Rohingya diaspora community invoking universal jurisdiction at an Argentine court. The lawsuit named Daw Aung San Suu Kyi as one of the culprits to have caused the Rohingya's plight. Myanmar has ignored these proceedings, and they are ongoing as of the end of 2019.[6]

Despite international criticism of her defence of the Tatmadaw during the ICJ proceedings, Daw Aung San Suu Kyi accumulated enormous political capital at home. Across Myanmar, billboards proclaiming "We Stand with Daw Aung San Suu Kyi" were erected, and rallies in support of her were held across the nation.[7] The NLD government and supporters framed her presence at the ICJ as her defence of Myanmar or Myanmar's national interest. However, not *all* the peoples of Myanmar were with *Amay Suu* (Mother Suu), as she is nicknamed. Some ethnic minorities, many of whom have suffered under the repression and crackdowns of the Tatmadaw, viewed the ICJ case as evidence of her complicity with the Tatmadaw, and they even openly supported The Gambia.[8] The ICJ case, which will take a long while to finalize, will be a double-edged sword for Daw Aung San Suu Kyi. On the one hand, she has been and will be able to accumulate sympathy from supporters, and she may be able to reach a political compromise with the Tatmadaw that she has had to defend at The Hague. On the other hand, her continued defence of the Tatmadaw risks further opprobrium towards her global image. She may also face diplomatic and economic repercussions if Myanmar's denial remains entrenched and repatriation does not begin soon.

The Ethnonationalist Arakan Army's Insurgency

Rakhine Buddhists, who constitute *the* absolute ethnic majority in Rakhine state, consider themselves the rightful and necessary masters of the political fate of their state. Rakhine ethnonationalism originated from three critical junctures of Rakhine history: the invasion and annexation in 1785 of the Kingdom of Mrauk-U (1429–1785) by the Burmese Konbaung Dynasty (1752–1885) and the consequent Burmese rule until 1826 prior to the British annexation of Rakhine (then Arakan); the long period of British colonization from 1826 until 1948; and the chronic neglect and marginalization of Rakhine ethno-identity and the "Rakhine nation" at the hands of various Burmese or Myanmar regimes for more than seven decades since independence in 1948. In the eyes of Rakhines, two agents threaten the Rakhine nation: the central Bamar-dominated state of Myanmar (or "the Bamar majority") and the Rohingya.

From 2012 until now, Rakhine ethnonationalists have ardently partaken in the production of an anti-Rohingya narrative within Myanmar that alienates, discriminates and securitizes the Rohingya and legitimizes the exclusion of the Rohingya from Myanmar's political and social life. Rakhines view the Rohingya as a demographic threat because the latter made up about a third of the Rakhine state's total population prior to the 2017 mass exodus. In contrast, Bamar and other Buddhists construct the Rohingya as a religious threat to Myanmar's Buddhism and Buddhists. The Rakhine ethnonationalist Arakan National Party (ANP) has been at the forefront of the anti-Rohingya campaign since 2012, and the party successfully weaponized the campaign in the 2015 elections.[9] However, the Rohingya have been increasingly deprived of their political, civil, social and economic rights since 2012, and less than half of the Rohingya population now remains in Rakhine state. Thus, Rakhine ethnonationalists in 2019 do not seem to view the Rohingya as the level of threat they did previously, although many remain opposed to repatriating Rohingya refugees stranded in Bangladesh.

With the Rohingya as no longer important in the Rakhine state's demographic and ethnonational calculus, Rakhine nationalists are now focusing on their other project: to strive by insurgency for self-determination, autonomy or secession from the central state of Myanmar, which Rakhines allege to be Bamar-dominated. It is for such a purpose that the United League of Arakan (ULA) and its armed wing, the AA, were founded—by no more than thirty young, educated Rakhines in Laiza, Kachin State—in April 2009. Although the AA was dormant in its first few years of existence, the situation changed for the ethnonationalist army from 2010 onwards. The transition that liberalized both the state and the society of Myanmar gave the AA unprecedented access to Rakhines in the Rakhine state and elsewhere in Myanmar.

The AA reportedly infiltrated into southern parts of Chin State first and later into the far north of Rakhine State after 2014. Many factors led to the rise in popularity of the AA among Rakhines. They include but are not limited to the difficult relations between the ruling NLD and the ANP, increased distrust of Rakhines in Myanmar's electoral democracy after extremely popular Rakhine civilian nationalist Aye Maung's resignation from his chairmanship of the ANP in November 2017, the killing of seven Rakhine protesters by the police in January 2018, and the immediate arrest of Aye Maung and well-known Rakhine writer Wai Hin Aung for alleged high treason. The AA hijacked these festering grievances and launched offline and online ethnonationalist campaigns such as "Arakan Dream 2020" and "The Way of *Rakhita* (Patriot)"—which imagine Rakhine's "independence", "freedom" or "self-determination" from the Bamar in 2020.[10] The appeal of the AA among Rakhines grew when Aye Maung and Wai Hin Aung were sentenced to twenty years' imprisonment for high treason in March 2019.[11]

The current exact size of the AA is not known; it is assumed though—under the young, eloquent and media friendly commanders Tun Myat Naing and Nyo Tun Aung—to be in the region of 10,000 or more in strength. It has also reportedly been successful in recruiting among young people, despite its humble origin as a twenty-nine-member "army" in April 2009. The year 2019 has so far been the deadliest for both the AA and the Tatmadaw, after the AA launched surprise attacks on four police outposts in Buthidaung township in northern Rakhine State, killing thirteen policemen on 4 January 2019. Although the AA has often boasted about the large numbers of casualties among Tatmadaw troops to have resulted from the non-stop fighting between the two sides throughout 2019, the Tatmadaw does not provide details of these numbers. What is probably more important than the loss of lives of the combatants is those of about 100 people caught in the crossfire, lawsuits against about 200 "civilians" for alleged contact with the AA, and the internal displacement of over 100,000 people in 2019.[12]

Furthermore, partly because of the NLD government's "complicity" with the Tatmadaw and its criticism of the AA, and partly because of the AA's ultimate aim of taking control of Rakhine State, the AA has increasingly opposed and challenged the government. NLD-AA relations reached a nadir when the AA detained NLD member of parliament Hawi Ting in November 2019[13] and NLD branch chair of Buthidaung township Ye Thein in December. Ye Thein was subsequently killed during an armed assault by the Tatmadaw.[14] Those events might have been motivated on the part of the AA by the arrest and deportation of AA chief Tun Myat Naing's brother Aung Myat Kyaw from Singapore in July 2019,[15] the arrest of Tun Myat Naing's sister Moe Hnin Phyu and brother-in-law Kyaw Naing in Yangon in October,[16] and that of Tun Myat Naing's wife Hnin Zar Phyu and two children in Thailand in December,[17] all accused of assisting and/or funding the AA.

In December 2019, the AA announced they were going to establish "people's rule" and tax large businesses in townships in Rakhine and Chin under their control.[18] As such, the 2020 elections would require their "permission".[19] All these signal that 2020 will herald more difficult developments of the Rakhine problem.

Constitutional Reform: The NLD's Attempt to Reform Civil-Military Relations

Undeniably, without the present Constitution of the Republic of the Union of Myanmar, known as the 2008 constitution, which was adopted in May 2008 and came into operation in January 2011, the ongoing transition to civilian rule would have not occurred. The previous military regime—the SLORC/State Peace and Development Council (SPDC)—only transferred their near-absolute power to the ex-SLORC/SPDC, pseudo-civilian Union Solidarity and Development Party (USDP) government in 2011 because of constitutional provisions that entrenched the leading role of the Tatmadaw in politics. Civilians and citizens neither played a role nor had a voice in all three important processes that activated the constitution: the long, intermittent process of drafting the constitution from 1993 until 2007; the questionable referendum in May 2008 that approved the constitution; and the flawed general elections in November 2010, which were boycotted by the popular NLD and leading ethnic parties such as the Shan Nationalities League for Democracy (SNLD) party.[20]

Important sections of the constitution that give the Tatmadaw undue powers include, but are not limited to, the following: unelected Tatmadaw officers hold a quarter of the seats in the lower and upper houses, giving them veto power to block any constitutional reform; the Tatmadaw bloc in parliament gets to appoint one of the three presidential candidates, who would then, at the least, become one of the two vice-presidents; the Tatmadaw's commander-in-chief is the one to nominate the three security-related cabinet portfolios of defence, home affairs, and border affairs; the Tatmadaw is free from civilian oversight in military affairs and justice; with the police placed under Home Affairs, it often makes it difficult for a civilian government to directly order the police and hold it accountable for any misconduct; and Tatmadaw officers dominate the supreme executive National Defence and Security Council, with the power to declare emergencies and to transfer all executive, legislative and judiciary powers to the commander-in-chief.

These constitutional provisions that continue to militarize politics serve as a constant reminder to Daw Aung San Suu Kyi, the NLD and ethnic minorities that the "Green Book", as it is often called by critics of the constitution, must be amended or repealed sooner or later. Civilians and the NLD contend that the constitution disproportionately empowers the Tatmadaw and thus marginalizes civilians. Ethnic minorities accuse the document of favouring Union-level institutions such as the Union government, Pyidaungsu Hluttaw and Tatmadaw, all of which are Bamar-dominated in their view.

Due to continued tensions over the constitution, all political sides, including the Tatmadaw, are now in agreement *in principle* that Myanmar must build a "democratic federal union". In writing, this general principle is expressed in both the Nationwide Ceasefire Agreement (NCA) that was concluded in 2015 and the so-called "Pyidaungsu (Union) Accord".[21] The Pyidaungsu Accord is being developed at the Union Peace Conference – 21st Century Panglong (UPC) that the NLD has convened three times so far. The UPC is the most inclusive political process where principles for a future democratic federal union of Myanmar are being developed with an eye towards being more than simply a ceasefire between the Tatmadaw and the ethnic armed groups. There was no UPC meeting in 2019 despite plans for one.

On a side note, the more focused peace process was largely stalled by an unprecedented attack on 15 August 2019 targeting Pyi Oo Lwin, which was home to a Tatmadaw academy, by three Northern Alliance members—the Ta'ang National Liberation Army (TNLA), the Myanmar National Democratic Alliance Army (MNDAA), and the AA. The attack resulted in the casualties of nine soldiers, four policemen and one civilian.[22] Notably, that attack occurred in spite of the Tatmadaw's announced ceasefire from December 2018 until September 2019.

Going back to constitutional reform, the NLD has not forgotten the promise it made in the 2012 by-elections and the 2015 general elections that the party would amend the constitution, and it has remained committed to this in its statements over the past four years. The party had joined hands in 2014 with the 88 Generation Peace and Open Society—a popular movement-type network of ex-student activists and former political prisoners—and mobilized a popular movement, though unsuccessfully, to demand the amendment of Section 436 that grants veto powers to the Tatmadaw bloc in parliament, allowing it to obstruct constitutional reform.

As seen above, the NLD also included constitutional reform as one of the aims of the UPC. However, there is no end of the UPC in sight yet. Thus, the ruling party chose another platform and moved to seek constitutional amendment within parliament from 29 January 2019 onwards. Despite strong opposition from the USDP and the Tatmadaw bloc, the NLD-dominated Pyidaungsu Hluttaw proceeded to form a forty-five-member Union of Myanmar Constitution Amendment Joint Committee (UMCAJC) by bringing in representatives from the USDP, the military, ethnic parties, other parties and independents. The UMCAJC finished collating 3,765 recommendations for amendment, repeal and addition in July and proceeded to draft constitutional amendment bills (at the end of 2019, these had not yet been submitted to the Pyidaungsu Hluttaw). On the other hand, the USDP and military representatives in parliament submitted several draft amendment bills on their own, seemingly to obstruct the NLD-led process, but these efforts were carried out in vain.

The process and the resultant hundreds of recommendations laid bare the formation of three political groups within and outside parliament. The ruling NLD prioritizes democratization over federalization and suggests gradually reducing the power of the military and increasing that of civilians, apparently seeking a more balanced and proper form of civil-military relations first. This position of the NLD has angered ethnic parties and groups, many of whom were once allies of the NLD. The military and the USDP, on the other hand, would like to maintain the constitutional status quo and only want to enable region or state *hluttaws* to appoint chief ministers—who are now directly nominated by the president and have to be approved by respective region or state *hluttaws* unless they can prove any disqualification of those nominated for the positions. Ethnic parties seek the immediate removal of the military bloc from parliament, and also demand federalist reforms to empower ethnic groups and their respective states.[23]

The NLD-led high-profile process within parliament resulted in pro-charter reform rallies by NLD supporters and counter-rallies by the other side across Myanmar throughout 2019. Despite the continuation of the process until the end of 2019, State Counsellor Daw Aung San Suu Kyi herself admitted in October that the charter reform necessary for "complete democracy" seemed unlikely before the next elections due in November 2020.[24] Her comments provoked questions about why her party initiated the process in the first place, which sparked controversy within and outside parliament. These questions also evinced the realization of the party that charter reform is impossible without the Tatmadaw on board. It is common knowledge within Myanmar that the constitution cannot be reformed easily, and that the Tatmadaw will not give in until the time is right. This has held true at least since the ongoing transition that began in 2010. For the Tatmadaw to permit charter reform, there need to be at least three favourable conditions in place: the cessation of fighting between the Tatmadaw and ethnic armed groups; the creation of a perfect balance between the solider and the civilian; and mutual guarantees that the power base and interests of the Tatmadaw will be protected or at least left untouched by civilians. None of these are in place at the moment.

Hence, considering everything, the NLD most likely initiated the constitutional amendment process for four possible reasons. First, the NLD wanted to "show" the party's voters that it is keeping its promise of charter reform, and it can have a clear conscience. Second, the party was able to shine a spotlight on the actions of the Tatmadaw that stand in the way of charter reform. Third, the NLD was able to remind the Tatmadaw that the latter should not always be complacent because the status quo is not sustainable; and last but not least the process was able to collate the first set of recommendations for constitutional reform in writing at the Pyidaungsu Hluttaw. Charter reform is, therefore, a political project for the NLD, and the party will use obstacles to the project as an excuse in the next polls due in November 2020.

Election Fever: Parties Gear Up Early for the 2020 Polls

In 2019 the NLD made two important but rather early announcements about the next general elections. In June 2019,[25] NLD spokesperson Myo Nyunt said that President U Win Myint and State Counsellor Daw Aung San Suu Kyi—who remains chair of the party but may not publicly participate in party activities—would run in the 2020 polls. Again, on the thirty-first anniversary of the founding of the party, which fell on 27 September 2019, the party claimed it would not enter any alliances with other parties and would instead stand alone in the next polls.[26]

These announcements triggered an early onset of election fever and resulted in a chain reaction among myriad politicians and parties who were left with no option but to position themselves as the opposition. In general, there are three types of political party that would contest the next election. The first is the ruling NLD. The second is the loose league of national opposition parties that includes but is not limited to the former ruling but now opposition USDP party, the Union

Betterment Party (which was established by the former chair of the USDP and former Speaker of the lower house Thura U Shwe Mann), and the People's Party chaired by former student activist and ex-political prisoner Ko Ko Gyi. The third comprises more than fifty ethnic political parties—accounting for more than half of all registered parties—that position themselves as representatives of ethnic minority groups such as the Kachin and the Kayin and which accuse the NLD of being *the* Bamar-dominated party.[27]

Many old and new parties in the second and third groups were established or are chaired by former allies of Daw Aung San Suu Kyi or the NLD, such as the UBP, the PP and the SNLD. Having been left to stand on their own, parties in the second and third groups now position themselves as the opposition. Despite suspicion of the NLD's unilateralism and criticism that the ruling party has failed to strike a deal or form an alliance with them for the next general elections, the national opposition parties such as the USDP, the UBP and the PP remain standalone themselves. Although the NLD has formed "loose" alliances with parties such as the SNLD before, and has jointly demanded political and social changes such as constitutional reform, the ruling party has never entered a formal bi-party or multiparty alliance with those parties. Nor has the NLD brought people such as Thura U Shwe Mann or Ko Ko Gyi in for leadership positions or senior membership in the party.

None among these "national" parties (the NLD, USDP, UBP, PP) would accept the claim made by ethnic parties that they are Bamar parties or representatives of the Bamar majority, who according to the 1983 census constitute sixty-nine per cent of the total population of Myanmar. Instead, these national parties would claim they are multi-ethnic and represent all the people or peoples of Myanmar. However, it is undeniable that the former ruling USDP and the current ruling NLD have won the most seats in the seven Bamar-dominated regions and far fewer in the seven ethnic states in the 2010 and 2015 polls. Of course, both ruling parties have won significant numbers of seats in some ethnic states, but the overall picture is that they fare best in Bamar-dominated regions. Thus, in electoral terms, it is reasonable if the NLD does not ally, let alone merge, with national parties such as the UBP or the PP because they will fight for votes in the same constituencies. Also, the NLD remains confident that the star power of Daw Aung San Suu Kyi, who remains highly popular, at least in the seven regions, will be helpful for them in the next polls, in addition to their incumbency.

Incumbency since 2016 has both benefitted and disadvantaged the NLD. As the ruling party, they have the resources and finances at their disposal to deliver public services and thus legitimize their performance. However, a lack of skills, economic mismanagement, corruption and the poor political communication of some NLD officials have also led to increased public scrutiny. Nonetheless, the NLD government is undeniably a lot more popular than its predecessor, which had to grapple with a legacy of rampant corruption and severe repression in its previous life as the military junta in the 1990s and the 2000s.

Last but not least, only Rakhine and Shan states among seven ethnic states posed obstacles to the USDP in 2010 or the NLD in 2015. Additionally, the two biggest ethnic winners in those states—the ANP and the SNLD—remain stand-alone parties. Further, the ANP—which won the most seats in Rakhine State in 2015, a merger between the winner of the 1990 elections the Arakan League for Democracy (ALD) and the winner of the 2010 elections the Rakhine Nationalities Development Party (RNDP)—split in 2017 after the ALD faction left the merger. Likewise, the SNLD, now the most popular Shan party in Shan State, has not merged with the Shan Nationalities Democracy Party (SNDP), which was the biggest ethnic winner in Shan State in 2010. Therefore, in the eyes of the NLD, the supposed competitive advantage of ethnic parties in states seems unlikely and questionable.

For their part, the ethnic parties seem to have learned a lesson from the 2015 elections. They believe that they did not win as many seats as they should have in the ethnic states because they were not united and because more than one ethnic party representing a single ethnic group ran against one another in constituencies in states. Thus, they have sought unity in two ways. First, many Kachin, Kayah, Kayin, Chin and Mon parties have merged into united parties, although one or more ethnic parties in Kachin, Kayah, Kayin, Chin and Mon states remain stand-alone or unmerged with the former. Second, those merged Kachin, Kayah, Kayin, Chin and Mon parties hold discussions among themselves and form alliances with two broad ethnic political party alliances—the twelve-member United Nationalities Alliance and the fifteen-member Nationalities Brotherhood Federation.[28]

Hence, the ruling NLD, opposition national parties and ethnic parties are now engaged in intense politicking and jostling for the 2020 polls. Another issue has further compounded this electoral politicking. A proposal made by the Union Election Commission in October 2019 sought to reduce the time limit of residence for internal migrant workers so that they would be able to vote in constituencies different from those of their habitual residence prior to migration. In 2015, migrant workers who had lived in a new constituency for more than 180 days were made eligible to vote. The NLD-appointed election commission wanted to reduce this qualifying period to 90 days. Several ethnic parties protested because internal migration over the past few decades has been huge and might have changed the demographics of constituencies in ethnic states.[29] The issue, as of the end of 2019, remained unresolved.

Increased Mistrust in the Police and the Judiciary

Besides the military, the two institutions that the people of Myanmar have a deep distrust of are the police and the judiciary. The police may seem to be a civilian institution, but it is highly militarized in the eyes of the people as it is under the Ministry of Home Affairs, which is headed by a military officer. In contrast, the judiciary is a civilian institution, but people lack trust in it because of the chronic lack of rule of law for decades, and the situation has not significantly improved since the transition. Because the police and the judiciary work in tandem to deliver criminal justice, the wrath of people often falls on both institutions.

The actions of the police lead to public outcries in relation to criminal cases the people care the most about. One of the most prominent recent cases was the assassination of Muslim lawyer and the NLD's constitutional advisor Ko Ni at Yangon International Airport on 29 January 2017; comments made by Police Chief Maj. Gen. Zaw Win and Home Affairs Minister Lt. Gen. Kyaw Swe on 25 February opined that the act was motivated by extreme nationalism and personal grudges.[30] Another significant case was the dropping in July 2018 of the murder case of Facebook comedian Aung Yell Htwe on the advice of Yangon Region Attorney-General Han Htoo, who received a bribe from the suspects.[31]

In relation to police misconduct, what has angered people most to date took place on 16 May 2019, when a two-year-old girl, later nicknamed "Victoria" to protect her identity, was raped at a private nursery in Nay Pyi Taw—the capital of Myanmar. Despite conflicting evidence, the police arrested school bus driver Aung Gyi in July, who was later found to be innocent and released on 18 December. The police thus suffered a public outcry between July and December. They were also faced with more popular wrath after they disclosed the name of the girl, intentionally or otherwise, at a police press conference about the case held the next day. Countless protests against the police took place in relation to the Victoria case across Myanmar until late December 2019.[32] Despite enormous public pressure, the case is still pending as of the end of 2019.

While public anger has focused on police misconduct and delayed justice, the anger has been intensified by arguments that such things would not have occurred if the police had been under civilian control.[33] Therefore, 2019 was the most difficult year for the police force, and by extension the judiciary, which was accused of corruption and inefficiency. Among three ministries whose chiefs are directly nominated and effectively appointed by the commander-in-chief of the Tatmadaw, the Ministry of Home Affairs and its subsidiary the police have received the greatest attention from civilians, and have hence been at the brunt of public outcries. People, rather correctly, view the police as a proxy of the military. Tensions therefore between the police and the Ministry of Home Affairs on the one hand and the people on the other have only increased, especially after the democratically elected NLD government came to power, and fuelled by the above-mentioned cases. Tensions are likely to remain high or to even increase in 2020 if the Victoria case lingers and if similar cases occur.

The Economy

Myanmar's economic growth rate in 2018/19 was 6.3 per cent, compared to 6.2 per cent in the previous year, according to the World Bank. Myanmar's ranking in the World Bank's Doing Business report rose from 171 to 165 out of 190 countries.[34] Myanmar reported the first fall in trade deficit in six years, which stood at US$1.1 billion in the fiscal year 2018/19, from more than US$3 billion in the previous year.[35]

Significant reforms and improvements were also seen in the insurance and banking sectors and in the domestic treasury bond market. Five foreign companies—including Britain's Prudential, Canada's Manulife and Hong Kong's AIA—and six joint ventures were licensed in November 2019 to operate in Myanmar's budding insurance market.[36] In the same month, the Central Bank of Myanmar announced that foreign banks may apply for branch licences for wholesale banking and subsidiary licences for both wholesale and retail banking, which will start operating from January 2021.[37] The government treasury bonds market also gained momentum, and reportedly covered the government deficit in 2018 (the deficit-to-GDP ratio was 4.6 per cent in 2018) and is expected to do the same in 2019 (the deficit-to-GDP ratio is expected to be 5.9 per cent in 2019).[38] In November, the Treasury Department announced it was considering selling 10-year bonds. Myanmar currently sells treasury securities with maturities of 3 months, 6 months, 1 year, 2 years and 5 years.[39]

The most drastic economic reform by the NLD government in 2019 was probably the hike in electricity tariffs—the lowest in the region—in July, under which private consumers and businesses would pay up to triple and double, respectively, of what they paid before. It was clearly unpopular among citizens and businesses, who responded by demanding better service. But, by the end of 2019, public criticism of the new tariff had subsided, and private users have reportedly reduced their electricity consumption accordingly. The government had also sought to electrify 50.09 per cent of total households across Myanmar, up from 34 per cent in 2016. Largely because of the increased electricity tariffs and the consequent higher prices, inflation stayed high, reaching 10.9 per cent and 10.4 per cent in July and August 2019, respectively, according to the World Bank. By December, inflation was still at 8.8 per cent, according to the Central Statistical Organization of Myanmar.[40]

In spite of initial jubilation over a small number of high-profile anti-corruption cases against certain senior government officials,[41] no significant improvements in corruption were seen during the year. Myanmar only scored 29 out of 100 and occupied the 130th place out of the 180 countries ranked in the Corruption Perceptions Index 2019. Despite the overall good economic picture, inequalities among diverse peoples geographically spread across Myanmar remain an issue of considerable magnitude, with impacts on both economics and politics.

The 2017 Myanmar Living Conditions Survey conducted by the Ministry of Planning and Finance found a dramatic decline in the proportion of people living below the national poverty level, from 48.2 per cent in 2005 to 24.8 per cent in 2017. In other words, the number of poor people fell from 18.7 million to 11.8 million. Despite this overall rosy picture of poverty reduction, significant urban-rural and region-state disparities exist. For example, the survey found that 58 per cent and 41.6 per cent of the total populations of Chin State and Rakhine State, respectively, were poor, while only 13.2 per cent, 13.2 per cent and 13.7 per cent of the populations of Tanintharyi Region, Mandalay Region and Yangon Region, respectively, were living below the poverty line. Likewise, 30.2 per cent of rural residents were poor, while only 11.3 per cent of their urban counterparts were poor. In terms of numbers, the figure for the rural poor is 6.7 times higher than that of the urban poor.[42]

That said, the economic outlook for the election year of 2020 and the years to come remains positive, in the views of the World Bank, the Asian Development Bank, the Economist Intelligence Unit and several other private risk assessment firms.

Conclusion

To conclude, the Rohingya problem and the AA insurgency—two sides of the same coin of the Rakhine problem—posed significant challenges to the NLD government and the Tatmadaw, both of which also faced increasing domestic and international repercussions in 2019. As it has been in power for more than three years, the ruling NLD has become more confident than ever. It has even played a calculated political game and used charter reform to challenge the continued dominance of the Tatmadaw in politics. In truth, the Rakhine problem and charter reform are "old" problems that have long existed before the NLD came to power. But the problems, and their new aspects and dimensions, posed bigger challenges in 2019. On the economic front, Myanmar was working quite well, with some challenges remaining in place while the economic reforms and policies of the NLD government gained momentum. Whether those reforms and policies will be beneficial for Myanmar as a whole in the medium to long term remains to be seen.

The year 2019 also saw the early rise of electoral politicking that had not subsided by the end of the year—a fever that will only increase in the election year of 2020. An unexpected benefit from this early electoral politicking is that the political positioning of actors—including parties, ethnic armed groups and the Tatmadaw—has become clearer than in previous years. The NLD will aim to win at the polls unilaterally in a landslide again. The party will only strike a deal with one or more parties if it does not obtain enough seats on its own—a scenario that is unlikely.

Notes

1. United Nations Office for the Coordination of Humanitarian Affairs, "Rohingya Refugee Crisis", https://www.unocha.org/rohingya-refugee-crisis.
2. For quite a comprehensive list of those domestic and international bodies, see Human Rights Watch, "Myanmar's Investigative Commissions: A History of Shielding Abusers", September 2018, https://www.hrw.org/sites/default/files/supporting_resources/201809myanmar_commissions.pdf.
3. United Nations Human Rights Council, "Report of Independent International Fact-Finding Mission on Myanmar (27 August 2018)", https://www.ohchr.org/EN/HRBodies/HRC/MyanmarFFM/Pages/ReportoftheMyanmarFFM.aspx.
4. "Myanmar Rejects ICC Probe into Alleged Crimes against Rohingya", Al Jazeera, 16 November 2019, https://www.aljazeera.com/news/2019/11/myanmar-rejects-icc-probe-alleged-crimes-rohingya-191115180754984.html.
5. International Court of Justice, "Application of the Convention on the Prevention and Punishment of the Crime of Genocide (The Gambia v. Myanmar)", https://www.icj-cij.org/en/case/178.
6. AFP, "Aung San Suu Kyi Named in Argentine Lawsuit over Crimes against Rohingya", *Frontier*, 14 November 2019, https://frontiermyanmar.net/en/aung-san-suu-kyi-named-in-argentine-lawsuit-over-crimes-against-rohingya.
7. Naw Betty Han, "Standing with Mother Suu", *Frontier*, 13 December 2019, https://frontiermyanmar.net/en/standing-with-mother-suu.

8. Phyo Thiha Cho, "Ethnic Groups Show Support for Gambia at ICJ", *Myanmar Now*, 13 December 2019, https://myanmar-now.org/en/news/ethnic-groups-show-support-for-gambia-at-icj.
9. Than Tun, "Ethnicity and Buddhist Nationalism in the 2015 Rakhine State Election Results", in *Conflict in Myanmar: War, Politics, Religion*, edited by Nick Cheesman and Nicholas Farrelly (Singapore: ISEAS – Yusof Ishak Institute, 2016), pp. 177–98.
10. Ye Min Zaw, "What Does the Arakan Army Bring to Rakhine State?", *The Irrawaddy*, 11 January 2019, https://www.irrawaddy.com/opinion/guest-column/arakan-army-bring-rakhine-state.html.
11. Ye Mon, "Aye Maung, Wai Hin Aung Handed 20-year Sentences for High Treason", *Frontier*, 19 March 2019, https://frontiermyanmar.net/en/aye-maung-wai-hin-aung-handed-20-year-sentences-for-high-treason.
12. Soe Thu Aung, "Arakan Army Say Gov't Should Be Concerned about Civilian Casualties after MP's Death", *Mizzima*, 28 December 2019, http://mizzima.com/article/arakan-army-say-govt-should-be-concerned-about-civilian-casualties-after-mps-death.
13. "Arakan Army Detains NLD MP Accused of Tatmadaw Collaboration", *Myanmar Now*, 5 November 2019, https://myanmar-now.org/en/news/arakan-army-detains-nld-mp-accused-of-tatmadaw-collaboration.
14. Thant Zin Oo, "Local NLD Leader Killed by Mortar Blast in Myanmar's War-Ravaged Rakhine State", *Radio Free Asia*, 26 December 2019, https://www.rfa.org/english/news/myanmar/local-nld-leader-killed-12262019160625.html.
15. Moe Myint, "AA Chief's Brother, Several Arakanese Arrested in Singapore", *The Irrawaddy*, 10 July 2019, https://www.irrawaddy.com/news/burma/aa-chiefs-cousin-several-arakanese-arrested-singapore.html.
16. Khin Myat Myat Wai, "Arakan Army Decries Arrest of Leader's Sister, Husband", *Myanmar Times*, 21 October 2019, https://www.mmtimes.com/news/arakan-army-decries-arrest-leaders-sister-husband.html.
17. "Wife, Children of Leader of Myanmar's Arakan Army Detained in Thailand", *The Irrawaddy*, 6 December 2019, https://www.irrawaddy.com/news/burma/wife-children-leader-myanmars-arakan-army-detained-thailand.html.
18. Nan Lwin Hnin Pwint, "Arakan Army to 'Tax' Large Projects in Myanmar's Rakhine, Chin States", *The Irrawaddy*, 10 December 2019, https://www.irrawaddy.com/news/burma/arakan-army-tax-large-projects-myanmars-rakhine-chin-states.html.
19. Kyaw Thu Htay, "Vox Pop on Arakan Army's 2020 Election Cooperation Proposition", *Development Media Group*, 31 December 2019, https://www.dmediag.com/interview/1010-vox.
20. Nyi Nyi Kyaw, "Putting their Guns on the Scale: Constitution-Making in Burma/Myanmar under Military Command", *Chinese Journal of Comparative Law* 7, no. 2 (2019): 309–32.
21. "37 Points Signed as Part of Pyidaungsu Accord", *Global New Light of Myanmar*,

30 May 2017, pp. 7, 9; "14 Points Signed as Part II of Pyidaungsu Accord", *Global New Light of Myanmar*, 17 July 2018, p. 6.
22. AFP, "At Least 14 Dead in Unprecedented Northern Alliance Attacks", *Frontier*, 15 August 2019, https://frontiermyanmar.net/en/at-least-14-dead-in-unprecedented-northern-alliance-attacks.
23. Nyi Nyi Kyaw, "Democracy First, Federalism Next? The Constitutional Reform Process in Myanmar", *ISEAS Perspective*, no. 2019/93, 8 November 2019.
24. Wataru Suzuki and Yuichi Nitta, "Suu Kyi: Myanmar Constitution Must Change for 'Complete Democracy'", *Asian Nikkei Review*, 23 October 2019, https://asia.nikkei.com/Editor-s-Picks/Interview/Suu-Kyi-Myanmar-constitution-must-change-for-complete-democracy.
25. Moe Moe, "Aung San Suu Kyi Announces Plan to Contest in 2020 Election", *The Irrawaddy*, 10 June 2019, https://www.irrawaddy.com/news/burma/aung-san-suu-kyi-announces-plan-contest-2020-election.html.
26. Htun Htun, "NLD Celebrates 31st Anniversary, Says Myanmar's Democracy Not Yet 'Genuine'", *The Irrawaddy*, 27 September 2019, https://www.irrawaddy.com/news/burma/nld-celebrates-31st-anniversary-says-myanmars-democracy-not-yet-genuine.html.
27. Nyi Nyi Kyaw, "Old and New Competition in Myanmar's Electoral Politics", *ISEAS Perspective*, no. 2019/104, 17 December 2019.
28. Ibid.
29. Lawi Weng, "Ethnic Parties in Myanmar Worried Proposed Voter Registration Changes Will Hurt Their Election Chances", *The Irrawaddy*, 18 November 2019, https://www.irrawaddy.com/news/burma/ethnic-parties-myanmar-worried-proposed-voter-registration-changes-will-hurt-election-chances.html.
30. Associated Press, "Myanmar Police Blame Grudge, Not Army, for Lawyer's Murder", *Wall Street Journal*, 25 February 2017, https://www.wsj.com/articles/myanmar-police-blame-grudge-not-army-for-lawyers-murder-1488033995.
31. San Yamin Aung, "Analysis: Why Was the Comedian's Murder Case Dropped?", *The Irrawaddy*, 24 August 2018, https://www.irrawaddy.com/news/burma/analysis-comedians-murder-case-dropped.html.
32. Nyan Hlaing Lin and Tin Htet Paing, "Myanmar Explodes in Anger over Police Disclosure of Child Rape Victim's Name", *Myanmar Now*, 20 December 2019, https://myanmar-now.org/en/news/myanmar-explodes-in-anger-over-police-disclosure-of-child-rape-victims-name.
33. "The 'Victoria' Rape Case Exposes Myanmar's Missing Rule of Law", *The Irrawaddy*, 12 July 2019, https://www.irrawaddy.com/dateline/victoria-rape-case-exposes-myanmars-missing-rule-law.html; Aung Theinkha, "Hundreds Protest Police Naming of Child Rape Victim in Myanmar", *Radio Free Asia*, 23 December 2019, https://www.rfa.org/english/news/myanmar/naming-12232019170954.html
34. World Bank, "Myanmar Economic Monitor December 2019: Resilience Amidst

Risk", 22 January 2020, https://www.worldbank.org/en/country/myanmar/publication/myanmar-economic-monitor-december-2019-resilience-amidst-risk.

35. Thiha Ko Ko, "Declining Imports, Trade Deficit Not a Cause for Concern: Experts", *Myanmar Times*, 21 October 2019, https://www.mmtimes.com/news/declining-imports-trade-deficit-not-cause-concern-experts.html.
36. John Liu, "Myanmar Awards Insurance Licences to Five Foreign Providers, Six Joint Ventures", *Myanmar Times*, 28 November 2019, https://www.mmtimes.com/news/myanmar-awards-insurance-licences-five-foreign-providers-six-joint-ventures.html.
37. John Liu, "First Round of Bank Licences under Suu Kyi Govt Announced", *Myanmar Times*, 7 November 2019, https://www.mmtimes.com/news/first-round-bank-licences-under-suu-kyi-govt-announced.html.
38. Kyaw Lin Htoon, "Treasury Bonds Gain Momentum", *Frontier*, 19 December 2019, https://frontiermyanmar.net/en/treasury-bonds-gain-momentum.
39. Thiha Ko Ko, "Myanmar to Commence 10-year Bond Auctions 'Soon'", *Myanmar Times*, 20 November 2019, https://www.mmtimes.com/news/myanmar-commence-10-year-bond-auctions-soon.html.
40. Thiha Ko Ko, "Myanmar Inflation Peaks at 8.8% in December 2019", *Myanmar Times*, 11 February 2020, https://www.mmtimes.com/news/myanmar-inflation-peaks-88-december-2019.html.
41. Nyi Nyi Kyaw, "Frying Just A Few New 'Big Fish'? Combating Corruption in Myanmar", *ISEAS Perspective*, no. 2019/71, 9 September 2019.
42. Ministry of Planning and Finance, *Myanmar Living Conditions Survey 2017: Poverty Report*, June 2019, https://www.csostat.gov.mm/InformationAndReport/SurveyReport.

THE 2020 MYANMAR GENERAL ELECTION:
Another Turning Point?

Ye Htut

According to the Constitution of Myanmar, a general election is to be held every five years in order to elect parliamentarians to the two legislative chambers, the lower house (Pyithu Hluttaw, or house of representative) and the upper house (Amyotha Hluttaw, or house of nationalities). Twenty-five per cent of the seats in both houses are reserved for military-appointed representatives. After parliamentary elections, the lower and upper houses will sit together in the Pyidaungsu Hluttaw (Assembly of the Union) to serve as an electoral college for the presidential election.

The coming general election in 2020 will be an important milestone for Myanmar. The elections in 2010 brought about the "Myanmar Spring" under President Thein Sein, while the 2015 elections witnessed Aung San Suu Kyi and her National League for Democracy (NLD) coming to power. The 2015 general election marked the very first peaceful transfer of power from one elected government to another since the country gained independence from the British in 1948.[1] The year 2015 was also the first time Aung San Suu Kyi and her party were able to form the government since winning the election in 1990.[2]

In the three years since assuming power, the NLD government has introduced reforms of the economy, banking and finance; implemented a crackdown on corruption; and initiated the 21st Century Panglong Conference, a new peace process aimed at settling the country's various ethnic insurgencies. However, these efforts have been overshadowed by an economic slowdown, the Rohingya

---

YE HTUT was Visiting Senior Research Fellow at the ISEAS – Yusof Ishak Institute from 2016 to 2019. His book, *Myanmar's Political Transition and Lost Opportunities (2010–2016)*, was published by ISEAS in October 2019.

crisis and a lack of progress in the peace process. In particular, the failure of the reforms to translate into tangible benefits at the grass-roots level has led many people to feel that the NLD government has under-delivered on expectations.

The upcoming general election in 2020 will be the first electoral test for the NLD government. It will also be a judgement of Aung San Suu Kyi's leadership and legacy. Meanwhile, the opposition parties in Myanmar have sought to capitalize on voter dissatisfaction with the NLD's performance in government. The Union Solidarity and Development Party (USDP), which lost power in the 2015 elections, has been reorganizing itself and replacing its old generation of party leaders, including former President Thein Sein. Ethnic-based parties have also sought to consolidate their electoral strength by merging into single parties in their respective states to avoid splitting their share of the vote, as happened in 2015. The following is an analysis of the plans and prospects of the different political parties for the 2020 elections.

National-Level Parties

The National League for Democracy

The by-elections of 2017 and 2018 revealed the extent of voter dissatisfaction with the NLD. In the various by-elections in 2017, the NLD only managed to win 9 out of 18 seats. In the by-elections of 2018, it emerged victorious in only 7 out of 13 seats. In comparison, the NLD was able to win 43 out of 45 seats in the by-elections of 2012.[3] Recognizing the recent by-election results as a warning sign, Aung San Suu Kyi and the NLD leadership have pursued a reorganization of the party in preparation for the coming election.

Although the formal election campaign remains more than a year away,[4] the NLD has already begun its unofficial campaign. Between February and August 2019, Aung San Suu Kyi has travelled fourteen times to visit twelve different states and regions. During her visits, Suu Kyi delivered speeches at public rallies, inaugurated infrastructure development projects, and conducted talk shows with youths, farmers and the local communities. The primary thrust of her message was that the NLD needed to secure another election victory in order to continue with its current reform programmes and to sustain the democratization process.

The NLD also started the constitutional amendment process on 6 February 2019. It did so despite objections from the military members of parliament (MPs), who hold enough seats in the Pyindaungsu Hluttaw to prevent the passage of the amendments.[5] Stifled legislatively, the NLD instead took the opportunity to hold mass rallies across the country over the issue in order to mobilize mass support and galvanize their followers prior to the official campaigning period. The NLD had used a similar tactic in the run-up to the 2015 elections when it mobilized its supporters with a public campaign to amend Section 436 of the constitution.

Aung San Suu Kyi is also responding decisively to the sense of public dissatisfaction with the NLD government. She has removed Union ministers as well as regional and state chief ministers.[6] NLD spokesperson Myo Nyunt also announced that the party disciplinary committee has taken action against forty-five of its MPs in response to public complaints; they will also be barred from standing as NLD candidates for the 2020 general election.[7] Another party spokesperson, Monywa Aung Shin, has shared that the NLD may replace more than half of its current batch of parliamentarians in the forthcoming elections.[8] The NLD also announced the formation of the 2020 campaign team led by vice chairman (1) Dr Zaw Myint Maung, with secretariat members Nyan Win, Hanthar Myint and Aung Moe Nyo.[9]

All said, Aung San Suu Kyi, who occupies the official role of state counsellor, remains the biggest asset for the NLD. According to the results of a survey on "Citizens' Political Preferences for 2020" conducted in July 2019 by the People's Alliance for Credible Elections (PACE), 70 per cent of respondents revealed their confidence in the state counsellor (while 10 per cent indicated no confidence), positioning her as the politician with the highest level of confidence among those surveyed. However, public confidence in Aung San Suu Kyi varies across the regions and states. Confidence for her is around 78 per cent in the Bamar-majority regions, but it falls to 49 per cent in the states with large ethnic majorities.

Because of Aung San Suu Kyi's popularity and the hatred for the military, the NLD may be able to win the majority of seats in Bamar-dominated regions. However, it faces substantial electoral risks in ethnic-dominated states. In particular, the NLD remains vulnerable in 71 lower house seats and 23 upper house seats that were closely contested in the 2015 elections.[10]

The Union Solidarity and Development Party

The USDP easily won the general election in 2010, with 259 lower house seats and 129 upper house seats. The victory was the consequence of the NLD boycotting the election, which meant that the USDP did not enjoy genuine public support. The weakness of the USDP was clearly revealed by its 2012 by-elections record, when the party managed to secure only a single seat out of the 45 it contested.

Before the 2015 general election, the USDP leadership aimed to secure 26 per cent of the elected parliamentary seats, given that they could rely on the military-appointed MPs (who constitute 25 per cent of the legislative membership) in order to form a parliamentary majority. However, this hope failed to materialize, as the USDP won a meagre 41 out of 498 elected seats. After this electoral defeat, the USDP chairman Thein Sein resigned.

On 22 August 2016, the party congress elected Than Htay, a former railways minister, as the USDP chairman. Than Htay sought to re-energize and mobilize a party that has been deeply demoralized, not only by the electoral defeat but also having been fractured by the power struggle between two of its party elders, President Thein Sein and Hluttaw Speaker Shwe Mann. Over the period from January to August 2019, Than Htay visited eight regions and states, holding a total of forty-nine meetings with the party's grass-root members. The USDP held a Youth Conference in May 2018 and a Women's Conference in November 2018 for its members to formulate party policies. Since January 2017, the party started conducting capacity-building training courses in order to strengthen its grass-roots organization. The USDP also began holding central committee meetings in September in order to firm up its electoral strategy for 2020.

For the coming general election, the USDP is planning to use the economic slowdown and the Rohingya issue to discredit the NLD government. There has also been some discussion about relying on nationalism and Buddhism in order to mobilize the Buddhist majority. However, this approach has been a double-edged sword: while it could win over rural Buddhist voters, it also has the possibility of alienating the support of the educated middle-class and of the ethnic voters, who still remember the Burmanization policy under the military government. That the USDP has to contend with the legacy of the military government points to how the public still views the USDP as a military-backed political party, despite efforts by the party to show that it is gradually transforming into a true civilian party. For instance, a USDP spokesperson, Nandar Hla Myint, has clarified that while former military officers sit in the party's central executive committee (CEC), more than 300 members of the central committee are civilians. He acknowledged that the USDP is not only seeking to defend the record of the Thein Sein administration but also the legacy of the military government that ruled Myanmar from 1988 to 2010.[11]

Respondents to the same July 2019 PACE survey indicated a range of attitudes towards the USDP: 26 per cent held a positive view of the party, 19 per cent held a negative one, whilst 29 per cent were indifferent. Unlike the case with the NLD, there was no substantial difference between the states and regions with regard to how the respondents felt about the USDP. In the ethnic-majority states, 23 per cent of respondents were positive about the party while 18 per cent were negative; in the Bamar-dominated regions there was a similar ratio of 27 per cent positive and 19 per cent negative. Respondents from the city of Yangon also had a similar response to the USDP: 25 per cent were positive and 23 per cent negative.

In the 2015 elections, the USDP received more than 25 per cent of the votes for the 158 lower house seats and 85 upper house seats that they eventually lost to the NLD. For 28 of the lower house constituencies and for 12 upper house seats, the USDP's margin of loss was as small as between 2 and 10 per cent of the votes.[12] Hence, if the USDP succeeds in re-branding its image and in removing the perception of it being a military-backed party, it stands a good chance of regaining these seats in the 2020 general election.[13] However, the USDP faces the challenge of defending the 18 lower house seats and the 9 upper house seats it won in ethnic-majority states during the 2015 elections. These seats will be vigorously contested by the ethnic parties in the coming election. Furthermore, if the USDP were to lose all the seats in the ethnic states whilst failing to gain more seats in the Bamar-majority regions, the party may end with fewer seats in the new parliament.

The People's Party

Led by Ko Ko Gyi, a prominent student leader of the 8-8-88 Uprisings, the People's Party (PP) is often regarded as a potential third force in Myanmar politics. When the student leaders of the 88 Generation were released in 2012 under President Thein Sein's national reconciliation policy, there were expectations that they would eventually enter politics under the leadership of Aung San Suu Kyi. These hopes were diminished when the NLD refused to select Ko Ko Gyi and some other student leaders as candidates for the 2015 elections. After nearly a year of public consultations, Ko Ko Gyi and some of the 88 Generation student leaders decided to form the People's Party on 17 December 2017, receiving the approval of the election commission on 23 August 2018. As of December 2019, the PP has opened nearly 50 township offices and 100 ward/village offices across the country.[14]

The People's Party has been the subject of much criticism, especially from NLD supporters who view the party as a potential threat to the NLD. In particular, they have accused the People's Party of potentially splitting the pro-democracy votes and thus hurting the NLD's prospects in the 2020 elections. Minn Ko Naing, another leader of the 88 Generation, has been vocal in refusing to join the People's Party. However, Ko Ko Gyi has rejected such criticisms, arguing that the risks of vote-splitting can be tempered if an alliance policy is implemented between the

NLD and the other pro-democracy parties.[15] He has also countered that if people believe in democracy, they should not be afraid of pluralism in politics.[16]

Significantly, Ko Ko Gyi recognizes that ethnic voters are losing trust in Bamar-majority parties. He has pointed out that the NLD committed a grave mistake in neglecting the ethnic parties after its election victory in 2015. According to him, the NLD's electoral victory in 2015 did not mean that the NLD had received the political mandate of the ethnic people. Furthermore, he has argued that the NLD needs to further understand the nature of identity politics in Myanmar.[17]

The National Unity Party

The National Unity Party (NUP) was founded in September 1988 to succeed the former ruling party, the Burma Socialist Program Party (BSPP), after the military coup. It contested the 1990 election and won only 10 seats. It contested again in the 2010 elections—which was boycotted by the NLD—and won 5 seats in the Amyotha Hluttaw, 12 seats in the Pyithu Hluttaw and 47 seats in the various regional and state *hluttaws*. However, in the 2015 elections the party was reduced to a single seat in the Amyotha Hluttaw.

After the 2015 election defeat, the party reorganized itself and elected a new central executive committee and central committee. Boasting a membership of over four hundred thousand, the NUP has also formed 293 local organizations in the 330 townships.[18] The main challenge for the NUP is reputational: most of the public see the party as a proxy of the military, while ethnic voters view the NUP as a Bamar party. Although the NUP is working closely with the USDP, including issuing joint statements after the 2015 elections on issues of importance such as the Rakhine situation and the state of Myanmar's economy, the vice-chairman of the NUP has revealed that the party does not have a coordinated election strategy with the USDP for the 2020 elections.[19] The major challenge for the NUP is differentiating itself from the USDP so that the party becomes an attractive proposition in its own right. Currently, voters who are against the NLD would prefer to vote for the USDP rather than the NUP.

The National Democratic Force

The National Democratic Force (NDF) was founded by Than Nyein and some leaders of the NLD after they disagreed with Aung San Suu Kyi's decision to boycott the 2010 elections. These defectors believed that participating in the 2010 elections was crucial because it was the only way to move the democratization of Myanmar forward.[20] The party was registered on 27 May 2010 and approved on 9 July 2010. In the 2010 elections, the NDF contested 261 seats, winning 2 in the Amyotha Hluttaw, 10 in the Pyithu Hluttaw and 4 in regional *hluttaws*.

However, after the elections, a dispute between Than Nyein and Thein Nyunt led to a split in the leadership of the NDF. Thein Nyunt and two other NDF parliamentarians defected to form the New National Democracy Party (NNDP) in 2011. After the NLD's by-election victories in 2012, another three NDF parliamentarians defected to the NLD. In the 2015 elections, the NDF contested in 265 seats but failed to secure even a single one. Khin Maung Swe, the chairman of the NDF, admitted that the party severely underperformed in 2015 because Bamar-majority regions voted overwhelmingly for the NLD out of sympathy for Aung San Suu Kyi. Moreover, in the ethnic-majority states, voters believed that Aung San Suu Kyi was the only person who could promote ethnic interests. The NDF also made the mistake of overstretching itself by contesting nationwide in 2015. For the 2020 general election, the NDF plans to concentrate its resources in the constituencies that it has previously done well in.[21]

The New National Democracy Party

The New National Democracy Party (NNDP) is a breakaway faction of the NDF. It is led by Thein Nyunt, who was previously a central committee member of the NLD until he defected in order to contest the 2010 elections under the NDF banner. Despite being a small party, the NNDP was very active during the First Hluttaw (2010–16) on account of Thein Nyunt's industrious parliamentary performance. Over the course of those years, Thein Nyunt gained public support as he proposed 28 bills, tabled 32 resolutions and submitted 143 questions to the government.[22]

In the 2015 elections, the NNDP contested more than 20 seats but failed to win any. Thein Nyunt has said that it was a mistake to spread his finite resources over that many seats in 2015. For the 2020 elections, the NNDP will concentrate on 4 seats in the Yangon region. He also believes that the 2020 elections will be more favourable as voters are losing confidence in the ability of the NLD's MPs to serve their constituencies. Instead, voters will be more discerning in electing more qualified candidates from the other parties. He also stated that Aung San Suu Kyi's slogan in 2015, in which she encouraged the electorate to "vote for the NLD, whoever the candidate is", will not work in 2020.[23]

The Union Betterment Party

The Union Betterment Party (UBP) was founded and is led by the former Speaker of the lower house, Shwe Mann. Shwe Mann had previously served as the chief of the general staff (Army, Navy and Air Force) and was the third-highest-ranking official in the military junta, the State Peace and Development Council (SPDC). In the run-up to the 2010 elections, he was expected to succeed Than Shwe, but the latter surprised everyone by selecting Thein Sein as the new president. Shwe Mann was instead given the speakership of the lower house. Since constitutional restrictions prevented Thein Sein from serving as the chairman of the ruling USDP, Shwe Mann was instead installed as the acting chairman. However, during Shwe Mann's chairmanship of the USDP, he attempted to undermine Thein Sein's authority. The power struggle between the two USDP leaders deeply affected the party's grass-root organizations, eventually leading to the removal of Shwe Mann as the chair of the USDP.

After the NLD's victory in the 2015 elections, the NLD-controlled Pyindaungsu Hluttaw, with the approval of Aung San Suu Kyi, formed the Legal Affairs and Special Cases Assessment Commission. Shwe Mann was appointed as the chairman of the commission over the fierce opposition of the military representatives in the Pyindaungsu Hluttaw. Since then, while NLD MPs have consistently voted to extend the commission's mandate, the military representatives in parliament have regularly voted against the annual extension.

On 5 February 2019, Shwe Mann announced that he would be forming his own party to contest the 2020 elections. On 28 February, when the Hluttaw was deliberating over the annual extension of Shwe Mann's commission, NLD parliamentarians received an unexpected order from the party's chief whips: they were instructed to vote against renewing the mandate of the Legal Affairs and Special Cases Assessment Commission.[24] When the Speaker called for a vote, a total of 555 lawmakers voted against the motion. Other than 10 abstentions, there were only 20 votes in favour of extending the commission. Both military MPs and USDP MPs were surprised by the NLD's last-minute decision.

Shwe Mann was also taken by surprise. On the evening of 27 February, commission members were celebrating the commission's third anniversary and had no doubts about the commission's future. On the morning of 28 February, Shwe Mann was caught off guard by the Hluttaw vote while at the commission's office. When journalists met him that afternoon, he admitted that there had been no prior discussion about the future of the commission with either the Hluttaw or Aung San Suu Kyi. Later he told *Frontier Myanmar* that although the vote caught him by surprise, it was a good thing for him, the NLD and the people. "It is important to distinguish between politics and personal relations", he said.[25]

After receiving the Union Election Commission's approval on 25 April 2019, Shwe Mann has travelled across the county to open party township offices, accept applications for party membership and deliver speeches. The UBP currently has nineteen members in its central executive committee, with most of them being former military officers and defectors from the USDP. One of the CEC members, Ko Ko Naing, shared with Khit Thit media on 28 July that the UBP is looking to contest at least 207 constituencies in Bamar-majority regions.[26]

The sudden abolition of Shwe Mann's commission has led to rumours that a plot has been hatched between Aung San Suu Kyi and Shwe Mann, and that the UBP is a subordinate vehicle to serve the interests of the NLD. However, Shwe Mann has rejected these allegations, asserting that the UBP is not under the influence of the NLD. Instead, the UBP will seek to cooperate with other political parties based on the national interest. He also said that the UBP will emphasize its presence in the regions while coordinating with ethnic parties in the ethnic states.[27]

Since the leadership of UBP consists of former military officers and USDP members, there is the likelihood the UBP could syphon some of the USDP's grass-roots support. However, USDP spokesperson Nandar Hla Myint has said this will not happen, since USDP supporters will not vote for a turncoat.[28] Shwe Mann, for his part, aims to position the UBP as a prospective partner in a future coalition government, since he believes it will be difficult for a single party to win a clear parliamentary majority in the 2020 elections.[29]

Tatmadaw (Armed Forces)

The constitution of Myanmar grants legislative privileges to the Tatmadaw by reserving 25 per cent of seats in Union, regional and state houses for military MPs appointed by the commander-in-chief. Another privilege afforded to the military MPs is that they are able to nominate their own candidate for president, who will then face off with the two other candidates respectively nominated by the lower house and the upper house.[30] Hence, the military-nominated presidential candidate stands a good chance of becoming either president or at least vice president. This has led to speculation as to whether the current commander-in-chief, Senior General Min Aung Hlaing, would enter the presidential election after the 2020 general election.

Min Aung Hlaing can hold his cards until the results of the 2020 elections emerge, since there is at least a gap of three months between the parliamentary elections and the presidential election. If the NLD does not win a majority in both the upper and lower houses, the Tatmadaw will be in a position to broker a deal with the USDP and other parties to support a Min Aung Hlaing presidency.

During a press conference on 28 September, the Armed Forces spokesperson, Major Gen Tun Tun Nyi, stated that Min Aung Hlaing "will serve the country by one way or another. He will make the decision and we have to wait and see."[31]

Ethnic Parties

According to the 2014 census, ethnic groups make up a third of the country's 51.5 million people. Of the 92 registered parties in Myanmar, 50 of them are ethnic parties.[32] However, the ethnic parties have not been able to win any sizeable numbers of seats during the 1990, 2010 and 2015 elections. The dominance of the USDP and the NLD in the parliaments of 2010 and 2015 were at the expense of the ethnic parties. In the 2015 elections, for instance, the NLD achieved a landslide victory both in the Bamar-majority regions and in the ethnic-majority states, with the exception of Rakhine and Shan. The ethnic people had voted for the NLD because they believed that only the NLD, which had campaigned on the slogan "Time for Change", would be able to deliver peace and development for ethnic people. The NLD was also the practical choice as they recognized that their ethnic parties were too small to be able to form a government.

However, the expectations of the ethnic voters were never matched by the NLD. For example, although the Arakan National Party (ANP) secured a majority in the state *hluttaw*, the NLD refused to offer the post of chief minister to the ANP and instead appointed one of their own party members. Furthermore, the NLD limited participation in the 21st Century Panglong peace process to only political parties that had managed to win at least one seat in the 2015 elections, thus effectively sidelined many of the ethnic parties. The NLD's decision was criticized for going against the Nationwide Ceasefire Agreement,[33] which had stipulated that future political dialogues must include representatives from all registered political parties.[34] Such developments have led the ethnic population of Myanmar to the realization that only their own elected ethnic party representatives will be able to properly advance and promote the rights of their people. This has prompted efforts to consolidate the different ethnic parties into a single party in order to contest effectively in the 2020 general election.

Kayah State

Among the ethnic political parties, those in Kayah state were the first to consolidate after the 2015 elections. The Kayah Unity Democracy Party and the All Nationals' Democracy Party (Kayah State) merged into the Kayah State Democratic Party (KSDP). This merger was approved by the Union Election Commission on

8 September 2017. Another Kayah party, the Kayan National Party, had chosen to decline a merger in favour of pursuing a strategic alliance with the new KSDP instead.[35]

Kachin State

In Kachin, four ethnic political parties (the Kachin State Democracy Party, the Kachin Democratic Party, the Kachin National Congress, and the Unity and Development Party of Kachin State) have merged to form the Kachin State People's Party (KSPP). The new party received approval of the Union Election Commission on 7 June 2019. For the 2020 general election, the KSPP hopes to secure a majority in the state house and to also win enough seats in the Pyindaungsu Hluttaw in order to be in a position to join a coalition government.[36]

Chin State

Three Chin parties (the Chin National Democratic Party, the Chin Progressive Party, and the Chin League of Democracy) have also merged to form the Chin National League for Democracy Party (CNLD). The CNLD was approved on 11 July 2019. Another Chin party, Zomi League for Democracy, did not join the alliance, but the CNLD is committed to find means of cooperating with the Zomi League in the 2020 general elections.[37]

Mon State

After more than two years of negotiations, two Mon Parties (the Mon National Party, or MNP, and the All Mon Region Democracy Party) joined forces to create the Mon Unity Party, which received official approval on 11 June 2019. However, the Mon Women's Party did not enter the alliance. Nai Soe Myint, a spokesperson of the MNP, stated the merger is the first step to a better future for the ethnic Mon:

> We can combine not only political parties but political groups. The public, especially Mon people, are satisfied with the merger and will support us in the election.[38]

Kayin State

The situation facing Kayin political parties is unique. Initially there were four ethnic parties in Kayin State. However, given the sizeable presence of the Kayin population in the Yangon and Ayeyarwady regions, there exist an additional two

Kayin parties outside Kayin State. Three of the four parties in Kayin State (the Karen Democratic Party, the Karen State Democracy and Development Party, and the United Karen National Democratic Party) have merged to form the Karen National Democratic Party (KNDP), gaining official approval on 22 February 2018. The fourth party, the Phalon-Sawaw Democratic Party (PSDP), turned down the opportunity to join the new party. The PSDP has however indicated it will not run candidates against the KNDP in Kayin State. Meanwhile, the two Kayin parties based outside Kayin—the Karen People's Party and the Karen National Party—are committed to contesting only seats outside the state.[39]

Rakhine State

The circumstances facing ethnic parties in Rakhine are somewhat more complex as a result of the elections in 2015. Prior to the 2015 general election, the two major Rakhine parties, the Arakan League for Democracy (ALD) and the Rakhine National Development Party (RNDP), merged to form the Arakan National Party (ANP).[40] The ANP was the most successful ethnic party in the 2015 elections: it secured 22 of the 35 elected seats in the Rakhine State House, won 12 seats in the lower house and a further 10 seats in the upper house. After the elections, the ANP leadership and its parliamentarians met with Aung San Suu Kyi and the leaders of the NLD at Naypyitaw to discuss the allocation of appointments in the Rakhine State government.[41] As mentioned above, the ANP, which had secured a majority in the state house, wanted to lead the state government. However, Aung San Suu Kyi rejected this request, having decided to appoint the NLD's Nyi Pu as chief minister of Rakhine State, even though the NLD only had 9 seats in the state house.[42] As a result the ANP declared it would not only refuse to cooperate with the NLD-led state government in Rakhine but would also reject any ministerial posts in the Union and state governments.

However, in 2016 the ALD decided to separate from the ANP with the expectation that they would be contesting the 2020 elections on the ALD party platform. This decision was precipitated by actions from the RNDP that broke the gentlemen's agreement between the two parties. Currently, the prospect of the ALD rejoining the alliance is small.[43] The ANP also suffered a setback when its chairman, Aye Maung, resigned to form the Arakan Front Party (AFP). The AFP managed to secure one seat in Rakhine during a by-election in 2018.

If the three Rakhine parties are not able to merge into a single party for the 2020 elections, the NLD and the USDP may have a good chance of taking some seats, especially in southern Rakhine. Moreover, there are concerns that security considerations may compel the election commission to cancel the elections for some constituencies in Northern Rakhine. This will reduce the number of available seats for Rakhine MPs in the Union and state houses.

Shan State

Shan State vividly represents the complex ethnic politics of Myanmar. Shan is the only state with five ethnic self-administered areas (Danu, Kokang, Pa-O, Palaung, and Wa), all of which have their own parties and local governments. Since 1988 the Shan Nationalities League for Democracy (SNLD) has emerged as the major Shan party. The SNLD won 23 seats in the 1990 elections that the military government refused to recognize. The SNLD formally boycotted the 2010 elections, but some SNLD members formed the Shan Nationalities Democratic Party (SNDP) to contest in the elections and they managed to win 18 seats in the lower house and 4 seats in the upper house. After the implementation of President Thein Sein's political reforms, the SNLD decided to contest the 2015 election, securing 12 seats in the lower house and 3 seats in the upper house. The SNDP was however reduced to a single seat in the state *hluttaw*.

The complexity of Shan State politics is reflected in the 2015 electoral results for the state house (see Table 1). The Shan State's *hluttaw* was fractured among many political parties, including the major national parties, the major ethnic parties and other small and minor parties.

TABLE 1
Composition of the State Hluttaw in Shan State after the 2015 Elections

Party	Seats
USDP	33
SNLD	24
NLD	23
Ta'arng (Palaung) National Party	7
Pa-O National Organization	6
Wa Democratic Party	2
Wa National Unity Party	1
Kokang Democracy and Unity Party	1
SNDP	1
Lisu National Development Party	1
Akha National Development Party	1
Independent	1

Source: "The Ethnic Parties' Dilemma: Merger or Strategic Alliance?", *Frontier Myanmar*, 18 April 2018.

According to Sai Nyunt Lwin, vice chair of the SNLD, there is very little prospect of a merger between the SNLD and the SNDP. However, the SNLD is looking at reaching some form of strategic agreement with the SNDP before the 2020 elections. The SNLD is also planning to consult with other ethnic parties in Shan State to hammer out an agreement on electoral strategy, with the aim of all ethnic parties in the state working together to deny an NLD or USDP victory there.[44] During its party congress on 6 June 2019, the SNLD also decided to transform the SNLD from an ethnic-based party to a regional and policy-based one that will seek cooperation with any political party that endorses the federal principles of self-determination.[45]

Conclusion

The coming general elections will not only determine the division of power in the legislature but also the election of the next president. Myanmar has a unique process of electing the president. The Pyidaungsu Hluttaw, which is the joint sitting of both the lower and upper houses, will act as an electoral college for the election of the president. The process commences with the nomination of vice presidential candidates by three electoral groups: the elected members of the lower house, the elected members of the upper house, and the military representatives from both houses. Each group can select a vice presidential candidate either from within or without the ranks of parliament. The Pyidaungsu Hluttaw then elects the president from among these three vice presidential nominees. The two runners-up will then become vice president 1 and vice president 2 in line with the number of votes they receive.

There will be 664 members in the Pyidaungsu Hluttaw, with 440 MPs drawn from the lower house and another 224 from the upper house. Since the Tatmadaw holds 25 per cent of seats in both houses, the Pyidaungsu Hluttaw is divided between 498 elected members and 166 military appointees. Given this arrangement, the party that secures a majority of the 498 elected seats will be able to control the legislature and stands a good chance of elevating its nominee to the presidency. This is especially true if the party is able to win more than 333 seats in total across both houses, in which case it can elect its nominee as president without having to rely on the support of other smaller parties or the military representatives. This happened in 2010 and 2015 when the parliamentary dominance of the USDP and NLD ensured that the parties could easily elect their nominees as president and vice president.

In the 2015 general election, the NLD won 255 out of 323 elected seats in the lower house[46] and 135 out of 168 elected seats in the upper house. In total, the NLD won 390 seats in both houses, which amounts to 79.4 per cent of the elected seats in the Pyidaungsu Hluttaw. Taking into account the reserved seats for the military, the NLD eventually held 59.4 per cent of the total seats in the Pyindaungsu Hluttaw.[47] This commanding margin of victory was driven not only by its strong performance in Bamar-majority regions but also in ethnic-majority states. The question however is whether the NLD can sustain this winning streak in the 2020 elections.

After the 2015 elections, the NLD has found itself in greater confrontation with ethnic political parties. The SNLD and ANP have already declared that they will refuse to join an electoral alliance with the NLD. During the NLD central committee meeting on 21–22 September, the NLD vice chairman Zaw Myint Maung stated that the NLD must win the coming elections by a landslide in order to avoid having to form a coalition government. At stake are the 498 elected seats in both the upper and lower houses. A total of 291 of those seats are in the seven Bamar-majority regions, while a further 207 seats are located in the seven ethnic-majority states. The NLD has to fight on two fronts: it faces stiff opposition from ethnic parties for the 207 upper and lower house seats in the ethnic states, while also confronting the possibility that the USDP, NDF, NUP, NNDP, PP and UBP may capture some of the 291 upper and lower house seats in the Bamar-majority regions. If the ethnic parties are able to win at least 150 seats (they currently hold around 50 seats across the two houses), it will prove to be very difficult for the NLD to break the threshold of 333 seats in the Pyidaungsu Hluttaw.

This is something that the USDP is aware of and which has prompted the party to try to cobble together a future parliamentary majority through a coalition with ethnic parties and the military. Nandar Hla Myint, a USDP spokesperson, has said that the USDP will not form a formal political alliance but will instead cooperate with other parties based on the national interest.[48] In the 2018 by-elections, the USDP worked with ethnic parties in Chin and Kachin States in order to ensure the loss of two NLD seats to the Chin Party and the USDP. The USDP will likely adopt the same approach in the 2020 elections in order to deny the NLD victory in ethnic states.

For the ethnic parties, the major challenge is to form an electoral alliance before the 2020 elections. There will also be a need to form a united front in the Pyidaungsu Hluttaw after the elections. Currently, there are two ethnic alliances: the Nationalities Brotherhood Federation (NBF), consisting of 14 parties; and the United Nationalities Alliance (UNA), consisting of 23 parties. There is little chance of an electoral alliance between the two organizations, as they have major policy differences relating to the structure of the federal union. Moreover, both ethnic alliances comprise different ethnic parties, each with their own interests, rendering an agreement on electoral strategy and seat allocations in ethnic areas difficult to achieve. Furthermore, a true ethnic alliance will only be able to emerge after the results of the 2020 election, as the victorious ethnic parties would seek to politically align themselves with partners that can offer them the greatest political leverage.[49] Another challenge, more pronounced among Rakhine and Shan ethnic parties, is whether the respective leaders of the ethnic parties will be able to overcome their differences, which are often more personal than ideological.

All things considered, only the NLD has a chance of winning an outright majority in the Pyidaungsu Hluttaw. Aung San Suu Kyi's star power should not be underestimated, especially in the Bamar-majority regions. Her decision to personally lead the country's legal team to The Hague to defend Myanmar against genocide charges has proven to be popular and may rally voters to her side in an election year. In order to deny the NLD such a majority, the best strategy for the USDP and the other parties would be to coordinate at the level of each constituency and to nominate the best single candidate from among them to stand against the NLD. They would otherwise run the risk of benefitting the NLD in each constituency by splitting the opposition vote.

Should the NLD secure fewer than 333 seats across both the upper and lower houses, it would be compelled to pursue a national coalition government with other parties. Such a coalition would help to advance the democratic transition along with national reconciliation and the federalism of Myanmar. This would be the best scenario for Myanmar politics after the 2020 General Election. It remains for the Myanmar people to decide this.

Notes

1. The first democratic government of Myanmar (then Burma) lasted from 1948 to 1962, when it was ended by a military coup on 2 March. The one-party socialist government that began in 1974 was ended by a military coup on 18 September 1988.
2. After the coup in 1988, the military junta held an election in 1990. Although the NLD won that election, the military government refused to transfer power to the NLD.
3. The NLD contested 44 seats.
4. The Union Election Commission allowed a campaign period of one month for the 2015 general election.

5. According to Section 436 of the 2008 Constitution, all constitutional amendments require the approval of more than seventy-five per cent of the representatives of the Pyidaungsu Hluttaw. This means that even if all elected MPs were to support a proposed amendment, at least one vote from the military parliamentarians would also be necessary for the amendment to pass.
6. The Union minister for finance and revenue, Union minister for energy and industry, and the chief ministers of Ayeyarwady and Mon States were forced to resign. The chief minister of Tanintharyi Region was arrested under the Anti-Corruption Act.
7. *Democratic Voice of Burma*, 9 June 2019.
8. "NLD to Replace Many 2020 Candidates", *Myanmar Times*, 16 October 2019, https://www.mmtimes.com/news/nld-replace-many-2020-candidates.html.
9. *Irrawaddy Magazine* (online), 29 October 2019.
10. Maug Maug Soe, "2020 Ywekaukpwe Nint Tineyinthar party Myar" [2020 Election and Ethnic Parties], *The Irrawaddy*, 14 September 2018.
11. Interview by the author with Nandar Hla Myint (USDP spokesperson), 13 August 2019.
12. Based on the official election results published by the Union Election Commission.
13. Interview by the author with U Thein Nyunt (New National Democracy Party chair), 25 August 2019.
14. Interview by the author with U Ko Ko Gyi (People's Party chair), 12 December 2019.
15. Interview with Ko Ko Gyi, *Frontier Myanmar*, 23 January 2018.
16. Interview with Ko Ko Gyi, *Voice of America*, 26 November 2018.
17. Interview by the author with Ko Ko Gyi, 24 September 2019.
18. Myanmar electoral constituencies are based on townships.
19. Interview by the author with Han Shwe (NUP vice-chair), 28 August 2019.
20. Interview with Dr Than Nyein, *Yangon Times*, 12 August 2010.
21. Interview by the author with Khin Maung Swe (NDF chair), 4 September 2019.
22. Interview by the author with Thein Nyunt (NNDP chair), 25 August 2019.
23. Ibid.
24. "Is Shwe Mann Out in the Cold?", *Frontier Myanmar*, 25 March 2019.
25. Ibid.
26. http://www.khitthitnews.com, 28 July 2019.
27. Speech delivered by Shwe Mann at Mandalay, 20 June 2019, press release, Union Betterment Party, https://web.facebook.com/UBP.Party.Official/.
28. Interview by the author with Nandar Hla Myint (USDP spokesperson), 13 August 2019.
29. Interview with Shwe Mann, *7days Journal*, 15 March 2019.
30. Section 60 of the Constitution on Election of the President by Pyidaugsu Hluttaw.
31. "Bogyokemugyi Min Aung Hlaing Thamada Pyit Hlar Mar Lar" [Will Senior Gen. Min Aung Hlaing become president], *Irrawaddy Magazine*, 4 October 2019.

32. Data from the Union Election Commission website, https://www.uec.gov.mm/index.php.
33. The National Ceasefire Agreement was signed by the government and eight ethnic armed organizations on 15 October 2015.
34. Article 22(A) of the National Ceasefire Agreement.
35. "The Ethnic Parties' Dilemma: Merger or Strategic Alliance?", *Frontier Myanmar*, 18 April 2018.
36. Interview with Dr Tu Ja, chairman of the KSPP, *The Irrawaddy*, 24 September 2019.
37. Interview by the author with Pu Zo Zam (NLD chair), 15 August 2019.
38. "Three Political Parties Merge under Mon Party Banner", *Myanmar Times*, 26 September 2018.
39. "Ethnic Parties' Dilemma".
40. The ALD boycotted the 2010 elections, enabling the RNDP to win 18 seats in the state house and 16 seats in the upper and lower houses.
41. Interviews by the author with U Oo Hlaw Saw (ANP leader), 12 September 2019, and Daw Htoo May (ALD parliamentarian), 15 September 2019.
42. According to the constitution, it is the president who appoints the chief minister of a state, and not the state *hluttaw*.
43. Interviews by the author with U Hla Myint (member of the ALD central executive committee), 6 September 2019, and Daw Htoo May Htoo (ALD parliamentarian), 15 September 2019.
44. Interview by the author with Sai Nyunt Lwin (SNLD vice-chair), 23 August 2019.
45. Interview with Sia Nyunt Lwin, *Nyang News*, 19 October 2019.
46. Of the 330 elected lower house seats, polling was suspended in 7 constituencies because of armed conflicts.
47. International Crisis Group, "The Myanmar Elections: Results and Implications", briefing no. 147, 9 December 2015, https://www.crisisgroup.org/asia/south-east-asia/myanmar/myanmar-elections-results-and-implications.
48. USDP press conference, 15 September 2019.
49. Interview by the author with U Oo Hlaw Saw (ANP leader), 12 September 2019.

Philippines

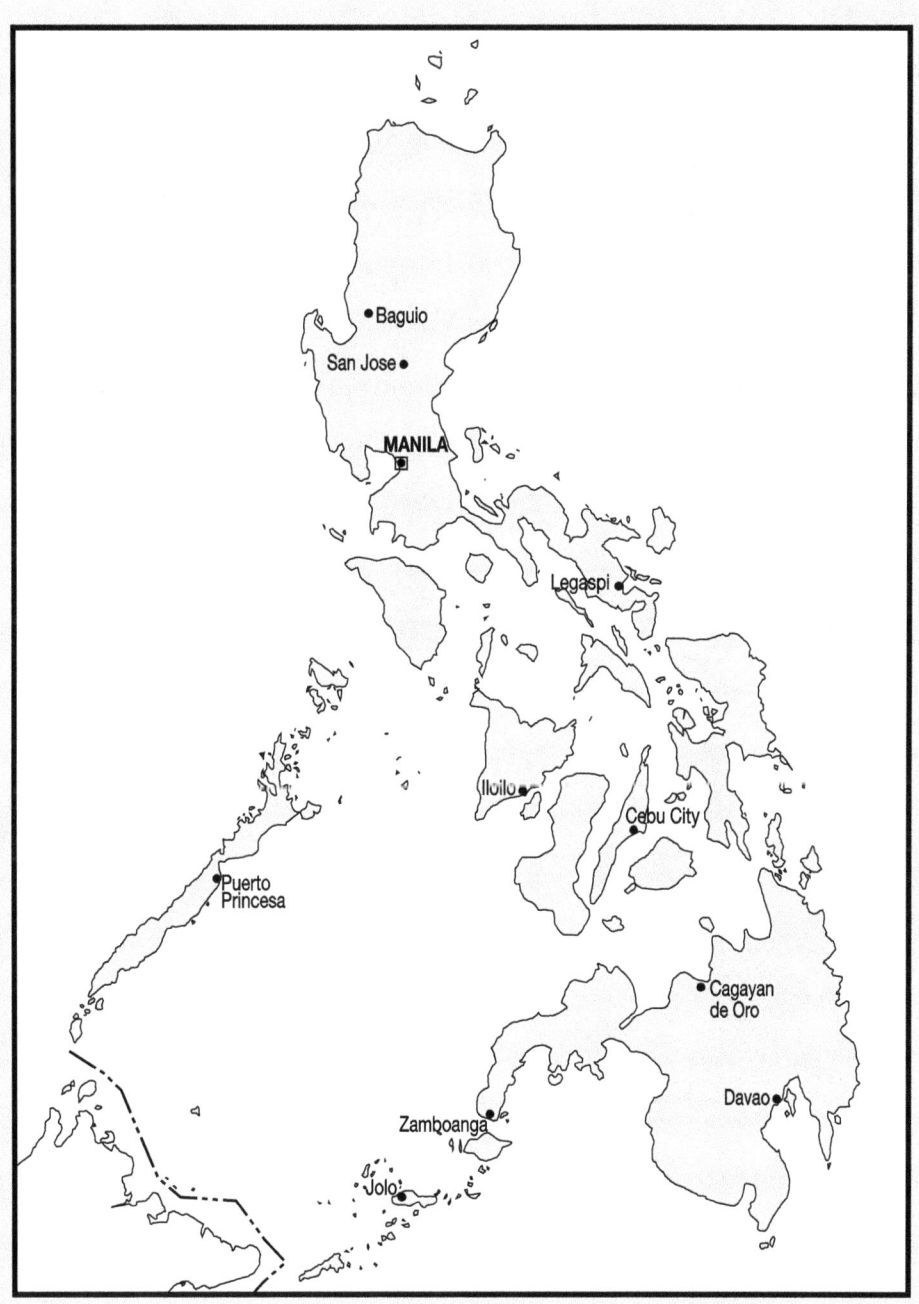

THE ONES WHO DON'T WALK AWAY FROM THE PHILIPPINES

Lowell Bautista

Back in 1974, renowned writer Ursula Le Guin won the Hugo Award for Best Short Story for "The Ones Who Walk Away from Omelas". Omelas was a peaceful, prosperous and blissful city. However, every child in the city, as a rite of passage, is made aware that their utopia depends on one child being locked and tortured in a basement. While the author frames the ending of the story in terms of those few who cannot stomach it and thus walk away from Omelas, a more instructive aspect is the part of those who did not—the ones who, no matter how begrudgingly, made the conscious decision to accept the price of paradise.

Halfway into his term, Philippine President Rodrigo Duterte, with his concomitant strongman approach to "get things done in the wake of democratic dysfunction",[1] continues to enjoy a "very good" approval rating from as much as 78 per cent of the population. While it is lower than the 86 per cent rating he held in 2016, it is still exceptionally high compared to those of other post-1986 Philippine presidents.[2] Duterte's popularity notably endures despite delays in infrastructure projects, a widely criticized rapprochement with China, doubt about the credibility of the Philippine National Police over the "ninja cops" issue, brewing unrest from farmers arising from competition with rice imports following the passage of the Rice Tariffication Law, and growing international criticism over the country's human rights record as evidenced by the so-called Iceland resolution in the United Nations Human Rights Council last June. During this year's midterm election, which was seen as a referendum on Duterte's illiberal

---

LOWELL BAUTISTA is Senior Lecturer at the School of Law and a Staff Member at the Australian National Centre for Ocean Resources and Security (ANCORS), University of Wollongong, Australia.

approach to politics, the opposition failed to gain a single seat in the Senate.[3] One writer despaired that the elections proved that "the Philippines just became more authoritarian, thanks to the people".[4]

This chapter joins the chorus of other reviews that have described the Philippine political trajectory as heading towards greater illiberalism and the centralization of power with the executive, which undermines the integrity of democratic politics as a modus vivendi.[5] However, as a way forward it also takes stock of Duterte's broader policy agenda, in addition to his governance style and its corrosive impact on democratic institutions, which many writers have emphasized. The novelty of Duterte is not so much in his illiberal approach to politics but in his exclusive focus on the goal of state-building fundamentals (e.g., public order, infrastructure and services) over a values-based agenda (e.g., human rights and anti-corruption) that previous administrations have not openly challenged.

As the Philippines enters its critical period of economic take-off, the reality is that it is beginning to confront more questions of "stateness"—levels of street crime, the presence of vital infrastructure, and issues of social services—which precisely reinforce the logic of Duterte's preference for state-building concerns over high-brow, values-based reformism. This can be seen in the increasing salience of urban development issues in the Philippines' 2019 headlines such as transportation and traffic problems, low-quality interconnectivity infrastructure, and drug proliferation over traditional news staples such as big-ticket corruption during the Arroyo administration, or coup d'etat attempts under Corazon Aquino. Such a focus is not inherently wrong, as state building fundamentals are necessary to the functioning of any society.

Like the moral dilemma of citizens in Le Guin's city of Omelas, the challenge for the Philippines is how to walk away from such an ugly, if not false, belief in a trade-off between state power and liberalism being marketed by no less than the president. The chapter concludes with two observations. First, the shift from a values-based agenda to method-agnostic state-building efforts will likely persist beyond Duterte. Exclusivist focus on intangibles or values will likely suffer electoral defeat, as the Otso Diretso slate learned in this year's elections. Second, the current administration's weak links in the coming years will be coalitional infighting in a bid to secure Duterte's endorsement, and the unevenness of its efforts and accomplishments vis-à-vis its three core priority areas of infrastructure, basic services and public order. Finally, one cannot help but think that—regardless of the academic point as to whether this public sentiment will turn out to be transient or more enduring (i.e., cultural)—there is the unmistakable reality of a grass-roots demand for strong executive leadership.

Consolidating the Illiberal-Majoritarian Nexus

Duterte's majoritarian coalition is consolidating its grip on power in a largely legitimate fashion. Not a single member of the oppositionist "Otso Diretso" slate—dominated by the Liberal Party—won a seat in the midterm senatorial elections. Despite not being on the ballot, Duterte himself framed the election as a confidence vote on his approach: "if you agree with me, you can vote for my candidates".[6] Traditional politicians flocked to Duterte-supported political parties, the regional Hugpong ng Pagbabago coalition led by presidential daughter Sarah Duterte and the ruling PDP-Laban party of the president.

Furthermore, Duterte's former vice presidential running mate Alan Peter Cayetano became Speaker of the House of Representatives and urged fellow lawmakers to join the "Die-hard Duterte Supermajority". The brazen and unapologetic pitch indicates just how asymmetric executive-legislative relations have become. The Supreme Court too is increasingly being brought under the president's influence. Between June and December 2019, the president shall appoint five more justices, and will have appointed a majority of magistrates to the Supreme Court.[7] Senior Associate Justice Antonio Carpio, an eminent critic of the president's policy on territorial conflict with China, has retired. Judicial independence will once again be of national importance, especially in light of a pending high court decision on the election protest of Ferdinand Marcos Jr. against Vice President Leni Robredo, who President Duterte has personal animus towards.

High on its public legitimacy, the administration is likewise doubling down on its ends-justify-the-means discourse. Duterte's script has been characterized as an "order over law" rather than a "law and order" agenda in holding out "the promise of making the Philippine government work."[8]

In July, Iceland initiated a resolution in the United Nations Human Rights Council to investigate the human rights situation in the Philippines. The government responded with a memorandum in August that ordered executive agencies to reject millions of dollars worth of loan and grant offers from the forty-one countries that supported the UN probe resolution.[9] In October, the administration openly called on courts to not hamper anti-narcotic operations with "very stringent requirements on the handling of evidence and the chain of custody rule", which has resulted in 60 per cent of drug cases from 2016 to 2017 being either dismissed or resulting in acquittal due to a weak case build-up or non-compliance with inventory of seized drugs.[10] Beyond the drug war, the president has alarmingly threatened the non-renewal of the franchise of ABS-CBN, which has been one of the more oppositionist media outlets thus far.

Sadly, efforts by external and internal political institutions to check excesses of executive authority will likely fuel the Duterte constituency's logic that views constraints on executive power, in the form of courts and human rights activists, as roadblocks to development and public order. An apt characterization of the emerging Philippine political system is what the political scientist Guillermo O'Donell calls "delegative democracy": because of his popular mandate, the president is entitled to "govern as he or she sees fit, constrained only by the hard facts of existing power relations and by a constitutionally limited term of office".[11] The shell of nominal democratic institutions—the courts, legislatures, and elections—remains in place, but these institutions are subject to the strong influence of one person.

The challenge from Duterte is that in having illiberalism backed or tolerated by a majority of the population, he pits his popular mandate against liberal restraints, even as both are central and sometimes conflicting principles of democracy.[12] The clamour for a popular voice, known in the literature as "vertical accountability", is different from the erstwhile focus of Filipino democrats on the liberal or "horizontal accountability" component of democracy, understood as the prevention of an excessive concentration of unaccountable power, particularly in the political executive.[13] The challenge of Duterte is not that he is entirely anti-democratic, but that he speaks to this historically recurring contest over what democracy means to people, which can lead to political polarization. Moreover, Borja's[14] analysis of data from the Asian Barometer Project (Wave 4: 2013–16) shows that while Filipinos remain somewhat committed to representative institutions, they hold some leader-centric, anti-pluralistic values that support a strong executive:

> For 56.4% of the respondents, the system of checks and balances between executive and the legislature may be detrimental to the capacity of the former to "accomplish great things". Thus, though they have weak anti-institutional tendencies, most are attached to the ideals of a strong executive.... [T]hough majority of the respondents does not consider government leaders in a paternalistic manner, most of them agree (61.4%) with the notion of giving absolute authority to leaders who they consider as *morally upright*. Regarding anti-pluralism, 64.3% of the respondents perceive the multiplicity of *ways of thinking* as a threat to social harmony.

Such a discussion, while appearing to be a theoretical one, has direct relevance to broader questions about how to make sense of Duterte's relationship with the political order. Despite his anti-elite rhetoric, the president has shown "a level of comfort to preserve the status quo he promised to meaningfully change".[15] The opposition has interestingly fielded political outsiders against the administration's line-up of scions of dynasties, business moguls, entertainment stars, and some who have been accused of corruption. With a victory for more-of-the-same candidates, it is questionable, using the president's own 2016 slogan, whether change truly came.

However, existing takes on the elections as more-of-the-same miss the broader qualitative change: Duterte's outcome-oriented style is gradually manifesting itself in electoral choice. Duterte's men—his former police chief and drug war implementer Ronaldo "Bato" Dela Rosa and long-time aide Christopher "Bong" Go—clinched the fifth and third highest senatorial votes, respectively, and even leapfrogged traditional dynasts such as Imee Marcos, Ramon Revilla Jr. and former Senate president Aquilino "Koko" Pimentel III. These "insurgent" candidates not only prevailed over liberal politicians but also against traditional dynasties. They are broadly representative of what may be a trend in favour of candidates with experience in the executive branch of government—the political equivalent of the nouveau riche in the outcome-oriented environment that the Duterte administration has fostered. As such, Duterte's effect on the political system is more textured than a mere return to traditional politics. What is being consolidated by his illiberal-majoritarian coalition is not just illiberalism as a method of governance per se, but a political system that is paradigmatically concerned with state-building fundamentals, as opposed to values-based reformism. It is to this year's developments in these aspects which we turn to next.

The Philippines Three Years Hence

It is worth noting that Duterte campaigned and eventually governed on two important but distinct platforms: anti-elite politics and state-building. His anti-elite rhetoric at present appears unfulfilled. Duterte has no large-scale redistributive agenda that is comparable to other populists such as Hugo Chavez or Evo Morales. His weakest moments were those related to challenging entrenched economic interests, such as the non-confirmation of staunch anti-mining advocate Gina Lopez as secretary of the environment and natural resources, and the inability to pass effective measures to end labour contractualization, which he had originally promised. The Duterte coalition has drilled down on its state-building agenda through centrepiece programmes on peace and order, public infrastructure, and basic services. In particular, the first two components are popularly known as the War on Drugs and the Build, Build, Build programme, aimed to usher in a "golden age of infrastructure".

Public Order

Much has been documented and said regarding the Duterte administration's frontier-style war on drugs. Midway through 2019, the Philippine government "acknowledged at least 6,600 killings at the hands of police" and even more thousands by unknown assailants that have led to possible human rights violations.[16] A study by the Stabile Centre for Investigative Journalism found that there is a wide, systematic discrepancy between the police-declared count of drug-related killings and an alternative accounting from civil society.[17]

The Supreme Court stands as one bulwark against an unaccountable police force, though its reputation has been tainted since the past two chief justices have been known to side with the president on key rulings. Interestingly, the current chief justice, Diosdado Peralta, wrote a 2018 ruling on the need for judicial conduct by demanding such strict compliance in the *People v. Lim* decision. In 2019, the Supreme Court granted a petition from the Free Legal Assistance Group and the Centre for International Law to provide access to police drug war documents.[18] These modest victories, while paling in comparison to the scale of increasingly unaccountable anti-narcotic operations, are constructive steps moving forward.

The reality however is murky. Polls from the Social Weather Station showed that the midterm view of the drug war three years in is "excellent", with 82 per cent satisfied. It is worth noting that under the current administration, crime victimization is actually at its historic lowest since 1998 (Figure 1), although the long-run trend has actually decreased and even hit single digits since 2012 under President Aquino.

Furthermore, by the police's own records, the volume of index crimes and total crimes have significantly declined since Duterte assumed office, and crime solution efficiency has gone up (Table 1). The *combined* presence of improving government statistics and public surveys on crime victimization attest to the sobering reality that the Philippines has an improving public order situation

TABLE 1
Anti-Criminality Accomplishments

	2016	2017	2018	Trend (2016 vs. 2018)
Index crimes	139,577	107,538	81,413	Decrease (41.67%)
Total crime volume	584,883	520,641	490,393	Decrease (16.16%)
Crime solution efficiency	57.03%	61.11%	74.42%	Increase (30.49%)

Source: President's Report to the People 2019; data from the Philippine National Police.

FIGURE 1
Crime Victimization of Family Members, 1989–2019

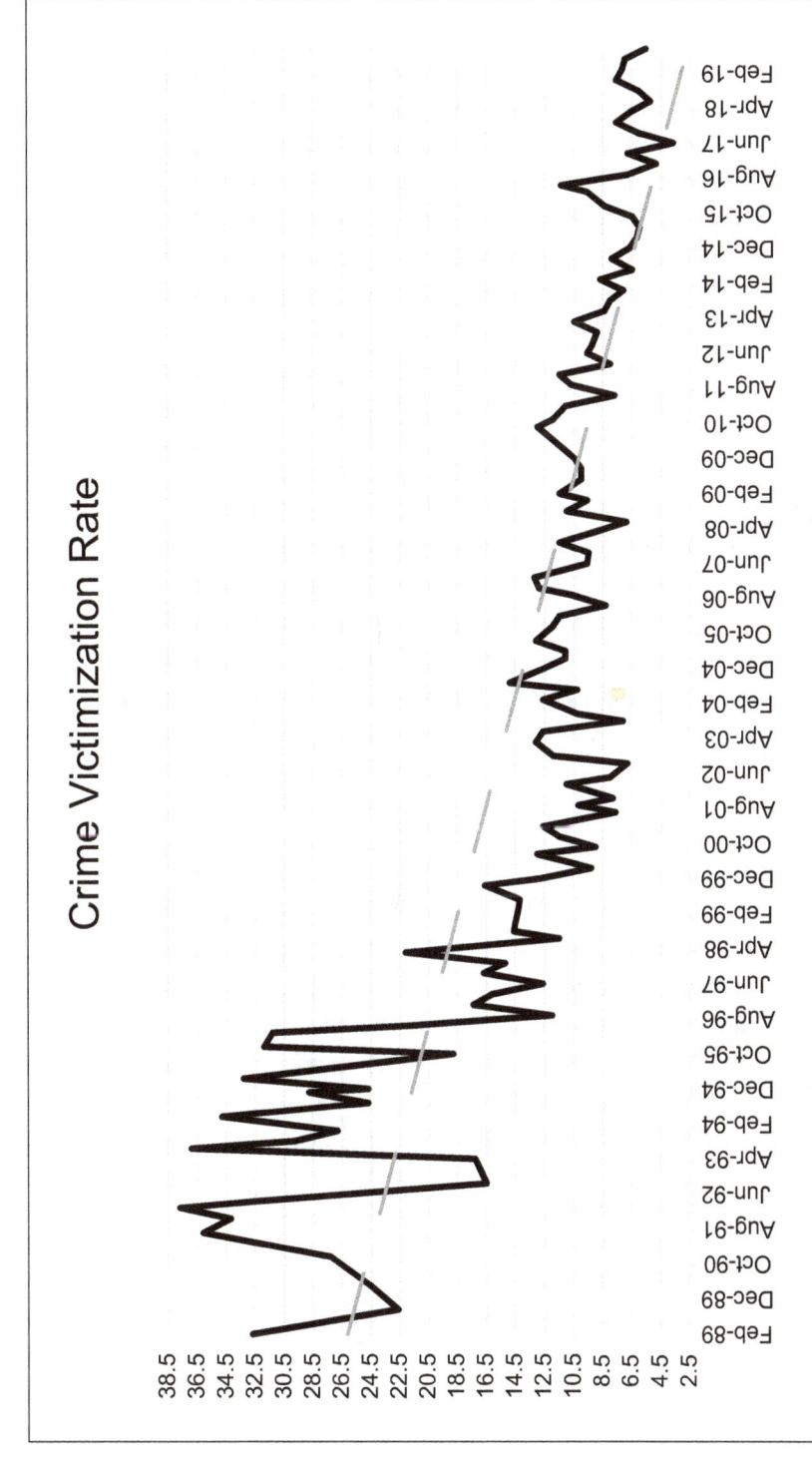

Note: These figures reflect victimization by common crimes, particularly property crime and physical violence. Source of data: Social Weather Stations, "Third Quarter 2019 SWS Survey: Families Victimized by Common Crimes Subside to 5.6%", 30 October 2019, https://www.sws.org.ph/swsmain/artcldisppage/?artcsyscode=ART-20191030164733 (accessed 1 November 2019).

insofar as criminality is concerned. However, this must be taken with a grain of salt, given the long-run effects of vigilantism among the police force on the quality of law enforcement, as well as the possibility that such improvements are not causally attributable to executive action but rather a secular trend concomitant to the Philippine's economic development and relatively improving funding for essential state functions (education and order). Nevertheless, it stands to reason that—whether by intelligent design or fortune—the administration benefits from the reality of decreased criminality.

On the aspect of armed insurgency, despite the president's militaristic and polarizing rhetoric, the government has quietly provided 2,129 former rebels with financial, livelihood and housing assistance under the Enhanced Comprehensive Local Integration Program.[19] Moreover, martial law in Mindanao has been extended by Congress until end-2019 and the government has so far avoided the wide-scale abuses it was initially feared would trail its declaration.[20] Another perspective is that big-picture public order strategic initiatives like the drug war and martial law are precisely what make Duterte popular. The implementation of the latter has led to more military checkpoints, liquor bans and troop deployments, which normalize military presence in public life in a way that can undermine democracy and increase the probability of abuse. But pending such long-run deteriorations, they have the more immediate effect of projecting government responsiveness and decisive leadership.

It is easy to dismiss Duterte's coercive approach to governance, and it is a very legitimate response to be wary of it, but such opposition has to be tempered with an understanding that projecting state power may actually be beneficial in places described in the literature as having "weak states, strong societies", where the absence of a governmental monopoly on the means of violence has permitted space for drug lords, warlords and rebels to the detriment of citizens. Known oppositionist Vice President Leonor Robredo concedes as much, that the drug war needs to be "tweaked" and re-assessed, but not necessarily abandoned. A broader focus on state-building as opposed to values-based politics means that the problem has more to do with conflicts over Duterte's questionable methods to address otherwise non-contentious goals.

However, one principal downside of Duterte's almost tunnel vision regarding public order is that he prefers men of such background to serve under his command. Consequently, seeds of future conflict over civil-military relations are being planted. True to his brand, Duterte lambasted his own ally Senator "Dick" Gordon over the latter's criticism regarding his militarization of the government and his penchant for appointing military officials to key government posts. The president has stated that he perceives military generals as able and loyal administrators with a "can-do" attitude which aligns with his governance style.[21] As such, the presence of former military and police generals in the Cabinet has increased from just four in 2016 to eleven in 2019.[22] They notably hold the top posts in non-defence related profiles such as the Department of Social Welfare and Development, the Department of Environment and Natural Resources, and the Technical and Education Skills Development Authority. This development has to be contextualized within the Philippine's long post-1986 struggle to return the military to the barracks after directly wielding executive power under Marcos. This appointment pattern may cultivate political ambitions of uniformed personnel and undermine civilian control of the military and the government more generally.

Build, Build, Build and Necessary Evils?

The Build, Build, Build (BBB) programme is the Philippine government's answer to its laggard status behind neighbouring Southeast Asian countries (Indonesia, Malaysia, Singapore and Thailand) in both direct foreign investment net inflows and infrastructure quality, both cited as contributing to sub-optimal economic development.[23] Historically, the Philippines has vastly missed its needed 5 per cent of gross domestic product that should be allocated for infrastructure construction, rising from a meagre 2 to 2.9 per cent from presidents Arroyo (2001–10) to Aquino (2010–16).[24] This is mainly attributed to a "disciplinary" economic policy of budget balancing, economic reform and inflation fighting.[25] One of the Duterte administration's selling points is its original commitment to roll out 8.4 trillion pesos (US$158 billion) in infrastructure spending over its term from 2016 to 2022, seen as both economically necessary to plug the infrastructure gap and politically popular to make citizens feel and see active government intervention.

Three years in, such projects are experiencing delays. First, there is now mounting scepticism regarding the BBB, seeing it as being too ambitious. The National Economic Development Authority admitted in the third quarter of 2019 that some big-ticket infrastructure megaprojects are not, after all, feasible. The administration is now planning to scrap some of the 75 original BBB projects, but increased the number of priority projects with smaller-scale force multiplier projects to bring the total to 100. Second, despite its supermajority in congress, implementation of projects is delayed. This is in addition to the debacle at the onset of the year where the government, for the first time in almost a decade, operated on a re-enacted budget after legislators squabbled over controversial last-minute insertions for pork-barrel funds.²⁶ As of July, the government will complete by 2022 only 21 projects worth 187.6 billion pesos (US$3.7 billion) out of the 75 flagship projects amounting to 2.4 trillion pesos (US$47 billion).

Third, there is mounting criticism against the possibility of a return to Marcos-era debt-driven development, or "borrow, borrow, borrow" as critics point out. In theory, the administration's spending bonanza derives from two planks: increased Chinese investment, and revenue from its tax reform programme. Punongbayan notes that the BBB has become dependent on foreign loans and grants for as much as 75 per cent of its projects, in contrast to the statements made by economic managers in early 2016 that it would be locally funded.²⁷ In particular, Chinese involvement has actually had a lukewarm reception because of collusion allegations between governments and the lack of transparency in bidding processes. Moreover, senators have raised concerns over the practice of Chinese firms of bringing in their own nationals as workers, since this undermines the Keynesian logic of BBB to spur growth by employing the local population.

Related to this, the government's controversial tax reform programme, known locally as the "TRAIN law" (Comprehensive Tax Reform Package 1), was accepted by some sectors as a "necessary evil"—despite warnings of an inflationary impact arising from its levy of additional excise taxes—because of expected benefits from the infrastructure spending spree.²⁸ The reality however is that revenue from TRAIN only constituted a paltry 8 per cent of total infrastructure disbursements in 2018.²⁹ A study³⁰ released in 2019 by the state-run think tank the Philippine Institute for Development Studies estimated that the "TRAIN law"—which slapped a higher excise tax on oil, which is a key factor of production—actually increased the incidence of poverty by 1.72 percentage points, though admittedly this was somewhat offset by the conditional cash transfer programmes of the administration.

Whither Anti-elite Credentials?

At this point the Duterte administration and the political system as a whole do not quite live up to the image of a "rebellion against the present order" or a "visceral rejection of the status quo"³¹ in the sense that traditional writings of Philippine populism understand it as having a redistributive agenda. If anything, the illiberal movement called by sociologist Randy David as "Dutertismo" has sought to greatly buttress the prevailing capitalist economic order.³² Duterte's main platforms—crime reduction and infrastructure spending—are in theory undertaken to boost the country's extant economic growth trajectory. As mentioned in the previous section, the Duterte administration had promised two distinct kinds of policies—anti-elite politics and state building—but has so far only significantly acted on the latter.

In the political sphere there has been little progress on the president's promise of a constitutional transition to federalism (from the current unitary set-up) as a way to decentralize power away from his much-criticized "Imperial Manila". In July, Duterte mentioned he would be fine if the legislature did not proceed with a transition to a federal system, and in October he intimated reservations about federalism.[33] Land redistribution, which is a good litmus test to how far an incumbent will tackle elite interests to pursue redistributive politics, is at a historic low under the Duterte administration.[34] There have also been no attempts to nationalize key industries despite the president's stern, flamboyant rants against key public utilities (e.g., transport, electricity, water). Moreover, last July, Duterte vetoed an already watered-down anti-labour contractualization bill despite said legislation being his own campaign promise. The hot-topic legislation—which would have prohibited the abusive practice of short-term labour contracting in order to circumvent statutory employee benefits—was rejected by the president on the grounds it was too restrictive on businesses for a country that is "at a disadvantage already in terms of cost and flexibility of labour use compared to its peers in the region".[35]

Another interpretation is that such developments reflect the voice of the country's economic managers, and it could even be viewed as sobriety on the part of the president. On the upside, the Duterte administration has made headway into progressive social programmes; namely, universal healthcare and free tertiary education, albeit these are now undergoing birthing pains over questions of how to source funding. Congress has also continued the previous administrations' lauded conditional cash transfer programme to poor households through a law providing for regular appropriations.

Here, the distinction between Duterte's anti-elite and state-building agenda becomes paramount. While not necessarily mutually exclusive, his insistence on state-building has trained his energy on administrative improvements that foster "state capacity". In contrast, an anti-elite agenda and one against the status quo deals more with the question of "state autonomy" from vested interests. The case could be made that Duterte's behaviour of not meddling in congressional squabbles and his realistic co-optation of key business magnates, notably the Villar family, are tacit concessions to the country's political elites.

Notably, Duterte's administration has been much less willing than the previous one to expend its tremendous political capital to try to discipline the behaviour of political elites in the legislature. The present government has strikingly kept anti-corruption campaigns *within* the executive branch, unlike Benigno Aquino III who marshalled resources to oust former ombudsman Merceditas Gutierrez and then chief justice Renato Corona on corruption charges. On the one hand, this is in keeping with constitutionally prescribed behaviour from a chief executive. But, on the other, one cannot help but raise eyebrows as to the motivation behind the out-of-brand moderation by a president so willing to exceed the bounds of law in other matters.

Aside from the drug war, the administration only flexed its political muscle and risked political capital when it fought and won to jail Senator Leila De Lima and former chief justice Ma. Lourdes Sereno, who were vocal about their criticism of the president at the onset of his term. The criteria here seem to be loyalty more than any principled stance against elite actions detrimental to public good. One angle to this is that leaving non-oppositionist elites alone allowed him to govern more smoothly in order to focus on delivering concrete policies and projects on public order, infrastructure and social programmes that do not threaten the existing politico-economic order. At this stage of self-propelling growth for the Philippines, more roads, better infrastructure, less street crime and more social security in the form of education and healthcare can exist without radically confronting the dominance of dynasties. In retrospect, this is starkly different from the previous administration's anti-corruption centrepiece, which was inherently bound to create enemies among political elites because they are the object of reform.

Duterte's House of Cards

Nevertheless, there are structural problems that indicate rough seas ahead. First, there are two problems inherent in Duterte's ruling coalition that may create political noise in the years ahead. One is that there has been no formally organized mass movement fostered by the administration.[36] The Duterte coalition's actual operation in government still relies heavily on alliances with political families whose temporary loyalty is motivated more by self-interest to bandwagon with a popular president than genuine ideological commitment. It may even be said Duterte is a "demobilizing populist" as a result of his "let me take care of everything" branding.[37]

This dovetails another coalitional weakness: the absence of a clear successor. His daughter, Sarah Duterte, is shaping up to be a viable contender, but such dynastic succession will throw a monkey wrench into the restorationist plans of

Ferdinand "Bong Bong" Marcos Jr., who is also gunning for the presidency. The elder Duterte's conundrum is therefore choosing between naming a successor—a deeply factionalizing effort, as seen in this year's race for Speaker of the House between Duterte supporters—and not naming one, which will surely also accelerate the collapse of the ruling coalition. This of course need not necessarily be seen as a "problem" per se, considering the illiberal agenda of this coalition, and it may even be a blessing in disguise for the opposition.

Second, there is a growing perception that Philippine foreign policy towards China is becoming more defeatist and submissive.[38] The administration has downplayed two national headlines on the Philippines-China maritime territorial dispute in the South China Sea: the Reed Bank incident in June and the denial of innocent passage to a Filipino-manned foreign vessel in Scarborough last October. Notably, data from a Pulse Asia survey prior to the president's State of the Nation Address showed that members of the middle-upper class most frequently raised sovereignty disputes with China as something they would like the president to address, which—at 21.3 per cent—is higher than wages, inflation and employment.[39]

However, a different facet of the China policy will likely stain Duterte's credibility because it is one that is more tangible for the population: economic interaction. On the one hand, it is correct that the Philippines has benefitted in absolute terms from synergized relations with the Middle Kingdom: Chinese tourist arrivals jumped by 39.16 per cent from the previous year, and offshore gaming operators that set-up shop in the Philippines three years ago are projected to provide the government with 8 billion pesos (US$158 million) in taxes, an increase of 33 per cent from 2018, and they will also overtake the information-technology business process management (IT-BPM) industry as the leading market for office space in Metro Manila.[40] But on the other hand, greater interaction with China has also given birth to its own novel set of problems, particularly immigration control, employment grievances as a result of China's use of its own nationals for construction projects, and an upsurge in local real estate market prices, which are already starting to crowd out locals from commercial and residential property. The economic aspect of the China question will "hit home" in ways that previously were only abstract when talking of sovereign jurisdiction over territories in the South China Sea.

Finally, Filipinos may get "buyer's remorse" and start to distrust the current illiberal ruling coalition because of its ineffectual handling of some state-building matters. In a spectacular fall from grace, national police chief General Oscar Albayalde resigned over mounting credibility issues because of his alleged involvement in a case of drug "recycling" way back in 2013.[41] Though the issue occurred under the previous administration, the scandal has rallied scepticism regarding the wisdom of handing the national police a blank cheque in anti-narcotics operations when they themselves are corrupt. Furthermore, there is the problem of unevenness in the Duterte administration's handling of public order, infrastructure and basic services.

Issues other than matters of law enforcement are proving to entail challenges for the administration. The government's official denial of a "transportation crisis" amid ever-worsening traffic congestion has earned it a lot of flak. Despite massive government expenditure, economic growth, while still comparatively good, slowed to 5.6 per cent, which is below the government's own target of 6–7 per cent. Inflation has slowed to normalcy after last year's alarming price increases, but this was achieved by curbing inflation through cheap rice imports under the Rice Tarrification Law signed in February 2019. This came at the cost of farm-gate prices of rice in the Philippines, which have reached an eight-year low, and this has hurt rice farmers. As Venzon writes, "some experts say farmers need to be patient, but it is hard to be patient when you cannot pay your bills".[42] Other problems will be fiscal-administrative in nature: providing higher pay for professionals in government, keeping debt levels appropriate to the size of the economy to avoid a debt trap, and paying for populist measures like universal healthcare.

Conclusion

Thus far I have contended that it may be misleading to see Duterte's illiberalism as the most defining aspect of his presidency. It is equally important to understand the strategic paradigm that governs such behaviour: the transition from values-based reformism towards a state-building agenda where noble goals such as human rights, due process and constitutionalism are no longer viable stand-alone primary electoral platforms. To be sure, state building is not inherently illiberal; it is simply a different tier of issues altogether concerning ends rather than means. For Duterte, the die is cast that the means will be illiberal ones. Much has been written about the implications of growing illiberalism, and rightfully so.

But, if anything, the challenge of Duterte goes beyond his methods that undermine democratic institutions. In having a governance script that addresses national modernization in basic, non-contentious areas of state power—monopoly of violence, economic stimulus, and welfarism—any challenger to the incumbent will have difficulty assailing the very validity of Duterte's goals. Problems that are specific to the modernization process (i.e., traffic congestion, affordability of housing, and economically motivated criminal activities) obtain higher salience than before.

It can be argued that Duterte has largely been faithful to this governance script—he has not been particularly "populist" in the sense of pandering to electorally convenient policies. He has allowed economic managers to push through with Rice Tarrification, even at the expense of rice farmers; he has done the same with the poor, who have been hurt by the inflationary impact of the TRAIN Law. His ability to evade serious criticism regarding these issues resides in the broader narrative that state-building, which is the common interest of society, should and can prevail over sectoral interests. Short-run and group-specific costs are legitimized as necessary sacrifices for otherwise uncontestable endeavours—low crime, good infrastructure, and better social services. Much can be tolerated in the pursuit of paradise.

Finally, the shift from a values-based agenda to method-agnostic state-building efforts will likely persist beyond Duterte. An exclusivist focus on intangibles or values will likely suffer electoral defeat, as the Otso Diretso slate learned in this year's elections. One need only look at a rising-star politician—Manila City mayor Francisco "Isko" Moreno—as the poster boy for this broader trend. Not necessarily as illiberal as Duterte, he is equally popular because of his focus on the concrete rather than the abstract: a free dialysis facility, clearing pavements of illegal vendors, a city-wide clean-up, and subsidies of all sorts. The coming years will be plagued by coalitional infighting in a bid to secure Duterte's endorsement and by public dissatisfaction over the unevenness of the administration's efforts and accomplishments relative to its three core priority areas of infrastructure, basic services and public order. Nevertheless, neither will liberal reformism be a sufficient antidote to public anger.

The political analyst Ramon Casiple once forecast that "[Duterte's] co-optation will essentially result in the preservation of the status quo. There may be some cosmetic reforms but these will not address the current inequalities and powerlessness regnant in society. The Duterte administration in this scenario—while starting with a bang—will end with a proverbial whimper".[43] But is this to be reasonably expected three years later? A state-building agenda ipso facto reinforces the status quo rather than radically changes it, but at the same time such improvements—if achieved—are not to be downplayed. Duterte, who has vowed to "go down fighting", could both not subvert the prevailing socio-economic order and still end with a bang: popular and vindicated. All these however depend on his ability to deliver the terms of his social contract in the next three years. The crux is whether Duterte's illiberal political choices today can credibly deliver.

Whereas Ursula Le Guin's short story focused its cautionary tale on those who walked away from the temptation that is Omelas, the Philippines has much to learn from those who did not.

Notes

1. Lowell Dittmer, "Asia in 2017: Return of the Strongman", *Asian Survey* 58, no. 1 (2017): 1–9.
2. Pulse Asia, "September 2019 Nationwide Survey on the Performance and Trust Ratings of the Top Philippine Government Officials", 2019, http://www.pulseasia.ph/september-2019-nationwide-survey-on-the-performance-and-trust-ratings-of-the-top-philippine-government-officials/ (accessed 15 October 2019).
3. Richard Heydarian, "Philippine Midterm Elections: Duterte Must Find an Heir—Or Face the Music on His Drug War", *South China Morning Post*, 30 March 2019, https://www.scmp.com/week-asia/opinion/article/3003885/philippine-midterm-elections-duterte-must-find-heir-or-face-music (accessed 1 October 2019).
4. Vergel Santos, "The Philippines Just Became More Authoritarian, Thanks to the People", *New York Times*, 24 May 2019, https://www.nytimes.com/2019/05/24/opinion/philippines-duterte-election-senate.html (accessed 1 September 2019).
5. For comprehensive reviews on the consequences of Duterte for liberalism and democracy in the Philippines, see Björn Dressel and Cristina Bonoan, "Southeast Asia's Troubling Elections: Duterte versus the Rule of Law", *Journal of Democracy* 30, no. 4 (2019): 134–48; Nicole Curato, "Toxic Democracy? The Philippines in 2019", in *Southeast Asian Affairs 2019*, edited by Daljit Singh and Malcolm Cook, pp. 260–74 (Singapore: ISEAS – Yusof Ishak Institute, 2019); and Mark Thompson, "Bloodied Democracy: Duterte and the Death of Liberal Reformism in the Philippines, *Journal of Current Southeast Asian Affairs* 35, no. 3 (2017): 39–68.
6. Regine Cabato and Shibani Mahtani, "Philippines Midterm Elections Expected to Boost Duterte and his Agenda", *Washington Post*, 13 May 2019.
7. Edu Punay, "Duterte to Appoint 5 More SC Justices in 2019", *Philippine Star*, 29 May 2019.
8. Thomas Pepinsky, "Southeast Asia: Voting against Disorder", *Journal of Democracy* 28, no. 2 (2017): 123.
9. Andreo Calonzo, "Duterte Rejects Millions of Dollars in Aid to Defend Drug War", Bloomberg, 26 September 2019.
10. Lian Buan, "Guevarra to Courts: Don't Dismiss Weak Drug Cases Outright", *Rappler*, 3 October 2019, https://www.rappler.com/nation/241705-guevarra-calls-courts-do-not-dismiss-weak-drug-cases-outright.
11. Guillermo O'Donell, "Delegative Democracy", *Journal of Democracy* 5, no. 1 (1994): 59.
12. Matthew Ordoñez and Anthony Lawrence Borja, "Philippine Liberal Democracy under

12. Siege: The Ideological Underpinnings of Duterte's Populist Challenge", *Philippine Political Science Journal* 39, no. 2 (2018): 139–53.
13. For discussions of this compelling approach to democracy as essentially contested because of competing notions of democratic accountability, read Dan Slater, "Democratic Careening", *World* Politics 65, no. 4 (2013): 729–63; and Aries Arugay and Dan Slater, "Polarization without Poles: Machiavellian Conflicts and the Philippines' Lost Decade of Democracy, 2000–2010", *The Annals of the American Academy of Political and Social Science*, 2019.
14. Anthony Lawrence Borja, "Intolerant Leaders for Intolerant Citizens: Illiberal Values in the Philippines", *New Mandala*, 3 October 2018, https://www.newmandala.org/intolerant-leaders-intolerant-citizens-illiberal-values-philippines/.
15. Aries Arugay, "The 2019 Philippine Elections: Consolidating Power in an Eroding Democracy", Heinrich Böll Stiftung Southeast Asia, 21 June 2019, https://th.boell.org/en/2019/06/21/2019-philippine-elections-consolidating-power-eroding-democracy.
16. Amnesty International, "Philippines: UN investigation Urgently Needed into Duterte Administration's Murderous War on Drugs", 8 July 2019.
17. Sheila Coronel, Mariel Padilla, David Mora, and the Stabile Center for Investigative Journalism, "The Uncounted Dead of Duterte's Drug War", *The Atlantic*, 19 August 2019, https://www.theatlantic.com/international/archive/2019/08/philippines-dead-rodrigo-duterte-drug-war/595978/.
18. Jim Gomez, "Philippine Supreme Court Orders Release of Drug War Evidence", Associated Press, 3 April 2019, https://apnews.com/b4f1653e558749f29862848d105d6bf6.
19. Office of the President—Presidential Management Staff, the Philippines, "The President's Mid-Term Report to the People, 2016–2019: Sustaining Transformational Reforms towards a Comfortable Life for All".
20. Although there have been reported incidents of harassment by state security forces, notably against "Lumad" groups (indigenous people). Nevertheless, systematicity pertains to a regular frequency of instances of abuse over numerous geographic locations.
21. Danny Manalo, "Duterte Explains Penchant for Having Military Men in his Cabinet", GMA News, 22 July 2019.
22. Pia Ranada, "Evolution of the Duterte Cabinet", Rappler, 19 August 2019, https://www.rappler.com/newsbreak/in-depth/237745-evolution-duterte-cabinet.
23. Jose Patrick Rosales, "Financing Infrastructure Projects in the Philippines", July 2017, https://www.unescap.org/sites/default/files/Financing%20Infrastructure%20Projects%20in%20the%20Philippines%20revised%20draft%2020170921.pdf.
24. Edwin Santiago, "Risk and Uncertainty of Build Build Build Program", *Philippine Star*, 29 March 2019, https://www.philstar.com/other-sections/news-feature/2019/03/29/1905606/commentary-risk-and-uncertainty-build-build-build-program.

25. Richard Javad Heydarian, "Duterte's Ambitious Build, Build, Build Project to Transform the Philippines Could Become his Legacy", Forbes, 28 February 2018.
26. Ben De Vera, "DBM Issues Rules to Implement Delayed 2019 National Budget", *Philippine Daily Inquirer*, 21 May 2019, https://business.inquirer.net/270986/dbm-issues-rules-to-implement-delayed-2019-national-budget.
27. J.C. Punongbayan, "The Pipe Dream That Is Build, Build, Build", *Rappler*, 24 July 2019, https://www.rappler.com/thought-leaders/236177-analysis-pipe-dream-build-build-build-program.
28. Curato, "Toxic Democracy?"
29. Punongbayan, "The Pipe Dream".
30. Ben De Vera, "More Filipinos Dragged into Poverty by Higher Taxes under TRAIN", *Philippine Daily Inquirer*, 30 October 2019.
31. See Ramon Casiple, "The Duterte Presidency as a Phenomenon", *Contemporary Southeast Asia* 38, no. 2 (2016): 179–84; and Nicole Curato, "Flirting with Authoritarian Fantasies? Rodrigo Duterte and the New Terms of Philippine Populism", *Journal of Contemporary Asia* 47, no. 1 (2016): 142–53.
32. Randy David, "Dutertismo", *Philippine Daily Inquirer*, 1 May 2016.
33. Pia Ranada, "Still About Drugs: Duterte's Other Reason for Giving up on Federalism", *Rappler*, 29 October 2019.
34. Jonathan Mayuga, "Group: CARP Land Distribution under Duterte Lowest in History", *Business Mirror*, 2 October 2019.
35. Ian Nicolas Cigaral, "Why Duterte Vetoed the Anti-endo Bill", *Philippine Star*, 26 July 2019.
36. As noted by David Timberman, "Philippine Politics under Duterte: A Midterm Assessment", Carnegie Endowment for International Peace, 10 January 2019.
37. Ibid.
38. Dindo Manhit, "3 More Challenging Years—For Duterte and PH", *Philippine Daily Inquirer*, 28 June 2019, https://opinion.inquirer.net/122247/3-more-challenging-years-for-duterte-and-ph.
39. Pulse Asia, "June 2019 Nationwide Survey on the State of the Nation Address (SONA) of President Rodrigo Roa Duterte", http://www.pulseasia.ph/june-2019-nationwide-survey-on-the-state-of-the-nation-address-sona-of-president-rodrigo-r-duterte/.
40. For a comprehensive analysis, see Aaron Jed Rabena, "The Chinese Wave in the Philippines", Working Paper (Manila: Asia Pacific Pathways to Progress Foundation, 2019).
41. Rambo Talabong, "From Tough Cop to Coddler: Oscar Albayalde's Fall from Grace", *Rappler*, 14 October 2019, https://www.rappler.com/newsbreak/in-depth/242529-oscar-albayalde-fall-from-grace-strict-cop-coddler.
42. Cliff Venzon, "Duterte's War on Inflation Hammers Philippine Farmers", *Nikkei Asian Review*, 29 October 2019.
43. Casiple, "The Duterte Presidency".

Singapore

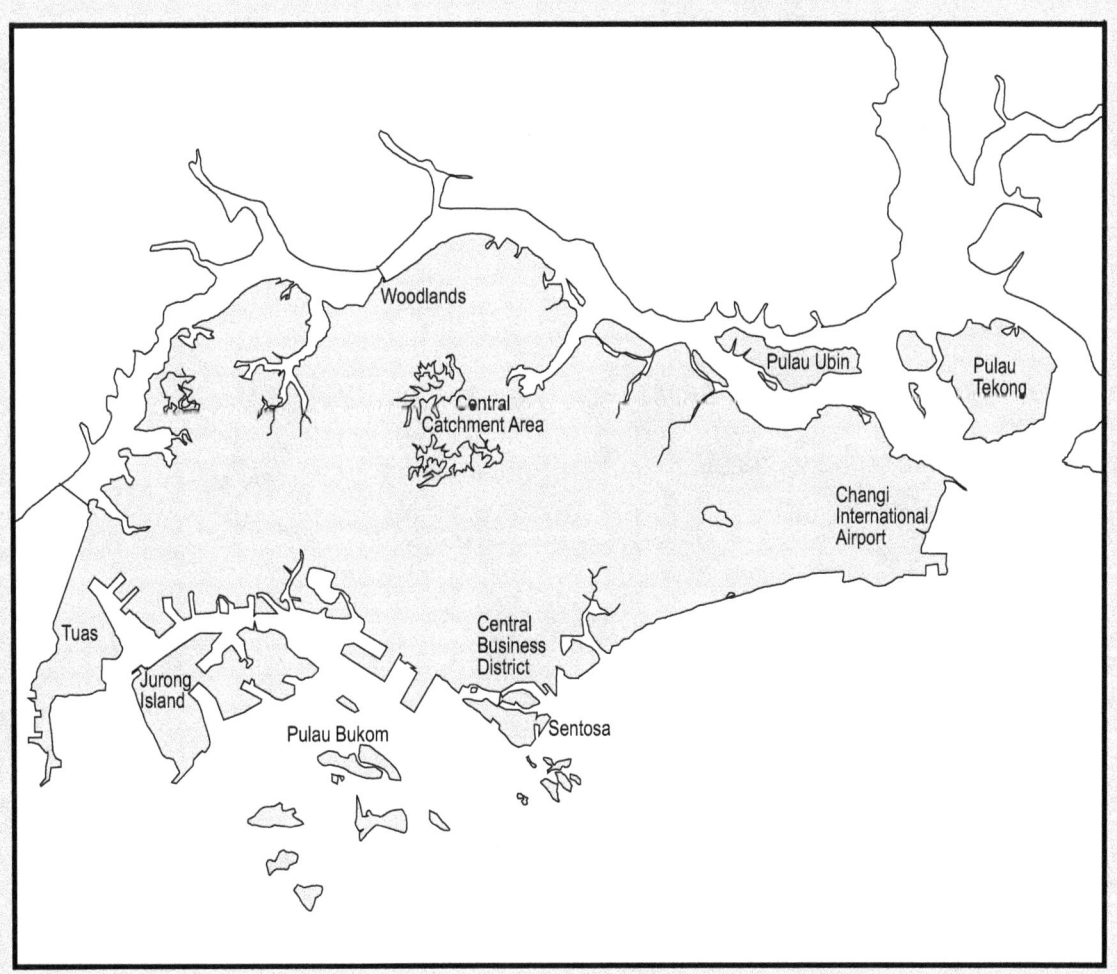

SINGAPORE IN 2019:
In Holding Pattern

Khairulanwar Zaini

A Nation Awaits

Frequent travellers flying to Changi Airport may occasionally find their aircraft caught in a holding pattern, as their flight circles the airport while waiting for clearance to land. Singapore in 2019 appears to be in a similar holding pattern as the country awaits an election that is coming sooner rather than later. Although the current parliamentary term only expires in April 2021, the Election Department's announcement on 4 September 2019 about the formation of the Electoral Boundaries Review Committee (EBRC) was the first—and clearest—sign of an impending election. Convened by the prime minister prior to every general election, the EBRC is tasked with determining the number of parliamentary seats and delineating the electoral map of constituencies, taking into account demographic changes and shifts in the residential housing populations.[1] The committee of five senior civil servants was also instructed to increase the number of single-member wards while reducing the average size of Group Representation Constituencies (GRCs).[2] In the past, the committee has taken between three weeks and seven months to issue its report to the prime minister, who would then generally call for an election soon after.[3] This time, however, the committee was reported to be still in the midst of deliberations as of early January 2020,[4] suggesting that the next election will only be likely to be called in the second quarter of 2020 or later, after the conclusion of the Budget and Committee of Supply debates in February 2020.

The PAP Continues Apace with Its Leadership Transition

As part of its preparations for the elections, the ruling People's Action Party (PAP) has taken steps to consolidate its fourth-generation (4G) leadership as

---

Khairulanwar Zaini is Research Officer at the ISEAS – Yusof Ishak Institute, Singapore.

Prime Minister Lee Hsien Loong moves ahead with his plans to step down after the next election. After being appointed as the PAP's first assistant secretary-general in November 2018, Finance Minister Heng Swee Keat was elevated to deputy prime minister in April 2019, in a further affirmation to the public and the international community of his status as heir apparent.[5] In order to facilitate this leadership renewal, the two incumbent deputy prime ministers—Teo Chee Hean and Tharman Shanmugaratnam—relinquished their positions and were appointed as senior ministers, while retaining their roles as coordinating minister for national security and coordinating minister for social policies, respectively. By convention, the Cabinet is generally served by two deputy prime ministers, but this particular reshuffle makes Heng the first solo deputy prime minister since 1985, firmly indicating his position as *primus inter pares* in the 4G leadership team. In his new role, Heng is expected to review the long-term policy challenges confronting Singapore, including managing an ageing population and future-proofing the country's economy.[6] He has also mooted the Singapore Together movement, which is intended "to allow regular citizens to play a part in the policymaking process".[7] Heng will be hoping that this new platform will be able to reprise the success of the Our Singapore Conversation, the consultative dialogue exercise held under his leadership in 2012 and which positioned him as a frontrunner in the prime ministerial race.

Prior to his entry into politics, Heng was a senior mandarin in the bureaucracy, rising to the rank of permanent secretary at the Ministry of Trade and Industry in 2001 before serving as the managing director of the Monetary Authority of Singapore, Singapore's central bank, from 2005 to 2011. Lauded for his leadership potential when he was introduced as a PAP candidate in the 2011 elections, he was then immediately appointed as education minister, thus being only the second person in Singapore's political history to be directly elevated to a full ministerial role upon being elected as a Member of Parliament (MP).[8] His political ascendancy was temporarily interrupted by a stroke in May 2016, but he was able to recover and resume his duties by August 2016. Since assuming the finance portfolio from Shanmugaratnam in 2015, Heng has designed government Budgets reflecting "a shift away from a top-down model of government to one that seeks to develop stronger partnerships" with the private sector and institutes of higher learning in an effort to give them "more skin in the game in transforming the economy".[9] A recurrent feature of Heng's Budgets are "co-investment schemes" that allocate matching government funding in order to grow local enterprises. For instance, in the 2019 Budget, Heng provided a further injection of S$100 million (US$72 million) to the Co-Investment Programme (CIP) to nurture "deep enterprise capabilities" in the domestic corporate sector.[10] The expanded CIP follows the International Partnership Fund introduced in the 2017 Budget that allocated SG$600 million (US$430 million) for the government to "co-invest with Singapore-based firms to help them scale-up and internationalise",[11] as well as the implementation of a working capital loan scheme for small-and-medium local enterprises (SMEs) in the 2016 Budget.[12] As Lin Suling, executive editor of Singapore's Channel NewsAsia, writes, the preference to "rally others towards common goals" emblematic of Heng's Budgets indicates that citizens can expect a "collaborative" style of governance under his future premiership.[13]

However, while Heng is often touted as "a safe pair of hands",[14] there have been minor concerns expressed by some observers that he has yet to sharpen his political instincts to complement his technocratic acumen. An Australian-based Singaporean academic once described Heng as a "political cleanskin" who "does not usually play the role of an attack dog in parliament",[15] and his seeming inexperience with such a role briefly emerged in a November 2019 parliamentary sitting. Upon the conclusion of a civil trial in October 2019 that found three opposition Workers' Party (WP) MPs liable for the misuse of their town council funds, Heng advanced a parliamentary motion on 5 November 2019 calling upon two of the MPs to recuse themselves from the town council's financial matters.[16] His performance was however seen as unconvincing, with one news editor recounting that Heng "hummed and hawed, flipping through his folder",[17] while another online media platform reported that Heng "appeared unsure" and was forced to call for a recess soon after introducing the motion when it was suggested that the matter may be *sub judice* since the WP MPs planned to appeal the judgment.[18] Heng took a backseat after the recess, allowing his junior parliamentary colleagues to instead front the assault against the WP. While the motion passed comfortably given the PAP's significant parliamentary majority, it prompted a commentary pleading for Heng to "raise his game".[19] With Heng expected to play a leading role in the upcoming elections, and the emergence of an increasingly sophisticated and demanding electorate, it behoves him and his fellow 4G leaders to be as politically nimble as they are economically astute.

The WP Fights for Its Future

In 2019, the Workers' Party, the only parliamentary opposition party, had its preparations for the elections complicated by legal woes arising from its appointment of FM Solutions & Services (FMSS) without a tender in 2011.[20] The party had picked FMSS to serve as the managing agent of the newly established

Aljunied-Hougang town council (AHTC) almost immediately after winning the multi-member Aljunied ward in the May 2011 elections.[21] The PAP government raised concerns about possible conflicts of interests since the two shareholders of FMSS—a husband-and-wife team who were supporters of the WP and who had previously worked with the party's Hougang town council—also held crucial appointments in the new town council.[22] Audits by the Auditor-General's Office and accounting firm KPMG flagged issues with the town council's governance and the possibility of "improper payments", eventually leading to a civil suit against five of Aljunied's town councillors,[23] including a trio of WP parliamentarians—party chair Sylvia Lim (who was also chair of the town council during the relevant period of FMSS's tenure from 2011 to 2015), secretary-general Pritam Singh (chair of the town council from 2015 to 2018), and former secretary-general Low Thia Khiang—for breaching their fiduciary duties.[24]

The first tranche of the proceedings was held over seventeen days in October 2018 to determine whether the town councillors could be held liable for the "improper payments" to FMSS, amounting to some S$33.7 million (US$24.2 million). A final summation was conducted in April 2019. The High Court released its 329-page judgment in October 2019, determining that Lim and Low had "failed to act in the best interests of the town council and breached their fiduciary duty" in hiring FMSS without a tender, while finding Singh lacking in his duty of care and skill in not questioning the decision.[25] In particular, the judge declared that the trio was responsible for "systemic control failures" in the town council.[26] Consequently, the three parliamentarians are personally on the hook for damages suffered by the town council arising from the payments to FMSS, although the exact quantum that can be exacted from the trio has to be determined in a second tranche of hearings. During the trial, lawyers for the WP MPs insisted that only S$15,710 (US$11,000), rather than the full S$33.7 million, is recoverable since the payments from the town council's purse to FMSS were for services that the town council did indeed receive.[27] The precise amount that Lim, Low and Singh are personally liable for will have significant repercussions on their own political futures and that of their party's—if they are not able to pay, the three will be declared bankrupt and thus disqualified from Parliament. However, the timeline for the second round of hearings has not been decided, especially since the three WP parliamentarians have filed their appeal against the High Court judgment on 11 November 2019.[28] This increases the likelihood that the WP will have to contend with a cloud of legal uncertainty while contesting the forthcoming election, with the PAP expected to capitalize on the issue and accuse the WP of financial mismanagement.

Following the November 2019 parliamentary motion calling for Lim and Low to withdraw from AHTC's financial affairs, the town councillors held a secret ballot and voted 17–1 against the need for the duo's recusal.[29] (Lim and Low did not participate in the vote.) However, the two were eventually issued with a rectification order by the minister for national development, Lawrence Wong, on 3 January 2020 to restrict their financial involvement in the town council,[30] which they have agreed to comply with despite reservations about "the propriety of the order".[31] In facing such political headwinds, the WP can however take comfort that there is no indication of widespread dissatisfaction or anger against the party among its constituents. Interviews conducted by national broadsheet the *Straits Times* with twenty Aljunied and Hougang residents after the release of the judgment revealed that most "were not surprised by the verdict, but hoped that the outcome would not disqualify the trio from being MPs".[32] Such sentiments fall in line with the success of the three parliamentarians in raising more than S$1 million (US$717,000) in a span of four days following an October 2018 "online crowdsourcing appeal" to defray their legal costs.[33] This suggests that while the WP may take a temporary hit from the outcome of the trial, it still retains a popular following and a reservoir of goodwill among supporters who are sympathetic to the difficulties that a relatively small opposition party such as the WP would encounter, especially given the logistical magnitude of running a large town council.

The Rest of the Opposition Chases an Alliance

Beyond the WP, the opposition scene was galvanized by the formal registration of the Progress Singapore Party (PSP) in April 2019. The new party is led by former PAP parliamentarian Tan Cheng Bock, who, in representing the single-member ward of Ayer Rajah from 1980 until his retirement in 2006, had consistently secured at least 70 per cent of the vote in each of his electoral contests.[34] Despite being a member of the PAP's all-important central executive committee from 1987 to 1996, he developed a reputation as a maverick with an independent streak, particularly for his vocal opposition to the Nominated Member of Parliament (NMP) scheme introduced by the PAP government.[35] In 2011 he resigned from the PAP in order to contest the non-partisan presidential election, facing off against one-time colleague and former deputy prime minister Tony Tan, the government's preferred candidate. In a four-way contest, Tan Cheng Bock managed to muster 738,311 votes (34.85 per cent) against Tony Tan's 745,693 votes (35.20 per cent), thus only losing by the narrow margin of 7,269 votes (0.34 per cent). This formidable electoral performance, achieved without the backing of the PAP's party machinery, testifies to Tan's enduring popularity and credentials as one of the best-performing political candidates in Singapore's election history.

Tan's formal entry into opposition politics has thus kindled considerable optimism and excitement, with some drawing parallels to Mahathir's defection to the Pakatan Harapan coalition in neighbouring Malaysia and expecting Tan to "split the People's Action Party's vote".[36] However, it is more likely that the PSP will find it difficult to make a significant dent in the PAP's parliamentary dominance, let alone displace the ruling party, even if it stands a fighting chance in the constituencies of western Singapore surrounding Tan's former stronghold of Ayer Rajah.[37] During the PSP's public launch in June 2019, Tan dismissed talk of regime change or prime ministerial aspirations, stating instead his modest hope of denying the PAP a two-thirds parliamentary majority, the threshold required to amend the constitution.[38] Throughout the year, comparisons to Mahathir also fed intense speculation that Tan could lead a grand alliance of opposition parties against the PAP in the coming election. However, despite a much-publicized "opposition alliance meeting" between Tan and the leadership of seven other opposition parties in November 2019,[39] there remains little indication that Tan has the appetite to helm a coalition of often-fractious minor opposition parties. The lack of progress has prompted four of these parties—the Singaporeans First party, the Reform Party, the People's Power Party and the Democratic Progressive Party—to announce in early January 2020 their plans to register a formal alliance in order to contest the next election under a unified banner. The four parties have also indicated that they welcome the participation of other opposition parties and remain open to Tan leading the alliance if he is so willing.[40] Thus far, the Singapore People's Party (SPP) has formally declined to join the alliance, as the party seeks to regroup under its new leadership after Chiam See Tong, a veteran opposition MP who represented the ward of Potong Pasir from 1984 to 2011, relinquished his position as secretary-general in October 2019 because of ill health.[41] The SPP's decision to sit out the new alliance highlights the party's dwindling fortunes since its heyday in the early 2000s when Chiam spearheaded the Singapore Democratic Alliance (SDA), the most recent attempt at an opposition coalition prior to the one mooted in January 2020.[42]

As the election looms, the frantic pursuit of a grand opposition alliance may prove to be the equivalent of political busywork: fostering merely the illusion of progress rather than substantively improving the electability of the opposition or expanding the country's democratic space. This is especially so as the more established opposition parties such as the WP and the Singapore Democratic Party

(SDP) remain absent from such arrangements. While the SDP had affirmed the need for an alliance under Tan Cheng Bock as recently as August 2019,[43] and has participated in inter-party talks, it remains to be seen whether party chief Chee Soon Juan would be willing to follow the directions of the head of a different opposition party, especially if it entails reining in his and his party's autonomy and downplaying the distinctive identity that the SDP has cultivated over the years as a champion of liberal democracy and human rights. The WP, meanwhile, remains sceptical of opposition alliances, preferring instead to organically grow itself on its own terms and stead.

The PAP Government Works to Burnish its Performance Legitimacy

Competent economic stewardship and effective governance are crucial ingredients for the legitimacy of a political regime that promises material security in return for strict political and social control. Singapore, however, experienced only tepid economic growth in 2019, narrowly avoiding a technical recession in the third quarter.[44] Flash government figures also revealed that the economy expanded by only 0.7 per cent year-on-year in 2019, the slowest pace since the meagre growth of 0.1 per cent in 2009.[45] The slowdown in the country's growth was attributed to an "external, manufacturing, trade-driven weakness" wrought by global uncertainties arising from the trade dispute between the United States and China.[46] The effects of the economic slowdown was most evident in the manufacturing sector, which generally contributes around 20 to 25 per cent of the country's annual gross domestic product, as it shrank by 3.5 per cent on a year-on-year basis by the third quarter of 2019.[47] Prime Minister Lee however assured citizens in his annual New Year's remarks on 31 December 2019 that the "economy is still growing, [albeit] less vigorously than we would like".[48] Although many challenges remain, the trade and industry ministry has forecast growth of between 0.5 and 2.5 per cent for 2020,[49] prompting expectations that the government will pursue "a highly expansionary fiscal policy" in order to reach the forecasted rates in the coming year.[50] The fiscal pump-priming will likely be done in tandem with the provision of monetary handouts to the citizenry that has often characterized the government's pre-election Budgets.

The 2019 Budget was initially viewed by some as an "election Budget" because of its generous provisions,[51] including the Bicentennial Bonus that disburses a total of S$1.1 billion (US$787 million) in cash vouchers, tax rebates, top-ups to citizens' education accounts, and pension supplements, with the benefits mostly accruing to lower-income and older Singaporeans.[52] The cornerstone of the 2019 Budget was however the Merdeka Generation Package (MGP), an S$8 billion (US$5.7 billion) healthcare aid programme aimed at subsidizing the medical expenses of the 500,000-odd Singaporean senior citizens born in the 1950s.[53] First announced by Prime Minister Lee in August 2018, the MGP extends and complements the S$9 billion (US$6.4 billion) Pioneer Generation Package (PGP), a similar social welfare scheme unveiled in 2014 to assist citizens born prior to 1950 with their retirement and healthcare needs. The implementation of the MGP and PGP could create the expectation, as George Wong and Woo Jun Jie reflect in *Southeast Asian Affairs 2019*, that "there will be future packages waiting for succeeding generations".[54] The packages may also be signalling a gradual evolution of the country's social welfare regime. In the fifty-odd years since independence, the PAP government has adopted a strict "anti-welfare development model",[55] in which direct welfare support is eschewed and social expenditures are channelled in a "productivist" direction towards education and workfare schemes that could stimulate economic growth.[56] In such a "productivist" welfare regime, the primary purpose of social policies is enhancing human capital rather than ensuring social security. However, programmes such as the PGP and MGP are "protective" in the sense of being more concerned with preserving the social welfare of citizens and mitigating the financial risks that they have to bear.[57] The need for structural changes to Singapore's welfare regime appears unavoidable as issues of socio-economic inequality become increasingly salient and visible. Although household income inequality was reported to be at its lowest level since 2001,[58] cracks remain. Results of the first-ever academic study of homelessness released in November 2019 revealed that there are around a thousand rough sleepers in Singapore.[59] Education, instead of being an opportunity for social mobility, remains in danger of becoming inequitable as children of the rich are able to move further ahead with the benefit of private tutoring.[60] Concerns also remain about the impact to less-well-off Singaporeans of an impending hike in the regressive goods and services tax from 7 to 9 per cent.[61] The Singapore political leadership have reiterated that they recognize the danger that inequality, if unaddressed, can undermine the country's social cohesion.[62] Less often discussed is how inequality also poses a threat to the PAP government's performance legitimacy and its ideology of meritocracy. Refining the country's welfare regime towards a more "protective" orientation—which means responding to the needs of vulnerable and marginalized citizens rather than questioning whether they are deserving of help—may thus be the pragmatic move for the PAP as they seek to retain the affective loyalties of the Singaporean public.

Another significant element of the 2019 Budget was the reduction in the foreign worker quota for the services sector. In 2019, firms in the services sector could fill up to 40 per cent of their workforce with foreigners. This will however be reduced to 38 per cent in 2020, and to 35 per cent in 2021.[63] Other than reducing the economy's reliance on cheaper foreign labour, the PAP must be hoping that the quota cut could forestall immigration from becoming an election issue. During the 2011 elections, anger over the PAP government's open immigration policies, among other things, led to the party's worst-ever performance in the polls, with its share of the total vote plummeting to 60.1 per cent.[64] To its credit the ruling party has since learnt its lessons and has sought to address these issues by carefully calibrating the immigration spigot and ramping up public infrastructure to cope with increases in the resident population.

The Singapore leadership also found itself tightening some bureaucratic processes in 2019 after three major incidents occurred that blemished its reputation for efficient administration. These steps were taken presumably in part to avert the loss of public confidence and trust in the PAP government machinery. The first incident was the death of 28-year-old popular actor Aloysius Pang on 23 January 2019 while he was serving his reservist duty in New Zealand.[65] Coverage of his passing in both the mainstream press and social media prompted concerns about the safety of the military's peacetime training, especially for a conscript army. In a move to reassure the public, the defence ministry announced on 1 February 2019 the formation of an Inspector General's Office with the power to "scrutinise and enforce safety processes and practices at all levels" of the armed forces.[66]

The two other incidents involved the leaks of confidential medical data. The health ministry revealed on 28 January 2019 that the "confidential information of 14,200 people with HIV, including their names, contact details and medical information, has been stolen and leaked online".[67] The person responsible for the leak, American citizen Mikhy Farrera-Brochez, was able to get hold of the data through his partner, Ler Teck Siang, a Singaporean doctor who, as head of the National Public Health Unit between March 2012 and May 2013, had access to the national HIV Registry.[68] The authorities believe that Ler had downloaded the content of the registry into a thumb drive. As a result of the incident, the health ministry has introduced additional safeguards, which include requiring the permission of at least the director of the Communicable Diseases Division to download the HIV Registry, instituting a "two-person approval process" for access to the HIV Registry, and establishing a dedicated workstation for managing HIV Registry data.[69] However, the health ministry faced criticism for not being forthright with the public after it emerged that the authorities had been aware as early as

2016 that the registry had been compromised. In Parliament, health minister Gan Kim Yong defended the "judgment call" not to go public about the breach—a decision taken twice, in 2016 and 2018—on the grounds that the ministry wanted to protect the interests and well-being of the people on the registry.[70]

The second data leak concerned the personal information of around 800,000 blood donors in Singapore. The Health Science Authority, which supervises the national blood bank, disclosed on 15 March 2019 that one of its third-party vendors had accidentally released the database online for close to two months; no sensitive medical information was however divulged.[71] These two incidents, as a former technology correspondent for the *Straits Times* argued, seem to indicate a "systemic issue" in which "measures you expect the government to take to protect confidential data are not there".[72] The data leaks came on the heels of the June 2018 cyberattack on SingHealth, the country's largest public health organization. The hackers, which IT security research firm Symantec later identified to be from "a state-sponsored espionage group" called Whitefly,[73] collected the personal information of 1.5 million patients, while specifically targeting Prime Minister Lee's personal particulars and prescription records.[74] These vulnerabilities suggest that as Singapore embraces digital technology in its pursuit of becoming a "Smart Nation", and more information about citizens are collated and held by the government, commensurate efforts must be undertaken to preserve the security and privacy of the data.

POFMA Is the Law of the Land

Following from the March 2018 public hearings by the parliamentary select committee on "deliberate online falsehoods", the PAP government introduced a bill empowering it to combat fake news in April 2019. The Protection from Online Falsehoods and Manipulation Act (POFMA) enables ministers to issue either a correction or takedown order against a "false statement of fact"—statutorily defined as "a statement of fact that is false or misleading"—that would be against the public interest to be left unchecked.[75] Ministers can also bar access to websites or accounts propagating falsehoods. There are also provisions allowing individuals to appeal to the courts to overturn the executive orders. In the parliamentary debate, the WP argued that the judiciary is the proper body to determine whether a falsehood has indeed been perpetrated. Accordingly, instead of issuing executive orders, the government should be filing an application with the courts if it wants action to be taken.[76] This was however rebuffed by home affairs and law minister K. Shanmugam, who insisted that the government may sometimes need to take prompt and immediate action to prevent the viral spread of falsehoods.[77] After two days of hectic deliberations, the bill was passed by Parliament by a 72–9 margin.[78]

After taking effect in October 2019, the law was first invoked on 25 November 2019 against PSP member Brad Bowyer for a 13 November Facebook post of his implying "that the Government controls Temasek and GIC's commercial decisions".[79] As of January 2020, there have been at least thirteen POFMA executive orders,[80] dashing hopes that the legislation would be used lightly. Most of these orders have been directed at opposition politicians or anti-establishment critics, prompting debate about whether the law is "protecting the truth" or "restricting free debate".[81] Instead of complying, some recipients of the executive orders have filed challenges in court,[82] while others—such as blogger Alex Tan and Malaysian human rights group Lawyers for Liberty (LFL)—have chosen to ignore them. Tan, a former opposition candidate based in Australia, runs a website known more for the vehemence rather than the accuracy of its frequent diatribes against the PAP government.[83] After Tan's refusal to obey a correction direction, the PAP government instead compelled Facebook to issue a correction notice on his website's Facebook page.[84] After Tan ignored two further correction orders on separate issues, the government designated the Facebook page as a "declared online location", barring Tan from benefitting monetarily through the page.[85] The social media platform eventually revoked local access to the website's Facebook page after receiving another POFMA directive, albeit with some reluctance as a Facebook spokesperson expressed concerns that POFMA was becoming a "censorship tool".[86] In the case of the LFL, a correction order was issued against its website after the group published a statement in January 2020 alleging the use of "brutal execution methods" in Singapore's Changi Prison.[87] The group's non-compliance with the order prompted the government to block access to the LFL website in Singapore.[88] The LFL retaliated by filing a civil motion against law and home affairs minister Shanmugam in the Kuala Lumpur High Court. According to the group, it is seeking a judicial declaration that the Singaporean minister "cannot take action against Lawyers of Liberty (LFL) in Malaysia under POFMA".[89]

Singapore Balances its Foreign Relations

On the external front, Singapore tried to keep an even keel as it navigated the increasingly tense rivalry between China and the United States. The country did so, as one defence correspondent observed, by being frank in public and private with both the Americans and Chinese "about the risks of more confrontational U.S.-China relations".[90] Prime Minister Lee reiterated this theme during the annual Shangri-La Dialogue in June 2019, highlighting how the "mutual lack of strategic trust" hampers the prospect of a "compromise or peaceful accommodation" between the two superpowers.[91] He however emphasized the imperative for both "to reach such an accommodation", especially since neither country is able to effectively contain, isolate or defeat the other.[92]

On its part, Singapore continued its deep engagement with China and the United States. In April 2019, Lee attended the second Belt and Road Initiative (BRI) Forum,[93] while identifying how Singapore could "play a constructive role in financial services, third-country investments and human resources development".[94] This comes after he was snubbed for the first summit in 2017 as a signal of Chinese displeasure at what they saw as Singapore's public affirmation of the 2016 South China Sea arbitration ruling. Relations have clearly improved since that nadir. Singapore upgraded its defence pact with China in October 2019, establishing the possibility of more "frequent high-level dialogues and larger-scale military exercises" between the two countries.[95] A new visiting forces agreement to enable troop exchanges and a mutual logistics support arrangement were also included. This was however not a shift in Singapore's defence posture in China's favour. Shortly before signing the Chinese defence pact, Singapore, in September 2019, also extended for another fifteen years the 1990 memorandum granting American forces access to Singapore's air and naval facilities. The Singapore defence ministry stated that the "milestone renewal" of the agreement "reaffirmed the importance of the US' continued engagement of the region".[96] In a similar vein, foreign affairs minister Vivian Balakrishnan had called for a "sustained U.S. presence" in Southeast Asia, especially one with a "more active economic agenda", during a May 2019 speech to a think-tank in the American capital.[97]

While relations with China and the United States may have consumed the bulk of public attention, Singapore did not neglect its commitments to and partnerships with other external powers. In November 2019, the free trade agreement (FTA) between Singapore and the European Union came into force, after close to a decade in the making.[98] Various Singapore ministers also assiduously tried to cajole India's participation in the Regional Comprehensive Economic Partnership (RCEP),[99] ASEAN's ambitious bid to consolidate the grouping's several FTA partners into one gargantuan trade pact. Singapore was also offered access to India's missile testing facility at Chandipur, which promises to help meet the city-state's need for overseas training grounds to conduct live-firing exercises with its military assets.[100] In June 2019, Singapore also received the honour of being one of the eight non-G20 (Group of Twenty) countries to attend the G20 summit in Osaka, at the invitation of host Japan,[101] testifying to the warm relations between Japan and Singapore as well as the island nation's dogged efforts to ensure the relevance of small states.

In terms of regional ties, Singapore was able to smoothen an ongoing maritime and airspace row with Malaysia as it was heading into 2019. The maritime dispute had been triggered by Malaysia's decision on 25 October 2018 to extend the Johor Bahru port limits into what Singapore deemed its territorial waters.[102] After filing a "strong protest" with the Malaysian government, Singapore extended its own port limits to cover the disputed area on 6 December 2018.[103] A month later, on 8 January 2019, in an effort to de-escalate tensions, the foreign ministers of both countries met and established a "working group" to examine the legal and operational aspects of the dispute. Subsequently, in March 2019, both countries reached an agreement to suspend the new port limits and allow the previous boundaries to again apply.[104] While the maritime quarrel was playing out, Malaysia was also raising a hue about the "delegated airspace" of southern Johor, which is under the supervision of Singapore's air traffic control as a result of two agreements signed in 1973 and 1974.[105] The Malaysian transport minister told his parliament on 4 December 2018 that Malaysia was intending to reclaim the southern Johor airspace because of sovereignty concerns.[106] This was on account of the planned implementation by Singapore of Instrument Landing System (ILS) procedures—which provide guidance for flights descending and approaching a runway—for the island state's Seletar Airport. According to the Malaysian transport minister, the ILS procedures would impose height limits on developments in Johor's Pasir Gudang area and they would also affect the shipping operations of the Pasir Gudang Port. In part to prevent the ILS procedures from taking effect, Malaysia designated the airspace over Pasir Gudang as a "permanent restricted area" on 2 January 2019.[107] However, at the same 8 January meeting between the two foreign ministers, both countries consented to a one-month suspension of the ILS procedures and the restriction of the Pasir Gudang airspace.[108] In April 2019 this suspension was made permanent, with the civil aviation agencies of both countries collaborating to develop alternative GPS-based instrument approach procedures for Seletar Airport.[109] Throughout the kerfuffle, Singapore adopted a measured resolve, continually counselling restraint and seeking de-escalation without conceding its interests, while relying on face-to-face ministerial exchanges to rectify the issues. Calmer relations also allowed a modicum of progress on the proposed Rapid Transit System (RTS) link between Johor Bahru and the northern Singapore town of Woodlands. After suspending the project in May 2019 because of fiscal concerns, the Malaysian prime minister announced on 31 October 2019 that the country would proceed with the cross-border subway connection after being able to reduce the projected costs by a third.[110] However, a few days later, Singapore revealed that Malaysia has requested a further six-month suspension until the end of April 2020,[111] this time "to ensure that the relevant agreements can be amended and signed".[112] This means that the resumption of the RTS project will come around the same time as Malaysia's final decision about the fate of the Kuala Lumpur–Singapore high-speed rail (HSR), the construction of which has been postponed to end-May 2020.[113]

Singapore was also briefly embroiled in a diplomatic spat with two fellow ASEAN member states after Prime Minister Lee expressed his condolences on the death of Thailand's former prime minister Prem Tinsulanonda in June 2019. In his tribute, Lee described how, in the aftermath of Vietnam's 1978 intervention in Cambodia to depose the Khmer Rouge regime, Prem "worked with ASEAN partners to oppose the Vietnamese occupation in international forums", which "prevented a military invasion and regime change from being legitimised, and protected the security of other Southeast Asian countries".[114] References to "invasion" and "occupation" irked both Vietnam and Cambodia: a Vietnamese foreign affairs ministry spokesperson expressed "regret" that Lee's statement did not "objectively reflect the historical truth",[115] while Cambodian prime minister Hun Sen accused Lee of supporting the Khmer Rouge genocide.[116] Beyond the rhetorical bluster, however, there was no lasting damage to Singapore's relationships with the two countries.

The Kids Are Alright

While lamentations about the political apathy of young Singaporeans may have been de rigueur a few years ago, the online and offline episodes of civic engagement and activism by youths in 2019 on issues of gender, ethnicity and climate change should arrest such complaints. In April 2019, twenty-three-year-old National University of Singapore (NUS) undergraduate Monica Baey took to Instagram to call for a "zero-tolerance policy towards any form of sexual misconduct" after she was filmed in a hostel shower by a fellow student.[117] She revealed that the police gave the perpetrator a twelve-month conditional warning, while the university merely required him "to write an apology letter" and "undergo mandatory counselling". He was also barred from the hostel and suspended for a semester. The ensuing public outcry following her social media posts impelled NUS into convening a review committee to assess the existing "disciplinary and support frameworks".[118]

The case also attracted the intervention of education minister Ong Ye Kung, who described the penalties imposed by the university on the perpetrator as "manifestly inadequate".[119] In June 2019 the university announced it was accepting all the committee's recommendations, including stiffer penalties.[120]

The second episode took place in June 2019 when controversy erupted over an advertisement featuring a Chinese actor, Dennis Chew, dressed in different costumes to represent characters from Singapore's major ethnic groups. Chew's skin was darkened in his portrayal of an Indian man, leading to the accusation that the ad was insensitive to Singapore's ethnic minorities by peddling in "brownface".[121] Attention to the ad, which was part of a campaign by local e-payment service provider NETS to encourage cashless transactions, was first flagged on Instagram before going viral on Twitter.[122] The uproar prompted apologies from Chew, state broadcaster Mediacorp (Chew's employer), NETS, and Havas Worldwide (the creative agency commissioned by NETS and responsible for casting Chew in the ad campaign).[123] Amid the brouhaha, the sibling duo of Preeti and Subhas Nair released a polemical three-minute rap video in response to the ad, which drew the ire of home affairs and law minister Shanmugam. The minister stated that the video "insults Chinese Singaporeans, uses four-letter words on Chinese Singaporeans, vulgar gestures, pointing of middle finger, to make minorities angry with Chinese Singaporeans", and social media platforms were instructed by the authorities to take down the video.[124] The siblings were issued with a twenty-four-month conditional warning in August 2019 after police investigations.[125] Nonetheless, the "brownface" saga had the value of advancing the national discourse on race relations and reflecting the changing expectations and norms of intercultural sensitivity, especially with respect to the representation of Singapore's multi-ethnic and multicultural diversity. The conversations that ensued highlighted how diversity requires more than the tokenistic presence of minority identities, and the importance of respecting the capacity and autonomy for persons to articulate their ethnic and cultural identity on their own terms—to *represent* themselves rather than be *re-presented* by others.

The third major instance of youth activism occurred on a hazy Saturday afternoon in September 2019 when a group of young Singaporeans in their late teens and early twenties organized the inaugural physical mass rally calling for climate change action at Hong Lim Park, the only gazetted area for demonstrations in Singapore.[126] To an audience of two thousand people, including government politicians, speakers at the Singapore Climate Rally (SCR) demanded the government do more in reducing its economic reliance on the fossil fuel industry and in establishing a more robust carbon tax system.[127] The timing of the climate rally was somewhat fortuitous as it took place shortly after the prime minister's annual national day rally (NDR) speech in late August 2019 that elevated the policy signature of climate change. Although a National Climate Change Secretariat has existed since 2010, Lee's speech elevated climate action into a national priority as he described climate change defence as an "existential" matter for Singapore on par with its military defence. There were however differences in priorities between the prime minister's NDR and the youths' SCR. The former primarily concentrated on *adapting* to the effects of climate change (particularly rising sea levels) through engineering techniques such as land reclamation and empoldering.[128] The latter, meanwhile, emphasized the urgency of *mitigating* climate change through structurally driven reductions in greenhouse emissions.[129] The diverging priorities are best symbolized by the "battle" over Jurong Island, the site of Singapore's petrochemical and refinery facilities. While the PAP government values the offshore island as a crucial component of the Singapore economy, climate activists view it askance for being "responsible for nearly half of national greenhouse emissions".[130] Although the youth climate activists recognize they are unlikely to prevail in their quest to shutter Singapore's petrochemical and refinery sector, one of the SCR organizers revealed that the government has readily engaged environmental groups in discussions and remains open to collaborations.[131] This augurs well for both Singapore's climate and civic futures, even if there is always more to be done.

2020 Clarifies

If Singapore in 2019 was about waiting, such patience might bear some fruit, especially if, as widely expected, the country heads to its thirteenth post-independence general elections in 2020. Elections are often clarifying moments, and we will find out whether the PAP government has sufficiently delivered on its promises of efficient and competent governance—in spite of the occasional hiccup—to retain the trust of the electorate. It will disclose whether Heng and his fellow 4G leaders have convinced Singaporeans that they are worthy successors to previous generations of PAP leaders and deserve the mantle of leadership. Thus far, the anointment of Heng as prime-minister-in-waiting has been an internal party affair, but an election will confirm if the succession has the imprimatur of the public. We shall also discover whether the opposition in Singapore will have, if not their own "Mahathir moment", a stronger showing in terms of their popular vote and representation in Parliament despite the significant structural hurdles confronting them. It may also reveal whether the country's fake news law—one of the first such pieces of legislation in the world—is worthy of emulation or merely another unfortunate instance of the ruling party overreaching. In all, 2020 promises to demonstrate, with some degree of clarity, the state of the body politic in Singapore.

Acknowledgement

This chapter benefitted from the research assistance of Rachel Qiu Kexin.

Notes

1. "Electoral Boundaries Review Committee Formed: Prime Minister's Office", *Today*, 4 September 2019, https://www.todayonline.com/singapore/electoral-boundaries-review-committee-formed-prime-ministers-office.
2. The five members of the EBRC are the Cabinet secretary (who is also the secretary to the prime minister and chairs the committee), the heads of the Elections Department, Housing Development Board, and Singapore Land Authority, and the government's chief statistician. Also, there are two types of electoral divisions in Singapore: the Single Member Constituency (SMC) and the Group Representation Constituency (GRC). Introduced in 1988 to ensure minority representation, parties are required to run a slate of four to six candidates in a GRC, with at least one candidate being from a minority ethnic group. Given the resources and funds needed to field a competitive multi-member team of candidates, the opposition has often criticized the GRC scheme for providing an unfair advantage to the incumbent People's Action Party (PAP), and it was only in 2011 that the first (and only) GRC was won by an opposition party. In the most recent 2015 parliamentary elections, there were 12 SMCs and 15 GRCs (2 four-member GRCs, 11 five-member GRCs, and 2 six-member GRCs).
3. "Electoral Boundaries Committee Formed: What Does It Mean and When Will Singapore's GE Be?", *Straits Times*, 4 September 2019, https://www.straitstimes.com/politics/electoral-boundaries-committee-formed-what-it-means-and-what-to-expect-now.
4. "Parliament: Electoral Boundaries Committee Still Deliberating Report, says Chan Chun Sing", *Straits Times*, 6 January 2020.
5. "Cabinet Reshuffle: Heng Swee Keat to be Appointed Deputy Prime Minister; DPMs Teo Chee Hean and Tharman to Become Senior Ministers", *Straits Times*, 23 April 2019, https://www.straitstimes.com/singapore/heng-swee-keat-to-be-appointed-deputy-prime-minister-dpms-teo-chee-hean-and-tharman; "Cabinet Reshuffle: Strong Message on Who Will Be in Charge Next, Say Observers", *Straits Times*, 24 April 2019, https://www.straitstimes.com/singapore/strong-message-on-who-will-be-in-charge-next-say-observers.
6. "As DPM, Heng Swee Keat Will Support PM Lee in Reviewing Policies on Ageing Population, Economic Restructuring", *Straits Times*, 28 April 2019, https://www.straitstimes.com/singapore/as-dpm-heng-swee-keat-will-support-pm-lee-in-reviewing-policies-on-ageing-population.

7. "Singapore Together Movement 'A Cornerstone' of Nation Building Where Citizens, Leaders Find Common Cause: Heng Swee Keat", *Today*, 20 January 2020, https://www.todayonline.com/singapore/singapore-together-movement-cornerstone-nation-building-where-citizens-leaders-find-common.
8. Richard Hu was the first person to be directly appointed as a minister upon his election as an MP in 1985 when he was handed the health portfolio.
9. Lin Suling, "Commentary: The Singapore Budget and Heng Swee Keat's Shift away from Big Government", Channel NewsAsia, 24 February 2019, https://www.channelnewsasia.com/news/commentary/heng-swee-keat-leadership-style-finance-minister-budget-2019-11282666.
10. "Budget 2019: Measures Worth S$1 Billion to Help Businesses Build 'Deep' Capabilities", Channel NewsAsia, 18 February 2019, https://www.channelnewsasia.com/news/budget-2019-measures-1-billion-help-businesses-capabilities-11252898.
11. "Budget 2017: Businesses to Get Help in Financing When Scaling Up Globally", Channel NewsAsia, 20 February 2017, https://www.channelnewsasia.com/news/budget-2017-businesses-to-get-help-in-financing-when-scaling-up--7595470.
12. "Budget 2016: SMEs Can Loan up to S$300k under New Working Capital Loan Scheme", *Business Times*, 24 March 2016, https://www.businesstimes.com.sg/government-economy/singapore-budget-2016/budget-2016-smes-can-loan-up-to-s300k-under-new-working.
13. Lin, "Commentary: The Singapore Budget".
14. "Singapore's Next Prime Minister Heng Swee Keat: A Safe Pair of Hands, 'There's Just One Pity' (Said Lee Kuan Yew)", *South China Morning Post*, 23 November 2018, https://www.scmp.com/week-asia/politics/article/2174743/singapores-next-prime-minister-heng-swee-keat-safe-pair-hands.
15. Ibid.
16. "Parliament Votes in Favour of Motion Calling on WP MPs Sylvia Lim and Low Thia Khiang to Recuse Themselves from AHTC Financial Matters", *Straits Times*, 5 November 2019, https://www.straitstimes.com/politics/parliament-dpm-heng-calls-on-workers-party-mps-sylvia-lim-and-low-thia-khiang-to-recuse.
17. Nicholas Yong, "Comment: Heng Swee Keat Needs to Raise His Game against Workers' Party", *Yahoo! News*, 6 November 2019, https://uk.news.yahoo.com/comment-heng-swee-keat-needs-to-raise-his-game-against-workers-party-120616036.html.
18. "Heng Swee Keat & Other PAP 4G Leaders Whacked WP in Parliament, Explained", *Mothership*, 7 November 2019, https://mothership.sg/2019/11/heng-swee-keat-ahtc-sylvia-lim/.
19. Yong, "Comment: Heng Swee Keat Needs to Raise His Game".
20. On top of being legislative representatives, parliamentarians in Singapore are also vested with the responsibility for estate management through their constituencies' town councils. On account of the complexity of such service provision, most town councils hire managing agents to run the town councils on a day-to-day basis. However, opposition-held town councils often face difficulties in retaining the services

of managing agents hired by PAP town councils. The WP has claimed, for instance, that its appointment of FMSS without a tender was partly precipitated when CPG Facilities Management, the managing agent of PAP-held Aljunied GRC, requested for early termination of its contract after the WP won the ward. (This account was however disputed during court proceedings.) It is also the norm for the town councils of small, single-member constituencies (such as Hougang) to be subsumed within a larger neighbouring ward's town council to achieve economies of scale. For further details about the possible politicization of town councils and the potential difficulties facing opposition parties in managing town councils, see "Town Council Management Should be Depoliticised: Low Thia Khiang", *Today*, 12 February 2015, https://www.todayonline.com/singapore/town-council-management-should-be-depoliticised-low-thia-khiang.

21. After being appointed without a tender for a one-year term in July 2011, FMSS served as AHTC's managing agent for a further four years until July 2015 when it was the only bidder to answer a tender from the town council in June 2012. Since July 2015, the WP has been directly managing the town council after no managing agent responded to its tender request. For details, see "Sylvia Lim's Open Letter to Residents", *Good Neighbours* town council newsletter, June 2015, https://www.ahtc.sg/sylvia-lims-open-letter-to-residents/.

22. "AHTC Lawsuits: All $33.7m Paid to Managing Agent Improper, Illegal, Say Lawyers", *Straits Times*, 10 April 2019, https://www.straitstimes.com/singapore/all-337m-paid-to-managing-agent-improper-illegal-lawyers.

23. Although the Workers' Party currently retains control of the Aljunied-Hougang town council, the civil suit was brought on behalf of the town council on the direction of an independent panel established in February 2017 to review the audit report by KPMG. The independent panel was formed at the behest of the Housing Development Board, the regulatory agency responsible for overseeing the country's town councils, with the agreement of the WP-run town council. For further details, see "Independent Panel Appointed to Look into Improper Payments Made by AHTC", *Straits Times*, 17 February 2017, https://www.straitstimes.com/politics/independent-panel-appointed-to-look-into-improper-payments-made-by-ahtc.

24. "AHTC Case: Timeline of Civil Suit against Workers' Party Leaders", *Straits Times*, 11 October 2019, https://www.straitstimes.com/singapore/timeline-of-aljunied-hougang-town-council-ahtc-civil-suit.

25. "AHTC Case: Workers' Party Leaders Put Political Interests above That of Town Council and Residents, Says Judge", *Straits Times*, 11 October 2019, https://www.straitstimes.com/politics/ahtc-case-wps-pritam-singh-sylvia-lim-and-low-thia-khiang-found-liable-for-damages-suffered.

26. "AHTC Case: Judge Says Risk of Overpayment Due to Conflicts of Interest, Lack of Safeguards", *Straits Times*, 12 October 2019, https://www.straitstimes.com/politics/risk-of-overpayment-due-to-conflicts-of-interest-lack-of-safeguards-judge.

27. "AHTC Trial: Only S$15,710 Recoverable, Not S$33.7 Million, Say Lawyers for Workers'

Party MPs", *Today*, 9 April 2019, https://www.todayonline.com/singapore/ahtc-trial-only-s15710-recoverable-not-s337-million-say-lawyers-workers-party-mps.; "Workers' Party MPs Found to have Breached Duties, Liable for Damages Suffered by AHTC", *Yahoo! News*, 11 October 2019, https://uk.news.yahoo.com/workers-party-m-ps-found-to-have-breached-duties-liable-for-damages-suffered-by-ahtc-031234106.html.

28. "Workers' Party Leaders, Town Councillors Have Filed Appeal in AHTC Case: Sylvia Lim", Channel NewsAsia, 11 November 2019, https://www.channelnewsasia.com/news/singapore/workers-party-leaders-town-councillors-have-filed-appeal-in-ahtc-12083114.
29. "Workers' Party MPs Low Thia Khiang and Sylvia Lim Do Not Need to Recuse Themselves: AHTC", *Straits Times*, 30 November 2019, https://www.straitstimes.com/singapore/workers-party-mps-low-thia-khiang-and-sylvia-lim-do-not-need-to-recuse-themselves-ahtc.
30. "MND Orders AHTC to Limit Powers of WP MPs Low Thia Khiang, Sylvia Lim in Some Financial Matters", *Straits Times*, 3 January 2020, https://www.straitstimes.com/politics/national-development-minister-lawrence-wong-orders-ahtc-to-limit-powers-of-two-wp-mps-in.
31. "AHTC to Comply with Order to Limit Powers of MPs Sylvia Lim and Low Thia Khiang", *Straits Times*, 18 January 2020, https://www.straitstimes.com/politics/ahtc-to-comply-with-order-to-limit-powers-of-lim-low.
32. "AHTC Case: Work Continues at Town Council as WP MPs Study Court's Decision, Says Pritam Singh", *Straits Times*, 12 October 2019, https://www.straitstimes.com/singapore/pritam-work-continues-at-ahtc-as-wp-mps-study-courts-decision.
33. "Workers' Party MPs End Fund-Raising Appeal as Public Donations Cross Million-Dollar Mark", *Straits Times*, 27 October 2018, https://www.straitstimes.com/politics/workers-party-mps-end-fundraising-appeal-as-public-donations-cross-million-dollar-mark.
34. In his last parliamentary hustings in 2001, Tan won his ward with 88 per cent of the vote.
35. Various reports have asserted, with Tan himself advancing such claims, that he once broke the party whip to vote against the NMP scheme. However, the two times that Tan voted against the continuation of the NMP scheme (which had to be renewed every parliamentary term before it was made permanent in a 2010 constitutional amendment), in 1997 and 2002, were instances when the party whip was lifted. When the NMP scheme was first mooted in 1989, Tan's backbench opposition to the proposal was widely recognized in the press. However, the whip was not lifted in the 1989 vote and the Hansard records his assent to the passage of the bill for both its second and third readings. The only vote against the 1989 bill was from opposition MP Chiam See Tong.
36. "Proposed Opposition Alliance Hoping Tan Cheng Bock's Progress Singapore Party Will Split PAP Vote in Election", *Straits Times*, 19 January 2020, https://www.straitstimes.com/politics/new-opposition-group-hoping-dr-tan-cheng-bocks-progress-singapore-party-will-split-ruling.

37. The single-member ward of Ayer Rajah was absorbed into West Coast GRC upon Tan's retirement in 2006.
38. "PSP Wants to Be a 'Credible Alternative' to PAP, But No Regime Change Expected in Next Election: Tan Cheng Bock", *Today*, 26 July 2019, https://www.todayonline.com/singapore/psp-be-credible-alternative-pap-no-regime-change-expected-next-election-tan-cheng-bock.
39. "How Did the 'Opposition Alliance Meeting' with Tan Cheng Bock Go on Saturday Morning?", *Mothership*, 4 November 2019, https://mothership.sg/2019/11/tan-cheng-bock-opposition-alliance-meeting/.
40. "Proposed Alliance of Smaller Opposition Parties to Contest GE under Single Banner, Other Parties 'Can Join Anytime'", *Today*, 5 January 2020, https://www.todayonline.com/singapore/proposed-alliance-smaller-opposition-parties-contest-ge-under-single-banner-other-parties.
41. "Chiam See Tong Steps Down as SPP Chief, Ending Storied Political Career That Spanned More Than Four Decades", *Straits Times*, 16 October 2019, https://www.straitstimes.com/politics/chiam-see-tong-steps-down-as-spp-chief-ending-storied-political-career-that-spanned-more.
42. At its height, the SDA consisted of the SPP, the National Solidarity Party (NSP), the Singapore Justice Party (SJP), and the Singapore Malay National Organisation (PKMS). The NSP and SPP have since withdrawn from the alliance.
43. "SDP Chief Chee Soon Juan Repeats Call for Opposition Alliance", *Today*, 4 August 2019, https://www.todayonline.com/singapore/sdp-chief-chee-soon-juan-repeats-call-opposition-alliance.
44. "Singapore Narrowly Dodges Technical Recession as Economy Grows 0.1% in Q3: Flash Data", *Straits Times*, 14 October 2019, https://www.straitstimes.com/business/economy/singapore-narrowly-dodges-technical-recession-as-economy-grows-01-in-q3-flash-data.
45. "Singapore's Economy Grew 0.7% in 2019, down from 3.1% in 2018: Flash Data", *Straits Times*, 2 January 2020, https://www.straitstimes.com/business/economy/singapores-economy-grows-07-in-2019-flash-data.
46. "Singapore Narrowly Dodges Technical Recession".
47. Ibid.
48. "Singapore Slump: Economic Growth Falls in 2019 on Trade Woes", *Al Jazeera*, 2 January 2020, https://www.aljazeera.com/ajimpact/singapore-slump-economic-growth-falls-2019-trade-woes-200102020959543.html.
49. Ibid.
50. "S'pore Set for Full-year Expansion for 2019, but Growth Prospects Remain Weak: Economists", 14 October 2019, https://www.todayonline.com/singapore/spore-set-record-full-year-economic-expansion-2019-growth-prospects-remain-weak-economists.
51. "Singapore's Government Will Likely Spend Big ahead of an Upcoming Election", CNBC, 15 February 2019, https://www.cnbc.com/2019/02/15/singapore-budget-preview-higher-spending-ahead-of-possible-election.html; "Is Budget 2019 an Election

Budget? 'I Don't Plan on That Basis,' Says Heng Swee Keat", Channel NewsAsia, 20 February 2019, https://www.channelnewsasia.com/news/singapore/budget-2019-an-election-budget-heng-swee-keat-11259404.

52. "Budget 2019: S$1.1 billion Bicentennial Bonus for Singaporeans", Channel NewsAsia, 18 February 2019, https://www.channelnewsasia.com/news/singapore/budget-2019-bicentennial-bonus-income-tax-rebate-gst-voucher-11252934.
53. "Budget 2019: Building a 'Strong, United Singapore'; Merdeka Generation Package, Healthcare Take Spotlight", Channel NewsAsia, 18 February 2019, https://www.channelnewsasia.com/news/budget-2019-merdeka-generation-package-healthcare-spotlight-11253018.
54. George Wong and Woo Jun Jie, "Singapore in 2018: Between Uncharted Waters and Old Ghosts", in *Southeast Asian Affairs 2019*, edited by Malcolm Cook and Daljit Singh (Singapore: ISEAS – Yusof Ishak Institute, 2019), p. 310.
55. Yen Kiat Chong and Irene Y.H. Ng, "Constructing Poverty in Anti-welfare Singapore", *Social Identities* 23, no. 2 (2017): 146.
56. Soo Ann Lee and Jiwei Qian, "The Evolving Singaporean Welfare State", *Social Policy and Administration* 51, no. 6 (2017), p. 917.
57. Ibid., pp. 930–31.
58. "Income Inequality in Singapore Drops to Its Lowest since 2001", *Today*, 20 February 2020, https://www.todayonline.com/singapore/income-inequality-singapore-drops-its-lowest-2001.
59. "About 1,000 Homeless People Sleeping Rough in Singapore, First-Ever Academic Study Finds", *Today*, 8 November 2019, https://www.todayonline.com/singapore/about-1000-homeless-people-sleeping-rough-singapore-first-ever-study-finds. The full report, *Homeless in Singapore: Results from a Nationwide Street Count*, is available at https://lkyspp.nus.edu.sg/docs/default-source/faculty-publications/homeless-in-singapore.pdf.
60. "Education Arms Race Fuelling Inequality; Solution to Improve Income alongside Access", *The Edge Singapore*, 4 June 2018, https://www.theedgesingapore.com/news/print-week/education-arms-race-fuelling-inequality-solution-improve-income-alongside-access. See also Teo You Yenn, "We Don't See Inequality in S'pore's Education Race because We're Conditioned to Focus on Our Own Lanes", *Mothership*, 9 February 2019, https://mothership.sg/2019/02/teo-you-yenn-education-inequality-meritocracy/.
61. The goods and services tax is set to be increased between 2021 and 2025, as announced in the 2018 Budget.
62. Heng Swee Keat, "Confronting the 3 Major Challenges to Social Cohesion", *Straits Times*, 23 September 2019, https://www.straitstimes.com/opinion/confronting-the-3-major-challenges-to-social-cohesion; K. Shanmugam, "Singapore Cannot Let Inequality Destroy Its Social Cohesion", *Today*, 20 April 2018, https://www.todayonline.com/commentary/singapore-cannot-let-inequality-destroy-its-social-cohesion.
63. "Budget 2019: Foreign Worker Quota in Services Sector to Be Cut to 35% by 2021",

Channel NewsAsia, 18 February 2019, https://www.channelnewsasia.com/news/budget-2019-foreign-worker-quota-in-services-sector-to-be-cut-to-11252904.

64. "Factbox – Main Issues in Singapore's 2011 General Election", Reuters, 6 May 2011, https://uk.reuters.com/article/uk-singapore-election-factbox/factbox-main-issues-in-singapores-2011-general-election-idUKTRE74513L20110506; "Singapore Opposition Stirs up Anti-foreigner Sentiment", *The Telegraph*, 5 May 2011, https://www.telegraph.co.uk/expat/expatnews/8494772/Singapore-opposition-stirs-up-anti-foreigner-sentiment.html.

65. "Aloysius Pang was Crushed When Caught between howitzer's Gun Barrel and Cabin", *Straits Times*, 24 January 2019, https://www.straitstimes.com/singapore/aloysius-pang-was-crushed-when-caught-between-howitzers-gun-barrel-and-cabin.

66. "New Inspector-General's Office to Ensure SAF Safety after Aloysius Pang's Death", *Straits Times*, 1 February 2019, https://www.straitstimes.com/singapore/new-inspector-generals-office-to-ensure-saf-safety.

67. "Data of 14,200 People with HIV Leaked Online by US Fraudster Who Was Deported from Singapore", *Straits Times*, 28 January 2019, https://www.straitstimes.com/singapore/data-of-14200-singapore-patients-with-hiv-leaked-online-by-american-fraudster-who-was.

68. "Data of 14,200 with HIV Leaked Online: What You Need to Know about the Case", *Straits Times*, 28 January 2019, https://www.straitstimes.com/singapore/health/data-of-14200-with-hiv-leaked-online-what-you-need-to-know-about-the-case.

69. "HIV Data Leak: Security Safeguards for HIV Registry in 2012–2013 in Line with Prevailing Government Policies", *Straits Times*, 12 February 2019, https://www.straitstimes.com/politics/hiv-data-leak-security-safeguards-for-hiv-registry-in-2012-2013-in-line-with-prevailing.

70. "HIV Data Leak: Gan Rejects Allegations of Cover-up, Says Chief Concern Was Well-being of Affected People", *Today*, 12 January 2019, https://www.todayonline.com/singapore/hiv-data-leak-gan-rejects-allegations-cover-says-chief-concern-was-well-being-affected.

71. "Personal Information of over 800,000 Blood Donors was Accessible Online for 2 Months: HSA", *Straits Times*, 15 March 2019, https://www.straitstimes.com/singapore/health/personal-information-of-over-800000-blood-donors-exposed-online-hsa.

72. Alfred Siew, "HSA Blood Donor Data Leak: When 'Sorry' May Not Be Enough", *Today*, 21 March 2019, https://www.todayonline.com/commentary/hsa-blood-donor-data-leak-when-sorry-may-not-be-enough.

73. "Cyber Espionage Group Whitefly behind SingHealth Hack: Symantec", Channel NewsAsia, 6 March 2019, https://www.channelnewsasia.com/news/singapore/singhealth-hack-whitefly-cyber-espionage-group-symantec-11317330.

74. "Singapore Health System Hit by 'Most Serious Breach of Personal Data' in Cyberattack; PM Lee's Data Targeted", Channel NewsAsia, 20 July 2018, https://www.channelnewsasia.com/news/singapore/singhealth-health-system-hit-serious-cyberattack-pm-lee-target-10548318.

75. "Parliament: 7 Things to Know about Singapore's Proposed Law to Combat Online Fake News", *Straits Times*, 1 April 2019, https://www.straitstimes.com/politics/7-things-to-know-about-singapores-proposed-law-to-combat-online-fake-news.
76. "Parliament: Workers' Party Opposes Proposed Law on Fake News, says Pritam Singh", *Straits Times*, 7 May 2019, https://www.straitstimes.com/politics/parliament-workers-party-opposes-proposed-law-on-fake-news-pritam-singh.
77. "Parliament: Fake News Law Passed after 2 Days of Debate", *Straits Times*, 8 May 2019, https://www.straitstimes.com/politics/parliament-fake-news-law-passed-after-2-days-of-debate.
78. The nine parliamentarians who voted against the bill were from the WP. Three NMPs abstained.
79. "Fake News Law Invoked for the First Time over Facebook Post", *Straits Times*, 25 November 2019, https://www.straitstimes.com/singapore/pofma-office-directs-opposition-member-brad-bowyer-to-add-correction-notice-to-facebook.
80. The full list of the POFMA orders can be found at https://www.pofmaoffice.gov.sg/media-centre/.
81. "Singapore's Fake News Law: Protecting the Truth, or Restricting Free Debate?", *South China Morning Post*, 21 December 2019, https://www.scmp.com/week-asia/politics/article/3043034/singapores-fake-news-law-protecting-truth-or-restricting-free. See also Kirsten Han, "Want to Criticize Singapore? Expect a 'Correction Notice'", *New York Times*, 21 January 2020, https://www.nytimes.com/2020/01/21/opinion/fake-news-law-singapore.html.
82. "SDP's Pofma Appeal to be Heard in Chambers", *Straits Times*, 15 January 2020, https://www.straitstimes.com/singapore/sdps-pofma-appeal-to-be-heard-in-chambers; "Judgment Reserved in TOC's POFMA Challenge, Arguments on Whether Falsehoods Can be Republished", 6 February 2020, https://www.channelnewsasia.com/news/singapore/court-toc-pofma-challenge-the-online-citizen-12400776.
83. Singapore's Fake News Law: Protecting the Truth, or Restricting Free Debate?", *South China Morning Post*, 21 December 2019, https://www.scmp.com/week-asia/politics/article/3043034/singapores-fake-news-law-protecting-truth-or-restricting-free.
84. "Facebook Issues Fake News Correction Notice on User's Post", *Straits Times*, 30 November 2019, https://www.straitstimes.com/singapore/facebook-issues-fake-news-correction-notice-on-users-post.
85. "States Times Review Facebook Page Barred from Receiving any Financial Benefit under Pofma", *Straits Times*, 15 February 2020, https://www.straitstimes.com/politics/states-times-review-facebook-page-barred-from-receiving-any-financial-benefit-under-pofma.
86. "Facebook Blocks Access in Singapore to States Times Review Page for Breaching Pofma", 18 February 2020, https://www.straitstimes.com/politics/facebook-blocks-access-to-states-times-review-page.
87. "Singapore Invokes Online Falsehoods Law against Malaysian Rights Group's 'Preposterous' Claims on Execution Methods", Channel NewsAsia, 22 January 2020,

https://www.channelnewsasia.com/news/asia/pofma-malaysia-lawyers-for-liberty-drugs-execution-falsehoods-12299384.
88. "Government Orders That Lawyers for Liberty's Website be Blocked in Singapore", Channel NewsAsia, 24 January 2020, https://www.channelnewsasia.com/news/singapore/lawyers-for-liberty-website-block-pofma-12321200.
89. "Malaysian Rights Group Lawyers for Liberty Files Motion in KL High Court against Shanmugam over Correction Direction", Channel NewsAsia, 24 January 2020, https://www.channelnewsasia.com/news/asia/pofma-singapore-malaysia-lawyers-for-liberty-shanmugam-execution-12322456.
90. Prashanth Parameswaran, "Why the New China-Singapore Defense Agreement Matters", *The Diplomat*, 23 October 2019, https://thediplomat.com/2019/10/why-the-new-china-singapore-defense-agreement-matters.
91. "Shangri-La Dialogue: China, US Must Avert Conflict or Fallout Will be Damaging, Says Lee Hsien Loong", *Straits Times*, 1 June 2019, https://www.straitstimes.com/singapore/china-us-must-avert-conflict-or-fallout-will-be-damaging-pm.
92. Ibid.
93. "PM Lee Hsien Loong in China to Attend Belt and Road Forum, Meet Xi Jinping", *Straits Times*, 25 April 2015, https://www.straitstimes.com/asia/east-asia/pm-lee-hsien-loong-in-china-to-attend-belt-and-road-forum-meet-xi-jinping.
94. "Singapore Can Make 'Modest Contribution' to China's Belt and Road Initiative: PM Lee Hsien Loong", *Straits Times*, 23 April 2019, https://www.straitstimes.com/asia/east-asia/singapore-can-make-modest-contribution-to-chinas-belt-and-road-initiative-pm-lee.
95. "Larger-Scale Military Exercises in Store as Singapore and China Upgrade Defence Pact", *Straits Times*, 20 October 2019, https://www.straitstimes.com/asia/east-asia/larger-scale-military-exercises-in-store-as-singapore-and-china-upgrade-defence-pact.
96. "PM Lee, Trump Renew Key Defence Pact on US Use of Singapore Air, Naval Bases", *Straits Times*, 24 September 2019, https://www.straitstimes.com/world/pm-lee-trump-renew-key-defence-pact-on-us-use-of-singapore-air-naval-bases.
97. "Edited Transcript of Minister for Foreign Affairs Dr Vivian Balakrishnan's Remarks on 'Seeking Opportunities amidst Disruption – A View from Singapore' at the Center for Strategic and International Studies (CSIS), 15 May 2019", Ministry of Foreign Affairs, https://www.mfa.gov.sg/Newsroom/Press-Statements-Transcripts-and-Photos/2019/05/20190516_FMV-Washington---CSIS-Speech.
98. "EU-Singapore Free Trade Agreement Comes into Force", *Straits Times*, 21 November 2019, https://www.straitstimes.com/business/economy/eu-singapore-free-trade-agreement-comes-into-force.
99. See, for instance, "Ambitious Regional Economic Pact Will Be Richer If India Signs Up: Iswaran", *Straits Times*, 20 June 2019, https://www.straitstimes.com/asia/south-asia/ambitious-regional-economic-pact-will-be-richer-if-india-signs-up-iswaran; "India Could Face Stark Future outside RCEP: Shanmugam", *Straits Times*, 2 September 2019, https://www.straitstimes.com/asia/south-asia/india-could-face-stark-future-

outside-rcep-shanmugam; "RCEP Will be Game Changer, Says Vivian Balakrishnan, Urging India to Join the Mega Trade Deal", *Straits Times*, 9 September 2019, https://www.straitstimes.com/singapore/rcep-will-be-a-gamechanger-says-vivian-balakrishnan-urging-india-to-join-the-mega-trade.

100. "Singapore and India Discuss Plans on Use of the Chandipur Live-Firing Range in India", *Straits Times*, 20 November 2019, https://www.straitstimes.com/singapore/singapore-and-india-discuss-plans-on-the-use-of-the-chandipur-live-firing-range-in-india.

101. "Singapore and Japan Reaffirm Excellent Relations ahead of G-20 Meeting", *Straits Times*, 27 June 2019, https://www.straitstimes.com/asia/singapore-and-japan-reaffirm-excellent-relations.

102. "Singapore, Malaysia Maritime Dispute: A Timeline", Channel NewsAsia, 8 April 2019, https://www.channelnewsasia.com/news/singapore/singapore-malaysia-maritime-dispute-port-limits-timeline-11006762.

103. "Singapore Extends Port Limits off Tuas, Won't Hesitate to Take Action against Malaysia Intrusions: Khaw", Channel NewsAsia, 6 December 2019, https://www.channelnewsasia.com/news/singapore/singapore-extend-port-limits-malaysia-khaw-boon-wan-11006710.

104. "Singapore-Malaysia Maritime Dispute: Both Sides Agree to Suspend Overlapping Port Limits", Channel NewsAsia, 14 March 2019, https://www.channelnewsasia.com/news/singapore/singapore-malaysia-maritime-port-limits-dispute-11343048.

105. "Singapore, Malaysia Airspace Dispute: What We Know and Timeline", Channel NewsAsia, 8 April 2019, https://www.channelnewsasia.com/news/singapore/singapore-malaysia-southern-johor-airspace-seletar-airport-10997022.

106. "Malaysia Wants to 'Reclaim Delegated Airspace' in Southern Johor", Channel NewsAsia, 4 December 2018, https://www.channelnewsasia.com/news/singapore/malaysia-wants-to-reclaim-delegated-airspace-in-southern-johor-10994982.

107. "Singapore Raises Concerns with Malaysia over Establishment of Permanent Restricted Area over Pasir Gudang", Channel NewsAsia, 1 January 2019, https://www.channelnewsasia.com/news/singapore/singapore-raises-concerns-with-malaysia-over-establishment-of-11077966.

108. "Malaysia, Singapore Agree to Suspend Permanent Restricted Area over Pasir Gudang, ILS for Seletar Airport", Channel NewsAsia, 8 January 2019, https://www.channelnewsasia.com/news/singapore/malaysia-singapore-permanent-restricted-area-seletar-airport-11098662.

109. "Singapore, Malaysia to Develop GPS-based Instrument Approach Procedures for Seletar Airport to Replace ILS", Channel NewsAsia, 8 April 2019, https://www.channelnewsasia.com/news/singapore/singapore-malaysia-seletar-airport-gps-based-instrument-approach-11422582.

110. "JB-Singapore RTS Link to Proceed with 36% Cost Cut: Malaysia PM Mahathir", Channel NewsAsia, 31 October 2019, https://www.channelnewsasia.com/news/singapore/malaysia-singapore-rts-link-mahathir-johor-12051132.

111. "JB-Singapore RTS Link to Go Ahead but Further Suspended to April 2020: Khaw", Channel NewsAsia, 4 November 2019, https://www.channelnewsasia.com/news/singapore/singapore-jb-malaysia-rts-rail-link-agreement-12062794.
112. "Six-Month Suspension for JB-Singapore RTS Link is to Ensure Relevant Agreements Can be Amended: Loke", Channel NewsAsia, 5 November 2019, https://www.channelnewsasia.com/news/asia/singapore-malaysia-rts-latest-suspension-agreements-12064268.
113. "'Good Progress' Being Made on RTS, Malaysia Needs Time to 'Review Some Details': Vivian Balakrishnan", Channel NewsAsia, 8 November 2019, https://www.channelnewsasia.com/news/asia/vivian-balakrishnan-cna938-rcep-rts-hsr-malaysia-12075004.
114. "PM Lee Sends Condolence Letter on Death of former Thai Premier Prem Tinsulanonda", *Straits Times*, 1 June 2019, https://www.straitstimes.com/singapore/pm-lee-sends-condolence-letter-on-death-of-former-thai-premier-prem-tinsulanonda.
115. "Lee Hsien Loong's Facebook Post on 1978 Vietnam-Cambodia Issue Upsets Both Countries", *Straits Times*, 6 June 2019, https://www.straitstimes.com/singapore/pm-lees-facebook-post-on-1978-vietnam-cambodia-issue-upsets-both-countries.
116. "Hun Sen Accuses Singapore PM Lee Hsien Loong of 'Supporting Genocide' as War of Words over Cambodia's Khmer Rouge-era Escalates", *South China Morning Post*, 6 June 2019, https://www.scmp.com/week-asia/politics/article/3013336/did-vietnam-invade-cambodia-or-save-it-singapore-pm-lee-hsien.
117. "NUS to Convene Review Committee after Student Calls for Tougher Action against Man Who Filmed Her in Shower", *Straits Times*, 20 April 2019, https://www.straitstimes.com/singapore/nus-to-convene-review-committee-after-student-calls-for-tougher-action-against-man-who.
118. Ibid.
119. "NUS' Penalties for Sexual Misconduct Case Were 'Manifestly Inadequate': Ong Ye Kung", Channel NewsAsia, 22 April 2019, https://www.channelnewsasia.com/news/singapore/ong-ye-kung-moe-penalties-sexual-misconduct-nus-monica-baey-11468688.
120. "NUS Accepts Recommendations for Tougher Penalties on Sexual Misconduct; Minimum 1-year Suspension for Serious Offences", *Straits Times*, 10 January 2019, https://www.straitstimes.com/singapore/education/nus-accepts-all-recommendations-by-committee-on-sexual-misconduct-cases.
121. "Singapore Broadcaster in Hot Water after 'Brownface' Advert Sparks Anger, Apology", *South China Morning Post*, 29 July 2019, https://www.scmp.com/news/asia/southeast-asia/article/3020480/singapore-broadcaster-hot-water-after-brownface-advert.
122. Ruby Thiagarajan, "Brownface and Racism in Singapore", *New Naratif*, 1 August 2019, https://newnaratif.com/journalism/brownface-and-racism-in-singapore/.
123. "'I Feel Terrible': Dennis Chew Apologises over Controversial E-Pay Ad", Channel

NewsAsia, 7 August 2019, https://www.channelnewsasia.com/news/singapore/dennis-chew-apologises-over-controversial-e-pay-ad-11789480.

124. "Rap Video by Local YouTube Star Preetipls on 'Brownface' Ad Crosses the Line, Not Acceptable: Shanmugam", *Straits Times*, 30 July 2019, https://www.straitstimes.com/politics/rap-video-by-local-youtube-star-preetipls-on-brownface-ad-crosses-the-line-not-acceptable.

125. "YouTuber Preetipls and Brother Subhas Given Conditional Warning by Police over Rap Video on 'Brownface' Ad", *Straits Times*, 14 August 2019, https://www.straitstimes.com/singapore/youtuber-preetipls-and-brother-subhas-given-conditional-warning-by-police-over-rap-video.

126. "Big Turnout at Hong Lim Park for First Singapore Climate Rally", *Straits Times*, 21 September 2019, https://www.straitstimes.com/singapore/environment/hundreds-turn-up-in-red-at-hong-lim-park-for-first-singapore-climate-rally.

127. "More than 1,700 Turn Up at First Singapore Climate Rally", Channel NewsAsia, 21 September 2019, https://www.channelnewsasia.com/news/singapore/1700-participants-sg-climate-rally-die-in-11930486.

128. "National Day Rally 2019: Land Reclamation, Polders among Ways S'pore Looks to Deal with Sea-level Rise", *Straits Times*, 18 August 2019, https://www.straitstimes.com/politics/national-day-rally-2019-land-reclamation-polders-among-ways-spore-looks-to-deal-with-sea.

129. "Singaporeans Push Government to Set Tougher Emissions Targets in First Ever Climate Rally", *Eco-Business*, 23 September 2019, https://www.eco-business.com/news/singaporeans-push-government-to-set-tougher-emissions-targets-in-first-ever-climate-rally/.

130. Angel Hsu, "Commentary: Forget Bamboo Straws. Let's Name the Elephants in the Room of Singapore's Climate Debate", Channel NewsAsia, https://www.channelnewsasia.com/news/commentary/singapore-climate-change-action-un-madrid-oil-refinery-petrochem-12178838.

131. "Young Climate Activist Wants to Phase Out Fossil Fuels, Move to Cleaner Energy, but Is Realistic", *Today*, 29 September 2019, https://www.todayonline.com/singapore/young-sg-climate-activist-wants-phase-out-fossil-fuels-and-move-towards-cleaner-energy.

THE BICENTENNIAL COMMEMORATION: Imagining and Re-imagining Singapore's History

Terence Chong

In early 2019 I was dining with a Japanese diplomat in the company of two fellow Singaporeans. When the conversation turned to the Bicentennial Commemorations, the diplomat asked inquisitively, "Why do Singaporeans find it necessary to celebrate two hundred years of colonialism?" After a moment's pause the Singaporeans around the table took random stabs at answering our dinner companion's question. Our replies ranged from the pedantic ("It's not a celebration, it's a *commemoration*"), the cynical ("It's for the feel-good factor to help with upcoming elections"), to the dismissive ("you know Singaporeans, they love nostalgia"). As we spoke I sensed that we were ourselves struggling to understand the event as much as we sought to explain it to our Japanese friend. Like most Singaporeans, we had felt that the Bicentennial Commemorations simply did not embody the same significance or emotional heft as SG50 in 2015 when we celebrated fifty years of independence. The country's Golden Jubilee was easier to embrace because it was an unabashed and unambiguous celebration of the nation-building project and the undeniable progress we had made as one people. But what were the Bicentennial Commemorations—or SG200—supposed to commemorate? Was it to mark the arrival of English rogue gentleman Stamford Raffles and the East India Company and, by implication, the unplugging of the island from the Malay world and its ascension into the global economy? If so, then it's understandable that the celebration of colonial capitalism and globalization did not exactly tug at the heartstrings of Singaporeans. The unthinking celebration of

---

TERENCE CHONG is Deputy Director of the ISEAS – Yusof Ishak Institute, Singapore and Head of the Temasek History Research Centre at the institute.

colonialism would also certainly be out of step with our sensibilities. Or was SG200 a knowing wink at the island's distinction from a region still mired in its internal political and economic squabbles and thus a marker of the nation's discrete sense of self, or what we would describe today as Singapore exceptionalism? The more we mulled over the question, the more uncertain we became. Then, somewhere between the fourth and seventh cup of sake, a particular remark from one of us, I forget who, struck me—"We don't have history, so we imagine it." Unlike ancient civilizations padded with multiple layers of epochs and ages, Singapore had but two popular dates committed to memory—1819 and 1965 (and 2004 if you want to count the year we implemented the five-day work week). But, of course, all societies, regardless of age and civilization, imagine their history. They tell themselves stories about who they are and where they came from, and then rewrite them over and over again. History-writing is an aspirational exercise that demands imagination. This imagination and re-imagination melds itself with the zeitgeist of each political and ideological cycle. Singapore is no different.

It is tempting to think of national history as a static and unyielding narrative, but that would be a mistaken assumption. National histories are constantly re-imagined in order to remain relevant, first and foremost, to the evolving interests of the political elite. How the political elite view the external environment, its opportunities and dangers has a profound influence on how national history is narrated. Geopolitical shifts, rising powers and the evolving regional architecture make it necessary for a small state like Singapore not only to be economically and politically nimble in catching the winds of opportunity but also historically imaginative in how it narrates the grand story of a small nation of immigrants hailing from China and India within the Malay world. For instance, when the People's Action Party (PAP) government came to power in 1959, Singapore's destiny was imagined as deeply intertwined with that of the Malayan peninsula. The imagination of the political elite at that time had no room for a self-sufficient Singapore severed from its Malayan hinterland because of the island's lack of natural resources. This was why merger with Malaysia was deemed vital to the survival of the island. The fact that Singapore has arisen from its circumstances and charted an economic upward trajectory from 1965 clearly demonstrates that such imaginations are underpinned by contemporary realities and open to evolution.

To understand the Bicentennial Commemorations, I explained to our Japanese friend, we have to recognize how Singapore has imagined and re-imagined its own history. The Bicentennial Commemoration was an exercise in redefining our position and place in the world; and it certainly will not be the last time we do it. Singapore's national history has undergone three major imaginations. The first was the imagining of our history as *tabula rasa* through self-inflicted amnesia in 1965; the second was the imagination of the great civilizations of China and India as the cultural homelands of our Chinese and Indian communities in the 1980s; and most recently, the attempt to imagine Singapore with a history of over 700 years, of which the Bicentennial Commemorations are part.

Tabula Rasa in 1965

Singapore's national history was first imagined as a *tabula rasa*. This meant marking 1819 as ground zero when Stamford Raffles landed. In this imagination, Singapore was born fully formed as a modern colonial entity without a past. Indeed, seminal history texts like Mary Turnbull's *A History of Singapore, 1819–1975*[1] did little to locate Singapore as a regional port or as part of the Malay world. Early historians like Turnbull helped perpetuate this truncated imagination either because historical evidence of pre-1819 communities was insufficient for further scholarly investigation or these communities were just not thought significant enough to warrant investigation. This modern colonial entity, as the story goes, proceeded to attract waves of immigrants from south China and India as coolies, indentured workers and traders who joined the Malay communities already here, thus giving rise to our present conception of a "multicultural society". This imagination of history as a clean slate was also shaped by the visceral and contentious ethnic politics between Singapore and Malaysia during the merger from 1963 to 1965. At stake during these two years of political and ideological experimentation was the political role of ethnicity in the organization of these two multicultural societies. On one hand, the ruling United Malays National Organisation (UMNO) in Malaysia championed *bangsa Melayu* to express Malay ethnic and political identity, and to distinguish the indigenous community from non-Malays. The thrust of UMNO's message was that national politics must be decided by the Malay community and the Malay community alone. On the other, the PAP in Singapore argued "that Malay privileges provided for in the Constitution were economic and social but not political; hence Malays had no special right to rule".[2] Instead, the PAP called for a "Malaysian Malaysia" at the Malaysian Solidarity Convention in 1965, just months before expulsion, which essentially appealed for national politics to be free from ethnic demands or communal interests; a call subsequently rejected by UMNO.

Upon independence, the PAP proceeded to erect multiculturalism and meritocracy as central pillars of the nation-building project in the effort to leave ethnic-based politics behind. For some within the PAP intelligentsia, this demanded a new way of imagining the national community. After all, UMNO's insistence on Malay dominance was merely a reflection of the wave of anti-colonialism sweeping across the globe at that time, which was heightening ethnic differences and creating distinct identities. Watching this closely was then culture minister S. Rajaratnam, who began to worry how emerging forms of national identities in postcolonial societies were taking on more and more exclusive characteristics. For him, the primordial desire of communities to distinguish themselves from each other was going to be a perennial challenge. In a 1968 speech, Rajaratnam observed that "People who were once united are becoming political archaeologists. They are rummaging among ancient myths, doubtful legends and historical records to find reasons why they are entitled to be distinct and separate from the rest of the national community".[3] Rajaratnam went on to explain the reason for history's dawn in 1819:

> Singapore's genealogical table, alas, ends as abruptly as it begins. However we could have contrived a more lengthy and eye-boggling lineage by tracing our ancestry back to the lands from which our forefathers emigrated—China, India, Sri Lanka, the Middle East and Indonesia.
>
> The price we would have to pay for this impressive genealogical table would be to turn Singapore into a bloody battleground for endless racial and communal conflicts and interventionist politics by the more powerful and bigger nations from which Singaporeans had emigrated.[4]

The young nascent country, shaken by the bloody racial riots of July 1964 that left twenty-three people dead, did not need political archaeologists searching for distinct threads of identity that would stretch the fabric of the multicultural society to breaking point. And while newly decolonized societies elsewhere had ridden the waves of indigenous and ethnic forms of nationalism, then prime minister Lee Kuan Yew made clear on 9 August 1965 that "This is not a Malay nation; this is not a Chinese nation; this is not an Indian nation. Everybody will have his place. Equal."[5]

In sum, Singapore's history had to begin from 1819 for three broad reasons. Firstly, the early generation of historians did not believe that there was significant historical and archaeological evidence to warrant the imagination of a Singapore before 1819. Secondly, in light of the multicultural complexion of the island and the different origins of the Chinese and Indian communities, beginning national history from 1819 was akin to cutting the Gordian knot. Finally, the ideological imperative to form a new society that vaunted the principles of meritocracy, multiculturalism and egalitarianism made it necessary to banish political archaeologists from the scene.

Looking to the Great Civilizations of China and India

And this was so for a few decades until the 1980s. By which time Singapore had achieved significant economic development. The local population were enjoying higher levels of education and qualifying for more professional vocations, while the economy was transitioning from a lower manufacturing base to a higher value-added one. This growth also saw greater numbers of Singaporeans owning their own homes as well as household items such as televisions and refrigerators, prompting then prime minister Lee Kuan Kew to declare confidently that "This means 80 per cent of our population are the bourgeoisie or middle-class."[6] Unsurprisingly, this new found middle class status came with conspicuous consumption, and greater familiarity and comfort with Western culture as Singaporeans travelled more widely for leisure and education. Nevertheless, this familiarity with the West sparked government concerns that the population had become too "Westernized" and out of touch with their Asian roots. In fact, this anxiety over "Westernization" was already present by the late 1970s. Two milestone reports were written on national education[7] and moral education[8] by Dr Goh Keng Swee and Mr Ong Teng Cheong, respectively, warning of increasing "Westernization" and "deculturalization" amongst younger Singaporeans. For the political elite, growing Westernization and deculturalization was disconcerting for two reasons. Firstly, it implied that the electorate would embrace liberal ideologies and values such as the prioritization of free speech and human rights, which would in turn result in a more confrontational and fractious relationship with the government. Secondly, and more existentially, Lee Kuan Yew had long feared that the English-educated Chinese, in mimicking Western practices and values, were less culturally confident and resolute in contrast to those who were firmly rooted in Chinese or Asian culture.[9] Ong Teng Cheong's report led to the introduction of Religious Knowledge (RK) as a mandatory programme in secondary schools in 1984. RK was designed to provide a moral ballast and to "support the moral values the government wanted to inculcate in the young".[10] The programme offered Bible Studies, Buddhist Studies, Hindu Studies, Islamic Religious Knowledge, Sikh Studies and, later on, Confucian Ethics as subjects, but was later withdrawn in 1989.

It was clear to the political elite that Singaporeans needed a cultural-ethnic ballast. This demanded a re-imagining of national history. Shifting from its initial *tabula rasa* position, the government made the decision to extend Singapore's history beyond 1819 in order to lengthen the cultural roots of our immigrant population. Singaporean Chinese were exhorted to understand China and appreciate Chinese history in order to develop a sense of cultural lineage to withstand the ills of an American-driven globalization. As scholars have observed, it was a massive ideological exercise that entailed the tapping of the "histories of the civilisations from which the migrant population could trace their origins".[11] The hope was that the different ethnic communities in Singapore would be able to draw on the culture, history and legacies of the civilizations that their forefathers came from and, in so doing, would have the cultural confidence to withstand Western influences.

This re-imagination certainly went beyond the rhetorical. For example, the Asian Civilisations Museum (ACM) was originally meant to have a Southeast Asian focus when it was conceived in the late 1980s.[12] However, when George Yeo took over the arts and culture portfolio as acting minister of the Ministry of Information and the Arts in 1990, he widened the scope of the ACM to include broader Asia. In explaining his decision to change ACM's mandate, Yeo noted that Singapore has "historical links not only to Southeast Asia but to a wider Asia—China, South and West Asia—from where Singapore's multi-ethnic population emanated".[13] Political archaeology was back in vogue. As a museum, the ACM not only served as a repository of cultural artefacts from Southeast Asia, South Asia, and East Asia but also as a concrete monument to Singapore's imagined position at the crossroads between China and India.

However, the government's attempt to move Singapore's history beyond 1819 was not welcomed by all. And the most prominent critic was none other than S. Rajaratnam himself. Rajaratnam, who was by then retired from office, wrote several letters to the press as a private citizen in 1990–91 to argue against pushing Singapore's collective history beyond 1819. He argued that the immigrants whom Raffles attracted to Singapore belonged to "different lands, different times" and "different histories".[14] Such cultural lineages were, according to Rajaratnam, "ancestral ghosts" that had to be exorcised from collective memory.[15] More important, for Rajaratnam, were the collective joys, sorrows, disappointments and achievements of the post-1819 and, more crucially, post-1965 period.

The Bicentennial Commemorations and 700 Years of History

By the late 2000s the geopolitical landscape had once again evolved. China had not only emerged as an economic powerhouse but it was also believed by many to be flexing its political muscles in Southeast Asia. For example, the economic dependence of a few Southeast Asian countries on China has hindered ASEAN from speaking with one voice on important issues, thus weakening ASEAN centrality. Its military build-up and claims over the South China Sea have alarmed the region and beyond. In November 2016, nine Terrex military vehicles belonging to the Singapore Armed Forces were embargoed in Hong Kong as they made their way back from Taiwan after military exercises. The official reason for the embargo was that the vehicles were listed as "civilian vehicles" and thus did not have the required licence.[16] However, others suggested that this was Beijing's way of expressing displeasure with Singapore for its response to the International Tribunal ruling that favoured the Philippines with regard to the South China Sea dispute.[17] To top it all, Beijing's call to all overseas Chinese, regardless of citizenship, to be loyal to China and contribute to its growth and serve the country's interests has been viewed with trepidation.[18] It is thus no surprise that, according to ISEAS's *State of Southeast Asia Survey: Report 2020*, fewer Southeast Asian opinion-makers see China as a "benign and benevolent power" or trust it to "do the right thing" when it comes to contributing to global peace and security. Quite clearly, the infatuation with all things China had quickly evaporated. While sections of the Singaporean Chinese community continue to gaze upon it as their cultural motherland, China was taking on a more aggressive demeanour in the eyes of many. When the China Cultural Centre was opened in 2015 in downtown Singapore to promote Chinese culture and history, the Singapore government promptly set up the Singapore Chinese Cultural Centre two years later in the business district to underline the fact that Singaporean Chinese culture was different from Chinese culture. In short, China's rise and its subsequent behaviour was changing the geopolitical landscape, and so too our imagination of history had to be revised once again.

While this was developing on a broader geopolitical scale, there were regional developments as well. Southeast Asia was experiencing rapid growth and had begun to be viewed as a region of opportunity. One of the positive outcomes of China's rise was the shift of economic gravity towards Asia, much to the benefit of Southeast Asia. Vietnam, with its rapidly growing middle class, strong manufacturing industry and ready adoption of technology, has been touted by observers to be entering its "golden period",[19] while Indonesia's robust consumer trends, vibrant start-up industry and entrepreneurship culture, as well as technological trends, have filled investors with some optimism.[20] These have prompted government leaders to look at the region with greater interest, with some exhorting Singaporeans to develop a deeper understanding of the diverse region.[21] At the national level, Singapore had grown in confidence in terms of national identity and its place in the world. The country's Golden Jubilee celebration in 2015 was an important milestone for allowing Singaporeans to dwell on the country's remarkable journey. Beyond its many well-documented economic successes, Singaporeans also took stock of the country's multicultural complexion and the way it has managed to maintain religious and ethnic harmony over the years, the occasional hiccup notwithstanding. When contrasted with other postcolonial or multicultural societies, Singaporeans began to realize that, whilst far from perfect, the country's careful management of ethnic and religious identities has been more fruitful and effective than that in most other societies, liberal or otherwise.

Meanwhile, on the scholarly front, much research had been conducted in the fields of history and archaeology to highlight the island's regional position and role over the centuries prior to 1819. Key texts include *Seven Hundred Years: A History of Singapore*[22] and *Studying Singapore Before 1800*,[23] both of which bring together the work of historians and archaeologists past and present to offer a collective body of evidence that asserts the vibrancy and connectivity of the various communities living on and around the island long before the arrival of Raffles. Perhaps more pertinently, this body of work underlines the importance of regionalism to the island by arguing that Singapore's identity and place in the world cannot be understood in a vacuum. It locates Singapore's past and culture within the immediate region, or what is popularly known as the "Malay world". The Singapore Stone found at the mouth of the Singapore River, for example, suggests fourteenth-century linguistic influence from the surrounding cultural centres. Meanwhile, archaeological material from Fort Canning Hill points strongly to cultural and political engagement with parts of Java and Sumatra. Collectively, such work offer a linear trajectory from the fourteenth century onwards, exploring the island's status as part of the Malacca Sultanate in the fifteenth century and, later, the Johor Sultanate. More recently, archaeological digs at downtown Empress Place conducted by the Archaeological Unit from the ISEAS – Yusof Ishak Institute in 2015 surfaced artefacts dating back to the thirteenth century suggesting that the island was a hub of commercial activity. In contrast to the concepts of internationalism and globalization that often portray Southeast Asia as merely a necessary trading pathway between larger civilizations, regionalism accentuates the importance of Southeast Asia as a coherent sphere of influence and meaning making. It was with this growing body of scholarship, together with China's rise and the re-energization of Southeast Asia, that made it possible, perhaps even necessary, to re-imagine Singapore's history as more deeply intertwined with the region.

And the Bicentennial Commemorations leverage heavily on this sense of regionalism. The Bicentennial Experience, a multimedia interactive exhibition at Fort Canning Hill, is divided into five acts that chart the island journey from the fourteenth century to the arrival of Raffles, its rise as a metropolis, the Japanese Occupation from 1942 to 1945, and its eventual formation as a nation. The first act was crucial in setting the narrative for the fourteenth to seventeenth centuries. It announces that "Singapura was a thriving maritime emporium under the rule of Sang Nila Utama and his successors. Being connected to the region brought Singapore waves of fortune and prosperity, but it also put her at the centre of regional disruptions".[24] The broader point was Singapore's varying positions, first under the Sriwijaya Empire, then the Majapahit Empire, followed by the Malacca and Johor Sultanates over the centuries, and how it has always been economically, politically and culturally influenced by its surroundings. In essence, the Bicentennial Commemorations seek to give Singapore history deeper roots in local soil.

The overarching message of the Bicentennial Commemorations is twofold. Firstly, the networks and influences from the region have shaped Singapore's culture and fortunes; and secondly, while it must always be a global city open to the rest of the world, it will remain a Southeast Asian city because of geography. The latter may sound banal to many, but to the more observant students of Singapore this represents something of a mindset change. Not too long ago, Southeast Asia was viewed by the country's political and business elite as an inconvenient reality that had to be put up with. It was not unusual for commentators to note how Singapore "suffers its region" and had to "leapfrog" it to achieve security and prosperity[25] or, more evocatively, a "good house in a bad neighbourhood".[26] This perspective has evolved for the reasons laid out above, with the Bicentennial Commemorations and its supporting exhibitions, events and collaterals underlying this point.

Conclusion

When visitors reach the end of the Bicentennial Experience at Fort Canning they are invited to choose from three of Singapore's "DNA traits" they identify most with. The choices offered are "self-determination", "multiculturalism" and "openness". When the exhibition finally closed its doors at the end of 2019, the total vote count was taken and "self-determination" was by far the most popular "DNA trait", with 234,000 votes, followed by "multiculturalism" with 176,500 votes and "openness" with 130,000 votes.[27] Nothing speaks of self-determination more than the purposeful imagination and re-imagination of one's national history. To be able to design and re-design one's story in order to envisage different pathways for a national community in an ever-changing world requires both political will and innovation. In many ways, the Bicentennial Commemorations of 2019 is a celebration of the ways that Singapore has, over the decades, managed to reinvent itself in response to global challenges. This is perhaps the best lesson one can distil from the year-long commemorations.

Notes

1. C. Mary Turnbull, *A History of Singapore, 1819–1975* (Singapore: Oxford University Press, 1977).
2. Michael Hill and Lian Kwen Fee, *The Politics of Nation-building and Citizenship in Singapore* (London: Routledge, 1995), p. 60.
3. Chan Heng Chee and Obaid Ul Haq, eds, *S. Rajaratnam: The Prophetic and the Political* (Singapore: Institute of Southeast Asian Studies and Graham Bash, 2007), p. 132.
4. Ibid., p. 139.
5. Lee Kuan Yew, "Transcript of a Press Conference Given by the Prime Minister of Singapore, Mr. Lee Kuan Yew, at Broadcasting House, Singapore, at 1200 hours on Monday 9th August, 1965".
6. Lee Kuan Yew, "Speech by Prime Minister Lee Kuan Yew at the Tanjong Pagar National Day Dinner Held at the Tanjong Pagar Community Centre On Thursday, 13 August 1987".
7. Goh Keng Swee, *Report on the Ministry of Education* (Singapore: Ministry of Culture, 1978).
8. Ong, Teng Cheong, *Report on Moral Education* (Singapore: Ministry of Culture, 1979).
9. Lee Kuan Yew, *The Singapore Story: The Memoirs of Lee Kuan Yew* (Singapore: Singapore Press Holdings, 1998).
10. Charlene Tan, "From Moral Values to Citizenship Education: The Teaching of Religion in Singapore Schools", In *Religious Diversity in Singapore*, edited by Lai Ah Eng (Singapore: Institute of Policy Studies and Institute of Southeast Asian Studies, 2008), p. 324.
11. Hong Lysa and Huang Jianli, *The Scripting of a National History: Singapore and its Pasts* (Hong Kong: Hong Kong University Press, 2008), p. 53.
12. Advisory Council on Culture and the Arts (ACCA), *Report of the Advisory Council on Culture and the Arts* (Singapore: ACCA, 1989), p. 6.
13. Kwa Chong Guan, "Redefining the National Museum: New Reflections on Heritage", in *Impressions of the Goh Chok Tong Years in Singapore*, edited by Bridget Welsh, James Chin, Arun Mahizhnan, and Tan Tarn How (Singapore: NUS Press, 2009).
14. Hong and Huang, *The Scripting of a National History*, p. 54.

15. Ibid.
16. Claire Huang, "Seized SAF Terrex Troop Carriers Listed as 'Civilian Vehicles' in Shipping Firm's Paperwork, HK Court Told", *Straits Times*, 12 October 2018.
17. Minnie Chan, "How Singapore's Military Vehicles Became Beijing's Diplomatic Weapon", *South China Morning Post*, 3 December 2016.
18. Amy Qin, "Worries Grow in Singapore over China's Calls to Help 'Motherland' ", *New York Times*, 5 August 2018.
19. Diana Ngo, "Vietnam is Entering Its 'Golden Period' ", *Business Times*, 30 December 2019.
20. Chng Kai Fong, "Jakarta Ticks All My Boxes as a Vibrant City", *Straits Times*, 8 January 2020.
21. Seow Bei Yi, "Singaporeans Need to Understand the Region Better, Says Chan Chun Sing", *Straits Times*, 28 November 2018.
22. Kwa Chong Guan, Derek Heng, Peter Borschberg, and Tan Tai Yong, *Seven Hundred Years: A History of Singapore* (Singapore: National Library Board and Marshall Cavendish, 2019).
23. Kwa Chong Guan and Peter Borschberg, eds., *Studying Singapore Before 2018* (Singapore: NUS Press, 2018).
24. https://www.bicentennial.sg/the-bicentennial-experience/.
25. Amitav Acharya, *Singapore's Foreign Policy: The Search for Regional Order* (Singapore: World Scientific, 2008), p. 8.
26. Linda Low, "The Singapore Developmental State in the New Economy and Polity", *Pacific Review* 14, no. 3 (2001): 434.
27. Timothy Goh, "Bicentennial Experience Closes, but Parts Will Remain at Fort Canning", *Straits Times*, 2 January 2020.

Thailand

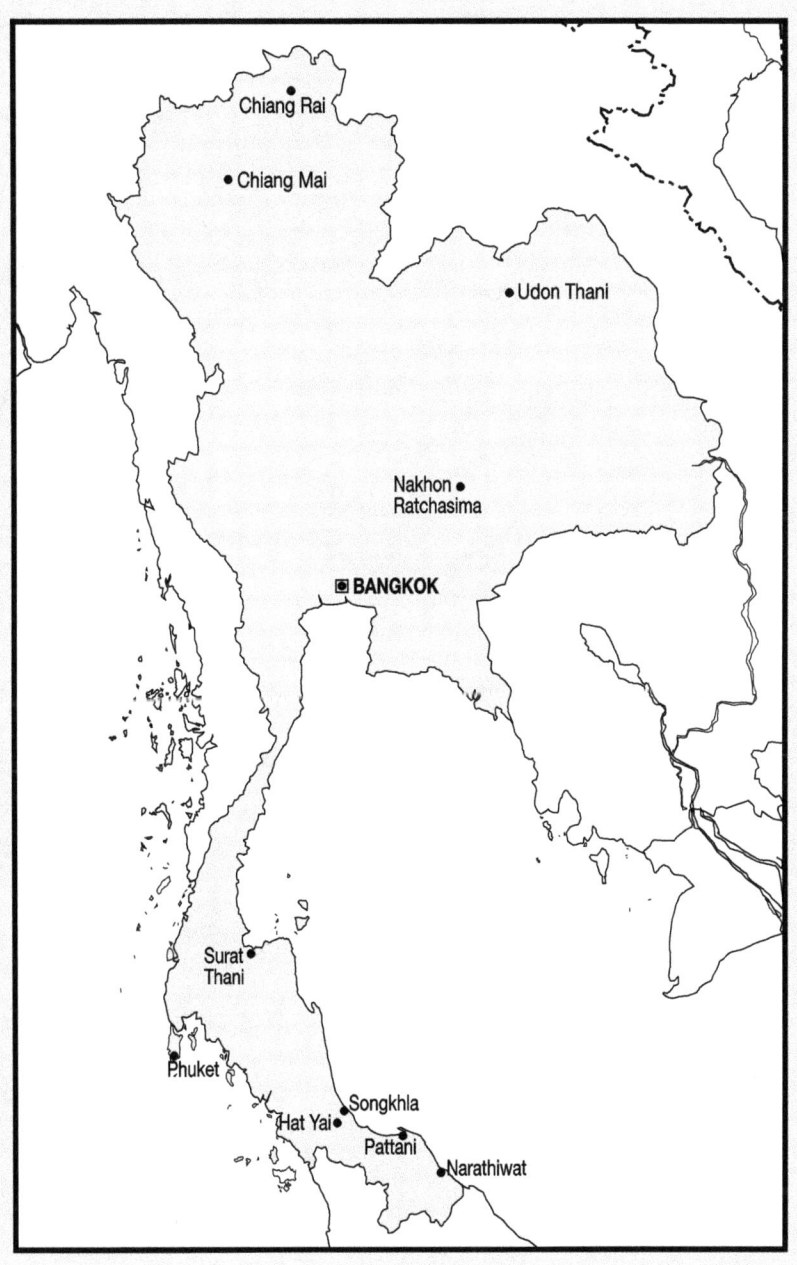

THAILAND IN 2019:
The Year of Living Unpredictably

Kanokrat Lertchoosakul

What happened in Thailand throughout 2019 was different from anything that had gone before in contemporary Thai politics. Prior to the March general election there were many questions. Was the election going to happen, and, if it was, what were the results going to be? The process leading up to the election was also intriguing. On the one hand, there were many new political parties. On the other hand, politicians faced many challenges and constraints caused by the pro-military constitution introduced in 2017.

The result of the election was even more startling. It saw the decline of the urban middle-class Democrats, the oldest party in Thailand, as well as the rural mass-based Pheu Thai, the latest incarnation of Thaksin-inspired parties, which had won every election this century. The election also witnessed the emergence of the "new kids in town": Future Forward and Palang Pracharat. The latter was a pro-military party that recruited from the ranks of existing politicians with existing patronage networks. Palang Pracharat nominated General Prayut Chan-o-cha, the leader of the 2014 coup and head of the junta, as its choice of prime minister. Even though Palang Pracharat was only the second-largest party in parliament, Prayut was still voted by a joint sitting of the House of Representatives and the military-appointed Senate to be the prime minister. Palang Pracharat also managed to form a coalition government of nineteen political parties to hold a slim parliamentary majority of 254 out of 500 seats, confronting an opposition bloc of seven political parties with 246 parliamentary seats. Given the economic downturn, strained relations with Western democracies, and the rise of a popular opposition in the form of Future Forward, the government was expected to

---

KANOKRAT LERTCHOOSAKUL is Lecturer at the Department of Government, Faculty of Political Science, Chulalongkorn University, Bangkok, Thailand.

be vulnerable and short-lived. But, after more than half a year, the pro-junta government has successfully maintained its upper hand, taming its medium- and small-sized coalition partners and suppressing the opposition. There have so far been no robust challenges to the pro-military government.

Peculiar Pre-election Conditions

In the decade following the 1992 democratic transition, Thailand was considered one of the most democratic countries in Southeast Asia. The subsequent campaign for reform led to the 1997 constitution, one of the most democratic in Thai political history. After this came two overwhelming electoral victories of Thai Rak Thai ("Thai Love Thai"), a new party led by Thaksin Shinawatra that was popular among the rural poor. In 2006, democracy was temporarily terminated by a coup d'état. The military claimed that the coup was necessary to protect democracy from the abusive, populist and corrupt government of Prime Minister Thaksin Shinawatra and to prevent the outbreak of violence stemming from the protracted conflict between the "Red Shirt" supporters of Thaksin and the anti-Thaksin "Yellow Shirt" movement led by the People's Alliance for Democracy (PAD). After the junta-appointed government stepped aside a year later, the conflict resumed. The People's Power Party, successor to the court-dissolved Thai Rak Thai, won the 2007 election under the leadership of Samak Sundaravej. Thaksin was then in self-imposed exile, while the anti-Thaksin movement, led by former politicians of the Democrat Party, re-emerged as the People's Democratic Reform Committee (PDRC). The confrontation between these forces continued from 2007 to 2014. Two prime ministers of the People's Power Party were dismissed by the courts, and later the party itself was dissolved. This then enabled the military to engineer a Democrat Party–led government in 2008, even though the Democrats had not won an election in two decades. Mass protests against the Democrat government in April and May 2010 were violently suppressed by the military, leading to around a hundred deaths. In 2011 the Democrats again lost a general election to the Pheu Thai Party led by Thaksin's sister, Yingluck. The red-yellow conflict reached another peak in 2013 when the anti-Thaksin PDRC movement mobilized one of the biggest mass protests in Thai political history. However, instead of promoting democracy—like the previous mass movements of 1973, 1976 and 1992—the PDRC campaigned for the suspension of electoral democracy and called for the military to intervene in parliamentary politics in order to uproot Thaksin's legacy. After nearly seven months of protest, the military seized power from the elected government of PM Yingluck Shinawatra in May 2014. In doing so, it established the National Council for Peace and Order (NCPO), which would go on to remain in power for nearly five years.

The 2014 coup meant that Thailand experienced its first long-term authoritarian government since the democratic movement overthrew a military dictatorship in 1973. During the period from May 2014 to March 2019, Thailand went through nearly five years without an election, while the junta consolidated its power by suppressing an opposition composed of Red Shirts and other democratic forces. Despite repeated calls for a return to electoral democracy, progress was slow and uncertain. There were countless demonstrations calling for elections by former Red Shirts and student activists critical of the government, even though there was a virtual ban on public assembly and the junta had significant powers to suppress dissent. While the junta promised elections from the outset, it repeatedly postponed the process.[1]

After three years of military rule, Thailand's twentieth constitution was promulgated in 2017. Far from being a product of reconciliation and compromise, the constitution instead enhances the power of the military, bureaucracy, judiciary and other non-elected independent state institutions. At the same time, it constrains the power of elected politicians, major political parties and anti-military pro-democratic forces.[2] The 2017 constitution also introduced a novel electoral system. Since 1997, voters were provided with two ballot papers: one to elect the member of parliament (MP) for their constituency and another for their choice of party, which would determine the allocation of party-list MPs. The new constitution however introduced a single ballot, which means that each vote would count towards the election of the constituency MP and the selection of the party-list parliamentarians. This was done because the drafters of the constitution had calculated that such a mechanism would increase the number of seats allocated to medium-sized parties at the expense of major parties such as Pheu Thai. Moreover, with no minimum threshold of votes necessary for a parliamentary seat, it also guarantees the presence of a large number of micro-parties in the legislature and increases the likelihood of a weak and unstable multi-party coalition government. This system is also virtually cast in stone, since amendments would require the support of one-third of the military-appointed Senate, twenty per cent of MPs from each opposition party, and a public referendum to confirm the changes.[3]

This constitution seems designed to bring Thai politics back to the semi-democratic system of the 1980s. Although members of the House of Representatives are elected, the members of the Senate are appointed, and the prime minister does not have to be an elected MP. This means that significant united power can be concentrated in the hands of an unelected prime minister and military-appointed senators while political parties and elected politicians remain divided.[4]

The timetable for elections however remained unsettled, even after the pro-military constitution was approved in 2016 before being promulgated in April 2017. Right afterward, a junta spokesman told journalists that the election could happen nineteen months after the coronation of King Rama X,[5] without announcing the exact date. The junta later corrected this to nineteen months after the promulgation of the constitution because of the lengthy process of preparing bills related to the election.[6] In September 2018 the palace endorsed the last two bills required for a general election. It was then reported in January 2019 that the Election Commission would announce 24 February as the polling day. However, the junta eventually declared yet another delay of a month in order to avoid conflict with the recently announced coronation schedule.[7]

Once the election campaign got under way, more peculiar incidents took place. The first thunderbolt was the nomination of former princess Ubolratana Mahidol (who had technically become a commoner as a result of her earlier marriage) as a prime ministerial candidate by Thai Raksa Chart, one of three sister parties created by Pheu Thai to circumvent the new voting system. This led to the first time in modern Thai history in which the palace openly and explicitly intervened in politics. Within less than twenty-four hours, a royal announcement from His Majesty King Vajiralongkorn asserted that the nomination of Princess Ubolratana was not only inappropriate and in violation of tradition but was also unconstitutional. Within a month the Constitutional Court dissolved Thai Raksa Chart and banned its executives from politics for ten years.

In spite of a custom-built constitution, the advantage of incumbency and questionable use of state mechanisms in its favour, the weak popularity of Palang Pracharat, the rise in support for Future Forward and the reported fragmentation among military groups in the weeks before the election gave rise to rumours of a possible military coup or a suspension of the election.[8] Most startlingly, on the eve of the election, the king made an unexpected announcement calling on the electorate to choose "good people" to rule the country. The royal announcement was interpreted as support for the junta, as the term "good people" is not neutral in the Thai political context; it has long been used by conservatives and the elite against their opponents, especially against Thaksin's supporters. The story did not however end there. Following the announcement, the #โตแล้วเลือกเองได้ ("We are grown up already and can choose for ourselves") became the top-trending hashtag on Twitter in Thailand,[9] as a critical (and clever) mass response from Thai youth against paternalism.

The Unanticipated 2019 Electoral Results: A Changed Political Landscape?[10]

The drama in the lead-up to the election on 24 March 2019 was not the end of the surprises. The competition was stiff between two political poles—one that supported coup leader Prayut and the other opposed to dictatorial power—each backed by a large enough popular base that it was difficult to predict who would ultimately enjoy a majority in the legislative assembly. Prior to the election, many sources predicted that out of 500 seats, Pheu Thai would come first and maintain their hold over 180 to 220 seats. The Democrats were expected to come second with about 100 seats in their traditional strongholds of Bangkok and the south. Palang Pracharat were to come third with no more than 80 to 100 MPs owing to the decline of the junta's popularity before the election. Other small and medium-sized parties were predicted to gain around 50 to 60 seats in total, while Future Forward would get no more than 30 to 50 seats at most.[11]

In contrast to these forecasts, the election results were a bombshell (see Table 1). Pheu Thai emerged first, as it has since the 2001 election, but won only 136 seats (22.24 per cent). This was the party's worst performance, having lost 129 seats since the last election. The party previously secured 248 seats (40.6 per cent) in 2001, 375 seats (56.4 per cent) in 2005, 460 seats (61.1 per cent) in the nullified 2006 election, 233 seats (36.63 per cent) in 2007 and 256 seats (48.41 per cent) in 2011. The total votes received by Pheu Thai plummeted dramatically from 15,744,190 to 7,920,630. This was less than the number of votes garnered by Palang Pracharat, which received the largest share with 8,433,137 votes. The number of seats secured by Pheu Thai in Isaan, the party's stronghold, fell from 104 in the previous election to 84.

The failure of the Democrat Party at the polls was unprecedented. As Thailand's oldest political party, the party has achieved high levels of institutionalization, commanding arguably the country's most loyal network of party members, with a stable, middle-class voter base in Bangkok, various other cities across the country and nearly all of southern Thailand outside the Muslim-majority Deep South. In 2019 it was resoundingly rejected in its former strongholds. In the previous election in 2011, the Democrat Party received the second-highest share of votes and gained 159 seats. Since 1992 the party has never dropped below second place in votes or secured less than 79 seats in any national election. However, for the 2019 election the Democrat Party was fourth with only 53 seats (11.17 per cent) secured through both constituencies and the party list. The party was also fourth in terms of its share of the vote (3,927,726). Most unexpected were the

TABLE 1
Thailand 2019 General Election Results

Party	Popular vote Count	%	Constituency	Seats Party list	Total
Palang Pracharat Party	8,441,274	23.74	97	19	116
Pheu Thai Party	7,881,006	22.16	136	0	136
Future Forward Party	6,330,617	17.80	31	50	81
Democrat Party	3,959,358	11.13	33	20	53
Bhumjaithai Party	3,734,459	10.50	39	12	51
Thai Liberal Party	824,284	2.32	0	10	10
Chartthaipattana Party	783,689	2.20	6	4	10
New Economics Party	486,273	1.37	0	6	6
Prachachart Party	481,490	1.35	6	1	7
Puea Chat Party	421,412	1.19	0	5	5
Action Coalition for Thailand	415,585	1.17	1	4	5
Chart Pattana Party	244,770	0.69	1	2	3
Thai Local Power Party	214,189	0.60	0	3	3
Thai Forest Conservation Party	134,816	0.38	0	2	2
Thai People Power Party	80,186	0.23	0	1	1
Thai Nation Power Party	73,421	0.21	0	1	1
People Progressive Party	69,431	0.19	0	1	1
Palang Thai Rak Thai Party	60,434	0.17	0	1	1
Thai Civilized Party	60,354	0.17	0	1	1
Thai Teachers for People Party	56,633	0.16	0	1	1
Prachaniyom Party	56,264	0.16	0	1	1
Thai People Justice Party	48,037	0.14	0	1	1
People Reform Party	45,420	0.13	0	1	1
Thai Citizens Power Party	44,961	0.13	0	1	1
New Democracy Party	39,260	0.11	0	1	1
New Palangdharma Party	35,099	0.10	0	1	1

Source: Election Commission.

Democrat Party's losses in past voter strongholds in Bangkok and the south of Thailand. The party lost in all the Bangkok constituencies that it contested, in comparison to its victories in 23 out of 33 constituencies in 2011. The Democrats also only prevailed in 22 constituencies in the south, a drop from the 50 out of 52 constituencies that it won in the previous election.

In contrast, the newly emerged parties obtained more support than had been predicted by any poll or political analyst. While an earlier survey was pessimistic about the success of either the pro-junta Palang Pracharat or the youth-oriented Future Forward,[12] the two parties returned extraordinary results. Palang Pracharat won the largest share of the popular vote, which translated into 116 seats, making it the second-largest party in parliament. An even more interesting development was the success of the progressive Future Forward. The party ran on a policy platform opposed to the continuation of the NCPO's rule, and it was openly in favour of military reform. The party was expected to receive no more than 50 party list seats, and at best would win in 3 to 5 Bangkok constituencies. Instead, Future Forward managed an electoral breakthrough by coming in third with 81 seats through a combination of 50 party list seats and 31 constituency seats. With 6,265,950 votes in total, the party had the third-highest share of the popular vote, overtaking the older and more-established Democrat Party.

There are four key explanations for the surprise results of the 2019 election. First is an electoral system designed to undercut large political parties such as Pheu Thai and the Democrat Party to the advantage of middle-sized parties such as Future Forward and Palang Pracharat. Second is the matter of the misguided campaign strategies of the Democrats and Pheu Thai, who restricted themselves to their existing voter strongholds and failed to accommodate new voter demographics. Third is the related shift in the electoral demographics, including the emergence of a new generation of first-time voters who came out in support of parties explicitly opposed to military rule, such as Future Forward, while turning their backs on parties who previously represented the middle-class, such as the Democrats. Last is the success of the junta in capitalizing on the conservatism of many Thai voters and on its ability to utilize state mechanisms and the constitution to maintain its power in electoral politics.

Pheu Thai's Disappointment

The drop in votes for Pheu Thai, which had dominated preceding elections with very little close competition, resulted firstly from the constitution introduced by the junta that reduced the chances of a large political party achieving a landslide victory. Secondly, the party's efforts to maintain a voter base of the lower-middle class placed limitations on its ability to expand its base to encompass new demographics.

Parties with strong voter bases across several constituencies were highly disadvantaged by the design of a new electoral system that bound votes for constituency MPs with the computation of party list seats. If a party were to receive a high number of constituency seats, this would simultaneously entail a reduction in its party list seats. To counteract this limitation, Pheu Thai decided to split the party to create Thai Raksa Chart, both to increase their chances of scoring party list seats and to serve as a safety mechanism in case the government or courts dissolved Pheu Thai. Pheu Thai contested in most constituencies but ceded 100 constituencies where it did not perform well in 2011 to Thai Raksa Chart. The two parties hoped that by coordinating their campaigns they would be able to overcome the institutional hurdles against large parties in the new constitution.[13] However, when Thai Raksa Chart was dissolved, Pheu Thai forfeited the votes that Thai Raksa Chart would have otherwise received in the 100 constituencies where it did not field candidates. The end result left Pheu Thai with 137 constituency seats in the preliminary tally, but it did not receive any party list seats at all.

Decline of the Democrats

A factor even more important than the Democrat Party's misevaluation of the electoral system was its misguided campaign strategy. Over the past decade, the Democrat Party has departed from its history as an advocate for electoral democracy. During the "yellow-red" political conflicts of the past ten years, the Democrats, under the leadership of Abhisit Vejjajiva, changed course and pursued an undemocratic path to power. The Democrats chose to join hands with conservative movements opposed to Thaksin, campaigning against the holding of elections, displaying nationalist, conservative or royalist attitudes, and even calling upon the military to intervene against elected pro-Thaksin regimes. Yet, during the final period of campaigning this year, Abhisit made a fundamental reversal by refusing to enter into a governing coalition with General Prayut Chan-o-cha as prime minister. Abhisit's decision likely stemmed from the tide of public opinion turning against Palang Pracharat in the lead-up to polls, as well as being an attempt to attract younger voters dissatisfied with the military regime. This reversal, however, ultimately made a substantial contribution to the Democrat Party's defeat at the polls. The party's popular base both in urban areas and the south—which has for years been made to believe that the military alone can eradicate Thaksin and bring peace to the country's politics—abandoned the party and evolved into strategic voters who marked their ballots in support of military parties such as Palang Pracharat. Meanwhile, young voters dissatisfied with the NCPO remained unconvinced by the Democrat Party's equivocal stance towards military rule and chose instead to support parties with a more explicit stance against prolonging the NCPO's power, such as Future Forward and Pheu Thai.

Future Forward's Electoral Breakthrough

The immense success of Future Forward was partly the result of the new electoral system, the dissolution of Thai Raksa Chart and the demographic introduction of first-time voters. To a considerable degree, the new conditions laid down by the 2017 constitution benefited Future Forward. The party had decided to field candidates in all 350 electoral districts in order to secure a high number of party list seats by amassing votes from young voters dispersed across all constituencies in the country. Future Forward was however also able to pick up a number of seats in constituencies where the Thai Raksa Chart candidates had been disqualified as a result of their party being dissolved. In several constituencies, former Thai Raksa Chart candidates urged their supporters to vote for Future Forward instead.

Future Forward experienced great success in mobilizing the support of many first-time voters, who comprised approximately eight million out of fifty-one million eligible voters, a number large enough to collectively win some one hundred constituency seats. From the very beginning of the election campaign, no other political party took this group of new voters as seriously as Future Forward did, which targeted its policies directly at this demographic. The party presented policies that no major party had ever attributed importance to, such as the abolition of military conscription, the promotion of LGBT rights, and decentralization. This is not to mention Future Forward's explicit opposition to the "old politics" of patronage and its clear antipathy towards the NCPO, both of which spoke directly to young voters who were dissatisfied with military rule.

While Future Forward made being anti-establishment cool and modern, no other political party elevated young voters as a priority. Most parties already had fairly reliable voter bases, whether based on political ideology or territory. On the pro-democracy side, the policies of Pheu Thai and Thai Raksa Chart were largely intended to appeal to the pool of voters who were already inclined to choose them. Pheu Thai campaigned around the same voter base that had previously propelled the party to landslide victories over the past ten years: the lower middle class and the rural and urban poor. Meanwhile, parties favouring the continuity of the military regime, such as Palang Pracharat, courted the followers of anti-Thanksinite movements such as the PDRC, the People's Alliance for Democracy (PAD) and other conservative groups.

Victory of Palang Pracharat

In spite of the unpopularity of the junta prior to the election, Palang Pracharat did much better than most observers predicted. It succeeded at both cashing in on the conservative population and in deploying state mechanisms and institutions to its advantage in the electoral battle. Approximately a quarter of Thai voters (8,441,274 voters, or 23.74 per cent of the popular vote) voted for Palang Pracharat, whose explicit purpose was to maintain the junta's grip on power.[14]

While "vote buying" through canvassers and support from local *chao pho* ("bosses") might have contributed to Palang Pracharat's victory, the manipulation of state mechanisms and the constitution were arguably the more visible factors enabling the party's triumph. Prior to the election, General Prayut and his cabinet actively harnessed state resources for self-promotion.[15] "Palang Pracharat", the name of the military party, was taken from ongoing populist "Pracharat" policies introduced by the junta. The Election Commission, which is effectively appointed by the military, was accused of both political bias as well as incompetence in handling the election, with countless complaints lodged over poll manipulation, miscounted ballots and inconsistent and delayed results. More importantly, the Election Commission also tweaked the allocation of party list seats in order to shore up Palang Pracharat's parliamentary position. Instead of adhering to its pre-election announcement that 71,000 votes would be needed to secure a single party list seat, the commission revised its requirements to allow pro-military micro-parties that had garnered 30,000 to 40,000 votes to gain a seat each.

Post-2019 Election: Signs of a Short-lived Government

Initially, many thought that the elected pro-military coalition government would be vulnerable and short-lived. It was quite clear that the election would bring about a fragmented multiparty coalition with a slim majority. In addition, the downturn in the economy—which some blamed on the incompetence of the previous junta-led government—and the fragile relationships with other powerful democratic countries were expected to threaten the legitimacy of the new government.

Weaknesses in Prayut's New Government

By the time the elected Prayut government was installed, critics foresaw that the junta would lose absolute power over both the army and society. First, after the election, Prayut would no longer rule as the junta chief. This meant having to govern without the special powers under Section 44 of the interim 2014 charter. He would not be able to act unopposed, pass laws without the agreement of parliament or suppress those who think differently. Second, the junta leader–turned–prime minister would lose his influence over the armed forces once he retired from the army and the junta came to an end. Third, there were several signs of internal fragmentation within the junta. General Prawit Wongsuwan, a senior and influential figure in the military and mentor to Prayut, had become a burden on the government because of allegations of graft stemming from his possession of a large number of expensive watches. Instead of allowing Prawit to continue with the defence portfolio he had held in the junta cabinet, Prayut took the position of defence minister for himself following the election. Fourth, neither Prayut nor Prawit were thought to have a charismatic following within the military or strong connections to the palace. They were compared unfavourably to General Prem Tinsulanonda, the longest-serving non-elected prime minister, who was appointed to serve under elected governments from 1980 to 1988. Prem had a strong influence over the military and solid connections to the palace, particularly through his close personal ties with the revered King Bhumibol Adulyadej. Prem was able to strategically exploit these advantages in his dealings with parliament. However, lacking these advantages, it appeared as though Prayut and Prawit would face a difficult struggle, especially given Palang Pracharat's slim majority in parliament.[16]

Ongoing Economic Downturn

As the Thai economy slowed throughout 2019, many political observers felt this might be one factor to bring down the government.[17] Over the past decade of political conflict and military government, annual GDP growth averaged only 3 per cent, in comparison to the almost 4 per cent annual growth over the previous decade. This ranked Thailand lower than its neighbours such as Indonesia and Vietnam. Prior to the election it seemed that there would be only a temporary disruption in Thailand's economic growth. After a few months it appeared that the slowdown would be more likely to be prolonged.

The Thai economy did not do well in the first half of the year, registering its worst performance since the 2014 coup. Thailand's year-on-year GDP growth fell to 2.3 per cent in the second quarter of 2019, the lowest in nearly five years.[18] Agricultural output dropped 1.1 per cent, exports fell 6.1 per cent and imports declined by 2.7 per cent in the second quarter compared to the same period in 2018.[19] Consumer confidence in May dropped to its lowest level in nineteen months, and first-quarter growth was a paltry 2.8 per cent from a year earlier. Furthermore, the ongoing trade tensions between the United States and China could weaken demand for Thai exports and discourage private investment in Thai export-oriented industries.[20] On top of that, the problem of a strong currency remained unresolved, damaging the competitiveness of Thai exports.[21]

Uneasy Relationships with Democratic Countries

During the earlier years of junta rule, the junta tried to reclaim the country's legitimacy on the regional and international stages. Nevertheless, pressure from the international democratic community continued. The first two years after the 2014 coup proved to be the most arduous because of the harsh reactions from the United States and the countries of Western Europe. However, most other countries did not place direct pressure on the military government prior to the election. China, Russia, Japan, India and South Korea adopted a "business as usual" approach. All maintained their bilateral relations at the "status quo", with economic and diplomatic engagement not disrupted.[22] In contrast, diplomatic relations with the United States and countries in the West stagnated. The United States halted several Thai-US initiatives, except for the annual Cobra Gold military exercise. Similarly, the relationship with the European Union reached a low point because of issues relating to the fishing industry.[23] After the 2014 coup, the European Union discontinued FTA negotiation with Thailand to protest the suspension of democracy.[24] On 6 April, diplomats from Australia, Belgium, Canada, Finland, France, Germany, the Netherlands, the United Kingdom and the United States, as well as human rights officials from the European Union and the United Nations, were in attendance at the police station in Bangkok when Thanathorn Juangroongruangkit, the leader of Future Forward, was charged with sedition, with helping a suspect escape and with organizing an assembly of more than ten people that caused unrest. The Thai government reacted negatively to this show of diplomatic force. The US Embassy however stated that attendance by embassy officials at legal prosecutions is merely standard practice.[25]

In terms of Thailand's regional collaboration, the country assumed the chairmanship of ASEAN in 2019. Given bitter memories of the previous time

Thailand hosted the summit,[26] as well as the political uncertainty of the post-election period, there was a lack of confidence that Thailand would be able to carry out the task. However, under the new Palang Pracharat government, the 35th ASEAN Summit in Bangkok and Nonthaburi was conducted smoothly in early November without any political disruption. Nevertheless, there were several disappointments, as the Thai hosts were unable to conclude the Regional Comprehensive Economic Partnership amidst news of India's departure from the trade pact. The absence of the United States was also keenly felt, as the Americans were only represented by national security advisor Robert O'Brien at both the ASEAN-US Summit and the East Asia Summit.[27]

Post-election: Anti-climax

Surprisingly, in light of earlier predictions, there are still no signs of a collapse of the government as 2019 comes to an end. The appointed prime minister and his government have been able to consolidate power within the coalition. The suppression of the opposition has also continued.

Triumph and Control over a Fragmented Coalition

Against expectations, the Palang Pracharat government has effortlessly managed to maintain control over its coalition partners and has passed major pieces of legislation in the lower house. The two major parties in coalition with Palang Pracharat—Bhumjaithai and the Democrats, which obtained 51 and 53 seats, respectively—readily accepted key cabinet positions in exchange for shoring up the pro-junta alliance.[28] The pre-election promise by Democrat leader Abhisit—who resigned after the election—to avoid partnering the junta vanished. The new party leader, Jurin Laksanawisit, instead joined Palang Pracharat in nominating Prayut as prime minister. The negotiation process with small parties was complicated. Initially, a bloc of eleven micro-parties (ten of them with a single MP each) asked to be allocated cabinet seats, threatening to withdraw their support for the coalition government otherwise. After a few days of negotiations, the micro-parties eventually received positions in the cabinet and thus committed their support to Palang Pracharat and Prayut.[29] Most of the crucial bills, including the partial transfer of army units and their budgets to a royal security command unit, and the annual government budget were passed. While Pheu Thai and Future Forward performed well in debates and succeeded in controlling the opposition, they were unable to stop the passage of government bills.

Crippled Opposition

The seven-party opposition coalition of Pheu Thai, Future Forward, Seri Ruam Thai, Prachachart, Puea Chat, New Economics and Thai People Power were not able to effectively challenge the Palang Pracharat government. So far, they have slowly and painfully campaigned to amend or replace the 2017 constitution.[30] Pheu Thai also seems reluctant to fight wholeheartedly against the military and the Thai traditional elite. In several cases, Future Forward was left to battle alone. One major example is the vote to approve an emergency decree to transfer the command of the Bangkok-based 1st and 11th Infantry Divisions from the army to the king. The bill was passed by 376 to 70 votes, with only Future Forward voting against this executive decree. The rest of the opposition, including Pheu Thai, voted in favour of the decree.[31] For its efforts, Future Forward was immediately berated by army chief General Apirat Kongsompong for supposed disloyalty to the throne.[32]

Future Forward is growing increasingly isolated as it confronts both external and internal threats. Party leader Thanathorn and other Future Forward members are facing numerous legal allegations relating to contempt of court, violations of the Computer Crimes Act, sedition, illegal donations and loans, violations of shareholding rules, and undermining the monarchy.[33] In early February the Election Commission alleged that Thanathorn held shares in V-Luck Media Co, a media firm, while being registered as a candidate. This violates Section 98(3) of the charter, which prohibits owners and shareholders of media or publishing firms from applying to become MPs. Although he was initially sworn in as an MP, the court issued an interim order suspending Thanathorn from his duties on 23 May. On 20 November the Constitutional Court ruled to disqualify Thanathorn as an MP.[34] The numerous other cases against Future Forward could yet lead to its dissolution.[35]

Conclusion: More Surprises Yet to Come

The year 2019 promised to be one where political conflict could be resolved as military rule ended and an election took place. However, the year was marked by bizarre episodes. Before the election, we witnessed the first instance of direct royal interference into the realm of electoral politics since the end of the absolute monarchy. This was followed by the shock outcome of the election. Because of provisions in the 2017 pro-military constitution and as a result of their misguided election campaigns, two formerly established parties, the Democrats and Pheu Thai, experienced unprecedented losses, while the liberal Future Forward Party gained double the predicted number of seats by tapping into the spirit of rebellion among the youth. The pro-military Palang Pracharat was also successful in exploiting state mechanisms to mobilize the support of conservative Thais. Above all, as intended by the pro-military constitution, Palang Pracharat managed to form a slim majority government. Many have questioned how long a coalition government of nineteen parties commanding a thin majority of 254 MPs out of 500 could survive while confronting an economic decline. However, the government managed to stay in power as 2019 came to a close. Thai politics in the coming year is likely to be unpredictable. Many are now asking whether the military and Thai traditional elite have succeeded in legitimizing themselves through the electoral process. Or will the opposition parties turn to mass mobilization to strike back at the Palang Pracharat government?

Notes

1. Panarat Thepgumpanat, "Thailand Must Postpone Election Again, until March: Officials", Reuters, 15 January 2019, https://www.reuters.com/article/us-thailandpolitics/thailand-must-postpone-election-again-until-march-officials-idUSKCN1P90Y5 (accessed 11 November 2019); "'We Want to Vote' Activist Charged with Various Offences", Thai Lawyers for Human Rights, 7 June 2018, https://www.tlhr2014.com/?p=7730 (accessed 15 November 2019).
2. "Thailand's New Constitution: What You Need to Know", *Straits Times*, 6 April 2017, https://www.straitstimes.com/asia/se-asia/thailands-new-constitution-what-you-need-to-know (accessed 10 November 2019).
3. Kongpob Areerat, "The Devil in the Details: Thailand's New Constitution in a Nutshell", *Prachatai English*, 9 April 2017, https://prachatai.com/english/node/7062 (accessed 9 November 2019); Jonathan Head, "Thailand's Constitution: New Era, New Uncertainties", BBC News, 7 April 2017, https://www.bbc.com/news/world-asia-39499485 (accessed 9 November 2019); Jacob I. Ricks, "Thailand's 2019 Vote: The General's Election", *Pacific Affairs* 92, no. 3 (September 2019): 447.
4. Ricks, "Thailand's 2019 Vote".
5. King Vajiralongkorn, 66 years old, has been head of state since his father, King Bhumibol Adulyadej, died in 2016 following a 70-year reign. However, he was not officially crowned until after a lengthy mourning period.
6. Oliver Holmes, "Thailand's King Signs Constitution that Cements Junta's Grip", *The Guardian*, 6 April 2017, https://www.theguardian.com/world/2017/apr/06/thailand-king-signs-constitution-path-polls-election (accessed 10 November 2019).
7. Panarat, "Thailand Must Postpone"; Masayuki Yuda, "5 Things to Know about Thailand's Long-Awaited Election", *Nikkei Asian Review*, 4 January 2019, https://asia.nikkei.com/Politics/Turbulent-Thailand/5-things-to-know-about-Thailand-s-long-awaited-election (accessed 11 November 2019).

8. Nyshka Chandran, "The Latest in Thailand's Political Drama: Ruling Government Dismisses #ThaiCoup Rumors", CNBS, 11 February 2019, https://www.cnbc.com/2019/02/11/thailand-political-drama-military-vehicles-and-the-royal-family.html (accessed 11 November 2019).
9. Duncan McCargo, "'We Are Grown-Up Now and Can Choose for Ourselves'", *New York Times*, 29 March 2019, https://www.nytimes.com/2019/03/29/opinion/thailand-election-thanathorn-future-forward-youth-vote.html (accessed 11 November 2019).
10. This part of the article has been modified from the article written by the author, "Explaining the Surprises and Upsets of Thailand's 2019 Election", *New Mandala*, 30 April 2019, https://www.newmandala.org/explaining-the-surprises-and-upsets-of-thailands-2019-election/ with the permission of *New Mandala* (Kanokrat Lertchoosakul 2019).
11. Yuda, "5 Things to Know".
12. Bangkok Poll, Phon Samruad Rueang "Nab Thoy Lang Sipsi Wan Su Kan Luenktang" [Survey: Counting Down 14 Days to the General Election], Bangkok University Research Center, 9 March 2019; FT Confidential Research, "Political Risk Soars ahead of Thailand's Election: Survey Finds Little Support for Pro-junta Faction ahead of Tumultuous Poll", *Financial Times*, 15 February 2019, https://archive.md/q3SqR#selection-1921.72-1921.96 (accessed 4 Novembers 2019).
13. Ricks, "Thailand's 2019 Vote".
14. Ibid., p. 454.
15. Aim Sinpeng, "Campaigning without Vote Canvassers", *Thai Data Point*, 19 June 2019, https://www.thaidatapoints.com/post/campaigning-without-vote-canvassers-part-i-of-the-futurista-campaigning (accessed 14 November 2019).
16. Supalak Ganjanakhundee, "Why the 'Prayuth Regime' Will Fail to Prevail", *New Mandala*, 16 September 2019, https://www.newmandala.org/why-the-prayuth-regime-will-fail-to-prevail/ (accessed 14 November 2019).
17. Joseph O'Connor and Son Nguyen, "Economy to Decide the Fate of Prayut's Government as Opposition Begins Charter Push", *Thai Examiner: Thailand's News for Foreigners*, 23 August 2019, https://www.thaiexaminer.com/thai-news-foreigners/2019/08/23/economy-to-decide-the-fate-of-prayuts-government-as-opposition-begins-charter-roadshow/ (accessed 14 November 2019); Zsombor Peter, "Thai Government May Beat Legal Threats, But Flagging Economy Looms", Voice of America, 15 September 2019, https://www.voanews.com/east-asia-pacific/thai-government-may-beat-legal-threats-flagging-economy-looms (accessed 14 November 2019).
18. Peter, "Thai Government May Beat Legal Threats"; Chartchai Parasuk, "Economy Faces 4 Key Hurdles This Year", *Bangkok Post*, 1 August 2019, https://www.bangkokpost.com/opinion/opinion/1722403/economy-faces-4-key-hurdles-this-year (accessed 14 November 2019).

19. David Hutt, "Can Prayutnomics Help Thailand's Economy? A Look at What the Prime Minister's Tenure May Mean for the Country's Economic Prospects", *The Diplomat*, 22 August 2019, https://thediplomat.com/2019/08/can-prayutnomics-help-thailands-economy/ (accessed 14 November 2019).
20. Somruedi Banchongduang, "Politics Key Threat to Thai Outlook, World Bank Warns", *Bangkok Post*, 8 July 2019, https://www.bangkokpost.com/business/1708943/politics-key-threat-to-thai-outlook-world-bank-warns (accessed 14 November 2019).
21. William Pesek, "Thai Baht Races Ahead of Prayuth's Slow Progress: The Strong Currency is Hurting Thailand's Competitiveness and Threatens Further Damage", *Nikkei Asian Review*, 8 July 2019, https://asia.nikkei.com/Opinion/Thai-baht-races-ahead-of-Prayuth-s-slow-progress (accessed 14 November 2019).
22. Kavi Chongkittavorn, "Post-poll Policy: Dynamic Continuity", *Bangkok Post*, 26 March 2019, https://www.bangkokpost.com/opinion/opinion/1651196/post-poll-policy-dynamic-continuity (accessed 14 November 2019).
23. Ibid.
24. Ibid.
25. "US Defends its Presence at Police Station in Thanathorn Case", *The Nation*, 10 April 2019, https://www.nationthailand.com/politics/30367503 (accessed 19 November 2019).
26. In April 2009 the anti-government Red Shirt protest jeopardized the ASEAN Summit held in Pattaya. The meeting was eventually cancelled, humiliating the Democrat-led government.
27. Prashanth Parameswaran, "Assessing the Outcomes of the 2019 ASEAN Summits", *The Diplomat*, 1 December 2019, https://thediplomat.com/2019/11/termsak-chalermpalanupap-on-aseans-year-in-review/ (accessed 17 January 2020); Supalak Ganjanakhundee, "Asean Worries about Thailand's Ability to Lead Grouping amid Political Challenges", *The Nation*, 1 January 2019, https://www.nationthailand.com/politics/30361455 (accessed 17 January 2020); Rajiv Bhatia, "Assessing The 35th ASEAN Summit – Analysis", *Eurosia Review*, 29 November 2019, https://www.eurasiareview.com/29112019-assessing-the-35th-asean-summit-analysis/ (accessed 17 January 2020).
28. Supalak, "Why the 'Prayuth regime' Will Fail".
29. "Small Parties Back Thai Military Government Chief after Rule Change Gave Them Seats", Channel NewsAsia, 13 May 2019, https://www.channelnewsasia.com/news/asia/thai-election-2019-result-parties-11528646 (accessed 15 November 2019); Supalak, "Why the 'Prayuth Regime' Will Fail".
30. O'Connor and Nguyen, "Economy to Decide the Fate".
31. Teeranai Charuvastra, "Abandoned by Allies, Future Forward Votes against Royal Transfer Decree", *Khaosod English*, 17 October 2019 http://www.khaosodenglish.com/politics/2019/10/17/abandoned-by-allies-future-forward-votes-against-royal-transfer-decree/ (accessed 15 November 2019).

32. Wasant Techawongtham, "Future Forward Party Makes Fearless Stand for Principles", *Bangkok Post*, 19 October 2019, https://www.bangkokpost.com/opinion/opinion/1775494/future-forward-party-makes-fearless-stand-for-principles (accessed 19 November 2019).
33. Chairith Yonpiam and Aekarach Sattaburuth, "Future Forward on Thin Ice", *Bangkok Post*, 11 November 2019, https://www.bangkokpost.com/thailand/general/1791424/future-forward-on-thin-ice (accessed 15 November 2019).
34. Ibid.
35. Ibid.

FUTURE—FORWARD?
THE PAST AND FUTURE OF
THE FUTURE FORWARD PARTY

James Ockey

In 2019, Thailand held its first election in eight years, a period that included five years of military rule. While Pheu Thai won the most seats—as it has in every election since 2001, under several different guises—in second and third place were two new parties. The second-placed party, Palang Pracharat (PPRP), was a party supported by the military regime, comprised largely of former members of parliament (MPs) who had been members of other political parties in the past. Palang Pracharat thus tended to replicate the campaign tactics that had previously secured victory for its MPs in past elections, while also relying on strong support from the state. Although Palang Pracharat garnered the most votes overall, it fell behind Pheu Thai in terms of parliamentary seats. In third place was another new party, Anakhot Mai (*lit.* New Future), known in English as the Future Forward Party.

Future Forward pursued a campaign strategy that was largely novel in Thai politics. Analysts have observed that the party carefully cultivated an image centred on its leader, Thanathorn Juangroongruangkit, as representative of the party's aspirations. According to these analysts, many cast their votes for Future Forward candidates because of the image of the leader and the policies of the party, while the qualifications of the individual Future Forward candidates were of little import. Future Forward was also seen as banking its chances for electoral gold on the use of social media to court young voters.[1]

Some analysts would thus describe Future Forward as a new type of party: one built for social media, particularly the young people who spend significant time on it. If this is the case, we may expect to see substantial changes in how

---

JAMES OCKEY lectures in the Department of Political Science and International Relations at the University of Canterbury, New Zealand.

other political parties operate, given the success of Future Forward. And since the government is composed of political parties, these changes may eventually reshape the political system in Thailand. In this chapter, I will examine the novelty of Future Forward, the role of Thanathorn, and the function of social media in the party's campaign. I will conclude by considering the future of Future Forward and whether it establishes a new model for political parties in Thailand.

The 2019 Election

The 24 March election was the first since 2011 and the 2014 military coup. The eight-year interval between the elections meant that over seven million of the fifty-one million eligible voters (around 13 per cent) were new voters with weak party loyalties, thus forming a large number of potentially persuadable voters. With a constitution carefully designed to benefit small and medium-sized parties, eighty parties registered to contest the election, nominating a total of 13,310 candidates between them.[2] Major parties include the Pheu Thai party, the pro-Thaksin vehicle that had, in different incarnations through the years, won the most seats in every election since 2001; the Democrat party, which has a strong base in the South and in Bangkok; and Bhumjaithai, a regional party with deep roots in the lower North East. Among the new parties were the pro-junta Palang Pracharat party, and Future Forward.

The major political parties in the 2019 election can be loosely categorized into three types. The first type consists largely of powerful local politicians, who are generally former MPs with extensive ties to their local community. These powerful local figures leverage their strong community ties to gain votes. They often rely heavily on traditional patron-client relationships, which was a style of campaigning common in the 1980s and 1990s. The junta-backed Palang Pracharat was the most prominent example of such a party. Needing resources to maintain their hold on power, many local notables were enticed to join the government-affiliated party in order to gain access to resources that could sustain their patronage networks. Having been cut off from government largesse since the coup, many of these local politicians would have otherwise struggled to be electorally competitive if they were left to rely on their own resources.

The second type of party also consisted primarily of powerful local politicians, but who were running under a party brand that was also influential with voters. There were two parties that had developed such voter loyalty over the years: Pheu Thai in the North and Northeast, and the Democrat party in Bangkok and the South.

The third type of party was represented by Future Forward. Because it sought to create a new style of politics, Future Forward ran first-time candidates while rejecting experienced politicians. The party instead focussed on its policy platforms, on transparency and participation for its supporters, and on its charismatic leader, Thanathorn Juangroongruangkit. Thanathorn, a young auto parts tycoon, was widely known as the "billionaire serf" in acknowledgement of both his wealth and his support for the lower classes. A nephew of a former cabinet minister, Thanathorn was himself new to politics and determined to shift Thai politics in a new direction.

Thanathorn, the Billionaire Serf

Thanathorn was born in 1978 in Bangkok as the second child of Phatthana and Somporn Juangroongruangkit. Thanathorn's grandparents, of Teochew origin, had migrated to Bangkok from Swatow, where Thanathorn's father, Phatthana, was born. While still young, Phatthana established a small business to make seat cushions for motorcycles with his brother and a friend. Their business, Thai Summit, received its big break when it secured a contract to make seat cushions for Yamaha. Other motorcycle manufacturers such as Suzuki and Honda would also turn to Thai Summit for seat cushions later. This enabled Thai Summit to expand its business to cars and other vehicles, as well as supplying a wide range of motorcycle and automotive parts.[3] By the time Thanathorn was born, the business was thriving.

Thanathorn studied at Saint Dominic School before enrolling at the prestigious Triam Udom Suksa School. There, his sister reports, he adopted a "*hi so*" (high society) image, going out with friends every night, wearing designer clothes, and frequently changing cars. He was also the first student of the school to purchase a mobile phone.[4] Upon graduation from Triam Udom Suksa, his love for expensive automobiles led him to enrol in the engineering programme at Thammasat University,[5] a decision that must have pleased his parents since it suited the family business. His engineering degree at Thammasat was divided into two years in Bangkok and a further two years at Nottingham University in England.

It was at Thammasat that Thanathorn first entered the public eye. In August 1999, Supara Janitchfah of the *Bangkok Post* wrote about the efforts of a group of Thammasat students seeking to help Karens in Prajuab Khirikhan who were facing eviction.[6] The students organized a fundraiser for the evicted Karens in the area around the university. They later contributed to the funds themselves when the collection drive proved insufficient. One of the students was Thanathorn, who described how "[t]he evicted Karens in Ban Pah Maak now only have one meal a day. Many of them go to bed on empty stomachs. Their huts have no roofs and walls. We don't mind sharing our own allowances to help people in misery."[7] During his time in Thammasat, Thanathorn often worked with groups focused on social justice, including joining demonstrations with the Assembly of the Poor. With the support of his friends, he was elected vice president of the student union at Thammasat University and later became the deputy secretary-general of the Student Federation of Thailand.[8] Although Thanathorn was only in Thammasat for two years before leaving for Nottingham, the friendships he formed at Thammasat were long-lasting, and he would continue to support his activist friends long after his return from England.

During the last two years of his engineering programme at Nottingham, Thanathorn sought to continue his student activism. He subscribed to *Matichon Weekly* to keep up with Thai politics and remained in touch with his activist friends during his visits home. At Nottingham, he took courses in critical theory and joined the Socialist Workers Party Student Society. Developing an interest in civil society and poverty in Africa, he briefly pondered the possibility of heading to Algeria with a non-governmental organization (NGO) after his graduation.[9] However, during his last year at Nottingham, his father Phatthana had become ill. Phatthana received medical attention in San Francisco and took six months to recuperate, with Thanathorn present to provide support to his father. Subsequently, Thanathorn gave up his plan to work in Algeria, and instead returned to Thailand to be near his family. In Thailand, he worked for a short time with an NGO called Friends of the Poor. Around this time Thanathorn also supported his activist peers to establish the *Fa Diaw Kan* (Same Sky) journal with 200,000 baht (US$5,000) in start-up funds.[10] First published in 2003, the journal has since served as a platform for critical, academic essays on Thai politics and society.

A crucial juncture was the passing of Thanathorn's father in April 2002. After the funeral, Thanathorn was named a vice president of Thai Summit Group, while his mother Somporn served as the company's president. When Thanathorn joined Thai Summit, the company had total sales of around 16 billion baht (about US$370 million). Despite its growth, it was still a traditional family-orientated business that was largely confined to the Thai domestic market. Thai Summit's foreign operations were limited to Malaysia, with direct exports only amounting to 0.36 per cent of sales and indirect exports only slightly higher.[11] However, by 2016, Thai Summit had expanded its operations to China, India, Indonesia, Japan, the United States and Vietnam, with about 25 per cent of its sales coming from these overseas operations.[12] By the end of 2017, the last full year before Thanathorn left to form the Future Forward party, Thai Summit boasted sales of about 80 billion baht (US$2.5 billion), a fivefold increase in baht terms (and more than an eightfold increase in US dollar terms). The company employed around twenty thousand workers and its profits were about 6 billion baht (US$180 million).[13] By any measure, Thanathorn's tenure as vice president of Thai Summit was highly successful.

When Thanathorn took up his position, Thai Summit was run in a traditional Sino-Thai fashion. He described how:

> [Thai Summit] did not have any kind of system. It did not have a budget system, no knowledge of how much each division spent. It did not have benchmarking with competitors. It did not have a business plan. It did not have goals. It did not have a strategy to manage human resources. It was an organisation where all plans were in the head of the *thaokae* [owner].[14]

Thanathorn modernized the business operations of Thai Summit by establishing clear organizational structures and processes. In developing these structures and processes, he sought to decentralize Thai Summit, which would be crucial when the company later expanded its international operations, as he believed decisions should be made by those with local knowledge. He also sought to place Thai Summit at the cutting edge of technology, expanding the budget for research and development. However, despite the modernization, Thai Summit remained very much a family business at the top, with Thanathorn's mother Somporn serving as president, while Thanathorn and his sister worked as vice presidents. When he left Thai Summit, Thanathorn turned his responsibilities over to his two younger brothers.

Under Thanathorn, Thai Summit went global. He inherited a company that was primarily a domestic business endeavour, save for its exports of parts to major overseas corporations and a limited joint production venture with Proton in Malaysia. Thai Summit first invested in India, producing parts for both motorcycles and motorized trishaws, before eventually opening six factories in a joint venture with Jay Bharat Maruti.[15] Thanathorn then expanded Thai Summit's operations in the ASEAN markets, particularly Indonesia and Vietnam. Thai Summit was however more cautious moving into the Chinese market, which Thanathorn believed presented unique challenges.[16] The purchase of Ogihara, a leading company in die manufacturing, allowed Thai Summit to acquire cutting-edge production facilities in Japan and the United States. It later invested in a second factory in the United States to support the production of Ford Trucks.[17]

In modernizing and globalizing the business, Thanathorn paid close attention to governmental and regional policies in order to take advantage of the opportunities provided. At the time he took over Thai Summit, the Thai Board of Investment had identified automobiles as a priority sector for investment, which proved to be fortuitous timing for Thai Summit. Later, as ASEAN began to move towards establishing a free trade area, Thanathorn established factories in Indonesia and Vietnam, the two largest ASEAN countries by population. The rapid growth of the middle class in both countries also meant a promising demographic for Thai Summit's growth. At the same time, Thanathorn hoped that his investment in Indonesia and Vietnam prior to the opening of the ASEAN Free Trade Area would provide Thai Summit with a buffer to stem the development of powerful rivals in the Thai market.[18] Thai Summit was also at the forefront of attempts to develop parts for electric cars in Thailand. Through the years, Thanathorn actively participated in university seminars on investment and the economy, and was often quoted in the press for his views on the automobile industry.

Last, during Thanathorn's time at Thai Summit, the family invested in print media. In 2003, Somporn, the family matriarch, began buying shares in Nation Multimedia Group (NMG), the publisher of *The Nation*, *Kom Chad Luek* (a Thai daily) and *Krungthep Turakij* (a business-orientated broadsheet). Over the course of the year, she increased her holdings to 10.51 per cent. Thanathorn held another 1.57 per cent, while his sister and Thai Summit co-vice president, Chanaphan, held a further 1.26 per cent. This made the family one of the largest shareholders of the company.[19] This period coincided with Thanathorn's sponsorship of *Fah Diaw Kan* as discussed above. The family held on to its NMG shares through 2010, selling them only because Somporn "saw no future in the group".[20] Just three years later, the family bought heavily into Matichon Plc, which publishes *Matichon* (a Thai language daily), *Khaosod* (another Thai language daily that has since begun an English language edition) and *Prachachart Turakij* (a business newspaper).[21] Matichon also publishes books, which includes a recent hagiography of Thanathorn. On his own, Thanathorn also built up his social media profile, sharing his exploits in adventure tourism (mountain climbing and an Antarctic expedition) and extreme sports (ultra-marathons).[22] His acute awareness about the importance of the press would stand Thanathorn in good stead when he left Thai Summit for politics.

Founding Future Forward

In May 2015, nearly four years before the election, Thanathorn was invited to join a seminar about the "Thai Economy, Hope and Future" at his alma mater, Thammasat University. The goal of the seminar was to consider the causes and possible remedies for the weak economic outlook. Thanathorn focused on the political system, arguing that the crisis could be traced back to 2006: the year of the first military coup since 1991 and a precursor to the longer-lasting 2014 coup. He noted that "We have prime ministers who stay in power one year and five months on average. If we cannot establish sustainable democracy, the country's economy will continue to perform poorly."[23] A month later he was at Pathumwan police station when fourteen student activists came to file a complaint against the police for allegedly abusing their power in an arrest. The authorities, seeking a mastermind behind the scene, as is their wont, appeared to consider Thanathorn a suspect, prompting him to post on his Facebook page that "I was there not because I'm the puppet master of them as accused, but because I'm a citizen who has every right to think and believe differently. I want to give them what they needed most: encouragement and mental support."[24] Thus, well before the election, Thanathorn made clear his preference for democracy and his opposition to the military junta. Later, as the election neared, Thanathorn would collaborate with an anti-junta professor from Thammasat University, Piyabutr Saengkanokkul, to establish the Future Forward party.

Piyabutr Sankanokkul was born in Bangkok to a lower-middle class Sino-Thai family. His father sold house paint, and, through hard work, managed to put all four of his children through Assumption, a Christian private school. Piyabutr went on to study law at Thammasat, focusing on civil law and constitutional law. Upon graduation, he taught at Thammasat for a year before securing a scholarship to study in France, completing his MA at Nantes and his PhD at Toulouse. He returned to Thammasat to teach in 2010, with his PhD officially awarded in 2011.[25] Piyabutr helped to form Nitirat, a group of legal scholars from Thammasat who would discuss and react to constitutional reforms before or as they happened.[26] The participants of Nitirat were concerned that legal decisions with long-lasting ramifications were being issued so rapidly that there was no opportunity for the wider community to understand and participate in the decision-making process. One of the proposals to emerge from Nitirat was particularly controversial as it suggested a reform of Thailand's *lèse-majesté* law. Nitirat argued that the *lèse-majesté* law had been abused in recent years to attack political rivals, and that using it in such a way damaged both civil rights and respect for the monarchy. Although Nitirat was seeking to reform the *lèse-majesté* law to prevent its abuse, the group was subsequently accused of seeking to undermine the monarchy. Piyabutr thus had a mixed reputation as a strong supporter of civil rights and democracy to some, and, despite his denials, as an anti-monarchist to others.

As preparation to establish a new political party, both Thanathorn and Piyabutr gave multiple press interviews, advancing the goals and broad outlines of the new party to build interest and support. Thanathorn stated that the party would seek to "reclaim" the future from the junta, adding that, "If I go ahead with setting up the party, it will not be an *ad hoc* one. I would not settle for anything less than changing the face of the country."[27] He also indicated that the party would focus on "young blood" voters, referring to "those of all ages who refuse to give up hope of true democracy".[28] Thanathorn actively promoted the party on social media, including a notable two-hour Facebook Live interview with The101.world site on 5 March 2018. That interview was viewed more than 100,000 times and shared over 3,000 times in the first two days it was available. It also led to the hashtag #HelpThanathornNameParty on Twitter. This approach proved highly effective in stirring up interest, while also provoking the junta to issue a statement that the interview might violate the ongoing ban against electoral campaigning.[29]

Thanathorn continued to develop public interest and support for his yet-to-be-established party on social media. Two days before his Facebook Live interview, he had written on Facebook that he had cleared another hurdle in establishing the party by securing his mother's permission.[30] He also announced on Twitter during that same two-day period that he was challenging another progressive politician, Sombat Boonngamanong, to a battle on *Realm of Valor*, a mobile game. This stirred discussion about who would win, while further generating online interest in Thanathorn.[31] As the game was broadcast on Facebook Live, Thanathorn took the opportunity to point out that online gaming might provide an entry into technology and programming for young people.[32] Although he lost the game, he was successful in reaching out to young voters on social media before his party was founded and before campaigning was allowed. These social media activities were also reported in the mainstream press, which meant that Thanathorn was able to reach beyond his online audience.

Having built up interest in the proposed party, Thanathorn issued an invitation on his Facebook page for medical practitioners to attend a "Friends of Thanathorn" coffee session and press conference on the morning of 15 March 2018. This was the day that he and party founders would officially register their party. The junta issued a warning, arguing that the coffee session amounted to campaigning, which was still banned. Thanathorn insisted, through his Facebook, that the session would only be limited to introducing the party, discussing the future of the country, and answering questions. The savvy social media campaign as well as the frequent warnings by the junta helped Thanathorn to establish his fledgling party as a credible and potentially dangerous opposition party, even before it was officially registered.

A New Approach

In seeking to establish a new type of political party in Thailand, Future Forward sought to avoid the traditional politics of patronage and declined to recruit former MPs or prominent politicians into the party. Instead, the party aimed itself at a new generation: 16 of the 26 founding members were under the age of 30, while party leaders Thanathorn and Piyabutr were both under the age of 40.[33] The party also hoped to establish a new funding stream based on small donations from its members, instead of donations from party leaders, so that the party would belong to members rather than the party leadership. Future Forward also set out a new style of party organization that relied heavily on social media to allow ordinary members the opportunity to participate in its decision-making. Future Forward adopted policies that were bold, progressive, anti-junta and pro-democracy, although it was not unique in doing so. As we will see, these new methods were all interconnected and were largely responsible for the party's positive election results. However, the party was also reliant to some degree on support it received through more traditional methods of electoral politics.

Candidate Selection

Future Forward rejected former politicians in its selection of founding members as well as election candidates. Thanathorn believed that because former politicians were too entrenched in the patronage system, the only means of circumventing it was to seek out new faces.[34] Future Forward turned instead to civil society for support. The founding and leading members of the party included a textile union leader, a printers' union leader, a "digital farmer" activist who teaches other farmers how to use technology to improve crop yields, human rights advocates, including a former head of Amnesty International in Thailand, a transgender rights campaigner, a disabled rights activist, a leader of a Muslim student group, and a computer technician. The party also recruited former student leaders and academics. Recruitment for local constituencies followed the same pattern, with civil society and former student activists filling many of the positions. While few, if any, of these members had national name recognition, what they had was influence in specific sectors of civil society, either locally or in Bangkok. Only Thanathorn and Piyabutr could be said to be well known nationally.

To select constituency candidates, Future Forward established an open online primary, with candidates chosen locally then vetted nationally. Members were encouraged to volunteer in each district. The prospective candidates were asked to provide their qualifications and political views, which were made available to members through the party website. In addition to the online primary, potential candidates were vetted by the party to ensure they met the requirements of the Election Commission. Local party leaders were chosen using a similar process. While this created a grass-roots process, it also meant that many of the candidates had limited campaigning experience. In particular, sustaining volunteer enthusiasm proved a problem. Combined with the shortage of funding, constituency candidates generally struggled in their campaigning, relying heavily on visits from national party leaders and the party's social media efforts.[35]

Campaign Funding

Generally, in Thailand, the bulk of the campaign funding comes from party leaders or their families. However, save for the exception of Thanathorn, party leaders of Future Forward were not able to donate large amounts to the election campaign. Thanathorn himself quickly reached the maximum campaign donation limit of 10 million baht, after having donated 8 million in October 2018 and another 2 million in November 2018. His wife Rawiphan donated a further 7.2 million baht in December 2018. While the donations represented a substantial contribution from his family,[36] it accounted for only a small portion of the estimated minimum of 350 million baht necessary to run a credible nationwide campaign. To overcome this, the party pursued a new "crowdfunding" approach, which also helped to ensure that the party belongs to the people, and not to financiers.[37] In practice this meant funding the party's election campaign through a combination of small-scale donations, membership dues, merchandising sales, the Election Commission's subsidies for parties, and interest-free loans from party supporters. Initially, the party employed social media to boost its fund-raising efforts, particularly through the online sales of Future Forward merchandise. However, the Election Commission prohibited the online sales of merchandise. The party was instead allowed to use social media to advertise its merchandise, but these could only be purchased at party offices. According to one party leader, merchandising sales, along with party memberships and donations, tended to rise whenever party leaders were accused of improprieties.[38] Merchandise sales in some months reached 2 to 3 million baht. The party also relied on small-scale donations through membership dues. At the rates set by the Election Commission, one year of dues raised 200 baht for the party, while lifetime dues provided 2,000 baht. Some new members donated more, generally around 10,000 to 20,000 baht.[39] On the first day after its registration, Future Forward signed up 712 members, with many paying lifetime dues. By the end of the week, the party had received some 20 million baht.[40] The party also held a few fund-raising dinners, aimed at ordinary people, with the admission cost set at a 1,000 baht donation. Encouraging small-scale donations while recruiting party members enabled Future Forward to eventually grow to 60,000 members, second only to the much older Democrat Party.[41]

With the party having to mostly rely on small-scale donations, constituency candidates often struggled to meet basic costs, such as the rental of campaign vehicles and drivers, as well as petroleum. Constituency candidates thus sought low-cost means of voter outreach, such as joining seminars sponsored by universities or debates sponsored by the Election Commission. One of the best low-cost methods for the candidates was social media, although some complained that confusing and unclear regulations from the Election Commission deterred them from relying on social media outreach except in very limited and careful ways.[42] Given the minimal experience, limited name-recognition and restricted funds of Future Forward's candidates, most analysts saw little chance for it to win constituency seats, expecting instead for the party's victories to come through the 150 party-list seats.[43]

Campaigning

Under the circumstances, the most important campaigning was left to Thanathorn and the central party leadership, through their visits to the provinces, provocative policy announcements, and social media. Soon after registering the party, Thanathorn embarked on a tour to the provinces, putatively to listen to the people, since the junta had not yet approved the start of campaigning. Such high-profile visits by party leaders to major provinces became a staple of the campaign, with mainstream media carefully cultivated to nationalize coverage of local visits. Visits to markets and other events were also broadcast on social media. In January 2019, I observed a campaign visit in Chiang Mai. The party leaders and candidates, accompanied by a small group of volunteers, visited a market to chat with vendors and shoppers while handing out leaflets that featured Thanathorn on the front and other key party leaders on the back. The leaflet also included QR codes linking to Thanathorn's own Facebook page, followed by links to the party's Facebook page, the party's Line account, and the party's website. A team from Singapore's

Channel NewsAsia covered the visit, which helped a local campaign event to become a larger newsworthy spectacle.

Despite the ban on campaigning during this early period, preventing parties from formally articulating its policies, Future Forward took every opportunity to make its stands known. Through social and mainstream media, both domestic and international, Thanathorn and Piyabutr were able to set out the aims of the party. First and foremost, they depicted the party as being pro-democracy and anti-military. In a seminar at Thammasat University, shortly after the party applied for registration, Piyabutr announced that the party would seek constitutional changes to curtail the power of the military and review the legality of all orders of the National Council for Peace and Order, the official name of the junta. In addition, he proposed adding to the constitution the right and duty of Thai citizens to resist coups, and to criminalize those who carry out a coup.[44] The attack on the legitimacy of the junta and the role of the military in politics was again taken up a few days later by Thanathorn. In an interview with the *Bangkok Post*, he stated that the party would seek to "restructure the organisation of the military, change the constitution that was drafted by the military government" and "eliminate undemocratic elements in Thai society".[45] The party would later call for large cuts to the defence budget, including halving the size of the military and eliminating conscription.[46] The cuts to the defence budget would be diverted to fund the initiatives designed to bring about greater equality, which is the other primary policy preoccupation of the party.

Future Forward thus became part of a broader narrative that placed competing political parties into two camps. One camp was pro-regime, which included not only the Palang Pracharat but also Bhumjaithai and some smaller parties. The other was anti-regime, and included Pheu Thai, Thai Raksa Chart (a party closely affiliated with Pheu Thai), and Future Forward. The party leaders of the anti-regime camp frequently attended the same academic seminars, while their parties were subjected to similar attacks from the junta, often simultaneously. This was not a narrative that Future Forward could control, since it was also encouraged by both the junta and the mainstream press. However, its leaders did take a strong position in the pro-democracy camp. Only the Democrat Party, deeply divided over whether to support the regime, tried to remain outside these two camps, which perhaps contributed to its losses in the election. More importantly, the binary division between pro-regime and anti-regime parties meant that, both in the press and in voters' minds, Pheu Thai, Thai Raksa Chart and Future Forward were seen as advancing similar positions and sharing a pro-democratic vision of the future. This would become important with the subsequent dissolution of Thai Raksa Chart.

Social Media

The need to circumvent the initial ban on formal campaigning, the structure of the party, and the party's focus on young voters all contributed to the heavy use of social media in Future Forward campaigning. The party made extensive use of Facebook, which is pervasive in Thailand. Facebook had around 49 million Thai users as of 2017, ranking it the eighth highest in the world. This is a rather remarkable level of penetration given that the total population of Thailand above the age of six is about 63 million.[47] Table 1 shows the Facebook following of the major Thai parties and their leaders. The Pheu Thai and the Democrat parties and their leaders have had Facebook pages for many years, while the Palang Pracharat and Future Forward parties and their leaders are relatively new to Facebook. Despite its newness, Future Forward has more followers than either of the older parties, and nearly six times as many followers as its contemporary, the PPRP party. It is also worth noting that, in every case, party leaders have more followers than their parties. However, with Future Forward the difference is much less, indicating the effectiveness of the party's use of social media to develop support.

The party also has an active YouTube channel with some 300,000 followers. The channel is primarily devoted to campaign footage and academic seminars where party leaders have participated, with Thanathorn playing a leading role. The channel also includes discussions of political issues and policies as well as short clips of news about the party. Thanathorn—or perhaps his social media team—has also demonstrated an ability to interact effectively with others on YouTube. In October 2018, ten Thai rap artists collaborated under the name Rap Against Dictatorship to produce a video called "Prathet Ku Mee" (My Country Has It). The song, which is harshly critical of the military regime, quickly went viral, gaining some twelve million views in less than a week and some 65,000 comments. Among those 65,000 comments was one from Thanathorn's personal account, stating that the song "showed tribute to a fighting spirit". It became the

TABLE 1
Facebook Followers (as of September 2019)

Party	Followers on Facebook	Leader	Followers on Facebook
Pheu Thai	493,000	Thaksin	2,670,000
Democrat	730,000	Abhisit	2,290,000
Future Forward	804,000	Thanathorn	1,100,000
Palang Pracharat	142,000	Prayut	746,000

most "liked" comment for the video, with some 29,000 users liking it.[48] The party thus creatively and effectively linked itself to a YouTube video far more popular than any of its own.

Compared to Facebook or YouTube, the party made relatively limited use of Twitter. However, individual candidates and party supporters used Twitter extensively, to some effective degree.[49] A wide variety of hashtags associated with the party trended during the campaign period. The two most effective hashtags came from party supporters. On 9 February 2019, some six weeks before the election, Thanathorn attended the annual football game between Chulalongkorn and Thammasat, where a fan called out "Fah rak pho" (Fah loves father). This is a line from a popular Thai soap opera involving Fah, a poor girl, who cultivated a wealthy patron she referred to as "father". As the *Bangkok Post* explains, "Fah utters the line as a way of expressing admiration for an older man who makes her feel safe and secure".[50] That same day, an anonymous Twitter user tweeted out the hashtag #fahrakpho, which rapidly trended. The hashtag was further boosted after Thanathorn acknowledged it with his own tweet stating that "Fah loves father, and father loves all Thais".[51] The social media interaction was picked up by the mainstream press, enabling its coverage to spread well beyond the online domain. In mid-February, Thanathorn was notified of a summons by the Criminal Suppression Division to respond to a complaint that claimed that he was responsible for false information in his biography on the party website. That led to a supporter tweeting out the hashtag #savethanathon, which spread rapidly, becoming the top trending hashtag on 21 February. Occurring shortly before the election, the trending of these hashtags were important in raising awareness of the party, especially among the young voters it was targeting for support.

As with Twitter, the party made minimal direct use of Instagram. However, the party was aware of the possibilities that the platform offered for spreading the party message. Thanathorn would spent long hours after rallies for selfies with supporters, in the knowledge that many would then upload those pictures on their Instagram and Facebook feeds for their friends to see.[52]

In relying extensively on social media, Future Forward was also forced to respond when it was under attack on Twitter and other platforms. Among the most notable attacks on the party was the release of a pair of amateurishly doctored videos: one seeking to tie Thanathorn to Thaksin (which was later picked up by a television station) and another of a lecture by Piyabutr on the monarchy held at Thammasat. Both doctored videos sought to provide "evidence" for accusations by critics of the Future Forward party leaders and to undermine their electability. The accusation against Piyabutr was particularly damaging, as he would later be investigated for *lèse-majesté*. The party sought to overcome such attacks through social media, with one party leader sharing that such online platforms allowed the party to quickly counter false accusations.[53]

For the purposes of organizing and communicating with members, Future Forward made extensive use of Line. Anyarat Chattharakul has described the social media-based recruitment and integration process through an analysis of one Future Forward party member named Somchai.[54] Somchai first became interested in Future Forward through mainstream media, after viewing an interview with Thanathorn on television. He then visited the party's Facebook page, leaving his email address and expressing his willingness to be contacted. Within a week a party member from his province contacted him to join the private Line chat for his area. He then began to attend physical meetings and joined the party. After becoming a member, he frequently watched the party's Facebook Live broadcasts, sometimes doing so multiple times in the hope that more viewings would, through Facebook algorithms, help spread the broadcast to more feeds. With encouragement through the Line chat group, he also retweeted and reposted Future Forward–orientated content, some of which was produced by the party but often curated by other party members and supporters. In this way, social media reinforced supporters internally, primarily through locally orientated Line chat groups, while helping to recruit additional members and supporters, primarily through Facebook, Twitter and Instagram. It is also significant to note that while most of the social media interactions around Future Forward were not limited to specific electoral regions and were best suited to party-list campaigning, the Line chats were distinctly local in character and helped to form loose-knit local community structures, which may support the development of a local grass-roots branch organization in the future.

Future Forward and Thai Raksa Chart

As noted above, Future Forward placed itself firmly in the pro-democratic camp, along with Pheu Thai and Thai Raksa Chart. Pheu Thai and Thai Raksa Chart were informally affiliated parties, as Thai Raksa Chart was created to secure the party list seats that would have been virtually impossible for Pheu Thai to win under the new constitution written by the junta.[55] Pheu Thai and Thai Raksa Chart tried to avoid direct competition with each other, with Pheu Thai contesting in only 250 of the 350 constituency seats and Thai Raksa Chart contesting in just 178 constituencies. In general, Thai Raksa Chart ran in the South, hoping to earn votes in Democrat territory for party list seats, as well as Bangkok and its nearby provinces. Future Forward contested nationwide, and thus competed directly with Pheu Thai and Thai Raksa Chart. In early February 2019, parties were required to submit the names of the candidates that they would support for prime minister. While Future Forward nominated Thanathorn, Thai Raksa Chart nominated Princess Ubolratana (who was technically a commoner as a result of her marriage). Later that week the king issued a statement barring Princess Ubolratana from running for office, as she had been carrying out the responsibilities of a member of the royal family since her return to Thailand. The Election Commission subsequently began an investigation, and after a hastened process dissolved Thai Raksa Chart, just seventeen days before the election, for having involved the royal family in politics.

The dissolution of Thai Raksa Chart meant that in many election districts neither Pheu Thai nor Thai Raksa Chart had candidates contesting the election. Vote canvassers for Thai Raksa Chart were now free to back candidates from other parties. Future Forward, the third major party in the pro-democratic camp, became the natural choice. This was reinforced when, on 7 March, Piyabutr criticized the dissolution of the party.[56] The following day the junta filed a complaint against Piyabutr, even as #dissolvedtodeathyetIstillwontvoteforuncle (in reference to Prayut) trended on Twitter.[57] The junta's threat against Future Forward for its public opposition to Thai Raksa Chart's dissolution instead galvanized supporters of Thai Raksa Chart to switch their support. For example, Thitima Chaisaeng, the Thai Raksa Chart candidate for Chachoengsao, called on supporters to vote for Future Forward,[58] enabling the party to win two seats in the province that was previously expected to go to Thai Raksa Chart.

Table 2 sets out the winners in the constituency seats where candidates from Thai Raksa Chart were registered to contest prior to the party's dissolution. The Democrat Party won 30 of its 33 constituency seats in areas that Thai Raksa Chart would have contested. This was expected, since Thai Raksa Chart's presence in the South, a stronghold of the Democrat Party, was primarily intended to boost its chances in the party list system. To understand the importance of Thai Raksa Chart canvassers, it is helpful to compare the respective performance of Palang Pracharat and Future Forward in the constituencies that should have been contested by Thai Raksa Chart. Palang Pracharat won 44 out of its 97 constituency seats (about 40 per cent) in districts that Thai Raksa Chart was intending to contest, while Future Forward won 24 out of 30 constituency seats (about 80 per cent) in such districts. In short, Future Forward appears to have successfully "borrowed" Thai Raksa Chart's election networks in a number of districts, thus contributing to the party's unexpectedly large number of victories in constituency seats.

TABLE 2
Winning Parties in Thai Raksa Chart Constituencies

Party	Seats won in constituencies contested by Thai Raksa Chart	Total number of constituency seats won
Pheu Thai	49	136
Palang Pracharat	44	97
Democrat	30	33
Future Forward	24	30
Bhumjaithai	19	39
Chat Thai Phatthana	5	6
Prachachat	4	6
Ruam Palang Prachachat Thai	1	1

Source: Election Commission of Thailand data.

Future Forward and the Election

The 2019 election took place under a new constitution, which was carefully designed to undermine the power of large parties while securing electoral legitimacy for the ruling military junta. Central to these attempts was a mixed party list and constituency system, in which voters would only cast a single vote, instead of separate ballots as they did in the past. The new voting system benefited medium-sized parties, particularly those that emerged second and third in individual constituencies, at the expense of the parties that won constituency seats.[59] Indeed, the anti-junta Pheu Thai, which had the second-highest vote total despite contesting only 250 of the 350 seats, was not awarded any party list seats, while the pro-junta Palang Pracharat received 18 party list seats (see Table 3). In addition to the advantageous electoral system, the pro-junta party had other advantages, including support from its nominee for prime minister, junta leader General Prayut Chan-o-cha, as the party campaigned heavily on continuity with the policies of the military government.

In an election marred by widespread irregularities,[60] Future Forward and Palang Pracharat outperformed most projections. The Democrat Party, which refused to join either the pro-junta or the pro-democratic camp, badly underperformed. Election results for parties with five seats or more are presented in Table 3. In addition, two parties won three seats each, one party won two seats, and, based on initial calculations, only two parties appeared to meet the threshold for one seat. As the unofficial results were announced, Pheu Thai and Future Forward moved quickly to form a majority coalition in the lower house with several minor parties.[61] They

TABLE 3
Election Results

Party	Constituency seats	Party list seats	Total
Pheu Thai	136	0	136
PPRP	97	18	115
Future Forward	30	50	80
Democrat	33	19	52
Bhumjaithai	39	12	51
Seriruamthai	0	10	10
Chatthaiphatthana	6	4	10
Prachachart	6	1	7
Setthakitmai	0	6	6
Pheuchart	0	5	5

Source: Election Commission of Thailand data.

did this despite being unable to enforce their choice of prime minister, since the post is determined in a joint sitting with junta-appointed senators. However, they hoped that in forming a majority coalition in the House it would prevent the junta from governing, since it would lack the numbers to pass legislation.

Subsequently, the junta-appointed Election Commission adopted a controversial formula, lowering the minimum threshold so that thirteen parties would secure one parliamentary seat each, even though eleven of those parties did not meet the initial minimum threshold.[62] Those eleven parties announced their support for the pro-junta coalition, thus shifting the balance of power and allowing PPRP to establish a razor-thin majority in the House.

All these manipulations to ensure the survival of the military regime largely denied it the electoral legitimacy it sought. Nevertheless, it has managed to perpetuate its rule for now, albeit with the constant risk of defections that might undermine its slim parliamentary majority.

Future Forward under Siege

From its beginnings, Future Forward and its leaders have faced a series of legal challenges, both from the junta and conservative activists, with most of these challenges still under investigation. The tactic of legal harassment has been frequently advanced against progressive parties since Prime Minister Samak Suntharawej of Phalang Prachachon (the former incarnation of Pheu Thai) was removed from office in 2008 for appearing on a cooking show. The most serious charges were levelled against Thanathorn: he was charged with sedition, abetting the escape of a suspect, and organizing an assembly of more than ten people for events that took place in 2015. He was also accused of spreading false information online and instigating public disorder for a Facebook Live broadcast and a Facebook post critical of the government. During the election he was investigated by the Election Commission for entering false information in his biography on the party website, which turned out to be a minor mistake made by a staff member. Both Thanathorn and Piyabutr were also accused of undermining the monarchy, while Piyabutr was investigated separately for cybercrimes for his speech criticizing the banning of Thai Raksa Chart. The Election Commission also declared that Thanathorn violated election law by holding shares in a media company while running as a candidate. The party was also investigated for undue outside influence for gaining help from Thai Raksa Chart. In addition, a host of other complaints were filed by conservative activists.[63] Not surprisingly, most of these cases, described by the *Bangkok Post* as "very weak",[64] were taken up by the authorities shortly after the election when it appeared that the opposition had enough seats to form a coalition government. In a speech to the Foreign Correspondents Club of Thailand, Thanathorn, prefacing his story by noting it was a "bad joke",[65] alleged that his mother had been contacted by a leading member of the government party and told that all the cases would go away if Future Forward transferred twenty members to Palang Pracharat. Despite his mother's urging, he refused to do so.[66]

Meanwhile, the Election Commission sped through its processes to quickly level charges that Thanathorn had violated election law by holding shares in a media company. The investigation and decision to prosecute came when Thanathorn was put forward by Future Forward as a candidate for prime minister. The case was then sent to the Constitutional Court for review before parliament was convened. While the case awaited the decision of the court, Thanathorn was sworn in as a member of parliament, although he was immediately suspended from his duties.[67] During that period, Thanathorn remained as the leader of Future Forward and an MP, yet he was not able to take up any post or participate in parliament. In mid-November the Constitutional Court ruled that Thanathorn had violated election law and retroactively stripped him of his MP status. It did not however impose any additional penalties, which could have included up to ten years in prison and a twenty-year ban from participating in politics, although the junta-appointed Election Commission may yet choose to levy criminal charges seeking such penalties. Thus, Future Forward will have to move forward in parliament without its charismatic leader and most important financial backer. The party itself faces additional legal proceedings, with the most serious involving charges that the party tried to overthrow the monarchy and that it violated party funding laws in accepting a large loan from Thanathorn for the election campaign. Either of these charges could lead to the dissolution of the party.

The Future of Future Forward

The success of Future Forward in the 2019 election was in many ways unprecedented. As a new party with no politicians with national-level experience, it managed to finish third, with 80 seats. It did so by gaining the support of young voters who will be voting for decades to come. From this perspective, the future of Future Forward seems bright. At the same time, the party faces many challenges. First and foremost are the many legal challenges facing its party leaders. The charges could lead to political bans on key leaders, including Thanathorn, who has been the driving force of the party through his leadership, his personality and his financial resources. The possibility that the party might be dissolved cannot be ruled out. At the same time, Future Forward faces structural challenges as it moves to consolidate its success. Future Forward has created a new style of party that features charismatic party leaders who are savvy in their social media outreach and a willingness to encourage grass-roots participation, primarily through the use of social media. It is a party that is well organized at the top and enthusiastic at the bottom, but is lacking anything except technology in between. To be sure, political parties in Thailand have always had weak formal organizational structures, with only the Democrat Party having an extensive branch structure. However, most parties have organized informally, generally around regional factions, constituency MPs, and powerful local politicians who control campaign organizations at the local level and are thus able to turn out the vote. Future Forward has none of this infrastructure; most of its successful constituency MPs appear to have benefitted from the voting networks of the dissolved Thai Raksa Chart. Lacking that level of infrastructure, Future Forward is entirely dependent on generating grass-roots enthusiasm through social media. Yet, such enthusiasm has generally been short-lived and fickle—like how hashtags "trend" on Twitter before quickly disappearing. Future Forward seems to be aware of this problem and has announced that it will compete in local elections across the country, which would allow it to develop the missing party infrastructure. Yet it will face a dilemma. If it chooses to compete against powerful experienced local politicians and their campaign organizations, it may struggle to win and develop that crucial infrastructure. However, if it brings powerful local politicians into the party, Future Forward may come to resemble other parties, dependent on informal campaign structures and powerful local notables embedded in patronage networks.

Pioneering a new style of politics is always challenging, with many hurdles to overcome. Future Forward, even if it survives without its leader in parliament, is just starting on that complex task.

The model established by Future Forward may be emulated by new parties in the future. Established parties will not be able to take the same approach. They may adapt the social media techniques of Future Forward, but they have well-established patronage networks of the type decried by Future Forward and its supporters. Nonetheless, these patronage networks also provide the infrastructure between party leaders and voters that Future Forward is currently lacking, and thus can be seen as an advantage, not a liability. Whether established parties can effectively integrate social media techniques with their current patronage structures in ways that appeal to voters, or, alternatively, whether Future Forward can survive and develop a better infrastructure, may determine whether we see a more extensive shift in the nature of Thai political parties.

Acknowledgements

I would like to thank Pinsuda Wonganan and her colleagues at Chiangmai University and Suthikarn Meechan and her colleagues at Mahasarakham University for their contributions to the research for this article.

Notes

1. "Dissecting Parties' Poll Game Plans", *Bangkok Post*, 30 March 2019.
2. Duncan McCargo, "Anatomy: Future Backward", *Contemporary Southeast Asia* 41, no. 2 (2019): 153.
3. Jenwit Cheuasawathi, *Pakthong Anakhot: The Future is Ours* [Plant a future flag: The future is ours] (Bangkok: Matichon, 2018), pp. 29–33.
4. Ibid., pp. 38–39.
5. Ibid., p. 39.
6. Supara Janchitfah, "We Care—Lessons in the University of Life", *Bangkok Post*, 10 August 1999.
7. Ibid.
8. Chachawanan Santidet, *Luak Yu Khang Wela* [Choose to be on the side of time] (Bangkok: Se-Education, 2018), pp. 19–20; Jenwit, *Pakthong Anakhot*, pp. 46–49; "A Risk-Taker Billionaire Pursuing Social Justice", *The Nation*, 9 April 2018.
9. Jenwit, *Pakthong Anakhot*, p. 59.
10. "Politics: Firebrand Vows to 'Break this Regime'", *Bangkok Post*, 2 April 2018.
11. Chachawanan Santidet, *Luak Yu Khang Wela*, pp. 51–52; "Automobiles: Local Parts Giant to Invest D2bn", *Bangkok Post*, 7 October 2003.

12. "Automotive: Thai Summit Targets Overseas Markets", *Bangkok Post*, 13 August 2016.
13. Chachawanan, *Luak Yu Khang Wela*, p. 52.
14. Ibid., p. 48.
15. "Asia Focus: Investment sans frontieres", *Bangkok Post*, 21 October 2006.
16. Ibid.
17. "Thai Summit Cuts Investment", *Bangkok Post*, 9 March 2009; Thai Summit Ogihara, "The Perfect Impression: Taking Your Project from Concept to Production: About", http://ogihara.com/about.php (28 September 2019).
18. Chachawanan, *Luak Yu Khang Wela*, pp. 58–59.
19. "Publishing: Minister's Family Quietly Builds up a Big Shareholding in Nation", *Bangkok Post*, 8 November 2003; "Family Raises Stake in NMG", *The Nation*, 8 November 2003.
20. "Somporn: Matichon Stake 'Purely an Investment'", *Bangkok Post*, 4 May 2013.
21. Ibid.
22. Jenwit, *Pakthong Anakhot*, p. 8.
23. "'Democracy is Best'", *The Nation*, 25 May 2015.
24. "Probe into Students 'Backers'", *The Nation*, 29 June 2015.
25. Kwanchai Dumrongkwan, "Chak chiwit khanat yao kap khwamfan nok muak nakwichakan khong Piyabutr Saengkanokkul" [Extended life story and dreams beyond the scholar cap of Piyabutr Saengkanokkul], *The Matter*, 8 May 2019, https://thematter.co/pulse/long-interview-with-piyabutr/76766.
26. Ibid.
27. "Thanathorn Mulls Youth-Oriented Challenge to the Establishment", *Bangkok Post*, 4 March 2018.
28. "Old Guard Warn Newbies", *Bangkok Post*, 5 March 2018.
29. "Regime Rattles Sabre at Young Bloods", *Bangkok Post*, 8 March 2018.
30. "Young Blood Party Plans Take Shape", *Bangkok Post*, 12 March 2018.
31. "Young Bloods Draw Phones for Online Duel", *Bangkok Post*, 13 March 2018.
32. "Online Battle Rages: Thanathorn, Sombat Broadcast Gaming Session in Apparent Cheeky Swipe at Prawit", *The Nation*, 20 March 2018.
33. "New Key Party Opposes Outside PM", *Bangkok Post*, 16 March 2018.
34. "The Future According to Thanathorn: Exclusive Interview", *Bangkok Post*, 1 March 2019.
35. Interview with a local FFP leader, 17 January 2019.
36. By way of contrast, members of the Silipa-acha family donated 27,600,000 baht to the more regionally focused Chatthaiphatthana party in December alone. See Election Commission of Thailand, "Khomun ngoenborijak phakkanmuang" [Money donated to political parties], https://www.ect.go.th/ect_th/news_all.php?offset=0&cid=22&filename=).

37. "Thanathorn Sets Eye on Premier's Job", *Bangkok Post*, 28 May 2018.
38. Phone interview with a party leader conducted by Pinsuda Wonganan, September 2019.
39. Election Commission of Thailand data shows a number of donations in the 5,000–50,000 baht range. Future Forward and the Democrats were the only major parties to list any donations in this range, with the Democrat party generally at 50,000 baht and up. See Election Commission of Thailand, "Khomun ngoenborijak phakkanmuang".
40. "New Party Pulls in B20 Million in One Week", *Bangkok Post*, 11 October 2018.
41. Phone interview with a party leader conducted by Pinsuda Wonganan, September 2019.
42. Interviews with three Future Forward constituency candidates, January–February 2019.
43. See, for example, "Pheu Thai No 1 Choice, But Well Short of Majority", *The Nation*, 6 March 2019.
44. "'Talk Show' Debate Sets Tone for Election", *Bangkok Post*, 28 March 2018.
45. "Politics: Firebrand Vows to 'Break this Regime'", *Bangkok Post*, 2 April 2018.
46. "The Future According to Thanathorn: Exclusive Interview", *Bangkok Post*, 1 March 2019.
47. "Thailand Makes Top Ten in Social Media Use", *Bangkok Post*, 1 March 2018, http://www.bangkokpost.com/business/news/1420086/thailand-makes-top-10-in-social-media-use (accessed 18 February 2019); National Statistical Office (Thailand), *The 2018 Household Survey on the Use of Information and Communication Technology (Quarter 1)* (Bangkok: National Statistical Office, [2018]).
48. Rap Against Dictatorship, *Prathet Ku Mee* [My country has it], https://m.youtube.com/watch?v=VZvzvLiGUtw (accessed 19 November 2019); "The Big Issue: The Kids Are All Right", *Bangkok Post*, 28 October 2018.
49. Anyarat Chattharakul, "Social Media: Hashtag #Futurista", *Contemporary Southeast Asia* 41, no. 2 (2019): 172.
50. "Hashtags on the Hustings", *Bangkok Post*, 17 February 2019.
51. "Fah Loves Her Dad, Num's Cuffed Up, Boss Skirts Booze Test", *Bangkok Post*, 17 February 2019.
52. Phone interview with a party leader conducted by Pinsuda Wonganan, September 2019.
53. "NBTC to Look into Airing of Doctored Clip", *Bangkok Post*, 22 March 2019; "Fanning Flames of Hate Speech Will End In Tears", *Bangkok Post*, 4 April 2019; Phone interview with a party leader conducted by Pinsuda Wonganan, September 2019.
54. Anyarat, "Social Media", pp. 173–74.
55. "When Alliances Bear Fruit", *Bangkok Post*, 9 February 2019.

56. "Pheu Thai Challenged with Disbandment, NCPO after FFP", *Bangkok Post*, 9 March 2019.
57. "TRC's Loss No Win for Pro-Regime Camp", *Bangkok Post*, 11 March 2019.
58. "Abhisit's Charm Offensive", *Bangkok Post*, 16 March 2019.
59. Details of the calculations for party list seats can be found at "Lakkaen lae witthikan kankhamnuan So. So. baeb banchi raichue" [Principles and methods of calculating party list MPs], https://www.ect.go.th/ect_th/news_all.php?cid=24.
60. Pavin Chachavalpongpun, "Fraud, Irregularities and Dirty Tricks", FORSEA [Forces of Renewal, Southeast Asia], May 2019, https://FORSEA.co; "Will Political Rats Follow the Prayuth Piper", *The Nation*, 27 March 2019.
61. The planned coalition had 255 seats and included Pheu Thai, Future Forward, Seri Ruam Thai, Prachachat, Puea Chat, Phalang Puangchon Thai and Setthakit Mai. See "Pheu Thai Announces 7-Party Coalition with 255 MPs", *Bangkok Post*, 27 March 2019.
62. "Election-Party-List Row Engulfs EC", *Bangkok Post*, 2 April 2019; "Election-Key Political Parties Attack 'Unfair' Party-List Formula", *Bangkok Post*, 8 April 2019.
63. The article, "Stop Salvo against FFP", *Bangkok Post*, 28 March 2019, summarizes a few of the complaints.
64. "Targeting FFP Boss Sets Bad Precedent", *Bangkok Post*, 2 May 2019.
65. While Thanathorn did not explain this reference, presumably it was an attempt to avoid charges of libel.
66. "PPRP to Sue Thanathorn over MP Poaching Claim", *Bangkok Post*, 17 May 2019.
67. "MP Freeze Order Irks FFP Boss", *Bangkok Post*, 24 May 2019.

Timor-Leste

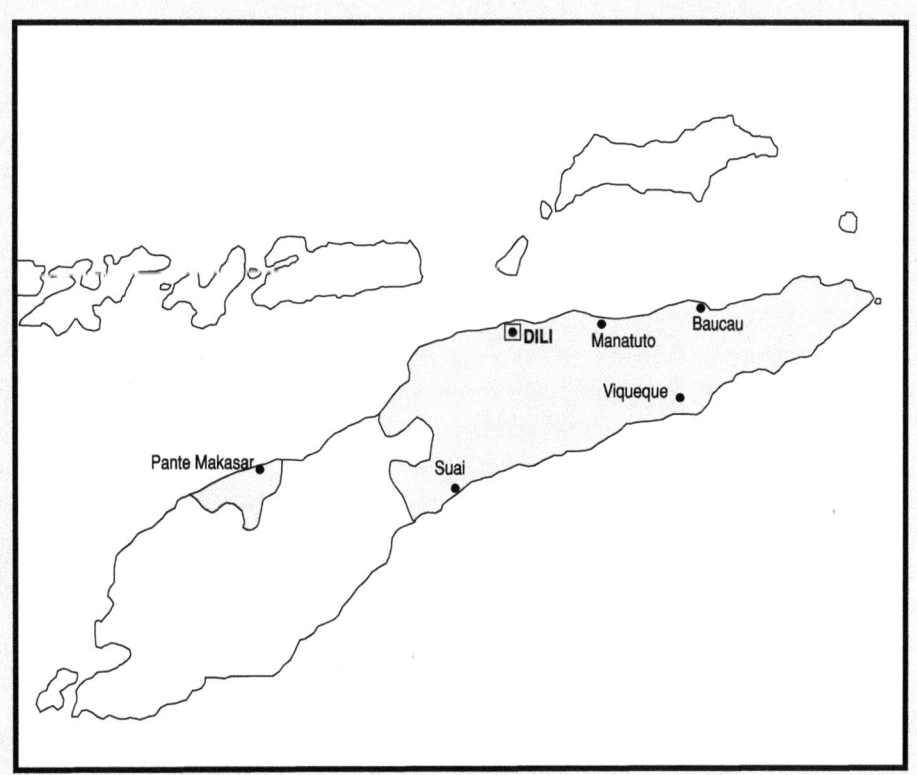

TIMOR-LESTE:
Twenty Years after the Self-Determination Referendum

Rui Graça Feijó

Frontiers and Sovereignty

On 30 August 2019, Timor-Leste commemorated the twentieth anniversary of the self-determination referendum when 98.6 per cent of registered voters chose by a very wide margin (78.5 versus 21.5 per cent) to break away from the Republic of Indonesia and open the way to independence. Since 20 May 2002, the Democratic Republic of Timor-Leste has been an independent country, recognized by the international community, and a member of the United Nations. High-ranking representatives from friendly nations headed to Dili for the celebrations. Amongst these, the Australian prime minister was a special guest.

Timor-Leste and Australia formally exchanged confirmation notes that brought to full fruition the treaty that had been negotiated in the preceding years, which was to put an end to the "Timor Gap" issue. The maritime borders of Timor-Leste were thus established after a turbulent period of negotiations and juridical claims in international courts. It was highly symbolic that the treaty could be signed in Dili on such a prominent date. In fact, the authorities of Timor-Leste, and chiefly the main negotiator, the once resistance leader, president of the republic (2002–7) and prime minister (2007–15), Xanana Gusmão, presented his efforts as destined to complete the recovery of sovereignty. He placed the agreement on par with the referendum, claiming that full sovereignty could only be achieved when the maritime borders were fixed for good and access to the

---

RUI GRAÇA FEIJÓ is Research Fellow at the Centre for Social Studies, University of Coimbra (contract supported by the Foundation for Science and Technology under the Transitional Provisions of Law 57/2016/CPO1341/CT0006) and Associate Researcher at the Institute for Contemporary History, NOVA University of Lisbon, Portugal.

plentiful natural resources—especially oil and natural gas—firmly placed at the disposal of the people of Timor-Leste. The East Timorese had a fundamental reason to rejoice.

At the time Timor-Leste became independent (20 May 2002), the country was among the poorest on Earth. The first time the United Nations Development Program Human Development Index included data on Timor-Leste (2004, with data for 2002), the country was ranked in 162nd place, included in the group of Low Human Development, with a rating of 0.436. Fifteen years later, Timor-Leste had moved to 132nd place and its performance had risen to 0.625, which permitted its inclusion in the group of Medium Human Development. Much of this tremendous improvement was due to the growth of the country's wealth. The World Bank estimates that the gross national product per capita (in purchasing power parity terms) rose from US$2,578 in 2003 to US$7,645 in 2018, having peaked at US$10,370 in 2012. An analysis of the yearly series shows that a significant jump was the result of the country beginning the exploitation of fossil fuels in the Timor Sea, and the fluctuations in this indicator are associated with the levels of oil production and its price on the world market. At present, Timor-Leste ranks among the countries in the world that depend most heavily on oil revenues.

The exploitation of fossil fuels was initially linked to the establishment of agreements between the governments of Timor-Leste and Australia in 2002–5, culminating in 2006. The treaty on "Certain Maritime Arrangements in the Timor Sea" (CMATS) was signed on 12 January 2006, and it provided for an equal share for both countries of the resources of the so-called Greater Sunrise oil field and for a 90/10 share of the Joint Petroleum Development Area (JPDA). The treaty also stipulated that both countries would refrain from border disputes or the settlement of permanent frontiers—an issue that divided these governments—for a period of fifty years, during which oil and gas reserves were supposed to be depleted.

However, in 2016 the authorities of Timor-Leste brought a case against Australia to the International Court of Justice in The Hague, claiming that in 2004–5 the Australians had negotiated in bad faith, on account of spying activities that had been uncovered. In the wake of this decision, Timor-Leste declared the treaty not to be valid, and negotiations were initiated under the United Nations Convention on the Law of the Sea (UNCLOS). These negotiations would eventually lead to the new treaty ratified by an exchange of notes in Dili on 30 August 2019, which stipulates a permanent and definitive frontier at the median line between the coasts of the two countries. It also grants a much larger share of the oil and gas fields to Timor-Leste.

The new treaty allows for an expectation of the extraction of fossil fuels for no less than twenty more years. The new fields are expected to yield at least 200 million barrels of crude and more than 5 trillion cubic feet of natural gas. Further investigation is currently under way in the region, and there is an expectation that more hydrocarbons will be discovered, both offshore and inland. The benefits of the known resources are to be shared between the two countries in a manner still to be decided, but already contemplated: if Timor-Leste manages to establish a processing plant in its territory, then the split will be 70/30 in its favour; however, if oil and gas are channelled to the Australian Northern Territory, then the split will be 80/20. In the fields under current exploitation, the peak extraction was attained in 2014 and has been declining since, although the rise in oil prices in the world market has somewhat disguised this downward turn in terms of wealth cashed by Timor-Leste.

The importance that Timor-Leste attributes to the strategic decisions to be made in relation to the Greater Sunrise hydrocarbons fields is mirrored in its decision to invest a substantial sum in the acquisition of shares in the consortium owned by Conoco-Phillips (30 per cent for US$350 million) and Shell (25.56 per cent for US$300 million). This move stirred controversy in Dili. President Lu Olo raised objections to the inclusion of this sum in the 2019 state budget, and the government then sidestepped those issues by financing it directly from the Petroleum Fund. Timor-Leste is also considering a very substantial investment in order to be in a position to install a processing plant on the south coast, and exploratory contacts are known to have been developed with prospective foreign investors. A substantial question mark still hangs over the wisdom and feasibility of such an enormous investment effort compared to the size of the currently known reserves to feed the venture.

To have an idea of the importance of hydrocarbons for Timor-Leste, a cursory glance at the "Petroleum Fund" established back in 2005 is revealing. The most recent figures for this fund (September 2019) indicate that it has now US$17.55 billion in assets. This amount corresponds roughly to twelve annual state budgets, which have hovered around US$1.5 billion in the last few years. The Petroleum Fund could grow faster if the local authorities limited the withdrawal of money to finance the state budget to the ESI—estimated sustained income (calculated on the basis of portions of new cash from oil plus revenues from financial investments). In fact, they have gone for sums well above the ESI. The state budget for 2019 anticipated two transfers from the Petroleum Fund: one amounting to US$533 million (36 per cent of the global budget) from ESI, and another US$667 million (45 per cent) *above* the ESI. However, its current level is testimony to the importance this sector plays in the livelihood of the country. The signing of the treaty was thus a fact of paramount importance for the future of Timor-Leste.

If the southern frontier has been thus established, the technicalities of the border negotiations with Indonesia mean that no final agreement has yet been met. In July, General Wiranto, on behalf of Indonesia, and Xanana Gusmão, representing Timor-Leste, issued a statement confirming the intention of both countries to settle the very small land disputes still on the table and to start working on the maritime limits (which have been impacted by the treaty with Australia) in order to have a final draft ready in 2020.

Relations with Indonesia remain peaceful and are not hindered by the delays on the frontier. Indonesia remains Timor-Leste's most significant economic partner (about a third of all imports come from the neighbour), and several Indonesian companies operate with success in the new country.

Timor-Leste made a highly symbolic gesture in August during the celebrations of the referendum: the public inauguration of a new bridge in Dili over the Bidau river named after the former Indonesian President B.J. Habibie. A few weeks later, as Habibie lay on his deathbed, Xanana Gusmão made a point of visiting him to thank him for the decision that allowed the referendum to be called. Although a private visit, it was widely reported on social media, with highly emotional images of Xanana embracing Habibie and weeping at his fast-approaching death. This episode epitomizes the state of good relations between the two countries—despite there being some pending issues, even of symbolic relevance, such as the refusal by the Indonesian authorities to disclose details about the death of resistance leader Nicolau dos Reis Lobato, shot while fighting in the mountains of Timor-Leste on 31 December 1978. Locating the whereabouts of his remains is still a major goal for the East Timorese.

The giant southern neighbour—Australia—also entertains good relations, as the signing of the maritime boundaries treaty epitomizes. However, Timor-Leste is campaigning very hard on behalf of the so-called "Witness K" and their attorney, Bernard Colleary. The two were instrumental in revealing the spying scandal of 2004–5 and they are now undergoing legal action at home. Timor-Leste insists the Australian authorities should drop the allegations levelled at them in order to finally put the incident to rest.

A Long Political Tug-of-War

The Constitution of the Democratic Republic of Timor-Leste (CRDTL) provides for a semi-presidential political system for the country. The basic feature of this kind of system is the twin election by universal, direct suffrage of the president of the republic and the national parliament, from which the prime minister emerges. Presidents of the country are not heads of government but share power with prime ministers, who are doubly responsible before the assembly and the head of state (CDRTL Section 107).[1] Presidential powers are not "executive" in most cases, as these are attributed to the government, although the concurrence of the head of state is necessary in matters of defence and security or in foreign relations. Presidents dispose of the *pouvoir d'empêcher* (the power to prevent) vis-à-vis the competences of government. This may be exercised through their prerogative to sign—or to veto—all legislation emanating from either the government or parliament, or through their discretionary power to nominate—or not to—individuals proposed by the government for a number of important positions in the public administration (military commanders, ambassadors, etc.). They also have some *pouvoir se statuer* (power of initiative), such as their capacity to address the nation or to summon a special meeting of the national parliament, where they can address it and make proposals. Presidents also have a free hand in appointing important public servants, including to the judiciary.

The duality of powers, based on individual strong legitimacies derived from direct popular suffrage, has been regarded in the literature as prone to generate instability when presidents and prime ministers come from different political families, as they may compete for the political agenda.[2] The first three presidential mandates after independence mostly avoided this pitfall, largely because of the fact that those presidents presented themselves to the electorate as "independent" figures without formal association with any political party, and thus capable of acting as "moderators" or "referees" in the political game.[3]

In 2017 the scenario changed with the election of Francisco Guterres Lu Olo, chairman of FRETILIN (Frente Revolucionária de Timor-Leste Independente; Revolutionary Front for an Independent Timor-Leste), as president of the republic. Even though he was elected with the backing of several parties—including Xanana's party, which was then in an informal coalition to form a "Government of National Inclusion" comprising all parliamentary parties—he chose to break with tradition and align his positions with those of his party.

The regular legislative election that followed Lu Olo's inauguration returned a hung parliament in which the president's party had the largest number of seats (23 out of 65). The president read the constitution, which states that the head of government is indicated by the largest party or coalition of parties (section 106), and appointed the leader of FRETILIN to form a government. Mari Alkatiri managed to engage the support of one party (Partido Democrático; Democratic Party) with 7 parliamentary seats, but this was not enough to overcome the opposition of the three other parties present in the 65-seat assembly. The opposition tabled and won a motion to reject the government's programme, and Mari Alkatiri became a caretaker prime minister. The law allows the prime minister to try a second reading of the government's programme, but Alkatiri could not alter the parliamentary arithmetic and preferred to fight an early election.

For the first time in Timor-Leste's history, the national parliament was dissolved and fresh elections called for May 2018. In these polls, a coalition of three parties—Xanana Gusmão's CNRT (Congresso Nacional para a Reconstrução de Timor-Leste; National Congress for the Reconstruction of Timor-Leste), Taur Matan Ruak's PLP (Partido da Libertação do Povo; People's Liberation Party) and KHUNTO (Kmanek Haburas Unidade Nasional Timor Oan; Enrich the National Identity of the Sons of Timor), the party of the "disenfranchised youth"—obtained the majority of seats (34). Lu Olo invited the coalition to nominate a prime minister, and so Taur Matan Ruak (who had been president of the republic between 2012 and 2017) was sworn in by the president and invested in parliament.

The new prime minister presented the president with a list of the proposed members of his government in June 2018. However, Lu Olo was of the opinion that a number of the individuals cited had insufficient "moral standing" to be made members of the government. He also argued some were under judicial investigation. Taur Matan Ruak, backed by all the coalition parties, refused to replace nine of the would-be ministers—including those named to important portfolios such as finance, health and natural resources—and insisted they be appointed. Up to December 2019, both actors have kept to their initial positions. Eighteen months into its term in office, the VIII Constitutional Government lacks nine ministers, almost all of them from Xanana's CNRT party. The largest party in the coalition (with 21 of its 34 seats) has thus a very small representation in the government. The would-be ministers are currently acting as "advisors" to the interim ministers holding the portfolios they were supposed to have, but they do not sit in the Council of Ministers. One of the CNRT's few ministers "coordinates" between the absent colleagues and those who are provisionally in their place. In the meantime, no judicial decision against any of the nine has been brought, reducing the president's room for manoeuvre. But his power to decide on who has the right to become a member of government is clearly stated in CRDTL (section 86h). In November, Prime Minister Taur Matan Ruak suggested that elections ought to take place in order to end the tug of war, but so far the president has not agreed to dissolve the national parliament for a second time in his first term in office.

This clear opposition between the president of the republic and the prime minister has other consequences. Arguing that a political stalemate prevents the country from running smoothly, the national parliament has refused to give its agreement to presidential trips abroad (CRDTL section 95h). Lu Olo filed for several authorizations; namely, to visit the Pope in Rome, to address the UN General Assembly in New York, to make a state visit to Portugal, and to attend a meeting of heads of state at the invitation of UN Secretary General António Guterres (who was the prime minister of Portugal at the time of the 1999 referendum and was critically involved in the process of Timorese self-determination).

The government also proposed to amend the law regulating the Special Administrative Zone of Social Market Economy in the enclave of Oecusse. This had been approved in 2013 and—without a constitutional amendment—attributed to the president the power to nominate its leader. Now, this power has been removed—and the president has sent the law to the Constitutional Court for review. He failed to stop the change, as the court ruled that this precise competence was not inscribed in the letter of the constitution. Mari Alkatiri, the leader of FRETILIN, who had been the chairman of that body since its inception, lost his position and was replaced by José Luís Guterres, appointed by the prime minister. Guterres has been a fellow traveller of Xanana Gusmão, a former member of FRETILIN, and the leader of a small party who has been an ally of CNRT.

The president, on his part, has withheld the appointment of a significant number of new ambassadors (CRDTL section 87b), thus depriving many embassies of a permanent high-ranking officer.

Political stalemate continues. Timor-Leste lives in times of uncertainty. This uncertainty, and the impediments to the current government that prevent it from performing at its optimum level, have severe implications for the well-being of the population. First, it impacts negatively on the process of democratic consolidation that requires the construction of a "common house", which is difficult to see taking place among the acrimony of the relevant political actors. Official institutions appear to be in a stage of shadow play: the real decisions are being made out of the sight of the people. But equally important is the economic impasse of this uncertainty.

In the meantime the solidity of the coalition sustaining the VIII Constitutional Government has been put to the test. The government approved a proposal for the 2020 state budget and submitted it to the national parliament. Among those who support the executive, and mainly in the seats occupied by CNRT and KHUNTO, voices were raised against the wisdom of having the second-largest budget in the history of the country. The opposition parties mostly stood by, allowing the fractures within the ruling coalition to grow. Faced with the likelihood of parliamentary defeat, the prime minister withdrew the document. A senior CNRT minister was tasked with preparing a more modest budget, which the cabinet approved and forwarded to the House. Full parliamentary procedures were then reinitiated, and the discussion and voting on the new budget slipped into 2020. For the time being the country will live with duodecimal instalments of the 2019 budget, although no withdrawal from the Petroleum Fund is contemplated.

Economy in Uncertain Times

The economy of Timor-Leste is suffering from the protracted period of uncertainty that followed the election of Lu Olo to the presidency. All major international institutions monitoring the evolution of this small economy converge on noting that they years 2017 and 2018 were marked by negative GDP growth rates. A World Bank report issued in late 2019 suggests the country has lost about US$350 million in forfeited growth over those two years.

The Asian Development Bank computed the growth rates for GDP per capita as −7 per cent (2017) and −2.3 per cent (2018). The International Monetary Fund found growth rates for real GDP to be −3.5 per cent (2017) and −0.2 per cent (2018). As for the World Bank, figures for the rate of growth of GDP per capita are −10.9 per cent (2017) and +0.8 (2018).

Two factors come into the picture: the declining stocks of hydrocarbons in JPDA (more visible in the curve of physical production than on that of financial gains because of the rise in prices) and, above all, the reduced capacity of public authorities to implement the policies agreed in the state budget. Government expenditure is a critical economic factor in a country where the primary sector—i.e., agriculture, forestry and fisheries—contributes less than 10 per cent to the wealth produced in a year (although it accounts for more than three quarters of the country's manpower), the secondary one—including hydrocarbons—close to 60 per cent, and the tertiary sector—services—where public spending is paramount, around a third. Fluctuations in public spending therefore affect severely the performance of the economy.

In the two preceding years, difficulties in enacting the state budget were regarded as important causes for the dire performance of public spending. This year, despite some issues over the state budget between the president and the national parliament, the budget was ready to be implemented early in the year. However, the coalition supporting the government has made several critical remarks on the president's decision not to appoint some ministers, holding him responsible for the inability of the government to execute the budget. In November, in a meeting destined to put pressure on the president and to discuss the implications of the economic performance for the 2020 state budget, the coalition admitted that perhaps not more than US$1 billion would be spent this year instead of the planned US$1.45 billion. The World Bank estimated that public spending would effectively grow compared with previous years, contributing to a modest increase of about 2 per cent in the GDP per capita in 2019

International institutions had predicted a significant growth of the economy for 2019. However, indicators available before the end of the year suggest otherwise. Public expenditure, even though it may be higher than in 2018, has remained below expectations, and foreign investment has mostly been put on hold. For instance, the announced cement factory in Baucau has not got off the ground, nor has significant investment in a tourist resort close to Dili taken place. The government, however, maintains the same economic strategy. Public mega-projects continue, both in Oecusse on the south coast and in the new port in Tibar, but their implementation is running slower than anticipated.

Regarding one aspect of public expenditure that has been criticized for being above sustainable levels—namely, the very generous pension schemes for veterans of the liberation struggle (amounting to 7 per cent of the state budget for 2019, the same as for health and agriculture combined, and an expense that will certainly be fully met)—the government has initiated a revision to its application. It is unclear whether this will be reflected in next year's budget.

Other Issues

The Catholic Church is an institution of critical importance in Timor-Leste, where 96.9 per cent of the population are self-classified as such.[4] As the CRDTL recognizes, "[i]n its cultural and humane perspective, the Catholic Church in East Timor has always been able to take on the suffering of all the People with dignity, placing itself on their side in the defence of their most fundamental rights." The state is officially secular, but in 2015 it signed a Concordat with the Vatican. Relations between the local Church and the Holy See have not always been peaceful over the last half-century, but right now they seem to be on a normal basis.

In this context, in September the Pope decided to upgrade the Diocese of Dili to the status of an archdiocese. The Bishop of Dili, the Salesian Virgilio do Carmo da Silva (born in Venilale in 1967), was promoted to metropolitan archbishop. The diocese was created in 1940, severing the ties it had with Macao, and covered the whole of the territory. After the Indonesian invasion, the diocese was placed under direct administration from Rome. In 1996, when the diocese was headed by Nobel Peace Prize laureate D. Carlos Filipe Ximenes Belo, it was divided in a move widely regarded as an attempt to curtail the prelate's influence, and a new one was created in Baucau. Later, the diocese of Maliana was also created from Dili's territory. Now the process has been essentially reversed, and the two more recent dioceses have become hierarchically dependent on the new archbishopric. All of them report directly to the Vatican, but the Apostolic Nuncio (the Vatican's ambassador, so to speak) is the same one that discharges this function in Indonesia, where he resides. The recent move can be interpreted as recognition of the influence the local Catholic Church has in the daily life of Timor-Leste.

The upgrading of the rank of the Catholic Church of Timor-Leste has been a contributing factor to strengthening the notion of the individuality of the country in the context of Southeast Asia. Not only is it the country with the highest percentage of Catholics in its population (above the 83 per cent of the Philippines), it has chosen Portuguese as an official language, together with Tetum. It also boasts its recent history of the struggle for self-determination and human rights, and its original decision to create simultaneously a new state administration over the ashes of the devastation that followed the announcement of the referendum results in 1999 and a democratic polity upholding the rule of law. Taken together, these characteristics configure a highly individualized country with a strong national identity.

Notes

1. For a discussion of Timorese semi-presidentialism, see Rui Graça Feijó, *Dynamics of Democracy in Timor-Leste: The Birth of a Democratic Nation 1999–2012* (Amsterdam: Amsterdam University Press, 2015).
2. See Robert Elgie, *Semipresidentialism: Sub-types and Democratic Performance* (Basingstoke: Palgrave Macmillan, 2011).
3. I expand on this issue in Rui Graça Feijó, "Dangerous Semi-presidentialism? On the Democratic Performance of Timor-Leste Government System", *Contemporary Politics* (2017), https://doi.org/10.1080/13569775.2017.1413504.
4. *Population and Housing Census of Timor-Leste, 2010*, vol. 3, *Social and Economic Characteristics*, p. xvi.

Vietnam

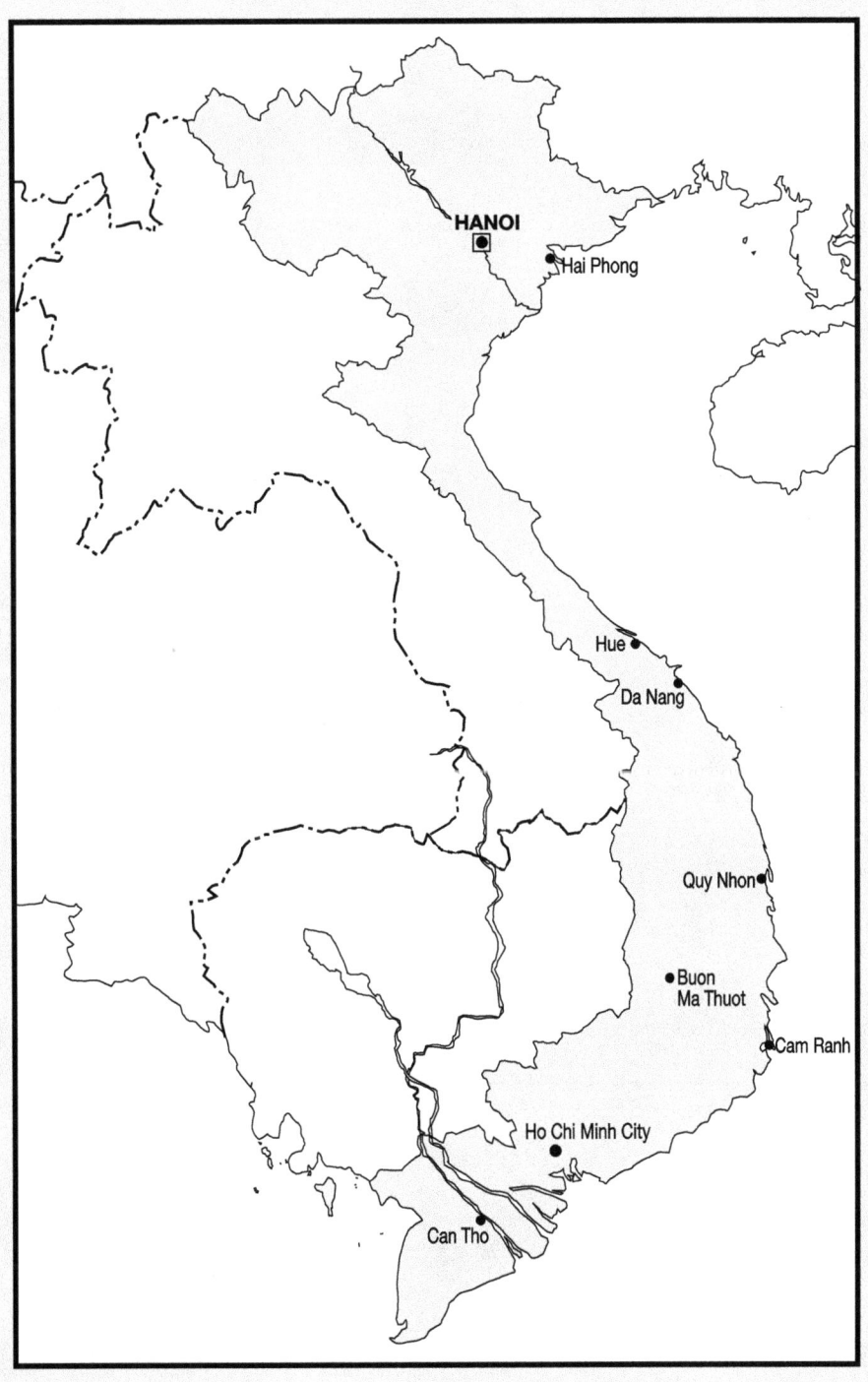

VIETNAM IN 2019:
A Return to Familiar Patterns

Paul Schuler and Mai Truong

While Vietnam is often proclaimed to be at a "crossroads", in retrospect the period between 2014 and 2016 was genuinely an inflection point. Given heightened anxiety over Chinese assertiveness in the South China Sea and a desire to join the Transpacific Partnership (TPP), Vietnam signalled a greater desire to side with the United States than ever before. This led to a flurry of high-profile visits of Vietnamese leaders to the United States as well as an unprecedented agreement to allow independent trade unions in exchange for TPP membership.[1] It also led to a reduction in political repression.

With President Donald Trump's decision in 2017 to pull out of the TPP, the dynamics have changed. Nearly three years after that decision, Vietnam has returned to its previous political and foreign policy orientations. As this chapter will discuss, the top contenders for power have returned to the previous hedging strategy of maintaining friendly ties with the United States while avoiding antagonizing China. The most likely successors to General Secretary Nguyen Phu Trong have maintained a generally balanced approach to political reforms and alignment with the United States. In short, it does not appear that there will be an elite-led liberalization on the horizon. If there is a question about significant elite-led political reforms in Vietnam, it is whether it is going to further centralize power in the hands of the party. On this question, we also believe that Vietnam is likely to revert to its previous collective-leadership pattern.

Although party-led political reform is largely off the table, this does not mean social pressures that could possibly force change from the outside have remained static. A number of important developments continue to challenge the

---

PAUL SCHULER is Assistant Professor of political science at the University of Arizona.

MAI TRUONG is a doctoral candidate in political science at the University of Arizona.

regime. On the South China Sea, Vietnam's relationship with China continues to represent a volatile mobilizing issue for collective action. The environment also remains a potent social concern. Additionally, social media continues to inject a new dynamic into these issues, providing both the opportunity for citizens to challenge the regime but at the same time allowing the regime to respond more quickly and shift blame to local governments.

In addition to these social issues, the structure of Vietnam's economy also continues to change in important ways that provide opportunities and challenges for the regime. Foreign direct investment surged in the wake of US trade disputes with China, and economic growth remains robust. At the same time, the trade wars may not have had a universally beneficial effect. In particular, farmers, who rely more heavily on the Chinese market than on the United States, have suffered a decline in imports from China, damaging their profits.[2] Additionally, although the tragedy involving thirty-nine Vietnamese citizens in the United Kingdom has complex roots, it has brought attention to potential differences in economic conditions outside Vietnam's major industrial areas. A final important economic change is the continued rise of large domestic conglomerates, particularly Vingroup, which has generated increased attention, both positive and negative, from political elites and civil society.

This chapter reviews each of these developments. It focuses first on elite politics in the wake of the lost opportunity of 2015 and 2016. It then turns to the major issues inflaming public opinion, including the South China Sea and the environment. Finally, the chapter focuses on the structure of Vietnam's economy and the degree to which the rising tide continues to lift all boats. In particular, it will look at whether the trade war and Vietnam's growth have disproportionately impacted urban versus rural areas. The overarching message from this review is that while elite politics and management of dissent has returned to the pre-TPP equilibrium, social and economic changes may challenge that pattern.

Politics: A Return to Familiar Patterns

Prior to the 2016 Party Congress, political change seemed a real possibility. In part because of Chinese pressure in the South China Sea, Vietnam was more firmly committed than ever to joining the TPP. The greater degree of alignment towards the United States was most explicitly evidenced by unprecedented US visits from General Secretary Trong and then minister of public security Tran Dai Quang. The most important concrete political concession included the decision to allow the formation of independent trade unions. Additionally, the ongoing negotiations compelled Vietnam to relax political repression. Between 2013 and 2015, while Vietnam was negotiating the agreement with the United States, it reduced the number of political arrests.[3]

This changed in January 2017 when Trump pulled out of the TPP. This was a momentous decision for Vietnam because US pressure was the key to the political reforms. With US pressure and leverage removed, the trade union side agreement and heightened tolerance of dissent disappeared. In terms of political repression, the number of dissident arrests returned to previous levels.[4] Some notable arrests in 2019 included former party member and blogger Pham Chi Dung,[5] lawyer Tran Vu Hai,[6] and blogger Truong Duy Nhat.[7] In sum, despite some suggestions that Vietnam continues to liberalize its politics,[8] in many ways Vietnam is back where it started with regards to its treatment of dissidents and organized civil society. As a former US ambassador to Vietnam said: "[Pulling out of the TPP] pulled out the rug from under the reformers."[9]

With regard to elite politics, the big question heading into 2019 was whether Vietnam would follow the Chinese model of centralizing power under the party. Since Doi Moi, Vietnam has differed from China in that the prime minister in Vietnam has far greater independence from the general secretary than is the case in China, particularly with regard to the management of the economy and social service delivery.[10] The Vietnamese Communist Party (VCP) signalled a potential desire to move in China's direction in 2018 by selecting Trong to simultaneously hold the positions of general secretary and president after President Tran Dai Quang's death.

The key question emerging from this change was whether this decision signalled a conscious desire to centralize power or if it was simply a matter of expedience.[11] While many argued that Trong was never likely to centralize power to the same degree as Xi Jinping, it is important to note that the decision to merge the positions did not occur in a vacuum. When the decision was made, the VCP was also carrying out a series of experiments led by Politburo member and Central Organization Committee chair Pham Minh Chinh to streamline the party-state apparatus. Chinh, for example, supported merging the district and commune People's Committee chairs with the party secretary positions. He also advocated for the elimination of People's Councils at the district level, an experiment that was tried and rejected by the National Assembly (VNA)[12] but which has since been revived as a possibility in urban areas.[13] In this context, the "unification" (*nhất thể hoá*) of the presidency and the position of general secretary was likely seen by some in the regime as part of a larger effort to follow the Chinese centralized management model.

The possibility that unification would remain permanent at the national level received a blow when Trong fell ill because of what was likely a stroke suffered during a visit to Kien Giang Province on 14 April 2019.[14] While the regime has been characteristically silent on the source or severity of the illness, Trong has made fewer public appearances since his illness,[15] which has possibly slowed the pace of his signature anti-corruption campaign.[16] His illness also throws into doubt the unification project. Although it is impossible to know at this stage whether unification will continue and whether the presidency and the position of general secretary will remain combined, a few pieces of evidence suggest that unification may face serious setbacks.

First, the VNA, largely at the behest of the government, strengthened the institutional position of the prime minister. In particular, the revised law on the Organization of the Government grants the prime minister the power to direct the human resource management in government administrative agencies as well as public service institutions. According to the revised law, the prime minister also has authority in establishing, merging and dissolving other agencies under provincial People's Committees.[17] Alongside the strengthening of the prime minister's position, VNA chair Ngan also oversaw legislation bolstering the ability of the VNA to oversee infrastructure projects proposed by the government.[18]

While some may consider this evidence of political liberalization,[19] our interpretation is that the VNA is an arm of the party apparatus designed to check the state.[20] From this perspective, the simultaneous strengthening of the prime minister's office and the VNA's oversight duties could signal that Vietnam is returning to its previous pattern of having a relatively independent prime minster checked by the party through the VNA. This, of course, would go against the "unification" push. What does this mean for the party congress in 2021? The simultaneous strengthening of the authority of the VNA adds further support to the notion that rather than consolidating power under a powerful general secretary, Vietnam will continue to have a relative balance between the prime minister and the general secretary. Furthermore, we should expect that the VNA will continue to play a role in overseeing the prime minister and the office of the government on behalf of the general secretary and the party.

Hedging on the South China Sea

Outside of elite politics, perhaps no issue impacts more areas of concern—from economics to security to mass mobilization—than the South China Sea. The issue of the South China Sea and the broader relationship with China place regime elites in a delicate position, where some desire increased cooperation with China to take advantage of Chinese investment and trade. At the same time, elites are keen to avoid the appearance of seeming too close to China, for fear they will look subservient to a country that inspires animosity amongst many in Vietnam.

That said, some recent works suggest that we should not take this anti-Chinese sentiment as a given. In the past few years, a number of studies have argued that the historical rivalry between the two sides is overblown, and that Chinese hegemony may even be welcomed in Vietnam and the region.[21] While it is a matter of debate as to whether the ancestors of those living in present-day Vietnam harboured resentment towards China, survey results from the Asian Barometer Survey between 2014 and 2016 show that the Vietnamese people have the lowest approval rating of China in East Asia. Furthermore, the differential in approval between the United States and China is also the widest in East Asia. This survey evidence is consistent with the speed with which anti-Chinese protests spread in 2014 and again in 2018. In short, whatever the nature of the historic relationships between the political entities in the Red River delta and their neighbours to the north, the distrust Vietnamese feel towards China in present-day Vietnam appears real.

The economic dependency and public mistrust generates a complex balancing act for regime elites. The explosion of the SEZ issue in 2018 perfectly encapsulates Vietnam's dilemma in managing the relationship. The issue emerged in June when the VNA considered a bill to allow special economic zones in three provinces in Vietnam. The most controversial element of the proposal was to allow foreign companies the ability to lease land for ninety-nine years in the strategically important Quang Ninh, Khanh Hoa and Kien Giang provinces. Supporters of the proposal, like Chinh, promoted the SEZ law in order to attract investment to their provinces.[22] However, they were forced to distance themselves from the project once protests spilled on to the streets. Despite this setback, commentators in Vietnam still acknowledge the need to establish a stable economic relationship with China, given that China provides an important market and source for processed materials that the Vietnamese export-oriented industries depend on.[23] These competitive incentives suggest that Vietnam is likely to face similar protests in the future.

Though not nearly as contentious as in 2018, the regime's dilemma vis-à-vis China was again exposed in July 2019 as China challenged Vietnam's ability to engage in oil and gas exploration in its own Exclusive Economic Zone (EEZ). In an echo of the 2014 oil rig crisis, which also sparked nationwide protests, China again inflamed nationalist sentiments by moving an oil exploration rig in a zone near current Vietnamese drilling operations. More problematically,

FIGURE 1
Public Sentiment towards the United States and China in East Asia

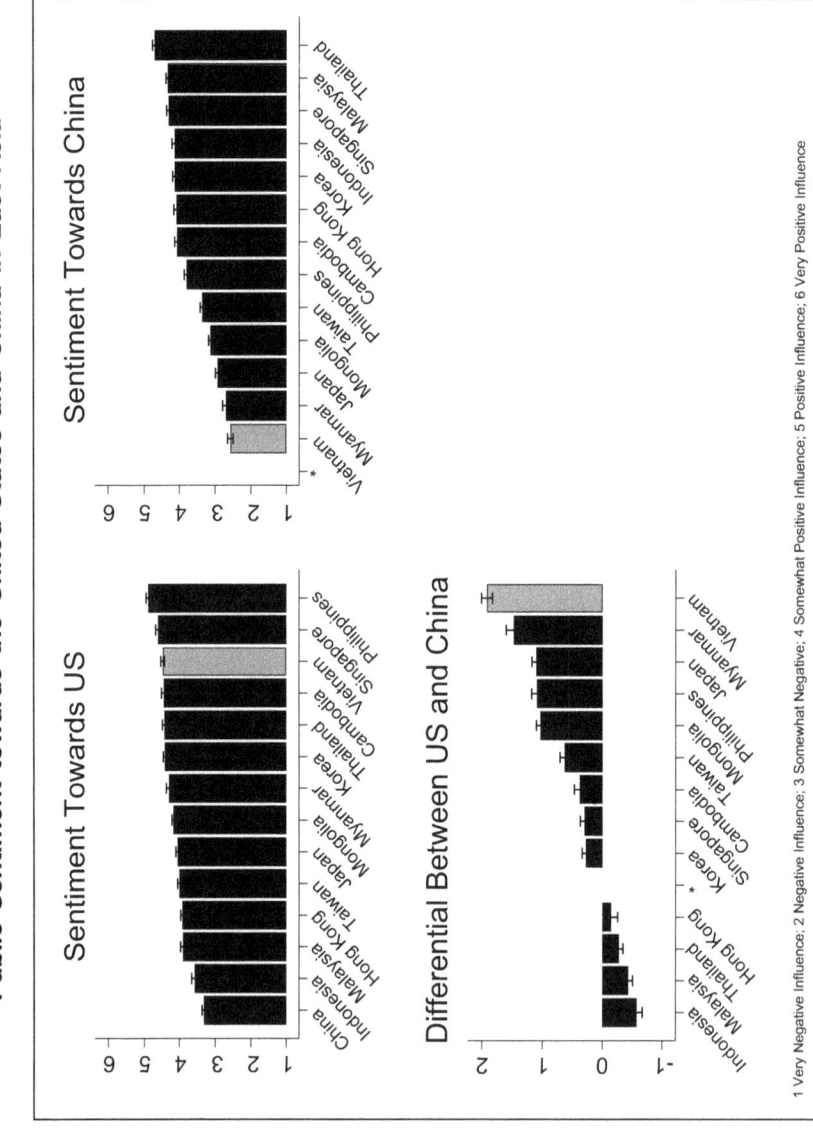

1 Very Negative Influence; 2 Negative Influence; 3 Somewhat Negative; 4 Somewhat Positive Influence; 5 Positive Influence; 6 Very Positive Influence

Note: Data from the 4th Wave of the Asian Barometer Survey taken from 2014 to 2016. The question asked whether China or the United States had a positive or negative influence in your country. The black lines indicate 95 per cent confidence intervals.

a Chinese coastguard vessel also harassed a Japanese oil rig that was drilling on behalf of Vietnam's joint venture with Russia's Rosneft. The Chinese vessel left in October, claiming to have completed its duties, but the Japanese rig had also left by then.[24]

Some Vietnamese officials speculated that China's goal in the standoff was to expand the zone of what is considered "disputed" territory as China pushes for a revised Code of Conduct in the South China Sea.[25] While the Spratly Islands chain and the Paracel Islands remain contested, the most recent incident, like the 2014 crisis, took place within two hundred miles of Vietnam's coast. Vietnam obviously does not want to concede this territory as "contested", as it is only disputed to the extent to which China's nine-dash line is deemed legitimate or to the extent that the disputed Spratly Islands are deemed to have their own EEZs. The UN Convention on the Law of the Seas (UNCLOS) tribunal struck down both of these claims in July 2016.

Regardless of Chinese motivations, the manner in which Vietnam approached the standoff and the result of the dispute reveal several differences between the situations in 2019 and 2014. In 2014, Vietnam took a relatively robust approach to opposing China when then prime minister Nguyen Tan Dung suggested Vietnam might take legal action.[26] In contrast, throughout the 2019 dispute, Vietnam maintained close contact with Beijing and continued to make several high-level visits to Beijing.[27] Unlike in 2014, Vietnam was also unable to force China to remove its vessel until it too had ceased operations in the area.

The regime's approach in 2019 has implications for Vietnam's relationship with both China and the United States. Although General Secretary Trong and Prime Minister Phuc consistently emphasized Vietnam's firm commitment to protecting Vietnam's sovereignty in the South China Sea, they were less aggressive in inviting US involvement in the issue. While Trong and Minister of Defense Tran Dai Quang visited the United States after the 2014 incident, in 2019 Vietnam instead took important measures to reassure China that it is not considering dramatically altering its military relationship with the United States. Indeed, in November it released a defence White Paper reaffirming its commitment to the "Three No's" policy of no foreign bases, no military alliances and no siding with one country against another. This is largely perceived as a measure to reassure China that Vietnam is not looking to join the United States as a military ally.[28]

In sum, despite intense public animosity towards China, Vietnamese leaders have largely returned to a strategy of attempting to reassure China while retaining the ability to drill in areas within its EEZ. Much like the developments in elite politics, this represents a return to normal.

Environmental Concerns: The Emergence of Post-Materialist Vietnam?

While elite politics and international issues have returned to previous patterns, Vietnamese society is changing in important ways, which may challenge the status quo. In this section, we discuss how environmental challenges continue to pose an important concern capable of galvanizing anti-regime dissent. Protests against the "tree-felling" project in urban Hanoi in 2017 and against a massive fish kill in coastal provinces in 2016 are prominent examples showing that concerns over the environment may mobilize citizens and challenge the legitimacy of the party.

Consistent with Inglehart and Welzel's notion of "post-materialist values",[29] Vietnamese citizens are increasingly concerned with environmental issues. The fish kill crisis of course played a key role in galvanizing citizen concern about the issue. A recent UNDP report, for example, shows that 6.5 per cent of the population in 2018 thought that the environment was the most important issue facing Vietnam. This represented a sustained increase from about 2 per cent in 2015.[30] In addition to the fish crisis, the increase could result from other severe environmental issues facing Vietnam such as in the Mekong Delta, where droughts, diminished water flows and rising sea levels present a triple threat to Vietnam's fruit and rice basket.[31]

In 2019, while there were no major disasters, the issue continued to simmer, showing the continued potency of environmental concerns. The ability of relatively isolated environmental events to spark collective action reveals how social media has helped to channel greater attention to environmental concerns. In the last quarter of 2019, Hanoi witnessed two pollution issues, including the contamination of tap water in southeast Hanoi and a fire at a light bulb factory in Thanh Xuan district, also near Hanoi. The tap water issue impacted approximately 250,000 households in the southeast section of the capital city.[32] The light bulb factory fire damaged approximately six thousand square metres of the warehouses of the Rang Dong Light Source Vacuum Flask JSC, creating serious pollution problems for nearby residents.[33]

The responses to these incidents show the importance of social media in shaping collective action and regime responses to these incidents. On 10 October 2019, residents in southeast Hanoi posted on Facebook about a strange smell similar to burned plastic bags in their tap water. Immediately, state media reported that the central government had ordered the government of Hanoi to investigate the problem. Social media clearly provided citizens with an avenue to raise their concerns and mobilize public sentiment. At the same time, it served as a good monitoring tool for the government. Because social media helped residents in the affected areas to report on issues affecting them in real time, both the central and local governments were able to respond to the challenges more quickly than they could have otherwise. Similarly, after the fire at Rang Dong factory on 28 August 2019, residents posted videos and information on social media, drawing considerable attention from the public. Such attention motivated the local government to respond quickly to residents' concerns by immediately issuing official health warnings.

These incidents also revealed the party's tactics in protecting its legitimacy in the face of environmental crises. Upon being informed of the issues, the central government shifted the blame to the local governments via state media. Many high-ranking leaders in the central government directed public attention to the local government's weaknesses in handling essential public services in times of difficulties, including their lack of timely response to residents' concerns and the lack of transparency in decision-making and information sharing.

For example, it took five days after residents reported the pollution in their tap water for the government of Hanoi to confirm that the water was contaminated. One day later, the Song Da Water Investment Joint Stock Company (Viwasupco), which is responsible for supplying water to the area, announced that it would stop providing water to residents until the system was cleaned. The chairman of the Office of the Government, Mai Tien Dung, criticized the Hanoi local government for failing to provide adequate and timely accommodation to residents' needs.[34] In addition to the slow response, the local government was accused of not being transparent in how it handled the situation, especially in terms of information sharing. Regarding the fire at Rang Dong company, while the immediate local government was quick in responding to residents' concerns, there was disagreement within the government on how to handle the crisis. On 30 August, the People's Committee of Thanh Xuan District ordered the ward to withdraw the health warnings, stating that such advice on potential health risks were groundless and were issued without consultation with higher authorities.[35]

In sum, these two pollution issues show that collective actions around environmental issues will continue to pose a threat to the party's legitimacy. At the same time, these challenges have shown the party's tactics and capability in utilizing social media—a seemingly threatening tool—to protect its legitimacy.

Economy: Does the Rising Tide Lift All Boats?

From a macro-level perspective, Vietnam's economy performed well in 2019. Although projected to see a slight decrease from 2018, the GDP growth rate should remain above six per cent.[36] Vietnam also attracted more foreign direct investment (FDI), in part thanks to the US-China trade war, which has led to greater investment in manufacturing facilities from its Asian neighbours. At the local level, Hanoi and Binh Duong have been the greatest beneficiaries of the increased investment.[37] All these indicators point to a robust economy.

Despite the relatively rosy picture, a number of concerns remain. As several analysts have noted, Vietnam remains ill-equipped to fully realize the benefits of the trade war because of its low-skilled labour force,[38] which remains primarily employed in the agricultural sector.[39] Additionally, the tragic death of thirty-nine migrants in the United Kingdom in October highlighted a possible concern that Vietnam's economic growth is not distributed equitably throughout the country. Because most of the migrants were from the relatively poor Yen Thanh Commune in Nghe An, one narrative from the international media on this incident held that the migrants were driven to the United Kingdom by the dire economic conditions outside of Hanoi, possibly made worse by the fish kill crisis in north central Vietnam.[40] Indeed, some basic facts are consistent with this narrative. According to 2016 data from the Vietnam Statistics Department, Nghe An is the tenth poorest province in Vietnam on a per capita basis, although Ha Tinh is closer to the national average.

Other accounts tell a more complex story of the tragedy, suggesting that it is not the simple fact of poverty that drove the migrants. Indeed, as other studies of migration to Europe have shown, it is not the poorest residents but rather the middle class of developing countries who are most likely to migrate.[41] While this is not true of all migration flows, it is a better explanation for Vietnamese migration. The simple reason for this is that the journey from Vietnam to Europe along the smuggler routes costs thousands of dollars, a sum not available to the poorest of the poor. In short, it is only because of the improving economic situation in north central Vietnam that its residents are able to afford the perilous journey to Europe.

With all that said, it is worth considering whether economic growth has been distributed equitably, and whether conditions in rural areas are perceived differently than in urban areas. There are some suggestions that the economic gains in 2019 may not have accrued to rural agricultural communities to the same degree they have for labourers and urbanites. Perspectives on this are mixed. Some highlighted the unusually good harvest, which drove up rural incomes, while others have noted that China's imposition of more stringent food standards have dramatically increased the difficulty of exporting agricultural products to what had previously been seen as an "easy" low-standards export market.[42] For example, fruits, which used to be packed in straw, now require foam packaging.[43]

A simple measure to assess the potentially diverging prospects in rural and urban Vietnam is the level of economic satisfaction by employment sector. If the economy is booming for all residents, then we should see parallel trends in the level of economic satisfaction. Using data from the UNDP's PAPI survey, Figure 2 shows that from 2013 to 2018 both agricultural and non-agricultural workers saw similar improvements in their personal economic situations. Although agricultural workers reported a lower overall level of economic satisfaction, their improving assessments have largely tracked those of non-agricultural workers.

This trend however diverged in 2019, when non-agricultural workers maintained their assessment of an improving economic situation, while agricultural workers saw no improvement. This suggests that after the record harvest of 2018, perhaps the trade war, environmental factors, tightening market access restrictions in China, or decreasing land availability are indeed impinging on the growth of Vietnam's most important employment sector. One year, however, could be a blip, so this indicator will bear watching in the coming years.

Vietnamese Conglomerates: A Force for Good?

A final economic development of importance is the rise of large domestic enterprises in Vietnam, some of which have been increasingly investing abroad.[44] Some of these companies, such as the military-owned Viettel, have managed to become globally competitive.[45] Others, such as the private Vingroup—which is primarily focused on real estate but is rapidly expanding into other sectors such as car manufacturing, healthcare and education—have also cracked into international lists of major global companies.[46]

A key question is the impact of the rise of these companies on economic development, politics and society in Vietnam. Some see large conglomerates like Vingroup as the key to Vietnam's development. No one, for example, seems more enamoured with Vingroup than Prime Minister Phuc, who attended the opening ceremony of the Vinfast factory in 2017. Since then, he, along with General Secretary Trong and VNA chair Ngan, has made several additional visits to the factory, with Phuc praising the company's contribution to Vietnam's economic development.[47] Indeed, it is easy to see why there is so much hope for Vingroup, given its enormous capital resources and Vietnam's need for technological upgrading.

Despite this hope, there are several concerns surrounding the rise of Vingroup and other state-linked firms. First, there are concerns that large corporations like the state-linked Viettel and the privately owned Vingroup are using privileged access to the government to crowd out investment from small and medium-sized

FIGURE 2
Pocketbook Economic Satisfaction by Employment Sector

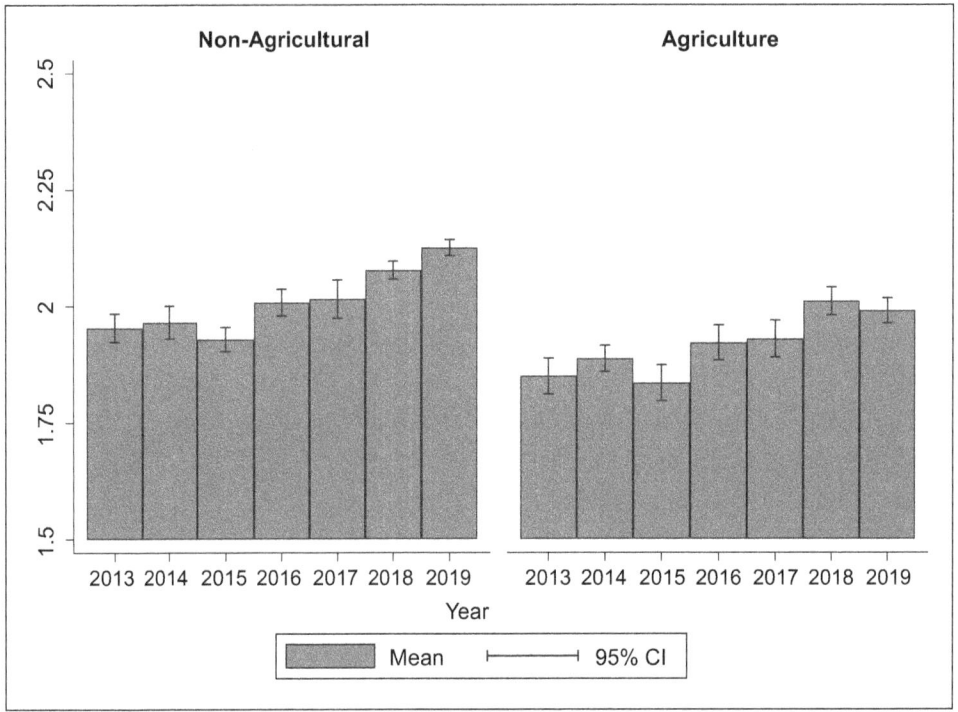

Note: The data is from the 2019 PAPI survey (PAPI 2020). The survey question asked whether the respondent's economic situation is 0 = "Very Bad"; 1 "Bad"; 2 "Normal"; 3 "Good", 4 "Very Good". Panel 1 includes all respondents working in non-agricultural professions and Panel 2 agricultural workers.

companies.[48] The same concern has been levied against state-owned enterprises (SOEs), with the major difference now being that a large private conglomerate is drawing the attention. There is also the related issue of Vingroup relying on its access to the state in order to gain market share in Vietnam without having to sharpen its business efficiency to compete globally. To date, Vingroup has proven profitable in its real estate enterprises. Despite its stated ambitions to be globally competitive in the tech and auto sectors, it remains to be seen whether it will realize these ambitions.

On this question, a recent book comparing growth trajectories in East and Southeast Asia offers some potential insights. As Studwell lays out in his 2014 analysis of South Korea and Malaysia, while both countries started their paths to development by devoting private capital to large real estate and construction firms, only South Korea was able to use these resources to nurture globally competitive companies.[49] He credits then president Park Chung Hee with forcing South Korean *chaebols* to compete for state benefits by proving their competitiveness on the export market. By contrast, Malaysia did not force its steel and auto conglomerates to compete, and they have never been able to expand internationally. Applied to Vietnam, the question is whether Vingroup will be able to make the transition from real estate to higher-value-added industries. It remains to be seen whether Vingroup can buck this trend or if it will face domestic competition.

Aside from concerns about the economic impact of the increasing dominance of Vingroup, other critics have focused on the social and political effects of the rise of the company. In particular, given the strong state control of the media, many have expressed concern that Vingroup's close connections to the regime allow it to stifle any criticism of the company, thus potentially shielding the company from any accountability.[50] Some dissidents in Vietnam have reportedly faced trouble for questioning the price Vingroup has paid to acquire and develop state-owned land.[51]

Regardless of which scenario plays out, what seems clear is that Vietnam's development will be impacted to a great degree not only by the efficiency of Vietnam's SOEs but also increasingly by how Vingroup and other real estate conglomerates use their vast wealth and connections.

Conclusion

Our major contention is that, in many respects, 2019 represented a return to familiar patterns. Vietnam has reaffirmed its long-standing neutral foreign policy, and remains steadfastly committed to reforming its political system without allowing any political challenger to the Vietnamese Communist Party to emerge. While the confluence of the TPP negotiations and Chinese aggression in the South China Sea has threatened to upend that pattern in previous years, the demise of the TPP has allowed Vietnam to revert to its previous political strategies. At the same time, as this chapter lays out, other developments outside of the party's control have evolved in ways that will continue to challenge the party. In particular, the environment is increasingly an issue of concern capable of mobilizing collective action. More importantly, nationalism and the South China Sea disputes with China are only increasing in their salience to the Vietnamese population. As the issue becomes more heated, the VCP, which has long touted its nationalist credentials, will increasingly find itself pressured to take a harder line on China, while seeking to preserve its vital economic relationship with the country. This will prove all the more difficult for Vietnam as China is not shy about using economic leverage to achieve strategic aims.

Economically, Vietnam has benefited in the short term from the trade war in terms of foreign direct investment. What remains to be seen is whether the country can upgrade its labour force and move its industrial production higher up the value chain. While the state has some responsibility for this, particularly in the realm of education, Vietnam's economic future will also increasingly depend on efforts by large domestic corporations to translate their market influence into increased productivity, rather than securing rent. More so than in the past, Vietnam's large private sector will have a huge hand in determining the economic trajectory of the country.

Notes

1. Simon Denver and David Nakamura, "Ripple Effect: How A Trump Administration Decision on Trade Became a Setback for Democracy in Vietnam", *Washington Post*, 11 October 2018, https://www.washingtonpost.com/graphics/2018/world/how-a-trump-decision-on-trade-became-a-setback-for-democracy-in-vietnam/; "Vietnam Was Set for Reform – Until Trump Cancelled a Trade Deal", *Washington Post*, 21 October 2018, https://www.washingtonpost.com/opinions/vietnam-was-set-for-reform--until-trump-canceled-a-trade-deal/2018/10/21/ff9d78e8-d0b4-11e8-8c22-fa2ef74bd6d6_story.html; Mike Ives, "The US Ambassador Who Crossed Trump on Immigration", *New York Times*, 7 September 2018, https://www.nytimes.com/2018/09/07/world/asia/ted-osius-trump-vietnam-ambassador.html.
2. "Vì sao nông sản nhận 'quả đắng' từ thị trường TQ?", BBC Vietnam, 24 October 2019, https://www.bbc.com/vietnamese/vietnam-50162998.
3. Denyer and Nakamura, "Ripple Effect".
4. John Boudreau. "Amnesty Urges U.S. to Press Vietnam on Rights as Arrests Rise", Bloomberg, 12 May 2019, https://www.bloomberg.com/news/articles/2019-05-13/amnesty-asks-u-s-to-press-vietnam-on-rights-amid-rising-arrests.
5. An Hai, "Vietnam Arrests Prominent Blogger Pham Chi Dung", Voice of America, 22 November 2019, https://www.voanews.com/east-asia-pacific/vietnam-arrests-prominent-blogger-pham-chi-dung.
6. "Vietnamese Lawyer Who Offered to Defend Dissident Blogger is Sentenced to Term of House Arrest", Radio Free Asia, 15 November 2019, https://www.rfa.org/english/news/vietnam/sentenced-11152019155826.html.
7. "RFA Blogger Who Disappeared in Bangkok is Being Held in Hanoi, Says Daughter", Radio Free Asia, 20 March 2019, https://www.rfa.org/english/news/vietnam/blogger-hanoi-03202019175732.html.
8. Pham Duy Nghia, "The Puzzles of Political Reform in Vietnam", *East Asia Forum*, 12 November 2019, https://www.eastasiaforum.org/2019/11/12/the-puzzles-of-political-reform-in-vietnam/.

9. Denyer and Nakamura, "Ripple Effect".
10. Edmund Malesky, Regina Abrami, and Yu Zheng, "Institutions and Inequality in Single-Party Regimes: A Comparative Analysis of Vietnam and China", *Comparative Politics* 43, no. 4 (2011): 409–27; Paul Schuler and Mai Truong, "Leadership Reshuffle and the Future of Vietnam's Collective Leadership", *ISEAS Perspective*, no. 2019/9, 22 February 2019.
11. For a different perspective, see Schuler and Mai Truong, "Leadership Reshuffle".
12. Chu Thanh Van, "Dừng thí điểm không tổ chức Hội đồng Nhân dân huyện quận, phường" [Halting the experiment to dissolve district and ward people's councils], *Vietnam+*, 30 March 2016, https://www.vietnamplus.vn/dung-thi-diem-khong-to-chuc-hoi-dong-nhan-dan-huyen-quan-phuong/378816.vnp.
13. Hoang Thuy and Anh Minh, "Đề xuất không tổ chức HĐND cấp phường ở TP HCM" [Proposal to disband district people's councils in Ho Chi Minh City", *VietnamNet*, 29 October 2019, https://vnexpress.net/thoi-su/de-xuat-khong-to-chuc-hdnd-cap-phuong-o-tp-hcm-4004113.html.
14. Hai Hong Nguyen, "Who Will be Vietnam's Next Party Boss", *East Asia Forum*, 18 November 2019, https://www.eastasiaforum.org/2019/11/18/who-will-be-vietnams-next-party-boss/.
15. David Hutt, "Is Vietnam's Trong Still Going Strong?", *The Diplomat*, 27 September 2019, https://thediplomat.com/2019/09/is-vietnams-trong-still-going-strong/; Ha Hoang Hop and Lye Liang Fook, "Change Awaits Vietnam's Leadership", *ISEAS Commentaries*, 2019/37, 29 April 2019, https://www.iseas.edu.sg/medias/commentaries/item/9563-change-awaits-vietnams-leadership-by-ha-hoang-hop-and-lye-liang-fook.
16. David Dapice, "Is Vietnam Swimming Naked?", *East Asia Forum*, 21 July 2019, https://www.eastasiaforum.org/2019/07/21/is-vietnam-swimming-naked/.
17. Communist Party of Vietnam, "Quốc hội tăng quyền cho Thủ tướng", 23 November 2019, http://dangcongsan.vn/nong-trong-ngay/quoc-hoi-tang-quyen-cho-thu-tuong-543430.html.
18. Pham Chi Dung, "Từ 'tăng quyền cho Thủ tướng' đến 'thêm quyền cho Quốc hội'" [From 'increasing the prime minister's power' to 'adding power for the National Assembly'], Voice of America, 4 June 2019, https://www.voatiengviet.com/a/từ-tăng-quyền-cho-thủ-tướng-đến-thêm-quyền-cho-quốc-hội-/4944264.html.
19. Pham Duy Nghia, "The Puzzles of Political Reform".
20. Paul Schuler, "Position Taking or Position Ducking? A Theory of Public Debate in Single Party Legislatures", *Comparative Political Studies* (2018).
21. David Kang. *American Grand Strategy and East Asian Security in the Twenty-first Century* (Cambridge University Press, 2017); Keith Taylor, *A History of the Vietnamese* (York: Cambridge University Press, 2013).
22. Cat Linh, "Phạm Minh Chính và Đặc khu Vân Đồn", Radio Free Asia, 19 June

2018, https://www.rfa.org/vietnamese/in_depth/pham-minh-chinh-and-van-don-sez-part1-06192018143537.html.

23. Le Hong Hiep, "Vietnam's Infrastructure Development Dilemma: The China Factor", *ISEAS Commentaries*, 2017/82, 8 October 2019, https://www.iseas.edu.sg/medias/commentaries/item/10494-vietnams-infrastructure-development-dilemma-the-china-factor-by-le-hong-hiep; Lam Thanh Ha, "Chinese FDI in Vietnam: Trends, Status, and Challenges", *ISEAS Perspective*, no. 2019/34, 24 April 2019.

24. Laura Zhou, "Chinese Survey Ship Involved in South China Sea Stand-off with Vietnam Back Home, Tracker Says", *South China Morning Post*, 25 October 2019, https://www.scmp.com/news/china/diplomacy/article/3034645/chinese-survey-ship-involved-south-china-sea-stand-vietnam.

25. Do Thanh Hai, "Vietnam Confronts China in the South China Sea", *The Diplomat*, 6 December 2019, https://www.eastasiaforum.org/2019/12/06/vietnam-confronts-china-in-the-south-china-sea/.

26. Romemarie Francisco and Manuel Mogato, "Vietnam PM Says Considering Legal Action against China over Disputed Waters", Reuters, 21 May 2014, https://www.reuters.com/article/us-vietnam-china/vietnam-pm-says-considering-legal-action-against-china-over-disputed-waters-idUSBREA4K1AK20140522.

27. Derek Grossman, "Vietnam Needs to 'Struggle' More in the South China Sea", *The Diplomat*, 15 November 2019, https://thediplomat.com/2019/11/vietnam-needs-to-struggle-more-in-the-south-china-sea/.

28. Le Hong Hiep, "New Defense White Paper Reveals Little Change to Vietnam's Defense Policy", *ISEAS Commentaries*, 2019/103, 10 December 2019, https://www.iseas.edu.sg/medias/commentaries/item/10977-new-white-paper-reveals-little-change-to-vietnams-defence-policy-by-le-hong-hiep.

29. Ronald Inglehart and Christian Welzel, *Modernization, Cultural Change, and Democracy: The Human Development Sequence* (Cambridge University Press, 2005).

30. CECODES, VFF-CRT, RTA, and United Nations Development Programme. The 2018 Viet Nam Governance and Public Administration Performance Index (PAPI): Measuring Citizens' Experiences. A Joint Policy Research Paper by the Centre for Community Support and Development Studies (CECODES), Centre for Research and Training of the Viet Nam Fatherland Front (VFF-CRT), Real-Time Analytics, and United Nations Development Programme (UNDP). Ha Noi, Vietnam (2019).

31. Tom Fawthrop, "Something is Very Wrong on the Mekong River", *The Diplomat*, 16 August 2019, https://thediplomat.com/2019/08/something-is-very-wrong-on-the-mekong-river/.

32. "Lời xin lỗi "đãi bôi" của Công ty nước sạch sông Đà tới 250.000 hộ dân Thủ đô!", Dan Tri, 25 October 2019, https://dantri.com.vn/xa-hoi/loi-xin-loi-dai-boi-cua-cong-ty-nuoc-sach-song-da-toi-250000-ho-dan-thu-do-20191025124925060.htm.

33. "Company Found Lying about Mercury Leak after Hanoi Fire", Tuoi Tre News,

9 September 2019, https://tuoitrenews.vn/news/society/20190909/company-found-lying-about-mercury-leak-after-hanoi-fire/51221.html.
34. "Vụ nước nhiễm dầu thải: 'Thủ tướng không hài lòng việc che đậy sự cố'", Zing.vn, 16 October 2019, https://news.zing.vn/vu-nuoc-nhiem-dau-thai-thu-tuong-khong-hai-long-viec-che-day-su-co-post1002209.html.
35. "Authorities Issue, Then Retract Health Warning after Lightbulb Factory Fire in Vietnam", Radio Free Asia, 6 September 2019, https://www.rfa.org/english/news/vietnam/vn-light-bulb-factory-fire-09062019174951.html.
36. "IMF Sees Vietnam's Growth Rate Slowing to 6.5% in 2019", Reuters, 16 July 2019, https://www.reuters.com/article/us-imf-vietnam/imf-sees-vietnams-economic-growth-slowing-to-65-in-2019-idUSKCN1UB2VU.
37. Fawthrop, "Something is Very Wrong".
38. Joelyn Chan, "Unfulfilled Potential: Trade War has been a Boon for Vietnam, but Opportunities have been Missed", *ASEAN Today*, 11 December 2019.
39. "Labor Market Trends in Vietnam", *Vietnam Briefing*, 29 June 2018, https://www.vietnam-briefing.com/news/labor-market-trends-vietnam.html/.
40. Michael Tatarski and James McAuley, "Vietnamese Families Say Migrants Were Lured to Europe with Promise of Work – and Found Tragedy Instead", *Washington Post*, 28 October 2019.
41. Tim Worstall, "Europe's Migration Crisis Isn't about Poverty: It's about Rising Wealth", Forbes, 15 September 2015, https://www.forbes.com/sites/timworstall/2015/09/05/europes-migration-crisis-isnt-about-poverty-its-about-rising-wealth/#26cf172a6f7e.
42. "Vì sao nông sản nhận 'quả đắng' từ thị trường TQ?", BBC Vietnam, 24 October 2019, https://www.bbc.com/vietnamese/vietnam-50162998.
43. Anh Tu, "Vietnam Wants More Northern Border Gates to Process Fruit Exports to China", *VNExpress*, 25 October 2019, https://e.vnexpress.net/news/business/industries/vietnam-wants-more-northern-border-gates-to-process-fruit-exports-to-china-4001681.html.
44. Pritesh Samuel, "FDI in Vietnam – Where is the Investment Going?", *Vietnam Briefing*, 7 June 2019, https://www.vietnam-briefing.com/news/fdi-in-vietnam-investment-by-sector.html/.
45. Hung Le, "Viettel Sole Vietnamese Brand in Global 500 Listing", *VNExpress International*, 25 January 2019, https://e.vnexpress.net/news/business/companies/viettel-sole-vietnamese-brand-in-global-500-listing-3873470.html.
46. Pritesh Samuel, "FDI in Vietnam – Where is the Investment Going?", *Vietnam Briefing*, 7 June 2019, https://www.vietnam-briefing.com/news/fdi-in-vietnam-investment-by-sector.html/.
47. See Le Hong Hiep, *Vietnam's Industrialization Ambitions: The Case of Vingroup and the Automotive Industry*, Trends in Southeast Asia, no. 2/2019 (Singapore: ISEAS – Yusof Ishak Institute, 2019), p. 16.

48. David Dapice, "Is Vietnam Swimming Naked?", *East Asia Forum*, 21 July 2019, https://www.eastasiaforum.org/2019/07/21/is-vietnam-swimming-naked/.
49. Joe Studwell, *How Asia Works* (Grove Press, 2014).
50. John Reed, "The Rise and Rise of a Vietnamese Corporate Empire", *Financial Times*, 26 June 2019, https://www.ft.com/content/84323c32-9799-11e9-9573-ee5cbb98ed36.
51. Ibid.

SUCCESSION POLITICS AND AUTHORITARIAN RESILIENCE IN VIETNAM

Nguyen Khac Giang[1]

On his seventy-fifth birthday, on 14 April 2019, Nguyen Phu Trong visited the southern province of Kien Giang, a practice he had adopted since being re-elected as secretary general of the Vietnamese Communist Party (VCP) in 2016. This time it did not go well; it was rumoured that Trong suffered a stroke, and he was subjected to a lengthy hospital stay.[2] He appeared fragile during his first public appearance a month later, and in June he had to delegate National Assembly (NA) chairwoman Nguyen Thi Kim Ngan to visit China on his behalf. There was only limited coverage of these events in the tightly controlled Vietnamese media, as they tried to downplay the significance of Trong's deteriorating health.

In 2021 the VCP will hold its 13th National Congress, at which Trong—who will be seventy-seven by then—is expected to step down. However, this is only a high possibility, not a certainty. When re-elected in 2016, Trong hinted that he would retire in the middle of his term to make room for younger leaders. In the two years following his re-election, however, he consolidated power to become the most powerful figure in Vietnamese politics in decades. The sudden health incident will have likely put an end to any wish of his to remain in power for longer. What is more important however is whether Trong's illness has any implications for Vietnamese succession politics. As the head of both the party and the state, Trong's preference will weigh heavily in the candidate selection process for the hot seat in 2021. The tradition in Vietnamese politics is for party elders to have strong opinions over who will assume their posts (or even who

---

NGUYEN KHAC GIANG is a doctoral candidate at Victoria University of Wellington, New Zealand, and a senior research fellow at the Vietnam Institute for Economic and Policy Research (VEPR), Hanoi, Vietnam.

should step down). The rise and fall of Secretary General Le Kha Phieu vividly illustrated that. Phieu was promoted to the party's supreme position in 1997 when he gained the support of both Le Duc Anh and Do Muoi after a long tug of war between two camps. He was nevertheless dethroned four years later when the party elders opposed his re-election.[3]

Tran Quoc Vuong, the executive secretary of the party's Secretariat—the fourth most powerful member of the party—was considered Trong's right-hand man and his favoured candidate for the top post. Vuong, however, is not a perfect choice. In addition to his lack of governance experience, he will exceed the age limit by the time the 13th Party Congress takes place. If health issues prevent Trong from maintaining his influence, it would be difficult for him to push ahead with his selection. In addition, Vuong is competing with other strong candidates, most notably the prime minister, Nguyen Xuan Phuc, and the head of the VCP's Central Organization Commission, Pham Minh Chinh.

The situation will likely lead to a heated political struggle during the next congress, similar to what was seen in 2016. At that time the contest between the then prime minister Nguyen Tan Dung and Secretary General Nguyen Phu Trong proved to be unpredictable until the very last minute. Both were over the age limit, but Trong secured the only exemption for an overaged candidate and won the race. The defeat exacted a heavy toll on Dung's allies; the anti-corruption campaign—known as the "hot furnace"—burned down many of their political careers. Dinh La Thang was dismissed as Ho Chi Minh City's party secretary and became the first Politburo member to be tried under criminal law for corruption. He was sentenced to thirty years in prison by a Hanoi court in 2018.[4] A series of southern provincial leaders, former central officials, and managers of state-owned enterprises deemed to be Dung's supporters were also disciplined.[5] A key technocrat under Dung's government, Nguyen Van Binh, was sidelined to the largely ceremonial position of head of the Central Economic Commission. Most of the new key posts were occupied by Trong's allies, giving him unprecedented power to impose his policy. It is not an exaggeration to say that, through the use of the "hot furnace", Trong has transformed himself from an obscure theoretician into the most powerful leader in Vietnam since the era of Le Duan.

The rise of Trong illustrates how leadership change maintains its relevance even in a highly institutionalized mechanism of collective leadership. The communist state could not have gone through the Doi Moi era if the conservative Le Duan had lived long enough to exert his control over the 6th National Congress. The accelerating economic reforms of the late 1990s and early 2000s were mostly credited to the reformist prime ministers Vo Van Kiet and Phan Van Khai. Accordingly, the key question is how new leaders are chosen in Vietnam and whether this could have any impact on the country's long-term prospects. This chapter first discusses the politics of succession in Vietnam with particular reference to the VCP's upcoming 13th Congress. It then evaluates Vietnam's leadership transition and provides a comparative institutional analysis with China, which has always been considered as the model for Vietnam's political development. Last, the chapter briefly examines the way forward to avoid the risk of a succession crisis in Vietnam.

The Institutionalization of Leadership Transition

Given the importance of leadership succession, it is surprising that the VCP has, since its establishment in 1930, only had a handful of vague specialized regulations on the issue. In each national congress, organized every five years, the VCP's top delegates review and suggest possible amendments to the Constitution (the VCP has passed constitutional amendments in all but two national congresses). However, there are only a few details pertaining to party elections, with the most prominent being the obscure principle of "democratic centralism", which dictates that all leadership positions of the party must be elected through "democratic elections" (*bau cu dan chu*).[6]

At the central level, the principle guarantees a voting procedure that is nominally democratic: congress delegates vote to select the Central Committee (CC), which in turn votes to select the Politburo and the secretary general among the newly elected Politburo members.[7] However, because the party constitution stops short of giving detailed instructions, the rules of the game can be changed during each congress. The institutionalization of succession was not very important prior to the 8th Congress, as the top position had previously been occupied by the independence hero (Ho Chi Minh), the supreme leader during the Vietnam War (Le Duan) and revolutionary leaders (Nguyen Van Linh and Do Muoi), who were all powerful enough to arrange the top positions among themselves. However, the influence of the party elders gradually waned in the 1990s, particularly when the advisory commission to the CC—which consisted of retired leaders—was disbanded in 2001.

As there was no dominant figure arising from the new generation of leadership, the need for an institutionalized process of succession increased. In 2000 the Politburo issued Decision 77-QD/TW regulating intra-party elections (later replaced by Decision No. 220-QD/TW in 2009 with some minor changes). This document specifies the procedures for preparing for elections, the rules for nomination and self-nomination, the election and vote counting process, and disciplinary actions for wrongdoings. It is important to note that these regulations were issued by the Politburo, which meant that they could only apply to the party cells under the supervision of the CC, and not to the Politburo or the CC themselves. For elections at the central level, regulations were still decided on an ad hoc basis by the CC. Nevertheless, the three congresses (8th, 9th and 10th) that followed the introduction of Decision 77 largely followed its procedure.

Decision 244–QD/TW, introduced in 2014, formalized such a procedure for high-level party elections. The decision was issued directly by the CC, which enabled it to cover all elections from the grass-roots party cells to the CC, as well as the elections of party members to positions in the state system and mass organizations.[8] Decision 244 was seen as a game changer, not just because it eventually helped Trong to win the fierce race against Dung[9] but also because it institutionalized the election process for the VCP's high-level positions.

Decision 244 strictly follows the principle of democratic centralism embedded in the party constitution, while also providing more details for the process. Specifically, Decision 244 requires the election of the secretary general to have two candidates, who would be nominated by the outgoing CC and the new Politburo, respectively. The incoming CC retains the right to nominate other candidates. If there are more than two candidates running for the post of secretary general, a preliminary vote will then be carried out in the new CC in order to choose the two most popular candidates. This is the first time that the election procedure for the secretary general has been explicitly stated in a party regulation.

While Decision 244 institutionalizes the voting procedure, Regulation 90 QD/TW issued in 2017 formalizes the criteria for candidature. To be eligible for the post, a candidate must hold at least one term of Politburo membership (ideally two terms) and have an "excellent" record in governance (either as a provincial party chief or head of one of the party's central commissions). In particular, the candidate must have the ability to "steer and administrate the Central Committee, the Politburo, and the Executive Secretariat", which has led to suggestions that the candidate must have served as one of the "top four" offices (secretary general, prime minister, chair of the National Assembly or state president) that are allowed to moderate a CC plenum.[10] Health is also considered a critical precondition, which places candidates with bad health records at a disadvantage for the top post.

In addition to written regulations, succession politics in Vietnam is heavily influenced by quasi-institutionalized norms, which are not clearly stated in official documents but are consensually accepted among the ruling elites.

The most widely discussed norm is the regional allocation among the leadership. Since the 6th VCP Congress, the "troika" within the Politburo (secretary general, president and prime minister) has generally been divided equally among three regions. The secretary general has always been a northerner (in this case, hailing from north of the 17th Parallel, the old border between North and South Vietnam). There is however more flexibility for the posts of prime minister and president (see Table 1). There is no clear reason for this norm, but a common explanation among party members revolves around the idea that northern communists are more ideologically committed and thus less likely to endanger the regime's socialist orientation.

Another norm is the age limit. There is no fixed threshold for election or re-election to the Politburo in written documents, although the CC usually discusses this issue before each congress. In the 9th Congress, for example, the CC set the appointment age at sixty-five, meaning that anyone exceeding the limit could not be re-elected to the Politburo.[11] This principle was reasserted at the 10th Congress[12] and has been considered a norm ever since. However, if one were to look closely at the ages of secretaries general when they first took the post, this norm has not been strictly adhered to. In fact the only party chief who qualified for the criterion of being under sixty-five was Nong Duc Manh at the 9th Congress (he was sixty-one). The norm seems to apply more strictly to other posts. Since the 10th Congress, all elected prime ministers and presidents have been within the age limit. In the recent 11th Plenum, the Politburo issued Conclusion 60-KL/TW on the age requirement of re-elected officials. However, the conclusion does not regulate CC members.[13]

A third norm revolves around the expectation that a secretary general should ideally have solid experience in governance, or as stated in Regulation 90, "a deep and wide knowledge on politics, economics, culture, society, defence, security, and foreign policy". A candidate should have experience governing a province as either the party chief or the people's committee chairman/chairwoman. It is however not a must, since Regulation 90 states that a candidate could also have served as the head of a central commission. However, not having governing experience is seen as a severe weakness. The only candidate promoted to the top post without such experience was Le Kha Phieu in 1997. Nevertheless, Phieu was by then already among the five members of the short-lived Standing Committee of the Politburo and held a key position in the military. Despite this, his selection was fiercely protested by many CC members.[14] In addition, although Phieu did get elected, his lack of governing experience and political connections isolated him, eventually leading to his failure to secure a second term.[15]

In sum, for the past three decades, succession politics in Vietnam has been characterized by a combination of increasingly institutionalized rules on the one

TABLE 1
Regional Allocation and Age of Top 3 Positions in Vietnamese Politics since the 6th Congress

VCP Congress	Position	Name	Age when elected	Origin
6th (1986)	**Secretary General**	**Nguyen Van Linh**	**72**	**Hung Yen (North)**
	Prime Minister	Pham Hung[a]	75	Vinh Long (South)
	President	Vo Chi Cong	75	Quang Nam (Central – South)
7th (1991)	**Secretary General**	**Do Muoi**	**74**	**Hanoi (North)**
	Prime Minister	Vo Van Kiet	69	Vinh Long (South)
	President	Le Duc Anh	71	Hue (Central – South)
8th (1996)	**Secretary General**	**Le Kha Phieu**	**67**	**Thanh Hoa (Central – North)**
	Prime Minister	Phan Van Khai	64	HCMC (South)
	President	Tran Duc Luong	60	Quang Ngai (Central – South)
9th (2001)	**Secretary General**	**Nong Duc Manh**	**61**	**Bac Kan (North)**
	Prime Minister	Phan Van Khai	68	HCMC (South)
	President	Tran Duc Luong	65	Quang Ngai (Central – South)
10th (2006)	**Secretary General**	**Nong Duc Manh**	**66**	**Bac Kan (North)**
	Prime Minister	Nguyen Tan Dung	57	Ca Mau (South)
	President	Nguyen Minh Triet	64	HCMC (South)
11th (2011)	**Secretary General**	**Nguyen Phu Trong**	**67**	**Hanoi (North)**
	Prime Minister	Nguyen Tan Dung	62	Ca Mau (South)
	President	Truong Tan Sang	62	Long An (South)
12th (2016)	**Secretary General**	**Nguyen Phu Trong**	**72**	**Hanoi (North)**
	Prime Minister	Nguyen Xuan Phuc	62	Quang Nam (Central – South)
	President	Tran Dai Quang[b]	60	Ninh Binh (North)

Notes: a. Pham Hung (1912–88) was initially the prime minister (known then as the president of the Council of Ministers). Hung was from Vinh Long (the South). After he died in office in 1988, Vo Van Kiet was chosen to be the acting PM. However, in the subsequent vote, Kiet lost to Do Muoi.
b. Tran Dai Quang (1956–2018) died in office. Nguyen Phu Trong replaced him as president in 2018.

Source: Compilation by the author.

hand and informal, implicit norms on the other. To an extent, the system has a degree of democratic elements, particularly in the election process and the criteria for nomination. However, for an authoritarian regime, democratic practice means a lack of predictable outcome for leadership transition and the risk of political infighting, especially when there is no clear favourite for the top post. The next section discusses such risks for the 13th Congress.

Candidature Uncertainties in 2021

Vietnam differs from China in lacking a position designating the heir apparent, thus making it extremely difficult to determine the identity of the next leader. If institutionalized rules are considered, theoretically all the currently active Politburo members are eligible to be candidates for the top post.[16] However, informal norms rule out certain people. Female Politburo members such as NA chairwoman Nguyen Thi Kim Ngan, vice NA chairwoman Tong Thi Phong and head of the Central Mass Mobilization Commission Truong Thi Mai will prove to be unlikely choices in the male-dominated politics of Vietnam. Minister of Public Security To Lam and Minister of Defence Nguyen Xuan Lich are not favoured due to fears about the over-centralization of power in the security sector. The party constitution dictates that a secretary general cannot hold the position for more than two terms.[17] Given that the CC is not recommending any changes to the party constitution in the coming congress in 2021,[18] it is very unlikely that Trong will stay at the top post beyond the 13th Congress. Not to mention that his deteriorating health and old age would also prove to be huge disadvantages if he wished to remain.

Trong, however, holds the power to introduce his preferred choice in his capacity as the incumbent secretary general and the head of the Personnel Subcommittee for the 13th Congress, which is responsible for preparing nominations for membership to the CC and Politburo. It was rumoured that Dinh The Huynh was initially his first choice, before Huynh withdrew from politics, citing health reasons. His replacement as the executive secretary of the party's Secretariat, Tran Quoc Vuong, is seen as even closer to Trong. Vuong had championed the Vietnamese anti-corruption campaign as head of the Central Inspection Commission (CIC). However, Vuong is not a "perfect" candidate if norms are taken into account. He has never governed a province, either as a provincial party chief or chairman of the People's Committee. Like Phieu, Vuong has spent most of his career in the Central Party Office and the Supreme People's Procuratorate of Vietnam before leading the CIC. These experiences have familiarized him with party politics but will also likely have created more enemies than friends for him. Another disadvantage is his age: Vuong will exceed the party's age limit for Politburo membership by 2021. This means that if he fails to secure the top post and thus becomes the "special candidate" to stay on, Vuong will have to retire.

As an experienced technocrat and two-term Politburo member, Prime Minister Nguyen Xuan Phuc is a clear frontrunner. For the last two years, Phuc has shown his ambition by touring the country tirelessly to promote himself as a reformist. He has also tried to be more involved in ideological and theoretical issues such as party building, the ideology of Ho Chi Minh, and "building successful socialism" in Vietnam,[19] something that had been less evident during the tenures of his predecessors, who concentrated mostly on governance. As the regime depends on economic performance for its legitimacy, his key advantage is the much-improved economic situation witnessed during his premiership since 2016. However, he will reach the age of sixty-six by 2021, and, more importantly, he is originally from the South. As noted above, no one from the former South Vietnam has ever become the VCP's supreme leader. Sustained rumours about his alleged corruption since the last congress might also damage his potential candidacy. In addition, his selection might destabilize the system in the sense that he is too powerful in comparison to his peers.[20] This was seen as the reason why his predecessor, Nguyen Tan Dung, was not supported by the CC during the 12th Congress.[21]

Pham Minh Chinh, who heads the Central Organization Commission (COC), is a younger candidate. Chinh has a solid record in governance as the former party chief of Quang Ninh, one of Vietnam's wealthiest provinces. During his time in that post he was known for promoting various economic and administrative reforms, including the much-discussed "unification" of party and government positions at the same administrative level. His current position, however, might weigh against him: there has never been a secretary general who was previously the head of the COC. A former COC head, Ho Duc Viet, was a favourite choice for the top post in the 11th Congress, but he eventually lost the race to Trong.[22] Looking further back in history, Le Duc Tho was also prevented from taking the top post in 1986 because of fears over manipulation from other CC members. Tho, a Politburo member of thirty-one years, led the COC for more than twenty years and successfully controlled the whole cadre management system to the point that both Ho Chi Minh and Le Duan complained about his accumulated power.[23] Furthermore, the failure to put forward the Law on Special Economic Zones (SEZs), which sparked violent protests in Vietnam last year, has dented Chinh's credibility. Chinh was seen as the main promoter for the draft law, which involves building an SEZ in his stronghold of Quang Ninh.

There are other potential candidates, although the likelihood of them succeeding is minimal. Standing deputy PM Truong Hoa Binh is a southerner who exceeds the age limit and lacks local governing experience, since he only ascended through the ranks of the police force. In addition, it would be unlikely that he could leapfrog Phuc in the pecking order. Another deputy PM, Vuong Dinh Hue, had been clearly groomed for the premiership. Deputy PM and foreign minister Pham Binh Minh is a career diplomat, which would traditionally rule him out from the race. Hoang Trung Hai and Nguyen Thien Nhan, the party chiefs of Hanoi and Ho Chi Minh City, respectively, are veterans of the system, but they have both suffered damage to their reputations. The former is said to have close connections with China, and has had his name implicated in some anti-corruption cases; the latter has been criticized for lacking the capability to govern effectively. Nhan will also exceed the age limit by 2021. The head of the Central Propaganda Commission, Vo Van Thuong, and the head of the Central Economic Commission, Nguyen Van Binh, are relatively young, and they may have to wait for their turn during the 14th Congress in 2026.

As such, the VCP seems to lack the "perfect" candidate for the post of secretary general in the upcoming congress. Most of the prominent choices have weaknesses, and selecting from among them would necessitate some bending of the formal and informal rules of succession. Breaking rules is not necessarily a bad thing, however, provided that the new ones are more institutionalized and guarantee fair competition for the top post. Unless Trong uses his power to push forward his preferred choice without adhering to the existing institutional framework, the likely outcome of this uncertainty will be a more competitive intra-party election mechanism in the VCP. In this sense, the Vietnamese regime seems to have more of an institutionalized power-sharing scheme than its communist neighbour China.

Vietnam's Succession Politics: A Comparative Analysis with China

For survival, authoritarian regimes must solve the "twin problems" of power control and power sharing.[24] The former refers to how rulers control their population, while the latter refers to how ruling elites manage the relationships among themselves. Succession politics lies at the centre of power sharing and is among the most significant factors that determine authoritarian resilience. Political crises often arise in autocracies as a result of succession quarrels. On the other hand, the longevity of party-based authoritarian regimes is often attributed to the existence of a norm-bound process of succession politics.[25] Both Vietnam and China, as the two longest-ruling communist regimes to survive, have each built a solid institutional arrangement for leadership transition since the late 1980s. Yet, a closer look reveals marked differences between the two regimes.

Succession politics in China tends to emphasize stability: the heir apparent is known well ahead of the National Party Congress at which the individual is supposed to be elected. For instance, Hu Jintao held the positions of successor-apparent (vice chairman of the Chinese Communist Party's [CCP] Central Military Commission and vice president) prior to replacing Jiang Zemin as the supreme leader in 2002.[26] There was a similar pattern for Xi Jinping in the run-up to the CCP's 18th Congress.

There are two symbiotic steps for leadership transition: the first deals with how the incumbent steps down, and the second with how the new leader is selected.[27] In China, the first step of leadership transition is institutionalized, but not the second. Since the third generation took power in 1992, exits from power in China have been smooth and orderly, thanks to term and age limits, as well as the balance of power among the ruling elites.[28] However, the selection of leaders is more unpredictable. The first two supreme leaders after the Tiananmen Square incident, Jiang Zemin and Hu Jintao, were handpicked by Deng Xiaoping. The promotion of Xi Jinping in 2007 was a largely unknown process. Some observers have credited his ascension to the support he enjoys among party elders,[29] his alleged popular image,[30] his princeling origin,[31] or even to luck.[32] No matter the reason, it is unlikely this process will be repeated in the next congress, given the fact that the term limit for the presidency was abolished in 2018, which paves the way for Xi Jinping to retain his hold on power. Xi Jinping has also abandoned the practice of appointing the heir apparent, which was seen in the case of Hu Jintao and himself. The institutionalization of succession politics in China is therefore fragile and more vulnerable to personal manipulation.

On the other hand, leadership transition in Vietnam is more rule-bound and increasingly more impervious to personal intervention. The death of Le Duan at the threshold of the VCP's 6th National Congress, and the subsequent retirement of revolutionaries such as Nguyen Van Linh and Pham Van Dong, had the effect of freeing Vietnamese politics from the influence of party elders. There is no leader like Deng Xiaoping in Vietnam who enjoys such paramount influence to determine the next generation of leadership. The selection of leaders in Vietnamese politics is usually the outcome of hard-won bargains and competition among the ruling elites rather than an imposition from the top. It is much more unpredictable in the sense that no one would be able to claim to know the results until the very last minute. Indeed, if we were to look at the various VCP congresses after Doi Moi, succession politics in Vietnam has been no less remarkable than those in a vibrant electoral democracy. Zachary Abuza has detailed the political struggle before the 8th Party Congress, where all the frontrunners were dismissed due to a lack of consensus over an acceptable candidate.[33] The VCP had to wait for another year after the 8th Congress to choose the new leader. The one chosen—Le Kha Phieu—eventually failed to even secure a post in the CC during the 9th Congress in 2001, as he lost support from all sides.[34] The compromise among ruling elites also led to the selection of Nong Duc Manh in the next two congresses (in 2001 and 2006). Malesky, Schuler and Tran have illustrated the race in the 11th Congress between the then NA chairman Nguyen Phu Trong and the head of the VCP's Central Economics Commission Truong Tan Sang,[35] while Vuving has described how a strong candidate like Ho Duc Viet can fall out of favour.[36] The most recent congress witnessed one of the most intense competitions in history, between the outgoing PM Nguyen Tan Dung and the incumbent party chief Nguyen Phu Trong.[37]

Furthermore, exits from power in Vietnam have been smooth. Outgoing secretaries general respect the norms of term limits and generally abstain from meddling in party affairs after their retirement. This has been particularly true since 2001, when the powerful advisory commission to the CC—which had consisted of retired leaders with widespread influence—was abolished. The situation is different in China—for instance, Jiang Zemin continued to hold on to the chairmanship of the Central Military Commission two years after his retirement.

Since 1989, Vietnam has had five different party secretaries general, and only two among them have managed to be re-elected (Nong Duc Manh and Nguyen Phu Trong). Over the same period in China, however, there have only been three secretaries general, who have each ruled for ten years.

When discussing leadership change in one-party regimes, it is also important to examine not only the supreme leader but also the ruling elites, or what De Mesquita et al. call "the winning coalition",[38] who collectively share power. In Vietnam the "winning coalition" refers to the Politburo, while in China it is the Politburo Standing Committee (PSC).[39] In the last six party congresses in the respective countries, the rate of holdover in Vietnam's ruling coalition has remained relatively stable, while for China it has fluctuated periodically according to the ten-year cycle that dictates when most of the PSC members would step down for a new generation of leadership. This pattern had clearly deteriorated by the 18th CCP Congress, when only two out of the seven PSC members retained their seats (President Xi Jinping and Premier Li Keqiang).

Thus it can be argued that while Vietnam maintains a stable ruling coalition and shuffles its leaders, China stabilizes the top posts and alternates the coalition. These characteristic have a huge impact on how power is shared among the ruling elites in Vietnam and China: the VCP seems to uphold the principle of collective leadership, while the CCP, particularly under Xi Jinping, tends to move towards more personalization.

What Is To Be Done?

Trong's tenure has been one of the most exciting periods in Vietnamese politics for decades. His rule is illustrated by two contradictory tendencies: while power is being increasingly consolidated in his hands, Trong has been laying the foundation for a more norm-bound process of succession politics. He was the mastermind behind Decision 244, which institutionalizes party elections at all levels, as well as Regulation 90, which determines the criteria for candidates aspiring for the top leadership position. Although there have been some concerns that Decision 244 has a negative effect on the VCP's intra-party democracy, particularly in emphasizing majoritarian views and enhancing the power of the outgoing steering committee in nominating candidates, it has the benefit of making the election to the top party post more procedural and competitive.

Trong's legacy, however, will depend on the person who succeeds him. The new leader might continue Trong's agenda for further intra-party democracy, but he could also imitate his quest of centralizing power. The latter scenario would destabilize Vietnam's relative balance of power among the elites and put the regime at risk of intense infighting. Trong is a committed party loyalist and a relatively clean politician, or at least he is widely perceived to be by his comrades. He has exercised power not for personal gain but to purify a party decaying from corruption and abuses of power. However, a younger successor with a longer time horizon might not be as committed to such ideals. Instead, he might take advantage of his position to enrich his family and cronies, as most autocratic rulers are wont to do.

Trong is aware of this risk. During his tenure the VCP has tried to uphold the principle of collective leadership by introducing different mechanisms for checks and balances, such as confidence voting for the top leadership[40] and increasing the supervisory power of the Central Inspection Commission. However, as previous congresses have shown, the ultimate tool to hold a leader accountable is the fear of being voted out. As a result, the key to maintain the regime's stability is to implement and adhere to a highly institutionalized election procedure that

FIGURE 1
Holdover Rates in Ruling Coalitions in Vietnam and China, 1991–2017

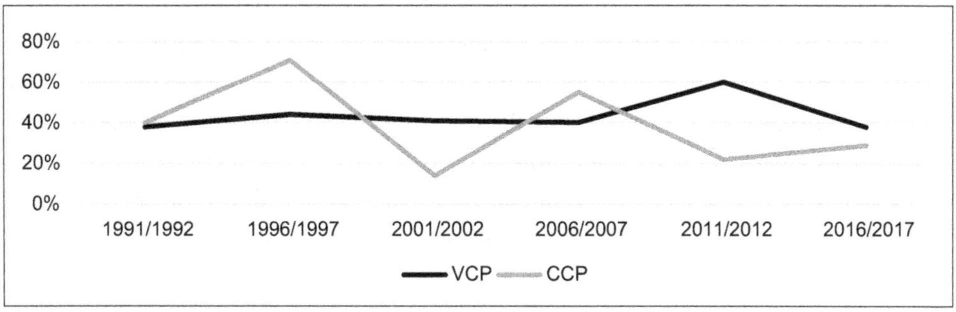

```
80%
60%
40%
20%
 0%
     1991/1992   1996/1997   2001/2002   2006/2007   2011/2012   2016/2017
                          ——VCP  ----CCP
```

Note: Ruling coalitions are the Politburo in Vietnam and the Politburo Standing Committee in China.
Source: Compilation by the author.

provides the "selectorate" with the necessary tools to elevate good leaders and eliminate bad ones. The VCP has been deliberating on a potential rule that would allow congress delegates to vote directly for the secretary general,[41] instead of the current delegate mechanism. Such a move has been trialled in several provinces since 2010,[42] but it has yet to be applied at the central level. If Trong can push through this practice at the 13th Congress or, even better, institutionalize it in the party constitution or through a CC regulation, it might prove to be his biggest legacy, along with his popular anti-corruption campaign.

Notes

1. The author would like to thank Xavier Marquez, Xiaoming Huang, Roberto Rabel and Malcolm McKinnon from Victoria University of Wellington for helpful comments on earlier drafts of this chapter. All remaining errors are my own.
2. Ông Nguyễn Phú Trọng không khỏe nhưng, "sẽ sớm trở lại làm việc" [Trong is not well but will soon return to work], BBC Vietnamese Service, 25 April 2018, https://www.bbc.com/vietnamese/vietnam-48051716.
3. Zachary Abuza, "Leadership Transition in Vietnam since the Eighth Party Congress: The Unfinished Congress", *Asian Survey* 38, no. 12 (1998): 1105–21.
4. Duc Minh, "Ông Đinh La Thăng chịu mức án chung 30 năm tù" [Dinh La Thang is sentenced 30 years in prison], *Phap luat*, 27 June 2018, https://plo.vn/phap-luat/ong-dinh-la-thang-chiu-muc-an-chung-30-nam-tu-778546.html.
5. Le Dan, "Vụ Trịnh Xuân Thanh: kỷ luật bí thư, nguyên bí thư tỉnh ủy Hậu Giang" [Trinh Xuan Thanh case: Discipline the party chief and former party chief of Hau Giang], *Tuoi tre*, 2018, https://tuoitre.vn/vu-trinh-xuan-thanh-ky luat bi thu-nguyen-bi-thu-tinh-uy-hau-giang-1243477.htm.

6. Article 10, VCP Constitution at 4th Congress (1976). This article was kept until the 7th Party Congress (1991), when it was rewritten in mostly the same way, but the word *dan chu* (democratic) was removed. There is no clear explanation for this change, but the Central Committee's Report on party building and the amendment of the party institution of the VCP 6th Congress suggests that there were concerns of "overly-democratic" tendencies that might lead to chaos. This implies a more cautious approach of the 7th Congress on political reforms after five years of Doi Moi. Indeed, in the 6th VCP institution *dan chu* appeared fifteen times, but it only appeared five times in the 7th VCP institution.
7. Article 17, VCP Constitution at the 11th Congress (2011).
8. Nguyen Duc Ha, "Một số điểm mới của Quy chế bầu cử trong Đảng" [Some new amendments on the party's election regulation], Vietnam Communist Party, 18 July 2014, http://www.cpv.org.vn/tieu-diem/mot-so-diem-moi-cua-quy-che-bau-cu-trong-dang-257568.html.
9. Alexander Vuving, "The 2016 Leadership Change in Vietnam and its Long-term Implications", in *Southeast Asian Affairs 2016*, edited by Malcolm Cook and Daljit Singh (Singapore: ISEAS – Yusof Ishak Institute, 2017), pp. 421–35.
10. Truong Xuan Danh, "Những ai sẽ vào 'tứ trụ' tại Đại hội Đảng 2021?" [Who will be in the "big four" at the 2021 Party Congress?], *Nghien cuu Quoc te*, 5 May 2019, http://nghiencuuquocte.org/2019/05/05/nhung-ai-se-vao-tu-tru-tai-dai-hoi-dang-2021/.
11. Abuza, "Leadership Transition in Vietnam".
12. David Koh, "Leadership Changes at the 10th Congress of the Vietnamese Communist Party", *Asian Survey* 48, no. 4 (2008): 650–72.
13. Conclusion 60-KL/TW, VCP Politburo, 2019.
14. Huy Duc, *Ben thang cuoc (The Winning Side Part II: Authority)* (Boston, MA: OsinBook, 2012).
15. Abuza, "Leadership Transition in Vietnam".
16. Hai Hong Nguyen, "Who Will Be Vietnam's Next Party Boss?", *East Asia Forum*, 18 November 2019, https://www.eastasiaforum.org/2019/11/18/who-will-be-vietnams-next-party-boss/.
17. Article 17, VCP Constitution at the 11th Congress (2011).
18. Ha Vu, "Trung ương quyết định không sửa đổi, bổ sung Điều lệ Đảng" [The Central Committee decides not to amend the party constitution], *VnEconomy*, 12 October 2019, http://vneconomy.vn/trung-uong-quyet-dinh-khong-sua-doi-bo-sung-dieu-le-dang-20191012203524958.htm.
19. "Các bài phát biểu của Thủ tướng" [The prime minister's speeches], Vietnam Government Office update, 26 November 2019, http://www.chinhphu.vn/portal/page/portal/chinhphu/trangchu/cacbaiphatbieucuaThutuong.
20. Paul Schuler and Mai Truong, "Leadership Reshuffle and the Future of Vietnam's Collective Leadership", *ISEAS Perspective*, no. 2019/9, 22 February 2019.

21. Vuving, "The 2016 Leadership Change".
22. Vuving, "Vietnam in 2012: A Rent-Seeking State on the Verge of a Crisis", in *Southeast Asian Affairs* 2012, edited by Daljit Singh (Singapore: Institute of Southeast Asian Studies, 2013), pp. 323–47.
23. When commenting on Tho's power, Ho Chi Minh allegedly said, "Our cadre policy depends on comrade Tho. He reported positively for who he favours, and negatively for those who he hates. The Politburo cannot know it all." Huy Duc, *Ben thang cuoc (The Winning Side Part I: Liberation)* (Boston, MA: OsinBook, 2012), p. 239.
24. Milan Svolik, *The Politics of Authoritarian Rule* (Cambridge: Cambridge University Press, 2012).
25. For more on this, see Jennifer Gandhi, *Political Institutions under Dictatorship* (New York: Cambridge University Press, 2008); and Barbara Geddes, "What Do We Know about Democratization after Twenty Years?", *Annual Review of Political Science* 2 (1999): 115–44; and Andrew Nathan, "Authoritarian Resilience", *Journal of Democracy* 14, no. 1 (2003).
26. Li Cheng and Lynn White, "The Sixteenth Central Committee of the Chinese Communist Party: Hu Gets What?", *Asian Survey* 43, no. 4 (2003): 553.
27. Erica Frantz and Stein Elizabeth, "Comparative Leadership in Non-democracies", in *Comparative Political Leadership*, edited by Ludger Helms (London: Palgrave Macmillan, 2012), pp. 292–313.
28. Zeng, Jinghan, "Institutionalization of the Authoritarian Leadership in China: A Power Succession System with Chinese Characteristics?", *Contemporary Politics* 20, no. 3 (2014): 294–314.
29. Richard McGregor, "The Party Man: Xi Jinping's Quest to Dominate China", *Foreign Affairs*, 14 August 2019, https://www.foreignaffairs.com/articles/china/2019-08-14/party-man.
30. Melinda Liu, "A People's Princeling", *Newsweek*, 27 October 2007, https://www.newsweek.com/china-peoples-princeling-103083.
31. Joseph Fewsmith, "The 19th Party Congress: Ringing in Xi Jinping's New Age", *China Leadership Monitor* 55 (2018): 1–22.
32. K. Brown, *CEO, China: The Rise of Xi Jinping* (London: Tauris, 2016).
33. Abuza, "Leadership Transition in Vietnam".
34. David Koh, "The Politics of a Divided Party and Parkinson's State in Vietnam", *Contemporary Southeast Asia* 23, no. 3 (2001): 533–51.
35. Edmund Malesky, Paul Schuler, and Anh Tran, "Vietnam: Familiar Patterns and New Developments ahead of the 11th Party Congress", *Southeast Asian Affairs* 2011, edited by Daljit Singh (Singapore: Institute of Southeast Asian Studies, 2012), pp. 339–63.
36. Vuving, "Vietnam in 2012".
37. Vuving, "The 2016 Leadership Change".

38. De Mesquita, Bruce Bueno, Alastair Smith, James D Morrow, and Randolph M Siverson, *The Logic of Political Survival* (London: MIT press, 2005).
39. Regina Abrami, Edmund Malesky, and Zheng Yu, "Vietnam through Chinese Eyes: Divergent Accountability in Single-Party Regimes", In *Why Communism Did Not Collapse: Understanding Authoritarian Regime Resilience in Asia and Europe*, edited by Martin Dimitrov (New York: Cambridge University Press, 2013), pp. 237–76.
40. Hoang Thuy, "21 thành viên Bộ Chính trị, Ban Bí thư được lấy phiếu tín nhiệm" [Confidence voting on the members of the Politburo and Secretariat], *VnExpress*, 25 December 2018, https://vnexpress.net/thoi-su/21-thanh-vien-bo-chinh-tri-ban-bi-thu-duoc-lay-phieu-tin-nhiem-3859117.html.
41. Le Hiep, "Trợ lý Chủ tịch Quốc hội: 'Nếu bí thư do đại hội bầu, mọi thứ sẽ khác" [National Assembly chairwoman's secretary: If the party chief is elected by the congress, everything changes], *Thanh nien*, 25 September 2019, https://thanhnien.vn/thoi-su/tro-ly-chu-tich-quoc-hoi-neu-bi-thu-do-dai-hoi-bau-moi-thu-se-khac-1130205.html.
42. Nguyen Hung, "Bí thư tỉnh đầu tiên được bầu trực tiếp tại đại hội Đảng" [The first provincial party chief elected by the congress], *VnExpress*, 9 September 2010, https://vnexpress.net/thoi-su/bi-thu-tinh-dau-tien-duoc-bau-truc-tiep-tai-dai-hoi-dang-2174776.html.

www.ingramcontent.com/pod-product-compliance
Lightning Source LLC
Chambersburg PA
CBHW081420160426
42814CB00039B/199